D0881098

ALEXANDER THE GREAT

II

Sources and Studies

ALEXANDER THE GREAT

II

Sources and Studies

BY

W. W. TARN

CAMBRIDGE UNIVERSITY PRESS

CAMBRIDGE

LONDON · NEW YORK · MELBOURNE

Published by the Syndics of the Cambridge University Press
The Pitt Building, Trumpington Street, Cambridge CB2 1RP
Bentley House, 200 Euston Road, London NW1 2DB
32 East 57th Street, New York, NY 10022, USA
296 Beaconsfield Parade, Middle Park, Melbourne 3206, Australia

Copyright Cambridge University Press 1948

First published 1948
Reissued 1979

Printed in Great Britain at the University Press, Cambridge

ISBN 0 521 22585 X

To all the friends, living and dead, who have
helped me over many years

PREFATORY NOTE

As the two volumes of this work can be bought separately, I may here call attention to the fact that the preface to the whole will be found in Volume I (the narrative volume); but there are a few points which concern this volume only. The Table of Contents largely explains itself, and some such examination of sources as is made in Part I is long overdue. As to the studies which compose Part II, they do not claim to cover all the problems raised by the Alexander-story; they only deal with matters on which I thought I had something to say which needed saying. Two or three are on subjects on which I wrote long ago, but, except for the use made of a recent article of mine in Appendix 24, all these are new studies. As I realise that some readers may desire to read some particular section apart from the rest, I have not hesitated to repeat points made in other sections if they are relevant to the matter under discussion; this has primarily been done for the convenience of readers, but also the same fact in a different setting may disclose a new facet. Putting aside the military section, the other studies do nevertheless form a certain unity; they build up Alexander's character by (I hope) clothing in flesh and blood various things which could only be glanced at in the narrative, and do thus lead up to the most important thing about him, which is considered in Appendix 25. That Appendix naturally draws upon former writings of mine, besides other relevant matter; but I hope the subdivisions will make for clarity in a difficult subject, and I have been able in subdivision VI to go a good deal farther than I have previously done.

The map of Alexander's route to illustrate the narrative in Volume I has been included in this volume also, for, though it does not contain all the places mentioned, its inclusion may save a reader trouble. There are some Addenda at the end of this volume, and there is one other thing to be said. It has been my lot, in Part I, to differ very considerably from Dr F. Jacoby; I should like therefore to acknowledge, once for all, the great amount of help and lightening of labour which I have derived from his admirable work *Die Fragmente der griechischen Historiker*.

W. W. TARN

MUIRTOWN HOUSE
INVERNESS
September 1947

vii

CONTENTS

ix

Contents

Contents

Appendices 18–21: PERSONAL

Appendices 22–25: THE MAIN PROBLEMS

CONTENTS OF
VOLUME I (*NARRATIVE*)

ABBREVIATIONS

Berve. H. Berve, *Das Alexanderreich*, 2 vols., 1926.

C.A.H. *Cambridge Ancient History.*

Jacoby. F. Jacoby, *Die Fragmente der griechischen Historiker* (*FGrHist*). In progress.

Kornemann. E. Kornemann, *Die Alexandergeschichte des Königs Ptolemaios I von Aegypten*, 1935.

Pliny. C. Plinius Secundus, *Naturalis Historia.*

Rostovtzeff, *Soc. and Econ. Hist.* M. Rostovtzeff, *The Social and Economic History of the Hellenistic World*, 3 vols., 1941.

Susemihl. Fr. Susemihl, *Geschichte der griechischen Literatur in der Alexandrinerzeit*, 2 vols., 1891, 1892.

S.V.F. H. von Arnim, *Stoicorum Veterum Fragmenta*, 3 vols., 1903–5.

Tarn, *Hell. Civ.*² W. W. Tarn, *Hellenistic Civilisation*, 2nd ed., 1930.

Tarn, *Bactria and India.* W. W. Tarn, *The Greeks in Bactria and India*, 1938.

ALEXANDER THE GREAT

SOURCES & STUDIES

*

PART ONE

THE SO-CALLED 'VULGATE' AND ITS SOURCES

*

A. THE PROBLEM

I N writing Hellenistic history, one of the modern historian's most powerful weapons should be source-criticism. It has taken more than one form, though its failures need not be noticed here. Its real business, as I understand it, should be to attempt to find the original source, the beginning, of the statements made by the secondary writer under investigation; and as it is certain that in many cases the original source cannot be found, then at least to attempt to get clear the school or type of thought which such source represented; it may, for example, in the Alexander-story, be of more importance to know that some item originated with the Stoics or with Cassander's friends the Peripatetics or with some group of poets than to know what writer actually started it or through what channels it has been transmitted to us, for in this way one can get at its tendency and evaluate its worth.

This study deals with the three extant writers who have long been classed together as having certain common characteristics and as representing the 'vulgate', viz. Diodorus, book XVII, Curtius, and Justin's Epitome of Trogus (with Trogus' Prologues); they have generally been distinguished as a body from the 'good' tradition, meaning primarily Arrian, though this excessive simplification has often been subject to various qualifications. Arrian will naturally figure largely in some Appendices (Part II), but the question of *his* sources, with one exception, seems in its general lines to be well settled; I take it as certain now that his principal source was Ptolemy and that he only used Aristobulus to supplement Ptolemy; that Ptolemy, who had better opportunities of knowing than most people, was also able to use the *Journal* and other official material; that, though the military part of

I

Arrian comes from him, he wrote a real history of Alexander and not merely a military study; and that Arrian's λόγοι, stories prefaced by the statement 'so they say', are neither from Ptolemy nor from Aristobulus, but may be from anybody, their authority, if any, depending on their source in each particular case. The matter which is not settled, and which will require careful consideration, is what sort of writer Aristobulus was and what is his real place among the Alexander-historians. In the same way, I am not here considering Plutarch's *Life* of Alexander, which belongs neither to the 'good' nor to the 'vulgate' tradition, but stands apart; I am dealing with certain aspects of it in App. 16.

The subject of this study, then, is essentially the three writers I have named—their characteristics, their sources, and the question whether there is, or ever was, such a thing as the so-called vulgate tradition; but the source-problems involved have come to centre primarily on Cleitarchus of Alexandria, and to a certain extent on Arrian's second source, Aristobulus, and in a sense Cleitarchus will be the central figure in what I have to say. The thorny group of questions connected with the vulgate writers was investigated many years ago by that brilliant critic Eduard Schwartz,[1] and the results he reached have dominated nearly all study since (including my own before I looked into the matter properly). When he wrote, it was believed that, generally speaking, Diodorus in each book took one source and copied it; and as he found a few cases in Diodorus XVII of the use of Cleitarchus, whom he regarded as a primary authority, he said that he had no hesitation in taking Diodorus XVII directly back to Cleitarchus.[2] This theme has been well worked up since; its most modern expression is that we can get a pretty good idea of the contents of Cleitarchus' history from the direct excerpt (*das direkte exzerpt*) Diodorus XVII, which with care can be supplemented from Curtius,[3] and that the vulgate is in essence Cleitarchus worked up;[4] indeed it is sometimes called the Cleitarchean vulgate. This is one branch of Schwartz' theory; the other relates to Aristobulus. His work, it is laid down, was not original; he was only a secondary source, and was in no wise independent of the Alexander-Romance (here meaning Cleitarchus); he is nearer to the vulgate than

---

1 Arts. 'Aristobulos' (14), 'Curtius' (31), and 'Diodoros' (38) in PW.
2 'Diodoros' (38) in PW, 683: 'auf Kleitarch direkt zurückzuführen.' He gave a second reason, for which see § F, p. 86.
3 Jacoby, 'Kleitarchos' (2) in PW, 629; repeated *F.Gr. Hist.* BD, p. 484.
4 Jacoby, *F.Gr. Hist.* BD, p. 484: Cleitarchus' book 'beherrscht die vulgata, die im wesentlichen ein immer wieder bearbeiteten K(leitarchos) ist'

to the good tradition, and was a sceptical rationalist, who wrote late and made it his business to explain things away.[1] Through all changes and chances these views have substantially held the field since, whatever else may have happened meanwhile. It has never, for example, been explained why, if this view of Aristobulus be correct and he sometimes copied Cleitarchus, Arrian, a sensible man who knew far more about the Alexander-writers than has been vouchsafed to ourselves, chose Aristobulus as his second source. Few now believe that Diodorus' method of work was what Schwartz supposed, even if there be small agreement as to what it really was. Some, including the chief modern exponent of Schwartz' view, Dr F. Jacoby, have come to doubt whether Cleitarchus did accompany Alexander, i.e. whether he was really a primary source at all. None of this has made any difference, any more than the fact that so little is really known of Cleitarchus himself. To turn from the enormously swollen figure of modern literature to the thirty-six slight fragments which are all that remain of him is to court something of a shock. Naturally I entirely agree with the view that the named fragments of a lost writer are only a starting-point for the study of that writer, seeing that Greek authors all too seldom name their sources. But one's deductions about a lost writer must follow the indications given by the named fragments; it is no use proceeding against or across the direction they indicate; and one trouble with the Cleitarchus fragments is that so few of them point in any recognisable direction at all. Instead of patiently proceeding from this, items from Diodorus XVII have merely been quoted, copiously quoted, as being Cleitarchus himself. Thus a figure called Cleitarchus has been built up from Diodorus XVII, with help from Curtius and others, and been used in its turn to show that Diodorus XVII *is* Cleitarchus.

The time is ripe, and over-ripe, for a fresh detailed examination of the whole subject. I may just indicate the contents of what follows. Section B examines the question whether Cleitarchus is a primary or secondary authority, and § C his date; the answers to both questions largely depend on Greek knowledge of the Caspian and Aral being arranged in the order of its historical development, which has never been attempted and which is done in § B. Section D deals with Aristobulus, and in particular with Cleitarchus' relation to him. Section E attempts to see what can be made of Cleitarchus' book from the named fragments; § E' examines a neglected source, the poetasters contemporary with Alexander. Section F gives a long analysis of Diodorus XVII; in § F' a single chapter is dissected to exhibit, in part, his method

1 'Aristobulos' in PW, 916.

of work. Section G contains a similar analysis of Curtius; § G′ gives the proofs that he knew and used Diodorus XVII. Section H is Trogus-Justin. Probably few people really read this sort of analytical study, for it is wearisome, though (as I see it) it is the only way of approximating to the truth; I have, therefore, in § J given a summary of results, which is rather more than a mere summary.

One general remark. It is impossible to suppose that a source can be found for everything given by our extant writers; for, other things apart, it is known that a considerable number of writers on Alexander must have perished without trace, over and above those whose names, but nothing more, have survived. They were, of course, not all formal historians; every kind of monograph on special points, long or short, good or bad, must have existed; we have the names of one or two,[1] and such writing became a regular feature of Hellenistic literature. I give one or two pieces of evidence. The name, though not the contents, of a monograph on Hephaestion's death has survived.[2] But Arrian (VII, 14, 2 *sqq.*) mentions, without any names, either eight or nine different versions of Alexander's grief for Hephaestion, and for each version he gives a plurality of writers, ἄλλοι—ἄλλοι. Though in any one case a plural of this kind may denote a single writer, this can hardly be so in every one of a number of consecutive cases; the number known to Arrian must have exceeded eight or nine. How does it stand with ourselves? Plutarch (*Alex.* LXXII) gives one of Arrian's versions; Diodorus (XVII, 110, 8) partly agrees with another, but the rest of his account is quite different; Justin (XII, 12, 11) does not agree with any of them, and adds yet another version; Curtius is missing. Here then is a whole mass of writers of whose existence and names we know nothing. To take another instance. Diodorus (XVII, 118, 2) says that many historians (or writers), συγγραφεῖς, did not dare to give the story of Alexander being poisoned for fear of Cassander. He therefore knew of many works dealing with Alexander's death which were written before Cassander's death in 298;[3] we, *perhaps*, know of just one, Ephippus. Add Strabo's remark that the historians of Alexander were very numerous.[4] It seems, therefore, that at every turn we are bound to run up against our own ignorance; we can only do our best with what material we possess.

1 As regards Alexander: Ephippus, περὶ τῆς ᾿Αλεξάνδρου καὶ ῾Ηφαιστίωνος τελευτῆς, Jacoby II, B, no. 126; Strattis, περὶ τῆς ᾿Αλεξάνδρου τελευτῆς, *id.* no. 118; Strattis on the Ephemerides; Amyntas on the work of the bematists. They soon became very numerous.   2 Ephippus (last note).
3 298, not 297; W. S. Ferguson, *Cl. Phil.* XXIV, 1929, p. 1.
4 XI, 5, 4 (505), τοσούτων ὄντων.

4

B. CLEITARCHUS[1] AND ALEXANDER'S EXPEDITION

I WILL consider first whether Cleitarchus accompanied Alexander or not; that is, whether he is a primary or a secondary source. Both views have always had supporters; the most authoritative of recent writers, Dr Jacoby, seems to think he did not, but says that there is no conclusive proof.[2] Proof, however, exists, though not where it has usually been sought; and the same proof will settle, not indeed the date at which Cleitarchus wrote, but a date before which he cannot possibly have written (see § C). To find this proof, one must first get the Caspian question into its proper order; and I mean by this the Caspian question, and not the Oxus problem or the northern trade-route problem,[3] which have nothing to do with the matter in hand. A great deal has been written about the Caspian, much of it of little value; I am not going through this, for no one has even attempted to get our information into its historical order, though that is the only way to understand it, and almost every one has neglected or mistranslated Aristotle,[4] not an author to neglect. What follows should clear up some points in the Alexander-story, apart from Cleitarchus. Two seas, which could also be called lakes, will come in question, a greater one which *we* call the Caspian and a smaller one which *we* call the Aral; but as the name 'Caspian' originally belonged to the Aral, I shall, to avoid confusion, usually call *our* Caspian by its original name, the 'Hyrcanian Sea'.

One or more of the Ionian geographers before Herodotus, who only knew of one lake, had thought it was a gulf of Ocean; Plutarch's statement to this effect is confirmed by the fact that both Herodotus and Aristotle are obviously combating some such theory.[5] There is much force in Gronovius' suggestion, made two centuries ago, that this theory came merely from the water of our Caspian being salt;[6] to this has recently been added, as another cause, the presence of seals.

---

1 I quote the Cleitarchus fragments throughout merely by their number in Jacoby II, no. 137.
2 'Kleitarchos' (2) in PW, XI, 1 (1921), 624.
3 The Oxus problem is a matter for science, Tarn, *Bactria and India*, App. 15; and the trade-route problem is settled, *ib.* App. 14.
4 P. Schnabel, *Berossos*, 1923, pp. 57 *sq.* is an exception.
5 Plut. *Alex.* XLIV. Herodotus' reference to the 'other sea' (*post*). Aristotle (*post*).
6 There is said to be a drinkable belt in the north, due to the inflowing Volga; but no Greek knew anything about the north.

Herodotus too knew of one lake only, which, however, he made too small for the Hyrcanian Sea;[1] he called it ἡ Κασπίη θάλασσα, and said of it ἐστι ἐπ' ἐωυτῆς, i.e. a lake (we shall meet this phrase again), and did not join the 'other sea', i.e. Ocean. But Aristotle, ultimately from Persian information, by whatever channel it reached him,[2] knew of *both* the seas, which he called the Hyrcanian and the Caspian, and said that both were lakes, which had no connection with Ocean: people dwelt all round both of them.[3] As his Hyrcanian Sea is identified with our Caspian by the known position of Hyrcania, his Caspian Sea is the Aral; and it has therefore to be borne in mind that, to Alexander and those about him, the word 'Caspian' did not mean what it means to-day. Aristotle's *Meteorologica* has sometimes been supposed to ante-date Alexander's expedition;[4] it is certain in any case that it was his tutor Aristotle's geography which Alexander had in his head when he started. A somewhat half-hearted attempt has been made to date the *Meteorologica* to the period 335–322 B.C.;[5] but whether it succeeds or not is quite immaterial, for Alexander got his geography, not from the *Meteorologica*, but from Aristotle himself (see App. 22, pp. 368 *sq.*). Consequently, when Alexander reached Hyrcania and saw the Hyr-canian Sea, he expected to find another lake also; and though he never saw the Aral himself, he heard, as we shall see, some things about it. As the knowledge that there were two lakes had died out by or before 284, the two becoming fused into one again, any primary source which knows of, and distinguishes, the two must be contemporary with, or not long after, Alexander.—See Addenda.

1 Herod. I, 203: ἡ δὲ Κασπίη θάλασσά ἐστι ἐπ' ἐωυτῆς, οὐ συμμίσγουσα τῇ ἑτέρῃ θαλάσσῃ, which shows that he was arguing against someone who had said that it was a gulf of Ocean. On the size, see § C, p. 18 n. 2.
2 His Persian information appears again in the *Liber de inundacione Nili*, which gives Ochus' views on the Indus.
3 *Meteor.* II, I, 10. There are seas which do not join one another anywhere. The Red Sea, indeed, has a narrow connection with the sea outside the Pillars, i.e. Ocean, ἡ δὲ Ὑρκανία καὶ Κασπία κεχωρισμέναι τε ταύτης καὶ περιοικούμεναι κύκλῳ, ὥστ' οὐκ ἂν ἐλάνθανον αἱ πηγαί, εἰ κατά τινα τόπον αὐτῶν ἦσαν. He polemicises against the old 'Gulf of Ocean' theory. The plural participles prove that he meant two lakes, not one, though (except Schnabel, p. 5 n. 4 *ante*) those writers who have not omitted Aristotle altogether have carelessly called it one lake; even Jacoby II BD, p. 490, talks of 'den binnensee' and an 'herodoteisch-aristotelische karte'.
4 See W. Capelle, 'Meteorologie' in PW Supp. Bd. VI, 1935, 339. He does not believe it himself.
5 W. Jaeger, *Aristoteles* (Eng. tr. 1934, p. 307). He is as muddled about the Caspian as anybody.

Our earliest document, after Alexander visited Hyrcania, is the Gazetteer, i.e. the list of the satrapies of his Empire, compiled in the last year of his life;[1] the proof of its date, which I gave briefly in 1923, is given in App. 17 in better shape and greater detail. I left it open before whether the document Diodorus gives is the official document or a compilation by Hieronymus made from official material of the year 324–323, but in fact we do not know that it came through Hieronymus at all; Diodorus was quite capable of reproducing a document himself (see § F, p. 87), witness Alexander's so-called Plans, and there is no real doubt that what we have is an official document, with some interpolations by Diodorus himself (see App. 14), an exact parallel to the reproduction by Isidore of Charax of the Parthian survey with comments of his own. The Gazetteer divides the Asiatic empire into two halves by the Taurus-Caucasus chain of mountains, a division which Eratosthenes borrowed later and made the best-known feature of his geography of Asia. It next gives the rivers flowing north and south from these mountains. Those flowing north are said (Diod. XVIII, 5, 3) to fall, some into the Caspian Sea, some into the Euxine, and some into the Arctic Ocean (literally 'the ocean beneath the Bears'). Then, after describing the rivers flowing south, the Gazetteer starts on the northern satrapies (5, 4)—Sogdiana beside (παρά) the river Tanais and Bactriane, and next to these Aria, and then Parthia 'by which there happens to be embraced the Hyrcanian Sea, being by itself'.[2] That is to say, to the compiler of this document the Caspian and Hyrcanian Seas were two different seas, as they were to Aristotle, and the equivalent phrase is used of the Hyrcanian Sea which Herodotus had used of his Caspian, to show that it was a lake and was not connected with any other sea. At the time of Alexander's death, then, the truth was still known. Of the rivers, those that fell into the Caspian (Aral) were the Oxus and Tanais (the lower Syr Daria, see *post*); those falling into the Euxine are the Halys and other rivers of Asia Minor; and the one falling into the Arctic Ocean is probably meant for the middle Syr (Jaxartes), a reminiscence of the time when it was not known whither it went; I shall return to this. One can hardly suppose hearsay of the great Siberian rivers; stories *could* have come to Bactra along the gold route, but it is not known if that route was still functioning in Alexander's day.

A little more information comes from our next document, a fragment

1 Diod. XVIII, 5, 2 to 6, 4. See App. 17.
2 δι' ἧς συμβαίνει περιέχεσθαι τὴν 'Υρκανίαν θάλατταν, οὖσαν καθ' αὑτήν.

7

of the historian and geographer Polycleitus,[1] a member of a well-known family in Larisa. His reference (fr. 10) to the great tortoises in the Ganges shows that he wrote later than Megasthenes;[2] that he was earlier than Patrocles is self-evident (see § C). He *wrote* therefore probably somewhere about 290–285; but his information is much earlier and admits of no doubt that he was with Alexander. For he has left one quite invaluable statement: the Caspian Sea bred snakes and its water was 'nearly sweet', ὑπόγλυκυ;[3] this can only apply to the Aral, or more accurately to that part of it dominated by the inflow of the two great rivers, and the word identifies the Caspian of the Aristotle-Alexander geography with the Aral without any doubt, if any could still persist. When Curtius (VI, 4, 18) and Diodorus (XVII, 75, 3) quoted Polycleitus' statement about the snakes, they added 'and fishes of strange colour'; this also may be from Polycleitus, though Strabo omits it; to-day the fishes in the Aral, in contradistinction from those in our Caspian, are said to be all fresh-water species, but I know nothing about their colour. From the sweetish water Polycleitus argued that his Caspian-Aral *was* a lake, as Aristotle had said. He gave one other fact: a river called Tanais flowed into it. It is improbable that any of Alexander's people ever saw the Aral; whence did Polycleitus get his information? Only one source is possible; it came from Pharasmanes king of Chorasmia (at this time Kwarizm) or someone in his train, when this king visited Alexander at Bactra.[4] Naturally Pharasmanes knew all about the Aral, on which his kingdom lay, and knew that the Oxus and another river, whose name he gave as Tanais, ran into it; Polycleitus, when he wrote, reproduced the statement about the Tanais, as did the Gazetteer when it made 'some rivers' fall into the Aral. There

---

1 Jacoby II, no. 128, fr. 7 = Strab. XI, 7, 4 (509): Πολύκλειτος δὲ καὶ πίστεις προφέρεται περὶ τοῦ λίμνην εἶναι τὴν θάλατταν ταύτην (i.e. τὴν Κασπίαν θάλατταν of three lines earlier), ὄφεις τε γὰρ ἐκτρέφειν καὶ ὑπόγλυκυ εἶναι τὸ ὕδωρ· ὅτι δὲ καὶ οὐχ ἑτέρα τῆς Μαιώτιδός ἐστι τεκμαιρόμενος ἐκ τοῦ τὸν Τάναϊν εἰς αὐτὴν ἐμβάλλειν (here Polycleitus ends). What follows, viz. that the Jaxartes comes down from the same Indian mountains as the Oxus and Ochus, and flows into τὸ Κάσπιον πέλαγος, is Strabo himself, as is shown by the change from 'oratio obliqua' to 'recta', and the use of the name Ochus, unknown to the Alexander-writers; Strabo himself took it from Apollodorus of Artemita, *c.* 100 B.C.; all this from Strabo XI, 7, 3 (509). It is this section which shows that the Ochus was the lower Arius (river of Herat); Alexander never saw the lower river.

2 Not because of the *name* Ganges, but because he made a statement, true or false, about it.

3 Defined, Athen. XIV, 625 A, τὸ μὴ γλυκὺ μὲν ἐγγὺς δὲ τούτου λέγομεν ὑπόγλυκυ.   4 Arr. IV, 15, 4.

is nothing in the Polycleitus fragment about the Hyrcanian Sea, though Pharasmanes must have known of it.

Before going on, I must consider the name Tanais. The Tanais which, Polycleitus was told, entered the Caspian-Aral could only be the Syr Daria; Tanais was therefore the local name of this river in its lower course.[1] But before Pharasmanes came to Bactra, Alexander had already reached, and for a moment crossed, the Syr in its middle course, near Chodjend; for this river he got a name which Ptolemy rendered as Jaxartes and Aristobulus in the fuller form Orexartes (Ar-yaxartes, the river Jaxartes), this being, says Aristobulus, the name given it by the local natives, τῶν ἐπιχωρίων βαρβάρων.[2] Where this Jaxartes went to Alexander's people did not know; here was a great river flowing *northward*, and they thought of the northern ocean, an idea probably preserved, as we have seen, in the Arctic Ocean of the Gazetteer. Later there came Pharasmanes with the information that a great river which he called Tanais flowed into the Aral; Alexander also had some communication with the Sacas across the Jaxartes,[3] and it became evident that this Tanais was the lower Jaxartes; before his death, as the Gazetteer shows, both names were being applied indiscriminately to the whole river. If the Gazetteer and Polycleitus be put together, it can be seen that it became known, during Alexander's lifetime, that both the Oxus and the Syr flowed into the Caspian-Aral; as they did, and do. Later writers, like Strabo and Arrian,[4] repeated that both rivers flowed into the 'Caspian', i.e. the same sea, without understanding what they were repeating; the Syr could never have entered our Caspian unless it ran uphill.

Then Polycleitus ceased recording and began to reason, with unhappy results. He argued (fr. 7) that if the Caspian were a lake of nearly sweet water and a river called Tanais ran into it, it could not be 'other than', ἑτέρα, the Maeotis (Sea of Azov) into which ran a river

---

1 Different names for different stretches of the same river are still common enough and must once have been much commoner.

2 Aristobulus, fr. 25 (I cite the fragments from Jacoby II, no. 139)=Arr. III, 30, 7, where MSS. give Ὀρξάντης; fr. 54=Arr. VII, 16, 3, where they give the well-known man's name Oxyartes; Plut. *Alex.* XLV has Ὀρεξάρτης, the correct form everywhere. Some of the MS. readings of Jaxartes in Pliny VI, 45 give corrupt forms beginning with IR. Ar-yaxartes=river Jaxartes: R. Roesler, *Wien S.B.* LXXIV, p. 256 n. 3, with many parallels. Demodamas later seemingly got another local name, Silis, for some part of the Syr: Pliny VI, 49.

3 Arr. IV, 15, 1 πρέσβεσιν; Curt. VII, 6, 12.

4 Strab. XI, 7, 4 (510), 11, 5 (518); Arr. VII, 16, 3.

9

called Tanais (the Don). It *was* very confusing; but whether he actually meant to identify the two cannot be said.[1] It must be remembered that Polycleitus, like Alexander, never saw the Aral. As far as Hyrcania and the bit of the Hyrcanian Sea which he saw, Alexander had plenty of guidance; he had the Persian roads, itineraries, satrapal boundaries, official documents, etc.[2] and knew where he was, but none of this applied to the Aral;[3] no one knew how far north it might extend, or where the Syr entered it, so Polycleitus was not really as futile as he sounds.[4] The important matter is that Polycleitus identified his and Aristotle's 'Caspian' as the Aral, and knew that the Tanais (Syr) ran into it; i.e he knew the truth. With him, true knowledge ended, to be alluded to again for an instant by Curtius, who in one passage distinguishes the Caspian and the Hyrcanian Seas,[5] and who must have read Polycleitus at first hand.[6]

At the very end of his life, about the time that the Gazetteer was compiled, Alexander sent one Heracleides to build warships and explore the Hyrcanian Sea.[7] Arrian's story comes in the middle of a number of extracts from Aristobulus, and has generally been ascribed to him.[8]

1 Note that Strabo XI, 7, 4 (509) distinguishes Polycleitus from the 'liars' (*post*).
2 On the Persian material cf. M. Rostovtzeff, *Soc. and Econ. Hist.* p. 1034.
3 The Persians had never ruled Chorasmia (Kwarizm); Tarn, *Bactria and India*, App. 11.
4 There is an almost exact parallel near my house. Into the Beauly Firth (Aral) runs a river of which the lower part (once Fraser country) is called the Beauly (Jaxartes), and the upper part (once Chisholm country) is called the Glass (Tanais). Somewhat farther to the north, another and different river Glass (Tanais) runs into the Cromarty Firth (Maeotis). Suppose that, in the illiterate period, a complete stranger from the Mediterranean (Polycleitus), hard put to it for an interpreter, had been trying to get at the lie of the country without seeing it; what are the chances that, confused by the two rivers called Glass, he would have identified the Beauly and Cromarty firths, which are anyhow much alike in character?
5 Curt. VII, 3, 21, the rivers from the Caucasus 'alia in Caspium mare, alia in Hyrcanium et Ponticum decidunt'.
6 He quotes Polycleitus in that strange mix-up, his formal account of our Caspian in VI, 4, 17 *sqq.* on which see § G, p. 104 n. 1. He knew no geography himself. On his possible knowledge of Aristotle's *Meteorologica* through Aristobulus, see *post*.
7 Arr. VII, 16, 1 = Aristobulus, fr. 54.
8 See Kornemann, *Die Alex.-Gesch. d. Ptolemaios I*, p. 166. But Jacoby on Aristobulus, fr. 54 (BD, p. 522), expresses reservations; to Kornemann himself the whole passage is a bad contamination of Ptolemy and Aristobulus. No one has noticed the quotation from Aristotle, or that Arrian is partly speaking in his own person, because no one has ever worked out the Caspian question properly.

The bare facts of the sending of Heracleides, and of Alexander's πόθος to explore the Hyrcanian Sea,[1] doubtless are from Aristobulus; the rest is Arrian's mix-up of the ideas of his own time with what Aristobulus said. Analysis shows this clearly. In Arrian VII, 6, 2 there is only one lake, called Caspian-Hyrcanian, the regular name used by Eratosthenes and the writers who followed him; this is far later than Alexander or Aristobulus. There follows the statement (16, 2) that Alexander wanted to know what sea the Caspian-Hyrcanian Sea was connected with, whether with the Euxine, or whether 'the great sea' (i.e. Ocean) which surrounded India flowed into the Hyrcanian Gulf, as he had found it did into the Persian Gulf. So put, this is much later, and belongs to the period when his speech at the Hyphasis was composed (see App. 15); but what follows shows that it may have contained a kernel of truth. For there follows[2] a quotation from Aristotle's *Meteorologica* (see p. 2 n. 3): Alexander wanted to know this because the beginnings of the Caspian Sea, ἀρχαί (πηγαί in Aristotle), had not yet been found, though many peoples lived there [so far Aristotle] and navigable rivers[3] ran into it, viz. the Oxus from Bactra, greatest of Asiatic rivers except the Indian (see p. 12 n. 1), and the Orexartes[4] through the Scythians [so far Aristobulus]; also the Armenian Araxes and smaller rivers [Arrian's own collection of various λόγοι].

There is much to be said about this passage in Arrian. Though some late writers, who all believed in the 'one lake' of Patrocles and Eratosthenes, called it indiscriminately Hyrcanian, Caspian, or Hyrcanian-Caspian, Arrian does not; he usually calls it Hyrcanian and once Hyrcanian-Caspian, but this is the only time he uses Caspian alone. The reason can only be that Aristobulus had called it Caspian; it was

1 V. Ehrenberg, *Alexander and the Greeks*, 1937, ch. II, has shown that πόθος cannot be used for source-determination.
2 Arr. VII, 16, 3: οὐ γάρ πω ἐξεύρηντο αἱ ἀρχαὶ τῆς Κασπίας θαλάσσης, καίτοι ἐθνῶν ταύτῃ οἰκούντων οὐκ ὀλίγων καὶ ποταμῶν πλοίμων ἐμβαλλόντων εἰς αὐτήν· ἐκ Βάκτρων μὲν Ὦξος, μέγιστος τῶν Ἀσιανῶν ποταμῶν πλήν γε δὴ τῶν Ἰνδῶν, ἐξίησιν ἐς ταύτην τὴν θάλασσαν, διὰ Σκυθῶν δὲ Ὀρεξάρτης (MSS. Ὀξυάρτης)· καὶ τὸν Ἀράξην δὲ τὸν ἐξ Ἀρμενίων κ.τ.λ.
3 Aristobulus' Ὦξος εὔπλους: Strabo XI, 7, 3 (509)=Aristobulus fr. 20, φησὶ δὲ καὶ εὔπλουν εἶναι καὶ οὗτος (Aristobulus) καὶ Ἐρατοσθένης παρὰ Πατροκλέους λαβών. What follows here about the 'northern trade-route' is Eratosthenes alone. Some have made Aristobulus jointly responsible, which is nonsense historically; he is only responsible for the statement that the Oxus was navigable. See generally Tarn, *Bactria and India*, App. 14.
4 The MSS. reading Oxyartes shows clearly that Orexartes, not Jaxartes, is correct here. This was Aristobulus' form, see *ante*, p. 9 n. 2.

Aristobulus who made the reference to Aristotle and who used the term Caspian for the lake which received the two navigable rivers Oxus and Orexartes (Jaxartes); that is, Arrian is using Aristobulus without knowing that, to the latter, 'Caspian' meant something quite different from what it meant to himself and to everyone since Patrocles, or anyhow since Eratosthenes.[1] The point is that Aristobulus, like everyone about Alexander, knew that the Oxus and Syr ran into the Aral; the importance of this will appear later. That to Arrian the term 'Caspian' meant the 'one lake' is shown by his tacking on to Aristobulus' statement some stories (λόγοι) of the Araxes and other rivers which really did run into the Hyrcanian Sea. As to the πόθος Arrian attributes to Alexander, Aristobulus' quotation from Aristotle, who was himself alluding to and refuting those early Ionian geographers who had said that the Hyrcanian Sea was a gulf of Ocean, may show that (in Aristobulus' view) Alexander, who of course knew what Aristotle thought, had by this time become puzzled as to whether, after all, Aristotle might not have been wrong in calling the Hyrcanian and Caspian Seas lakes; it may further show that the kernel of truth in Arrian's story, and the way it should have been put, is that Alexander wanted to find out which was true, Aristotle's 'lakes' or the older 'gulf of Ocean' theory; for nothing at all was known at first hand about the greater part of the Hyrcanian Sea, and Alexander too may have been puzzled by the salt water and the seals, which did not seem right for a lake.

Heracleides' mission has left no trace, and doubtless it was cancelled, like many other things, when Alexander died. The next notice is from Patrocles, who in 284 or 283[2] explored the Hyrcanian Sea for Antiochus I, then ruling the East as joint-king with his father Seleucus. The quotations which Strabo gives from Patrocles, via Eratosthenes, do not enable us to say specifically that he thought, or decided, that there was one lake only and not two; but the whole of his story implies that he did think, or decide, that there was only one, and that the Caspian-Aral was, and always had been, merely a part of the greater Hyrcanian Sea. Probably what led him to this belief was his taking the mouth of

---

1 In the parallel passage about the Oxus in Arrian, III, 29, 2, where he first gives the statement, explicitly from Aristobulus, that the Oxus was the greatest river which 'those with Alexander' saw in Asia except the Indian ones, Arrian has altered the word 'Caspian' (for the lake receiving the Oxus) into his usual 'Hyrcanian', which proves what I have said in the text.
2 For the date, see Tarn, 'Tarmita', *J.H.S.* LX, 1940, p. 93. The fragments of Patrocles have not yet appeared in Jacoby.

the Atrek, seen from the sea, for that of the Oxus;[1] and as the Oxus was known to enter the Caspian-Aral, this to him showed that the latter sea was only part of the Hyrcanian. With Patrocles, then, knowledge of the Aral vanished from the Greek world; and as Eratosthenes, whose geography was canonical for centuries, followed him, it became an article of faith that there was one sea only and that it was, as Patrocles had decided, not a lake but a gulf of Ocean; and in due course the 'sweetish water' of the Aral became transferred to this one lake, making pure nonsense.[2] Henceforth the one sea was indifferently called Caspian, Hyrcanian, or more usually Hyrcanian-Caspian, the two names being treated later as parts of the same sea, though not always the same parts,[3] for the tribe Caspii, if they ever existed, followed the name about; Pliny complains that he had never met such a confusion as the peoples about the Caspian,[4] while Strabo (XI, 4, 2 (502)) cut the knot by saying that the Caspii had ceased to exist.

I can now at last come to Strabo's setting of the Polycleitus fragment (fr. 7) and to Cleitarchus; and here I must premise that Strabo himself had not the faintest idea that there were two lakes or that anyone had ever supposed that there were, and he uses both names indiscriminately

1 Kiessling, 'Hyrkania' in PW, 465, saw this but did not give the proof. Eratosthenes in Strabo XI, 507 makes Patrocles give a measurement along the south coast of the Caspian from the μυχός (mouth of the Kizil-Usen or thereabouts) past the Anariakae, Mardi, and Hyrcanians to the mouth of the Oxus; but Pliny VI, 36 quotes the same passage of Eratosthenes as taking us past the Atiaci, Amardi and Hyrcanians to the mouth of the Zonus. *Praestat lectio difficilior*. Zonus cannot be a corruption of Oxus, so Eratosthenes had *both* names, and what Patrocles wrote was 'to the mouth of the Zonus, which is the (native name for the) lower Oxus', it being in fact the lost name of the Atrek. That Patrocles' list of the peoples he passed ends with the Hyrcanians confirms this; for if his river had lain farther north he must have mentioned the well-known Dahae, who had been in Xerxes' empire and had supplied troops to Alexander.

2 Curtius VI, 4, 18, 'mare Caspium dulcius ceteris, and grows huge serpents and fishes of strange colour...'. Some think the Maeotis falls into it, adducing the water, 'quod dulcior sit quam cetera maria' (all this from Polycleitus). It proves that Polycleitus did use the name Caspian (p. 8 n. 1 *ante*), for Curtius continues: 'Some call the sea Caspian, some Hyrcanian.' Pliny VI, 51: Alexander said the water of the sea (the 'one lake') was sweet. Plutarch *Alex.* XLIV, Alexander in Hyrcania saw the Hyrcanian Sea was γλυκύτερον τῆς ἄλλης θαλάσσης. Pliny VI, 51, Varro says Pompey was told the same. (Naturally: all Pompey got was the Greek geographers, see Tarn, *Bactria and India*, App. 14.)

3 Compare Pliny VI, 36 with Mela III, 5.

4 Pliny VI, 51: 'nec in alia parte maior auctorum inconstantia.'

unless he be quoting. He begins by saying that many lies had been imagined about the Hyrcanian Sea for the honour and glory of Alexander.[1] He continues that everyone knows that Europe and Asia are divided by the river Tanais (i.e. the Don) and that there is a great tract (πολὺ μέρος) of Asia between the Hyrcanian Sea and the Tanais-Don which was never conquered by the Macedonians (this is true); nevertheless, the liars brought together into one the Maeotis lake (Sea of Azov) which receives the Tanais-Don and the Caspian Sea, saying that the latter was a lake and the two were connected, each being part of the other. But Polycleitus[2]—and here follows Polycleitus' statement as given above, p. 8 n. 1; the word 'But' shows that Strabo is distinguishing Polycleitus from the liars. As to what Polycleitus meant by the 'Caspian' Strabo had not the least idea; to him, the Oxus and Jaxartes both entered the 'one sea' of his geography, compounded of the Hyrcanian and Caspian Seas. Strabo then, having said that Polycleitus' Tanais was the Jaxartes, returns to the liars; *they* named the Jaxartes Tanais from the Tanais-Don (this is untrue, for we have seen that part of the Syr *was* called Tanais), and said that Polycleitus' Tanais *was* the Tanais-Don;[3] and they added, as proof of this, that the Scythians beyond Polycleitus' Tanais had arrows of fir (ἐλάτη), a proof that across that river was Europe, for there were no firs in inner and eastern Asia. This *was* a lie, and no one who had been with Alexander could have told it; for, apart from the fir-trees so plentiful in N.W. India,[4] he had found firs enough near Chorienes' stronghold in Sogdiana.[5]

Who now were Strabo's 'liars'? He tells us himself in another place. Their principal lie had been to bring the Sea of Azov and the Hyrcanian-Caspian Sea close together, so as to get rid of the huge district between them which Alexander had neither seen nor conquered. Strabo describes

1 Strabo XI, 7, 4 (509): προσεδοξάσθη δὲ καὶ περὶ τῆς θαλάττης ταύτης (the Hyrcanian, i.e. the 'one sea') πολλὰ ψευδῆ διὰ τὴν 'Αλεξάνδρου φιλοτιμίαν.

2 Strabo *ib*. εἰς ἓν συνῆγον τήν τε Μαιῶτιν λίμνην τὴν δεχομένην τὸν Τάναϊν καὶ τὴν Κασπίαν θάλατταν, λίμνην καὶ ταύτην καλοῦντες καὶ συντετρῆσθαι φάσκοντες πρὸς ἀλλήλας ἀμφοτέρας, ἑκατέραν δὲ εἶναι μέρος τῆς ἑτέρας. Πολύκλειτος δὲ κ.τ.λ. as on p. 8 n. 1.

3 Strabo *ib*. (510): τοῦτον (the Jaxartes) οὖν ὠνόμασαν Τάναϊν, καὶ προσέθεσάν γε τούτῳ πίστιν ὡς εἴη Τάναϊς ὃν εἴρηκεν ὁ Πολύκλειτος. The πίστις is the fir-trees.

4 Strabo XI, 7, 2 (509)=Aristobulus, fr. 19, τὴν 'Ινδικὴν πληθύειν τούτοις, i.e. πεύκη, ἐλάτη, πίτυς; so Aristobulus in Strabo XV, 1, 29 (698), Alexander's fleet on the Jhelum built of ἐλάτη (principally), πεύκη, κέδρος (on this being Aristobulus see § D, p. 40 n. 6). Eratosthenes repeated this, Strabo XI, 7, 4 (510).   5 Arr. IV, 21, 3, ἐλάτας, many and very tall.

this district elsewhere,[1] in connection with the Tanais-Don, and says it is a sort of isthmus (χερρονησίζοντα), bounded west by the Tanais-Don, the Maeotis (Sea of Azov) and the Black Sea coast as far as Colchis, north by Ocean, east by the Caspian Sea and south by a line from the mouth of the Cyrus to Colchis; the isthmus is 3,000 stades across from the Black Sea to the Caspian, and those who contract it, συναγαγόντες, *to the extent that Cleitarchus does*, saying that it is flooded (ἐπίκλυστον) from either sea, are simply not worth a mention. Strabo's liar-in-chief, therefore, is Cleitarchus, though the plural may include any other writers known to Strabo who followed his statement about the isthmus;[2] and this colossal ignorance of the geography is definite proof that he was not with Alexander in Hyrcania, for the humblest soldier in the army knew at least one thing, that since leaving Asia Minor his feet had marched a very long way indeed. A second proof, equally cogent, that Cleitarchus was never in Hyrcania and had not accompanied the army thither from Asia Minor will be found in App. 19. Again, Cleitarchus on the fir-trees, noticed above, is conclusive proof that he was not with Alexander either in Sogdiana or in Northern India; and his identification of the warlike Iranian Oreitae with the primitive stone-age Fisheaters of the Makran coast shows that he was not with Alexander on his return from India.[3]

Cleitarchus then was not with Alexander in Hyrcania, in Sogdiana, in Northern India, or in Gedrosia;[4] that is, he was a secondary writer who did not accompany Alexander's expedition.

1 Strabo XI, 1, 5 (491) = Cleitarchus, fr. 13.
2 [Arist.] περὶ κόσμου πρὸς 'Αλέξανδρον, 393 b, l. 25, a very narrow isthmus separates the Hyrcanian and Pontic Seas (the date is not before the first century B.C., as part of the western Mediterranean is called τὸν Γαλατικὸν κόλπον). Curtius VI, 4, 17, on the left (of the Caspian), looking up from Hyrcania, are the Mosyni and Chalybes (of Asia Minor); VII, 4, 27, Bactria swept by wind from the Black Sea; VII, 3, 3, Arachosia on the Black Sea. No one else, I think; and Strabo could hardly have known Curtius.
3 Pliny VII, 30 = Cleitarchus fr. 27; repeated Pliny VI, 95, Ichthyophagos Oritas. There can be no real doubt that the confusion of the relative positions of the Arabitae or Arbies, the Gedrosi, and the Oreitae, which occurs in Curtius IX, 10, 5 *sqq.*, Diod. XVII, 104, 4 to 105, 3, Pliny VI, 95, also goes back to Cleitarchus.
4 I am not using Schnabel's argument that Cleitarchus had never seen Babylon (see § C, p. 20 n. 1), though it is a probable one.

C. THE DATE OF CLEITARCHUS

THERE has long been a question as to whether Cleitarchus wrote in the fourth century or whether he was away down in the third; the very little recorded of his personal relationships is too vague and conjectural to give any help. Everything that can possibly be said for an early date will be found summed up in Dr Jacoby's article,[1] which puts him about 300 B.C.; the evidence for a later date has never been put satisfactorily, and has chiefly consisted of matter and arguments which cannot be supported. As there exists one quite conclusive piece of evidence for a date before which Cleitarchus cannot have written, I will take that first. It depends again on a right understanding of the Greek evidence about the Caspian, and is indeed the principal reason why I have treated that matter so minutely; we have had a great deal too much mere opinion. I must now go back to Patrocles' exploration of the Caspian, which I began in § B.

Patrocles gives the distance which he sailed (or rowed) northward along the west coast of the Hyrcanian Sea from the mouth of the Kizil-Usen to the country of the Albanians and Cadusians as 5,400 stades (Strabo XI, 6, 1 (507)); and it is certain enough that, like other maritime explorers of the time, he used the Greek and not the short Macedonian (bematists') stade.[2] On the usual rough reckoning of 8 Greek stades to an English mile he therefore went some 675 miles northward, on his reckoning. But the total length of the sea to the στόμα or mouth, that is, the connection he supposed with Ocean, which he took to be the most northerly point, he made 6,000 stades,[3] 750 miles. The actual greatest length of our Caspian is 760 miles as the crow flies; but Patrocles was not as near to this measurement as he sounds, for, of course, he coasted. Still, on his reckoning, he was only 600 stades, 75 miles, from the στόμα when he turned back; he must have estimated

1 'Kleitarchos' in PW, to which he usually refers back in *F.Gr. Hist.*
2 Anaxicrates, in Alexander's service, made the length of the Red Sea, from Aelana, at the head of the Gulf of Akaba, 14,000 stades (Strabo XVI, 4, 2 (767); Tarn, *J.E.A.* XV, 1929, p. 13) which, if the bematists' stade be taken, is curiously close to the modern distance to Bab-el-Mandeb as the crow flies. But he coasted, of course, and also went far beyond Bab-el-Mandeb, though it is not said to what point he measured; so he must have used Greek stades. Ariston, in the service of Ptolemy II, made the distance greater (Strabo *ib.* εἴρηται δὲ ἐπὶ πλέον, from Eratosthenes), for he was exploring every inlet; Greek stades are not here in doubt. (See Tarn *ib.* on these voyages.) Whatever method of logging distances at sea Greeks had, all ships must have used the same.   3 Strabo II, 1, 17 (74).

the last 600 stades from native information. Even allowing for coasting, then, he got quite far enough to hear of the Volga mouth; what sort of interpreting he got among these northern tribes, and what sort of muddle he made of it, hardly bear thinking about. But he probably thought when he started that, on the analogy of everything he knew, he *might* find a connection with the outer sea, so he naturally found one; confused hearsay about the Volga would best account for some of the later descriptions of the στόμα, for all say it was a long and narrow strait, and Mela adds 'like a river'.[1] But the point I want to make is this. Patrocles was the only Greek who is recorded to have made a voyage on our Caspian; Eratosthenes knew no periplus of it but his;[2] nothing more, as we saw, had become known between Alexander's visit and his. He was the solitary expert on our Caspian; when Pompey wanted to know about a trade-route, he was given Patrocles' report to Antiochus I, for nothing more was known.[3] And Patrocles really had got so far to the north, which was totally unknown to Alexander and those about him, that he was justified in using native information to make an estimate of the size (length) of the sea; and the estimate he made was this: 'practically equal in size to the Black Sea'.[4] But Cleitarchus

1 Strabo XI, 6, 1 (507); Pliny VI, 38; Mela III, 5, who adds 'quasi fluvius'. The entrances Patrocles knew, or might have known, to other inland seas were all narrow—Dardanelles, Bosporus, Straits of Kertch, of Ormuz, of Bab-el-Mandeb. That his *stoma* lay in the extreme north is certain from Strabo II, 74 and 119, and XI, 507; nothing could be said about the tribes on either side but the vague term 'Scythians'. Patrocles' strait is therefore not to be confused with the second εἴσπλους given by Strabo. For after describing Patrocles' strait (XI, 507) he says (508) that one cannot always credit the old writers or most of the Alexander-writers; much more trustworthy are the later historians of Parthia, who had discovered and seen more (he means his regular source, Apollodorus of Artemita, see Tarn, *Bactria and India*, p. 44); 'therefore', and he goes on to describe another εἴσπλους, on the left of which, as you enter the Caspian, you pass the Dahae, now surnamed Parni; south of them is desert, and then Hyrcania. This is something quite different, and is the much discussed channel entering the Caspian at Balkan Bay; what it was, and whether it existed, are matters for science. Later references to this channel are Curtius VI, 4, 18, it is *intermittent*, and Pliny VI, 38, Scythians go to and fro across it. I need not discuss it here; but as it has always been confused, both by Roman and modern writers (including myself in 1901), with Patrocles' strait, I am putting the distinction on record.
2 Strabo XI, 6, 1 (507), φησὶ δ' Ἐρατοσθένης τὸν ὑπὸ τῶν Ἑλλήνων γνωριζόμενον περίπλουν κ.τ.λ. Note the definite article.
3 Tarn, *Bactria and India*, pp. 489 *sq.*
4 Strabo XI, 7, 1 (508), Πατροκλῆς ὃς καὶ πάρισον ἡγεῖται τὸ πέλαγος τοῦτο τῷ Ποντικῷ.

said the same thing: 'not smaller in size than the Black Sea'.[1] No two men could have made that identical statement and comparison independently. But, as we have seen, Cleitarchus was not with Alexander's expedition at any point, never even saw the Hyrcanian Sea, and was totally ignorant of the geography of all that part of Asia; he could not even have made the wildest guess at the size of that sea. Neither, for that matter, could Alexander or any of those with him; all they ever knew was part of the south coast. No one at all, since any Greek first saw the Hyrcanian Sea, could have made a guess, let alone a very good guess, at its size before Patrocles; it is curious how most modern writers have managed to slide over this elementary fact. Cleitarchus then, beyond any shadow of doubt, is quoting Patrocles. And this also happens to be common sense; for the expert does not take his facts from the romantic writer, but vice versa.

Certainly, long before Alexander, somebody *had* made a guess, a very bad one, at the size of the Hyrcanian Sea, which Herodotus recorded; and I suppose I must point out that Cleitarchus could not have taken his comparison from Herodotus, even if he knew that much neglected author, which is unlikely. Herodotus I, 203, or his source, gave the length of the Hyrcanian Sea as 15 days' journey for a 'ship using oars', and the breadth 8 days'. No one has any idea what this conventional expression means, or whether the ship intended were a trireme, a pentekontor (slower), or even something slower still, but it is clear that it made the sea far too small; the outside figure possible on his reckoning—and it is certainly too high—would give some 495 by 264 English miles[2] (it is really about 760 by 400). As in addition he enormously exaggerated the size of the Black Sea, making it some 1,387 by 412 miles[3] (it is really about 700 by 400), it is clear that no

1 Pliny VI, 36 = Cleitarchus fr. 12: 'non minus hoc esse quam Pontum Euxinum Cleitarchus putat.' Jacoby rightly emphasises that the rest of the passage, as Pliny says, is Eratosthenes.

2 W. Kroll, 'Schifffahrt' in PW 411, tried to estimate the length of such a day's journey from Herod. II, 11, the Red Sea is 40 days' journey long for a ship using oars; but no one will suppose that Herodotus knew the actual length of the Red Sea. If, however, he did, the day's journey would be about 33 miles, say 8 hours rowing at 4 m.p.h., which is too much; a fleet of triremes on passage only averaged some 2 m.p.h. (instances, Tarn, *C.R.* XXIII, 1909, p. 184), and Herodotus' expression may not even mean triremes. Kroll's figures, as he says, relate to short special efforts, but there is nothing better to be had. But even if one takes 33 miles a day, as I have done in the text for illustration, Herodotus' Hyrcanian Sea is still too short by one-third. Obviously nothing was really known about it.

3 Herod. IV, 86: 11,100 stades in length.

one could derive from Herodotus the statement that the two seas were much of a size, as in fact they are.

Cleitarchus therefore wrote later than Patrocles. There has never been much doubt about Patrocles' date; and it is now certain that his time as Seleucid general in Bactria-Sogdiana lies between 285, when he was in Syria, and 280 B.C., when he was back in Asia Minor.[1] I have to ascertain the *earliest* moment at which he could have written, not the most probable one. He could perhaps have explored the Hyrcanian Sea in the summer of 284; but his first year in his new and important post is so unlikely that 283, or even 282, must be the year. He then had to make a report[2] to Antiochus I on the trade-route question, which no doubt had to be done promptly, i.e. in the succeeding winter; finally he had to write his book. He may not, of course, have written it till many years later; many men of affairs in this age, like Ptolemy I and Hieronymus, did not write till life's active work was over. Some have supposed that he must have written by 280, because they believe that he was killed in Bithynia that year, but that is quite unfounded; Memnon's text, as every one admits, *says* that the man killed was his lieutenant Hermogenes, and the name has been altered to Patrocles on the ground that the latter was so important that he must have been heard of later, if alive, and he is not; but so little information remains about the reign of Antiochus I that the argument is worthless. Patrocles may well have written years after 280; but let us suppose that he wrote at the first possible moment, say 282, unlikely as it is. The book then had to get into circulation, which took far longer than to-day. No doubt the Alexandrian library, where Cleitarchus of Alexandria presumably worked, would get a new book as quickly as any one, but, even so, the hostility and perpetual wars between Egypt and the Seleucid Empire (they were at war in 280 and 279) must often have imposed a considerable time-lag on books coming from the Seleucid sphere. Certainly, taking everything at the very quickest, Cleitarchus would have had every sort of luck had he read Patrocles in 281; undoubtedly it was years later. However, I will take 281; and that enables us to say with absolute certainty that Cleitarchus cannot have written *before* 280, which is the thing that matters. To suppose that he could have written before Ptolemy I, who *died* in 283–282, is utterly out of the question.

Some of the arguments which have been used for a late date for Cleitarchus, like the Galatian embassy to Alexander or the time at which Ptolemy I got the name Soter, are worthless; and I need not

1 On this see Tarn, 'Tarmita', *J.H.S.* LX, 1940, p. 93.
2 On this report see Tarn, *Bactria and India*, App. 14.

consider the difficult question whether Cleitarchus used Berossus.[1] But there are two other points worth notice, the relation of Cleitarchus' date to those of Timaeus and Hegesias.

(1) Timaeus. Cleitarchus fr. 7 shows that he took a date from Timaeus, but the date must have come early in Timaeus' vast work. Again, in fr. 36 (= Suidas, ἔχετον), Suidas, to illustrate the use of ἔχετον as a dual form, quotes some unknown writer as saying λέγετον τοῦτο Τίμαιος καὶ Ἀναξιμένης, ἔχετον δὲ καὶ Κλείταρχον αὐτοῖς νοοῦντα ἐς μίαν καὶ τὴν αὐτήν, 'Timaeus and Anaximenes say this, and they have Cleitarchus agreeing with them'. (Anaximenes belongs to an earlier period.) To the writer, then, Timaeus was earlier than Cleitarchus, or he must have written 'Cleitarchus and Anaximenes say this, and they have Timaeus agreeing with them'. But what was the meaning of a statement, or an implication, that writer A was earlier than writer B? We rarely know. It could mean that A was dead before B appeared; or that A's book in question was published before B's book; or that A attained 40 (his *floruit*) somewhat before B, who therefore greatly overlapped him. All that these two fragments *necessarily* show is that Timaeus had published his early books before Cleitarchus wrote. Timaeus probably fled to Athens in 312, and according to Polybius finished his book in the Olympiad 264–260. If he published his book in sections as each was completed, it obviously does not bear upon Cleitarchus' date; if he published it as a whole in 264–260, then Cleitarchus cannot have written before *c.* 260, as Niese supposed on other and untenable grounds. And which Timaeus did we do not know.

(2) Hegesias. Philodemus[2] gives a list of authors who used metaphors in a certain way; it runs Alcidamas, Hegesias, Cleitarchus of Alexandria, Demetrius (breaks off), and Jacoby notes that Philodemus, whose rule is to give such lists in chronological order, has for once broken his rule and reversed the positions of Hegesias and Cleitarchus.[3]

1 P. Schnabel, *Berossos*, 1923, ch. III (this chapter had previously been published as a separate study); this would put Cleitarchus after 293. Jacoby, 'Kleitarchos' in PW, said Schnabel was wrong; this apparently frightened him, and in a note at the end of his book he withdrew what he had said. But what Jacoby did say (*ib.* 653), very fairly, was that Schnabel was wrong 'so lange als der oben gegebene Ansatz K.'s (Kleitarchos') auf gegen 300 nicht widerlegt ist'. As nobody, in view of the Patrocles fragment, can ever maintain a date of *c.* 300 for Cleitarchus again (I do not mean that somebody may not try to), Schnabel's argument can now be treated on its merits. But, though probably correct, it is complicated, and I do not need it.
2 See 'Kleitarchos', T. 12 in Jacoby, no. 137.
3 'Kleitarchos' in PW, 622.

This is not a scientific explanation; the list means what it says, that Hegesias was earlier than Cleitarchus, whatever 'earlier' may mean. Hegesias, says Cicero, wanted to imitate Charisius;[1] it was an acute observation of Susemihl's that Charisius was not important enough for any one to want to imitate him long after his death,[2] and that Hegesias must therefore have been a younger contemporary of his. Cicero makes Charisius a contemporary of Demochares,[3] whose public life lasted from 307 to 271, the most important part being from 288 onwards. It would seem on this that, however much we allow for Hegesias overlapping Charisius and Cleitarchus overlapping Hegesias, we get a definite possibility, though no more, that Cleitarchus cannot have written much before c. 260.

To sum up. Cleitarchus cannot have written *before* 280, and to reach even that year strains the evidence; and we have to allow for a possibility that may take us to c. 260. The right way to put it, evidently, is that he probably wrote in the decade 280–270, with the decade 270–260 possible.

So far so good. But it is advisable to consider the alleged evidence for an early date for Cleitarchus, which has been put forward with such unbounded, though unfounded, assurance. Everything will be found collected and discussed in Jacoby's article 'Kleitarchos' in PW, to which he refers back in his *F.Gr. Hist.* I have been through this article most carefully several times, and there are three points, and three only, with regard to Cleitarchus' date which I must notice. One is Schwartz' belief, which Jacoby, like many others, has adopted, that the succession of Alexander-historians was Cleitarchus—Aristobulus—Ptolemy; it has already been shown that Cleitarchus—Ptolemy is impossible, but the question of Aristobulus must be deferred to § D. The other two points, discussion of which (though so much has been written) has never been satisfying, are the story of the Roman embassy in Pliny III, 57, and the story of Ptolemy saving Alexander's life at the Malli town. Of the former, especially, Jacoby says that it is conclusive that Cleitarchus was earlier than Theophrastus,[4] and that that settles the matter.

(1) Cleitarchus fr. 31 = Pliny III, 57; I give Pliny's text in a note[5]

---

1 Cicero, *Brutus*, 83, 286.
2 Susemihl, II, p. 464 n. 40.
3 Cicero *ib.*   4 'Kleitarchos' in PW, 623.
5 Circeii once an island. 'Mirum est quod hac de re tradere hominum notitiae possumus. Theophrastus, qui primus externorum aliqua de Romanis diligentius scripsit (nam Theopompus, ante quem nemo men-

and must take it as read. Pliny, when merely copying out his notes, is one of the most elliptical of authors; he never uses a word more than he can help. The sentence in question is framed on the antithesis *diligentius—fama*, careful investigation[1] contrasted with the adoption of mere reports; and what Pliny says is this. Circeii, now standing on a plain, was once an island. 'It is astonishing what about this fact we are able to hand down to human knowledge. Theophrastus, the first Greek to write anything about the Romans from careful investigation (Theopompus, before whom nobody mentioned them, merely [following a *fama*, a report] said that the city had been captured by Gauls; Cleitarchus, the next after him [to mention Romans], only said [following a *fama*] that an embassy had been sent [by them] to Alexander, though Cleitarchus already had something more than *fama* to go on), even gave the measurement of the island of Circeii as 80 stades round', etc. There are two remarks to be made about this translation. When Pliny says that Cleitarchus was *already* giving something more than *fama*, he implies that Theopompus, whom he makes Cleitarchus' predecessor, gave a *fama* only, and that Cleitarchus too gave a *fama*, but that in his case he had something more than *fama* to go on. Again, Cleitarchus is only put next to Theopompus in the category *fama*; he is in no way connected with Theophrastus in the category *diligentius*; and the passage has no bearing at all on his date in relation to the date of Theophrastus. (On Pliny's text see also Addenda.)

So far Pliny's actual wording; we must now turn to the more important matter, the substance of his statement, and see what business he had, if any, to bring in Cleitarchus at all in this connection. Pliny, of course, can make very bad mistakes when he chooses; I need only instance his list of inventors, the extraordinary list of peoples which I had to investigate elsewhere,[2] the yarns about the circumnavigation of Europe-Asia in II, 67 (167–170). But to show that he makes bad mistakes does not prove that he made one here. Again, some of his statements in this passage are at best dubious; in the whole voluminous list of Theophrastus' writings it is impossible to find any title which even suggests an investigation connected with Rome, and in fact Pliny is contradicted flatly by the earlier author Dionysius of Halicarnassus,

tionem habuit, urbem dumtaxat a Gallis captam dixit, Cleitarchus ab eo proximus legationem tantum ad Alexandrum missam, hic iam plus quam e fama), Circeiorum insulae et mensuram posuit stadia octoginta', etc.

1 Pliny uses *diligentia* to mean historical investigation; e.g. VI, 59, 'non tamen est diligentiae locus, adeo diversa et incredibilia traduntur'.
2 Tarn, *Bactria and India*, p. 285.

who says that Hieronymus of Cardia was the first, so far as he knew, to give even a brief account of Roman ἀρχαιολογία, and Timaeus the second;[1] and Pliny may be wrong about Theopompus being the first to mention the taking of Rome by the Gauls, for both Heracleides Ponticus and Aristotle mentioned it[2] (though the former in strange guise), and we cannot decide the question of priority of date. But even if he made a mistake about Theophrastus or Theopompus, it would not prove that he was making one about Cleitarchus. Some have believed that he did, and that Cleitarchus' name is a mistake, two reasons being given. One is that Diodorus XVII does not give the Roman embassy among those he does give, and Diodorus XVII *is* Cleitarchus; the other is that Arrian names two writers, Aristos and Asclepiades, as giving the Roman embassy and does *not* name Cleitarchus; but the second reason is indeterminate and the first invalid, for, as we shall see (§ F), Diodorus XVII is not Cleitarchus. We must cut all this out for the present, and start afresh on a consideration of the Roman embassy.

It is certain that Rome never did send an embassy to Alexander; hardly any competent scholar now believes that she did. Every embassy had to be recorded in the *Journal* as a matter of course. Ptolemy gave, from the *Journal*, a list of the genuine embassies sent to Babylon, which included three from Italy (Bruttians, Lucanians, Etruscans), but he did not (Arrian says) give one from Rome.[3] He could not have omitted it from his list had he found it, so it was not in the *Journal*; that is, no such embassy was sent. Arrian begins with a list of the genuine embassies sent to Babylon. He continues with a number of others, not including Rome, which were alleged to have been sent (λέγεται), and adds that people say (λέγουσιν) that these envoys asked Alexander to settle their differences, so that he appeared to himself and to those about him to be ruler of the whole earth and the sea, γῆς τε ἁπάσης καὶ θαλάσσης κύριον (no embassy came from the sea). But (Arrian continues) Aristos and Asclepiades[4] say that the Romans sent an embassy also, and that Alexander was struck by the bearing of the

---

1 *Ant. Rom.* I, 5, 8 = Jacoby II, no. 154 (Hieronymos), fr. 13. Had Pliny continued the category *diligentius*, Hieronymus must anyhow have come next.
2 Plut. *Camillus*, XXII.
3 This and the following stories are Arr. VII, 15, 4–6.
4 Asclepiades is never mentioned elsewhere. Aristos is earlier than Strabo; fragments in Jacoby II, no. 143, p. 812, who rightly declines to identify him with the minister of Antiochus II, an identification for which no shred of evidence exists.

envoys and prophesied something of the future greatness of Rome, τι τῆς ἐσομένης ἐς τὸ ἔπειτα δυνάμεως μαντεύσασθαι. The story of the embassy cannot be separated from Alexander's prophecy, which is an essential part of it; I do not mean that the prophecy proves that there was no such embassy—that is already proved—but that, when its wording is considered, it shows that the story of the embassy is a very late one. What then exactly, in the story, did Alexander prophesy? Obviously the words given by Arrian in his introductory λόγος: Rome would be ruler of land and sea.

We now know where we are. It is the famous prophecy in the *Alexandra* of Pseudo-Lycophron that Rome would have γῆς καὶ θαλάσσης σκῆπτρα καὶ μοναρχίαν, sole rule over land and sea, 'sea' meaning the Mediterranean.[1] As no such prophecy, as regards the sea, could have been made until Rome had settled with Carthage (202 B.C.), and, as regards the land, till she had tried conclusions with Macedonia (Cynoscephalae, 197 B.C.), there can, to my mind, be no doubt that the *Alexandra* is later than 197 B.C. (I fully accept 196 B.C. as its date)[2] and that the prophecy attributed to Alexander presupposes, and is later than, the *Alexandra*. But here we have to bear in mind the great silence about Alexander in the second century B.C., and the revival of interest in him in the middle of the first century B.C., the age of Caesar, Pompey, and Crassus, who all (in literature at least) aspired to be new Alexanders. We here get two lines of thought, or invention, at work. The first century B.C. was an age of prophecies; and though doubtless most of those burnt by Augustus were prophecies of Rome's fall, there cannot fail to have been also prophecies *ex eventu* of Rome's greatness, following the lead given in the *Alexandra*; that document can hardly have stood alone, and indeed another prophecy of the sort, Melinno's ode *To Rome*, probably early first century,[3] has survived. That was one line; the other was the line taken by the famous *levissimi* against whom Livy polemicised,[4] the glorification of Alexander as against Rome. To this period belongs the document called Alexander's ὑπομνήματα, his fictitious Plans (see App. 24), designed to show that, had he lived, he would have conquered the whole Mediterranean and had what Rome

1 *Alexandra*, l. 1229. As no embassy came to Alexander from the *sea*, it is obvious that Arrian's phrase about Alexander appearing to be ruler of land *and sea* was not merely a result of the (land) embassies, but was taken from somewhere else. See *post*, and Note at the end of this section.
2 Ziegler's date in PW, art. 'Lykophron' (8), reached after a most thorough investigation. See further the Note at the end of this section.
3 On the date see A. Momigliano, *J.R.S.* XXXII, 1942, p. 54 n. 12.
4 See App. 24, p. 396.

in fact had later, rule over the Mediterranean and its lands; and also the document which gave the fictitious Embassies (see App. 23), designed to show that, even in life, he *appeared* (says Arrian) to be ruler of the Mediterranean and its lands, that is, *appeared* to be in the position which Rome in fact occupied but which he would have had had he lived. Now the story of the Roman embassy was not given in the document[1] which gave the other fictitious embassies, and must therefore be later. In this story Rome is made to honour Alexander with an embassy, but Alexander in his turn follows the line started in the *Alexandra* and prophesies (but *ex eventu*) the coming greatness of Rome; in other words, this, the latest[2] of these first-century inventions, is intended to combine both lines of thought in a sort of reconciliation, that reconciliation of East and West which some men hoped would follow Actium: Rome honours Alexander with an embassy, Alexander in turn honours Rome with a prophecy. Small wonder that, in an age which had 'rule by land and sea' in its mind, the phrase 'terra marique', by land and sea, played such a part in Augustus' story after Actium.[3]

To return to Pliny. If, then, the story of the Roman embassy and Alexander's prophecy was invented in the latter part of the first century B.C., it was not related by Cleitarchus of Alexandria in the earlier part of the third century; consequently Cleitarchus' name has no business in Pliny here at all, and the Pliny passage has no bearing on Cleitarchus' date; the form and the substance of that passage are at one in proving that much. How then did the name get there? Is this merely another of Pliny's unaccountable blunders? I doubt it; I think it can be seen what happened. Arrian ascribes the story to *two* obscure writers, one virtually, one entirely, unknown; both then, presumably, had a common source, and the author of that source, the original inventor, must be presumed to have ascribed his work to Cleitarchus. Nothing was commoner in the later Hellenistic period (and under the early Roman Empire also) than for obscure writers to tack their effusions on to some well-known name of the past;[4] and Pseudo-

1 On this document, which lies behind the accounts in Arrian, Diodorus, and Justin, see App. 23.
2 App. 23, p. 376.
3 The phrase 'terra marique' became especially attached to Octavian after Actium; Horace fixed it instantly (*Epode* IX, 27) and Augustus used it in *Res Gestae* 13 and on the temple at Nicopolis, 'Αρχ. Δελτ. IX, 1924–5, Παραρτ. p. 1; for other references see Momigliano, *op. cit.* p. 53 nn. 44, 45.
4 In the chapter-headings to his vol. II, Susemihl gives 59 names beginning with Pseudo-, including writers of forged letters; there are a few more in vol. I, or scattered about the notes, and new ones can now be added, as

Cleitarchus took in Pliny. That appears to be the only possible explanation of Cleitarchus' name in the Pliny passage in question.

(2) Cleitarchus' story of Ptolemy shielding Alexander at the Malli town is interesting, because it has often been treated as proof positive that Cleitarchus wrote before Ptolemy I, whereas it does show that he wrote after that king's death. Of the untruth of the story there is no doubt, because Arrian (VII, 5, 4 *sqq.*) gives, from the *Journal* through Ptolemy, the official list of the gold crowns bestowed at Susa (gold crowns were too important not to appear in the *Journal*); Peucestas and Leonnatus were crowned first, explicitly for shielding Alexander at the Malli town; then Nearchus and Onesicritus for their services at sea; then Hephaestion, and then the other Bodyguards (which would include Ptolemy).

Cleitarchus' story is given by Curtius[1] and Arrian.[2] Curtius reports Cleitarchus as saying that Ptolemy was present at the battle (at the Malli town). But, he continues, Ptolemy (in his book) has recorded that he was absent, sent on an expedition (note the rhetorical antithesis *adfuisse—afuisse*, which shows that Curtius is merely giving the tenor of what Ptolemy actually wrote). Arrian takes us a little further. All writers agree, he says, that Peucestas was one of the two who shielded Alexander, but there is no agreement about Leonnatus and Abreas. For, he continues, some (i.e. Cleitarchus primarily) wrote (aorist) that it was Ptolemy who went up the ladder with Peucestas and shielded Alexander as he lay, from which he got the name Soter; and yet Ptolemy has written (perfect) that he was not even present at the business, but that he, in command of an army (or expedition), was fighting other battles and against other barbarians. This has been taken to mean that Ptolemy *explicitly* contradicted Cleitarchus' account (*expressis verbis*),[3] but that is not in the Greek (or the Latin either). The words καίτοι ἀναγέγραφεν (perfect) show that it is Arrian

Pseudo-Aristippus, Pseudo-Isidore, Pseudo-Lycophron. Add to these the 13 names of 'Schwindelautoren' in the Plutarchean pseudepigrapha (Jacoby, III A, nos. 284 to 296).

1 IX, 5, 21: 'Ptolemaeum, qui postea regnavit, huic pugnae adfuisse auctor est Cleitarchus et Timagenes. Sed ipse, scilicet gloriae suae non refragatus, afuisse se, missum in expeditionem, memoriae tradidit.'

2 VI, 11, 8: Πτολεμαῖον γὰρ τὸν Λάγου ἔστιν οἳ ἀνέγραψαν ξυναναβῆναί τε Ἀλεξάνδρῳ κατὰ τὴν κλίμακα ὁμοῦ Πευκέστᾳ καὶ ὑπερασπίσαι κειμένον, for which he got the name Soter; καίτοι αὐτὸς Πτολεμαῖος ἀναγέγραφεν οὐδὲ παραγενέσθαι τούτῳ τῷ ἔργῳ· ἀλλὰ στρατιᾶς γὰρ αὐτὸς ἡγούμενος ἄλλας μάχεσθαι μάχας καὶ πρὸς ἄλλους βαρβάρους. It is certain from Curtius that ἔστιν οἳ means primarily Cleitarchus.

3 Jacoby's phrase, 'Kleitarchos' in PW, 625.

himself speaking: Cleitarchus said so-and-so *and yet* Ptolemy has written, i.e. *and yet* it can be read in Ptolemy's book. If anything more be implied in καίτοι, it is that Cleitarchus ought to have known this. What we have, in both Arrian and Curtius, are merely these authors' statements that two discrepant accounts existed, not statements that Ptolemy was contradicting Cleitarchus or any one else. Besides, Ptolemy never explicitly contradicted anybody; things that he believed to be wrong or unfounded he usually just omitted,[1] and his own statements never show that different versions of a thing existed, if they did.

I need not labour this, for every one can read what Ptolemy did say, though it seems to have escaped notice. Arrian (VI, 5, 5–6) gives Ptolemy's account of the Malli campaign. Alexander planned a great drive. Hephaestion with his command was sent down the Chenab 5 days in advance, to catch the enemy driven forward; Ptolemy with his command was to follow Hephaestion at 3 days' interval, to catch any enemy breaking westward across the Chenab; Alexander and Perdiccas with their forces were to cross the desert and round up the Malli from the east; Craterus was to follow down the Chenab to guard against a break back. Hephaestion was to halt when he reached the junction of the Chenab and the Ravi and wait till Alexander, Ptolemy, and Craterus all joined him. The main body of the Malli, however, spoilt the plan by breaking eastward across the Ravi (they were trying to join their allies the Oxydracae), though evidently Ptolemy did have some fighting; it was after driving them back across the Ravi that Alexander got his wound, which compelled his army on the Ravi to halt where it was; the original plan was now incapable of fulfilment, and word must have been sent to Hephaestion and Ptolemy to rejoin Alexander; it was presumably some days before Ptolemy arrived, and doubtless he recorded that fact. His account of the campaign sufficiently showed that he was not, and could not have been, at or near the Malli town when Alexander was wounded; no contradiction of any one who said otherwise was needed.

How has this been turned into a 'proof' that Cleitarchus wrote before Ptolemy I? The argument runs thus: one of them was contradicting the other (a false premise as regards Ptolemy); but Cleitarchus of Alexandria could not have contradicted his own king; therefore Ptolemy is contradicting *him*, which means that he wrote before Ptolemy. I am inclined to agree that Cleitarchus could not have contradicted his king *if* he wrote in that king's lifetime; but this is the point at issue, and it is merely assumed. But if he wrote under Ptolemy II,

1 H. Strasburger, *Ptolemaios und Alexander*, 1934, pp. 50, 55.

as we know he did (there is no getting over the Patrocles fragment), then the argument falls to the ground. For Ptolemy II, who honoured his father so greatly in the *pompe* described by Callixenus, would certainly have had no objection to Cleitarchus saying to him: 'Your great father was too modest about his own exploits. *We* all know that he was the hero of the day, though he omitted the incident from his book.' I am not making this up; it was what Cleitarchus did say, not of course to Ptolemy II but in his history. For readers will have noticed that, so far, I have omitted one clause in Curtius. Curtius says: 'Sed ipse (Ptolemy), *scilicet gloriae suae non refragatus*, afuisse se', etc.— 'of course not gainsaying (or denying) his own renown'. The reason Curtius put these words in can only have been that somebody had said that Ptolemy *was* gainsaying his own renown; and 'somebody' can only be Cleitarchus, whom Curtius is talking about. 'Your great father was too modest' is not myself but Cleitarchus; and Curtius is sarcastically contradicting Cleitarchus,[1] for he knew well enough that neither Ptolemy nor any other Macedonian or Greek was ever modest about his exploits. Witness Ptolemy's own description of his duel with the Indian chief;[2] doubtless it *was* a feat, and Ptolemy does not let you forget it. The principle underlying the 'vote of Themistocles', strange as it may seem in England to-day, was deep-seated in the Greek nature of twenty-three centuries ago.

Cleitarchus then was *not* earlier than Theophrastus (died in the Olympiad 288–284), and did *not* write before Ptolemy I (died 283–282); both these beliefs are baseless. But there still remains one matter to consider: Schwartz' view, so generally adopted since, that Aristobulus was later than, and used, Cleitarchus. If any one had happened to remember that a baboon is not a monkey (see § D), it could have been seen long ago that it was Cleitarchus who used Aristobulus.

Note on *Alexandra*, l. 1229 (see *ante*, p. 24 n. 1)

In a valuable study of the history of the phrase *terra marique*, *J.R.S.* xxxii, 1942, p. 53, Dr A. Momigliano has made it merely a formula, having little relation to facts. I am not too sure about this, and in any case I agree with Prof. F. W. Walbank, *C.Q.* xxxvi, 1942, p. 137, who also has doubts on the subject, that even a traditional formula (it can be traced back to after the siege of Rhodes in 304 B.C. *if Anth. Pal.* vi, 171 is of the date it professes to be) must not be too patently contradicted by the real situation; and as its use by and for Augustus was real enough, formula or no formula, so therefore may any other instance of its use be. Its use for Philip V, between

1 On Curtius' sarcasm see § G, p. 93.   2 Arr. IV, 24, 3 *sq.*

Lade and Cynoscephalae, was doubtless mere flattery; but the contradiction of that flattery by the author of the *Alexandra* some six years later, after Cynoscephalae, was real. Now there have always been scholars who have continued to believe that the *Alexandra* was written, much earlier than this, by the real Lycophron, Menedemus' friend, despite its new use of the old Greek invention of the Romans being Aeneadae, Trojans;[1] and Momigliano, who takes this view, has sought to connect the Alexandra prophecy with Rome's defeat of Pyrrhus *by land* in 274. But the prophecy says that Rome will have γῆς καὶ θαλάσσης σκῆπτρα καὶ μοναρχίαν, 'sole rule' over land *and sea* (i.e. over the Mediterranean at least); and not only is μοναρχία something new, but the sea cannot be left out, formula or no formula. Even in 196 the prophecy about the sea was a pretty long shot, seeing that Rome's μοναρχία over the Mediterranean was not really established till Pompey's time; still, a prophet might have considered it a good bet. But how about 274? I fear that, as regards the sea, I cannot follow Momigliano's version of the facts of the time (pp. 60 *sq.*) and must give my own. When the war with Pyrrhus began, Rome's navy consisted of two duumviral squadrons of ten small ships apiece; she could not face even Tarentum at sea. In her treaty of alliance with Carthage in 279 (Polyb. III, 25, 3–5) the whole of the sea-affair, warships and transports alike, was undertaken exclusively by Carthage; and in 276, in a great naval battle, Carthage destroyed Pyrrhus' Syracusan fleet, which ended Carthage's secular duel with Syracuse and left her sole mistress of the western Mediterranean, with an enormous naval reputation. How is it possible that in or soon after 274, with the great fleet of Carthage in firm control of the western Mediterranean, the still greater fleet of Egypt in control of the eastern, and Rome's sea-power hardly that of a second-class Greek city, somebody should prophesy that Rome would have the sole dominion over the whole Mediterranean? It is not possible. *We* know that a few years later circumstances were to force Rome to become a naval power. No one in 274 knew it.—I fear that, as regards Momigliano's dating, I have still not been convinced by his later study, *C.Q.* XXXIX, 1945, p. 49.

D. ARISTOBULUS AND CLEITARCHUS

STRABO speaks of monkeys in India.[2] In the wood near the Jhelum where Alexander cut timber for building his ships on that river there lived, he says, an enormous number of very large monkeys (κερκοπιθήκων), so that when the Macedonians once saw them on certain bare hills standing upright in rank and facing them, they got the impression of an army and prepared to attack, but Taxiles told them what it was. The latter part of this sentence has nothing to do with

1 On this see Momigliano, *J.R.S.* xxxv, 1945, pp. 99–104.
2 Strabo xv, 1, 29 (699). ἐν δὲ τῇ λεχθείσῃ ὕλῃ καὶ τὸ τῶν κερκοπιθήκων διηγοῦνται πλῆθος ὑπερβάλλον καὶ τὸ μέγεθος ὁμοίως· ὥστε τοὺς Μακεδόνας ποτὲ ἰδόντας ἔν τισιν ἀκρολοφίαις ψιλαῖς ἑστῶτας ἐν τάξει κατὰ μέτωπον

monkeys living in the woods; these were baboons, living in the open. The baboon, once numerous enough in India, is now said to be extinct there; but it is common in South Africa, and the appearance of a military formation adopted by a herd of baboons when expecting an attack is a well-known thing. Strabo then, having attributed the baboons' military formation to monkeys, returns to his monkeys and says they live in trees and are imitative and are caught in two ways. In one, the hunter washes his eyes in a basin of water and then retires, leaving a basin of bird-lime instead of the water; the monkeys wash their eyes in the bird-lime, and are blinded and so caught. In the other, the hunter puts his feet into sacks as if they were shoes and then retires, leaving sacks smeared inside with bird-lime; the monkeys put these on, and so are caught. (Whether monkeys are, or ever were, caught like this I do not know; it is immaterial for what I want.) Strabo's source, then, has mixed up baboons and monkeys and two totally different matters—the military formation of the baboons, who live in the open, and the ways of catching monkeys, who live in trees, through their imitativeness.

Now two writers could not, independently, have made this particular confusion of monkeys and baboons and at exactly the same point in their accounts of monkeys; but Strabo's story is given in a named fragment of Cleitarchus,[1] who never was in India, with the same confusion at the same point, though with certain differences later. Cleitarchus says that in India are races of monkeys, πιθήκων, very big. In mountainous places they are so numerous that Alexander with his army was astounded when he saw a crowd of them, thinking that he was looking at an army drawn up and lying in wait for him; for by some chance the monkeys (πίθηκοι) were standing erect when they appeared to him. These creatures are not caught with nets or hunting dogs; they will dance if they see a man dancing, or will try to play the

πολλούς... στρατοπέδου λαβεῖν φαντασίαν καὶ ὁρμῆσαι μὲν ἐπ' αὐτοὺς ὡς πολεμίους κ.τ.λ. ἡ δὲ θήρα τοῦ ζῴου διττή.—I note for completeness that this passage and that from Cleitarchus which here follows are given on p. 75 of W. C. McDermott, *The Ape in Antiquity*, 1938, but are not examined in any way; he has not noticed the reference to baboons, and is not concerned with sources.

1 Cleitarchus fr. 19 (16) = Aelian, *N.A.* XVII, 25. λέγει δὲ Κλείταρχος πιθήκων ἐν 'Ινδοῖς εἶναι γένη ποικίλα τὴν χρόαν, μεγέθει δὲ μέγιστα. ἐν δὲ τοῖς χωρίοις τοῖς ὀρείοις τοσοῦτον αὐτῶν τὸ πλῆθος εἶναι, ὡς 'Αλέξανδρόν φησι τὸν Φιλίππου καὶ πάνυ καταπλαγῆναι σὺν καὶ τῇι οἰκείαι δυνάμει, οἰόμενον ἀθρόους ἰδόντα στρατιὰν ὁρᾶν συνειλεγμένην καὶ ἐλλοχῶσαν αὐτόν· ὀρθοὶ δὲ ἄρα ἦσαν οἱ πίθηκοι κατὰ τύχην ἡνίκα ἐφάνησαν. θηρῶνται δὲ οὗτοι κ.τ.λ.

flute, and will imitate a man putting his shoes on or smearing his eyes with honey.[1] The confusion of baboons and monkeys is thus rather more complete than in Strabo, and the two stories have fused further. Cleitarchus then gives Strabo's two stories of catching monkeys through their imitativeness, but with differences; the shoes the monkeys put on are made of lead with nooses attached, and the man washes his eyes, not in water, but in honey, bird-lime being then substituted for the honey.[2] That this version and Strabo's are connected, and must both derive from a common source, is conclusively shown by the confusion of baboons with monkeys and by the identical reference to the baboons' military formation; that Cleitarchus' version is later than, and presupposes, Strabo's version, is conclusively shown by the fact that water, which makes sense, is replaced by honey, which makes nonsense (a man washing his eyes in honey would have them closed up), while for sacks bird-limed inside, which also makes sense, are substituted the difficult and expensive leaden shoes with nooses, with no explanation of how the nooses are supposed to work. This is all I need; but the nooses, in fact, belong to another story which follows in Cleitarchus, a story of mirrors and nooses with a rather corrupt text, which is not in Strabo; and Diodorus (XVII, 90, 2–3) has yet another version, based on Cleitarchus but with variations, which omits the baboons, gives Cleitarchus' story of the honey, but makes the monkeys caught by nooses, while in Cleitarchus they are blinded by the mirrors and so caught. I need not follow this story out, as it is immaterial for my purpose; but the nooses of Cleitarchus and Diodorus, which do not appear in Strabo's account and which have nothing to do with the imitativeness of the monkey, were brought in from some other account of how to catch monkeys, and Cleitarchus, who is embellishing Strabo's story for effect, has mixed them up both with the shoes and with the mirror story, which by itself is another example of imitativeness.

Cleitarchus' account, then, is obviously secondary, and, omitting the story of mirrors and nooses tacked on to it, *is* Strabo's account embellished and worsened; it was obviously taken from Strabo's account, that is, from the source which Strabo reproduced, and what we now have to do is to find the source of Strabo's account, which was earlier than, and was used by, Cleitarchus. There is, of course, not the least doubt that Strabo's source was Aristobulus; but as the matter is vital to the problem of the sources of the Alexander-vulgate, I am going

1 εἰ θεάσαιτό τινα ὑπογράφοντα τὼ ὀφθαλμὼ μέλιτι, καὶ τοῦτο δρᾶσαι θέλει.
2 δέλεαρ δὲ αὐτοῖς ὀφθαλμῶν πρόκειται ὑπὲρ (instead of) τοῦ μέλιτος ἰξός.

to analyse this part of Strabo step by step, however tedious it may be.
What Strabo is doing in the earlier part of book XV is giving the story
of Alexander's march across India from Aristobulus, with many
passages interpolated from other writers whom he names; Athenaeus
apart, there is hardly any work of antiquity better documented.[1]

In book XV, after he has finished with mythology and the shape of
India, Strabo gives (691 to 701) Alexander's expedition across India;
and in 702, where he changes sources and Megasthenes becomes the
main one, he names as his sources for 691–701 οἱ μετ' Ἀλεξάνδρου
στρατεύσαντες, which excludes Cleitarchus, whom indeed Strabo
himself hardly ever used (see App. 13, p. 274 n. 4). The beginning,
XV, 1, 17 (691)=fr. 35 in Jacoby, is ascribed to Aristobulus by name,
and contains three name-forms which are therefore all his, as they do
not occur in Ptolemy-Arrian.[2]

They are Hypanis, Hypasii, and Ἀσσακανός (in Ptolemy Ἀσσακηνός,
Arr. IV, 30, 5). Hypanis is Aristobulus' name for the Beas, which in
Ptolemy, and in the Alexander-writers generally (except Diodorus,
see § F, p. 76 n. 2), is Hyphasis, and is most important for identifying
Aristobulus-material.[3] Fr. 35 ends with 1, 19; fr. 36 is part of 1, 21;

1 Jacoby's fragments of Aristobulus, II, no. 139, do not fully represent the
   use made of this author in this part of Strabo; there are other passages
   shown to be Aristobulus' by the name-forms or other evidence. This is one
   of the reasons why I have to go through Strabo's text of XV, 1, 17–34 (691–
   701). It is strange that no one seems to have thought of using Aristobulus'
   well-marked nomenclature.
2 There is a named case of Ptolemy and Aristobulus using different names
   for a tribe in Arrian V, 20, 2=Aristobulus fr. 45: Γλαῦσαι Ptolemy,
   Γλαυγανῖκαι Aristobulus. The certain case of Jaxartes and Orexartes has
   been noticed, § B, p. 9 n. 2. I once thought that Arrian's use of Bactra
   and Zariaspa side by side was another case, but analysis shows this is *not*
   a case of different sources.
3 I showed in *Bactria and India*, p. 144 n. 3, that Hypanis was Aristobulus'·
   form, but I omitted to cite this passage in Strabo, which clinches it. But
   as the matter is important I will take the proof further, which will also
   explain an unexplained problem. A writer in Strabo XV, 1, 3 (686),
   repeated XV, 1, 33 (701) (see my note in *Bactria and India*, ante), who
   uses the form Hypanis, says that between Hypanis and Hydaspes were
   5,000 cities, 'none smaller than Meropid Cos'; the phrase is reproduced in
   Pliny VI, 59, 'nullum Coo minus'. It is of course an impossible exaggeration, as Strabo noticed (doubtless it is a mistake in transmission or interpreting for 500, i.e. the Indian use of 500 for 'a large number', see Tarn,
   J.H.S. XL, 1940, p. 84); but the point is, why did the writer take *Cos* as his
   basis of comparison? Obviously because it was his own home-town;
   see too the touch of local pride, *Meropid* Cos. Now Pliny says that the

what comes between is an excursus, Nearchus and Onesicritus (named) on plants. At the end of 1, 21, after the words καὶ τῶν ἐριοφόρων, the words φησὶν οὗτος ought, on every principle of construction, to mean Aristobulus, the person last mentioned, six lines previously; but the details show that Jacoby ('Onesikritos', no. 134 fr. 22) is right in making οὗτος refer throughout to Onesicritus, who therefore goes down to the named passage at the beginning of 1, 24. From that point to the middle of 1, 26 (697) we get another excursus, viz.: Onesicritus and Nearchus (named) on rains and rivers; then in 1, 26, with the words Ἀλέξανδρος γάρ, Strabo takes up again Alexander's progress, of which the beginning in 1, 17 was explicitly ascribed to Aristobulus, and this (with two lines about the Graeco-Bactrians inserted by Strabo himself in 1, 27) runs on to the end of the passage in 1, 28 about Taxiles and Taxila. This section is full of Aristobulus' peculiarities. In 1, 26 we get a city Γῶρυς, while Ptolemy (who does not mention the city) spells the river and tribe Γουραῖος and Γουραῖοι (Arr. IV, 23, 1; 25, 6 *sq*.). In 1, 27, besides Hypanis throughout, there are six names between Kophen and Indus which are all Aristobulus', for two of them, Assakanos and Hypasioi, we have already had in a named passage of Aristobulus; of the others, the Masianoi, like the Hypasioi, do not come in Ptolemy-Arrian; Masoga is Ptolemy-Arrian Massaga, and Astakenoi probably Assakenoi; Νυσαῖοι almost certainly did not occur in Ptolemy at all.[1] Taxila, in 1, 28, is from Aristobulus, as is shown by Strabo's long description of the town in XV, 714, ascribed to him by name; and the general statement in 1, 26 that Alexander kept near the hills so as to get narrower crossings can only be from Aristobulus, for Strabo does not use Ptolemy and it is also evident from Arrian (V, 20, 8 *sqq*.) that Ptolemy made no general statement on the subject; Ptolemy's actual account of the crossing of the Chenab bears Aristobulus out, while Arrian (V, 20, end of 9) is obviously arguing on his own account against some writer who had said that Alexander chose narrow crossings and who in the circumstances can only be Aristobulus.

writer was one of *Alexandri Magni comites*, and with one exception all their home-towns are known. Cleitarchus is excluded, as he was not a companion of Alexander; anyhow he was born in Colophon and worked in Alexandria. Ptolemy was a Macedonian prince, Nearchus a Cretan settled in Amphipolis; Chares came from Mytilene, Onesicritus from Astypalaea or Aegina; Callisthenes of Olynthus was dead. There is only Aristobulus of Cassandreia whose home-town is unknown, for he could not have settled at Cassandreia, founded not before 316, till it existed; he therefore is the writer who came from Cos and used the form Hypanis.

1 It is evident from Arrian V, 1 *sqq*. that Ptolemy did not mention Nysa.

The rest of 1, 28 is a digression on large snakes, with the views of Onesicritus and 'others'. With 1, 29 Alexander's progress is taken up again, after leaving Taxila. Between the Jhelum and the Chenab is Porus' country, containing 300 cities and 'the wood' where Alexander cut timber for his shipbuilding; next comes the foundation of Bucephala and Nicaea; and then, beginning with the words 'in the wood aforesaid', there follows the passage about the baboons and the monkeys which I have been considering. No one who has troubled to follow the foregoing analysis of Strabo can doubt for a moment that this passage is from Aristobulus; for the words ἐν δὲ τῇ λεχθείσῃ ὕλῃ dovetail the monkey story into Aristobulus' account of Alexander's progress, where 'the wood' has just been mentioned. It cannot be a digression, for Strabo gives his digressions as such and does not dovetail them into Aristobulus' basic narrative; also he gives their source. Aristobulus then is certain.

In fact there is no one else who it could be. As the Macedonian army *saw* the baboons, only an Alexander-writer can come in question, and most probably only one who was also interested in natural history, as Aristobulus is known to have been.[1] Strabo neither uses nor mentions Ptolemy; also Ptolemy is not known to have given any natural history, apart from his two snake stories, both propaganda for Sarapis. Eratosthenes is too late; the writer has to be earlier than Cleitarchus. Patrocles, like Ptolemy, is never mentioned, and there is no reason to suppose that he wrote on Alexander. Megasthenes, who from xv, 1, 35 (702) follows Aristobulus as Strabo's main source for a time, is cited once in the early part (1, 17 (693)) as saying that India produced two crops a year; but he certainly did not write on Alexander. There remain the two men who wrote both about Alexander and Indian natural history, Nearchus and Onesicritus. Nearchus is out of the question. He certainly described how to hunt monkeys;[2] but he has nothing about baboons and their military formation, and he said that some monkeys were *beautiful*, which took Arrian's fancy and which also shows that he was not the source of the Strabo passage under consideration.[3] The only writer who would really have to be considered is Onesicritus. Strabo on India quotes him several times, for geography,[4] native

---

1 He was interested in animals as well as in plants, frs. 38–40; see especially the understanding account of the tiny karaits in fr. 38.
2 Arr. *Ind.* 15, 8.
3 He might be the source for catching monkeys with nooses; see *ante* p. 31.
4 xv, 689, size of India; 693, 701, shore of the Indus Delta.

customs,[1] and natural history;[2] he might have written on monkeys, though we do not know. But Strabo only quotes him for digressions, usually as Ὀνησίκριτος δέ, 'but Onesicritus (says something different from the source he, Strabo, is following)'; he was rather contemptuous of Onesicritus as a romancer,[3] and never uses him for his account of Alexander's progress and doings, into which, as we have seen, Strabo's monkey story is dovetailed; it had to be, as the baboon incident is part of Alexander's *acta*. Indeed, it is improbable that Onesicritus ever wrote a consecutive account of Alexander's progress and *acta* at all; his book was not a history but a sort of romance, an imitation of Xenophon's *Cyropaedeia*,[4] a fact which too many modern writers, including Schwartz himself with his praise of Onesicritus as 'colourful', have overlooked. He was no more a liar than any historical novelist; he wrote a professed romance. It has always been a puzzle how a good practical seaman, who steered Alexander's ship and received a gold crown for his services with the fleet,[5] could have been such a hopeless historian; the answer is that he never professed to write history.

I may just finish my analysis of Alexander's progress. After the monkey story which has been considered comes a digression, xv, 1, 30, 31, giving the opinions of τινες and ἄλλοι on the location of the Cathaeans, together with Onesicritus' remarks on their customs; there follows another digression on Indian dogs, which recurs in many forms in many writers and might be from anybody.[6] In 1, 32 Alexander's

1 689, Cathaeans; 701, Musicanus' people.
2 690, hippopotami; 692, the grain βόσμορος; 694, the banyan; 695, colours of tropical creatures. I omit the rain falling ready boiled.
3 xv, 1, 28 (698); cf. ii, 1, 9 (70).
4 Diog. Laert. vi, 84=Jacoby ii, no. 134, T. 1, especially τῆι ἑρμηνείαι δὲ παραπλήσιος, 'in the interpretation of its subject it is like' the *Cyropaedeia*, that is, it bore the same relation to the historical Alexander as does Xenophon's work to the historical Cyrus. Why Strasburger, 'Onesikritos' in PW, should doubt this I cannot imagine. It is unfortunate that the recent Loeb edition of Diogenes should have translated ἑρμηνείαι by 'diction'. On this passage and Onesicritus generally see Tarn, *A.J.P.* lx, 1939, pp. 49–51.
5 Arr. vii, 5, 8. Jacoby BD, p. 470, followed by Strasburger *op. cit.*, doubts this, saying only *selbständige Befehlshaber* received gold crowns. This is incorrect; Peucestas and several Bodyguards, who received gold crowns at the same time, had never held independent commands. These gold crowns *must* come from the *Journal*.
6 See Aristobulus fr. 40, with Jacoby's note BD, p. 518, where the various versions and references are collected. Nothing can be made of them, as we have not Aristobulus' account in full.

progress is taken up again; we get his route from the Jhelum to the Hypanis, keeping to the foothills (both name and fact are, we have seen, Aristobulus'), and (1, 33) the '5,000 cities' between these two rivers, again Aristobulus' (p. 32 n. 3 *ante*); the nomenclature too throughout differs from that used in Ptolemy-Arrian, Συδρακαί for Oxydracae, Sabos and Sindomana for Sambos and Sindimana, Porticanos for Oxycanos.[1] That all this is still from Aristobulus is also shown later in 1, 33 on the distance between the two mouths of the Indus; Strabo begins Ἀριστόβουλος μὲν οὖν (i.e. his regular source to which he returns) says one thing, Νέαρχος δέ...Ὀνησίκριτος δέ say other things. Here Aristobulus and Alexander's progress alike end; in 1, 34 (701) there follow some remarks of Onesicritus on the swampy nature of the coast, and in 702 Strabo changes his main source and subject from Aristobulus to Megasthenes and a new world.

The foregoing analysis should be sufficient proof that Cleitarchus took from Aristobulus a passage which confused monkeys and baboons, made a rather more thorough confusion of them, and made nonsense of Aristobulus' stories of catching monkeys, most notably by the substitution of honey for water. This one proven instance suffices to show that Schwartz' scheme reversed the facts; it was not, as he supposed, Aristobulus who used Cleitarchus[2] but Cleitarchus who used Aristobulus; this of course was bound to be so on the dating of Cleitarchus established in § C, but it is well to have an independent proof, as it and the dating mutually support each other. With this, much of what Schwartz and his followers have written about Aristobulus falls to the ground, and many ideas will have to be revised in the light of the facts. Aristobulus can no longer be treated as a sceptical rationaliser, explaining things away; it was his plain statements of fact which others took up and embellished, or worse. I do not mean that everything he said was trustworthy; in certain spheres it sometimes was not. But he is what Arrian knew him to be, our best independent evidence for Alexander after Ptolemy.

There will be more to be said about this later; but first I must consider what has been put forward in support of Schwartz' idea. Jacoby on this matter[3] merely refers back to Schwartz' famous article 'Aristobulos' in PW; and Schwartz gave three reasons and no more, which must now be looked at. The principal one is that Aristobulus said that Alexander returned from Ammon by the way he had come,[4] i.e. to

1 Oxycanos in Arr. VI, 16, 1. Aristobulus' form Porticanos occurs again in Diod. XVII, 102, 5, Curt. IX, 8, 11.
2 'Aristobulos' in PW, 916.   3 BD, p. 509.   4 Arr. III, 4, 5.

Alexandria, while in fact, as Ptolemy says, he returned to Memphis; and Schwartz says that Aristobulus' version only makes sense in connection with the legend which put the foundation of Alexandria after, and not before, the visit to Ammon, and so gave to Alexandria a founder already legitimised as a god,[1] which would appeal to the Alexandrian Cleitarchus, from whom Aristobulus is supposed by Schwartz to have taken his version. All this is quite in the air. There is not a trace anywhere that any one ever considered Alexandria to have been founded by a god; there is nothing about it in Diodorus, Curtius, Justin, or in the valuable account of the founding of Alexandria in the Romance, A′; it is Schwartz' own guess, a brilliant one certainly—that goes without saying—but devoid of any foundation. Had there been a legend to this effect, it *must* have been alluded to in the Romance; on the contrary, in the Romance there was already a god on the site marked out for Alexandria, the old chthonian snake, later called Agathodaemon, whom Alexander killed by mistake, to whom he then built a temple, and who was certainly not identical with Alexander, though he may have become one of the constituents of Sarapis.[2] There is of course nothing about Alexandria being founded by a god in the fragments of Cleitarchus; and indeed Diodorus, whom Schwartz and his followers treat as Cleitarchus, does not even say that Alexander returned from Ammon by the way he came; he only says (XVII, 51, 4) that he returned to Egypt, which could equally well mean Memphis. Curtius, IV, 8, 1, might or might not mean that he returned straight to Lake Mareotis; Justin XI, 11, 13 gives no indication at all; the Romance alone *seems* to take him back by Paraetonium.[3] The common sense of the matter is that Aristobulus, who was not at Ammon and who wrote long after the event, has adopted some version of the itinerary which was mistaken; there is nothing anywhere in Aristobulus to show that he concerned himself in any way with the matter of Alexander's divinity.

Schwartz' other two instances are concerned with military matters, which were not Aristobulus' business and of which his knowledge was doubtless limited to the broad outlines; they are that he made Spitamenes hand Bessus over to Ptolemy,[4] whereas in fact Ptolemy captured him, and that he made Alexander's fight with Porus' son take place

---

1 He was not in fact made a god at Siwah; he was already one in Egypt, but nowhere else; see generally App. 22. So this argument is quite unfounded.
2 This story is given in A′, I, 32, 5 *sqq.* (p. 32 in W. Kroll, *Historia Alexandri Magni*, 1926). On it see Tarn, *J.H.S.* XLVIII, 1928, pp. 214, 218 *sq.*
3 A′, I, 31, 1 (p. 28, Kroll).
4 Arr. III, 30, 5 = Aristobulus, fr. 24.

directly he crossed the river, while in fact it took place a little later;[1] and these mistakes are supposed to show that Aristobulus was a late writer who took existing accounts and rationalised them, a writer who often followed the vulgate account, i.e. Cleitarchus (whereas in fact it was Cleitarchus who followed *him*). There is in fact little difference between Spitamenes handing over Bessus to Ptolemy and (as he did do) dropping Bessus in a certain village in order that Ptolemy, whom he knew to be hard on his heels, might capture him; in either version Spitamenes secured the same result. As to the battle with Porus' son, Aristobulus was not there and, many years later, made a mistake; but what the displacement of a minor engagement has to do with 'sceptical rationalising' I cannot imagine; no deductions were drawn from it, nor could they be. What these instances do show is, not that Aristobulus used the 'vulgate' (presuming that that means Cleitarchus), but that he had not read Ptolemy's book; *that* they do show very plainly indeed, and it is of the first importance. The supreme instance of his 'rationalising' is supposed to be the Gordian knot. I have considered this carefully in App. 10; the conclusions are that Ptolemy thought the matter too unimportant to notice; that all the versions we have, except that of Aristobulus, are mere propaganda; and that Aristobulus gave the true version, the only one not hopelessly at variance with Alexander's character. The incident *was* unimportant, as Ptolemy realised; and the way in which it was worked up later is only of interest as an illustration of human credulity.

How then do matters stand about Aristobulus? He wrote many years after the events which he records; presumably he had to trust to his memory and to such notes or diaries as he may have taken or kept himself; this amply accounts for any mistakes of fact in matters in which he was not particularly interested. He had not the advantage Ptolemy had of access to the *Journal* and official records, and he did not know Ptolemy's book; *that* is quite clear. By profession he was an architect and engineer; he knew little and possibly cared less about military, and perhaps political, matters, and as a Greek he was not in the inner circle, the circle of the great Macedonian generals whose interests were war, power, and personal feuds, restrained only by the king they at once loved and feared. It is obvious, if only from variations in place and personal names, that he and Ptolemy moved in different spheres and got their information in different ways; and we shall do well to keep those different spheres in mind, for here we get something really important.

1 Arr. v, 14, 3 = fr. 43.

For, to Alexander himself, the inner circle of hard-bitten Macedonian nobles, from whose ranks he drew his generals and governors, was by no means the end of the matter. He knew that he could not make the kind of conquest he wanted with them alone; he needed also what would now be called technicians and experts, and for these he had to go to Greece. We hear all too little about them. Diades of Thessaly, the expert in siege-machines, must have been of the first importance; later times knew him as 'the man who took Tyre with Alexander',[1] but none of our extant Alexander-historians even mention him, any more than they mention the other siege-engineers whose names have survived, Diades' colleague Charias and Poseidonius and Philippus.[2] We hear of Gorgos, water and mining engineer;[3] he was not the only water engineer with Alexander, and we just get indications later of the pitch to which the art of sinking wells had been brought by Greeks.[4] We hear but little more of Deinocrates, the town-planning expert who laid out Alexandria,[5] or of the bematists Baeton, Diognetos, and Philonides,[6] whose business was routes and camping grounds, and who made and kept the records which were to be the foundation of the geography of Alexander's Empire in the East. There must have been others whose names have perished—such may have been the two Greeks who were dining with Alexander on the night of Cleitus' murder[7]—apart from the well-known figures of Nearchus and Onesicritus, naval experts, and Eumenes, head of the secretariat. Of this company was Aristobulus, architect and engineer, with a vivid interest in geography and natural history. We cannot talk of a second circle alongside that of the great generals, for we do not know; but in the nature of things the relations of some of these Greeks with Alexander

1 See the papyrus, *Laterculi Alexandrini*: Diels, *Abh. Berl. Ak.* 1904, *Antike Technik²*, p. 30. His machines: Athenaeus περὶ μηχανημάτων. Other references in Berve II, no. 267.

2 Berve II, nos. 821, 656, 789.

3 Strabo xv, 1, 30 (700). For μεταλλευτής as a water engineer, see *id.* IX, 2, 18 (407); XV, 2, 3 (721), which shows that Alexander had several with him. This Gorgos cannot be the same person as Gorgos the ὁπλοφύλαξ, on whom see App. 22, p. 354 n. 2.

4 Tarn, *Bactria and India*, pp. 148 *sq.*, 311. For Alexander's wells, Arr. VI, 18, 1; Strabo, XV, 2, 3 (721).

5 Berve II, no. 249.

6 Jacoby II, nos. 119, 120, 121. Amyntas (Jacoby II, no. 122) is not called a bematist, and his descriptive work is probably later, using their material; see Jacoby II BD, pp. 406, 410, and Tarn, *Bactria and India*, p. 55 n. 1.

7 Plut. *Alex.* LI. περιπατεῖν shows that they were part of the expedition, not visitors.

must have been fairly close, since they took their orders from him and not from or through the generals. In the Romance the engineer Philippus dines with him;[1] and though this is not evidence for the fact (it is part of the poison story), it *is* evidence for a belief in the estimation in which Alexander might hold a Greek engineer.[2] The Macedonian nobles might have looked down on Aristobulus as a Greek architect; Alexander certainly would not have done so. He was struggling with inchoate ideas of something greater than war and power politics, ideas which his nobles could not understand; technical matters apart, he needed all the Greek help he could get, and the philosophers with him were of little use. That he thought well of Aristobulus is obvious from his giving him the, to himself, important commission to restore Cyrus' tomb, and other commissions also;[3] and in fact Aristobulus knew so much about Alexander that the relationship between them must have been closer than one would guess.[4]

He well understood the feelings of the generals; about Cleitus' murder he said that Cleitus had only himself to thank,[5] for he came back after Ptolemy had got him safely away; he knew, as the subsequent story was to show, that the murder of one of their number did not affect the attitude of the other generals towards Alexander. But far more important are the things he knew about Alexander himself. He knew the real nature, so soon obscured and garbled, of Parmenion's very intimate proposal to Alexander (App. 20, pp. 335 *sq.*), which he can only have heard from Alexander himself, Parmenion being out of the question. He knew beforehand of Alexander's intention to return home down the Hydaspes to the ocean, after he had reached (what he thought to be) the end of India;[6] Alexander must have told him. He knew

---

1 A', III, 31, 8 (p. 135 Kroll). It is the story of Medius' banquet, at which, in the Romance, Alexander was poisoned.
2 Berve I, p. 158 (a good section): an example 'welches Ansehens und welcher Gunst bei Alexander sich auch einzelne Ingenieure erfreuen konnten'. There are a good many items of truth in the Romance, A'; see my remarks, App. 22, p. 363.
3 Strabo xv, 1, 19 (693), πεμφθεὶς ἐπί τινα χρείαν.
4 The story in Lucian, *quom. hist. conscr.* 12 = Jacoby II, no. 139, T. 4, is naturally pure invention.
5 Arr. IV, 8, 9 = fr. 29.
6 Diod. XVII, 89, 4, which is from Aristobulus for certain; for the first part of the sentence, τῆς δὲ πλησίον ὀρεινῆς ἐχούσης πολλὴν μὲν ἐλάτην εὔτροφον, οὐκ ὀλίγην δὲ κέδρον καὶ πεύκην, ἔτι δὲ τῆς ἄλλης ὕλης ναυπηγησίμου πλῆθος ἄφθονον κατεσκεύασε ναῦς ἱκανάς, is identical with Strabo xv, 1, 29 (698) ἡ πρὸς τοῖς Ἠμωδοῖς ὄρεσιν ὕλη, ἐξ ἧς Ἀλέξανδρος κατήγαγε τῷ Ὑδάσπῃ κόψας ἐλάτην τε πολλὴν καὶ πεύκην καὶ κέδρον καὶ ἄλλα παντοῖα

(App. 10) that Alexander, being what he was, *could* not stoop to cheat, let alone to call heaven as his witness. He knew that Alexander did not put men to death for superstitious reasons, whatever stories might be told;[1] and he knew that he was a man to whom you could safely tell the truth.[2] To him too probably go back the statements we have that Alexander never put anything off (see § F, p. 75 n. 4). He knew that the stories of Alexander's excessive drinking, put about after his death by enemies or fools, were untrue; and he gave the truth, that the king sat long at dinner for the sake of conversation, not of wine.[3] Above all, when on the night of 17th–18th Daisios 323 B.C. Alexander did drink as hard as he could and his enemies asserted that he had drunk himself into the fever which killed him,[4] Aristobulus knew the true reason, borne out by the *Journal* (to which he had not access), that already on the 17th Alexander felt the shivering and *malaise* of the oncoming malaria (his illness was patent to the world, and officially recorded, on the 18th) and drank hard to try to check it.[5] How a man who knew as much as this could ever have been called a sceptical rationaliser, a secondary and unoriginal writer, passes my compre-

στελέχη ναυπηγήσιμα, ἐξ ὧν στόλον κατεσκευάσατο; and the analysis I have previously given of the early part of Strabo's book xv is conclusive that the Strabo passage here quoted is from Aristobulus, quite apart from the fact that no one else distinguished the different conifers in this way; see Strabo xi, 7, 2 (509) = Aristobulus fr. 19, Jacoby.

1 The stories of Alexander's diadem blowing away, and of the man who sat on the throne, which are examined in § F, p. 77.

2 Arr. vii, 18, 1 *sqq.* = fr. 54, the story of Pythagoras; see 18, 4 ὅτι ἀδόλως τὴν ἀλήθειάν οἱ ἔφρασεν. Also the story of Timocleia, Plut. *Mor.* 259 D *sqq.* = Aristobulus fr. 2.

3 Arr. vii, 29, 4 = fr. 62. He must sometimes have been present.

4 Ephippus, Jacoby ii, no. 126, fr. 3, ἐκ τούτου νοσήσας ἀπέθανε. The story has long been discarded by modern historians. A similar story was told by the unknown pamphleteer who took the female name Nicobule, *ib.* no. 127, fr. 1. Is it possible that Nicobule was represented as one of Roxane's women and that this pamphlet originated the story of Roxane preventing the dying Alexander from committing suicide in the Euphrates, her solitary appearance on the stage prior to Alexander's death?

5 Plut. *Alex.* lxxv = Aristobulus, fr. 59, where, however, Jacoby gives too much; only the last lines, from 'Αριστόβουλος δέ, are from Aristobulus. The *Journal*, as given by Arrian (see Jacoby ii, no. 117, p. 619) shows that on the 17th Daisios Alexander behaved normally, but drank hard that night; on the 18th it was known that he had a fever. Aristobulus gives the thirst induced by the (oncoming) fever as the cause of his drinking hard that night, 17th–18th Daisios. Plutarch on the *day* of 17th Daisios agrees neither with the *Journal* (which he only quotes as from the 18th) nor with Aristobulus.

hension. It was the kind of knowledge he possessed which made two late writers (Lucian is one) accuse him of flattering Alexander;[1] it only means that his book presented him in a favourable light.[2]

Finally, Aristobulus' date. He certainly did not know Ptolemy's book, as we have seen; it may therefore be taken for granted that his book was the earlier of the two. As Cleitarchus, we have seen, cannot have written before 280 at the very earliest, and as Ptolemy died in 283–282, this alone would make Aristobulus earlier than Cleitarchus, apart from the fact that, as has been shown, Cleitarchus used him. The tradition that Aristobulus was 84 when he wrote, even if true (and I have little faith in Pseudo-Lucian's *Macrobii* as a source), does nothing to fix his date, for it is not known when he was born; we only know that in 324 Alexander, who regarded the restoration of Cyrus' tomb as important, entrusted him with the work, which means that at the time he was a responsible man, well-known in his profession; but this might mean any age from 30 to 60. But perhaps something can be got on other lines. He could have settled in Cassandreia any time after its foundation, which was not earlier than 316. Cassandreia, though rather independent in feeling, was anyhow in the realm of its founder Cassander, and Cassander, whose connection with the Peripatetic school was a close one,[3] hated Alexander and his memory; Aristobulus could not have published a book favourable to Alexander while Cassander and his line ruled in Cassandreia. It is known that he did not in fact write, or anyhow publish, till some little time after 301 B.C. (battle of Ipsus);[4] and as Cassander died in 298 and his sons lost Macedonia to Demetrius the Besieger in 294, it may be taken as tolerably certain that Aristobulus cannot have published till after 294. Demetrius ruled Macedonia from 294 to 288, when he lost it to Lysimachus, Cassander's most intimate friend, who ruled till 281 and had at his Court all the surviving members of the houses of Cassander and Antipater. It hardly admits of doubt, therefore, that Aristobulus' book appeared in the period 294–288, when Cassandreia was under the more sympathetic Antigonid rule. This,

---

1 'Aristobulos', no. 139 in Jacoby, T. 4 and 5. See Jacoby's quotation from Schwartz II, BD, p. 509.

2 κόλαξ (flatterer) may have meant what it said in Alexander's time, but long before the close of the Hellenistic period it had lost all real meaning and had become a political and literary catchword signifying any one who thought well of a king, just as a king's minister was apt to be called his ἐρώμενος; Greek propaganda was not pretty.

3 On Cassander's circle see Tarn, 'Alexander the Great and the Unity of Mankind', *Proc. Brit. Acad.* XIX, 1933, pp. 140–5, 163 [20–5, 43]; *A.J.P.* LX, 1939, p. 59.　　　　4 Arr. VII, 18, 5 = fr. 54.

too, agrees with the common belief that Ptolemy I wrote at the end of his life; it was usual enough in this age for men of affairs not to write till their life's work was pretty well over, or, as we should say, till they had retired. Every Hellenistic king was worked to death; it may even be that *one* of the reasons why Ptolemy I made his son Ptolemy II joint king with himself in 285 was to secure leisure enough to write, or finish, his book. If Aristobulus published between 294 and 288, Ptolemy, writing later than he, could not have published till after 288; for he evidently had access to the archives at Pella, and that he could have had in the reign of Lysimachus but certainly not in that of Demetrius. Ptolemy then published his book somewhere between 288 and his death in 283–282.

The order of the Alexander-historians is therefore not Cleitarchus—Ptolemy—Aristobulus, as Schwartz and Jacoby have supposed, but quite certainly Aristobulus—Ptolemy—Cleitarchus.

E. CLEITARCHUS' BOOK

NO ONE can glance through the thirty-six fragments of Cleitarchus without being struck by one thing, how little we really know about the writer who in modern times has been magnified into such an influential and far-reaching source in the Alexander-story, and has attracted to himself most of the flotsam brought down by that somewhat muddy stream or streams, the so-called vulgate, till its very name is sometimes cited as the 'Cleitarchean vulgate'. We can only find Cleitarchus by following the lines indicated by the named fragments, and they give little indication of what line we ought to follow. Most of them relate to purely incidental matters, such as natural history, geography, stories that must have been excursuses or digressions; very few bear on what we want to know, Cleitarchus' attitude to Alexander and his acts. It is perhaps noteworthy how many of the fragments relate to just two subjects, Hyrcania and the Caspian, and India; while there are none for the important period after Alexander's return from India.

A little help as to what Cleitarchus' book was like can be got from later writers who had read it. Quintilian says he was clever but not honest.[1] Cicero classes him with the rhetoricians, and says he was

---

1 Jacoby II, no. 137, T. 6 = *Inst.* x, 1, 74: 'probatur ingenium, fides infamatur.'

quite ready to lie if it made a story more lively;[1] Strabo calls him a liar without more ado,[2] so we may have to reckon with a certain amount of pure invention in this writer. Demetrius[3] says he spoilt things which might otherwise have been good by over-writing, the example he gives being that he describes the wild bee of Hyrcania as though it were a wild bull (see § F', p. 90); at a later time, 'to write like Cleitarchus' became a synonym for exaggeration.[4] Very informative is that fine critic, the anonymous author of περὶ Ὕψους, *On the Sublime*;[5] Cleitarchus' writing, he says, was not sublime but only inflated; he was all outer husk, and the tunes he played were wild; what he himself took for flashes of divine light were only the 'purple patches' of immaturity. Lastly, Curtius names him twice,[6] once to show that he himself takes no responsibility for the statement he quotes from him, and once to refute him, saying that he possessed the twin vices of carelessness and credulity. One cannot in fact find any writer who has a good word for him, beyond the admission that he was clever. All this gives us a pretty good idea of the kind of writer he was, a type that can never die out, for it is attractive to the multitude. That Cleitarchus attracted them in the early Roman period is certain, and there is no need to multiply evidence; Pliny's reference (x, 136) to him as a 'much read author', *celebratus auctor*, will suffice. For the Hellenistic period there is no evidence, but probably he was read, or he could hardly have been taken up in the way he was later. It is our loss that Eratosthenes, who had very just notions about the third-century Alexander-literature, has left no remarks about Cleitarchus beyond the general statement that he himself disbelieved all the divinity stuff (τὸ θεῖον) in the Alexander-story.

What now did Cleitarchus say about Alexander? He related (fr. 25) the massacre of 80,000 Indians in Sambos' territory, which I shall come to later. He did *not*, as we have seen (§ C, pp. 22–6), relate the Roman embassy to Alexander (fr. 31). He lied about Ptolemy saving Alexander's life in the Malli town (fr. 24; see § C, p. 26), but it may not have been his own lie; it could have been Alexandrian gossip, one of

---

1 Jacoby, T. 7 = Cicero, *Brutus* 11,42; for rhetoric cf. also T. 12 (Philodemus).
2 Strabo XI, 7, 4 (509) πολλὰ ψευδῆ conjoined with XI, 1, 5 (491) = Cleitarchus fr. 13; see § B, p. 15.
3 Jacoby, T. 10 = *De eloc.* 304.
4 Κλειταρχικῶς = ὑπερβολικῶς: Tzetzes, *Epist.* 13; see Susemihl, I, p. 539 n. 46.
5 Jacoby, T. 9 = περὶ ὕψους 3, 2. Παίζουσι refers, not to childish play, but to immaturity like that of a παῖς.
6 IX, 5, 21 (see § C, pp. 26 *sqq.*); IX, 8, 15 (see p. 53 *post*). See § G, p. 102.

those reports which, as we know well to-day, arise and spread widely without their origin ever being discovered. He told, though he did not invent, the story of the Queen of the Amazons visiting Alexander, which is dealt with elsewhere (App. 19); probably he thought it romantic, and this story makes it probable that it was he who told the companion story[1] of Alexander's intrigue with the Indian queen Cleophis, who was in fact (see App. 18, p. 324) a middle-aged woman with a grown-up son old enough to govern and to lead in battle; but there can be no certainty about Cleophis, for Onesicritus might be as likely a candidate. This brings us to the two important fragments, nos. 11, Thais at Persepolis, and 17, which shows that Cleitarchus must have related Dionysus' conquest of India and the story of Nysa; it may be necessary here to consider also the reference to Semiramis in fr. 10. I will take Nysa first.

It is a commonplace that nearly everything in ancient art and literature relating to Dionysus' conquest of India derives from Alexander's expedition. But already by Euripides' day Dionysus, going eastward, had reached Bactra,[2] the *last* important stage on the main road into India; it is therefore conceivable that between Euripides' time and Alexander's he had reached India, or at any rate the Paropamisadae. Arrian (v, 1–2, 7) tells the story of Nysa at length as a λόγος—that is, Ptolemy did not give it—and only half believed it himself (v, 3, 1); Eratosthenes (*ib.*) called the story of Dionysus in India an invention. But Aristobulus names a people called Nysaeans, Νυσαῖοι, in the Paropamisadae,[3] which would import also the town Nysa and guarantees the bare fact that Alexander did come to a town whose Indian name sounded to Greek ears something like Nysa, the well-known mountain of Dionysus. This story is not from Cleitarchus, who (fr. 17) called Nysa a *mountain* in India, not a town; and it had already been called a mountain by Chamaeleon the Peripatetic (*ib.*), Theophrastus' friend and co-worker, who must have been independent of Aristobulus. We have then *two* early stories, that Alexander found a town and a people whose name suggested, and could be turned into, Nysa, and that what he found was not a town but a mountain.[4] Cleitarchus might have taken the mountain from Chamaeleon; but there is no real trace of any

---

1 Curtius VIII, 10, 35; Justin XII, 7, 9. 2 Eur. *Bacchae*, l. 15.

3 Strabo XV, 1, 27 (698). For evidence that the passage and name are from Aristobulus, see § D, p. 33.

4 There is a curious parallel in the story of Crassus after Carrhae. Plutarch, *Crassus* XXIX, calls Sinnaca a mountain, while it is certain, both from the story, the form of the name, and Strabo's express statement, XVI, 1, 23 (747), that it was a town.

affinity between himself and the Peripatetics, and more probably both drew on a common source, one of the poetasters to be considered in § E′. With the mountain came the story that on it grew a plant 'like ivy' called σκινδαψός; in the Arrian story it *is* ivy, which is probably again from Aristobulus. It would be natural for Chamaeleon, Theophrastus' fellow-worker, to mention the plant; but some one had played off a joke either on him or on the poet he took it from, for σκινδαψός is no transliteration of an Indian word; it is good Greek for 'thingummy', 'what-do-you-call-it', and the correct translation is 'a plant called So-and-so'.[1] One thing, however, may be noticed here about Aristobulus' Nysaeans. India west of the Indus (and indeed the Punjab also) contained various peoples of foreign origin who had come in through the passes, the peoples whom Indians called collectively Bāhlīkas (Bactrians),[2] and who have sometimes been termed Proto-Bactrians; and the Nysaeans may well have been a sept of some Bāhlīka people, still exhibiting differences from their Indian neighbours.

To continue Arrian's story. All the Akouphis part (v, 1, 3–6; 2, 2–4) is pure invention, one cannot say whose; but v, 2, 1 is on a different footing. Here we are told that Alexander *wanted* the story of the foundation of Nysa by Dionysus to be true (which may mean that he put it about himself), because it would make it easier for him to get the army to go on if they believed that they were going farther than the god had done. This practical military reason is an exact parallel to his becoming a god in Greek cities for a purely practical political reason (App. 22, III), and was given by some one who knew a good deal about him; and as Ptolemy does not come in question, this can only be Aristobulus, who *did* know a good deal about him (§ D, pp. 40 *sq.*). But as Cleitarchus told *his* story in a work about Alexander, he must have connected it with Alexander; Cleitarchus should therefore come in Arrian's λόγος somewhere, and there can be little doubt where it is; he is the οἱ δὲ καὶ τάδε ἀνέγραψαν of v, 2, 7, who related that some of the 'prominent Macedonians' became possessed by the god and held a Bacchic revel, crying εὖα—in other words a κῶμος to Dionysus. There is an exact parallel to all this in Arrian (VI, 28, 2), where he first describes Alexander's alleged Bacchic rout in Carmania, saying that

---

1 The later history of the σκινδαψός story may be noticed. A scholiast on Apollonius Rhodius repeated Cleitarchus' absurdity that it was a plant 'like ivy'. Suidas identified it with a plant ἄφανα, which was a tufted thorny affair, not in the least like ivy (R. M. Dawkins, *J.H.S.* LVI, 1936, p. 9). The end of all the confusion was Hesychius' Κινδαψοί· οἱ Ἴνδοι.

2 Tarn, *Bactria and India*, p. 169.

he does not believe it and that neither Ptolemy nor Aristobulus gave it, and then says that he follows Aristobulus, whose account (certainly the true one) was that Alexander sacrificed χαριστήρια (the thanksgiving for deliverance from danger)[1] and held the usual games (a necessary relaxation for the army after its sufferings in the Makran). Both these stories of Bacchic revels obviously came from the same source, and both grew out of a perversion of Aristobulus; Cleitarchus, we know, did use Aristobulus, and Cleitarchus has to come in somewhere in the Nysa story. It is not a mathematical proof, but it affords a very strong presumption indeed that both stories of Bacchic routs came from Cleitarchus. We can now get on, remembering always that we are only building on a strong probability, not a certainty.

All that we know about Cleitarchus' account of Thais at Persepolis is given in two lines of Athenaeus, in which Athenaeus, after suggesting that Thais was Alexander's mistress—this is not ascribed to Cleitarchus—goes on 'Cleitarchus says that Thais was the cause of the palace at Persepolis being burnt'.[2] This is a mere summary of Cleitarchus' story, whatever it was. Diodorus, Curtius, and Plutarch all give different versions. Diodorus' account (XVII, 72) is well known to every one through Dryden. Alexander is at dinner with his Companions, who get drunk; it is not said that Alexander was drunk. One of the 'women present', the Athenian Thais, exhorts Alexander to burn the palace as a noble act, κωμάσας—he is to lead a κῶμος. The drunken men applaud her, and say the king must lead a κῶμος of victory (ἐπινίκιον κῶμον) to Dionysus. Alexander catches fire at the idea. Torches are brought; the king heads a κῶμος of flute-girls and such, Thais leading the way; he throws the first torch, she the second, and Diodorus then proceeds to draw his moral: as Xerxes had burnt the Acropolis at Athens, so now an Athenian girl was burning his palace. It is a clever touch, and may remind us that Quintilian called Cleitarchus clever; Diodorus himself was not. Curtius (V, 7, 2 *sqq.*) differs. Alexander is already on the downward path, and has *pellices* present at dinner; he and Thais are both drunk; he throws the first torch, but there is nothing about her throwing the second; the army rush to put out the fire, but abstain when they see the king; finally, when sober again, Alexander repents

---

1 So Nearchus in Arr. *Ind.* 42, 8, Alexander sacrifices ἐπὶ τῶν νεῶν τε καὶ τῶν ἀνθρώπων τῇ σωτηρίῃ; *ib.* 36, 3 σωτήρια τοῦ στρατοῦ ἔθυε. I apprehend that σωτήρια and χαριστήρια mean the same thing.

2 Fr. 11 = Athen. XIII, 576 DE: περὶ ἧς (Thais) φησι Κλείταρχος ὡς αἰτίας γενομένης τοῦ ἐμπρησθῆναι τὰ ἐν Περσεπόλει βασίλεια. The use of βασίλεια for a single building is very common.

of the burning. The κῶμος to Dionysus, and Diodorus' moral, are alike omitted. Plutarch (*Alex.* XXXVIII) has points from both accounts, but mostly agrees with Curtius: Alexander is going downhill, and has his Companions' mistresses present at dinner; Thais makes a long speech, which brings in something like Diodorus' moral; the κῶμος is only a drunken revel, not a κῶμος to Dionysus; afterwards Alexander repents.

Which, if any, of these three accounts is that of Cleitarchus? If what I have said above about Dionysus be well founded, Diodorus must represent Cleitarchus, because of the κῶμος to Dionysus; but again I must emphasise that this is only a strong probability. Once the story got started, there would infallibly be many versions; Curtius and Plutarch are a long remove from Diodorus. But there is one other matter. Curtius (see § G) gives in his book, very thoroughly, the Peripatetic view of Alexander; in Curtius the cloven hoof shows for the first time at Persepolis, though his downward course actually begins with Darius' death. In Diodorus there is nothing about this; Alexander's feast is a mere rejoicing over victory. If then Diodorus' account be Cleitarchus', the latter did *not* take the Peripatetic view of Alexander's character. But the deduction is very far from certain.

I need hardly say that there is not a word of truth in the Thais story. Alexander burnt Xerxes' palace deliberately, as a political manifesto to Asia. No doubt Thais was with the army, for she was Ptolemy's mistress at the time (see App. 18, p. 324 n. 7); many of the generals, one supposes, had mistresses with them, though we only have the name of one other, Philotas' mistress Antigone.[1] Alexander habitually dined with his generals, but to suppose that he dined their mistresses too would be merely silly. We have in fact accounts of some of his dinners from our good sources; no woman is ever mentioned. As to the crowd of flute-girls and such, it *was* a Greek custom to have flute-girls in after dinner, but it was not a Macedonian custom and Macedonians did not practise it,[2] apart from the fact that such a practice would have been entirely out of keeping with Alexander's character. These girls belong to the circle of ideas which made him perpetually drunken; accusations of drunkenness became a standing feature of all abusive propaganda, as can be seen in the case of Antony, and of Cleopatra (VII) also. Aristobulus, who knew far more about Alexander than any popular writer did, said that he sat long at dinner, but for the sake of friendly conversation, not of wine;[3] that alone suffices to negative the flute-girls. What doubtless did happen was that, when the palace was fired, the

1 Plut. *Alex.* XLVIII. 2 Herod. v, 18 (very definite).
3 Arr. VII, 29, 4; see § D, p. 41.

women rushed out of their quarters to see; that would be quite enough for a Cleitarchus.

As Cleitarchus made Alexander lead a κῶμος to Dionysus three times —Persepolis, Nysa, Carmania—no doubt the fourth occasion is from him also. At Phaselis Alexander placed a wreath on the statue of Aristotle's friend Theodectes, whose writings he had read with Aristotle; this was turned into a drunken κῶμος.[1] The matter is not important.

Few legends spring absolutely out of the blue; and Cleitarchus, or rather perhaps his source, in attaching Dionysus stories to Alexander, did have two things to go on. In Macedonia there was a day sacred to Dionysus, and on that day, year by year, Alexander sacrificed to him;[2] for Alexander, outwardly and officially, always did the proper thing by any god, as he did about the gods' omens and oracles. And Dionysus *was* one of his ancestors, though Alexander never took any notice of the fact; he was not a vastly creditable one, and the ancestors whom Alexander did honour, Heracles and Achilles, were very different figures; the idea of Dionysus as a conquering warrior was merely taken from Alexander himself, and can have had nothing to do with any Indian stories about Śiva, who had been established on and west of the Indus for thousands of years. If my suggestion above be correct, one might also add that Alexander himself, for military reasons, had adopted the idea that Dionysus had reached Nysa. If, however, it was Cleitarchus who to some extent spread the legend of the connection of Alexander with Dionysus, it is to be remembered that he was only a secondary writer, who must have largely depended on others, and the probabilities are that both he and Chamaeleon borrowed from one of the poetasters to be presently considered (§ E').

Besides Dionysus, there is one other mythical figure in the Alexander-story whose connection with Cleitarchus can be traced, Semiramis.[3] Long before Cleitarchus wrote, Nearchus, who was a truthful writer, had recorded that one of Alexander's reasons for going home through the Makran was a desire to surpass the march of Semiramis,[4] who had returned from India that way and had lost her army. It does not follow that Alexander gave this out to the army; the words may merely have been spoken, half in jest, to Nearchus himself, for Nearchus gives at the same time his real reason, to support the fleet. If it *was* given out to the army, the reason must have been the same as the reason at Nysa, to put

1 Plut. *Alex.* XVII, ἐπεκώμασε μεθύων. See Berve II, p. 419, no. 27.
2 Arr. IV, 8, 1.   3 Cleitarchus fr. 10.
4 Nearchus in Jacoby II, no. 133, fr. 3 = Arr. VI, 24, 3 and Strabo xv, 1, 5 (686).

the army in better heart. It shows that Alexander knew Ctesias' story of Semiramis; not being a modern historical critic, he may well have believed both that she had existed and that she had returned from India through the Makran. So far the facts; but Semiramis was introduced further into the Alexander story, and it would seem that this was done by Cleitarchus. In the stories about Semiramis in Diodorus book II, Diodorus shows that his basis is Ctesias, but he uses Cleitarchus also, for in II, 7, 3 (= Cleitarchus fr. 10) he quotes that writer by name as differing from Ctesias over Semiramis' building of Babylon, and when in II, 16 he comes to Semiramis' invasion of India from Bactra, he attributes to her items from the Alexander-story which are too late for Ctesias and can only come from Cleitarchus, whom he has already named. In II, 16, 6 she gets shipwrights from Phoenicia, Syria, Cyprus, and the rest of the coastal districts, τῆς ἄλλης τῆς παραθαλαττίου χώρας, who are merely the shipwrights with Alexander's army;[1] in 16, 7 she has ships carried overland from Bactra to the Indus, which is copied from the ships built in Phoenicia for Alexander and carried overland in sections to the Euphrates;[2] in 16, 5 she sends orders to her *eparchs*, a word proper to the Seleucid organisation which Cleitarchus would know, though here it *might* be Diodorus' own. We get Semiramis again in Pliny's story of altars being set up on the Jaxartes by those conquerors who reached the river,[3] viz. Heracles, Dionysus, Semiramis, Cyrus, Alexander, and Demodamas, general of Antiochus I. The altars of Alexander and Antiochus I are historical, as those of Cyrus could perhaps be; but Semiramis is presumably again due to Cleitarchus, just as Heracles and Dionysus are presumably due originally to one of the poets he used (§ E′).

If then Alexander did say, before entering Gedrosia, that he meant to surpass the march of Semiramis, Cleitarchus has worked up the Semiramis motive to any extent; he has made Alexander imitate her in invading India from Bactria, and in Bactria itself he has made Alexander, in reaching the Jaxartes, follow in her footsteps. As we have seen that Cleitarchus also made Alexander imitate Dionysus in his invasion of India, it is evident that he made Alexander a very *imitative* character, as at least one poet had done before him.[4] That this makes complete

1 Arrian (VI, 1, 6) mentions Phoenicians, Cyprians, Carians, Egyptians; Arr. *Ind.* 18 (Nearchus) mentions Phoenicians, Cyprians, Egyptians, Ionians, Hellespontians, and men from the islands. There can be no doubt that Diod. II, 16, 6 is merely an abbreviated statement of this.
2 Arr. VII, 19, 3 = Aristobulus fr. 55.
3 Pliny VI, 49; see Tarn, *J.H.S.* LX, 1940, p. 92.
4 Strabo III, 5, 5 (171); see § E′.

nonsense of the character of one of the greatest of men was not likely to trouble Cleitarchus, any more than it has troubled a modern writer who has worked up Cleitarchus' theme.[1] But I must point out once again that, although the probability that this *was* Cleitarchus' theme (or one of his themes) is very high, and seems to be the best that can be done with what little evidence we have, the matter has not been strictly proved in the way that Cleitarchus' date and his use of Aristobulus have been proved.

As regards imitativeness, then, Cleitarchus is probably responsible for representing Alexander as imitating Dionysus and Semiramis. The connection with Dionysus, save for the existence of the 'Nysaeans', was the complete fabrication which Eratosthenes said it was,[2] and, as will be seen (in § E'), was taken by Cleitarchus from one of the poetasters; he was not actually the inventor of the Alexander-Dionysus myth which was to play such a part later, though he passed it on and perhaps formulated it. We have now to consider the question of Alexander's imitation of his other two ancestors, Heracles and Achilles. If it was Cleitarchus who reproduced the Dionysus stories, it was probably he who passed on stories about Heracles and Achilles also; but again there is no complete certainty.

Heracles is more difficult than Dionysus, for a number of things are true. It is known that Alexander *did* honour Heracles; he sacrificed to him after the defeat of the Getae,[3] and the procession of the Macedonian army (forerunner of the Hellenistic form of triumph) in honour of Heracles after the fall of Tyre was ordered by Alexander;[4] and even if Heracles here really meant Melkart, the army would take it to be the Heracles they knew. Callisthenes' story[5] that one of the reasons why Alexander wanted to go to Ammon was because (he had heard that) Heracles and Perseus had gone there before him might quite well be true, just as Curtius' story[6] that he wanted to see Ethiopia because it had been Memnon's kingdom might be true; we cannot say, but Curtius' remark that Alexander was 'eager to know about ancient times' rings sound. The story that Heracles had failed to take Aornos stands apart: it is not merely part of the invented story of Heracles' expedition to

---

1 G. Radet, *Alexandre le Grand*. I understand that the popularity of this brilliantly written work when it appeared was enormous.
2 Arr. v, 3, 1 *sqq.*; Strabo xv, 1, 7 (687).
3 Arr. I, 4, 5.
4 *Id.* II, 24, 6.
5 Jacoby II, no. 124, fr. 14 = Strabo XVII, 1, 43 (814). Cf. Arr. III, 3, 2.
6 Curt. IV, 8, 3, 'cognoscendae vetustatis avidum'.

India, for Alexander heard the story on the spot,[1] as he heard particulars of the 'rock'; the latter he heard from Indians and probably therefore the former also, in which case it can only have been (as has been suggested) some story about Krishna, which Alexander adopted as good propaganda for his army. So far, the only imitation of Heracles suggested is the visit to Ammon; we are not finding Cleitarchus at all; so we turn to the other stories concerning the supposed Indian expedition of Heracles, which Erastosthenes said were as untrue as those about Dionysus' Indian expedition, and were invented to magnify Alexander.[2] (We may omit the stories about Heracles' daughter Panchaea, as they obviously have nothing to do with Alexander.) One is that the name Caucasus, together with Prometheus' cave, was shifted from the real Caucasus to the Hindu Kush, so that it was in India that Heracles unbound Prometheus; Eratosthenes ascribed this to the Macedonians, i.e. the army. One may remark that Aristotle, and therefore Alexander, already knew, before Alexander went to India, the real name of the Hindu Kush (Parnasos[3] = Parapanisos or Paropamisos, whichever form be the more correct); while on the other hand the name Caucasus was already in use before Alexander died, as shown by its appearance in the Gazetteer,[4] and is still in use to-day (Kush). The story, then, that the name was given by the Macedonian army might be true; but it was taken up and spread by the poet of the *Heracleia* whom Strabo calls 'Peisander' and who, whatever his name, was Alexander's contemporary (§ E'). The other story which Eratosthenes expressly disbelieved was that the Sibi were the descendants of Heracles' followers. Once Heracles had reached India, the cattle branded with a club (naturally his club) were a gift to any writer, and this story too appeared in 'Peisander'. Strabo went further than Eratosthenes, for he included the story of Heracles at Aornos in the same category;[5] doubtless therefore 'Peisander' gave it, but, as has been explained, it stands on a different footing. In all this we have not found Cleitarchus. Probably he repeated, and helped to popularise, these stories of Heracles in India; but it is only a general probability, and he had little chance of making Alexander *imitate* Heracles, unless it were at Aornos.

The last figure, Achilles, is easier than Heracles. Alexander *did* honour Achilles, and, as in the case of Heracles, certain things are true.

1 Arr. IV, 28, 4, where the μῦθος about Heracles is included with the particulars of the 'rock' as things Alexander heard, ταῦτα ἀκούοντα.
2 *Id.* V, 3, 1 *sqq.*; Strabo, XV, 1, 7–8 (688).
3 Arist. *Meteor.* I, 13, 15. 4 Diod. XVIII, 6, 1 (see App. 17).
5 Strabo XV, 1, 8 (688).

Arrian gives as a known fact his ambition since boyhood to emulate Homer's hero,[1] and also as a fact his crowning of Achilles' tomb at Ilium.[2] One may also believe Onesicritus' story that he slept with a copy of the *Iliad* under his pillow,[3] for Onesicritus, who steered his ship, was in a position to know, and probably too Plutarch's story[4] that he put a copy of the *Iliad* in Darius' most valuable casket, saying that he knew no more worthy content for it. But there are also several untrue stories which made Alexander imitate, or connected him with, Achilles; these, or some of them, must come from another poet, Choerilus of Iasos, though as Cleitarchus made Alexander an imitative figure it was doubtless he who passed them on. These stories, and Choerilus, are considered in § E'.

I now turn to the one fragment of Cleitarchus relating to Alexander where we are on firm ground, fr. 25 = Curtius IX, 8, 15: Alexander killed 80,000 Indians in Sambos' kingdom, and also sold many captives. Diodorus (XVII, 102, 6) has the same story; no reason is given. In both writers Sambos has become a king, and in Curtius his capital has to be taken by siege works. The facts were that Sambos was a subordinate ruler of some sort (σατράπης), not a king, who fled on Alexander's approach because he feared, not Alexander, but Musicanus; his capital opened its gates and put everything, treasure and elephants, at Alexander's disposal; one town alone 'revolted' at the instigation of some Brahmans, always irreconcilable, and when Alexander took the town he put the Brahmans to death.[5] Diodorus (102, 7) alludes to this account of Arrian's immediately after Cleitarchus' account, and reconciles the two by making the whole 80,000 Brahmans; doubtless the killing of the Brahmans was the basis on which Cleitarchus' story was founded. Now what this fragment shows is that Cleitarchus had a taste either for inventing massacres or for retailing massacres invented by others; probably therefore the fictitious massacre of the Oreitae[6] and one version of that of the Branchidae (see App. 13) come from him, and he must also have described the Massaga massacre, for if he invented or related fictitious massacres he could not have omitted the one that really happened. Ptolemy records this terrible business, which is

1 Arr. VII, 14, 4 κατὰ ζῆλον τὸν ᾿Αχιλλέως, πρὸς ὅντινα ἐκ παιδὸς φιλοτιμία αὐτῷ ἦν.
2 Arr. I, 12, 1.   3 Jacoby II, no. 134, fr. 38 = Plut. *Alex.* VIII.
4 Plut. *Alex.* XXVI, on the authority of οὐκ ὀλίγοι τῶν ἀξιοπίστων.
5 Arr. VI, 16, 3–5.
6 Diod. XVII, 104, 6–7: country wasted by fire, and many myriads killed (see App. 8, 11). Curt. IX, 10, 7 has an identical account, with the fire, but omits the massacre.

discussed in Vol. I, p. 89; but what must be noticed here is that in
Diodorus' account (84, 1–2) Alexander not only massacres but *cheats*;[1]
this is a new feature, unknown to Ptolemy, and (in view of my examination of Diodorus' sources in § F) can only be attributable to Cleitarchus.
Now while Alexander never cheats in the good tradition—it would be
completely at variance with his type of character—in our inferior sources
he cheats several times: (*a*) over the Massaga massacre; (*b*) over the
Gordian knot;[2] (*c*) over Darius' letter after Issus;[3] (*d*) he contemplates
cheating over the Ammon oracle;[4] (*e*) he secures the names of dis-
affected soldiers by encouraging them to write home and then opening
their letters;[5] (*f*) he secures Darius' murderers by breaking his word,
using exactly the same quibble as Diodorus makes him use over the
Massaga massacre.[6] There can be no real doubt that (*a*), which carries
(*f*) with it, and (*d*) are from Cleitarchus, and little doubt about (*b*);
if so, all must be from Cleitarchus. This shows, as will appear independently when the massacre of the Branchidae comes to be considered (App. 13), that Cleitarchus' book was hostile to Alexander and
was intended to show him in a bad light. The view, which never had
any real foundation, that he wrote a sort of romantic glorification of
Alexander, cannot be maintained; it must rather be supposed that the
reason why he was much read under the early Roman Empire was just
because he chimed with the widespread hostility to Alexander's memory,
more especially exhibited in Stoic (i.e. Republican) circles; Alexander
was to them an early example of the tyranny which, in their view, they
themselves were enduring.

This seems about all that can be said about Cleitarchus till Diodorus
XVII and Curtius are examined. One can see the kind of romantic,
exaggerated, untrustworthy writer that he was, inventing stories or
repeating legendary ones provided that they served his purpose, or taking
a bit of fact from some competent historian and embellishing or working

---

1 The mercenaries leave the city under an agreement, ὁμολογία; Alexander
  then attacks them; they exclaim that he is breaking his oath; he replies
  that he agreed that they might leave, but did not agree to remain friendly
  with them. Curtius omits both mercenaries and massacre.
2 On this story, from a λόγος in Arrian, see App. 10, pp. 264 *sq.*
3 Diod. XVII, 39, 2, he suppresses the real letter and puts a forgery before his
  friends.
4 App. 22, 1, p. 356, ἢ φήσων γε ἐγνωκέναι; see Wilcken's reasons for
  assigning this sentence to Cleitarchus, *S.B. Berlin*, XXX, 1928, p. 588 [15].
5 Curt. VII, 2, 35–7; Justin XII, 5, 6–8.
6 Ps.-Callisthenes Α', II, 21, 22 *sqq.*; obviously from the same source as
  Diodorus on the Massaga massacre.

it up—a fairly well-known type. His ignorance of the geography of Asia has already been dealt with (§ B, pp. 14 *sq.*). But as to what he thought of Alexander, all we can see is, on the one hand, untrue and highly sensational stories, by no means creditable to Alexander, such as the Amazon Queen, Thais, Alexander in India imitating Dionysus, and so on, and, on the other hand, accusations of cheating and massacre which show a strong animus against the Macedonian king. More than this cannot be deduced about his book from the fragments, and I do not know that it would be of much value if it could be.

E'. THE POETASTERS

IT has been seen (in § E) that, in all probability, the connection between Alexander and Dionysus, and certain imitations of Dionysus and Semiramis by Alexander, appeared in and were handed down by Cleitarchus; he probably also recorded some imitations of the Achilles story, applied to Alexander, but whether he had much, or anything, to do with the Heracles stories is obscure, though in some cases it might be a natural supposition. Now that it is certain that Cleitarchus was not with Alexander's expedition, but was a secondary writer who wrote in the reign of Ptolemy II, his own sources have to be considered. Some of this has been done—his use of Aristobulus, for instance; but we still have to account for those of the stories connected with Alexander's three ancestors, Dionysus, Achilles, and Heracles, which are untrue and which appear in our extant writers. There is little doubt where they originated, even if in some cases it may be quite uncertain, and in no case completely certain, that it was Cleitarchus who adopted and passed them on; they originated with certain poets contemporary with Alexander, all or most of whom accompanied his expedition. It is a source which has been strangely neglected.

Curtius has an invaluable passage on the poets, or poetasters, who were with Alexander at Bactra:[1] Agis of Argos and Cleon of Sicily

---

1 Curt. VIII, 5, 8, speaking of the 'perniciosa adulatio' of Alexander as due to Greeks, not Macedonians, says: 'Agis quidam Argivus, pessimorum carminum post Choerilum conditor, et ex Sicilia Cleon...adulator, et cetera urbium suarum purgamenta, quae propinquis etiam maximorumque exercituum ducibus a rege praeferebantur—hi tum coelum illi aperiebant Herculemque et Patrem Liberum et cum Polluce Castorem novo numini cessuros esse iactabant.'

are named, the rest he lumps together as *cetera urbium suarum purgamenta*. Agis, whom he calls the worst of poets after Choerilus, wrote an epic on Alexander, and was one of those who were ready to make *proskynesis* to him;[1] Plutarch exhibits him as a type of those flatterers (κόλακες) who used blunt speech as an instrument of flattery, and makes him say to Alexander, who had given a present to a jester: 'You sons of Zeus all love flatterers and buffoons; Heracles rejoiced in the Kerkopes, Dionysus in the Sileni, and now look at yourself.'[2] Cleon[3] is called a regular *adulator* (κόλαξ), who in Curtius' story proposed that, following the precedents of Heracles and Dionysus, Alexander should be deified.[4] There were others also; collectively, says Curtius, they opened to Alexander the portals of heaven and were in the habit of boasting that Heracles, Bacchus, and the Dioscuri (the reference to the Dioscuri will be presently explained) would give place to the new deity.[5] These people constituted, or formed part of, what Plutarch calls Alexander's 'chorus' (χορός) of flatterers;[6] and it will be noticed that every general reference to them which has survived always brings in Dionysus and Heracles. But apparently they confined themselves to these two (except for the reference to the Dioscuri); also it is clear, from Curtius' statement that Heracles and Dionysus were to give place to the new deity, that they did *not* identify Alexander with Dionysus, which may have its bearing on the thoroughly discredited story that Alexander was made a New Dionysus at Athens.

What Curtius says is supported by stories, λόγοι, quoted by Arrian; these stories give the substance of some of the flatteries bestowed on Alexander at Bactra, but do not allude to the manner in which this stuff got handed down to posterity. The obscure reference in Curtius to the Dioscuri is explained by Arrian IV, 8, 3. Alexander, runs the λόγος, had neglected his usual sacrifice to Dionysus on his day and had sacrificed to the Dioscuri instead; and at the banquet at which Cleitus was killed some had recalled that the Dioscuri had become sons of Zeus, cutting out Tyndareus (meaning thereby to suggest that Alexander had become a son of Zeus, cutting out Philip); certain 'flatterers' thereon asserted that the Dioscuri had done nothing comparable to what Alexander

---

1 Arr. IV, 9, 9, where he is called κόλαξ and ἐποποιός.
2 Plut. *Mor.* 60 B, C, cf. 61 C (the treatise on κολακεία).
3 For conjectures about other writings of his see Berve II, no. 437.
4 Curt. VIII, 5, 10 *sqq.*
5 *Id.* VIII, 5, 8 (given p. 55 n. 1).
6 Plut. *Mor.* 65 C, where Medios is called the leader τοῦ περὶ τὸν Ἀλέξανδρον χοροῦ τῶν κολάκων. So Plut. *Mor.* 331 A, the poets who flattered Alexander's Fortune.

had done.[1] Another λόγος (Arr. IV, 10, 6) asserted that before the abortive προσκύνησις ceremony Anaxarchus had said that Alexander the Heraclid had a better right to be considered a god than Dionysus or Heracles. All this indicates that Curtius' poets reproduced and worked up the kind of talk that went on, some of it no doubt their own.

For the Achilles stories we have to turn to another poet, Choerilus, whom Curtius also mentions. Choerilus of Iasos,[2] not to be confused with the earlier and better known Choerilus of Samos, was also with Alexander in Asia and described his *opera* (i.e. his acts, πεπραγμένα);[3] this took the form of a poem in which in some way, though exactly how cannot be said, Alexander appeared as Achilles, as is evident from the story—whether true or otherwise is immaterial in this connection— that Alexander said he would sooner be Homer's Thersites than Choerilus' Achilles.[4] Some or all of the fictitious connections of Alexander with Achilles which we possess must be Choerilus' invention. The picturesque ride of the Thessalian cavalry round Achilles' tomb, while they called on Achilles' horses by name,[5] is not history (though one would like it to be), for the Thessalians were not there at all;[6] it is obvious poetry, and not bad poetry either, despite Choerilus' reputation. Alexander's fight with the river Acesines,[7] down which he did *not* sail, is poetical stuff also; it was imitated from one poet, Achilles' fight with the river Scamander in Homer, and passed on to another, the fight in Nonnus of Dionysus with the river Hydaspes, father of the Indian leader Deriades. When Alexander crowned Achilles' tomb, Hephaestion was said to have crowned that of Patroclus.[8] It was too early for Hephaestion, who was not one of Alexander's boyhood friends, to appear as his Patroclus; it may be from the source featuring

1 What the Dioscuri had done seems unknown, but Aëtius (*S.V.F.* II, 1009) says that they, together with Heracles and Dionysus, were raised to the gods for benefiting mankind.
2 Berve II, no. 829, with full references; Jacoby II, p. 828, no. 10.
3 Porphyry on Horace, *A.P.* l. 357.
4 *Ib.*, 'Alexander dixisse fertur, multum malle se Thersiten Homeri esse quam Choerili Achillem'. So, without naming Choerilus, Ps.-Call. A', I, 42, 13.
5 Philostratus, *Heroicus*, XX, 29; see G. Radet, *Notes critiques sur l'histoire d'Alexandre*, I, 1925, p. 12.
6 The cavalry crossed from Sestos to Abydos with Parmenion, Arr. I, 11, 6; Diod. XVII, 17, 1 implies the same. Plutarch, *Alex.* XV, makes Alexander too cross the Dardanelles and thence go to Ilium, which differs from the λόγος in Arrian.
7 Diod. XVII, 97, 3; Curt. IX, 4, 14; Addenda.   8 Arr. I, 12, 1, a λόγος.

Hephaestion which Diodorus used (§ F, p. 78), but whether from Choerilus originally cannot be said. Finally, there is the death of Batis, which is on quite a different footing and requires separate treatment (App. 11).

Apart from the poets mentioned by Curtius, another of the time is known who had a great deal to do with the Heracles stories, the author of the *Heracleia* known to Strabo. Heracles had naturally been a favourite subject for poets for centuries, and three other *Heracleias* were written later in Hellenistic times;[1] but Strabo calls the one in question '*the* Heracleia' as though no other were known,[2] which may mean that it was the only one known to him as bearing on the Alexander-Heracles stories he is discussing. The ascription of this poem to Peisander was usual, and in one place Strabo so cites it;[3] but in another place he expresses doubts whether the author was Peisander or someone else.[4] Naturally we are no wiser than he; conjecture has been rife,[5] and the name is not very material; I shall use the term 'Peisander', in inverted commas, to denote the author of the *Heracleia* cited by Strabo, which will beg no questions. It is certain, from Arrian's explicit statement,[6] that much of Strabo's criticism which I am about to cite was, in essence, taken from that genuine critic Eratosthenes, and it may be that the phrase '*the* Heracleia' is Eratosthenes' also; but I shall continue to call it Strabo's, for besides reproducing Eratosthenes he made additions of his own. Strabo then says first[7] that, to flatter Alexander, the name Caucasus (the 'end of the earth' to Greeks, Καύκασον ἐσχατόωντα) was transferred to the Indian mountains (i.e. to the new 'end of the earth'), and with the name were transferred the stories of Prometheus and his cave and of Heracles releasing him; the flattery here must lie in the suggestion that Alexander had gone farther than Heracles. In a later book[8] Strabo is more explicit; taking together the three Heracles stories in India which were connected with Alexander, viz. that Heracles had failed to take Aornos, that the Sibi were descendants of Heracles' troops, and the Prometheus-Caucasus story, he says it is clear that these stories are 'inventions of those who flattered Alexander'[9] (for which he gives two reasons) and then adds that the στολή of

1 See Gruppe, 'Herakles' in PW Supp. Bd. III, 1118, 1121.
2 Strabo XIV, 2, 13 (655); XV, 1, 9 (688).
3 *Id.* XIV, 655, Πείσανδρος ὁ τὴν Ἡρακλείαν γράψας.
4 *Id.* XV, 688, εἰ Πείσανδρος ἦν εἴτε ἄλλος τις.
5 Gruppe, *op. cit.* 1118. Not in Susemihl.
6 Arr. V, 3, 1–4, expressly from Eratosthenes.
7 Strabo XI, 5, 5 (505).   8 *Id.* XV, 1, 9 (688).
9 *Id.* XV, 1, 9 (688), πλάσματα τῶν κολακευόντων Ἀλέξανδρον.

Heracles, i.e. his Indian expedition, is 'an invention of the poet of the *Heracleia*, whether he were Peisander or someone else'.[1] These two phrases, both using the same word for invention, πλάσμα, and both referring to the same thing, the Indian expedition of Heracles, prove that 'those who flattered Alexander' and 'the poet of the *Heracleia*' are identical; and as you cannot flatter a dead man, it means that 'Peisander' was another contemporary of Alexander's. It does not prove that he was one of the 'chorus' who were with him in India, but it makes it very probable; otherwise how would he have flattered him?

Before leaving Heracles, there are two other points to notice. One is a small apparent discrepancy in our sources with regard to the transfer of the name Caucasus. According to Arrian, Eratosthenes attributed the transfer of the name to 'the Macedonians', i.e. the army.[2] According to Strabo, who is also following Eratosthenes, the transfer was due to flatterers of Alexander, whom he specifically identifies with 'Peisander'.[3] The poet, even if he was there, which is only a strong probability, certainly did not carry weight enough to make an invention of that sort stick; I imagine it means that the army started it and 'Peisander' then wrote about it and wrote it up. The other point is the Heracles-road. Alexander's fictitious Plans included an Alexander-road planned to run along the south coast of the Mediterranean to the Pillars of Heracles, i.e. from Egypt to the Straits of Gibraltar; there it would join the traditional Heracles-road through Spain and Liguria to Italy (see App. 24). Some connection of the two roads there must be; what it was I do not know.

The Achilles and Heracles stories, then, centre on two known poets respectively; the Dionysus stories cannot be taken so far, though it follows from Curtius that Agis and Cleon must both have had a good deal to say about Dionysus, and as regards Agis this is borne out by the story already cited from Plutarch (p. 56). It may also be noticed that, alike in Curtius, Plutarch and Strabo,[4] Dionysus and Heracles are always bracketed together, as though what was true of one was true of the other. Now Curtius' statement, that these poets as a whole boasted that Dionysus and Heracles would give place (*cessuros*) to the new deity Alexander, can only mean that the new deity must have done (or be

1 *Ib.*, πλάσμα τῶν τὴν Ἡρακλείαν ποιησάντων, εἴτε Πείσανδρος ἦν εἴτε ἄλλος τις. Τῶν ποιησάντων = ποιητής.
2 Arr. v, 3, 1–3.
3 Reading together Strabo xi, 505 and xv, 688. See p. 58, nn.
4 Taking the whole of Strabo's discussion in xv, 1, 7 to 9 both inclusive (687–688).

doing) things *of the same kind* as the two older deities had done but had surpassed (or was surpassing) them in the doing of these things; and there are no acts ascribed to either Dionysus or Heracles which can come in question here except their supposed Indian expeditions. In the case of Heracles we have seen that this was in fact so; the same thing therefore cannot fail to be true of Dionysus, and Alexander must have been represented as imitating and surpassing Dionysus' Indian expedition. This is borne out by the fact that Strabo, in another connection (which I shall come to), says that Alexander in India was imitating both Heracles and Dionysus.[1]

We have therefore four named poets—Agis, Cleon, Choerilus of Iasos, 'Peisander'—besides an unknown number of others (Curtius' *cetera purgamenta*)—who were contemporary with, and flatterers of, Alexander, and who were all with him in Asia, at least from Bactra onwards, except 'Peisander', in whose case there is a strong probability but not a certainty. These men wrote poems, not all necessarily before Alexander's death, in which, taking the license of poets, they connected him with, and to a large extent made him imitate, pretended exploits of Dionysus and Heracles, and made him imitate a recorded exploit of Achilles, together with other Achilles connections; that is, they made him an imitative character. But it has already been seen (§ E, p. 50) that Cleitarchus made him an imitative character (allowing that it is not a complete certainty, but only a very high degree of probability, that the writer in question *was* Cleitarchus); he made him imitate Dionysus and Semiramis; and in face of this there can be very little doubt that it was Cleitarchus who reproduced many of the stories invented by these poets, not only about Dionysus but about Heracles and Achilles also. (For Semiramis we have no evidence; probably most of her connection with the Alexander story, § E, p. 51, was Cleitarchus' own.) We can hardly suppose that all these poets told their stories in precisely the same form, and Cleitarchus' use of them would explain why Diodorus and Curtius sometimes have differing versions of the same story, a thing hard to understand when both writers were supposed to have drawn on Cleitarchus alone; Curtius, at any rate, may have read all or any of these poets—he certainly knew Agis, Cleon, and Choerilus— and that may account, not only for his sometimes differing from Diodorus, but for his occasional omission of something he might have been expected to give.

I have often had to speak of these poets as a body, in the way Curtius

---

1 Strabo III, 5, 5 (171), μιμούμενος τὸν Ἡρακλέα καὶ τὸν Διόνυσον. See p. 62 n. 5 *post*.

does, but they were really a fortuitous concourse of individuals who showed certain common tendencies; we do not possess the material to differentiate them as we should wish. Naturally some of the remarks attributed to, or of the personal stories told about, this or that member of the body by other writers may not be true; but the collective tendency of the group to write up Alexander on certain lines is unmistakable. Of course, as I have pointed out elsewhere (§ D, p. 42 n. 2), the word κόλαξ, flatterer, which in Alexander's day probably did mean a flatterer, had become, long before Strabo, Curtius (i.e. *adulator*), and Plutarch wrote, merely a common-form cliché of Greek propaganda, used to signify anyone who thought well of a king, just as some English expressions to-day have become mere party propaganda and have lost all real meaning; and our poetasters need not have been as worthless, whether as poets or as men, as they appear in the tradition.[1] Choerilus survived to be read by Horace;[2] Eratosthenes and Strabo, as we have seen, thought it worth while refuting 'Peisander'; Curtius must have read Agis and Cleon, which means that their poems were there for him to read. But their writing up of Alexander on the lines indicated by the tradition about them started inventions which were not only untrue and foolish but which have exercised an unhappy influence on history.[3]

Naturally, so long as it was believed that Cleitarchus was contemporary and primary evidence, it was impossible for anyone to isolate this group of poetasters and to put them in their right place among the Alexander-sources; but now that they have been isolated and that it has appeared that Cleitarchus was indebted to them, it is natural to ask whether other things in the tradition may not derive from them besides stories connecting Alexander with Dionysus, Heracles, and Achilles. It is of course impossible now to find out what Cleitarchus' real debt to them was, or whether other things which in § E are ascribed to Cleitarchus might not have originally come from them also; there is not the material. But one story at least exists which *must* belong to this group. Strabo in one place discusses the habit, or supposed habit, of Greeks of setting up pillars or altars to mark the farthest

1 Curtius' 'urbium suarum purgamenta'.
2 Horace, *A.P.* l. 357; cf. *Ep.* ii, 1, 232 *sqq.*
3 Instances are not wanting in Greek literature of poetic inventions becoming 'history'. Pausanias' account of the exploits of the Messenian hero Aristomenes is taken from Rhianus' epic; the nightmare horrors recorded of Apollodorus, tyrant of Cassandreia, probably come, as Niebuhr first suggested, from a tragedy of Lycophron's (see Tarn, *Antigonos Gonatas*, p. 171). Doutbless search would reveal other cases.

point reached;[1] and Alexander set up altars both on the Jaxartes,[2] his farthest point north, and on the Beas,[3] his farthest point east. Pliny records that Dionysus, Heracles, and Semiramis had all set up altars on the Jaxartes before him;[4] the Semiramis altars presumably come from Cleitarchus, those of Dionysus and Heracles from one of our poets, whether they were passed on by Cleitarchus or otherwise. Strabo records, as we have seen, that on the Beas also Alexander was imitating Heracles and Dionysus,[5] which presumably again comes from one of our poets, whoever passed it on. But the point I wish to make is that there is a story attached to the altars on the Beas, the story of Alexander's camp,[6] which is such a meaningless extravaganza that even a Cleitarchus could not have invented it; it must come from some poet, and a very bad poet at that. As given in the fullest version, that of Diodorus, Alexander orders a camp to be built three times too large, with two couches for each man five cubits long ($7\frac{1}{2}$ ft.) and two mangers for each horse twice the usual size, so that the camp might be ἡρωικήν (suitable for one who was imitating ἥρωες) and that the natives might think the Macedonians had been giants. This piece of nonsense of course no more invalidates Ptolemy's testimony to the building of the *altars* than does the failure of a modern attempt to find traces of them.[7]

1 Strabo III, 5, 5 (170–1).
2 Pliny VI, 49; Orosius I, 2, 5; Peutinger table. See Tarn, *J.H.S.* LX, 1940, p. 92. There is no reason to doubt the authenticity of these altars, though the Alexander-historians do not mention them.
3 Arr. V, 29, 1, from Ptolemy; the citation of Ptolemy runs on from 28, 4.
4 Pliny VI, 49; see § E, p. 50.
5 Strabo III, 5, 5 (171); see p. 60 n. 1 above. Diodorus and Justin do not mention Heracles and Dionysus in this connection, and Curtius only mentions them in one of his rhetorical speeches (IX, 2, 29); this may be against it having been Cleitarchus who passed on the notice given by Strabo, especially as Strabo hardly ever used Cleitarchus (App. 13, p. 274 n. 4), whom he considered a liar (§ B, p. 15; § E, p. 44 n. 2).
6 Diod. XVII, 95, 2; Curt. IX, 3, 19; Justin XII, 8, 16.
7 Sir A. Stein, *Archaeological Reconnaissances in N.W. India and S.E. Īrān*, 1937, chap. 1: the altars must have been long since washed away by the westward shift of the Beas, there examined.

F. DIODORUS XVII

I MUST now turn to Diodorus book XVII and consider it by itself as what it professes to be, an account of Alexander and his career written by Diodorus as a chapter in his Universal History.

It used to be believed that Diodorus was a mere conduit pipe, that is, that he took some particular writer for the chapter in hand and largely reproduced him. A more recent variant of this theory has maintained that he took *two* writers and corrected his principal source by the other one;[1] another, that he changed sources but only used one at a time and never conflated two;[2] another, that he added to his principal source from any and every source he chose.[3] As to these theories, it must be remembered that, in his own eyes, he was a historian, with all that that implied; he is never averse to giving his own personal view;[4] and it does not follow that each of his books was written in the same way. He was not a competent historian, but that he naturally did not recognise; he is personally rather stupid, but honestly in earnest; he writes what he *thinks* is history, and in book XVII, when he comes across some story which he doubts, he gives it as a λεγόμενον, 'so they say', exactly as Arrian does.[5] If modern source-analysis has led to one result more certain than others, it is that the main source of his books XVIII–XX, omitting the Sicilian parts, is Hieronymus of Cardia; but, even so, he inserts at his pleasure items from other writers or from his own knowledge, and his account of the affairs of old Greece is from a different writer altogether.[6] Again, take the remaining book which has a good deal to do with the Hellenistic world, book II. There is no principal source here at all; it is a medley of many sources, some of which leap to the eye—Ctesias, Herodotus, Aristobulus, Cleitarchus, Iambulus,

1 See R. Laqueur, *Timaios von Tauromenion und Nikolaos von Damaskos*, 1936 (offprint of two PW articles with an Introduction).
2 N. G. L. Hammond on book XVI, *C.Q.* XXXI, 1937, p. 79; XXXII, 1938, p. 137 (summary, p. 149).
3 R. Schubert, *Die Quellen der Geschichte der Diadochenzeit*, 1914, and see § F'.
4 E.g. 6, 3, Darius a worthy opponent; 38, 4–7, his personal view of Alexander and of the part played by τύχη and ἀρετή, an important passage; 52, 4 *sqq.*, Alexandria in his own day; 117, 5, he ranks Alexander above Julius Caesar.
5 See 4, 8; 65, 5; 73, 4; 85, 2; 96, 2; 110, 7; 115, 5; 118, 1.
6 If this be Diyllus in books XVI (Hammond, *op. cit.*) and XVIII (Schubert, *op. cit.*), XVII must follow.

Agatharchides, Poseidonius, to mention only a few. Obviously therefore one must not start looking at book XVII with any preconceived ideas. Whatever may be the case in the earlier books,[1] in the later books, where so much is covered by the κοινή, there is little aid to be got from style; in XVII, very occasionally, some unusual word may help,[2] but as a rule Diodorus covers up everything with his own style, pleasant, pedestrian, quite undistinguished. But the *personality* of the source may show through the style. Take the description of Arabia in book II; it has been called 'flaming', and flaming it is, but the flame is that of Poseidonius. No one, passing from XVII to XVIII–XX, can be insensible to the change of atmosphere when Diodorus begins to use Hieronymus, even though his own personal framework of history remains.

For Diodorus, in his later books, had a theory of history which can be summed up by naming that great Hellenistic goddess, Fortune. He gives his own philosophy of the ups and downs of Fortune in XVIII, 59, 5–6, using as an exemplar Eumenes of Cardia: the real marvel, he says, would be, not that the unexpected happens, but should it ever fail to happen, and history must be accepted on this basis—a convenient doctrine which can be invoked to cover any improbability or inconsistency. Fortune is the framework of, and dominates, book XVII; but as Diodorus' theory of Fortune is not set out till XVIII, it is obvious that this conception, though far from original, is his own; it cannot be taken from Cleitarchus or any other Alexander-historian. But Diodorus himself is inconsistent, for he distinguishes sharply between Philip and Alexander. In XVI, 1, 6 he dismisses Fortune from the story of Philip; Philip did what he did, not by τύχη but by his own ἀρετή, whereas (XVII, 38, 4) Alexander's victories were due rather to τύχη than to ἀρετή, though once (at Tyre, 46, 2) he rises superior to the envy of Fortune. Fortune runs all through book XVII; it is she who brings the Persian leaders together at Granicus (20, 1), who causes Memnon's death (29, 4), who cures Alexander at the Cydnus (31, 6) and reverses her former favours to Persia,[3] though Persians thought their treasures a refuge against her (66, 2). Various instances of her mutability are given;[4] Sisygambis refuses to trust such an unstable goddess (59, 7). She in-

---

1 Laqueur, *op. cit.* argues that in the earlier books the style *is* important for tracing the sources.
2 I have not found many; the Cleitarchus extract in 75 (see § F'), στρατηγία at Gaugamela for a τάξις of the phalanx (57, 2), the mention of argyraspids (see § G'), perhaps exhaust the list. But we shall find some instances of *sentences* quoted verbatim from Aristobulus.
3 At Issus, 35, 7 to 36, 3; the story of the weeping eunuch, 66, 4.
4 47, 6; 69, 6; 101, 2.

fluences ordinary events; the rains in India (94, 3), and Harpalus' benefits to Athens (108, 6), are alike her work. She even influences the gods; it is her doing that an oracle arrives from Ammon at an opportune moment (115, 6). Once, and once only, she has no share in events: Alexander's death is decreed, not by her, but by Fate.[1] It must be emphasised that Diodorus' 'Fortune' in book XVII is the universal goddess; it has nothing to do with Alexander's own special τύχη, the thing which, in Peripatetic eyes, as exhibited in Curtius (see § G), was his ruin; Diodorus knows nothing of the 'Fortune of Alexander', so his sources knew nothing either.

Within this framework Diodorus—and this is the important matter— has set two inconsistent and totally different portraits of Alexander, which run side by side throughout the book; the dominant portrait, which occupies the greater space, is favourable, the other unfavourable. It is curious that this fact, which leaps to the eye, seems never to have been noticed. I will take the favourable portrait first.

Speaking in his own person (38, 5–7), Diodorus says that, though Alexander's victories were due to τύχη rather than to ἀρετή, yet when once he had got power his compassion for the fallen was his own, whereas most men cannot stand good fortune and become overweening; so, though Alexander lived long ago, it is just and fitting that we to-day should give him the praise due to his own virtues. As this is the exact antithesis of the view given by Curtius (see § G), any idea that the two writers can have had the same main source vanishes from the very start. It is difficult to-day to realise how strange this trait of compassion in Alexander[2] must have seemed to his contemporaries, anyhow to Greeks; no public man throughout Greek history is, I think, recorded to have shown pity;[3] it was unmanly,[4] and best left to poets and

---

1 ἡ πεπρωμένη only comes on the stage at Babylon (116, 1 and 4), and may be due to Diodorus' source, here mainly Aristobulus (*post*). But Fate had also killed Philip, in whose career Fortune had no part (XVI, 1, 5). I do not profess to understand Diodorus' reasoning in the matter.

2 It is brought out by Arrian no less than by Diodorus: Alexander shows mercy at Ephesus, I, 17, 12, and pity (οἶκτος) at Miletus, I, 19, 6; he pities the Theban envoys, II, 15, 3, and pardons the hungry men who broke the seals on his food-dump in Gedrosia, VI, 23, 5.

3 Once of a Macedonian, Antigonus Gonatas, when he sent two slaves to nurse the dying Bion.

4 Note how, in the Mitylenaean debate in Thucydides (III, 48), Diodotus, while arguing that it is inexpedient to put the Mitylenaeans to death, indignantly disclaims all idea of pity (οἶκτος) or kindness (ἐπιείκεια), both for himself and his audience. Herodotus V, 92 has *one* story of men showing pity; they were assassins.

philosophers.[1] Diodorus' theme is illustrated by Alexander's pity for Darius' womenfolk[2] and for the maimed men at Persepolis,[3] and by the whole story of his relations (partly at any rate historical) with Darius' mother Sisygambis, who at the end refuses to survive him (118, 3); on one occasion (66, 6), he fears that he *has* been overweening. Throughout the book, in unstinted profusion, are attributed to him all the well-known qualities which went to compose the figure of the ideal Hellenistic monarch, as elaborated by the world of philosophy in its endless treatises on Kingship, that is, on the art of ruling: φιλανθρωπία or love for subjects;[4] εὐεργεσία, which brings benefits to subjects;[5] ἐπιείκεια, kindness to all, a kindness based upon reasonableness;[6] μεγαλοψυχία or greatness of soul;[7] χρηστότης, goodness;[8] σύνεσις, wisdom.[9] The connotation, in particular, of the three terms here put first is unmistakable. But though he can show compassion, which is no part of the equipment of the ideal Hellenistic king, he is anything but a soft character. His courage, ἀνδρεία, and energy, ἐνέργεια, are emphasised throughout;[10] daring and endurance are natural to him;[11] he enters Tyre and the Malli town all alone (the former feat is not historical); Granicus is his own personal victory (21, 4), and he hopes and intends that Issus and 'Arbela' will be the same;[12] he punishes his satraps severely for the (to philosophy) most grievous sin of ὕβρις, insolence (106, 2), the sin which the Stoic school attributed to Alexander himself. Nevertheless, in spite of his victories, he often brought peoples over to him by persuasion, not by force;[13] like Seleucus after him, he answered in this (though Diodorus may not have known it) not to the Hellenistic but to the Indian ideal conception of the supreme monarch.[14]

This is a consistent and understandable portrait of a hero; but beside it there runs through the book another portrait quite inconsistent with

1 Philosophers: Bion and Xenocrates pitied animals, Epicurus slaves. Poets: one or two stories in Homer; Aeschylus' *Prometheus*; Euripides, of course, all through. He stood alone.
2 Diod. XVII, 38, 3 and 5, ἔλεος.
3 69, 4; so Curt. V, 5, 8.
4 2, 2; 4, 1, 3, 9; 24, 1; 37, 3, 6; 38, 3; 104, 4.
5 24, 1; 69, 9; 94, 3.
6 38, 3; 66, 6; 69, 9; 73, 1; 76, 1; 91, 7.
7 69, 5; 74, 4; 84, 1.
8 79, 1.   9 σύνεσις, 1, 3; φρόνησις, 38, 5.
10 ἀνδρεία *passim*; ἐνέργεια, 4, 5; 7, 2; 30, 7.
11 82, 6, τῇ συνήθει τόλμῃ καὶ καρτερίᾳ.
12 33, 5; 57, 6; 60, 1.   13 3, 6; 24, 1; 73, 1; 91, 2; 104, 4.
14 On this feature of the Chakravartin, see Tarn, *Bactria and India*, p. 263 and references. Seleucus: App. *Syr.* 55.

the first one, that of a contemptible and bloodstained tyrant. I give this second portrait here as Diodorus gives it. Though Alexander desired an accommodation with Thebes, he nevertheless decided to destroy the city utterly;[1] and when the Thebans issued their counter-proclamation he became 'like a wild beast in his soul'.[2] At Tyre, besides the captives he sells (this was true), he hangs or crucifies 2,000 others (46, 4). At Persepolis he not only burns the palace, which was true, but sacks the town with every circumstance of murder and rapine (70, 2). He devastates the Mardi country with fire and threatens the people with extermination (76, 5, 7). He massacres the harmless Branchidae for the supposed treachery of their ancestors.[3] He utterly exterminates the first people he meets in India, to discourage the rest.[4] He massacres the surrendered mercenaries at Massaga (84, 1 *sqq.*). He burns the Agelasseis alive in their town (96, 5). He massacres 80,000 people in Sambos' country (102, 6). For no apparent reason he ravages the land of the Oreitae with fire and sword and massacres 'many myriads' (104, 6 *sq.*). His personal character is no better. Though the army has condemned Parmenion to death, Alexander does not execute the sentence but assassinates him,[5] just as he is said to have assassinated Attalus, though a proven traitor.[6] He has a concubine for every day of the year.[7] He does not know what common fairness means.[8] He can be at a loss, or indeed in an agony of distress and perplexity;[9] at Tyre he nearly gives up (42, 6; 45, 7). Above all, he is a trickster; he cheats over Darius' letter, submitting a forgery to the generals (39, 2); and he is made to cheat in very terrible fashion over the Massaga massacre (pp. 53–4).

That these two portraits cannot come from the same source is obvious. They are not even joined up. The statements that Alexander wanted accommodation with Thebes and decided to destroy the city utterly stand side by side in the same section. His μεγαλοψυχία is emphasised just before the terrible quibble at Massaga. Persian cities

---

1 Both in the same section, 9, 2–4.   2 9, 6, ἀποθηριωθεὶς τὴν ψυχήν.
3 Table of contents κ′. See App. 13.
4 Table of contents λβ′.   5 80, 1, 3, ἐδολοφόνησε.
6 2, 5, δολοφονῆσαι, though his treachery is given 3, 2. In 5, 2 Diodorus has a different story, even worse for Alexander; this is an accretion on the unfavourable portrait from some other source. For another such accretion see n. 9 below.
7 77, 6. See p. 82 n. 3 and App. 18 p. 323.
8 The story of Dioxippus' duel, 100 *sq.*
9 ἀμηχανία at Halicarnassus, 26, 7, and at Tyre, 42, 6; ἀγωνία in case Memnon invades Macedonia, 31, 4. This particular failing is not met with after the 'mercenaries' source' ceases, and should therefore come from it.

join him, *not* through fear, just after the (supposed) horrors of the sack of Persepolis. The vitally necessary punishment of the satraps for ill-treatment of subjects follows straight upon his own massacre of the Oreitae. Two completely different accounts of his treatment of the Oreitae, of which more presently, stand side by side (see App. 8, II, pp. 252 *sq.*). I really need not go on. It means that Diodorus personally, apart from his sources, was not a good historian; but that is well-known. Left to himself, he *can* say the most extraordinary things: Sisygambis warns Alexander of the Lyncestian long before he ever came across her (32, 1); when his men are swept away crossing the Tigris he devises the scheme of making them take hands, commonplace knowledge to everybody everywhere.[1] I do not of course mean that the one portrait could have been all light and no shadows, the other all shadows and no light; I mean that the two conceptions of Alexander which stand at the base of the two portraits, the king and the tyrant, are irreconcilable; we are dealing with two separate sources, and we have to find them.

There is no doubt about the secondary portrait, the unfavourable one. The source is some one who delighted in stories of massacres, whether his own or somebody else's invention or just the floating tales of popular belief, and this can only be Cleitarchus (see § E, pp. 53 *sq.*); in fact, one massacre, that in Sambos' territory, is explicitly ascribed to him.[2] There will be more to say about Cleitarchus later; meanwhile I need only point out that it follows that the dominant portrait, the favourable one, was *not* from Cleitarchus, who moreover was, as has been seen (§ E), in all probability hostile to Alexander's memory. But the dominant portrait, in a secondary writer, is almost bound to come from his main source (if he has one),[3] the source he used to give him, at the least, a connected outline of the story, however much he might embellish it or add incidents and details from elsewhere; and as we know that Diodorus did, for the connected story in books XVI and XVIII–XX, use a main source—i.e. Theopompus for Philip II in book XVI, Hieronymus for the Successors in books XVIII to XX—he must have had a main source for XVII also; and Cleitarchus was not, and cannot have been, his main source for that book, otherwise we should get the

1 55, 5, ἀντιμηχανώμενος. Taking hands 'like men crossing a river' is one of the two unforgettable illustrations in Agelaus' famous speech at Naupactus, Polyb. v, 104, 1, and he had to use an image universally known.
2 Cleitarchus fr. 25, Jacoby= Curt. IX, 8, 15.
3 Curtius (see § G) is an exception, as in so many things; he seems to have had no main source after Gaugamela, and his main portrait derives from Peripatetic tradition.

absurdity that the main source was only used for a secondary portrait, not for the primary one. What we really have to do, therefore, to get at Diodorus' main source in XVII, is to seek the origin of the main portrait.

It was favourable to Alexander, and portraits favourable to Alexander were anything but common. Literature, generally speaking, was in Greek hands, not Macedonian; and Greece, with the exception of one or two bodies of men who produced no literature—the aristocracy of Argos, for example—was hostile, often bitterly hostile, to Alexander; that needs no repeating. We do get, in Alexander's own generation, some individual Greeks who accompanied him and felt his influence, but these were the only Greeks favourable to him till a much later time, so far as our knowledge goes. Of the great schools of philosophy and learning who guided thought, two, the Stoics and the Peripatetics, were bitterly hostile to him from start to finish,[1] and that coloured the whole of the literature of Alexandria, which grew out of Peripateticism, just as the Stoics were responsible for the blind hatred of Alexander so vehemently expressed by the eclectic Stoics of the early Roman Empire, like Lucan and Seneca. Of the other two schools, the Epicurean neither sought nor exercised any influence on history, while the Academy seems to have been tolerably neutral. It is noteworthy that, of the only three later writers known (Diodorus apart) who on the whole represented Alexander in a favourable light, the affinities of Eratosthenes[2] and Plutarch were with the Academy; and the fact that the third and most important, Arrian, was a convinced Stoic and yet wrote the book he did, is evidence of a character whose desire for the truth could not be better proved by a dozen disquisitions. The question then has to be asked very seriously, who *could* have been responsible for the favourable portrait in Diodorus, it having to be somebody who wrote a history of Alexander from start to finish, to give Diodorus the outline of events. Not Nearchus; he only wrote on India and his own

---

1 I give this here once for all, as it will often be referred to. For the Stoic view see J. Stroux, *Die stoische Beurteilung Alexanders des Grossen*, Philol. LXXXVIII, 1933, p. 222, which supersedes all earlier work, though W. Hoffmann, *Das literarische Porträt Alexanders d. G.*, 1907, is still useful, and cf. Tarn, *A.J.P.* LX, 1939, pp. 51–6. To the Stoics, he was bad from the start; his *paidagogos* Leonidas ought to have knocked the τῦφος out of him, and did not. Justin may have some affinity with this view, see § H. The Peripatetic view has long been known, as Cicero gives it; it is clearly set out in Stroux, pp. 229 *sq.*: Aristotle turned out a perfectly good pupil, but he was ruined by his own fortune. This portrait is given at full length by Curtius, see § G.

2 This is certain. Evidence collected, Tarn, *A.J.P.* LX, 1939, pp. 53 *sq.*

voyage. Not Onesicritus; he did not write a history but a professed romance (§ D, pp. 34 *sq.*), and there is no sign of Diodorus having used him. Certainly not Chares the Chamberlain; one or two passages apart, like the *proskynesis* matter (which he presumably saw), the fragments only exhibit a trifler, immersed in Court ceremonies and dinners, the minutiae of his office; no influence on anybody can be traced. The scanty fragments of Marsyas of Pella, the only Macedonian writer known besides Ptolemy, tell us nothing, and no influence of his is traceable. Callisthenes of course is out of the question; he died at Bactra, and anyhow we know the kind of things he wrote, which Diodorus does not reproduce. Unless we are to postulate the use of some unknown writer whose history has perished without trace, which would be absurd, we are thrown back on Arrian's sources, Ptolemy and Aristobulus. Arrian is primarily Ptolemy; but Diodorus' complete lack of understanding of Alexander's military operations, after he ceases to have the 'mercenaries' source' to help him, shows that if he did use Ptolemy at all, it can only have been incidentally. He sometimes reproduces the 'good' tradition which we know from Arrian, but in such cases it is usually impossible to say whether he is reproducing Ptolemy, or Aristobulus, or the two in agreement. I can only say that I have not found anything myself which *must* show a knowledge of Ptolemy, though there are two things which perhaps *might* do so.[1] There is the figure of 1,000 ships on the Indus (95, 5). This is Ptolemy's figure;[2] but Aristobulus, or anybody else, might have given it also. And there is the story (103, 7) that in Sambos' country Ptolemy was wounded by a poisoned weapon and cured through Alexander dreaming that a serpent brought to him the proper remedial herb in its mouth. The serpent, like one of the snakes which, Ptolemy said, guided Alexander to Ammon, must have been Psois-Sarapis in his serpent form,[3] and the story is propaganda for Sarapis. Ptolemy did twice introduce propaganda for Sarapis, the god he had made, into the Alexander-story: the snakes on the way to Ammon, and the story that the god at Babylon whose oracle was sought by the generals when Alexander lay dying was Sarapis.[4] But it is more than doubtful if the story of the serpent in

1 Add perhaps that Diodorus (XVII, 17, 6) does once call Granicus a ἱππομαχία, which is Arrian's phrase (I, 17, 9; IV, 8, 6; VI, 11, 4; cf. VII, 9, 7). But he might have got it anywhere.
2 Arr. VI, 2, 4, where χιλίων for δισχιλίων is certain.
3 Tarn, *J.H.S.* XLVIII, 1928, p. 219. The other snake was Thermuthis-Isis.
4 Arr. VII, 26, 2; Plut. *Alex.* LXXVI. See Kaerst, *Gesch. d. Hellenismus* II², pp. 244 *sq.*; A. D. Nock, *J.H.S.* XLVIII, 1928, p. 21 n. 2.

Alexander's dream comes from Ptolemy at all. It is a dubious story, for there is another version which places Ptolemy's wound in the land of the Oreitae and makes Alexander dream that a man, not a serpent, brought the remedial herb;[1] more likely Diodorus got the serpent story from some writer (it could even be Cleitarchus, for it recurs in Curtius ix, 8, 26) who invented it to do honour to Ptolemy and his god, seeing that Diodorus follows it up with a formal 'Praise of Ptolemy', which Ptolemy could not have written himself. Another matter to notice, in regard to Ptolemy, is that Diodorus' favourable portrait of Alexander makes much use, as we have seen, of the terminology proper to the ideal Hellenistic king; this does not fit with what is known of Ptolemy and his portrait of Alexander, but it does fit with Arrian, and *may* therefore fit with Aristobulus.

The result is that, by a process of exhaustion, we are thrown back on Aristobulus as Diodorus' main source, that is to say, his main source from the point (which I shall come to) where he ceases to rely on the 'mercenaries' source'. I am not of course relying solely on a process of exhaustion; book xvii contains many recognisable items from Aristobulus, apart from the important but unnoticed fact that Diodorus uses Aristobulus' nomenclature, a good and certain test; for my analysis of part of Strabo xv in § D has shown that Aristobulus used a number of name-forms differing from those of Ptolemy-Arrian. I must now run through Diodorus, and examine his sources; I may say at once that we shall find that book xvii is a pretty complex work.

Diodorus begins by taking the 'mercenaries' source' as his principal guide down to Issus, and it will be well to see what this document, also largely used by Curtius, was.[2] Every one will have noticed two things: that Diodorus has very little about Alexander himself between his crossing to Asia and Issus, and that he dismisses the whole of the story in Asia Minor between Halicarnassus and Cilicia with the bald state-

1 Strabo, xv, 2, 7 (723).
2 Ranke, I believe, was the first to suggest that Diodorus had some information from the side of Darius' Greek mercenaries, and this was taken up by Kaerst, *Gesch. d. Hellenismus* I³, 544; but as long as it was believed that Diodorus xvii was Cleitarchus and that Cleitarchus was an early source who might have had verbal information, there was no temptation to go further. But now that it is certain (§ C) that Cleitarchus, at the earliest, is after 280 b.c., the position is altered, and Diodorus' omission of Alexander's march across Asia Minor is alone conclusive that he was using some *written* source which omitted it also; and only a 'mercenaries' source' could have had a reason (pp. 72–3) for doing this.

ment that 'Alexander subdued the coast as far as Cilicia',[1] thus omitting two incidents which bear strongly on Alexander's character, Mount Climax and the Gordian knot. The reason of both phenomena is that Diodorus is following the so-called 'mercenaries' source', an unknown Greek who wrote from the point of view of the Greek mercenaries in Darius' service. He was a capable and tolerably accurate writer, well versed in military matters; he does not abuse Alexander, who is merely the opponent of Darius; his object is to tell the story of the mercenaries. From him come the detailed numbers in Diodorus of Alexander's army (see App. I, IV), and the oft-repeated statement that the Macedonians fought in relays and replaced tired troops by ἔφεδροι,[2] a thing not mentioned elsewhere in our literature, not even by Ptolemy, to whom doubtless it was such an everyday matter that he never thought of describing it, just as Polybius never described the Achaean constitution. This writer's hero is the mercenary leader Memnon, who is well written up;[3] he intends to invade Macedonia itself, not Greece;[4] he is the hero of Halicarnassus,[5] and takes Mitylene himself,[6] though in fact it was taken after his death; that death is the supreme instance of Fortune's aid to Alexander.[7] From this writer also comes the favourable view given by Diodorus of the mercenaries' paymaster Darius; his bravery is praised[8] (he was really a coward) and his care for his troops[9] (which might be true for the invaluable Greeks); he has a good reason for fighting at Issus;[10] his flight at both Issus and Gaugamela is elaborately excused.[11] But what makes Diodorus' use of this writer certain is this. In the Aegean, Diodorus naturally takes the story down to Memnon's death. But shortly after that, the mercenaries with the Persian fleet were taken by sea direct to Issus; they were not concerned with

---

1 27, 7, τὴν παραθαλαττίαν πᾶσαν μέχρι Κιλικίας χειρωσάμενος. At first sight it looks as if Appian, *Mith.* 8, made Hieronymus say the same thing (Jacoby II, no. 154, fr. 3), ἀνὰ τὴν παράλιον τῆς Παμφυλίας καὶ Κιλικίας ἑτέραν ὁδὸν ἐπὶ τὸν Δαρεῖον τραπέσθαι; but the context shows that Appian is only giving the general gist of Hieronymus in order to show that he did not take Alexander by Amisus and the north.

2 Relays: 11, 1; 12, 2; 22, 1; 24, 4; 26, 4. The later references in Diodorus (67, 5 Uxii, 85, 6 Aornos) are probably only Diodorus himself putting in what he has learnt.

3 7, 2 and 9.   4 18, 2; 31, 3.

5 24, 25.   6 29, 3.   7 30, 1; 31, 4.

8 6, 1, his duel with a Cadusian champion. Roughly speaking, the formal duels in the Alexander-story are never true. Ptolemy doubtless did kill an Indian chief, and Eriguios may himself have killed Satibarzanes in their battle; but these were not 'duels'.

9 7, 2, ἐπιμέλεια.   10 32, 3 *sq.*   11 34, 6; 60, 3 *sq.*

Alexander's proceedings in Asia Minor prior to his arrival in Cilicia, so their writer omitted all this, and consequently Diodorus omitted it also; he disposes of Alexander between Halicarnassus and Cilicia in six words, though he could have got information elsewhere. The writer had some idea that at Granicus the Persian leaders had a plan to kill Alexander personally (20, 1 *sq.*) which Ptolemy could not know (note also his touch here that Spithridates, whom he calles Spithrobates, had a bodyguard of 40 kinsmen); but though Diodorus uses this, he himself attributes the gathering of the Persian leaders to Fortune, one of several things which may show that he never gave book XVII a final revision (see p. 80 n. 1). Another is the contradiction between Diodorus' own account of the slaughter of the Persians at Issus[1] and the account of the 'mercenaries' source', which says (35, 1) that the Persians escaped easily (this is true) and some of them brought over ἔθνη to Darius, raised a power, and proceeded to take appropriate action (48, 6); it is known from Curtius, certainly from the same source, that this reference is to the occupation of Cappadocia and its important sequel (§ G, pp. 110 *sq.*).

Very useful is this writer's account of the mercenaries' masterpiece, the defence of Halicarnassus; it permits us to have two long accounts of this siege, that of Ptolemy-Arrian and that of Diodorus following the 'mercenaries' source',[2] which agree wonderfully as to the actual military operations, but are written, the first from the point of view of the besiegers, the second from that of the besieged. Ptolemy gives details of the troops Alexander used and of the principal Macedonians killed, and Alexander's attempt on Myndus during the siege; these things would hardly be known to the garrison, and do not come in Diodorus. In the attack started by Perdiccas' drunken soldiers, Ptolemy (naturally) says the city was almost taken and then breaks off, while Diodorus, equally naturally and perhaps truthfully, says that the Macedonians were defeated outside the wall and that Alexander had to ask Memnon for a truce to bury his dead. In the last great sortie, Diodorus praises, while Ptolemy does not mention, the Athenian exile Ephialtes who led it; Diodorus adds that the young Macedonians were put to flight and were turned back by the veterans behind them,[3] which Ptolemy would naturally omit. Finally, while both relate that after the defeat of the last sortie Alexander recalled his men when practically in—so much the garrison would see—Ptolemy alone gives the reason for this strange

1 36, 6, over 110,000.
2 Arr. I, 20, 2 *sqq.*; Diod. 23, 4 *sqq.*
3 Diod. 27, 2; see also Curt. VIII, 1, 36 who also (see § G) made much use
   of the 'mercenaries' source'.

act,[1] and that reason the garrison could not know. It is certain that, like as the two accounts sometimes are, Diodorus was not using Ptolemy at all.

From this source too comes much of Diodorus' account of Gaugamela (57 *sqq.*). Diodorus himself has no understanding of the battle, and is very confused (see App. 5, pp. 182 *sq.*), with some rhetoric; but certain points show a source favourable to Persia.[2] The description and disposition of Alexander's troops, except the light-armed, are so correct, including the flanking columns, that it might almost look as if he were using Ptolemy, but two things negative this: the fifth battalion of the phalanx, that of Amyntas, is commanded, not by Simmias, but by Philippus son of Balacrus (57, 3); and Philotas, in command of the Φίλοι, whatever that may mean, is detached from the eight ἴλαι of his real command, the Companion cavalry. Diodorus' source (60, 1) makes Alexander's charge the answer to the charge of the Persian Guard, which was hardly the case; and Alexander's camp is captured, not by the Persian Guard, but by the Sacas. He says however, as is true, that the aim of the capture was to free the female prisoners, i.e. Darius' family;[3] the 'mercenaries' source' knew Darius' order, while Ptolemy naturally did not.

One of the striking things about this source is its peculiar references to the Thessalian cavalry. In it, Parmenion's call for help at Gaugamela never reaches Alexander; the Thessalians turn the battle on their side without his help, because they could use their ἴλαι (squadrons) far better than any other cavalry.[4] By the time this was written, the Thessalians had more than rehabilitated themselves in the eyes of Greece by their exploits on the Greek side in the Lamian war, when the world of mercenaries once again challenged Macedonia; and the curious reference to their ἴλαι, twice repeated, is probably connected somehow with the statement of a later Greek writer on tactics that, unlike all other cavalry, the Thessalians fought in a rhomboid formation.[5] But the exaltation of the Thessalians above the Companions (33, 2) is merely Greek patriotism.

1 Cf. Diod. 27, 4 with Arr. 1, 22, 7. The reason was a desire to save Halicarnassus.
2 Besides the excuses for Darius' flight, see expressions like 61, 1, Δαρεῖος τῇ στρατηγίᾳ διαφέρων.
3 59, 7, αἰχμαλωτίδων. See § G, p. 110, on Curt. IV, 14, 22, who is explicit.
4 60, 8, Parmenion ταῖς τῶν Θετταλῶν εἴλαις χρώμενος ἐμπειρότατα, previously explained in 57, 4, the Thessalians τῇ τῶν εἰλῶν ἱππασίᾳ πολὺ προέχοντες τῶν ἄλλων. Cf. 21, 4, ἄριστα ταῖς εἴλαις χρώμενοι.
5 Asclepiodotus, *Tactica* VII, 2.

I need not follow the 'mercenaries' source' further; it must have gone down to Darius' death, at the least.[1] But, after Issus, Aristobulus begins to come in as a source with the statement that Parmenion, who had already advised Alexander to marry and leave an heir before invading Persia,[2] now again advised him to marry Darius' elder daughter Barsine, one of his captives, and beget an heir,[3] an obvious course which Alexander did not take till much later, though as a general rule he never put things off.[4] After Gaugamela Aristobulus becomes Diodorus' main source throughout; but I am not going through Diodorus minutely, for I am not writing a commentary. We get Aristobulus again for certain in Diodorus' account of Alexander's treatment of Darius' family, of the return from Ammon (§ D, pp. 36 *sq.*) and of the handing over of Bessus to Ptolemy (§ D, p. 37), and almost certainly in several statements about Hyrcania (see § F'). The story in Bactria and Sogdiana is unfortunately missing, so it is not known if Diodorus used Aristobulus' name-form Orexartes for the Jaxartes; but in India there is plenty of material from Aristobulus, though mixed with another source, almost certainly Cleitarchus (*post*). Diodorus' account of Nysa is lost; but the table of contents, II, λγ', makes Alexander show kindness to the city of Nysa, τὴν Νυσίαν πόλιν; the account of Nysa was therefore from Aristobulus, who we know mentioned the people, Νυσαῖοι (§ D, p. 33, § E, pp. 45 *sq.*); for the only alternative would be Cleitarchus, and to Cleitarchus Nysa was not a city but a mountain (fr. 17). The passage on Alexander's shipbuilding on the Hydaspes (89, 4) is taken from Aristobulus almost verbatim.[5] In 91, 3, Diodorus mentions suttee, the only one of our extant Alexander-historians to do so. As in book XIX he reproduces from Hieronymus, who saw it, a famous description of a suttee ceremony in the army of Eumenes of Cardia, it might be suggested that in XVII, 91, 3 he is quoting back from himself, as he sometimes does;

---

1 See further under § G. There is no sign that it went down to what might have been its logical conclusion, the Lamian war.
2 Diod. XVII, 16, 2.
3 This is the real meaning of Parmenion's advice; see App. 20, pp. 335 *sqq.* and the Note at the end of that Appendix.
4 When Alexander refused Parmenion's advice the first time (XVII, 16, 2), Diodorus says of him πρὸς πᾶσαν πράξεως ἀναβολὴν ἀλλοτρίως διακείμενος. This would apply even better the second time; and as both incidents must be from the same source, this statement is probably, like the second incident, from Aristobulus. It is repeated in Ps.-Call. A', II, 7, 7, τούτῳ γὰρ πάντων περιεγένετο ὁ Ἀλέξανδρος, μηδὲν ἀναβαλλόμενος.
5 See § D, p. 40 n. 6, where both passages are set out.

but it is quite certain that he took the notice in book xvii from Aristobulus, since both agree as to the place (among the Cathaeans) and the reason (to prevent wives poisoning their husbands), and the two accounts are moreover almost identical verbally.[1] Very important for India is Diodorus' use of Aristobulus' name-forms already referred to (p. 71). On the only occasion in book xvii on which he mentions the Beas (93, 1) he uses Aristobulus' form Hypanis[2] and not the more common form of Ptolemy-Arrian, Hyphasis. He uses Συδράκαι in 98, 1 for the Ptolemy-Arrian 'Οξυδράκαι, a form known from Strabo to be Aristobulus';[3] and in 102, 4 he mentions a people called Μασσανοί, whom no one else but Aristobulus gives.[4] Diodorus' name Porticanus (102, 5), for the ruler called Oxycanus in Ptolemy-Arrian (Arr. iv, 16, 1), is also from Aristobulus.[5] The statement in 85, 3, that the Indus is the greatest river in India comes from some writer earlier than Megasthenes (Cleitarchus was later), and the context shows that it is not from Ptolemy, since the Aornos measurements differ from his as given in Arrian; and as Aristobulus was interested in, and has left one invaluable fact about, the Indus,[6] it is probably his.

It is certain, however, that no one, reading Diodorus through, can miss a certain deterioration in the narrative when India is reached, which can only mean less of Aristobulus and more of a source which is almost certainly Cleitarchus (I shall come to this later); it is not till after the Bacchic rout in Carmania that Cleitarchus drops out, and we get back to the more sober narrative of the earlier part of book xvii. What has been going on in the Indian section in Diodorus' mind is very well shown in his account of Alexander's dealings with the Oreitae; he gives two different accounts, one after the other, of Alexander's pro-

1 Diod. 91, 3, νόμιμον ἦν τὰς γυναῖκας τοῖς ἀνδράσι συγκατακαίεσθαι. Aristobulus (Strabo xv, 1, 30 (699)) ἴδιον δὲ τῶν Καθαίων καὶ τοῦτο ἱστορεῖται... τὸ συγκατακαίεσθαι τεθνεῶσι τοῖς ἀνδράσι τὰς γυναῖκας. In the Strabo passage (xv, 1, 30) the quotation from Onesicritus (φησιν Ο.) ends with the words φιλοκόσμους δέ, and with the words ἴδιον δὲ τῶν Καθαίων καὶ τοῦτο ἱστορεῖται Strabo (as the verb shows) turns to another source, which, being unnamed, can only be his main source for all this part of xv, Aristobulus (see § D).
2 See § D, p. 32 and especially n. 3. On the MSS. readings in Diodorus here, see App. 14, p. 280 n. 1. Diodorus uses Hypanis again, ii, 37, 4.
3 See § D, p. 36 and App. 14, p. 280 n. 1.
4 They are the Μασιανοί of Strabo xv, 1, 27 (698) misplaced. See § D, p. 33.
5 Strabo xv, 1, 33 (701); see § D, p. 36.
6 Aristobulus fr. 35, Jacoby, on which see App. 14, p. 285 n. 2.

ceedings, with no attempt at fusing them; one account is certainly from Aristobulus, the other almost certainly from Cleitarchus.[1] After Carmania is left behind Diodorus has much agreement with Arrian, and we get the same three narratives from Aristobulus which Arrian gives: the story of the Chaldaeans begging Alexander not to enter Babylon from the west;[2] the story of Alexander's diadem blowing off and lodging on a rush, when the sailor who swam out for it put it on his head to keep it dry;[3] the story of the man who sat on Alexander's throne.[4] As regards the Chaldaeans, Arrian (VII, 17, 4) says that they wanted to keep Alexander away so as to enjoy the temple revenues themselves, but he shows that this was not Aristobulus' version; Diodorus' more probable account (112, 3), that they told Alexander he would be safe if he rebuilt E-sagila, must then be Aristobulus' version, which has to come in somewhere. It is true that Alexander had already *ordered* the rebuilding, but in his absence the work was proceeding slackly.[5] In the diadem story, which Ptolemy did not give (Arr. VII, 22, 4), Arrian follows the usual λόγος that Alexander gave the man a talent and then beheaded him, which makes no sense and is not like Alexander; Aristobulus says the man got a talent and a whipping, and as in Diodorus nothing happens to the man, he was following Aristobulus. This story illustrates two things, the falsity alike of the modern accusation against Aristobulus that he minimised and rationalised incidents and of the ancient accusation that he 'flattered' Alexander;[6] for it is so entirely obvious that he was right. The man had worn Alexander's diadem, and the seers would demand some apotropaic rite; doubtless at one time he would have been put to death; the whipping he got was a symbolical act which replaced the death penalty, like those acts in Greece which had replaced what had once been human sacrifices. The λόγος that Alexander put the man to death for doing him a service is only one of the numberless stories told later to discredit him. The story of the man who sat on the throne is very similar, though this time it is Diodorus who has added to Aristobulus' story the λόγος that the man was put to death, which has no chance of being true. Aristobulus' statement that he was first put to the question and then

---

1 See on these two accounts App. 8, II, pp. 252 *sq.*
2 Diod, XVII, 112 = Arr. VII, 16, 5 *sqq.* (Aristobulus fr. 54, Jacoby).
3 Diod. 116, 5–7 = Arr. VII, 22, 2 *sqq.* (Aristobulus fr. 55).
4 Diod. 116, 2–4 = Arr. VII, 24, 1–3 (Aristobulus fr. 58).
5 Arr. VII, 17, 3, μαλθακῶς.
6 See § D, p. 42 and especially n. 2, on the meaning of 'flattery' as a Hellenistic catchword.

released cannot be wrong, for Alexander offered sacrifice to the Avenging Deities so that they might transfer to the man the evils indicated (by the seers);[1] that is, the man became a scapegoat, and the point of a scapegoat is that it must *not* be put to death, but must live to bear its burden.

This is probably far from being the whole of Diodorus' debt to Aristobulus (see e.g. App. 23, p. 378); but it may suffice for examples. No one, however, can say where many of the items in Diodorus XVII come from; some unique accounts, such as the long description of Hephaestion's tomb, perhaps drawn from some work of art (115), sunrise as seen from Mt Ida, professedly by an eyewitness (7, 4–7), the description of Persepolis (71, 3–8), and others, merely illustrate the fact that he drew material from many quarters. His long account of the siege of Tyre embodies sections applicable only to the siege of a land fortress, apparently taken from some later technical work on Hellenistic siege tactics.[2] Again, he used some source which wrote up Hephaestion. In this source Hephaestion appears much too early, for he was not one of Alexander's boyhood friends;[3] he is Alexander's Patroclus at Ilium (the Achilles motive) and crowns Patroclus' tomb;[4] Alexander entrusts to him the appointment of a new king of Tyre (47, 1); he conquers a large part of India (91, 1, cf. 114); there is a long and unique account of his tomb (115); and he becomes a god, not a hero (115, 6). This source possibly appears again in Plutarch's story (*Alex.* XXXIX) of Alexander sealing Hephaestion's lips and in the λόγος in Arr. (II, 12, 7) which makes Alexander say that Hephaestion was his second self; some of the material might ultimately derive from one of the poets examined in § E', but Diodorus' source itself may well be identical with the source, whether a monograph on, or a *Life* of, Hephaestion, which Arrian (VII, 14, 2–5) must have used for the great number of versions of Hephaestion's death given by him.[5] We have seen that Diodorus had a separate source, very likely Diyllus, for the events in old Greece; his knowledge of Persia, e.g. the history of Ochus (5, 3 *sqq.*) and the quenching of all fires in Persia when a king died (114, 4), ought to be from Deinon, the former being too late for Ctesias, whom he used in book II. He also incorporates in his text matter of a later day than Alexander's, like references to the Seleucid

1 Diod. 116, 4, ὅπως τὰ σημαινόμενα δυσχερῆ εἰς ἐκεῖνον τρέπηται.
2 Given in detail in § G'.   3 Plut. *Alex.* x.
4 Arr. I, 12, 1 (a λόγος). The Achilles-Patroclus motive recurs in an unnamed writer, Arr. VII, 14, 4.
5 See § A, p. 4 and App. 16, p. 306 n. 1.

organisation,[1] and quotes from his own later books (or from the material collected for them), e.g. the name Argyraspids for Alexander's hypaspists,[2] the praise of Ptolemy,[3] and the long reference to Agathocles (23). Very interesting is the statement put into Alexander's mouth that, as the universe (κόσμος) cannot hold two suns, so our world (ἡ οἰκουμένη) cannot hold two kings.[4] Darius was not king of the οἰκουμένη, and it is doubtful if the phrase was in use in Alexander's day at all;[5] the sentiment belongs, not to the historical Alexander, but to the Alexander of the world-conquest myth, invented not too long before Diodorus wrote (App. 24), and in my view is probably to be explained as a reference to the famous advice said to have been given by Areios to Octavian, that the world could not hold two Caesars.[6] (Whether that advice was really given or not is immaterial here; it corresponded to what Octavian *did*.)[7] This supposed saying of Alexander's is also given by both Curtius and Justin *and in identical words*,[8] which are a good deal shorter than Diodorus' Greek version. I know of nothing to show that either Curtius used Trogus or Trogus Curtius; in any case, one secondary writer did not usually quote another secondary writer *verbatim*. Both Trogus (§ H) and Curtius (§ G') did use Diodorus; but they are not translating from Diodorus or any other Greek original,

1 105, 8, the satraps of the eparchies; 65, 2, Sittakene an eparchy. Bagistane, 110, 5, is another good eparchy name, one of the missing eparchies of Media. It could be the missing name in Isidore 6, if Alexander was following the great road from Babylon to Ecbatana; this is probable, but Diodorus is not clear.

2 57, 2; see § G'.   3 103, 7, from XVIII, 28, 5.

4 54, 5: οὔθ' ὁ κόσμος δυεῖν ἡλίων ὄντων τηρῆσαι δύναιτ' ἂν τὴν ἰδίαν δια-κόσμησίν τε καὶ τάξιν οὔθ' ἡ οἰκουμένη δύο βασιλέων ἐχόντων τὴν ἡγεμονίαν ἀταράχως καὶ ἀστασιάστως διαμένειν ἂν.δύναιτο.

5 ἡ οἰκουμένη is Diodorus' own regular phrase for the 'inhabited world'. It is doubtful if it was in use in Alexander's day at all; in Demosthenes VII, 35 (85, 15) and XVIII, 48 (242, 1) it only means the Greek world, and the same can be shown for Hypereides *Eux.* 33, 42, but I need not go into that. Alexander and his contemporaries always called the Persian Empire 'Asia'; some references are collected in my *Bactria and India*, p. 153 n. 1, but there are many others in Arrian.

6 Plut. *Ant.* LXXXI, οὐκ ἀγαθὸν πολυκαισαρίη.

7 He killed Ptolemy-who-is-also-Caesar because of his name and parentage, but did not kill Cleopatra's sons by Antony.

8 Curt. IV, 11, 22, 'ceterum nec mundus duobus solibus potest regi nec ⟨orbis⟩ duo summa regna, salvo statu terrarum, potest habere'. Justin XI, 12, 15, 'ceterum neque mundum posse duobus solibus regi nec orbem summa duo regna, salvo statu terrarum, habere'. The word *orbis* has obviously fallen out in Curtius; the *mundus* could not have kingdoms.

for two independent translators could never have produced versions both abbreviated and absolutely identical, especially the strange phrase *salvo statu terrarum*; they are both reproducing an original written in *Latin*, not Greek, and it is Diodorus who is paraphrasing it in Greek and amplifying it. And a Latin original, which need not have been in a history, could not, if I am right about Areios, have been produced earlier than 30 B.C., or even if I am wrong, before the middle of the first century B.C.; there was no interest in Alexander before the time of Caesar.

We have now got together the framework of Diodorus XVII. For the main thread of his story, events in old Greece apart, he used two sources consecutively, the 'mercenaries' source' and Aristobulus, which overlapped between Issus and Gaugamela; and on this background he superimposed material drawn from many quarters, few of which can be identified. The book then is rather a complex structure; to show this further, I have in § F' minutely analysed a single chapter, on Hyrcania. It remains to see how Cleitarchus came into this structure.

The first thing is to consider the amount of Cleitarchus which Diodorus omits; for little as we know of Cleitarchus, the amount Diodorus omits of what we do know, or think we know, is startling, if it were the case that Cleitarchus was his main source. No stress can be laid on the fact that he omits just half of the known Cleitarchus fragments, for his book XVII must seemingly have been much shorter than Cleitarchus' book, and he had to omit a good deal. Besides, he also omitted things which have no bearing on Cleitarchus; not being a skilful historian, he fills part of his available space with matter .quite immaterial, while he leaves out important things like the pursuit of Darius and the crossing of the Hydaspes, and gives only one line apiece to the mutiny at the Beas and to Opis. One omission is most peculiar; in 110, 2 Alexander forms a mixed army ἁρμόζουσαν τῇ ἰδίᾳ προαιρέσει, 'in accordance with his own particular purpose', i.e. the fusion of races; but there is not a word anywhere to show what that purpose was.[1]

---

1 It does not appear how this purpose could have been mentioned in the lost chapters on Bactria and Sogdiana. Many things besides this omission suggest that book XVII never had its final revision: such are the two inconsistencies noted on p. 73 *ante*; the duplication of the account of the 'whirling wheels' in the siege of Tyre (43, 1; 45, 3); the whole account of that siege (§ G', pp. 120 *sq.*); the two accounts, side by side, of Alexander in the land of the Oreitae (App. 8, II, p. 253 n. 1); repetitions, close together, of some word or phrase (§ F', p. 90); the curious slip in the account of Alexander's line at Gaugamela, which he has given correctly just before (§ G', p. 118, ὄπισθεν).

But here any attempt to whittle down his omissions from Cleitarchus must end. What strikes one most, seeing that he does give certain stories which, as we have seen, are in all probability Cleitarchus', is that he omits so much of the highly coloured material of popular literature, some of it usually, whether rightly or wrongly, ascribed to that author, e.g. invented figures like Memnon's widow (App. 20 and 18) and the eunuch Bagoas, who is Dicaearchus' (App. 18 and § G, p. 98), and sensational incidents like Mount Climax (that is Callisthenes), the Gordian knot (App. 10), the torture of Batis (App. 11), the intrigue with Cleophis; it is as if working with writers like Aristobulus and Hieronymus had given him a measure of sobriety which is very noticeable if he be compared with Curtius and Justin, and which has nothing to do with Cleitarchus.

Again, Diodorus XVII contains a number of excursuses or digressions —I have counted 13, and there may have been others in the lost chapters— while the Cleitarchus fragments perhaps indicate 6;[1] but no items in the two lists correspond, and that is more important than the omission of little points. It is also important that, except when definitely quoting a story from Cleitarchus, like that of Alexander and the Acesines (p. 84), he takes not the least notice of the very incompetent Cleitarchean geography, which has been indicated in § B. Finally, he omits what was probably the most important statement in Cleitarchus, that it was Ptolemy who saved Alexander's life at the Malli town, and he follows the 'good' tradition of Arrian in giving Peucestas the honour; and most modern writers would, and do, add to this that he omits Cleitarchus' chief sensation, the Roman embassy to Alexander (this, however, never did come in Cleitarchus, see § C, pp. 21–23). There has been much searching of heart as to why Diodorus, if he were substantially Cleitarchus, should havé omitted these two items; but as Cleitarchus in reality was nowhere Diodorus' main source, the difficulty does not exist.

Diodorus, however, *had* read, and was to some extent influenced by, Cleitarchus. Turn back a moment to his two portraits of Alexander. It has been seen that the dominant portrait, the favourable one, is at bottom that of Aristobulus, though probably somewhat worked over; while the secondary portrait, the unfavourable one, must be based on Cleitarchus, for it embodies pretty well everything which in § E was deduced about Cleitarchus' portrait of Alexander. We get all the

1 Fr. 2, Sardanapalus; 9, Carthaginian religion; 20–22, Indian processions; 33, 34, Themistocles; 17, Dionysus' invasion of India; and perhaps 10, Semiramis (cf. the account of her in book 11).

massacres (§ E, pp. 53 *sq.*)—the Branchidae; that in Sambos' country (expressly ascribed to Cleitarchus); Massaga (which was true); the Oreitae, both the massacre and the destruction of the country by fire; and the extermination of the first people met with in India. Some other items from Diodorus, unknown to the 'good' tradition, must obviously come from the same source; such are the 2,000 men hanged or crucified at Tyre (46, 4); the destruction by fire of the Mardi country, with the threat to exterminate the people;[1] possibly the burning of the Agelasseis in their town;[2] possibly the sack of Persepolis. It is obvious therefore that Diodorus' secondary portrait came from some one who liked to relate stories of massacres and so forth; and though very little about Cleitarchus' book is absolutely certain, there is a very high degree of probability, seeing that the massacre in Sambos' country is known to be from him, that this was Cleitarchus, as has already been seen (§ E, p. 53). If we add various other things in Diodorus' secondary portrait —Thais at Persepolis (§ E, pp. 47 *sq.*), the story that Alexander had a concubine for every day of the year (which is shown by the figures to be from Cleitarchus),[3] and the fact that Diodorus gives two of the few alleged cases of Alexander cheating (see § E, p. 54), over Darius' letter and over the Massaga massacre (he necessarily omits altogether the story of the Gordian knot)—it becomes as near a certainty as one will get that Diodorus' unfavourable portrait is in essence from Cleitarchus. In fact there is no alternative, for it is a portrait definitely hostile to

1 76, 4, πυρπολοῦντος; 7, ὄψονται... πανδημεὶ κατεσφαγμένους.
2 96, 5. Curtius, however, IX, 4, 1–6, transfers the story from the unknown Agelasseis to the well-known Sibi and makes them burn themselves, while in Diodorus 96, 2 *sq.*, from the 'good' tradition, Alexander makes friends with the Sibi and leaves them free. This illustrates the slender basis on which many deductions about Cleitarchus rest.
3 The figures are instructive. In the tradition, the walls of Babylon were built at the rate of a stade for each day of the year. Ctesias (Diod. II, 7, 3) gave 360 stades, the old reckoning, while Cleitarchus (*ib.* = fr. 10) gave 365, the reckoning of his own time. Similarly, the Great King had a concubine for every day of the year; Deinon (*F.H.G.* II, p. 92, fr. 17 = Plut. *Artaxerxes*, 27) gave the old reckoning, 360; Diodorus (XVII, 77, 6) makes Alexander take them over and says the number was the days of the year, i.e. 365, which, by a comparison with the wall of Babylon, is almost certainly from Cleitarchus. It is of interest, as showing once more that similar stories in Diodorus and Curtius do not always mean that Cleitarchus was the common source, to note that Curtius mixes up the two reckonings anyhow, in his careless fashion: Darius' concubines were 360 (III, 3, 24) and 360 was the number Alexander took over (VI, 6, 8); but he makes the Persian year contain 365 days (III, 3, 10, 365 young men) and makes the walls of Babylon 365 stades round (V, 1, 26).

Alexander; and as it is not the Peripatetic portrait given in such detail by Curtius (see § G), we are narrowed down to two sources,[1] Cleitarchus and Stoic tradition, which also made Alexander bad from start to finish; and it is certainly not Stoic tradition. That tradition (p. 69 n. 1), though alluded to by other writers, does not appear ever to have been embodied in a full-length historical work; it remained the teaching or tradition of a School; but it is known that it put the blame on Alexander's *paidagogos* Leonidas, and attributed to Alexander the two vices which the Stoics especially condemned, τῦφος and ὕβρις, the typical vices of the tyrant; and neither Leonidas nor these two vices are mentioned by Diodorus, at least in connection with Alexander.[2]

So far as we have now got, it appears that a good many of the worst of the acts attributed by this source of Diodorus to Alexander relate to India; and in fact there is not much more, beyond what I have given, which appears to be from Cleitarchus till we come to India. Two unimportant fragments of Cleitarchus, 4 and 30, relating to old Greece, correspond with Diodorus, but another, fr. 1, though giving the same figure as Diodorus XVII, 14, 4, differs so entirely in its application that Diodorus cannot have been using Cleitarchus; the natural inference is that, in all three cases, both were using a common source, probably Diyllus, and that in fr. 1 Cleitarchus either misunderstood Diyllus or was deliberately being sensational. Except for the episode of Darius' letter, I can trace no more of Cleitarchus in Diodorus till Thais at Persepolis (fr. 11), followed in Hyrcania by two items of natural history (see § F') and the Queen of the Amazons story. The statements about Alexander being at a loss, or dismayed, in connection with some military operation cease to appear after the 'mercenaries' source' ends (p. 75 n. 1), and doubtless come from that source and not from Cleitarchus; the author of that source does not speak evil of Alexander, but it is natural enough that he should represent the opposing commander as in difficulties.

I now come to Diodorus' use of Cleitarchus generally in the Indian part of the history; only two of the stories, other than the massacres already given, seem to bear on Alexander's character, but evidently in India Diodorus made more use of Cleitarchus as a general source than elsewhere. In the story of Dioxippus' duel (100–1) Alexander is represented as a man who did not understand common fairness, and here Diodorus for once—I cannot recall another occasion—makes an

---

1 Because it must come from some full-length study or history, and most of the literature unfavourable to Alexander seems to have been episodic.
2 In 106, 2, ὕβρεις are attributed to some satraps.

epigram;[1] this is so foreign to his way of writing (or to that of Aristobulus either) that one naturally thinks of the clever Cleitarchus (*probatur ingenium*). The details of the camp, the beds, etc. on the Beas being so built as to make men think that the Macedonians were giants (95, 1 *sq.*) are given as an evidence of megalomania; the actual story (see § E′, p. 62) may have been invented by one of the poets with Alexander for a different purpose, the glorification of Alexander, but there is no sign of Diodorus knowing these poets at first hand; it can only have been Cleitarchus who passed on the story, which was also known to Curtius and Justin, but he altered its purport. Of other matters we know that Cleitarchus exaggerated, so doubtless from him comes the story (88, 5) that Porus could throw as hard as a catapult could shoot;[2] and as he made Alexander an imitative character (§ E, p. 50), from him must come the story (97, 3) of Alexander's fight with the river, in imitation of Achilles' fight with the Scamander; this is certain enough, for the river named is the Acesines (Chenab), whereas Alexander sailed down the Hydaspes (Jhelum), and the hopeless geographical confusion, combined with the Achilles motive, can be due to no one but Cleitarchus.[3] We get cases, too, in Diodorus of other writers being passed on to him through Cleitarchus; his 16 cubit snakes (90, 1) came originally from Nearchus (fr. 10, Jacoby) and were taken over by Cleitarchus (fr. 18); and his account of the Fish-eaters is a highly composite one.[4] The latest trace of the use of Cleitarchus which I have found is the κῶμος to Dionysus in Carmania, which is certain enough (§ E, p. 49). If Diodorus' single sentence on this extravaganza be compared with Curtius' florid and quite impossible account,[5]

1 101, 6, παρόντι μὲν οὐ χρησάμενος, ἀπόντα δὲ ἐπιποθήσας: 'pleasure to have it none, to lose it pain'.

2 For other exaggerations about Porus, see App. 2.

3 Diod. 97, 3, πρὸς ποταμὸν ὁμοίως Ἀχιλλεῖ διαγωνισάμενος, i.e. the Acesines (95, 3). So Curt. ix, 4, 14, 'cum amni bellum fuisse crederes'; Acesines, ix, 3, 20. See Addenda to p. 57.

4 105, 4–5. 5 is largely Nearchus (fr. 1, Jacoby, p. 693 = Arr. *Ind.* 12 and 16, but Nearchus has no reference to fish-scales used as tiles). 4, which agrees with Curt. ix, 10, 9 *sq.*, is not from Nearchus; it might contain elements from some later writer, like Agatharchides, or from Aristobulus, who described Alexander's march (Arr. vi, 22, 4; the ἀκάνθας τῶν ἰχθύων of 23, 3 is not from Nearchus), or even from Onesicritus through Cleitarchus (Diodorus is not known to have used Onesicritus directly).

5 Curt. ix, 10, 24–end. The army in reality lost all its baggage train in the Makran, even to Alexander's personal luggage; but for the κῶμος it casually produces gold craters, huge gold cups, and expensive tent-hangings, while every soldier has a stock (*copia*) of something.

we have a case of what I mean by speaking of Diodorus' (comparative) sobriety; another is his complete omission of the Cleitarchean thesis that Alexander in India was imitating Dionysus. To imitate his ancestor Achilles, vouched for by Homer, was one thing, to imitate the somewhat dubious exploits of a god was quite another.

We have seen (pp. 76 *sqq. ante*) that in India there are plenty of traces that Diodorus was still using Aristobulus as his main source, though he superimposes more of Cleitarchus than he does elsewhere. But Cleitarchus was only a secondary writer, like Diodorus himself, and Cleitarchus, too, made a good deal of use of Aristobulus, embellishing him in the process; one particular case (the baboons) has been proved in § D. It is of interest to see how Diodorus handles his two sources in conjunction. Sometimes they are put side by side without any explanation: two kings, Porus and Sopeithes, are both called exceptionally tall men, but Porus is called 5 cubits high and Sopeithes over 4 cubits; that is, Porus' height is given in short Macedonian cubits, as in Arrian, while Sopeithes' height is given in Greek cubits, which means Cleitarchus.[1] Again, among the Oreitae, as is shown elsewhere (App. 8,`11, pp. 252 *sq.*), the accounts of Aristobulus and Cleitarchus are both given, one after the other. Sometimes Diodorus tries to reconcile the two accounts; in Sambos' country the account given by Cleitarchus is reconciled with the 'good' tradition by supposing that the whole 80,000 massacred were Brahmans (102, 7). Sometimes he picks and chooses details from both. In the account of catching monkeys, treated at length in § D, *q.v.*, he follows in the main, not Aristobulus, but Cleitarchus' embellishments of him, as is shown by his giving the item of the honey; but he salves his conscience by omitting the mirrors and the whole of the passage referring to the military formation of baboons. The best example is his handling of the little karaits in 90, 5 *sqq.* Aristobulus (fr. 38, Jacoby=Strabo xv, 1, 45), who had seen them, gave a good account of their habit of hiding in tents and household utensils, and of what happened if one bit you; Cleitarchus (fr. 18), who had not seen them, confined himself to a long and exaggerated account of their colouring. Diodorus combined the two: his account (90, 6 *sq.*) begins with their colouring, taken from Cleitarchus, as the words ποικιλίαι and χαλκοειδεῖς show, but greatly abbreviated, and then gives the consequences of their bite from Aristobulus.[2]

1 This is fully considered in App. 2.
2 Aristobulus fr. 38, αἱμορροεῖν ἐκ παντὸς πόρου = Diod. 90, 6, ῥύσις ἱδρῶτος αἱματοειδοῦς; Ar. βοήθειαν διὰ τὴν ἀρετὴν τῶν ᾽Ινδικῶν ῥιζῶν καὶ φαρμάκων = Diod. 90, 7, παρὰ τῶν ἐγχωρίων μαθόντες τὴν ἀντιφάρμακον ῥίζαν.

One feature of Diodorus' India must be omitted here; the Ganges question is too important and too complicated not to have a study to itself (App. 14).

Why now did Diodorus in India make so much use of Cleitarchus, when elsewhere he only uses him for isolated incidents or stories? The reason, I think, must merely have been that he thought that India, unlike better known countries, wanted writing up, as he had written up Arabia from Poseidonius, and he could not get what he wanted from Aristobulus. We know from Strabo a good deal about Aristobulus on India; he had an earnest desire to understand the phenomena of that strange country, the rains, the great rivers, the unaccustomed animals and plants, things which he treated at some length. Diodorus wanted a touch of something more interesting, exactly as some modern historians of Alexander, attracted by the warmth and colour which they have thought to find in the 'vulgate' writers, have agreed that you *must* use their stories or you get an incomplete picture. This is why such a fine critic as Schwartz, in his various writings on Alexander, was always hankering after Onesicritus. Doubtless there *was* warmth and colour to be found in Cleitarchus; too much, maybe. But history is concerned with truth, and with nothing else; though the chances are that if you can approximate to the truth the colour will follow automatically. But it will not be the colour of an Onesicritus or a Cleitarchus.

Probably, in Diodorus xvii, there was more of Cleitarchus, as there was more of Aristobulus, than I have been able to identify; but enough has been said to make the general position clear. The book is a complex piece of work; every passage has to be taken on its merits, and often enough the source cannot now be detected; but Diodorus' use of Cleitarchus is entirely a secondary matter, and to say that the book is essentially Cleitarchus, and to use it as such, is not only wrong but impossible. I mentioned before (§ A, p. 2 n. 2) that Schwartz gave a second reason for his view that Diodorus xvii was essentially Cleitarchus, which now need hardly detain us; it was that Diodorus names Cleitarchus in II, 7, 3, and that this was his way of introducing his sources.[1] Even were that true, the passage he quotes would not sustain his thesis; for what Diodorus does name is not Cleitarchus but 'Cleitarchus and some of those who later (i.e. after Ctesias) crossed to Asia with Alexander'; and even so, Cleitarchus and some of the Alexander-writers are only brought in as differing from Ctesias over one single measurement. But the complicated sources of book xvii could not be brought in thus by a side wind in book II over the question

1 'Diodoros' (38) in PW.

of a single measurement. Consider, for example, the books on either side of XVII: the formal introduction of Diodorus' sources in XVI with particulars of their work—Callisthenes and Diyllus (XVI, 14, 4 and 5) and Theopompus (XVI, 3, 8)—and the frequent references in XVIII and XIX to Hieronymus.[1] In XVII Diodorus never names any writers at all, which bears out the deduction that it was a tolerably complex work.

Diodorus XVII then is not Cleitarchus, and the book gives no support to any theory of a 'Cleitarchean vulgate'. Ever since Freeman wrote, it has been rather a fashion to decry Diodorus; certainly his critical ability was small. But the Hellenistic historian, at any rate, must acknowledge that he owes him a very considerable debt of gratitude. He has preserved for us many documents which would otherwise have perished unknown: for example, Iambulus in book II, the fictitious (and other) Embassies to Babylon in XVII, Alexander's Gazetteer and his so-called Plans in XVIII; above all, but for him we should know little enough about the great historian Hieronymus of Cardia. How he came to unearth the 'mercenaries' source', unknown to Arrian, cannot be guessed; let him at least have credit for considerable diligence in his profession.

F′. DIODORUS' METHOD OF WORK

IT has been a matter of dispute whether Diodorus only used consecutive excerpts from his source, or whether sometimes he changed sources as he pleased, even in the same chapter. Probably my analysis in § F should have settled the question as regards book XVII; but as it is rather important to know which view is correct, I am here analysing closely a single chapter in book XVII, Diodorus' account of Hyrcania in ch. 75. Why some of the Alexander-writers paid so much attention to Hyrcania, a province which, as Strabo complains (XI, 7, 2 (509)), was much neglected later, is entirely obscure.

I take the items in ch. 75 in order, after Alexander has left Hecatompylos. 75, 2, the river Stiboites, which enters the earth in a foaming cataract and runs underground for 300 stades (roughly 37½ miles) before re-emerging, is the river of Polybius X, 48, 7 which he calls the Oxus, and which, after producing a miraculous waterfall, also runs underground for a sufficient distance to enable the nomads to raid Hyrcania across dry land. Curtius in VI, 4, 4 calls the river Ziobetis

1 Collected by Jacoby, Hieronymos, no. 154, T. 3–6.

and repeats Diodorus' story with embellishments after his custom, but in VII, 10, 1 he transfers the story to the Polytimetus in Sogdiana; finally Seneca (*N.Q.* III, 26, 4) transferred the story to the Tigris. All these stories are merely variations of some native yarn; how it reached our extant authors cannot be guessed.

In 75, 3 Diodorus alludes to the Caspian Sea, giving the double name, Caspian and Hyrcanian, which it had borne since Eratosthenes (see § B, p. 11); this is Diodorus himself speaking. There follows a reference to the snakes and fishes in it, which comes from Polycleitus on the Aral (§ B, p. 8). In Curtius VI, 4, 16 *sqq.* this passage has become a regular treatise on the Caspian, which will be considered elsewhere (§ G, p. 104 n. 1); he gives more of Polycleitus than Diodorus does, but mixed with matter from Patrocles and (probably) Apollodorus of Artemita,[1] and also some Cleitarchean geography.

In 75, 4, we come to some villages called Eudaimones, the Blest, which are not mentioned elsewhere. They were presumably invented to illustrate the fertility of the country, Εὐδαίμονας καὶ πρὸς ἀλήθειαν οὔσας; who invented them cannot be said.

In 75, 5 and 6 we get examples of the fertility of the country, which require to be carefully examined. There are four items. As given by Diodorus they are as follows: (*a*) a vine produces a μετρητής of wine; (*b*) a fig-tree produces 10 medimni of dried figs; (*c*) spilt corn grows and produces a crop; (*d*) a tree like an oak drips honey. Of these, Curtius VI, 4, 22 gives specifically only (*d*). Onesicritus gives two of them, (*b*) and (*d*), but in different shape; he says (*b*) that a fig-tree produces 270 modii (= 45 medimni)[2] and (*d*) that a tree like a fig, called occhus, drops honey;[3] Diodorus therefore is not using Onesicritus, and indeed it cannot be shown that he ever does. Strabo alone, XI, 7, 2 (508–9), gives all four: (*a*) and (*c*) as in Diodorus; (*b*) a fig-tree produces 60 medimni; (*d*) 'the trees' drop honey. Strabo's sources can be ascertained. It has been seen (§ C, p. 17 n. 1) that the writer meant in XI, 6, 4 (508) is Apollodorus of Artemita, one of his regular sources; οὖν at the beginning of XI, 7, 1 shows that Apollodorus is being quoted, and he is Strabo's basis down to the end of 7, 3, where he is named; but Strabo, as is his way, inserts items from other named sources,

1 Curt. VI, 4, 19 mixes up the connection with the outer sea in the extreme north, 'a septentrione', postulated by Patrocles, with some connection with another sea which is *intermittent* and can only be that of Apollodorus; see § C, p. 17 n. 1.

2 Fr. 4, Jacoby = Pliny XV, 68. It does not say whether green figs or dry are meant.

3 Fr. 3, Jacoby = Pliny XII, 34.

Patrocles twice, Aristobulus twice, while part of 7, 2 is his own. 7, 2 begins with a list of Hyrcanian towns, not one of which occurs in the Alexander-historians or in Polybius; the list therefore must be later, after Hyrcania had become Parthian,[1] which means that it comes from Apollodorus. As we do not know that Patrocles ever wrote on Hyrcania or was ever there, and as Aristobulus did write on it,[2] the two sober statements (*a*) and (*c*), on which Diodorus and Strabo agree, must come from Apollodorus or Aristobulus. Strabo used both freely; Aristobulus was Diodorus' basis (see § F) but there is no evidence that he ever used Apollodorus; statements (*a*) and (*c*) must therefore be from Aristobulus. If one compares (*b*) in Diodorus with the exaggerated statements in Onesicritus and Strabo—grossly exaggerated even if green and not dry figs are meant[3]—it is tolerably certain that (*b*) in Diodorus must come from Aristobulus also. It remains to consider (*d*), the tree that drops honey. Why does Onesicritus say a tree *like* a fig, and Diodorus a tree *like* an oak? Who uses that sort of phrase? We have met it before. While most writers talk of the ivy on Mount Nysa, Cleitarchus[4] said that it was a plant *like* ivy called σκίνδαψός. So Cleitarchus (fr. 14) called the mountain bee of Hyrcania (which I shall come to) a creature *like* a bee, ζῴου μελίσσῃ ἐοικότος. It would seem, then, that Onesicritus started the game of making things sound more romantic by calling the tree, not a fig, but a tree *like* a fig, with a strange foreign name which nobody could check, and Cleitarchus, whether he thought of it for himself or was copying Onesicritus, did the same thing, but not too successfully; his name for the mountain bee, ἀνθρηδών, is indeed only his own version of the usual name,[5] but his name for the plant like ivy, which he probably meant to be taken for an Indian word, is merely Greek for 'a what-do-you-call-it' (see § E, p. 46). Diodorus (*d*), therefore, must come from Cleitarchus[6] just as the mountain bee does. Aristobulus had called attention to the oaks in Hyrcania (fr. 19), and probably said that some dropped honey, and

---

1 Strabo almost says as much a few lines later; the latest rulers of Hyrcania are the Parthians. Cf. xi, 6, 4 (508), where he says that Parthian rule πλεῖόν τι προσεκκαλύπτει.   2 Fr. 19, Jacoby=Strabo xi, 7, 2 (509).

3 Dried figs are said to weigh some 40 per cent of green.

4 Fr. 17=Schol. Apoll. Rhod. II, 904.

5 The usual name, from Aristotle onwards, was τενθρηδών, with a dialectical π form πεμφρηδών; references in Jacoby II, BD, p. 491. Diodorus' ἀνθρηδών, with MSS. variants, must be Cleitarchus' own coinage; hence Hesychius' explanation, ἀνθρηδών· ἡ τενθρηδών.

6 This is almost certain from Curt. VI, 4, 21, 'arbor faciem quercus habet', which is Diodorus' παραπλήσιον δρυῒ κατὰ τὴν ἐπιφάνειαν (appearance).

Cleitarchus, as he often did (§ D, pp. 30 *sq.*, 36, cf. § F, p. 85), took Aristobulus and wrote him up. Strabo, finding different trees named by Onesicritus and Aristobulus, just took refuge in writing 'the trees'. Of Diodorus' four items, then, three come from Aristobulus and one from Cleitarchus.

Finally, in Diodorus, 75, 7 we get, from Cleitarchus, the mountain bee of Hyrcania,[1] already mentioned. Diodorus' words ἐπινεμόμενον τὴν ὀρεινήν (though ἡ ὀρεινή is a common phrase of his own) must represent Cleitarchus' κατανέμεται τὴν ὀρεινήν; but it is more important that the preceeding phrase in Diodorus, μεγίστην ἔχει τὴν ἐπιφάνειαν, must be Cleitarchus' own words, for the following reason. Demetrius *de elocutione* 304 (see n. 1) said that Cleitarchus spoke of the bee as if it were a wild bull or the Erymanthian boar; but the words quoted from Cleitarchus do not bear this out in the least. Evidently Demetrius' quotation had something more in it than the Tzetzes extract gives; Tzetzes has clipped the quotation, and what he has left out must be the words I have quoted, 'it has an immense appearance', even if the phrase was originally used only in the sense of *une apparence immense*. Dindorf, whom Fisher follows, missed this and altered ἐπιφάνειαν to the meaningless ὠφέλειαν, thus making Demetrius talk nonsense. Their reason was that Diodorus had used ἐπιφάνειαν in the sentence before, 'a tree like an oak in appearance', κατὰ τὴν ἐπιφάνειαν. So he had; but he has a worse jingle in the sentence I am considering, where he uses λειπόμενον twice over; all it means is what many other things in book XVII show,[2] that that book never had a final revision. That Diodorus on this bee is following Cleitarchus very closely seems certain enough, though there is a most curious difficulty,[3] which does not, however, affect my results in this study.

1 Demetrius *de elocutione* 304, from Tzetzes=Jacoby, 'Kleitarchos', T. 10 and fr. 14 together: ὁ Κλείταρχος περὶ τῆς τενθρηδόνος λέγων, ζῴου μελίσσῃ ἐοικότος, κατανέμεται μέν, φησί, τὴν ὀρεινήν, εἰσίπταται δὲ εἰς τὰς κοίλας δρῦς, ὥσπερ περὶ βοὸς ἀγρίου ἢ τοῦ Ἐρυμανθίου κάπρου λέγων ἀλλ' οὐχὶ περὶ μελίσσης τινός, κ.τ.λ. Diod. XVII, 75, 7: ἔστι δὲ καὶ ζῷον κατὰ τὴν χώραν ἐπτερωμένον, ὃ καλεῖται μὲν ἀνθρηδών, λειπόμενον δὲ μεγέθει μελίττης μεγίστην ἔχει τὴν ἐπιφάνειαν· ἐπινεμόμενον γὰρ τὴν ὀρεινὴν ἄνθη παντοῖα δρέπεται καὶ ταῖς κοιλάσι πέτραις καὶ τοῖς κεραυνοβόλοις τῶν δένδρων ἐνδιατρῖβον κηροπλαστεῖ κ.τ.λ. Diodorus may have expanded his original with a little verbiage, as seems to have been his habit; compare the 'two suns', § F, p. 80.
2 Several instances are collected in § F, p. 80 n. 1.
3 The sentence in Diodorus which I have examined combines the peculiar phrase μεγίστην ἐπιφάνειαν with the extremely rare verb κηροπλαστεῖν. He combines the two again in another passage (his only other use of

We find then that, in this one chapter, the sources of the statements made are, in order: a native yarn, transmission unknown; the common Eratosthenian geography of his own day; Polycleitus; a unique name for a group of villages, source unknown; Aristobulus thrice; Cleitarchus twice. This proves that, in book XVII, far from always using consecutive excerpts, Diodorus might make a mosaic of items from as many sources as he chose.

G. QUINTUS CURTIUS RUFUS

NOTHING is known about Q. Curtius Rufus. To us he is only a name at the head of the book *De gestis Alexandri Magni*; he is never mentioned anywhere, and no other writing of his is known or even referred to; possibly the name was not even the author's real name. He presents a mass of problems, and the first is, why his book was ever written. The reason for the existence of all the other extant works on Alexander is known; the reason for the existence of this one cannot even be guessed. Probably it was stated at the beginning of the work, but books I and II are lost. The only conjecture which has even seemed worth considering has been that of Wilamowitz, that the book was written merely for entertainment,[1] or, as we should say, was a 'popular' work. This would certainly explain one or two things about it—its extraordinary carelessness, for example—but there are many other things which it would not explain; for all its shortcomings, too much trouble and too much valuable material have gone to the making of it for it to be merely a popular work; so though some difficulties are inexplicable, I am treating it as an attempt at a serious history. But it is a self-revealing work and is undoubtedly coloured by the peculiar personality of the author. He corresponds pretty well to what our forefathers called a 'gifted amateur'. The amateurishness is obvious; he often cares nothing whether or not he gets events in their right order, whether his geography is confused, whether he gives the wrong names;

κηροπλαστεῖν) which has nothing to do with Cleitarchus but comes from Timaeus: XIX, 2, 9, a swarm of bees ἐκηροπλάστησεν on the statue of the boy Agathocles, and the seers said it meant that he would come εἰς μεγάλην ἐπιφάνειαν, 'to a great showing-forth' or 'manifestation' (like a god). Is the double occurrence of this combination just a coincidence? or was Cleitarchus copying from Timaeus? Or is Diodorus in XIX, 2, 9, by a common enough trick of the mind, unconsciously reproducing phraseology he has already used? I have no worth-while explanation to offer.

1 Wilamowitz, *Die griechische Literatur*[3], p. 171, Unterhaltungslektüre.

he is going to create a certain impression, and he creates it. But the gifts are equally undeniable; he is as clever as he can be, and is quite aware of the fact. He seems to have no interest in his subject, save that it enables him to show what a clever man Q. Curtius Rufus was; he stands outside it and apart, and plays with it like a virtuoso. He can make epigrams which might pass for Tacitus on a day when Tacitus was not feeling quite at his best.[1] He is steeped in rhetorical training and writes like a rhetorician, and that not merely in speeches and battle-pieces—for instance, both Alexander and the Macedonians weep on every possible occasion; but if he wants to, he can slough the rhetoric as a snake sloughs a dead skin. And one neglects the rhetoric at one's peril, for scattered through it, like pearls in a pig-trough, are some quite invaluable facts and strange pieces of insight; the book is both repellent and fascinating. So far as his purpose can be detected, it was to impress upon the world a particular view of Alexander, and he succeeded down to quite recent times; his work seems once to have been very popular. It is a strange fate which has led to his name being usually coupled with that of Diodorus—the honest plodding Greek, doing his best (and not so bad a best) to write a history to which, intellectually, he was unequal, and the brilliant careless Roman, who had it in him to be equal to almost anything, if only he had possessed any historical principle.

For one striking thing about this writer is his complete lack of historical principle. He advertises the fact. He says: 'I have copied from others more than I believe; for while I cannot assert that things which I doubt are true, at the same time I cannot leave out what is traditional.'[2] One may search the histories of the world in vain for any similar pronouncement; cynicism can go no farther. Yet a few pages later on he is blaming older writers for carelessness and credulity, 'the one vice being as bad as the other'.[3] His cynicism shows through at many points; one frequently feels that he is writing with his tongue in his cheek. He tells at length the story of the visit of the Amazon Queen to Alexander, because it puts Alexander in a bad light; but he cannot help at the end inserting a sentence which half stultifies

1 E.g. IX, 3, 11, 'omnium victores omnium inopes'; VII, 8, 21, 'bellum tibi ex victoria nascitur'; VIII, 4, 29, 'e captiva geniturus qui victoribus imperaret'; V, 11, 11, 'difficilius...damnare quam decipi'.
2 IX, 1, 34: 'Equidem plura transcribo quam credo; nam nec affirmare sustineo de quibus dubito, nec subducere quae accepi.' Cf. v, 6, 9, 'de aliis quoque dubitabimus aut credemus'. Herod. VII, 152 is quite different.
3 IX, 5, 21. The reference is primarily and explicitly to Cleitarchus.

his thesis,[1] because really it is so clever and unexpected. His story of the Gordian knot (see App. 10) comes to this: 'It may have happened this way, and it may have happened that way. Who knows? and who cares?' And that is largely his attitude throughout: 'Who cares?' He can insert bits of most effective sarcasm into his story. For instance, he tells Diodorus' story about Phegeus, but the conclusion is not quite the same; in Diodorus, Alexander calls in Porus because he doubts what he had heard,[2] but Curtius, in a separate sentence, remarks: 'All these things seemed incredible to Alexander',[3] with the innuendo 'as they do to you, dear reader'. Another case is the supposed slaughter of the Persians after Issus; Curtius (III, 11, 17) says of Alexander's pursuit, with a side-hit at Ptolemy: 'Think of that vast multitude of Persians being killed, when Alexander had only 1,000 horse with him'; and again (IV, 9, 11) before Gaugamela, 'after all that slaughter (at Issus) Alexander could not believe that Darius had collected a still larger army'. But his masterpiece of cynicism is the eunuch Bagoas, Alexander's supposed minion (VI, 5, 23). Curtius took this figure from Dicaearchus the Peripatetic, who invented it (see App. 18), and he made great play with it, as doubtless became a strict moralist; and then at the end of his book he tells his readers, in plain Latin, that there is not a word of truth in the whole business.[4]

For Curtius, in spite of his entire lack of historical principle, was as a writer a strict moralist. He apologises to his readers for describing the Babylonian strip-tease dance,[5] which seems to have been a very thorough performance; but he describes it nevertheless, though it had no bearing on his subject. His morality comes out in many places; his definition of a respectable woman is among the curiosities of literature.[6] Luxury he condemns whole-heartedly; his remarks about pearls, 'offscourings of the sea' (he thought they were washed ashore), as ministers of vice[7] recall, though apparently he could not have read, Pliny's famous remark on the silk trade[8] and Tacitus on Roman greed for pearls.[9]

1 VI, 5, 32, 'acrior ad Venerem feminae cupido quam regis'.
2 Diod. XVII, 93, 2, ἀπιστήσας τοῖς λεγομένοις.
3 IX, 2, 5: 'Incredibilia regi omnia videbantur.'
4 X, 5, 32: 'Veneris intra naturale desiderium usus nec ulla nisi ex permisso voluptas.'   5 V, 1, 38, 'honos auribus habitus sit'.
6 V, 7, 2, 'quas violari nefas esset'.
7 VIII, 9, 19, 'quippe aestimantur purgamenta exaestuantis freti pretio quod libido constituit'.
8 Pliny, VI, 54, silk brought from the ends of the earth 'ut in publico matrona traluceat'.
9 *Agricola* 12, 'ego facilius crediderim naturam margaritis deesse quam nobis avaritiam'.

Section G

Yet with all this he had the makings of a critic, if he had taken his history seriously. He understood that at Issus the Persian force was small, either equal to Alexander's or even outnumbered (p. 106); no wonder he was sarcastic about the number of the Persian slain. He is the only writer of antiquity to notice (III, 8, 8) the obvious fact that Darius could not have fed the vast armies attributed to him. He knew that magic was all a sham (VII, 4, 8) and that Alexander's supposed will was not genuine (X, 10, 5). I have mentioned that he could slough his rhetoric if he chose. His book is full of speeches. Many are the usual rhetorical stuff; the alteration of the real conclusion of Alexander's speech at Opis and its transfer to the speech on the Hyphasis are unforgivable.[1] But consider Cleitus' speech before his murder (VIII, 1, 28 *sqq.*). Cleitus defends Philip and Parmenion (doubtless this is true) and accuses Alexander of murdering Attalus; and there is nothing rhetorical about the tremendous effect of the riposte when Alexander runs him through, exclaiming: 'Go then to Philip and Parmenion and Attalus.' Indeed Curtius has a confusing habit of inserting into the rhetoric of his speeches bits of fact, or what he thinks is fact, which would have been more properly placed in the narrative, a thing one has to look out for, and in other respects too he may use a speech for some purpose of his own: the speech of Coenus at the Hyphasis[2] is practically a pacifist tract, that of Hermolaus[3] a tract on tyranny. The speech of the Scythian envoys to Alexander was certainly written by Curtius himself, for it includes one of his best epigrams and he cannot resist showing off his knowledge of the literature of fables;[4] but its tone is remarkable for the way in which it recalls a greater speech, and one wonders if Tacitus had it in mind when he wrote the magnificent appeal of the Caledonian chieftain Calgacus, especially as Tacitus' *ubi solitudinem faciunt pacem appellant* seems to show a knowledge of Curtius IX, 2, 24, where Alexander says to his army *postquam solitudinem in Asia vincendo fecistis*. But most noticeable are the two speeches at Philotas' trial. Philotas and a lesser general, Amyntas, were put on trial for treason before the army; Philotas was condemned to death and Amyntas acquitted; so much is matter of history. Philotas' speech in his own defence in VI, 10, 37 *sqq.* is rhetoric of the worst school type. At this point one imagines Curtius saying to a reader: 'So you don't like my speeches? They *are* rather terrible, aren't they? But I'll show you what I could do if I could be bothered', and he wrote the speech of

1 IX, 2, 34: 'Ite reduces domos', etc. (see App. 15). On the Hyphasis these words make no sense. 2 IX, 3, 5. 3 VIII, 7, 1.
4 VII, 8, 21; *ib.* 15, a lion was once eaten by very small birds.

Amyntas (VII, 1, 18 *sqq.*). Rhetoric is thrown to the winds; we have a plain soldier, conscious of his innocence, stating the facts quite simply in the belief that that should secure his acquittal—as it did.

What philosophy, if any, Curtius professed is unknown, but certainly he stood close to the Peripatetics (*post*). The goddess Fortune plays a certain part in Alexander's story, if only as the source of glory and fame,[1] but she is not the framework of that story, as in Diodorus XVII; in this respect the two histories are quite different, and in Curtius she is only part of the Peripatetic machinery; in one place (X, 5, 35–6) he seems to identify her with Fate. Curtius appears to believe in two rather inconsistent things. He specifically declares his belief in Fate,[2] which no one can escape, but Fate plays little part in the story; it causes Alexander's death (X, 5, 36) as in Diodorus and probably many others, and it causes civil war after his death (X, 9, 1); that is about all. What really runs through Curtius' book is something much more personal than the Hellenistic goddess Fortune or the Babylonian Fate, something which every man possesses; it is the man's own Fortune, which sometimes comes uncommonly near to being the man's own character. Every man has his own Fortune (VI, 4, 12), Darius (III, 12, 6) and Antigonus (IV, 1, 35) no less than Alexander. Alexander's own Fortune guards and helps him perpetually (IV, 9, 22), and never wearies of indulging him (VIII, 3, 1); it makes a way for him through the Cilician Gates and the sea at Mt Climax (V, 3, 22), saves him from attack when crossing the Tigris (IV, 9, 22) and when his army was helplessly drunk (VIII, 10, 18; IX, 10, 27), and rids him of Spitamenes (VIII, 3, 1). It turns all his rashnesses to success (VII, 2, 37; cf. IX, 5, 3), and all disadvantageous circumstances to his advantage (VIII, 13, 2); it even saw to it that there should be a convenient tree in the Malli town to shield him on one side (IX, 5, 3; 6, 12). When the Egyptians and Chaldeans embalmed him after death they put the insignia of his own Fortune on his head (X, 10, 13). Yet he was greater than his Fortune; he won Gaugamela by his valour (IV, 16, 27, *virtus*, ἀρετή) and he alone of mortals had his Fortune in his power.[3]

I have mentioned Curtius' carelessness. He cares nothing for self-contradiction; there is plenty of it, and it is not usually a case of two

---

1 VIII, 10, 18; IX, 10, 28.
2 V, 11, 10: let those mock who think that human affairs are conducted by chance (forte); I believe 'nexu causarum latentium et multo ante destinatarum suum quemque ordinem immutabili lege percurrere'. So IV, 6, 17; X, 1, 30: fate is inevitable.
3 X, 5, 35: 'quam solus omnium mortalium in potestate habuit'.

sources side by side. I give a few instances. In v, 6, 9 the treasure at Persepolis goes to the war-chest, but in v, 6, 20 it is distributed among his friends. In vI, 11, 8 Philotas listens to a speech when (vI, 10, 37) he was not there. Arachosia is on the Black Sea, vII, 3, 3, and suzerain of the Malli on the Ravi, IX, 7, 14. In IX, 2, 2 the Indian Phegeus tells Alexander about the Ganges, though (IX, 3, 8) India beyond the Beas is unknown even to Indians. In vIII, 2, 27, Oxyartes secures the surrender of Sysimithres (i.e. Chorienes) by enlarging on Macedonian good faith, as in Arrian; in Arrian this is true of Oxyartes' stronghold, but in Curtius the defenders of that stronghold, called Arimazes', had been crucified![1] Substitutions of names are very common. In vIII, 13, 17–27 Ptolemy is substituted for Craterus, though vIII, 14, 15 shows that Curtius knew the facts; so vIII, 11, 5, Mullinus *scriba regis* (a pure invention) for Ptolemy; x, 1, 43, Coenus for Antipater. Such confusions are a feature of many late writers. But the great instance of Curtius' self-contradiction is Alexander himself.

It may just be noticed that Curtius, like Diodorus, refers to things far later than Alexander. In III, 1, 13, Asia means the continent, not, as usually in Alexander's day, the Persian Empire. The references to the extent, populousness, and military power of Bactria[2] belong to Euthydemid times; the statement that Alexander's eastern cities are now slaves to those they once ruled (vII, 10, 16) belongs to Curtius' own day. The Roman *testudo* is alluded to more than once.[3] One could multiply instances; such things are inevitable.

This may suffice for Curtius himself; and the more pleasant task of estimating his real contribution to knowledge must be deferred till we have considered the main thing in his book, the portrait of Alexander. Like Diodorus, he uses two portraits, a main one and a subordinate one; but the main portraits given by the two authors differ greatly. About Curtius' main portrait there is happily no doubt, as he himself has been at pains to explain what it is.[4] It is the Peripatetic portrait of

---

1 VII, 11, 28. Curtius is fearfully confused over the Sogdian rock fortresses; but Arimazes' stronghold must be meant for that of Oxyartes, because of the 'flying men', though Roxane was somewhere else, vIII, 4, 23. Curtius has a certain number of correct items about the various strongholds, but ladles them out indiscriminately, with fictitious names. Diodorus is lost; but the table of contents, κ′ to κε′, indicates a story of events in Sogdiana very different from either Arrian or Curtius. Justin omits the whole story of events in Bactria-Sogdiana, though Trogus did not (*Prol.* xII).

2 v, 10, 3 and 9; vII, 4, 30. 3 v, 3, 9, 21, 23; vII, 9, 3.
4 III, 12, 18–20; vI, 2, 1–4.

Alexander, the one full account of it which we have. The outline of that portrait has already been noticed: Aristotle turned out a perfectly good and virtuous pupil, but he was ruined by his own fortune and became a cruel tyrant.[1] The portrait was the revenge of the school upon Alexander for putting Callisthenes to death, and revenge they have indeed had; for long they managed to hold the modern world in bondage. The portrait was assisted by the friendship which several members of the school felt for Alexander's enemy Cassander;[2] it took the shape it did because the school could not go back on Aristotle and say, as did the Stoics, that Alexander was bad from the start, though probably for the latter part of his life there was little difference between the two portraits. Curtius expresses his view in III, 12, 18 *sq.*: if only Alexander could have gone on as he had begun; he would have had a truer fortune than world-conquest had he conquered, as he never did, the twin evils of pride and anger; there would have been no murders of Cleitus and Parmenion. I have said some hard things about Curtius' 'morality', but this passage has a dignity of its own and a considerable element of truth; as Eratosthenes said of Bion, Curtius sometimes lets us see the real Odysseus under the beggar's rags. No one need deny that the Alexander of 324 was not the Alexander of 334; what is wrong with the Peripatetic portrait is that it exaggerates what was bad in Alexander's development and entirely omits what was good, a matter of much greater scope and importance.

I must just run through Curtius' portrait. In III, 6, 17–20 he gives his formal praise of the young Alexander, dearest and most admired of kings; and again, as late as Persepolis, V, 7, 1, he repeats a long list of his virtues,[3] though he adds that one evil thing has begun to show itself, an intolerable love of drink. Down to the end of book V there are many allusions to his good qualities: III, 5, 2, his pride in keeping his body fit; IV, 6, 26, his admiration of courage (*virtus*) in his enemies; III, 12, 13, after Issus he buries the Persians with equal honour; IV, 10, 4, he knows no fear; IV, 16, 33, he and his army are worthy of each other. Other things noted are his moderation and clemency among the Uxii,

---

1 See § F, p. 69 n. 1. It is well put by Cicero *ad Att.* XIII, 28, 3: 'Quid? tu non vides ipsum illum Aristoteli discipulum, summo ingenio, summa modestia, postea quam rex (i.e. Great King) appellatus sit, superbum, crudelem, immoderatum fuisse?'

2 Theophrastus and Demetrius of Phalerum certainly, Dicaearchus probably. See Tarn, 'Alexander the Great and the Unity of Mankind', *Proc. Brit. Acad.* 1933, pp. 140–5, 166 [20–25, 46] and *passim.*

3 'Indoles, constantia, velocitas (speed of action), fides, clementia, temperantia.'

v, 3, 15; his weeping in pity for the wretched;[1] the whole episode, fully written up, of his conduct toward Darius' family[2] and of his friendship for Darius' mother Sisygambis, part of which at least is true.[3] At the sack of Persepolis he issues the unique order, amazing for the fourth century B.C., that the women are not to be touched.[4] Finally, as opposed to Diodorus' account, he wins 'Arbela' less by fortune than by his own *virtus* and by his prudence, without which he might have lost it (IV, 16, 27 *sqq.*). If only he could have gone on as he had begun! But (III, 12, 20) his soul had not yet been swamped by his fortune.

Curtius dates the change in Alexander's character to a precise moment of time; it follows the death of Darius, which concludes book v, and the new state of things begins with a formal exposition in book vi, ch. 2 (ch. 1 relates to old Greece). The cloven hoof had already shown itself in his burning of the palace at Persepolis when drunk (V, 7, 1 *sqq.*); then in Hyrcania comes the change. He had stood war; he could not stand peace and success (VI, 2, 1), and deteriorates fast; he indulges his desires—banquets, drink, gambling, with a side glance at Darius' concubines; vi, 6, 1 *sqq.*, his continence and moderation turn into wantonness and pride; the eunuch Bagoas, invented by Dicaearchus the Peripatetic (see App. 18) to mark the change in Alexander, now comes into his life (VI, 5, 23) and is used later to exhibit his degradation, x, 1, 22–9. No longer content with being *called* the son of Zeus, he presently orders that it shall be *believed* also, as though he could control men's minds like their tongues, VIII, 5, 5. The man who knew no fear is now terrified, vi, 2, 18; the man who had wept in pity now weeps in terror (*ib.*). The man praised for *celeritas* and *constantia*, speed and resolution, now always hesitates in difficulties[5] and is devoid of counsel.[6] He dissimulates (VI, 8, 16), and pretends condonation, VI, 10, 11 (Philotas); believes slanderers, IX, 7, 24; is suspected of

1 V, 5, 8 and 24; III, 12, 6.
2 IV, 10, 23, 'kindness and continence'; *ib.* 34, 'iustus hostis, misericors victor'.
3 Ptolemy records that she begged off the Uxii, Arr. III, 17, 6. This is sufficient evidence for the friendship between her and Alexander, and one would like to believe the whole story—that at Gaugamela she refused to return to Darius when she appeared to have the chance, and that at the end she refused to survive Alexander. It is perfectly possible that she should have come to regard Alexander as more truly her son than the cowardly Darius. Cf. Curt. v, 2, 20–22.
4 v, 6, 8, 'corporibus et cultu feminarum abstinere iussit'. See App. 18.
5 VI, 6, 27; cf. IX, 2, 10.
6 'Inops consilii': at Aornos, VIII, 11, 3; facing Porus, VIII, 13, 17; at the Hyphasis, IX, 3, 18.

shamming illness, VII, 7, 7; boasts in his cups and belittles his father, VIII, 1, 22 *sqq.*; tries to strip Porus when he thinks he is dead, VIII, 14, 40. The account of his marriage to Roxane (VIII, 4, 25 *sq.*, 29), who was not of royal blood, is one scarcely veiled sneer; after Cleitus' murder he tears his face with his nails, i.e. he mourns like a woman, not a man, VIII, 2, 5. But all his *luxuria* is no bar to cruelty, IX, 10, 30. He orders or condones torture;[1] crucifies opponents;[2] indulges in massacres.[3] The man who had been called *misericors*, full of pity, now has no mercy for the conquered, and punishes regardless.[4] Curtius admits that some small traces of his original character remained for a time, VI, 2, 8; he was at first unwilling to believe the worst,[5] though he soon became the exact opposite;[6] he is called clement to those who surrendered (VII, 6, 17), notwithstanding the contrary examples above; he tries to control his temper with Cleitus (VIII, 1, 31 *sq.*), and does an unselfish act, VIII, 4, 15; Curtius cannot deny his treatment of Porus, and even seeks to relieve him of the guilt of the murder of Parmenion (see App. 12). Possibly we have here, generally speaking, bits of Aristobulus showing through the general picture Curtius is giving (*post*). But the general picture is clear: a worthy young man is turned by success into a cruel, mean, and sensual tyrant. What pulls him through now is his Fortune, and that alone. It had given him success from the start, though it had nearly failed him at the Persian Gates;[7] now it is merely his 'everlasting luck' which saves him from the consequences of his own mistakes and rashness, and, never weary of indulging him, turns every disadvantage to his profit.[8]

So far, then, we have a picture which hangs together; Curtius has drawn an Alexander which accords exactly with the Alexander of the Peripatetics. But this does not end the matter, for Curtius has also used a second and subsidiary portrait, just as Diodorus has done (see § F), which gives the view that Alexander was bad from the start. In this

---

1 Bessus, VII, 5, 40; Philotas, VI, 11, 9 *sqq.*; Callisthenes and the pages, VIII, 8, 20 *sqq.*
2 Arimazes, VII, 11, 28; Musicanus, IX, 8, 16.
3 The Branchidae, VII, 5, 35; on the Polytimetus (an order), VII, 9, 22; the first people met with in India, VIII, 10, 5–6; in Sambos' territory, IX, 8, 15. Curiously, the one genuine massacre, that of the mercenaries at Massaga, is omitted.
4 X, 1, 39; cf. VII, 6, 17, 'inexorabilis in devictos'.
5 VII, 1, 12, 'invitum deteriora credentem'.
6 X, 1, 39, 'praeceps ad deteriora credenda'; so IX, 7, 24.
7 V, 3, 22, 'tunc haesitabat deprehensa felicitas'.
8 VII, 2, 37; VIII, 3, 1; 10, 18; 13, 22; IX, 5, 3; 6, 12; 9, 2; 10, 28.

portrait, the young man who was called fearless[1] is everlastingly afraid;[2] he is superstitious (IV, 6, 12 and often) and terrified by an omen (IV, 2, 14). He lays a mean trap to destroy Sisines, III, 7, 11 *sqq.* The man praised for resolution is almost a 'quitter'; he twice thinks of giving up at Tyre (IV, 3, 11; 4, 1) and hesitates whether to give up before 'Arbela'. Above all, he is given to rage and cruelty.[3] That is, Curtius himself seems so anxious to display Alexander's unworthiness that he has contaminated his Peripatetic thesis with the thesis of Alexander's unworthiness from the start also used by Diodorus. It must be remembered, however, that, as in Diodorus, so in Curtius, this second thesis is only a subordinate one, added to the main portrait; and the main portrait in these two writers is so totally different that it is hard to understand how they ever came to be classed together.

Then Alexander dies. Curtius, X, 5, 26–37, sums up his character, and proceeds to contradict and stultify nearly everything he has said. Nothing can fit the summary to the body of the book; the long list of Alexander's virtues applies to his whole life, not to his youth only; the Bagoas story is flatly contradicted, X, 5, 32, as is Alexander's supposed attitude to Philip, *ib.* 31; and the only things ascribed to Fortune, except trifles like dress, are the assumption of divine honours and over-impatience with those who did not concede them. Certainly, says Curtius, we must confess that, however much he owed to his own *virtus*, he owed even more to his Fortune; but [this was in itself a sign of greatness, for] he was the only man of all men who had Fortune in his power. We have seen Curtius contradicting himself over details; but here he stultifies at the end the main thesis to which his book has been devoted. I shall return to this.

I come now to the question of Curtius' sources. If a secondary writer has a very definite portrait of his leading character running right through his book, like the Peripatetic character of Alexander in Curtius, then, if that writer has used one principal source, with whatever additions, the portrait of the leading character is almost bound, in its main lines, to be taken from that principal source. But there is no evidence to show that any writer before Curtius ever committed to writing the full Peripatetic portrait of Alexander; indeed no writer is even known who *could* have done so; the portrait depended on what might be called

1 IV, 10, 4, 'interritus ad omnia'.
2 III, 6, 5, 9, the Philippus story; III, 8, 20, Issus; especially IV, 13, 15–18, before Gaugamela.
3 At Tyre, with details, IV, 4, 13–14, 17; at Persepolis; Batis (see App. 11).

University teaching, a tradition of the Peripatetic school, often no
doubt alluded to in writing, possibly even to some extent expounded
(though this is not actually known), but never embodied in a full-
length history. It follows from this that Curtius cannot have had
any principal source at all, and this analysis, I hope, will make that
obvious; all he wanted was a background of some sort against which to
develop his view of Alexander, and he put it together in such ways as
occurred to him, using, as will be seen, various writers in the process.
Of course, Cleitarchus has been suggested as his principal source—
obscurum per obscurius—but this is quite out of the question. It has
been seen, in considering Diodorus xvii (§ F), that if Cleitarchus was
responsible for either of the two portraits in Diodorus it can only have
been for the unfavourable one, which is entirely subordinate to the
other; and as Curtius also used a subordinate portrait which was unfavourable throughout, it may be here that Cleitarchus comes in, but,
like most things connected with Cleitarchus, this is no more than a
strong probability; so little about that writer is certain that it has been,
and is, only too easy to make of him a dumping-ground for anything
which cannot be otherwise placed. These two subordinate portraits
only partially correspond; if I may refer back to my sketch in § F of the
one in Diodorus, Curtius omits the Massaga massacre, the Oreitae
massacre, the burning of the country of the Mardi, and has a very
different story about the death of Parmenion, besides a good deal
which is not in Diodorus at all; but there are sufficient common elements,
I think, in these two subordinate portraits to point to a common source
somewhere in the background which is almost bound to be Cleitarchus
(as he has to come in somewhere), though the two writers have treated
it in rather different ways, and Curtius has worked up the badness of
Alexander, with other material, far the more thoroughly of the two.
Another portrait is also known which made Alexander bad from start
to finish, that of the Stoic school; but this is certainly not the subordinate
portrait of Diodorus and does not appear to be that of Curtius, for
neither has anything corresponding to the two vices, ὕβρις and τῦφος,
which are the characteristics of the Stoic version and which appear in
Justin (see § H). But, of course, as regards Curtius, the loss of the
first two books does introduce an element of obscurity. His ten books
go down, not to Alexander's death, but to his final burial in Alexandria;
and as at the beginning of book iii Alexander has only reached Celaenae
in Phrygia, Curtius must have begun with, or before, his birth and
must have had plenty of room to describe his boyhood, as Plutarch
does; so without knowing Curtius' view of Alexander's *paidagogos*

Leonidas it cannot really be said whether or not his subordinate account may have borrowed something from the Stoics.

As regards Cleitarchus, Curtius does indeed mention him twice, but on one occasion (IX, 8, 15) only to show that he himself takes no responsibility for the statement he cites, and on the other (IX, 5, 21) with expressions of contempt;[1] and any part he may play in Curtius' narrative cannot therefore be a leading one. There are a good many stories and incidents common to Diodorus and Curtius; but as it is certain enough that Cleitarchus was not Diodorus' principal source, the basis for the belief that these portions of Curtius' narrative came from Cleitarchus is gone; some reason must be given for every item ascribed to Cleitarchus. No doubt some *are* from him, but the matter has ceased to be of any great importance, now that it is clear that he was only a secondary source; we have, for example, already met one story on which Diodorus, Curtius, and Justin agree, but which originated far later than Cleitarchus.[2] In many cases of agreement between Diodorus and Curtius, Curtius either adds or subtracts something; in some cases the variation may be due to Curtius using, not Cleitarchus, but one of the poetasters who were among Cleitarchus' sources (see § E'). But what seems to me strange, in this connection, is that, amid the almost universal preoccupation with Cleitarchus, I cannot recall any writer who has made the simple and obvious suggestion that Curtius may have read and used Diodorus. Proof is difficult, of course, while it is fatally easy to refer correspondence to the use of a common source of which nothing, or little, is known; but in spite of the difficulty, proofs do exist. I have relegated them to a separate section, § G'; but I may remark that, even if only those three cases can be really proved, then we cannot say how far the use of Diodorus by Curtius may or may not have extended.

Here may be noticed the difficult question of the proper names in Curtius, for he has many names unknown elsewhere. Where, over officials like satraps, he differs from Arrian, giving unknown names or wrong attributions of known men to satrapies, no difficulty arises, for Ptolemy was following the official documents and cannot be wrong. But Curtius too used Ptolemy, and sometimes to good purpose; why these apparently meaningless differences? It is even worse with those

---

1 He ascribes to him carelessness and its twin vice credulity, 'securitas vel par huic vitium credulitas'. See p. 92 n. 3.
2 The two suns, § F, p. 79. Jacoby, 'Kleitarchos' in PW 629, has very properly said that Diodorus + Curtius + Justin do not necessarily make Cleitarchus.

lesser people who appear nowhere else. Some seem to be inventions of Curtius' own; 'Plato the Athenian', commanding a detachment of troops, was too much even for Berve. Yet too much stress cannot be laid on inventions, with the example of Omphis before us;[1] and I am not going to guess what weird error in transmission lies behind 'Cohortandus'.[2] But some must be inventions; was this merely to create an illusion of detailed knowledge, or is it possible that one or more of the poetasters mentioned in § E' thought it advisable to conceal allusions to living people under fictitious names,[3] which Curtius took to be real? There are things in Curtius which look like pure impishness, designed to annoy serious readers.

One thing can be said. We get, in Curtius, Diodorus, and all 'vulgate' writers, certain substituted names regularly used, the two most notorious instances being Arbela for Gaugamela and Stateira for Barsine;[4] and it is possible that we have enough to show that in certain small respects, but in those only, there existed a definite tradition differing from the 'good' tradition of Arrian. It is easy to ascribe such names to Cleitarchus, but there is no proof, and if there were it would not take us far, for Cleitarchus was only one more secondary writer; the probabilities are that the names peculiar to the 'vulgate' writers generally are merely the popular names of common speech which had become established before Ptolemy wrote—how well established may be judged from this, that Arrian himself, notwithstanding all the trouble he took to show that the battle was not fought at Arbela but at Gaugamela, does once, when speaking in his own person, slip up and write Arbela (III, 22, 4).

It is certain, of course, that in putting together Alexander's itinerary after Darius' death Curtius did, to some small extent, use the Cleitarchean geography, especially for the Caspian country, where it is easy to trace (see § B). The Queen of the Amazons visits Alexander in Hyrcania, and the Thermodon, where she came from, is put next door to Hyrcania;[5] this is Cleitarchus beyond question (§ B, pp. 14 *sq.* and App. 19); so possibly are the statements that Arachosia is a country on

---

1 VIII, 12, 4; Omphis (Ambhi) is the personal name of the king for whom Arrian uses only the official name Taxiles, i.e. 'King Taxila'.

2 VIII, 4, 21. The context shows Oxyartes is meant, but the MSS. have Cohortandus. See App. 21, p. 341 n. 5.

3 This might account for the number of names in circulation as the original name of Alexander's mother Olympias; Plut. *Mor.* 401 A gives Polyxene and Stratonice as well as Myrtale.

4 This pair of names is fully considered in App. 20, p. 334 n. 4.

5 VI, 5, 24, 'Hyrcaniae finitima'.

the Black Sea (VII, 3, 4), and that it is a wind from the Black Sea which dries up Bactria, VII, 4, 27. But Curtius' own account of the Caspian is a mosaic from several sources,[1] and certainly much of his extraordinary geography has nothing to do with Cleitarchus or perhaps with anyone else; he had no particular guide to follow, and it was to him a matter of complete indifference. He makes a real hash-up of the Uxii, v, 3, 1 *sqq.* Alexander passes the Mardi of the Elburz on his way from Persis to Ecbatana (v, 6, 17), though Curtius knows where the Mardi really were (VI, 5, 11), and his account of their tree-fortresses rings true. In VI, 4, 2 Alexander goes through Parthiene to reach Hyrcania, which would mean going backwards. He reaches the Oxus after going through Sogdiana, VII, 5, 13. Curtius' account of the rock-fortresses taken by Alexander in Sogdiana is a jumble not worth disentangling, and he exhibits every phase of the 'Europe across the Jaxartes' muddle, which Cleitarchus gave, though he did not originate it. The Ganges I have dealt with separately (App. 14). How little sense there is in seeking 'sources' for much of this can be illustrated by the native story of an underground river in Central Asia, which Polybius (x, 48, 7) made the Oxus and Diodorus a river called Stiboetes in Hyrcania (§ F', p. 87). Curtius in one place, VI, 4, 4–7, follows, though he embellishes, Diodorus, calling the river Ziobetis and placing it in Hyrcania, but in another place, VII, 10, 1, he transfers the same story to the Polytimetus in Sogdiana. Who is going to follow the 'sources' of this native story? And Curtius would have said 'Who cares?'

No doubt, as regards India, Curtius took the Dionysus business largely from Cleitarchus, though he had probably read the poetasters (§ E') who were Cleitarchus' source or one of his sources; some of the differences between Diodorus and himself may necessitate this supposition. In Curtius, Dionysus had been in India before Alexander;[2] had founded Nysa, VIII, 10, 11, and had left boundary stones (*termini*),

---

1 VI, 4, 16–19. 17 appears to be Cleitarchean. 18 is practically Polycleitus down to 'cetera maria', and shows Curtius must have read him; Curtius is the last to mention the Aral as a separate sea (see § B, p. 10); alii, however, includes Cleitarchus. 19 begins with Patrocles on the northern connection with Ocean, perhaps through Eratosthenes. The source of the second sentence, that the strait is *intermittent*, is doubtless a confusion with the strait of Apollodorus (§ C, p. 17 n. 1; § F', p. 88 n. 1); the third sentence, beginning 'et quidam credidere', I do not understand, and I doubt if Curtius did either. Apollodorus' strait is given VII, 3, 19; *ib.* 21 is ultimately Aristotle, perhaps through Aristobulus, see Arr. VII, 16, 3 and § B, p. 12.

2 VIII, 10, 1; cf. IX, 2, 29; 4, 21; 8, 5.

III, 10, 5; in Carmania, Alexander is imitating Bacchus' triumph,[1] and at Nysa the army 'serves' Bacchus for ten days.[2] But we do not get actual religious service to Dionysus as in Diodorus and most probably in Cleitarchus (§ E, pp. 46 *sq.*); the idea of a Dionysiac κῶμος is absent alike at Persepolis, in Carmania, and at Nysa; for though at Nysa the word *operor* is used, which should mean religious service, what Curtius describes is mere 'mafficking' and what he calls it is *lascivia*; there is a good deal of difference. Of the Achilles motive we get very little. Like Diodorus, Curtius gives (IX, 4, 11 *sqq.*) Alexander's fight with the river Acesines, down which he did *not* sail, but he omits Diodorus' (XVII, 97, 3) comparison to Achilles, one of the few cases where he diminishes, rather than enlarges, Diodorus; this may mean that one of them, presumably Curtius, used Choerilus direct and not through Cleitarchus. Curtius (VIII, 4, 26) does bring in Achilles on his own account as part of his sneer at Alexander's marriage with a barbarian captive, the *ignobilis virguncula* Roxane; but he has to admit that Achilles is not a good precedent, for while Alexander did marry Roxane in proper Macedonian form, Achilles did not marry Briseis in any form at all.

I may here notice two of Curtius' sources which are easy to isolate, omitting events in old Greece, where Curtius is as sober as Diodorus and doubtless used Diyllus also (if Diodorus' source be Diyllus). The first is the excellent 'mercenaries' source', also used by Diodorus (see § F). Even though Curtius' first two books are lost, we get a good deal from this writer. We just get Memnon's death; he was Alexander's only anxiety.[3] The mercenaries are praised (III, 8, 1), and their get-away after Issus correctly given (III, 11, 18), with a long account of Amyntas' adventures, IV, 1, 27–33. Darius is whitewashed at great length, which I need not go through: he is *sanctus et mitis*, III, 8, 5; the massacre at Issus town was due to his generals, III, 8, 15; his plan at Issus was sensible, but was upset by Fortune, III, 8, 29; excuses are made for him at Issus (III, 11, 11), and at Gaugamela he fights till all is lost, IV, 15, 30 *sqq.* This long writing up of Darius (III, chs. 8–11) contains much which no one could ever have known, but the loyalty of the mercenary leader Patron must be from the 'mercenaries' source', and so probably must be part of Darius' death; Curtius explains the cup of water, which no one else does, but this must obviously come from elsewhere—it

---

1 IX, 10, 24; III, 12, 18.
2 VIII, 10, 17, '(Alexander) per decem dies Libero Patri operatum habuit exercitum'.
3 III, 1, 21, 'in quem omnes intenderat curas'.

cannot be said where. But the notable thing is that Curtius uses this source independently of, and differently from, Diodorus, which means that they did *not* get it through a common medium, and both must therefore have used the original for themselves; it was unknown to Arrian, and therefore to Arrian's two principal sources. For example, there is nothing in Curtius about Macedonians fighting in relays, which Diodorus so stresses, while he has much about Issus which is highly important but which Diodorus omits. By Darius' fault the Persian army at Issus was small, III, 3, 28; the two armies were equal, III, 7, 9, or else Alexander's was the larger, III, 10, 2. This does not prevent Curtius saying that vast masses of Persians were slaughtered like sheep in the pursuit, though he is sarcastic on the subject (*ante*, p. 93); but he has a very different story, taken from the 'mercenaries' source', to which I shall come later (pp. 110 *sqq.*).

Curtius' second much-used source, easy to isolate, is the work he used on Macedonian customs, ἤθη Μακεδονικά. Many philosophers described the ἤθη of this or that Greek, and sometimes barbarian, people, but I have not found in any list a work on Macedonian customs; it may therefore have been an Alexandrian compilation, i.e. in effect Peripatetic, a further sign that Curtius stood near to that school. The compilation was a thoroughly good one and therefore pretty early, certainly not later than the third century B.C. The character of the Macedonian monarchy (IV, 7, 31), so far as it goes, gives the one indispensable fact, the power of the people in arms, the army, to judge capital cases, murder and treason (VI, 8, 25)—a famous passage, the truth of which is established by many trials before the army under both Alexander and the Successors. It was Macedonian 'law', or rather custom, that if, in a trial for treason, the accused were condemned to death, his relatives should be put to death also; this is so important that I have had to treat it separately (App. 12). It was customary to stone the condemned,[1] but sometimes spears were used (VII, 1, 9), or javelins, as in Arrian III, 26, 3. Custom decreed that almost the most sacred duty of a Macedonian king was to bury his dead after a battle[2] [to let the enemy bury them was the sign of defeat]. The army was purified by passing between the two halves of a dog.[3] It was

---

[1] VI, 11, 10 and 38; VII, 2, 1.

[2] V, 4, 3. Compare the Hohenzollern custom, dropped in the war of 1914–18, that after a battle the king must ride over the battlefield and face his dead.

[3] X, 9, 12; further and more elaborately described in Livy XL, 6, *temp.* Philip V. The two accounts differ just enough to show that they come from different sources; Livy's account is from Polybius, who must have described it, see XXIII, 10, 17.

customary, in founding a city, to mark out the site with meal, IV, 8, 6, as in the accounts of the founding of Alexandria in Plutarch and the Romance. Curtius gives the only extant account, VIII, 4, 27, of the Macedonian marriage rite, rather like the Roman *confarreatio*; a piece of bread was divided by a sword, presumably by the bridegroom, and the couple each ate half, the bread denoting that they were not to seek luxury. In a changed world it is now the bride who cuts the cake, but she still uses her husband's sword, if he has one. It was customary to uncover when addressing the king, IX, 3, 4. The king might not hunt on foot, or alone, VIII, 1, 18. Any one anticipating him was flogged, VIII, 8, 3; but only the king could flog the royal pages, VIII, 6, 2–7.

Curtius is our invaluable source for Macedonian customs;[1] apart from him, I think only three are mentioned. The statements of Duris and Hegesander,[2] that Macedonians sat at meals instead of reclining like Greeks, might be true, though Duris is speaking of a special occasion and Hegesander's account is part of the anti-Cassander propaganda. Plutarch shows (*Alex.* XVI) that enough Macedonians still held the superstition that it was unlucky to commence military operations in the month Daisios for Alexander to have to take account of the feeling. The Macedonian custom of announcing the end of a banquet, i.e. the moment for the libation, by trumpet is thoroughly well attested.[3]

It has never been doubted that Curtius used the 'good' tradition to a certain extent, and I need not embellish the obvious. The use of Ptolemy is clear in his account of Gaugamela (see App. 5), of the siege of Tyre, and several other places; in IX, 5, 21 he is named. The capture of Bessus in VII, 5, 19 *sqq.* is Aristobulus' account written up, with the addition of Catanes to Spitamenes and Dataphernes; there is probably more of Aristobulus in Curtius than is immediately apparent, and the account in VIII, 2 of Alexander's grief over Cleitus' murder is pure Arrian, with the addition of Alexander's attempt at suicide and his tearing his face with his nails. But Curtius also has things which are entirely his own, like the invaluable account of the poetasters who were with Alexander in India (§ E'); and I may notice a few more instances of the peculiar knowledge, however obtained, which he occasionally displays. He knows and emphasises the difference between Parthava and Parthi,[4] which no other classical writer does. He knows that a

---

1 For another see p. 163 n. 4. 2 Athen. I, 17 F, 18 A.
3 For the evidence see Tarn, *J.H.S.* XLVIII, 1928, pp. 210 *sq.*
4 IV, 12, 11; he calls the Parthava Parthieni, and knows (VI, 2, 12) that the country of the Parthieni was occupied by the 'Scythian' Parthi. Certainly from Apollodorus of Artemita.

Persian satrap was properly called a slave,[1] and indeed knows a good deal about Persia; besides some Persian words,[2] he knows of the Persian custom that all lights should be extinguished when the king dies,[3] and he has an extraordinary account of a Persian royal procession, with the sacred fire on silver altars carried before a crystal image of the sun;[4] at Gaugamela the sacred fire is carried on altars before the army, and Darius swears by it and the sun, IV, 14, 24. Curtius knows that there were shirkers in Macedonia, as everywhere else, VII, 1, 37; that the name rhinoceros is only a Greek invention, IX, 1, 5; that when Alexander was overtaking Darius all that he saw was a dust-cloud, V, 13, 12. He gives the story of the statue of Hercules carried before Porus' army (VIII, 14, 11), which has played such a part in the discussion whether Indians ever made statues of their gods prior to Greek contacts. And he knows the story in the later versions of the Romance of Alexander's journey to the Land of Darkness.[5]

I come now to six items in which Curtius seems to fill up gaps in, and to explain omissions in, Arrian. Naturally Arrian has to omit, or does omit, many things; but five of these items, at least, are certainly given correctly by Curtius, while their omission by Arrian in each case renders something which follows incomprehensible. Four depend on the 'mercenaries' source'; I give first the two which do not.

(1) Arrian, VII, 8, 3, does not explain why, in the mutiny at Opis, the whole army clamoured to go home with the 10,000 veterans. Curtius explains: they thought Alexander meant to transfer the seat of government permanently to Asia (as apparently he did). I cannot guess Curtius' source; obviously it was neither Ptolemy nor Aristobulus.

1 IV, 11, 20; V, 12, 16; VI, 3, 13. The *locus classicus* is Ditt.[3] 22.
2 Kidaris, III, 3, 19; gangabas, III, 13, 7; the meaning of Tigris, IV, 9, 16.
3 X, 5, 16; also given by Diodorus, XVII, 114, 4. Doubtless it is from Deinon or Ctesias.
4 III, 3, 8–16. The source of this vivid account is a mystery. It is not from either Deinon or Ctesias, because both took the Persian year as 360 days (§ F, p. 82 n. 3) while in the procession are 365 noble youths representing the 365 days of the year. To say Cleitarchus is meaningless, for it only shifts the matter one peg backwards: what then was *his* source? Possibly Curtius used some Alexandrian collection of ἤθη Περσικά or βαρβαρικά, as he did one of ἤθη Μακεδονικά; but this is useless guesswork, for most of what he knew about Persia *could* have come from Deinon or Ctesias.
5 IX, 4, 18, the army fear that Alexander intends to take them to the land of perpetual night, which is described. This shows that Curtius knew the story that he did go there.

(2) Aristonous the Bodyguard. He is named once only by Arrian in the *Anabasis*, in the official list of the Bodyguards, VI, 28, 4; it is nowhere said what he had done to receive this honour. But in Arrian's τὰ μετ' 'Αλέξανδρον, which represents Hieronymus, he suddenly comes to life; that is, Hieronymus gave his actions, but Ptolemy, for some reason unknown, perhaps a personal one, omitted him altogether; the mere fact that after Alexander's death he adhered to Olympias' ally Perdiccas and subsequently to Olympias herself hardly seems a sufficient reason for this. Curtius offers an explanation of Aristonous' honours: he had helped to save Alexander's life at the Malli town, IX, 5, 15 and 18. The difficulty is the official list of gold crowns for the generals, as given by Ptolemy from the *Journal* (Arr. VII, 5, 4 *sqq.*). Had Aristonous really helped to save Alexander's life, his crown must have been named separately, with those of Peucestas and Leonnatus; instead, according to Ptolemy, Aristonous is merely included in the rubric 'the other Bodyguards', who all received crowns at the end without being named individually. Either then our sole, and very circumstantial, account of the reason for Aristonous' honours is untrue, or else Ptolemy doctored the official record, which is almost incredible. I cannot resolve the dilemma.

The next three items all relate to Gaugamela. Arrian's Gaugamela is from Ptolemy; Curtius uses both Ptolemy and the 'mercenaries' source', but though he has many of Ptolemy's incidents they are often in wrong places, his actual battle being an unintelligible confusion (see generally App. 5). But the three items which follow are from the 'mercenaries' source', and are certainly correct.

(3) In Arrian, Mazaeus is not mentioned in the battle, neither does he relate, as did Curtius, how when Mazaeus at Babylon came out to surrender to Alexander he was received with greater honour than any Asiatic except Porus; consequently, when Arrian mentions that Mazaeus was made satrap of Babylonia (no Asiatic having been made a satrap previously) the reader has not the least idea why. Curtius shows. Mazaeus commanded the Persian right, and it was he who came so near to making Gaugamela a Persian victory;[1] Alexander was honouring a worthy opponent.

(4) In Arrian it is impossible to understand the position and pretensions of Bessus after the battle. Curtius shows. Bessus was Mazaeus' counterpart; he commanded the Persian left,[2] opposite Alexander, and he and his Bactrians had, personally, not been defeated.

1 IV, 16, 1; see also V, 1, 18 on Mazaeus' 'fama' from the battle.
2 IV, 15, 2. It is Bessus who orders the Saca horse to turn Alexander's right, and nearly succeeds.

(5) In Arrian, after the Persian Guard have cut the phalanx in half, they incomprehensibly throw away their chance of victory by riding on to Alexander's camp and the baggage instead of taking the phalanx in rear; one is left to think of men out of hand, intent on mere plunder. Curtius shows what did happen. The army had Darius' express orders to rescue his family, who were in Alexander's camp,[1] and the Persian Guard deliberately threw away their success from a mistaken sense of loyalty.[2] As regards these three items, Ptolemy, one would suppose, *must* have known the commands of Mazaeus and Bessus, though it does not follow that he gave them, but he might very well have not known Darius' order about his family; Curtius got this, and presumably all three items, from the 'mercenaries' source', which knew, but which Arrian did not use.

(6) Antigonus. This is far the most important item of the six. In Arrian's story, Antigonus is made satrap of Phrygia and is never heard of again; Ptolemy was not going to relate the *acta* of one who had been his most bitter enemy, while Aristobulus was not concerned with purely military matters. Consequently, when after Alexander's death Antigonus suddenly appears as one of the most important people in the realm, we are quite in the dark as to the reason. Curtius gives the reason, and with it a great block of an otherwise lost story, never given by modern historians; it can only come from the 'mercenaries' source', and is certainly true. I have mentioned elsewhere (App. 3) that it must have been Antigonus who, from his central position at Celaenae in Phrygia, was in charge of Alexander's communications across Asia Minor by the Royal Road. Those communications had a bad bottleneck, where Cappadocia pressed upon the road from the north and the unconquered Isaurians of the Taurus from the south. Alexander, hurrying on to meet Darius, had not waited to subdue Cappadocia; he evidently trusted to Antigonus to keep the bottleneck open, which doubtless in the ordinary way Antigonus had force enough to do. Curtius now relates what happened.[3] He, i.e. his source, knew well enough, as we have seen, that the great slaughter of the Persians at Issus was nonsense; much of the Persian army, he says, was able to retreat into

---

1 IV, 14, 22: my family are captives; 'eripite viscera mea ex vinculis', etc. It illustrates Curtius' regular habit of inserting in his speeches facts that ought to come in the narrative.

2 In my original text I overlooked this and made the Persian Guard get out of hand. I corrected this in *Hell. Mil. Dev.* p. 65.

3 IV, 1, 34 *sq.* Lydia is of course a mistake for Phrygia, and Curtius himself does not know what the Persians were aiming at. But this is immaterial; he has preserved the facts.

Cappadocia, and the Persian generals, having raised Cappadocia and Paphlagonia, made a determined attack on the dangerous bottleneck, perhaps the most critical moment of Alexander's career; possibly the Isaurians co-operated from the south, for after Issus Alexander had made Balacrus satrap of Cilicia and he was killed in battle with them.[1] Antigonus mastered the main attack, though it cost him three battles to do so, and kept Alexander's communications open; Cappadocia he could not conquer, but he eased the position by annexing Lycaonia (Curt. IV, 5, 13). This is what gave Antigonus his great reputation. But the bottleneck, we know, remained a standing threat, and after Alexander's death Perdiccas' first act, when once firm in the saddle, was to get rid of it for good by conquering both Cappadocia and Isauria; the gravity of the task is seen in his taking with him the whole Imperial army. The preservation of the passage which elucidates this important matter is Curtius' best contribution to history. An interesting side of it is Alexander's faith, completely justified by the event, in Antigonus.

Now, if nothing were known of the dates of Arrian and Curtius, it would look, on what is given above, as if Curtius were deliberately explaining and supplementing Arrian's story; but on accepted views Curtius wrote long before Arrian, whose approximate date is certain. It will be advisable therefore to consider Curtius' date, of which, except that it must be earlier than A.D. 224 or 227 (p. 113), nothing is known beyond what he himself says, x, 9, 3–7. The Roman people, he says [more fortunate than the Macedonian], owe their safety, *salus*, to the present Emperor, *princeps*, who shone forth as a new star, *novum sidus*, on the night which was almost our last [note *habuimus*; it was every one, not certain people only]. It was he, not the sun,[2] who restored light to a darkened world, when without him the several parts of that world were at variance and tottering, *discordia membra trepidarent*. He caused many torches of war, *faces*, to be extinguished, many swords to be sheathed [*civil* wars],[3] and gave a sudden calm after the

1 Arr. II, 12, 2; Diod. XVIII, 22, 1. His death is only dated 'during Alexander's life-time'.

2 Diodorus, Curtius, and Justin all make Alexander compare himself to the sun; these stories are examined in § F, p. 79. Plutarch, *de Alex. fort.* I, 330 E, writing in his own person, says that that part of the world which never saw Alexander was an ἀνήλιον μέρος. But I am not too sure that the sun here *is* Alexander (see the phrase discussed App. 25, p. 422 n. 4); and even if it be, there is not enough to suggest that the sun in Curtius is Alexander.

3 Civil war is the real point (see *post*). No one cared about wars on the frontiers.

storm. The world not only grows green again but flowers [i.e. Curtius was writing quite a time after the Emperor's accession]. We hope there will be no envy of the Emperor, and that he will have a long line of descendants, *diuturna posteritas*. At present there is public happiness. This passage has to be considered, not only in itself but in relation to its context, the passage which precedes it, x, 9, 1–2. Civil wars, *bella civilia*, broke up the Macedonian empire after Alexander's death; it might have lasted under the rule of one man, but when many were seeking the supreme power, the body, *corpus*, of the realm had more than it could carry, while the members, *membra*, of the realm [i.e. the outlying portions, the provinces, as opposed to the central *corpus*] began to break off, *deficere* [literally, to fail for want of nourishment].[1] This passage shows plainly that the wars which Curtius' Emperor put an end to were *civil* wars; in fact *discordia membra* would alone suffice to show the same thing.

What Emperor now will these passages fit, bearing in mind that the position is being compared to what happened after Alexander's death? The reference to descendants shows that Curtius' Emperor was regarded as one of a dynasty, which gives three choices, Julio-Claudians, Flavians, Severans; I do not think *posteritas* can be used to show whether the Emperor in question already had a son (or grandson) or not. Claudius, Augustus, Vespasian have all been proposed, together with names far later, and at one time the world seemed to have settled on Claudius;[2] but the case for him has little substance. No doubt it was nearly certain people's 'last night' when Gaius was opportunely killed; but Curtius' expression refers to every one generally, not to certain people, and the absence of civil war puts Claudius completely out of court.

Before trying to decide between Augustus and Vespasian,[3] the Severans ought to be considered,[4] as a late date would remove a number

1 Curtius is drawing his imagery from the old Roman fable of the belly and the members.
2 A list of the supporters of Claudius is given by J. Stroux, *Philol.* LXXXIV, 1929, pp. 233 *sq.*
3 Stroux, *op. cit.* best gives the case for Vespasian. He rightly emphasised that the decision must rest entirely on Curt. x, 9, 1–7 and on the comparison with what happened after Alexander's death.
4 The time of Severus Alexander was advocated by R. B. Steele, *A.J.P.* XXXVI, 1915, p. 402, on an elaborate comparison of Curtius' style and phraseology with those of many writers, from Livy to Orosius. I think he showed a connection between the styles of Curtius and Livy—not more than that; but that leaves it open which of them used which, or if both wrote under some common influence. Curtius' date cannot be decided by style—few questions of fact can.

of difficulties. Technically, it is possible enough; the *terminus post quem non* for Curtius' book is the fall of the Parthian empire,[1] and the date of the defeat of Artabanus V by Ardashir is either A.D. 224 or 227 (there are different methods of reckoning). The book then *could* have been written for Caracalla, who believed himself to be a reincarnation of Alexander and acted accordingly, but not published till the accession of Severus Alexander in A.D. 222; the beginning of his reign was calm enough, and Alexander was among those he honoured. This, I think, and this alone would explain the hopeless crux why, at the end of his book, Curtius went back on nearly everything he had previously said; he is saying to Severus Alexander 'Alexander wasn't *really* like that, you know'. It would explain why the reference to the new Emperor comes right at the end of the book; why Curtius appears to know Arrian and perhaps Tacitus; why he is not included in Pliny's encyclopaedic list of his own sources;[2] one may perhaps add the story that a 'new star' appeared when Severus Alexander was born[3] (but the star metaphor had long become a commonplace). But I fear that there is no real possibility of such a date. There had been no civil wars for a generation, which is conclusive; there was no 'sudden calm' in 222, no 'last nights'; it seems far too late for any one to be putting together, for the first time, the Peripatetic portrait of Alexander. Above all, it would not agree with Curtius' main contention. For Curtius is preaching on the text οὐκ ἀγαθὴ πολυκοιρανίη: when, on Alexander's death, many rulers took the place of one, it meant the ruin of the empire, which under one ruler might have stood. But there was no question of πολυκοιρανίη in 222.

We are then thrown back on a decision between Augustus and Vespasian. The civil wars, the sudden calm, fit both; in either case the 'last night' must be taken as a general expression for coming ruin. The comparison with Alexander's generals struggling for the *corpus*, the actual empire, might suit the year of the Four Emperors better than that of Actium; indeed a purist might argue that the Actium campaign was not a civil war at all, since Octavian had declared war on Cleopatra alone, not on Antony. But it is not to be supposed that most people troubled themselves about the juridical distinction; to them Octavian's success meant the end of the whole series of civil wars since the Rubicon, and that no doubt would be how Curtius saw it. But three things have

1 v, 7, 9, the Parthians now rule Macedonian cities; v, 8, 1, they now hold Ecbatana; vi, 2, 12, they now rule everything beyond the Euphrates.
2 This is not important, for Pliny omits Aristobulus also.
3 *Hist. Aug.* XVIII, 13, 5.

decided me for Augustus. One is that Curtius seems to be referring to the institution of a *new* system, the rule of one man instead of the conflict of several. The second is the *discordia membra*; there was no question of Vespasian saving the realm from breaking into pieces,[1] while in the struggle between Octavian and Antony the Roman East was for a time separated from Italy *de facto* and might easily have become so *de jure*. And the third is the Emperor as a *novum sidus*, which I find difficult to dissociate from the *Iulium sidus*—a transfer of imagery from Caesar to his adopted son. It could perhaps be suggested from the context that a *new* star might mean a new Alexander. In Augustus' reign no such ambiguity would be possible, for Alexander had never yet, so far as I know, been a star. But by the time of Vespasian the star metaphor had become common, and Alexander *had* become a star; Lucan in his famous invective had called him the evil star of humanity,[2] and in view of this I do not see how Curtius could have called Vespasian a new star without some sort of explanation.[3] One apparent difficulty in the way of an early date for Curtius, as regards either Augustus or Vespasian—Curtius' knowledge of Alexander's journey to the Land of Darkness (p. 108 and n. 5)—does not really exist; for Teles shows that Alexander's journey to the Well of Life was known in the third century B.C.,[4] and the two stories cannot be separated.

This is how I see it; others may prefer Vespasian. But in either case Curtius cannot have known Arrian, and therefore was not correcting or supplementing him; what he was doing therefore, at least in my items (3) to (6), was correcting and supplementing Ptolemy from the 'mercenaries' source', though perhaps not deliberately. For if we take the most important item (6), Ptolemy's omission of any information about Antigonus would have struck a reader of Ptolemy and Hieronymus precisely as it now strikes a reader of Arrian and Diodorus XVIII. Curtius then, in his extended use both of the Peripatetic character of Alexander and of the purely Greek 'mercenaries' source', different as they are, may in a sense be said to represent the Greek tradition as against the Macedonian; but the main problem about him, why in his

1 The revolt of Civilis, and the Jewish war, did not threaten to break up the realm.
2 *Pharsalia* x, 35, 'sidus iniquum gentibus'.
3 Stroux, *op. cit.* dismissed the words relating to light and darkness as rhetorical commonplaces; but I cannot think that this would apply to *novum sidus*, at least till far later.
4 App. 22, p. 364 n. 1.

summary he went back on nearly everything he had written, remains unsolved and, to myself, insoluble.[1]

It may, in conclusion, be worth summing up what Curtius had read and used. For the Peripatetic tradition which he knew so well no one author can be quoted; it was a school tradition. Among primary sources, Ptolemy, Aristobulus, and the unknown author of the 'mercenaries' source' are obvious, as is some writer on old Greece, probably Diyllus, and on Persia Ctesias or Deinon or both; but he knew more about Persia than can be accounted for from these writers (p. 108 *ante*). He had certainly read some or all of the poetasters who accompanied Alexander (VIII, 5, 8), as well as Choerilus of Iasos (VIII, 5, 8; see § E'). Polycleitus he had read and quotes (VI, 4, 18; p. 104 n. 1). Nearchus is used very sparingly;[2] it is doubtful if he used Onesicritus at all;[3] he was critic enough to have known what his book was. He may have known Aristotle's *Meteorologica*;[4] but as Arrian's quotation (VII, 16, 3) of the same passage from this work probably came through Aristobulus (§ B, pp. 11 *sq*.), so may any knowledge of it which Curtius possessed, if he really had any. Of secondary writers, Cleitarchus, Dicaearchus (the eunuch Bagoas), and Timagenes, who is named, are certain, and Hegesias possible (see App. 11); that he used Diodorus XVII seems certain enough also (§ G'), but to what extent cannot be said. Of writers on other subjects he knew Patrocles,[5] but perhaps only through Eratosthenes; Apollodorus of Artemita he uses more than once;[6] the collection of Macedonian customs already referred

1 It has been suggested to me that Curtius' summary is connected with his statement 'I have copied from others more than I believe'; having done this liberally throughout his book, he says again at the end that he does not believe these things. This would explain the summary if we agree with Wilamowitz that Curtius only wrote for popular entertainment, but that, as I have said, I cannot believe; the whole of this study appears to negative it.
2 Items in IX, 10, 9 *sqq.*; X, 1, 10 *sqq.* His instructions, IX, 10, 3, are not the real ones.
3 It may depend on the plural, 'nuntiabant', in X, 1, 11.
4 VII, 3, 21, the Hyrcanian and Caspian seas as two separate lakes (see § B). This cannot be from the Gazetteer, which makes the rivers run differently.
5 VI, 4, 19, the entrance to the Caspian sea in the far north (see § C, p. 17 n. 1).
6 Curtius' knowledge of Euthydemid Bactria (p. 96 *ante*) and of the difference between Parthava and Parthi (p. 107 n. 3) is more likely to come from Apollodorus than from 'Trogus' source' (on whom see Tarn, *Bactria and India*, pp. 45 *sqq.*) because Curtius seems to allude to Apollodorus' strait into the Hyrcanian Sea (VII, 3, 19, where it is coupled with the Araxes-Oxus), which is certainly Apollodorus and not Patrocles; see the discussion in § C, p. 17 n. 1.

to plays a considerable part; he quotes from some book of fables (p. 94), gives two Bactrian proverbs (VII, 4, 13), and knew the beginnings of the Romance.[1] A complete analysis would produce more, but there would always be a large residue from unknown sources; who can say who first transferred the proposal, and some of the machinery, of the Alexander-tent from Eumenes to the meeting of the generals at Babylon (x, 6, 4, 15), who represented Philip III as in possession of his senses (x, 8, 16–21),[2] who invented the first (Curtius') version of a plan to conquer the Mediterranean (x, 1, 17; see App. 24)—all the things in fact which show that Curtius had *not* read Diodorus XVIII and XIX? As in addition there is no evidence that he knew Hieronymus of Cardia,[3] it seems evident that he took little trouble to read up the Successors; parts of book x, where they appear, are wild.

We seem to have travelled a long way from Cleitarchus. But anything one writes about Curtius can only be a second best, owing to the loss of the first two books.

G'. CURTIUS' USE OF DIODORUS

I SAID in § G, p. 115, that Curtius used Diodorus XVII. I now give the evidence.

(1) In describing Alexander's battle-line at Gaugamela, both Diodorus and Curtius use, for his hypaspists, the word *Argyraspids* (Silver Shields).[4] This word is considered in App. 1, III, pp. 151 *sqq.*; it was not in use during Alexander's lifetime, but is Hieronymus' name for Alexander's hypaspists; it plays a large part in the story of Eumenes of Cardia, but Hieronymus does not use it till Eumenes goes to Kyinda;

1 Besides the journey to the Land of Darkness already noticed, he knew of Alexander's *Testament*, and also knew that it was a fabrication, x, 10, 5. Probably VII, 8, 13 contains another allusion to the Romance.

2 Doubtless it was one more offshoot of Cassander's propaganda against Olympias, who was accused of destroying the boy's wits from jealousy, Plut. *Alex.* LXXVII.

3 For a definite reason against such knowledge see § G', p. 118. Also Curtius x, 6 to end, displays ignorance of Hieronymus.

4 Diod. XVII, 57, 2: ὄπισθεν δὲ τούτων (the Companion cavalry) ὑπετάγη τὸ τῶν ἀργυρασπίδων πεζῶν τάγμα, διαφέρον...τῇ τῶν ἀνδρῶν ἀρετῇ· καὶ τούτων ἡγεῖτο Νικάνωρ ὁ Παρμενίωνος. ἐχομένην δὲ τούτων (here follow the six battalions of the phalanx; the hypaspists were really in line between the Companions and the phalanx). Curt. IV, 13, 27, 'post phalangem (i.e. the battle-line, a well-known use of φάλαγξ; see App. 1, 1, p. 136) Argyraspides erant; his Nicanor, Parmenionis filius, praeerat'.

before that he uses the word hypaspists,[1] so the name presumably dates from Kyinda, whether the actual shields do or not. Now in book XVII Diodorus never uses the word hypaspists, though he does later;[2] in XVII, except for the passage now being considered, he never distinguishes the hypaspists from the phalanx, but groups them together as 'the infantry' or 'the phalanx'; and as he has no battle-pieces after Gaugamela, i.e. after his use of the 'mercenaries' source' ends (see § F), and has therefore no need to distinguish the two arms, it must have been the 'mercenaries' source' which did not distinguish them, for the reason given in App. 1, III, p. 153. Curtius, who also used the 'mercenaries' source', groups phalanx and hypaspists together in just the same way.[3] But at Gaugamela both Diodorus and Curtius distinguish the hypaspists from the phalanx as Argyraspids, identifying them by calling them Nicanor's command (he commanded the hypaspists); that is to say, both in effect give the hypaspists twice over. Ptolemy (Arrian), of course, did not use the word Argyraspids at Gaugamela; neither did the 'mercenaries' source', which does not distinguish the hypaspists from the phalanx, and also cannot have known this much later word; looking at its history, which I have given, the word cannot have come from any source but Hieronymus.[4] That is, Diodorus here is his own source; he had studied Hieronymus on Eumenes, and the too familiar word, which plays such a part in Eumenes' story in books XVIII and XIX, slipped in.[5] It was natural enough; the same word Argyraspids,

1 Diod. XVIII, 33, 6; certainly from Hieronymus.
2 Besides XVIII, 33, 6, see XIX, 28, 1; 40, 3 (Eumenes' hypaspists).
3 A good instance is III, 9, 7, at Issus: 'phalangem....Dextrum cornu Nicanor, Parmenionis filius, tuebatur.'
4 To talk of Cleitarchus here would be idle; it is not known if he even gave an account of Gaugamela, let alone what it was; it is not known if he had read Hieronymus or even if he could have done so, for Hieronymus went down at least to Pyrrhus' death in 272 and could not have published anyhow till after 270. Where Diodorus in his account of Gaugamela differs from the 'good' tradition without it being just some muddle or misunderstanding of his own, there he is certainly using the 'mercenaries' source'. One proof of this is his high praise of the Thessalians (57, 4 ἀνδρείᾳ...πολὺ προέχοντες τῶν ἄλλων; so at Issus, 33, 2, πολὺ τῶν ἄλλων διαφέροντες ταῖς τε ἀνδραγαθίαις καὶ ταῖς ἐμπειρίαις) and his apparent knowledge of their special tactics (§ F, p. 74); for the Lamian war, when the world of mercenaries again challenged Macedonia, had made the Thessalians heroes to all mercenaries. See also p. 119 n. 2.
5 This is confirmed by Diodorus (XVII, 57, 2) calling the Argyraspids διαφέρον τῇ τῶν ἀνδρῶν ἀρετῇ; for in the Eumenes story they are regarded as invincible, but while Alexander lived there is no record of one corps being more praised for courage or competence than others; it is assumed of all.

instead of hypaspists, slipped in once in just the same way in Arrian's *Anabasis*,[1] he having also studied Hieronymus for his τὰ μετ' 'Αλέξαν-δρον, precisely as Diodorus did. It must be remembered that, in Diodorus' own mind, his books XVII and XVIII–XX, though they seem so different to us, were closely connected, and that not merely because in XVII he quotes back from the later books, e.g. Agathocles' invasion of Africa (XVII, 23, 2); book XVII is built up on a framework of τύχη (see § F), but he does not explain his own idea of the working of τύχη till he comes to Eumenes in XVIII, 59, 5–6; he must have had Eumenes in his mind throughout.

But there is more than this. Diodorus, we have seen, says the phalanx was ἐχομένην τούτων, next in line to the Argyraspids; he regards the phalanx as prolonging the line to the left of the Argyraspids (as was true), just as the Argyraspids should have been prolonging the line to the left of the Companions. But, by some oversight, he has put the Argyraspids *behind* the Companions (ὄπισθεν τούτων), which makes nonsense of the position of the phalanx and of his own account of that position. It is perfectly clear from Ptolemy-Arrian that the phalanx was in line with the Companions, with the hypaspists in line between them, as at the Granicus and at Issus; and the 'mercenaries' source', which as we shall see (p. 119 n. 2) Diodorus was following in his account of the phalanx at Gaugamela, could not have said otherwise, for the author, or his informants, *saw* Alexander's line. Consequently the word ὄπισθεν, behind, is just a slip of Diodorus' own,[2] as is shown by his own account of the position of the phalanx (for *he* knew what the Argyraspids were); the slip would doubtless have been corrected had book XVII had a final revision (§ F, p. 80 n. 1).

How now about Curtius? *He* was not a student of Hieronymus; here is no evidence that he knew him at all (§ G, p. 116). But at Gaugamela he has used Hieronymus' word Argyraspids in the same context as Diodorus and has identified them with the hypaspists in the same way by calling them Nicanor's command. It is certain enough from this that he was copying Diodorus, but what clinches the matter is Diodorus' mistake, ὄπισθεν; for Curtius, who obviously did not know what Argyraspids were and has previously treated Nicanor's command as part of the phalanx (III, 9, 7; see p. 117 n. 3), has *copied Diodorus' slip also* and has put the Argyraspids '*post* phalangem',

---

1 Arr. VII, 11, 3, on which see App. 1, III, p. 152.
2 I once did exactly the same thing; with complete knowledge, I wrote 'across' for 'round', and published it.

behind the line; his *post* is Diodorus' ὄπισθεν.[1] This should be conclusive.

(2) The second instance also comes from Alexander's battle-line at Gaugamela, close in the text to (1). In XVII, 57, 3 Diodorus describes the phalanx and the cavalry on the left of it. He gives, right to left, the six battalions of the phalanx as those of Coenus, Perdiccas, Meleager, Polyperchon, Philippus son of Balacrus,[2] Craterus; the text here, from the fifth battalion, runs Φίλιππος δ᾽ ὁ Βαλάκρου τὴν συνεχῆ ταύτης (Polyperchon's) στρατηγίαν ἐπλήρου καὶ τῆς μετὰ ταύτην Κρατερὸς ἡγεῖτο. τῶν δὲ προειρημένων ἱππέων τὴν συνεχῆ τάξιν ἀπεπλήρουν (read ἐπλήρουν with Florentinus[3]) οἱ ἀπὸ Πελοποννήσου...ἱππεῖς under Eriguios. Curtius IV, 13, 28, giving the phalanx in the same way, right to left, gives it from the fifth battalion as follows: 'Philippus Balacri Stymphaeos regebat. Haec dextri cornus facies (the configuration, or appearance) erat. In laevo Craterus Peloponnensium equites habebat.' That is to say, Curtius' eye in reading the Greek text has slipped from συνεχῆ ἐπλήρου to συνεχῆ ἐπλήρουν, and he has run Craterus and the Peloponnesian horse together accordingly, leaving out Craterus' battalion of the phalanx and making him command the Peloponnesian horse; he was therefore writing from Diodorus' text. There is no alternative. Certainly Diodorus' account here comes from the 'mercenaries' source', as we have seen (Philippus for Simmias, the peculiar στρατηγία for τάξις), and certainly Curtius made liberal use of that source; but to suppose that Curtius' eye slipped in reading, not Diodorus but Diodorus' source, is out of the question. For it would mean that Diodorus here copied out his source exactly and minutely, word for word and letter for letter, which is not his way. The most that he does is, when describing some particular thing or perhaps in a story, to write a sentence sufficiently resembling the original to show where it came from,[4] and he *may* occasionally reproduce some rare or striking word;[5] but in narrative his method is very different. (I am speaking of the Hellenistic books only.)

1 'Post' cannot mean 'after', i.e. on the left of, as that position is explicitly assigned to the Peloponnesian horse.
2 The fifth battalion was really commanded by Simmias deputising for his brother Amyntas. Philippus' name, and στρατηγία for τάξις, show we are dealing with the 'mercenaries' source', and not Ptolemy.
3 Florentinus has usually been considered the best MS. for the Hellenistic books.
4 Some instances, § D, p. 40 n. 6; § F, p. 76 n. 1, pp. 79 *sq.* (the two suns); p. 85 n. 2 (the karaits).
5 As in the account of the mountain bee from Cleitarchus (§ F').

These instances, (1) and (2), which complement each other, prove that in one particular passage, Alexander's line at Gaugamela, Curtius was copying from Diodorus. I will now give another instance, which depends, not on language, but on sense, and which is unmistakable: in his account of the siege of Tyre, Curtius has introduced from Diodorus an isolated statement which in Diodorus makes sense but in his own account makes no sense of any kind.

(3) The siege of Tyre.[1] Putting aside certain incidental stories, like the chaining of Apollo, which is doubtless true,[2] Diodorus' main account, in which the mole never reaches the island and Alexander works from ships, keeps close enough to the 'good' tradition; this main account goes down to the end of 43, 4, where Alexander, working from ships, throws down part of the wall and breaks in, which is near enough to the truth; here the main account stops, but is taken up again and supplemented in 45, 5–6, the death of Admetus, which ought to have come earlier, where Alexander breaks in. However, Tyre is now really taken, as in Ptolemy-Arrian. But with 43, 5 Diodorus has begun a quite different story, which goes down to 45, 5, and which I will call the land siege account. In this, the mole reaches the wall and Tyre becomes an isthmus, χερρονήσου γενομένης, and we get a land siege, τειχομαχία (the word is repeated several times), with a description of all the wonderful machines proper to a land siege which the Tyrians used or invented. That is, an account taken in substance, with added stories, from the 'good' tradition, or anyhow in substantial agreement with the 'good' tradition, has had dovetailed into it an account which does not belong to Tyre at all. At the end, the two accounts are contaminated; though Tyre has really fallen with the death of Admetus and Alexander breaking in (which is what did happen), in 46, 1 Alexander retires from the city and starts afresh with the ships, so as to bring in the boarding-bridge, which ought to have come in before; but the boarding-bridge he enters by is not borne on shipboard, as in the 'good' tradition, but starts from a wooden tower up against the wall[3] (this is the point to bear in mind); the fall of Tyre is duplicated to get in the boarding-bridge as part of the τειχομαχία. Among the devices the Tyrians use in the land siege account are some things which, so far as I know, are never mentioned in any Hellenistic siege—fishing

1 Diod. XVII, 40, 2–46, 4; Curt. IV, 2, 2–4, 18.
2 See G. Radet, *Notes critiques sur l'histoire d'Alexandre I*, v, p. 51.
3 43, 7, towers as high as the wall are moved up to the wall (the regular land siege operation); in 46, 2 Alexander enters by a boarding-bridge from one of these towers.

nets to catch men,[1] whirling wheels of marble full of holes to catch or divert catapult bolts (45, 3), and sand heated red hot on metal shields (44, 1 *sqq.*). All these, indeed, may be only suggestions made in technical literature; the land siege account reads as if Diodorus were copying, as he probably was, from some text-book on Hellenistic siege warfare at large. The sole attempt he makes to combine his two accounts, the attack on the island of Tyre and the land siege, is that he has inserted the whirling wheels from the land siege account back into his main account (43, 1), so that they are described twice over. All this, of course, like the items out of their order in the main account, shows that his whole account of the siege is merely a draft, which never had a final revision, like some other things in book XVII (§ F, p. 80 n. 1); the land siege account was merely worked in for picturesqueness, like the mountain bee (§ F′), sunset as seen from Ida, and other passages. But our concern now is with Curtius.

Curtius keeps pretty close to the 'good' tradition and the main facts, with the same incidental stories as Diodorus; the mole never reaches the island, but only comes within shot of it, and the Tyrians' machines, various sorts of grapnels, are adapted for use against attacking ships. Then, without any warning or explanation, he brings in two items from Diodorus' land siege account—two and no more; one is the sand heated red hot in metal shields and poured down on the attackers (IV, 3, 25 *devolvebant*), which could only be done if the enemy were right under the wall, not on shipboard; the other (4, 10–11) is a tall wooden tower almost touching the wall from which Alexander spears the fighters on the wall. This is the tower of Diodorus' land siege account; but Curtius, who has throughout been talking of an attack from on shipboard, gives not the least explanation of how that tower got there, as Diodorus does; in Curtius it is a sudden bit of pure nonsense. That this tower, and the red hot sand, were copied by Curtius from Diodorus seems to be beyond all reasonable doubt. The chances against two writers independently sandwiching the same material from the same account of a land siege into the siege of an island fortress must be astronomical; but, putting this aside, had Curtius known and independently used Diodorus' source for a land siege, then he *must* have given some explanation of how that tower got there. He gives none.

Any suggestion that Curtius and Diodorus took their accounts here

[1] 43, 10, ἁλιευτικὰ δίκτυα. Aeneas Tacticus, XXXIX, 6, advocates the use of βρόχοι for catching besiegers, but whatever sort of net or noose is meant, it is something stronger and heavier than a fishing net.

from a common source, whether Cleitarchus or another, would be futile. It would mean that Curtius drew from that source a connected and tolerably reasonable account (save for the two items mentioned), fairly close to the 'good tradition', while Diodorus drew from it a muddled story which displaces some true incidents and tries to combine, very inadequately, the sieges of an island and of a land fortress. No more need be said.

If then, as seems certain, Curtius read and used Diodorus, how much did he use him? He had a perfectly independent outlook and took his own line; his main portrait of Alexander differs utterly from that of Diodorus; where both, for example, use the 'mercenaries' source', they make very different use of it. The conclusion must be that Curtius can only have used Diodorus much as he did so many writers—just as and when, and as much or as little as, he chose.

H. JUSTIN, BOOKS XI AND XII

JUSTIN'S Epitome of Trogus does not always represent Trogus exactly or correctly as regards details—so much is clear from a comparison with Trogus' *Prologues*; but no doubt in the main it represents him fairly well, except where a whole section is omitted, and one can use it for any question about sources. Trogus depends on his sources as much as, or even more than, Diodorus; it is the sources which decide whether he is tolerably good or very bad. But Trogus'— or perhaps one should call it Justin's—Alexander is so hopelessly bad that, except on one point, it is hardly worth considering sources at all. To Justin, Alexander is a conqueror and no more,[1] with all the traditional vices; his portrait bears no relation to the main portrait in Diodorus, and not much to the main (the Peripatetic) portrait in Curtius; for though, as in Curtius, Alexander's *luxuria* begins in Hyrcania after Darius' death (XII, 3, 8–10), what really made him worse in much more important ways was Ammon. That is, perhaps, as regards sources, the only thing of real interest in Justin, viz. that after his visit to Ammon his arrogance (*insolentia*) and false pride (*tumor animi*) increased;[2] for

[1] See the summary, XII, 16, 11: he never met an enemy he did not conquer, never besieged a city he did not take, never reached a people he did not trample down. That is all.

[2] XI, 11, 12: 'Hinc illi aucta insolentia mirusque animo increvit tumor.' 'Aucta' and 'increvit' show that these were no new things.

as *insolentia* is ὕβρις, and as *tumor animi* represents, I suppose, τῦφος, we get here the two vices which, in the Stoic view of him, were characteristic of Alexander,[1] and Justin's portrait of him may therefore be related, not so much to the secondary portraits in Diodorus and Curtius already described, which appeared to be connected with Cleitarchus, as to the teaching of the Stoics; for while τῦφος was, from the start, the primary feature of the Stoic portrait of Alexander, Justin does not give the characteristic Cleitarchean massacres nor the imitations of Dionysus and Achilles. For the rest, Justin often gives the impression that he is trying to go one better than Curtius or somebody else; his book is full of foolish exaggerations of things given elsewhere.

A few of these may be noticed. XII, 6, 14, Alexander murders his stepmother (Cleopatra) and his brothers (plural).[2] XI, 11, 5, the tension between Philip and Olympias becomes a divorce. XI, 10, 14, Tyre is taken by treachery. XI, 9, 13, Alexander after Issus visits Darius' family in person at the start; in every other account he first sends a general. XI, 11, 6, the priests of Ammon are bribed. XI, 11, 11, the generals are *ordered* by Ammon to worship Alexander as a god, while in Curtius (IV, 7, 28) they are *permitted* only. XI, 15, 4, Alexander fights many dangerous battles while pursuing Darius (there were none), and the dying Darius makes a long speech in the best theatrical tradition. XII, 5, 3, Parmenion is put to the torture no less than Philotas, while in Curtius it is Philotas alone. XII, 6, 4, Alexander *rejoices* over the murder of Cleitus. Curtius (VI, 6, 8) had objected to Alexander allowing Darius' concubines to stay in the palace; in Justin (XII, 3, 10) Alexander takes them about with him and sleeps with them. Curtius sneers at his marriage to Roxane; in Justin (XII, 10, 10) his marriage to the Persian Stateira is a crime (*crimen*). Justin does not use Peripatetic material, so we do not get the eunuch Bagoas; in his place, Hephaestion was once Alexander's minion (XII, 12, 11–12). On the army, Justin says (XI, 6, 4–6) that *all* the troops were elderly men, no file-leader in particular

---

1 I examined the two meanings of τῦφος at length in *Antigonos Gonatas*, p. 240 n. 70; it finally tended to become a word in which 'you sum up all that you dislike in those with whom you disagree'. It was a quality specially condemned by Zeno (*S.V.F.* I, no. 317). Though τυφόω and *tumeo* start from different ideas, τετυφωμένος, swollen up ('swelled head'), comes near to *tumidus* in meaning; and I do not see how *tumor animi*, conjoined with *insolentia* (ὕβρις), can here be a translation of anything but τῦφος. For the Stoic view, see Stroux' article, § F, p. 69 n. 1; Stroux also (*Philol.* 1933, pp. 233–8) treats *tumidus* as the Latin representative of τετυφωμένος.

2 There is no suggestion of this elsewhere. See generally App. 9.

being under 60. This story is told by Diodorus (XIX, 41, 2), but only of the hypaspists (the Argyraspids): in 316 B.C. the youngest was about 60 and the most about 70 or over, a passage actually repeated in various modern works in the belief that it came from Hieronymus. The story is first found in one of the Hellenistic components of the Romance, Ps.-Call. A′, 1, 25, 3–5, where Alexander tells Philip's elderly hypaspists, who claim to be too old for further service, that he needs them, not as fighters, but as instructors for the younger men, a perfectly sensible idea which might well be true. Diodorus has dropped the idea of instructors and has made the old men the actual fighting corps; Justin has followed this, though he (or Trogus) still retained some dim memory of the 'instructors', for he says *ut non tam milites quam magistros militiae lectos putares*. The point, however, is that while Diodorus, following the Romance writer, still makes the old men the hypaspists (Argyraspids), Justin with his usual exaggeration has extended, not only the great age, but also (XII, 7, 5) the name Argyraspids and the actual silver-washed shields, from the hypaspists to the whole army; and if Trogus, or Justin, has thus taken *three* things given by Diodorus about Alexander's hypaspists and extended them to the whole army, then Trogus (for it is unlikely to have been Justin on his own account) must have known and used Diodorus. With this crowd of ancients Alexander in Justin proceeds to conquer countries he never saw, first Chorasmia (XII, 6, 18) and later Magadha (XII, 8, 9), an appropriate conclusion to the Ganges legend (see App. 14), but one which the most extravagant of his predecessors had not dared to relate. Finally, Alexander does not die of a fever; he really *was* poisoned (XII, 13, 10).

To talk of sources for this mass of rubbish would be idle; it is merely somebody—perhaps not always Trogus himself—writing with the flowing pen of the popular historiographer. One can find bits of anybody; the voyage down the Acesines (XII, 9, 1) was originally Cleitarchus, the name Sudracas (XII, 9, 3) is Aristobulus' form, Craterus and Antipater changing places (XII, 12, 9) was originally Ptolemy; but probably none of this was first-hand, and one can hardly talk of sources, least of all of Cleitarchus, for, as has been noticed, we do not get the two things which seem to be characteristic of that writer. It has been seen that Trogus is almost bound to have used Diodorus; but I have found nothing to indicate either that Trogus used Curtius or that Curtius used Trogus, though there are a few cases where both seem to be using the same popular story. The passage in Justin XI, 12, 15 about the two suns, which agrees with Curtius word for word, stands alone; I have given what I believe to be the explanation elsewhere (§ F, p. 79). In any case, Justin's Alexander-books are, in essence, merely 'popular' history.

Is there any bread at all to this intolerable deal of sack? Not much. In xi, 3, 2, Alexander becomes head of the Thessalian League, as Philip had been; that he would take his father's place is obvious, but in fact no other writer mentions it. The mourning (xii, 3, 1) decreed for his brother-in-law Alexander of Epirus may be true, though not mentioned elsewhere; for the Lucanians and Bruttians, in battle with whom the Epirote had been killed, did later send embassies to put themselves right with Alexander (Arr. vii, 15, 4). The account in xii, 4 of the army, with wives and children, as a moving city exhibits knowledge of the later Hellenistic armies.[1] Alexander's promise (xi, 9, 15) to Darius' daughters that they should be called *reginae* (βασίλισσαι) is from Ptolemy or Aristobulus (Arr. ii, 12, 5). That I think is about all.

The substitution of one known proper name for another known proper name, presumably by mistake, is common enough in all our secondary writers (see App. 17, p. 315 n. 2); but Justin in this respect holds a place apart, not merely from the number of his blunders but from the ease with which he blunders even where Trogus, whom he is epitomising, gave the name correctly;[2] this can only be checked where the name occurs in Trogus' *Prologues*, but Trogus is known, as regards dynastic names, to have been careful never to leave any doubt which king he is talking about.[3] Justin, however, has two proper names worth notice. While other writers call the Queen of the Amazons Thalestris, Justin (xii, 3, 5) calls her 'Thalestris or Minythyia', showing that Trogus knew some version of the story now lost. And in xii, 9, 2, for the unknown Agelasseis whom Diodorus (xvii, 96, 3) couples with the Sibi, he substitutes the equally unknown name Agensonas; it may come from Graeco-Bactrian times, where Trogus had a good source behind him.

---

1 On these see Rostovtzeff, *Soc. and Econ. Hist.* i, pp. 146 *sqq.*
2 Some instances from the Hellenistic books, certainties only. xiii, 4, 6, Arridaeus rex for Arridaeus the general. xiii, 5, 8, Heraclea for Lamia. xiii, 8, 7, Polyperchon for Craterus (correct in Trogus). xiv, 6, 2, Hercule for Alexandro. xiv, 6, 13, Arridaei for Philippi. xv, 2, 3, Hercules and Barsine for Alexander (iv) and Roxane (correct in Trogus). xxiii, 3, 3, Helenus for Alexander. xxv, 4, 4, Chersoneso for Peloponneso. xxvi, 3, 3 and 7, Arsinoe for Apama. xxvii, 3, 1, rex Bithyniae Eumenes for Pergami Attalus (correct in Trogus). xxx, 1, 7, Eurydice for Arsinoe; so 2, 7.
3 See my analysis, *J.H.S.* xxix, 1909, pp. 265 *sqq.*

Justin is occasionally useful for comparisons; otherwise the modern historian of Alexander might neglect books XI and XII completely, but for one matter: he gives a more thorough-going account than any other writer of Alexander's alleged intention to conquer the world. Alexander from the start intends to conquer the whole earth, *universum terrarum orbem* (XI, 6, 3). As it was certain that he did not conquer it, some means had to be found of getting round this. He reaches the farthest bounds of Ocean in the East (XII, 13, 1) and in XII, 16, 9 he orders that he shall be *called* king of the universe, *terrarum omnium ac mundi*; but the real matter is the supposed embassies to Babylon.[1] A λόγος in Arr. VII, 15, 5 says that they made him *seem* to be king of the world, and Justin improves on this (XII, 13, 1–3) by saying that he had so terrified the whole earth, *universum terrarum orbem* (the phrase used at the start), that all nations were ready to worship him as their destined king; it was as if he were going to hold at Babylon a formal meeting of the whole earth, *conventus terrarum orbis*. This represents yet one more attempt to magnify Alexander as against Rome;[2] but this time Alexander does, not merely what Rome was to do later, but much more. We thus get two plainly inconsistent threads in Trogus on Alexander: the glorification of him as the supreme conqueror, and the condemnation of him as a cruel tyrant. Both throw light on Trogus' date. The latest event mentioned by Justin is the return of the eagles by the Parthians in 20 B.C. On the other side, Alexander in Trogus has not actually conquered the world, whereas by Nero's time he had;[3] Trogus therefore should come after 20 B.C. but before Nero. He was, as has been seen, dominated by, or anyhow close to, the Stoic view of Alexander which was fashionable in Nero's reign, but there is reason for placing him somewhat earlier than Nero. For there is still some measure in his account of Alexander's misdeeds; in Lucan and Seneca there is none.

1 These are considered in App. 23; see also § C, pp. 23 *sqq.*
2 The theme of Livy's *levissimi*, on whom see App. 24, p. 396.
3 Seneca, *Ep.* 119, 7, 'mundi claustra perrumpit'; *Ep.* 94, 62, 'toto orbe arma circumfert'; he goes 'ultra oceanum solemque'. Lucan, *Pharsalia* X, 31 *sqq.*, 'gladiumque per omnes Exegit gentes', etc. A little later Juvenal was to go still further: x, 168, 'Unus Pellaeo iuveni non sufficit orbis.' Did they know the story of Alexander's journey to the Land of the Blessed, which was not in this world at all (κόσμον ἄλλον κατέλαβε)? Our versions (Fr. Pfister, *Rh. Mus.* LXVI, 1911, p. 458) are late; but the story is not necessarily late.

J. SUMMARY

IT may be useful to summarise the foregoing sections. Three things have been proved for certain. The first, § B, is that Cleitarchus was not with Alexander at any point of his expedition, and was therefore a secondary writer. This section contains perforce a long examination of the Caspian question in its proper historical order; this has never before been done, but it happens to be the key to the linked problems of whether Cleitarchus was a primary authority or not and what was his date. The second, § C, gives the proof that Cleitarchus quoted Patrocles, and that therefore his book could not possibly be *earlier* than 280 B.C.; he probably wrote in the decade 280–270, but as late even as *c.* 260 is quite possible, though the reasons for this possibility are not those sometimes previously adduced, which have no value. This section also examines the reasons which have been put forward for assigning a much earlier date to this author. The third, § D, gives the proof that Cleitarchus used Aristobulus, the proof, which is conclusive, being independent of Cleitarchus' date; it also evaluates Aristobulus as a source (*post*). The fourth, § E, deals with what can be made out about Cleitarchus' book from the named fragments. They give little information, but two things are worth notice. The first is that, with the solitary exception of Quintilian's remark that he was clever, no later writer who mentions him has a good word for him; the other is that the fragments give little guide to his attitude towards Alexander. The only thing that can be got with certainty from the fragments in this respect is that Cleitarchus had a taste for inventing, or adopting inventions of, massacres (that he must have done a certain amount of inventing himself, whatever its nature, seems to follow from the testimony of later writers); but one other line of writing—extravagances such as are connected with the names of Dionysus, Achilles, Semiramis—though not certain, possesses a high degree of probability and can probably be fairly used in a reconstruction of Cleitarchus; if this be correct, he made Alexander an imitative character. There is no foundation for the belief that he wrote a sort of popular glorification of Alexander: what little can really be made out indicates rather a book hostile to him, as would be natural in an Alexandrian, seeing that Alexandrian learning was the great heir of the Peripatetic tradition. In § E' a neglected source, the group of poets, or poetasters, contemporary with Alexander, all or most of whom were with him in Asia, are considered as being the originators of some of the extravagant stories which have come down to us and which may have been passed on by Cleitarchus.

Section F gives an analysis of Diodorus book XVII, so far as is necessary for my purpose; I am not writing a commentary on Diodorus. This book contains two separate and distinct portraits of Alexander, one favourable, one the reverse; the favourable one is the basic one, the other having been added to it without much attempt at adjustment. We have the difficulty that all the chapters which narrated events in Bactria and Sogdiana are lost; but it is hardly likely that they could have affected the general conclusion, though they would have given us more details. As regards sources, I have tried to forget the various opinions which exist about Diodorus' methods of work and to treat book XVII merely as a document; I may add that his methods were not necessarily the same in the Hellenistic books, with the wealth of material to his hand, as in the earlier ones, where he had fewer authorities. Down to Issus his chief, if not his only, source (events in Greece apart) was the 'mercenaries' source', a well-informed writer who gave the point of view of the Greek mercenaries in Darius' service and is valuable in a military sense; he seems, not unnaturally, to have had little to say about Alexander himself, and there is consequently little in this part of Diodorus. It has of course been noticed before that Diodorus has some information from this angle. This source can be seen from Curtius to have gone down to Darius' death, its natural termination; but after Issus another source appears in Diodorus and ousts it as the principal source. This new source goes down to the end of the book, and from it must be taken, at least in outline, Diodorus' basic portrait of Alexander, the favourable one. There were never many favourable portraits of Alexander in existence; and several factors—direct internal evidence, the favourable portrait, Diodorus' contacts (often noticed) with the 'good' tradition, and a process of exhaustion—are practically conclusive that it must be taken from Aristobulus, for Diodorus does not use Ptolemy as a source. On this basic portrait is superimposed an unfavourable portrait from another source; this more or less bears out the contention of those who have maintained that Diodorus' habit was to use *two* sources, writing from the main one and correcting it from a second one, only in the case of book XVII there is little question of correction; two opposed statements may be left side by side. (There are, however, several indications that the book never had a final revision.) There is just enough to show that this second source is, in all probability, Cleitarchus; and there can be no doubt, both from the dates of the two writers and from the position of the second source, that the meaning of those occasional resemblances between Aristobulus and Cleitarchus which have led to the belief that Aristobulus used and rationalised Cleitarchus is really the precise opposite: it is Cleitarchus using and writing up Aristobulus. In one section, India, Diodorus has altered his method and seems to be giving the preference to Cleitarchus' versions over those of the older writer; the only explanation seems to be that Diodorus must have thought that India needed more colour than Aristobulus' sober and factual narrative would supply. The last trace of Cleitarchus is the Bacchic rout in Carmania; thenceforth Diodorus returns to Aristobulus. What this analysis, coupled with the earlier sections, brings out clearly is the complete lack of basis for the common belief that Diodorus XVII is substantially Cleitarchus; therewith much of the traditional figure of Cleitarchus, built up in modern times from Diodorus, vanishes. In § F' I have examined a single chapter of Diodorus XVII, which shows that over detail he would make a mosaic from any and every writer who occurred to him—a disputed point.

In § G Curtius is analysed in the same way as Diodorus; what I have said about this strange and interesting character himself does not lend itself to a summary. The loss of the first two books is serious, as it prevents us knowing why he wrote; there must have been an introduction giving his reasons. I am satisfied, however, from the quite invaluable pieces of information embedded in his rhetoric, that it was meant to be a serious history and not a work of entertainment. Like Diodorus, he had two distinct portraits of Alexander, but not the same two. There is no doubt about the main one, for he has taken much trouble to explain what it was; it is the Peripatetic portrait of Alexander (he does not actually use the word), the one full version of it which we possess: Aristotle's pupil was a thoroughly good king down to a point, which in Curtius is Darius' death; then he was ruined by his own Fortune, and became a cruel tyrant. But Curtius has also used a secondary portrait, as did Diodorus, and substantially the same one, though there are differences of presentation; in this, Alexander is bad all along. As to his sources, two things are quite plain. One is that, again like Diodorus, he used the 'mercenaries' source', and he made very good use of this valuable primary document; we should know more about it had we the first two books, in which it must have figured largely. His use of it continues to Gaugamela (it is especially enlightening for Issus and Gaugamela) and probably down to Darius' death, where it must have ended; his long narrative of Darius' flight and death, which does explain, e.g., the cup of water, rather obscure in Arrian, may suggest that the mercenary leader Patron supplied a good deal of the material to the author of this document, if indeed he was not the author himself. The other thing is that, apart from this document, Curtius had no single definite main source at all, or rather his source was the traditions of the Peripatetic school; there is no trace that these had ever been committed to writing in their entirety as a history, but they seem to have remained 'University teaching', perhaps with monographs on various points. He probably made rather more use of Cleitarchus than just the secondary portrait of Alexander (if that portrait be indeed from Cleitarchus); but he speaks of this writer with utter contempt, and his use of him must therefore have been limited. What seems certain enough, though it has been overlooked, is that he knew and used Diodorus' book XVII; proofs are given in § G'. We have, too, the curious basic facts that both writers begin by using the 'mercenaries' source', unknown to Arrian, and both apparently used the same secondary portrait of Alexander, though their main portraits are quite different; and where they give stories that agree, it is sometimes quite impossible to say whether both are using a common source or whether Curtius is using Diodorus. One remark attributed to Alexander (§ F, p. 79) is interesting in this connection. It is very late (time of Octavian), so no question of sources arises; Diodorus, Curtius, and Justin all give it, and in exactly the same context; and as Curtius and Justin agree word for word, the original was in Latin and Diodorus' Greek version is a (rather loose) translation. Curtius is not translating from Diodorus, as Justin shows; but the identical setting shows that he knew where to find Diodorus' Latin original. Indeed I can place little limit on Curtius' reading, till he comes to the Successors; I have given a list of what can be made out, but I do not suppose that it includes the half of it. Clever, careless, cynical, he is about the most maddening writer of antiquity; he could have told us so much, had he been in earnest; instead, like the Sibyl, he exacts the same price—to wade through his rhetoric—for a mere fraction of what he must have known.

Section H is Justin. He is very brief and incredibly bad and extravagant; there are passages where one might be reading the Romance, but he has some interest as exhibiting a certain kinship with the Stoic tradition; alone of our extant Alexander-historians he specifically ascribes to Alexander those typical Stoic catchwords, the vices of ὕβρις and τῦφος.

I have not discussed Callisthenes here, for (except for his invention of the massacre of the Branchidae, treated in App. 13) his influence upon the tradition seems confined to the questions connected with Alexander's deification; here he is important, but these matters are discussed fully in App. 22. He may perhaps have had some responsibility for a garbled account of the battle of Gaugamela which obtained some currency (App. 5, pp. 182 *sq.*); his account of Issus was heavily criticised by Polybius. It seems obvious that he was soon displaced by better sources; he may perhaps have been sometimes used by Cleitarchus, though their points of view were very different (see App. 13). His real importance to the tradition is as the unconscious cause, after his death, of the Peripatetic portrait of Alexander.

After the generation which had known Alexander had died out, no such thing as a favourable portrait of him appeared again for centuries (so far as we know) save for a few remarks surviving from that genuine critic Eratosthenes, himself a lost writer. The reason is not far to seek: literature was in the hands of Greeks, and Greeks were on the whole thoroughly hostile. Of the four great schools which guided thought, the Peripatetics, friends and allies of Cassander while he lived, hated Alexander wholeheartedly for Callisthenes' death, and to some extent carried Alexandria with them. *Their* hatred is comprehensible; but the Stoics, who became the most influential school of the four, hated him no less, while the reason is obscure; though this did not prevent both schools from borrowing his ideas. The Academy was neutral, the Epicureans indifferent. It was this widespread antipathy, and not Cleitarchus, which led Ptolemy I to write his book; but that book seems for long to have made little difference. Hate was succeeded by neglect; in the second century B.C. Alexander can hardly be traced in literature; Greeks now had Rome to think about. He first comes into view again in the age of Cicero and Caesar, largely as a legendary figure of extravagant ideas. This was the state of things, the background, which lay behind Diodorus, the earliest in time of our extant secondary historians; and Diodorus shows up much better than I expected when I began this investigation. There is plenty of rubbish in book XVII, but it is easy to detect and discard; and it speaks volumes for him that, in the circumstances, he should have turned to Aristobulus and the 'mercenaries' source', should have dragged the latter document (and, for all we know, Aristobulus' book also) out of obscurity, and should have done something, in however limited a degree, to start that rehabilitation of the real Alexander which was to culminate in Plutarch's youthful *De Alexandri fortuna* part I and in Arrian.

My other surprise, though I had long been suspicious, was to find what a large part in our tradition was played by Aristobulus; I trust that I have done something towards restoring him to his rightful position. How a man who knew so much of what needed knowing about Alexander should ever have been supposed to have been a late 'sceptical rationaliser' passes my comprehension; it seems to show that, if you once start on the wrong path, you must of necessity go on floundering deeper and deeper in the morass to which it leads. His three real mistakes, of which so much has been made, are in one case a blunder in an itinerary in which he had not shared, while the other two cases relate to military matters of minor importance in which he took no interest and on which he had not the guidance of Ptolemy and the official documents. For there is not the least doubt that the real order in time is not, as so often asserted, Cleitarchus—Ptolemy—Aristobulus, but Aristobulus—Ptolemy—Cleitarchus; it has in fact been found possible to define the two periods within which Aristobulus and Ptolemy must respectively have written.

As to Cleitarchus, with whom I began, I hope he is now reduced to his proper place and dimensions as a source. He is supposed to have been widely read. Certainly he was read under the early Roman Empire, say from Cicero onwards; his highly coloured work was doubtless fitted to attract the uncritical, while his unfavourable view of Alexander suited that part of society whose ideas on the subject can be read in Lucan and Seneca. But in the Hellenistic period there is little or no trace of any one reading Cleitarchus. He used and garbled Aristobulus, perhaps more than we know; some stories can be traced to one or other of the poetasters who were with Alexander; he must have relied largely on popular stories and beliefs and on a vivid imagination. I trust that less may be heard of him in future; but I fear that for many years yet he will haunt the courts of history, an unhappy gibbering shade, decked in the faded tinsel of the role once thrust upon him.

It follows that there never was any such thing as an Alexander-vulgate or 'Cleitarchean vulgate', exhibited by Diodorus, Curtius, and Justin. How two such totally different historians as Diodorus and ·Curtius, with such different points of view and such different main portraits of Alexander, ever got bracketed together is very hard to understand; Curtius, at least, is one of the most individualistic of writers. What we do get is not a 'vulgate tradition' but a number of stories and points of view, and to some extent names, which represent floating popular beliefs, the usual kind of uncritical stuff which we know so well to-day. Sometimes the origin of some story can be traced: there *was* a Saca girl (though Alexander never saw her), but she was not the Queen of the Amazons; Alexander *did* honour Achilles, but not as Choerilus and Hegesias represent. Sometimes the stories are just invented, whether by Cleitarchus or some other. There *was* an antithesis to the 'good' tradition (which means the tradition of Ptolemy and Aristobulus, of Arrian and Plutarch in his youth), but it was not the 'vulgate'; it was the feeling in Greece, fed and made vocal by two great philosophic schools, the Stoics and the Peripatetics. The Peripatetic tradition crystallised in Curtius. The Stoic, so far as is known, never crystallised in any historian, though Justin may perhaps claim kinship; we know the outline, and possess much abuse of Alexander; that is about all.

The practical problem for the conscientious modern historian has always been, how far can he use the 'vulgate' to supplement Arrian; of those who have merely used it for effect I need not speak. I trust that the foregoing analyses may have made it easier to see what of value, which means of truth, can be found in Diodorus and Curtius. But one thing, to myself, is certain: the more other writers are studied, the greater grows the sense of our enormous debt to Arrian. Arrian was a Stoic; but he was experienced in war and government, and there is no trace in his book of the tenets of the school or of their blind hatred of Alexander; he has written, not as a Stoic, but as a man, which is no less to his credit than is the clear-sightedness which made him select Ptolemy and Aristobulus as his guides. He had sat at the feet of Epictetus; it would seem that that great man taught his pupils something more than philosophy.

ALEXANDER THE GREAT

SOURCES & STUDIES

*

PART TWO: *APPENDICES*

*

Appendices 1–6: MILITARY

1. ALEXANDER'S MACEDONIAN TROOPS

(All citations in this Appendix are from Arrian's *Anabasis*
unless otherwise stated)

THE difficulties of this subject are notorious; no satisfactory account exists in spite of the labour expended on it, and no account will get rid of *every* difficulty, though they can be reduced to very small dimensions if a little trouble be taken to understand Arrian's terminology. The most recent full account, Berve's, is useful as a collection of material and earlier theories, though not always complete; unfortunately his deductions from his material are often sadly to seek. Nothing can be made out of our figures for Alexander's losses, of which there will be something to say later (p. 137), and only occasional details out of the figures for reinforcements (pp. 143, 159 n. 1, 168); Arrian rarely gives reinforcements, though all must have been entered in the *Journal*.

I. Terminology and Development

One's restoration must be based on Arrian, and on Arrian alone; it is as a rule useless trying to insert material of unknown value from Diodorus and Curtius. So long as these two writers are using the 'mercenaries' source', i.e. down to Darius' death, they give military information which is of real value but which is only indirectly concerned with Alexander's formations; for Bactria and India their value in this respect is small. Practically all of Arrian on this subject is Ptolemy. Ptolemy knew everything about it, but he knew it too well; it had been part of his daily life, and evidently he mentioned various things without giving such description or explanation of them as would be needed by a writer nearly 500 years later. Arrian in turn was a successful general and well informed on military matters, but they were those of his own time; and when writing of Alexander's army he found himself dealing with practices, formations, terminology of a day long dead, which he did not always understand. Mistakes therefore there must be; the wonder is that they are so few. But one has to take into account Arrian's habit of not confining one word to one thing, or one thing to one word.[1] He shared to the full the Greek dislike of technical terms, in our sense, and would write anything to avoid a jingle of sound, which was one of the basic reasons of that dislike. The worst jingle was to use the same word twice running, which he avoided like most Silver Greek writers—doubtless this was taught in the schools of rhetoric; every modern writer does it instinctively. Two instances may suffice. In III, 1, 3 Alexander sends some ships up the Nile from Pelusium to Memphis, with orders ἀναπλεῖν κατὰ τὸν ποταμόν, literally 'to sail up-stream down the river', simply because Arrian could not bear to write ἀναπλεῖν ἀνὰ τὸν ποταμόν; κατά no doubt is used in the sense of 'along',[2] but even so it is bad enough, looking at the regular use of κατά for 'down toward the sea-coast'. Even worse is VI, 11, 8, ξυναναβῆναι κατὰ τὴν κλίμακα 'to go up down the ladder', where κατά cannot mean 'along'. Of the principal military terms he uses, τάξις, which only means 'formation', is maid of all work; its most consistent meaning is a battalion of the phalanx, but it is also applied to archers (V, 23, 7), Balacrus' javelin-men (IV, 24, 10, p. 144), horse-javelin men (III, 24, 2), squadrons, ἴλαι, of the cavalry (I, 15, 4), and the later hipparchies (VII, 8, 2), and has other uses also. πεζέταιροι always means the phalanx, but πεζοί, 'foot-soldiers', though it usually means the phalanx, can mean all or any of the infantry. φάλαγξ can mean what we call the phalanx; but it can also mean a single battalion of the phalanx, and even the hypaspists (V, 23, 1 compared with 22, 6), and it is too common in the sense of 'battle-line' to need references.[3] The worst confusion of all is the word ἱππαρχία; it properly means one of the later hipparchies, but its use for a squadron (ἴλη) of the Companion cavalry is too common to be a mere blunder;[4] it must have been

---

1 See for example his use of ὕπαρχος, App. 3, p. 173 n. 1.
2 Cf. IV, 29, 4, where κατὰ τὸ ὄρος means, not 'downhill', but 'along the ridge'. We talk of going *up* from London to Scotland by the *down* train; are we any better than Arrian?—See Addenda.
3 Even cavalry in line could be called ἐπὶ φάλαγγος, V, 16, 4, as opposed to κατὰ κέρας, in column.
4 I, 24, 3. III, 29, 7. IV, 4, 6, 7; 24, 1. VII, 11, 6. The same use in Diodorus XVII, 57, 1, shows that it is not merely a blunder of Arrian's.

a popular variant for ἴλη, just as many people in England used once to call an infantry battalion a 'regiment'. The word will be examined later, as also ἑταῖροι (two senses), σωματοφύλακες (two senses), and ὑπασπισταί. Finally, it is worth remarking that Arrian wrote in the second century A.D., and that his use of ordinary words is not invariably that of a Xenophon or a Demosthenes.

This seems the place to say something about Ptolemy's figures for losses, which Arrian reproduces. Both Alexander's and the Persian losses are merely propaganda figures, of a type to which we are well accustomed to-day; when we read, for example, that at Gaugamela, a hard-fought battle, Alexander lost 100 men and Darius 300,000, it can only raise a smile. Ptolemy used his figures for the honour and glory of Alexander (and of himself as one of his principal lieutenants); that is all. Curiously enough, one exact proof remains. In the desperate fighting at the capture of Sangala, Alexander's dead are given as under 100, but the wounded, which means only the seriously wounded (light wounds were not counted), are given as over 1,200 (V, 24, 5), and Arrian, an experienced soldier, noticed at once that the proportion was impossible. This statement about the wounded is unique; how the truth for once slipped out I do not know. Ptolemy's figures for Alexander's *forces* are usually accurate enough, though I have given elsewhere (App. 6) a proven case where he greatly minimised the number of Alexander's troops in action to enhance the credit of the victory; it is safe to say generally that his figures for Alexander's army are never likely to be too *high*, and that, when he gives a round figure, he rounds it down rather than up.

I had now better sketch briefly the historical growth of Alexander's army, which will help with the terminology. The old Macedonian monarchy had retained some of the characteristics of the heroic monarchy, known from Homer and the Teutonic sagas:[1] the god-descended king, the idea of the Kin (which was not yet dead in Alexander's day),[2] and the retinue of nobles who rode with the king in battle and who formed his *comitatus*, his Companions (ἑταῖροι).[3] Part of their business was to guard the king's person in battle; if he wanted a general or governor, it was to them he turned. Macedonia, however, had never been purely an heroic monarchy; the Macedonian

1 H. M. Chadwick, *The Heroic Age.*
2 Arr. VII, 11, 6 *sq.*, after the mutiny at Opis.
3 Anaximenes fr. 4 (7), Jacoby II, no. 72, wrongly attributed the formation of this *comitatus* to Alexander II. It was coeval with the monarchy itself, and of its essence.

farmers and peasants were free men, who had certain rights of their own over against, and almost certainly older than, the monarchy,[1] rights which resided in the general body of farmers in arms, the national infantry levy. They too had to be considered; and some king formed from them a standing foot-guard, probably small, whose duty was to guard his person, not only in battle but at all times; they were called σωματοφύλακες, Bodyguards. We still find traces of the original idea in Alexander's day; for though any sort of a bodyguard was now normally called an *agēma*, Arrian (VI, 27, 2) still calls the bodyguard of Philip the satrap in India σωματοφύλακες (which must mean that Ptolemy did), and several times he uses that word for what had now become Alexander's foot-guard, the *agēma* of the hypaspists;[2] and that *agēma* still had the duty of safeguarding his person in peace time, which they fulfilled at Opis when most of the army mutinied.

The development from the original Companions took two lines. The original Companions were nobles, and also land-owners, for in a land of somewhat primitive economy like Macedonia a noble could be nothing else; one might, by analogy, call them the king's 'peers'. Under Alexander they formed a pool on which he drew for satraps, generals, and men to command on some special occasion or to fill some new office; from their ranks came the future kings. He is only once recorded (1, 6, 5) to have called on them (or those who were with him) to fight as a body, and that was before he crossed to Asia and in very special circumstances. It does not appear in what form they accompanied Alexander across Asia, but most certainly it was not as cavalry troopers; if only Ptolemy had recorded what he was doing himself during the earlier years of the invasion we should be a good deal wiser than we are. The two things certain are that during those years none of the great names appear as officers in the cavalry, and that the pool, the Companions, *was* there whenever Alexander wanted to draw on it,

---

1 Kaerst maintained that these rights were granted by the king, and opinion on the subject has been divided. There can really be little doubt, however, that the kingship was created by, or evolved from, the people, and on their own terms; no king would have given the people in arms the right to cut out his eldest son from the succession or to judge in cases of treason (which usually meant attempts on his own life), nor would he have arranged that on his own demise the crown should be in the hands of the people in arms till they had elected or confirmed a new king, an arrangement which meant that no treaty he made, however expressed, could be valid for longer than his own life; there are several instances.

2 IV, 3, 2; 30, 3. In III, 17, 2 they are called τοὺς σωματοφύλακας τοὺς βασιλικούς, corresponding to V, 13, 4, τὸ ἄγημα τὸ βασιλικόν.

which he did perpetually. But at some period unknown, prior to Alexander, the original Companions had been relieved as a whole from the duty of guarding the king's life in battle, and that duty had been transferred to a special portion of them, a body of horse which can only have been formed from the lesser nobility, the smaller land-owners, freeing the greater men; it was called the Royal squadron of the Companions, ἴλη βασιλική, with or without the addition of τῶν ἑταίρων.[1] As Alexander himself usually fought on horseback, not on foot, it was this squadron and not the foot-guard which did in fact look after him in battle, for example at the Granicus, where its commander saved his life; and the term ἴλη βασιλική became so well established in the meaning of 'Guard' that both Arrian and Plutarch use it for the Persian cavalry of the Guard.[2] This squadron grew (see IV) till under Alexander it had become eight squadrons, the famous Companion cavalry; all the squadrons were officially called Royal,[3] the whole body usually being under Alexander's personal leadership in battle, but the original Royal squadron remained distinguished from the other seven as Alexander's bodyguard, the *agēma* (Guard) of the Companions.[4] The word ἑταῖροι, Companions, in Arrian thus means two things indiscriminately, which can only be distinguished by the context: the Companions of the king, properly speaking, and the Companion cavalry.

The development of the σωματοφύλακες is more difficult. The name took two courses, as the name ἑταῖροι had done; but of one course we only see the result, not the development. The other can be traced. The

1 I, 18, 3; II, 5, 9; III, 1, 4; 11, 8. In I, 18, 3 and III, 1, 4 it is called the Royal ἴλη of the Companions.

2 III, 11, 6; Plut. *Alex.* XXXIII.

3 III, 11, 8, τελευταία δὲ τῶν βασιλικῶν ἰλῶν. This is the official account of the army as drawn up at Gaugamela, and the text cannot be altered arbitrarily to suit a preconceived theory, as was done by Hackman, whom Berve follows, I, p. 107 n. 1. It will be seen presently that βασιλικῶν is not only correct but necessary.

4 The name ἴλη βασιλική drops out after Bactra, and thenceforth Arrian only uses the terms *agēma* or *agéma* of the Companions. But this is not a new name, as Berve supposed, I, p. 109 n. 2. Alexander at Thebes, I, 8, 3, had τὰ ἀγήματα, which can only be the *agēma* of the Companion cavalry, i.e. the ἴλη βασιλική, and the *agēma* of the hypaspists, the cavalry and infantry guards, no other *agēma* being ever heard of (Berve's suggestion of unknown ἀγήματα, I, p. 124 n. 2, is out of the question). Cf. Curt. IV, 13, 26, at Gaugamela, 'equites, quos *agēma* appellabant. His praeerat Cleitus' (i.e. the Black). Cleitus' command identifies this *agēma* with the ἴλη βασιλική, and Curtius here may well be Ptolemy.

original foot-guard of the king must at first have been part of the territorial army formed from the Macedonian farmers; but by Alexander's time the connection between the two formations had come to an end. The foot-guard had grown, and was no longer part of the Macedonian levy; how it was recruited is unknown, but, though obviously recruited, or largely recruited, from the same class, the Macedonian farmers, it was recruited. It had changed its name to *agēma* (Guard), though the old name, σωματοφύλακες, was still occasionally used, as has been seen (p. 138 n. 2); it was now the *agēma* of the hypaspists (*post*), the latter word probably having something to do with its armament, though what it may have been is unknown. This *agēma*, like the original σωματοφύλακες from which it was derived, was the king's own force, as the name σωματοφύλακες shows; it is sometimes called the Royal *agēma* (v, 13, 4) or the Royal σωματοφύλακες (III, 17, 2). Like the Royal cavalry Guard, the Royal foot-guard continued to grow till it had become three battalions of hypaspists, though the original battalion, the *agēma*, continued to be Alexander's personal Guard. The same thing then happened as had happened when the Royal squadron grew into the Companion cavalry; as all the squadrons of the Companion cavalry could be called Royal, though the original squadron, Alexander's cavalry Guard, remained the Royal squadron *par excellence*, so all the battalions of the hypaspists became known as the Royal hypaspists; possibly the name Royal may have remained attached *par excellence* to the original battalion, the *agēma*, but there is no information on this point. In any case, the whole three battalions are called indifferently hypaspists and Royal hypaspists, and the battalion which was the *agēma* is mentioned both as part of, and as apparently separate from, the hypaspists; few phrases in Greek have led to more bad theorising than these unlucky 'Royal hypaspists'.[1]

The Royal Companion cavalry and the Royal hypaspists had thus given the king an army of his own, which is why the hypaspists are once called the hypaspists of the Companions.[2] This army was quite distinct from the native Macedonian army, the levy of the farmers, and was bound to strengthen the hands of the king as against the people. How far the process had gone, and what discontent it might have evoked, when it attracted the notice of some king, probably Philip II,[3]

1 This question is fully considered in part III of this Appendix.
2 I, 14, 2, οἱ ὑπασπισταὶ τῶν ἑταίρων, ὧν ἡγεῖτο Νικάνωρ. Nicanor commanded the hypaspists.
3 Because the first occurrence of the word πεζέταιροι is in Demosthenes II, 23, 2 (the second Olynthiac) and refers to Philip's army.

cannot be said; in any case, when Alexander quelled the mutiny at Opis by saying to the Macedonians 'I make you all my Kinsmen', he was copying what some earlier king, probably his father, had done when he made the national Macedonian levy of infantry his Companions. Thenceforth the national levy, the infantry of the phalanx, bore the name πεʒέταιροι, 'Foot Companions'. It made no real difference; but people will often welcome a name in place of a thing.

The other line of development of the term σωματοφύλακες seems lost. Though Arrian, as has been seen, sometimes uses the word for the *agēma* of the hypaspists, that use is a mere survival; its real meaning, to Arrian (and therefore to Ptolemy), is to designate a few great officers, the so-called Bodyguards, who formed Alexander's personal Staff. How they came to be called Bodyguards cannot even be guessed; we merely have the confusing fact.¹ The largest number known at once, for a moment (VI, 28, 4), is eight.² They were appointed by Alexander, who chose men he thought suitable for the work; they had to be actually with him, and if one was subsequently appointed to a distant post, like Balacrus son of Nicanor to the satrapy of Cilicia, or Menes to take charge of Alexander's sea-communications between Phoenicia and Greece, he ceased to be on the Staff.³ Thus, though a great honour, it was not a mere honour, but imported definite duties; so, while he appointed some men yet unknown, like Lysimachus and Peithon son of Crateuas, he did not appoint some of his ablest generals, like Antigonus and Craterus, because they could not be with him; any one appointed gave up his existing command, like Perdiccas. In India, however, two of the Staff, Hephaestion and Perdiccas, held commands in the cavalry also; it may show, as some other things suggest,⁴ that by that time Alexander was getting somewhat short of really good officers. The one appointment which appears to have been a mere honour was that of Peucestas, who had saved Alexander's life; Alexander

---

1 Twice (I, 24, 1; II, 12, 2) Arrian calls them τῶν σωματοφυλάκων τῶν βασιλικῶν, which in view of III, 17, 2 (see p. 138 n. 2 *ante*) is confusing enough.

2 If the unknown Aristophanes τῶν σωματοφυλάκων (Plut. *Alex.* LI) really existed, he was certainly not on the Staff, and the context shows that he was not a member of the σωματοφύλακες = *agēma*; the only resource would be to read στρωματοφυλάκων, Alexander's 'Gentlemen of the Bedchamber', mentioned again *ib.* LVII. But probably he is imaginary.

3 Balacrus, II, 12, 2. See p. 142 n. 1.

4 E.g. the failure to find a suitable satrap for Bactria, and the rapid promotion of Cleitus the White (p. 147).

did not wish him *not* to receive the honour, but he lost it again at once by being appointed satrap of Persis.[1]

II. The Phalanx

There was no such formation in Alexander's army as 'the phalanx'; both in Greek and English it is only a convenient expression for the sum total of the battalions of the πεζέταιροι, the heavy infantry of the line, each being a territorial battalion of 1,500 men with a separate commander (phalanx-leader); there was no general commander of all the battalions corresponding to Philotas' general command of all the squadrons of the Companion cavalry. Six battalions of the phalanx crossed with Alexander, and six were left with Antipater in Macedonia. There were six battalions, all specifically enumerated, at Gaugamela (III, 11, 9), where Alexander needed every man he had; this is a fixed point. But at his battle with Porus on the Hydaspes, where again he needed every man he had, there were seven, all named (App. 6); this is another fixed point. Battalions can be identified by their commanders' names. At Issus one phalanx-leader, Ptolemaeus, was killed, Polyperchon succeeding him (II, 12, 2), and at Gaugamela the six phalanx-leaders were Perdiccas, Craterus, Coenus, Amyntas, Meleager, and Polyperchon (III, 11, 9 *sq.*); Amyntas being absent recruiting, his brother Simmias deputised for him in the actual battle. Amyntas died in Drangiana (III, 27, 3), and his brother Attalus got his battalion (IV, 16, 1). Meleager, Polyperchon, and Attalus all survived Alexander, and no change in the commands of their battalions, all named in the battle with Porus, comes in question; they are fixed points. But between Alexander's attack on the Persian Gates and his return from India we have the names of six other phalanx-leaders, in alphabetical order Alcetas, Antigenes, Cleitus the White, Gorgias, Peithon, Philotas;[2] while the original leaders of the other three battalions, Perdiccas, Craterus, Coenus, all received promotion at various times, which meant new commanders for their battalions, and a seventh battalion fought on the Hydaspes. How is all this to be fitted together? Many writers have adopted the rough and ready conclusion that in India Alexander must have had far more than six battalions; a common guess has been

---

1 VI, 28, 3, Alexander had already decided to make Peucestas satrap of Persis, but wished him πρὸ τῆς σατραπείας μηδὲ ταύτης τῆς τιμῆς ἀπείρατον εἶναι, where πρό shows that he would lose the title on becoming a satrap.
2 Berve's table, I, 116, omits Antigenes and Peithon, but includes Philippus and Balacrus, IV, 24, 10.

ten, i.e. the three fixed names (Meleager, Polyperchon, Attalus) plus seven new names, Philippus being included; for this there is nothing to be said. Now Berve (1, 116), though he himself believed in either nine or ten battalions in India, pointed out very justly that, after 330 B.C., no reinforcements from Macedonia sufficient to form new battalions are heard of, and that, as opposition to Alexander came mainly from the phalanx, he was unlikely to increase it;[1] so I take it as another fixed point that the number of battalions in India must not be increased beyond the seven of the Porus battle without very clear evidence, as is indeed commonplace scientific procedure. Certain things must be borne in mind in any investigation. (1) The historical order of the mention of the several names must be carefully observed. (2) Simmias at Gaugamela shows that an isolated name may mean a temporary deputy. (3) Nearchus' command of a battalion of the hypaspists between leaving his satrapy and becoming admiral (IV, 30, 5) shows that an isolated name may mean an interim command. (4) A battalion could be called for a time by the name of a commander who had left it on receiving promotion. This is proved by the mention of Coenus' battalion at the battle with Porus (V, 12, 2), though Coenus himself was in command of a hipparchy. One reason for this, apart from the old commander's repute, would have been that the battalion still retained his σημεῖον, the badge or mascot which he had invented for it (VII, 14, 10). Alexander after Hephaestion's death (*ib.*) decreed that his command should not be filled up, but should bear his name and his badge for ever; this implies that other commands sometimes bore the old name for a time. Had this fact been recognised, we might have been spared some strange theorising.

I now take the separate battalions, omitting the three that are fixed.

Perdiccas' battalion. This is not mentioned again after Gaugamela, while Perdiccas had been promoted to the Staff before Sogdiana was reached (IV, 21, 4), doubtless after the battle; consequently this battalion must appear under another name, and when at the Persian Gates Philotas appears in command of a battalion it can only be that of

---

1 Berve (1, 116) tried to solve his dilemma by saying that the phalanx must have been diluted with native infantry or Greek mercenaries. There is no evidence for this anywhere; also Persia had no native infantry worth mentioning, and Alexander had been leaving Greek mercenaries in every province and new foundation and can have had but few in India; however, those he did have, horse and foot, are mentioned separately both in the battle with Porus (V, 12, 1) and again among the Oreitae (VI, 22, 3), so they were not incorporated in the phalanx or in anything else.

Perdiccas.¹ It cannot be a new battalion, as Berve (1, 116) supposed; for the only place between Gaugamela and the Persian Gates where Alexander stayed long enough to do any reorganisation, and the only place where he received any reinforcements from Macedonia, was Susa, and these reinforcements are specifically stated to have been inserted into the existing (six) battalions κατὰ ἔθνη (111, 16, 11).

When Ptolemy was sent to capture Bessus, he was given, beside other troops, Philotas' battalion of the phalanx (111, 29, 7), the only battalion of the phalanx he had; and this brings us to the difficulty in iv, 24, 10. Alexander is forming two columns beside his own, under Ptolemy and Leonnatus, for the attack on the Aspasii. Ptolemy is given much the same troops as he had for the pursuit of Bessus,² but instead of Philotas' battalion he is said to have had τὴν Φιλίππου καὶ Φιλώτα τάξιν. Grammatically, this could equally well mean one battalion or two; but this peculiar phrase, with the second definite article omitted, is used by Arrian a number of times and invariably means two battalions,³ so it must mean two battalions here: Ptolemy had the τάξεις of Philotas and of Philippus. But Philippus' command cannot have been yet another battalion of the phalanx, as Berve supposed; for seven battalions in the battle with Porus is a fixed point, and Arrian has already mentioned the seventh, Cleitus', iv, 22, 7. The solution is Arrian's already noticed use of τάξις as a general utility word. Leonnatus and Ptolemy are each said to have got two τάξεις, those of Leonnatus being Attalus' battalion of the phalanx and the τάξις of Balacrus, the latter being the well-known formation of javelin-men which Balacrus commanded;⁴ in the same way, Ptolemy, like Leonnatus, only got one battalion of the phalanx (Philotas') and the τάξις of Philippus, whatever it was—light-armed of some sort. It is useless to inquire who this unknown Philippus was; Berve lists sixteen of the name. By the time Massaga was reached,

1 III, 18, 6, Ἀμύνταν δὲ καὶ Φιλώταν καὶ Κοῖνον. Parmenion's son Philotas has been suggested; but the great general of the Companions could not have been thus casually mentioned between two phalanx-leaders as though of equal rank. In fact, Philotas' τάξις is specifically mentioned soon after, before Alexander reached Bactra, III, 29, 7.
2 Compare the details in III, 29, 7 and IV, 24, 10.
3 III, 24, 1, τὴν Κοίνου καὶ Ἀμύντου τάξιν; 25, 6, τὴν Ἀμύντου τε καὶ Κοίνου τάξιν; IV, 22, 1, τὴν Πολυσπέρχοντος καὶ Ἀττάλου (τάξιν); 24, 1, τὴν Κοίνου τε καὶ Ἀττάλου τάξιν; 25, 6, τὴν Κοίνου καὶ Πολυσπέρχοντος τάξιν; V, 12, 2, τὴν Κλείτου τε καὶ Κοίνου τάξιν; VI, 17, 3, τὴν Μελεάγρου καὶ Ἀντιγένους (τάξιν). So v, 12, 2, τὴν Περδίκκου τε καὶ Δημητρίου (ἱππαρχίαν).
4 III, 12, 3; 13, 5 (Gaugamela); IV, 4, 6 (Jaxartes). Berve made of Balacrus another phalanx-leader.

Perdiccas' brother Alcetas is found in command of this battalion[1] instead of Philotas, who is not heard of again; he may have been dead, or he may have been the Philotas who was sent to Cilicia as satrap; the name is too common to say. On the analogy of Amyntas and his brother Attalus, one would have expected Alcetas to have got his brother's battalion when Perdiccas vacated the command; there may be many reasons unknown to us why he did not,[2] such as absence or inexperience; he might even have still been in Macedonia. He survived Alexander.

Craterus' battalion. There was no change of command here till Bactra. When Alexander invaded Sogdiana the second time, he left Craterus in supreme command in Bactria to safeguard it (IV, 17, 1), and thenceforth Craterus regularly acted as Alexander's second-in-command, often with an independent commission. He cannot have held this post and commanded a battalion of the phalanx at the same time; his battalion must have been given a new commander. Four battalions were left with him in Bactria (IV, 16, 1), those of Polyperchon, Attalus, Meleager (the three that are fixed) and Gorgias, a new name; Gorgias must be the new commander of Craterus' battalion, which would certainly be one of those left with him, and might for a time be called by his name. For when Alexander returned, he sent Craterus to reduce Catanes and Austanes and the hill country; he had still four battalions with him, which must have been the same four, but which are called those of Polyperchon, Attalus, Alcetas and 'his own' (IV, 22, 1). 'His own' is obviously Gorgias', but the third, as we know, was Meleager's, not Alcetas'; and as Alcetas, we have seen, did not get a battalion till Gandhāra, and then must have got his brother's, not Craterus', there can be no doubt that 'Alcetas' here is a mistake for 'Meleager'. This is the sole mistake we have found, or shall find, in Arrian on the phalanx; and it may be only a mistake in transmission.[3]

Coenus' battalion. Coenus was still commanding his battalion in Gandhāra,[4] and was not promoted till at Taxila Alexander reorganised

---

1 IV, 27, 1; mentioned again IV, 27, 5; V, 11, 3. On IV, 22, 1 see *post.*
2 There is a parallel in the case of Amyntas' battalion; one would have expected it to have been given to his brother Simmias, who had commanded it at Gaugamela; the reason why it was given to his brother Attalus instead is unknown.
3 More probably it is connected somehow with the first of the two forged letters in Plut. *Alex.* LV; see App. 16, p. 301 n. 1. Of course, the substitution of one name for another is common in many writers; see App. 17, p. 315 n. 2; § H, p. 125 n. 2.
4 IV, 24, 1; 25, 6; 28, 8.

his cavalry into hipparchies (see IV), when Coenus received the command of the hipparchy which he commanded in the battle with Porus, and his battalion received a new leader. There are still three names of phalanx-leaders to be accounted for—Cleitus the White, Antigenes, and Peithon. Coenus' successor was certainly not Cleitus; for in Gandhāra Alexander had Coenus' battalion with him (IV, 24, 1), while Cleitus' battalion was sent with Hephaestion and Perdiccas (IV, 22, 7); Cleitus, as will be seen, commanded the new (seventh) battalion. Peithon is not mentioned till very much later, and there is no doubt that the new commander of Coenus' battalion was Antigenes. The seven battalions in the battle with Porus (see App. 6) are given by Arrian as those of Alcetas and Polyperchon (V, 11, 3), Meleager, Attalus, and Gorgias (12, 1), and Cleitus and Coenus (12, 2); but as Coenus was actually commanding his hipparchy, the battalion called Coenus' was in fact commanded by his son Antigenes, though the old name was used. We know that Antigenes did command a battalion of the phalanx (VI, 17, 3) and commanded it in the battle; and there is no alternative to it having been Coenus' battalion.[1] What Arrian says about the battle (V, 16, 3) is that the infantry line, τῶν πεζῶν τὴν φάλαγγα, was commanded by Seleucus, Antigenes, and Tauron; and as it is certain that Seleucus commanded the hypaspists (see III) and Tauron the archers (V, 14, 1)—possibly on this occasion he commanded all the light-armed—it is equally certain that Antigenes' command lay in the phalanx. As, however, there were five battalions of the phalanx in line against the elephants (see App. 6), what does Arrian exactly mean? He cannot mean that Antigenes' battalion had the ἡγεμονία, the right to lead, on that day (see App. 6, p. 192), for that (so far as is known) would not have given Antigenes the general command; he must mean that Alexander, unable (because of the elephants) to give orders to the infantry himself, had put Antigenes in temporary command of all five battalions. Doubtless he had already seen in Coenus' son something of his father's ability and steadfastness, the qualities for which later he was praised;[2] but as, later in life, Antigenes thwarted Ptolemy badly at Kyinda,[3] Ptolemy would say no more about him than he could possibly help, exactly as he said little about any other of his subsequent enemies, e.g. Antigonus. Coenus' battalion is mentioned twice again after the

---

1 I had written this before I discovered that Antigenes must have been Coenus' son (App. 17, p. 314), which makes it certain; but I have left the original deduction of Antigenes' command unaltered.

2 Diod. XVIII, 62, 6, of Antigenes, συνέσει καὶ πίστεως βεβαιότητι διαφέρων; cf. Arr. VI, 2, 1, of Coenus, ἐν τοῖς πιστοτάτοις.

3 Diod. XVIII, 62, 1–63, 6.

battle with Porus; as 'Coenus' battalion' it was left at the Acesines with Coenus[1] (v, 21, 1), already perhaps dying, and as 'Antigenes' battalion' (vi, 17, 3) it is named on its homeward march with Craterus.

Cleitus' battalion. This, the seventh battalion, appears for the first time soon after Alexander crossed the Hindu Kush (iv, 22, 7) and therefore dates from Bactra. As Alexander took it with him when crossing the Hydaspes together with that formerly of Coenus, the crack battalion of the phalanx,[2] it was no formation of young recruits; it might have been composed of details from the other battalions, if they were sufficiently over strength, which seems most unlikely, but much more probably it was a seasoned battalion sent out as a unit by Antipater,[3] who could spare troops after his crushing defeat of Sparta. On Coenus' death, which happened before Alexander started down the Indus, Cleitus was promoted to the command of his hipparchy (see iv), and Peithon, the last name on our list, took over the command of Cleitus' battalion of the phalanx, which appears as Peithon's in the Malli campaign (vi, 6, 1). This Peithon was not the son of Agenor, the future satrap of Sind, who is first mentioned later (vi, 15, 4; 17, 1), in each case with his title of satrap, clearly to distinguish him from the Peithon of the Malli campaign. At the same time, the Peithon of the Malli campaign was a sufficiently important person to be put in command of two hipparchies as well as his own battalion (vi, 7, 2), an impossibility for a mere phalanx-leader, who ranked below a hipparch; he was therefore no unknown man, but the Bodyguard, the son of Crateuas, holding (like Nearchus) the interim command of a vacant battalion. I have already suggested that Alexander may have been running short of good officers in India.

Everything then in Arrian, i.e. Ptolemy, works out quite well for six battalions of the phalanx up to, and seven after, Bactra, allowing for

---

1 Arrian does in one place, vii, 8, 2, use τάξις to mean hipparchy; but the instructions given to Coenus in v, 21, 1 forbid any supposition that his τάξις here means his hipparchy.

2 It was picked for the attacks at Tyre and Aornos.

3 This might explain Cleitus' rapid promotion over the heads of veterans like Meleager and Polyperchon; though this, as I have suggested, might be due to a dearth of good officers. But it is certain that Alexander promoted men for ability, not seniority. This battalion, and perhaps reinforcements for the other six, must be the 'army from Macedonia' of iv, 18, 3, which Sopolis, Epocillus, and Menidas were sent to bring to Alexander when he was at Nautaka. They were not of course sent ἐς Μακεδονίαν, as the text says—that has merely been put in from ἐκ Μακεδονίας; the dates show that they met it on the way, perhaps at no great distance.

the one certain mistake in Arrian's text which I have noted (p. 145); and most certainly it will not work out at all for anything else. But this study may serve to exhibit the endless difficulties caused to the historian by there being so few proper names in use in Macedonia.

III. THE HYPASPISTS

These were the infantry counterpart of the Companion cavalry; the full name was 'the hypaspists of the Companions' (I, 14, 2). They numbered 3,000 men (*post*), in three battalions of 1,000 each, called chiliarchies.[1] The development of the corps has been given; one of the battalions was Alexander's foot-guard, *agēma*;[2] it is sometimes mentioned by Arrian as though it was separate from the other hypaspists, but the official list shows that it was part of the corps.[3] All the three principal divisions of the Macedonian army had thus come to bear the name Companions (of the king). But the Companion cavalry and the hypaspists were the king's own troops, formed by himself, as has been seen, while the phalanx, though called 'foot-companions', was not the king's own troops, but was, or represented, the territorial levy of the Macedonian people, and probably ante-dated the monarchy (p. 138); the difference between the hypaspists and the phalanx comes out clearly on more than one occasion in India. Consequently, both the Companion cavalry and the hypaspists bore the appellation 'Royal'.

Had writers on the subject considered the historical development of Alexander's army, we might have been spared some unfortunate theories about the Royal hypaspists. For these it will suffice to refer to Berve's long examination of the subject (I, 123 *sqq.*); a favourite one has been that they were the Royal pages, the lads training to be officers. Berve took the trouble to refute this absurdity; it might suffice to say that Alexander did not send young boys to face the dreaded elephants

1 Chiliarchies: IV, 30, 6; V, 23, 7; probably I, 22, 7.
2 Usually called *agēma*; but called the foot-guard, τὸ πεζικὸν ἄγημα, V, 2, 5, and the *agēma* of the hypaspists, III, 11, 9. At Tyre and Opis (*post*) Arrian calls them merely 'the hypaspists'.
3 Nicanor held the same command, the hypaspists, at Granicus, Issus, and Gaugamela. In the official list at Gaugamela, from the *Journal* through Ptolemy, his command is called (III, 11, 9) τὸ ἄγημα τῶν ὑπασπιστῶν καὶ ἐπὶ τούτῳ οἱ ἄλλοι ὑπασπισταί, which is conclusive. At Issus (II, 8, 3) it is called briefly τὸ ἄγημα καὶ τοὺς ὑπασπιστάς, and at the Granicus (I, 14, 2) οἱ ὑπασπισταὶ τῶν ἑταίρων. These passages show that when Arrian talks of the '*agēma* and the hypaspists', as he sometimes does, it means 'the *agēma* and the other hypaspists', οἱ ἄλλοι.

on the Hydaspes. But though Berve cleared away some rubbish, he himself took the untenable view that the hypaspists and the Royal hypaspists (whom he rightly derived from the original σωματοφύλακες) were two different bodies of troops, the Royal hypaspists being the same as the *agēma*; and as he made the Argyraspids, whom I shall come to, a different body again, he managed to produce three formations out of one. There is no evidence that the *agēma* alone was ever called the Royal hypaspists; but so much has been written about this corps that I shall have to go through all the mentions of the Royal hypaspists and give the formal proof that they are merely the hypaspists, just as the Royal σωματοφύλακες (III, 17, 2) are the σωματοφύλακες and the Royal ἵλαι of the Companion cavalry are the ἵλαι (see IV).

I, 8, 3, at Thebes. Alexander sends the archers and Agrianians to help Perdiccas, but holds back τὰ ἀγήματα καὶ τοὺς ὑπασπιστάς, that is, the two ἀγήματα (the cavalry Guard, ἴλη βασιλική, and the foot-guard, one battalion of the hypaspists; there was never any other ἄγημα) and the rest of the hypaspists. The archers are put to flight, and the survivors (I, 8, 4) fled for refuge, κατέφυγον, to 'the *agēma* of the Macedonians and the Royal hypaspists'; that is, they returned whence they came. That the hypaspists of the first sentence and the Royal hypaspists of the second sentence are the same people is certain; to set up any theory to the contrary is about as hopeful as would be an attempt to prove that the Camerons and the Queen's Own Cameron Highlanders are different regiments.

IV, 24, 1, in Gandhāra. Alexander has with him a considerable number of specified formations, including 'the hypaspists'. In 24, 10 he divides these into three columns, to be commanded by Leonnatus, Ptolemy, and himself; the formations mentioned in 24, 10 can only be those mentioned in 24, 1, and in 24, 10 Ptolemy, among other troops, is given τῶν ὑπασπιστῶν τῶν βασιλικῶν τὸ τρίτον μέρος, 'the third part of the Royal hypaspists', i.e. one of the three battalions of 'the hypaspists' given in 24, 1.

III, 13, 6, at Gaugamela. Alexander had the hypaspists in line next the Companion cavalry, with some light-armed thrown well forward before the Companions to break up the charge of the chariots; but in advancing he inclined to the right all the time (twice repeated), bringing the chariots opposite to, and the light-armed in front of, the hypaspists. The light-armed broke up the charge of the chariots; only a few reached the hypaspists, who (it is said) opened their ranks to let them pass through. Whether this were so, or whether the chariots broke through, cannot be said; anyhow, a few penetrated, or passed through, the line, and were brought down by 'the grooms' (who would be behind the line somewhere) 'and the Royal hypaspists', which can only mean the troops they had charged, the hypaspists. Of course Arrian has the order wrong; a modern writer would have said 'the Royal hypaspists and the grooms'; but I think many parallels could be found if one sought for them.

v, 13, 4 is the fourth and last mention of the Royal hypaspists. This much discussed passage, which is really a tolerably simple matter, is fully considered in App. 6.

It is certain then that the Royal hypaspists and the hypaspists are the same thing. It is equally certain that the number of the hypaspists was 3,000, that is, three battalions including the *agēma*, and *not* three battalions plus the *agēma*; the evidence—the figures in Diodorus,[1] the arrangement at Issus,[2] the 'third part' put under the temporary command of Ptolemy, as already mentioned, and the number of the Argyraspids—is clear that there can have been no higher number. But there is a passage in Arrian which is badly written and might be a source of confusion, and which may be noticed here, IV, 30, 6. It is before Alexander reached the Indus, that is, at the time when Nearchus was holding an interim command as chiliarch of a battalion of the hypaspists. Alexander sends out Nearchus and Antiochus, chiliarchs of the hypaspists; to Nearchus he gives the Agrianians and light-armed, to Antiochus his own chiliarchy καὶ δύο ἐπὶ ταύτῃ ἄλλας. This, as a matter of Greek, might imply a total of *more* than three chiliarchies. But as Alexander is said to have *given* to the chiliarch Antiochus the leadership (ἄγειν) of his own chiliarchy, but is *not* said to have given to the chiliarch Nearchus the leadership of his own chiliarchy but only that of other troops, it is clear enough what it *means*: Antiochus had all the hypaspists (three battalions) and Nearchus all the light-armed. It is just a piece of bad writing on Arrian's part; instead of saying 'two others', he ought to have said 'the two others'; it is like the case we have already met (p. 148 n. 3) where he has altered the official and correct formula of Gaugamela, 'the *agēma* and the other hypaspists', to 'the *agēma* and the hypaspists'.

There is one other matter to notice before coming to the name

---

1 Diod. XVII, 17, 3 (on which see further under IV). Alexander's 12,000 Macedonian foot in 334 was phalanx 9,000 (six battalions), hypaspists 3,000.

2 II, 8, 3–4, the *agēma* and the rest of the hypaspists (Nicanor's command) occupy the same space as two battalions of the phalanx, i.e. 3,000 men. The detection of this was due to Beloch, *Gr. Gesch.* III², ii, p. 330.

Argyraspids. It has been mentioned (p. 148 n. 2) that Arrian some-times calls the *agēma* of the hypaspists, Alexander's foot-guard, simply 'the hypaspists'. That 'the hypaspists' of VII, 8, 3 who stood by him in the mutiny at Opis were his Guard is obvious; and there is another instance in the siege of Tyre, II, 23, 2. In the final assault, the two ships which carried the bridges carried also, the one Coenus' battalion of the phalanx, the other 'the hypaspists' under Admetus, together with Alexander himself. This cannot mean the whole 3,000 hypaspists, for one ship would not have taken them, and, if it had, Nicanor, and not the battalion-commander Admetus, must have been in command; it can only mean the battalion which was Alexander's Guard, for he was with them himself and could not have given another battalion the honour over their heads. It shows once more, what is anyhow certain, that the *agēma* was part of the hypaspists and not a separate body. In one passage here the *agēma* is called ἑταῖροι, Companions; this is quite correct.[1]

The name Argyraspids, the 3,000 'Silver Shields' who played such a part later in the war between Eumenes and Antigonus, is only Hieronymus' name for Alexander's hypaspists, as has often been recognised; indeed, but for Berve's arguments to the contrary, I need hardly have noticed it. The origin of the name is unknown; it was not in use in Alexander's lifetime, for Arrian still calls them hypaspists in the mutiny at Opis (VII, 8, 3), nor for some time after his death, for Hieronymus still calls them hypaspists when Perdiccas invaded Egypt;[2] Hieronymus does not use the name till Eumenes secured their services at Kyinda; he gives their number as 3,000.[3] I have shown elsewhere (§ G', pp. 116 *sq.*) that Diodorus XVII, 57, 2 furnishes complete proof that the Argyraspids were Alexander's hypaspists,[4] and there is an equally certain identification in Arr. VII, 11, 3. During the mutiny at Opis Alexander began to form a Persian army, using all the Macedonian names for the several formations; Arrian lists Persian πεζέταιροι (the phalanx), Persian Companion cavalry with a βασιλικὸν ἄγημα, and a

---

1 II, 23, 6: after Admetus falls, Alexander σὺν τοῖς ἑταίροις captures the wall. They were 'the hypaspists of the Companions'; see p. 148.
2 Diod. XVIII, 33, 6.
3 Diod. XIX, 28, 1. Fischer's text gives πλείους τρισχιλίων, which Berve and others have followed; but the best MS. for this period of Diodorus, Florentinus, gives οὐ πλείους, which is certainly correct.
4 In Diod. XIX, 41, 1, they claim to have conquered the world with Philip and Alexander. I am not using this, as it belongs to the exaggerated story of their great age, 41, 2, which cannot be from Hieronymus; on this story see § H, p. 124.

Persian infantry ἄγημα, but he does *not* name any Persian hypaspists; he says instead ἀργυρασπίδων τάξις Περσική, that is, the Argyraspids *were* the hypaspists. It does not of course mean that the name was then in use; the passages I have already quoted forbid that. What it means is that, just as the name Argyraspids slipped in once in Diodorus XVII through his familiarity with the word in Hieronymus (that is explained in § G′), so it has slipped in here in Arrian through *his* familiarity with the word in Hieronymus.[1] This is certain, because Arrian has done precisely the same thing in another passage where no doubt can even be hinted: after all the trouble he took to explain that Alexander's decisive battle was fought at Gaugamela and not at Arbela, and that to call it the battle of Arbela is wrong, *once*, when he was writing in his own person, the too popular name Arbela slipped in.[2]

Berve, however (I, 128), managed to misunderstand the passages in Diodorus and Arrian which mention the Argyraspids and advanced the view that the Argyraspids were a new corps formed by Alexander when he invaded India. There is no evidence for this, nor did he give any; but he quoted three passages which I will look at, though they have no bearing on the matter. Justin XII, 7, 5 says that, when Alexander invaded India, the *whole army*, horses and arms, shone with silver and were called Argyraspids; it may be noted that, when he comes to Eumenes, Justin uses the word correctly (XIV, 2, 6; 3, 7). Curtius VIII, 5, 4 has the same story as Justin, but amplifies it considerably: Alexander had heard that Indian soldiers shone with gold and ivory, so he adorned his own army with gold and silver in rivalry. But Curtius follows this arrant piece of nonsense with his invaluable account of the poetasters who were with Alexander;[3] there is no apparent reason for his bringing them in where he does, and it must have been his gold and silver army which reminded him of them; the whole story therefore was presumably invented by one of these poets as 'poetic colouring', for which such stories as the golden armour of Glaucus in the *Iliad* might provide an excuse. Neither Justin nor Curtius refers to a *corps* called Argyraspids, and Curtius does not even use the word at all. Berve's third passage is from Diodorus XIX, 28, 1 (battle of Paraetacene); he says it shows that Eumenes' Argyraspids cannot be the hypaspists (i.e. Alexander's), as both words occur there. So they do, but the hypaspists are those of Eumenes himself. Eumenes treated his army as that of the deified Alexander, present in the

1 Hieronymus is the main source of his *Successors*, τὰ μετ᾽ ᾽Αλέξανδρον.
2 III, 22, 4, Darius ἐν ᾽Αρβήλοις ἔφυγέ τε ἐν πρώτοις.
3 For these poets see § E′.

Alexander-tent, and copied his formations; he had Companion cavalry, a cavalry *agēma*, phalanx, hypaspists, and a corps of Pages.[1]

Everything about the hypaspists is then perfectly clear, if one attends to the evidence. They were called indifferently the hypaspists or the Royal hypaspists, and at a later date were known as the Argyraspids. Their number under Alexander was 3,000, divided into three battalions (chiliarchies) each of 1,000 men; one of the three battalions was Alexander's foot-guard. Their commander Nicanor died of illness not long after Gaugamela (III, 25, 4), and no other commander is mentioned till Seleucus in the battle with Porus; whether he directly succeeded Nicanor cannot be said.

As regards armament, they were heavy infantry, as heavily armed as the phalanx;[2] the difference between the two bodies was one of history, recruitment, and standing, not of armament. The once common beliefs that they were armed as peltasts,[3] or that their armament was intermediate between that of the phalangite and the peltast, have no evidence to support them and need not be noticed. The 'mercenaries' source' used by Diodorus and Curtius (see § F and § G) treated them as part of the phalanx (§ G', p. 117); that is to say, the men who had to face Alexander's line in the field could see no visible difference; if difference there was, it was in trifles, non-essential matters. They shared all the heavy infantry work; but the most important matter is that when Alexander had to mount some infantry to accompany his cavalry on his great forced march in pursuit of Darius, he took either phalangites or phalangites and hypaspists indiscriminately. When he started from Ecbatana he took both phalanx and hypaspists; many fell out before reaching Rhagae (III, 20, 1). Here (21, 2) he picked out the strongest and most active[4] τῶν πεζῶν, which normally means the phalanx but could include both, to accompany the cavalry. At the last village,

---

1 Diod. XIX, 27, 28.
2 On the much discussed question of the length of the spears of Alexander's phalanx, see App. 2; there is a simple proof that they were 13–14 ft. long.
3 The fact that Polybius calls the hypaspists of the later Antigonids peltasts, while as regards the Macedonia of their day he uses the term hypaspist for special officers only, has no bearing of any kind on Alexander. I am not discussing here what Polybius' words mean.
4 21, 2, τῶν πεζῶν τοὺς εὐρωστοτάτους καὶ κουφοτάτους. The latter word does not mean lighter-armed (had the hypaspists been lighter-armed he would presumably have taken them); it means the most active, see III, 23, 3, τῆς φάλαγγος τοὺς κουφοτάτους; IV, 6, 3, the same phrase; IV, 28, 8, τῆς ἄλλης φάλαγγος ἐπιλέξας τοὺς κουφοτάτους τε καὶ ἅμα εὐοπλοτάτους, which is conclusive, as is III, 18, 5, τῶν τοξοτῶν τοὺς κουφοτάτους.

where he took a short cut and the infantry could do no more, he dismounted 500 horsemen and put on their horses τοὺς ἡγεμόνας τῶν πεζῶν (file-leaders)[1] and those of the rank and file who were holding out best, armed just as they were;[2] the rest were ordered to discard all impedimenta and follow by road. It is obvious that there was no distinction between fully armed phalangites and hypaspists as regards the weight imposed on the weary horses.

IV. THE COMPANION CAVALRY

It has been mentioned (1, 1, p. 139) that the Royal squadron of the Companions, Alexander's bodyguard, had, by the time he crossed the Dardanelles, grown to eight squadrons by the addition of seven others, the whole body forming the famous Companion cavalry and all the squadrons being officially called Royal (i.e. the King's troops), though the original Royal squadron remained distinguished from the others as the Royal squadron *par excellence*, Alexander's cavalry Guard, also known as the *agēma* of the Companions. Before considering the numbers and development of the Companion cavalry, it has to be asked where the additional seven squadrons came from, assuming that the Royal squadron must still have been drawn from the smaller Macedonian landowners. Five of these seven squadrons are known to have been territorial,[3] so presumably all were; and we have to account for the fact that four of these squadrons were drawn from Chalcidice and the coastal districts, i.e. the lands recently conquered and added to Macedonia by Philip; the fifth bears the name of a district, Λευγαία, which is unknown, and the districts of the other two are not recorded; but there is nothing to show that any came from old Macedonia, and if the majority came from the newly conquered territory it is perhaps fair to assume, as is usually done, that all the seven did.[4] An explanation recently given,[5] which is certainly correct, is that these squadrons

---

1 Not 'commanders', who would have been mounted in any case; see Curt. VII, 1, 34 on the horses of the phalanx-leader Amyntas.

2 21, 7, τῶν ἄλλων ἐπιλεξάμενος τοὺς κρατιστεύοντας...οὕτως ὅπως οἱ πεζοὶ ὡπλισμένοι ἦσαν.

3 A convenient table in Berve I, p. 105.

4 This would seem to be the natural meaning of Arr. III, 16, 11 (see p. 160).

5 Fr. Hampl, *Der König der Makedonen*, 1934, pp. 66–77. His conclusion must be correct, in spite of the grave defects in its exposition. He imagines a Macedonian 'State' apart from Philip, who *was* the Macedonian state; there was no other. His attempt to distinguish between ἑταῖροι and ἑταῖροι τοῦ βασιλέως (or 'Αλεξάνδρου or Φιλίππου) breaks down on

(always called Macedonian) were formed from the Macedonians whom Philip had settled in the conquered districts; and as the one grant of land which we possess from those districts[1] shows that the king had reserved the right of escheat for failure of heirs, it may be presumed that these grants entailed the obligation to serve, that is, that they were *kleroi*. This territorial recruitment would not have precluded some of those who served in the cavalry from being, or having been, landowners in Macedonia also,[2] nor would it have precluded the inclusion of a few Greek oligarchs, friends of Macedonia, from what cities survived; but the force must have been essentially Macedonian settlers, who owed their land in the conquered territories to the king personally, and who were thus 'King's men' in a sense in which the Macedonian peasantry who served in the phalanx never were. There is nothing to be said for the view that there must have been an equal force of cavalry raised from old Macedonia and left with Antipater:[3] when the Lamian war broke out Antipater could only muster 600 horse, and it is not known what they were.

Unlike that of the phalanx and the hypaspists, the strength of the Companion cavalry, when Alexander crossed the Dardanelles, is unknown. It is known, from the three battles, Granicus, Issus, and Gaugamela, that it consisted of eight squadrons, as already mentioned, and that each squadron had a separate commander, the Royal squadron being commanded by Cleitus the Black; the whole body was under the command of Parmenion's son Philotas. Here, for the moment, certainty ends. The total strength of the force, and the strength of a squadron, are unknown and can only be ascertained by analysing backwards and taking into account the various reorganisations of the corps and such isolated figures as we possess. To give that analysis here would mean telling the story twice over, first backwards and then forwards; so

numberless passages in Arrian, besides presupposing that Arrian and others used technical terms in the way we do. And he bases his study on frs. 224 and 225 of Theopompus (Jacoby II, no. 115), some of the most worthless stuff in the Greek language; I need add nothing to the well-merited castigation given it by Polybius (VIII, 9 (11)–11 (13)), who had no axe to grind in the matter and who said what was necessary about writing history from personal prepossessions (VIII, 8 (10), 7 *sq.*). Macedonian history cannot be written from Greek propaganda.

1 Ditt.[3] 332; see M. Rostowzew (Rostovtzeff), *Gesch. d. römischen Kolonates*, 1910, pp. 251 *sqq.*; Tarn, *Antigonos Gonatas*, pp. 190 *sqq.*

2 I imagine that one could use the Norman settlement of conquered England for the understanding of Philip's settlement of these conquered Greek lands. 3 Berve I, p. 105.

I shall merely tell the story, with such digressions and explanations *en route* as are inevitable. Little help is to be got from Alexander's recorded losses, which are usually just propaganda figures, and little from his recorded reinforcements, unless those given by Arrian, which may be from the *Journal* through Ptolemy; taking the recorded reinforcements as a whole, they are certainly incomplete, often vague, and generally of dubious authority; in any case, there is very little which relates to the Companion cavalry.

Certainly Diodorus XVII, 17, 4 gives a list of the cavalry and infantry which crossed the Dardanelles with Alexander, and it has been tremendously discussed; but as it has not been noticed that this list must come from the 'mercenaries' source', on which Diodorus depends for his military material prior to Issus, the discussion has led to little result, for no distinction has been made between the things this source must have known and the things it could not be expected to know. It gives Alexander's cavalry as 1,800 Macedonians under Philotas (i.e. the Companions), 1,800 Thessalians, 600 (Greek) allies, and 900 Thracian *prodromoi* (see p. 157) and Paeonians, while 1,500 horse were left in Macedonia with Antipater. The numbers of the Thessalians and of the Greek allies cannot well be wrong, for these would either be within the personal knowledge of the Greek author of the 'mercenaries' source' or could be easily ascertained; but the same certainty would hardly apply to the Macedonian and the Balkan formations. For example, Alexander is said to have taken with him 12,000 Macedonian infantry and to have left 12,000 with Antipater; Alexander's 12,000— 9,000 phalanx and 3,000 hypaspists—is certainly correct, being borne out by everything that follows, but Antipater's 12,000 is certainly wrong, for he could have had no hypaspists in the nature of the case, and Alexander could not have given him *more* than half the phalanx, at best. Antipater's figure is merely made up to balance Alexander's figure; it is possible therefore that the figure of 1,800 Companion horse is merely made up to balance the 1,800 Thessalians by a writer who knew that the two did balance each other in the battle-line. The normal Thessalian cavalry levy was 2,000, the figure of the Lamian war; and as Alexander received a reinforcement of 200 Thessalian horse at Gordium (I, 29, 4), this means that he, as head of the Thessalian League, had naturally called out the full levy. But 1,800 for the Companions does not divide easily into eight squadrons. It will be shown later that the normal strength of a squadron of the Companions was 200; if so, what crossed may have been 1,600, or 1,700 if the βασιλικὴ ἴλη, Alexander's Guard, numbered 300, as it certainly did at a later time;

even 1,800 might be possible, if the squadrons were over strength; we cannot say which figure is correct. At Gordium Alexander received, besides the 200 Thessalians already mentioned, 300 Macedonian horse (I, 29, 4), which means reinforcements for the Companions, as he had no other Macedonian horse; and as the Thessalian reinforcement meant that their number was being raised (nominally) to 2,000, so the reinforcement for the Companions may mean that *their* numbers were being raised to 2,000 also; Alexander could not have had a smaller body of horse under his own hand than Parmenion.[1] He may have received further reinforcements for the Companions before Gaugamela, but they were a specially recruited corps, and his power of reinforcing them was limited. It is not very important to know what their numbers were when he crossed; what matters is that he knew that cavalry was going to be all-important, and that by Gaugamela he had raised the strength of the Companions to 2,000.[2]

I have said that Alexander had no Macedonian horse with him but the Companions. It is, however, in view of a theory which I shall come to, necessary to notice his corps of lancers, σαρισσοφόροι, who have often been supposed to be Macedonians, though they are never so called;[3] the idea arose solely from their lances being called, in our sources, σάρισσαι, probably on account of their length. They are often referred to as πρόδρομοι, i.e. scouts or advance troops, a term which some-times included the Paeonians also;[4] what matters is that Diodorus calls them Thracians,[5] and Thracian σαρισσοφόροι are heard of elsewhere.[6] They formed part, together with the Paeonians and the other Thracian cavalry, of Alexander's Balkan horse; to get the numbers of the three different formations is impossible, and juggling Diodorus' figures about does not get us anywhere; all that can be said is that while his

1 Parmenion's special relation to the Thessalians is shown by the fact that at Gaugamela one body of them, the Pharsalians, acted as an informal bodyguard for him, III, 11, 10.
2 I attach no importance to the number 2,000 for Alexander's Macedonian horse in Ps.-Call. A', 1, 26, 1, the whole section being very confused. But it is curious.
3 They cannot be the 'Macedonians' of II, 8, 9, τούς τε ἑταίρους καὶ τούς Θεσσαλούς καὶ τούς Μακεδόνας, for, as the Companions were Macedonians, the sentence as it stands is impossible, and Μακεδόνας has replaced some other word; there is a large choice.
4 References in Berve I, 129.
5 Θρᾶκες δὲ πρόδρομοι καὶ Παίονες. Beloch's emendation, III², ii, 325, obscures the sense.
6 For Didymus' mention of a mounted Thracian (Triballian) sarissophoros in Philip's reign see Wilcken, *S.B. Berlin*, XVIII, 1929, p. 298 n. 6.

figures for the Thessalian and Greek allied horse must be correct, those for the Macedonian and Balkan cavalry need not be so, but that the total reached by adding up his different formations, 5,100, cannot be far wrong.[1] The lancers at Gaugamela were a substantial body of horse;[2] later on, four squadrons of them, strength unknown, are mentioned on the Jaxartes (IV, 4, 6). As they are not heard of again, and as all the troops left by Alexander in Bactria were Greek mercenaries, they and the Paeonians must have been sent home from Bactria when Alexander started for India,[3] which shows once again that they cannot have been Macedonians.

My reason for referring to the lancers is Berve's theory that Diodorus' 1,800 Macedonian horse means 1,200 Companions and 600 lancers, based on a supposed proof that a squadron of the Companions numbered 150. This cannot be right, for many reasons: the whole 1,800 are called Philotas' command and he did not command the lancers; the lancers were not Macedonians at all but Balkan troops; we shall come to proof of a squadron-number of 200 for the Companions; and Berve's supposed proof of a squadron-number of 150, viz. that at Issus two named squadrons of the Companions are called 300 men, is a mere misunderstanding of Arrian II, 9, 3 *sq*. I had better give what it says. Alexander's main line, called φάλαγξ, was facing Darius. He weakened its extreme right by sending the Thessalians to Parmenion on the left, and remedied this by taking two squadrons out of the middle (ἐκ μέσου) of the Companions and sending them to the extreme right. To meet the Persians who were outflanking his right by stretching forward along the hill he formed another line which extended back from his right at an angle, ἐς ἐπικαμπήν, composed of light-armed troops and some horse, ἱππέων τινας, so getting his army into the shape of a right angle, thus: ⌐. As all his other cavalry formations have been mentioned, the horse in the line ἐς ἐπικαμπήν could only be mercenaries; in this battle he had all the mercenaries in reserve and none in the main line. The light-armed troops of the line ἐς ἐπικαμπήν drove the Persians on the hill out of action, whereon Alexander saw (ἔγνω) that it would

1 There is a useful table of the totals of various writers in Berve I, 177. Ptolemy's cavalry total (I, 11, 3) was 'over 5,000', and we cannot go behind it; Plutarch's total of 5,000 for Ptolemy (*de Alex. f.* I, 327 E) is only a round figure. The highest figure is Anaximenes' 5,500; the lowest, that of Callisthenes, no authority on military matters, 4,500. Diodorus repeated this figure, though his own detailed figures add up to 5,100.

2 III, 14, 1; cf. Curt. IV, 15, 18, which, except the plundering of the baggage, is also from Ptolemy.

3 The other Balkan horse was left in Media with Parmenion, p. 160 n. 1.

now suffice to leave 300 horse to watch them. These 300 are the ἱππέων τινας of the foregoing account, i.e. mercenaries; the two squadrons of the Companions, already posted at the end of the main line, had nothing to do with the line ἐς ἐπικαμπήν. Berve's squadron number of 150 vanishes if one just reads Arrian.

I can now get on with what matters, viz. Alexander's cavalry numbers at Gaugamela. Ptolemy says that Alexander had 7,000 horse in the battle (III, 12, 5), much the highest number he is ever recorded to have had; probably that is the official figure, but in any case it is not likely to be too high (see p. 137). He had therefore received heavy reinforcements since landing with 'over 5,000' horse, especially as the losses at Issus and the loss by wear and tear had to be made good; but as a rule there is nothing to be made of the recorded reinforcements, except the very few given by Arrian;[1] beside those of the Thessalians and Companions, already noticed, he received 150 Greek allied horse (Eleans) at Gordium (I, 29, 4), and 500 Thracians at Memphis (III, 5, 1). Now if Alexander's cavalry formations were ever going to be up to strength, they would have been so at the crucial battle, Gaugamela; the figure of 7,000 horse shows that, and it is not difficult to see how it was made up. The full Thessalian levy was 2,000, and it is therefore safe to take that number; and as Alexander's personal command could not have been smaller than Parmenion's that means 2,000 Companions also; I shall come to that later. He had two formations of mercenary horse, commanded by Menidas and Andromachus respectively; these were new since he crossed, though as shown above some 300 at least had been at Issus. Menidas' command, when attacked by 1,000 Sacas and the Bactrians who acted with them, probably 2,000 horse altogether (App. 5, p. 184 n. 3), is called 'a few men opposed to men far more numerous';[2] and as Alexander subsequently always used 1,000 as the standard figure of a body of horse, whether recruited or rearranged, it cannot be far wrong to take his mercenary horse as 1,000, divided into two bodies of 500 each. That leaves 2,000 for the Greek allied horse and the Balkan horse. The numbers known for the former are 600+150 less losses, which would leave some 1,300–1,400 for the four bodies of

1 Useful tables of the recorded reinforcements, chiefly infantry, are given by Berve I, pp. 179 *sqq.* Practically all come from Diodorus and Curtius; now and again one can be checked, but some are obviously very wild, and the sources are unknown. There is no way in which they can be used, except as illustrating the obvious fact that Alexander did receive large reinforcements, especially of mercenaries.

2 III, 13, 3, ὀλίγους ὄντας πολλῷ πλείονες.

Balkan horse at Gaugamela;[1] in the battle itself the lancers and Paeonians formed part of the right flanking column under Alexander, the Thracians (and Odrysians) part of the left one under Parmenion. This analysis of Alexander's 7,000 horse at Gaugamela cannot be far wrong; and as regards the number 2,000 for the Companions, which is what matters, we shall find good reason to believe that at one time the Companions must have numbered 2,000, which could only be at Gaugamela. This would mean that the squadrons were much over strength, for the number of squadrons, as will appear, was never increased.

The loss of Companions at Gaugamela was substantial; the Sacas and Bactrians got into their ranks from the flank, though the position was restored (III, 13, 4), and they had a desperate battle later with the Persian Guard; they lost over 500 horses in the battle and pursuit (III, 15, 6). At Susa Alexander received reinforcements for them, number unknown (III, 16, 11), which he divided among the squadrons κατὰ ἔθνη; he also divided each squadron into two *lochoi*, each with a *lochagos*, which must mean that he thought that the enlarged squadrons at Gaugamela had been insufficiently flexible. The normal strength of a cavalry *lochos* can be ascertained. When Alexander reached Carmania after his march through Gedrosia, where large numbers of baggage animals perished, his satraps Stasanor and Phrataphernes sent him a fresh supply of mules (ὑποζύγια) and camels, which he distributed (*a*) to the commanders individually, (*b*) by squadrons, ἴλαι, and ἑκατοστύες, (*c*) by *lochoi*.[2] The *lochoi* of (*c*) are obviously the well-known infantry λόχοι,[3] and the division (*b*) is the distribution to the cavalry, as indeed the word ἴλαι, squadrons, shows. The only cavalry with him were what remained of the Companions, the mercenary horse who had been with him in the land of the Oreitae having been left behind there with Leonnatus (VI, 22, 3); the distribution by squadrons and ἑκατοστύες must therefore correspond to the division of the Companions into squadrons and λόχοι, and the *lochos* was therefore a

---

1 The four are the lancers, Paeonians, Thracians, and Odrysians; these last (III, 12, 4) are not mentioned again either before or after the battle, but could have been included under 'Thracians', and were probably part of the 500 Thracian horse who came to Memphis. If Diodorus' figure of 900 Balkan horse at the crossing be approximately correct, 900 + 500 = 1,400; that is about right. The Thracians, as the name of their commander Sitalces shows (and presumably the Odrysians also), were left in Media with Parmenion, III, 26, 3; VI, 27, 4.

2 VI, 27, 6, τοῖς μὲν ἡγεμόσι κατ' ἄνδρα, τοῖς δὲ κατ' ἴλας καὶ ἑκατοστύας, τοῖς δὲ κατὰ λόχους.

3 References, Berve I, p. 119.

ἑκατοστύς, a company of 100 men; ἑκατοστύς may have been the regular term for the cavalry λόχος.[1] It does not, of course, mean that when the cavalry *lochoi* were first formed at Susa each contained exactly 100 men; the squadrons were possibly still over strength, and if so the *lochoi* were the same; what it does mean is that the basic organisation of the Companions had been the number 200 for a squadron. We shall meet this number again.

Following upon the reorganisation of the Companions at Susa, there was a second reorganisation in Drangiana after their commander Philotas had been executed for treason. Alexander appointed no new commander, but divided them into two hipparchies, commanded respectively by Hephaestion and Cleitus the Black as hipparchs (III, 27, 4); as Cleitus was commander of the Royal squadron, Alexander's Guard, his hipparchy must have included that squadron and three others, Hephaestion getting the other four. There is plenty of evidence, which we shall come to (pp. 165 *sq.*), that a hipparchy meant 1,000 men; the name therefore implies that at some period, which can only be Gaugamela, the Companions had numbered 2,000 or thereabouts, though it cannot be said what their exact strength was in Drangiana at the time; all we know is that, between the commencement of that battle and Alexander quitting Bactria, their strength was considerably reduced. Amid all the mass of troops that came to Alexander in Bactria, no reinforcements for the Companions are mentioned, and it is certain from the subsequent story that those that came out to Susa were the last.

After the murder of Cleitus the hipparch in Bactria Alexander appointed no new commander of his hipparchy, which means that he must have taken command himself; we shall see that he was commanding it in Gandhāra. It was the beginning of the process which in India made the Royal squadron Alexander's personal command. The name ἴλη βασιλική now vanishes from Arrian's text, and from and after Bactra the former Royal squadron, Alexander's cavalry Guard, is always called the *agēma*, fuller forms being the *agēma* of 'the cavalry' or 'of the Companions' or 'of the Companion cavalry'.[2] Before Alexander quitted Bactria, the Companions had come back to the normal figure of 200 men to a squadron. Alexander gave Coenus 400 Companions for the force with which he finally defeated Spitamenes (IV, 17, 3), and

---

1 VII, 24, 4, κατὰ λόχους καὶ ἑκατοστύας, presumably means infantry and cavalry subdivisions.
2 τὸ ἄγημα τῶν ἱππέων, IV, 24, 1; V, 13, 4. τὸ ἀ. τῶν ἑταίρων, V, 12, 1. τὸ ἀ. τῆς ἵππου τῆς ἑταιρικῆς, VI, 21, 3.

gave Craterus 600 Companions for his operations against Catanes and Austanes (IV, 22, 1); there can be no doubt that this means that Coenus was given two, and Craterus all three, of the three squadrons of the Companions at Alexander's disposal other than the *agēma*, without his drawing on Hephaestion's four squadrons.

There is another figure which must relate to the Companions in Bactria. After the Malli campaign Alexander is said to have taken on board, for the voyage down the lower Indus, 1,700 Companion cavalry (VI, 14, 4), which would mean the *agēma* of 300 (I shall come to that figure presently) and 1,400 men in the other seven squadrons, that is, 200 to a squadron. This figure cannot belong where it is placed; for the Companions who ultimately got back from India to Susa, the *agēma* apart, were only about 1,000 men, little more or less (p. 166), and they cannot have lost 400 men between the end of the Malli campaign and Susa; they are not recorded to have had any fighting, and as to Gedrosia, it is clear from Arrian's account of the march that, except for loss of baggage, the army got through pretty well. It was the non-combatants and camp-followers—γύναια, παιδάρια, merchants, and so forth—who lost so heavily; and while masses of baggage-animals perished or were killed for food, hardly any loss of cavalry horses is noted,[1] and the satraps who, at Alexander's order, collected and sent baggage animals to Carmania, as already noticed, to replace the losses, did *not* send any cavalry remounts. There can be little doubt that this figure of 1,400 Companions, 200 to a squadron, was the number in Bactria, where we have already seen two cases of squadrons being 200 strong. But the number 1,700 presupposes that the *agēma* was 300 strong, and a word must now be said about this.

For all we know to the contrary, the Royal squadron, Alexander's Guard, may have been 300 strong from the start. If not, Bactra was the last place where it could have been reorganised and raised to that total; and we have been considering a figure (1,700) which suggests that it *was* 300 strong in Bactria. What is quite certain is that in the latter part of Alexander's life, at the least, the number of his cavalry Guard was 300. The proof is simple, though I do not think it has ever been given. When Eumenes of Cardia was fighting Antigonus, his army, as already noticed, was a copy of Alexander's formations, and he treated it, not as his own, but as the army of the deified Alexander, present with them in spirit in the Alexander-tent. Eumenes had plenty

---

[1] See especially VI, 25, 5. The ἵπποι of 25, 1 and elsewhere are baggage animals; just a few cavalry horses may have been lost, 26, 5, though this is not actually stated.

of cavalry, and in theory could have made his personal cavalry guard, his *agēma*, any size he liked; but in fact, as it was really treated as Alexander's *agēma* and not as his own, it could only be the same size as Alexander's had been, and it was 300.[1] In the same way, Antigonus, who was claiming, before his Friends, to stand in Alexander's place and who already had Companion cavalry, made his *agēma* 300;[2] and the number was presently adopted by others.[3] Eumenes' action is conclusive.

The final, the third, reorganisation of the Companions did not take place at Bactra, or anywhere west of the Indus;[4] the proofs of this are, that in Gandhāra we meet the old division of the Companions into eight squadrons (including the *agēma*) still existing; that Coenus in Gandhāra was still commanding his battalion of the phalanx and had not yet been promoted (p. 145 n. 4); and that the reorganisation included horse from the Paropamisadae, which shows that Alexander had already conquered that province. When after crossing, or rather rounding, the Hindu Kush he divided his army in the Paropamisadae, sending Hephaestion and Perdiccas by the direct route to the Indus, Hephaestion had half the Companions (IV, 22, 7), that is, his own four squadrons; Alexander had with himself all the Companions that

1 Diod. XIX, 28, 3. 2 *Ib.* 29, 5.
3 *Ib.* 28, 3; and see Curtius X, 9, 18; Tarn, *Bactria and India*, p. 200.
4 Berve I; p. 107, put the final reorganisation in 329, between Maracanda and the Oxus, citing Arr. III, 30, 6, which says Ἀλέξανδρος δὲ ἀναπληρώσας τὸ ἱππικὸν ἐκ τῶν αὐτόθεν ἵππων (πολλοὶ γὰρ αὐτῷ ἵπποι ἔν τε τῇ ὑπερβολῇ τοῦ Καυκάσου κ.τ.λ. ἐξέλιπον); he seems to have read ἱππέων for ἵππων, which the context absolutely forbids, and said 'dass das ἱππικόν mit einheimischen Reitern ausgefüllt wurde'; and he believed that Arrian's description of the reorganisation in VII, 6, 3 *sq.* related to something at Susa in 324–3, instead of being (as Arrian shows) part of a catalogue of grievances extending far backwards in time. As, in addition, he did not know that Arrian uses ἱππαρχία in two senses, and did not understand the relations of Coenus and Cleitus the White (explained pp. 146 *sq.*, *ante*), his whole account in I, 107 *sq.*, with its six, seven, or eight hipparchies, is entirely misconceived. Arr. III, 30, 6 *is* interesting as being our only mention of cavalry remounts for the army, though the need must have been perpetual; Alexander can hardly have trusted solely to getting horses as he went along, and must have had some system of reserves. He lost 1,000 horses at Gaugamela alone, III, 15, 6; as they must have been replaced long before he reached Ecbatana, the sale in that town of their horses by the Thessalians before going home (III, 19, 6) would have given him a substantial reserve for the moment; otherwise no information about army reserves of horses remains. But a *general* might have as many as ten horses with him, and apparently a general who had lost his horses was by custom helped out from the stud of another (Curtius VII, 1, 32–34, who calls it a *mos*; he is good on Macedonian customs, § G, pp. 106 *sq.*).

remained (IV, 23, I), that is, the other four squadrons, including the *agēma*;[1] this shows, as I mentioned before, that he had himself taken command of the hipparchy (four squadrons) of Cleitus the Black. As the two divisions of the army did not again unite till the Indus was reached, it is clear that the reorganisation was not made in Gandhāra; and as it was made before the battle with Porus, where it appears in full working order, it is quite certain that it was made at Taxila. As Coenus already had some Iranian horse when he defeated Spitamenes, it is strange that no Iranian horse except the horse-javelin men[2] is mentioned in Arrian's detailed accounts of the campaigns in Gandhāra; some, one supposes, may have been raised by Alexander's satraps and sent direct to meet him at the Indus, but some must have accompanied him, or he would have been badly off for light horse, all his Balkan horse having been left in Media or sent home.

This final reorganisation is fully described by Arrian, VII, 6, 3, not in its place but by reference backward on a later occasion. Alexander separated the *agēma* altogether from the rest of the Companions as his own personal command, and divided the remainder of his cavalry (except the mercenaries and horse-archers) into five hipparchies, each of 1,000 men.[3] The first four hipparchies contained one Macedonian squadron apiece, formed from the Companions (VI, 21, 3); each hipparchy was filled up with Eastern Iranian horse, whose contingents comprised Bactrians, Sogdians, Sacas, Arachosians, Zarangians, Arians, Parthians (i.e. Parthava), and horse from the Paropamisadae.[4] The Iranian cavalry was not included among the Companions, and its losses were reckoned separately, V, 18, 3; once Arrian uses the term 'Companions' instead

1 IV, 24, I, called τὸ ἄγημα καὶ τῶν ἄλλων ἑταίρων ἐς τέσσαρας μάλιστα ἱππαρχίας, a clumsy phrase which might suggest that the *agēma* was not included in the four squadrons. Berve's 'nicht ganz vier Hipparchien', I, 108 n. 5, is a very old mistake. For Arrian's so common use of ἱππαρχία for ἴλη, see p. 136 n. 4.

2 This corps, strength unknown, had been raised in Hyrcania, III, 24, I, and was with Alexander in Swat, IV, 23, I, but is not mentioned again, even in the Hydaspes battle; it must therefore have been taken up into the reorganised hipparchies at Taxila.

3 For the number see pp. 165 *sq.*

4 Combining for the nationalities V, 11, 3; V, 12, 2; VII, 6, 3. The 'Scythians' of V, 12, 2 are Sacas from the country between the mountains north of Samarcand and the Jaxartes, the 'Saca-land beyond Sogd' of the gold plate of Darius I. In VII, 6, 3 some Persians called Euakes are also mentioned; these were not Eastern Iranians, whatever they were, and cannot belong here; their place must be at Susa later, when Alexander began to raise forces from the Western Iranians.

of hipparchies, v, 16, 4, but, with this exception, all through the rest of the story the name Companions belongs to the Macedonian squadrons only, the remains of the original Companion cavalry. The Iranians were merely brigaded with the Companions under the same hipparchs; in Arrian's phrase they were 'distributed among the Companions'.[1] The fifth hipparchy, says Arrian, differed somewhat from the others, but still was not 'wholly barbarian';[2] this must mean that it had a much smaller Macedonian squadron. The strength of the Macedonian squadrons is nowhere stated, but is not difficult to deduce. At some period in Bactria, as we saw, the Companions, exclusive of the *agēma*, numbered 1,400. By the time they reached Taxila they must have had some losses, and certainly received no reinforcements; the first four hipparchies must then have had a Macedonian squadron of 300 each, leaving a few Macedonians over for the fifth hipparchy. It was easy to turn the old squadrons of 200 into 300; it only meant adding another lochos, making three in the squadron instead of two. The five hipparchs in the battle with Porus (see App. 6) were Hephaestion, Perdiccas, Craterus, Coenus, and Demetrius; as the first four were officers of the highest consequence, while Demetrius apparently was only a promoted squadron-leader (ilarch),[3] it was presumably he who commanded the fifth hipparchy; he was often put under the command of some one else, of Coenus, v, 16, 3, Hephaestion, v, 21, 5, and probably Peithon the Bodyguard, vi, 8, 2 *sq.* When Coenus, perhaps already dying, was left behind on the Acesines, his hipparchy was taken over by Cleitus the White (v, 22, 6), at first no doubt as his deputy, and after his death as hipparch, vi, 6, 4.

The number 1,000 for a hipparchy is certain. By the time of this

---

1 VII, 6, 3, καταλοχισθέντας εἰς τὴν ἵππον τὴν ἑταιρικήν. The word had long ceased to have any connection with actual λόχοι; see Diod. XVIII, 70, 1, Plut. *Lycurgus* VII, *Sulla* XVIII. Elsewhere, VII, 8, 2, Arrian calls it ἀνάμιξις τῶν ἀλλοφύλων ἱππέων ἐς τὰς τῶν ἑταίρων τάξεις.

2 VII, 6, 4, καὶ πέμπτη ἐπὶ τούτοις ἱππαρχία προσγενομένη, οὐ βαρβαρικὴ ἡ πᾶσα. This makes it certain, apart from the battle with Porus (where Alexander needed every man he had), that there were five hipparchies and no more. Berve's statement (I, 109 n. 3) that there is no evidence that the hipparchies only numbered five is quite wrong.

3 Squadron-leader at Gaugamela, III, 11, 8. In IV, 27, 5 (Gandhāra) he is called hipparch; as there was then no hipparch but Hephaestion, it certainly means ilarch, squadron-leader, just as Arrian often uses ἱππαρχία for ἴλη, p. 136 n. 4 (most recently in IV, 24, 1). Another certain case of the commander of an ἴλη being called commander of a ἱππαρχία is the Callines of the mutiny at Opis, VII, 11, 6; Berve II, no. 405, saw that he could not be a hipparch.

reorganisation, or perhaps as early as the division of the Companions into two hipparchies in Drangiana, Alexander had formed the opinion that 1,000 was the right figure for a large cavalry unit; this is shown by the fact that he recruited 1,000 horse-archers from the Dahae,[1] for as they were his subjects[2] he could have had any number he wished. For the battle against Porus he took across the Hydaspes the *agēma*, four of the five hipparchies (the fifth was left with Craterus) and the 1,000 Dahae, nominally 5,300 horse (see App. 6); Ptolemy (V, 14, 1) gives it as a round figure, 5,000, and it is certain that he would level down, not up (p. 137), even if it be supposed that each formation was at paper strength. This makes it certain that the hipparchies numbered 1,000 men apiece; this is confirmed later, for when after returning to Susa Alexander collected all the Companions who remained, except the *agēma*, into one body under Hephaestion's command, Hieronymus called the formation a hipparchy,[3] while Ptolemy (VII, 14, 10) called it a chiliarchy, i.e. 1,000 men.

When he quitted India, Alexander sent most of his Eastern Iranian horse back to their satrapies; they reappear in the story of the Successors.[4] He took with him the *agēma* and the Macedonian squadron from each hipparchy,[5] and he took the 1,000 Dahae and what mercenary horse he had as far as the Oreitae (VI, 21, 3) where the Dahae must have been sent home also; the mercenary horse he left behind with Leonnatus (VI, 22, 3)[6] and only took the *agēma* and the Companions for the march through the Makran; fighting was over, for western Gedrosia was his already, III, 28, 1. The Companions who reached Susa must have been about 1,000 strong, as he formed them into one chiliarchy with Hephae-

1 V, 12, 2; the number 1,000, V, 16, 4.
2 The Dahae were included in the province-list of Xerxes (E. Herzfeld, *Arch. Mitt. aus Iran*, VIII, 1936, pp. 56, 61, l. 6) and were still subject to Darius III, as at Gaugamela they were brigaded with the Bactrians and Arachosians, III, 11, 3, and therefore were not allies.
3 Diod. XVIII, 3, 4, Σέλευκον δ' ἔταξεν (Perdiccas) ἐπὶ τὴν ἱππαρχίαν τῶν ἑταίρων, οὖσαν ἐπιφανεστάτην (therefore only one). ταύτης γὰρ 'Ηφαιστίων πρῶτος μὲν ἡγήσατο.
4 Diod. XVIII, 7, 3, where Peithon has 8,000 horse from the eastern satrapies to subdue the mutineers.
5 VI, 21, 3, τῆς ἵππου τῆς ἑταιρικῆς τό τε ἄγημα καὶ ἴλην ἀφ' ἑκάστης ἱππαρχίας.
6 Beside mercenary horse, Leonnatus had τῶν ἱππέων ἐστὶν οὕς. If there is any truth in Curtius' statement, IX, 10, 7, that Alexandria in Makarene (Alexandria among the Oreitae) had some Arachosian settlers, Alexander may have kept the Arachosian contingent with him so far; if not, the phrase must refer to part of the Dahae.

stion as chiliarch (vizier), VII, 14, 10; the Achaemenid vizier bore a title which Greeks translated as chiliarch because he commanded the 1,000 horse of the Persian Guard. At Susa Alexander began to replace the Eastern Iranian horse, whom he had sent home, by Western Iranians (called Persians), but as a separate army;[1] what broke down the mutineers at Opis was his giving the Macedonian names to the Persian formations, and especially his giving to the cavalry the name Companions, VII, 11, 3, which the Eastern Iranian horse had never borne. Prior to the mutiny he had also attached a few Persians of the highest nobility to the *agēma*, a further proof that it had become his personal command. After his death the *agēma* is not again heard of; Hephaestion's vacant hipparchy of the Companions was given to Seleucus, but is then not heard of again either. Both bodies must have dissolved, probably into the 'Friends' who gathered round the leading satraps; Macedonians of the upper and cleruch classes were too important in the new world that had arisen to act as mere troopers any longer. That was the end of the most famous cavalry force the ancient world ever saw.

V. Some Conclusions

The foregoing examination invites a few general remarks. In taking over 5,000 horse with him across the Dardanelles, Alexander had a cavalry force such as the Greek world had never even dreamt of; but though he knew beforehand that, against Persians, cavalry would be all-important, he soon saw that he would need more than he had, and despite losses he steadily raised the number till in the crucial battle, Gaugamela, he had 7,000 horse, though the great increase was partly due to the two bodies of mercenary horse, commanded by Menidas and Andromachus, which for once he used as first-line troops. The experiment failed; Menidas could not hold the Saca cataphracts, nor Andromachus Mazaeus' Cappadocians. But Alexander won his battle with the Companions and Thessalians, aided by the steadiness of his heavy infantry, and once it was won he felt secure; he sent home the Thessalians and allied horse, allowed the Companions' numbers to fall again, and relied on recruiting mercenaries; he had not foreseen what the Bactrian-Sogdian horse could do in their own country. Spitamenes' victory showed him his error; important work could not be left to mercenaries. His very typical reply to Spitamenes was, not to bring over more Macedonian cavalry, but to send home his foreign

1 It never progressed far; after Alexander's death it is never again heard of as a separate army.

Balkan horse, to keep only the Companions, i.e. the personal cavalry
of the new Great King, and, as Great King, to enlist the enemy horsemen. They served him well; probably his marriage to Roxane helped
him. In one sense it was the beginning of that policy of nursing
Macedonians at the expense of less important troops which, in a weakened
Macedonia, was to be practised perforce by Antigonus Gonatas and
his dynasty. In India he again had something over 6,000 horse (mercenary horse not included), but the greater part were no longer Europeans; they were Iranians. Though he expected, and got, some serious
infantry fighting in India, he still mainly relied on his cavalry as king
of the battlefield; he could, he thought, always outflank enemy infantry.
Again he did not foresee that he might meet an arm which would
paralyse his cavalry. Porus' elephants were a worse shock than
Spitamenes had been; for the first time, he could not help his men, and
could only leave his infantry to a hammer-and-tongs fight while he
prevented Porus' cavalry from interfering. He won his battle, but at a
price; it was the beginning of that change of feeling in the army which,
aggravated by the rains and other causes, showed itself in the mutiny
on the Beas and culminated in the great mutiny at Opis, where the
Macedonians did not see that his Iranian troops, far from being an
insult to them, were meant to spare them. But the two things that he
did not and could not foresee cannot be treated as a reflection on his
generalship; the point *there* is that, when they did happen, he nevertheless overcame them successfully.

The infantry numbers suggest one further reflection. He crossed the
Dardanelles with something over 30,000 foot, and despite losses in
battle and marching, and detachments left in conquered provinces, he
had by Gaugamela raised the number to 40,000, a number which has
to be accepted—for Ptolemy never puts Alexander's figures too *high*—
but which can only be made out by supposing a very large force of
mercenaries, who were only second-line troops. For the invasion of
India he raised the phalanx to seven battalions; but though he received
enormous reinforcements, notably at Bactra—Arrian calls them three
armies—we cannot as a rule check the details, and two of these 'armies'
(IV, 7, 2) were mercenaries;[1] he needed masses of men both as occupation
troops and new settlers, and is recorded to have left 13,500 mercenaries
in Bactria alone. He took a few mercenaries to India with him, but
they are scarcely mentioned and were finally left among the Oreitae
with Leonnatus. If we add up his known infantry formations in India,

1 For the third στρατιά, IV, 18, 3, see p. 147 n. 3.

taking the highest possible figures, they do not make more than 20,000–22,000, even taking paper totals;[1] and as he had much heavy fighting, many places to garrison, and received no more reinforcements after leaving Bactra, the numbers during his Indian campaign must have fallen steeply. His infantry figures show, what his Iranian cavalry shows, that by Bactra it had become impossible for him, with all the other calls on him, to keep his first-line European field army, both cavalry and infantry, up to strength; and while he could make good the cavalry, he could not make good the infantry, though it was said after his death that he had drained Macedonia of her native troops to fill up the gaps in his army,[2] a remark which, even if made by an enemy, throws some light on his real, as opposed to his propaganda, losses. But the important thing, clearly shown by the mere numbers alone, is that by the time he reached the Beas he must have practically shot his bolt; even without the mutiny he could have gone little farther; the mutiny was really a blessing in disguise. No wonder that after returning to Susa he began to raise a Persian army.[3]

2. THE SHORT MACEDONIAN CUBIT

In *Hellenistic Military and Naval Developments*, 1930, p. 15, I gave reasons for supposing that, just as there was a short Macedonian stade (the bematists' stade), so certain measurements which we possess seemed imperatively to demand a short Macedonian cubit, otherwise they made no sense. I should have known that there was proof of such a cubit; I now give the proof.

Arrian (v, 4, 4) says that Indians were the tallest race in Asia, most of them being 5 cubits tall, or a little less; the exact source cannot be indicated, but his account of India is from 'those with Alexander and Megasthenes', i.e. from good sources (v, 5, 1). In v, 19, 1, Alexander

1 Paper totals: phalanx 10,500, hypaspists 3,000, archers 2,000 (possibly 3,000), Agrianians and javelin-men 2,000 (possibly 3,000), the Thracian foot, the slingers, and a few mercenaries.
2 Diod. XVIII, 12, 2, ἐσπάνιζε γὰρ ἡ Μακεδονία στρατιωτῶν πολιτικῶν διὰ τὸ πλῆθος τῶν ἀπεσταλμένων εἰς τὴν 'Ασίαν ἐπὶ διαδοχὴν τῆς στρατείας. Usually supposed to be from Diyllus; the phrase 'citizen troops' for native troops as opposed to mercenaries clearly shows that it is from a Greek of some Greek city.
3 The 30,000 Epigoni brought to him at Susa, VII, 6, 1, were only boys, παῖδας ἡβάσκοντας.

marvels at Porus' height, he being over 5 cubits; the source here is Ptolemy or Aristobulus. This is given also by Diodorus (XVII, 88, 4), who says Porus was 5 cubits in height; he does not use Ptolemy, but his basis for book XVII was Aristobulus (see § F). It is obvious that these statements cannot refer to the Greek (Attic) cubit of 18¼ in.; 'most' Indians were not 7 ft. 7 in. high, neither was Porus, who is represented as a very strong man and a great fighter. We get the proof, as regards Porus, in Plutarch (*Alex.* LX), who, from some different source, calls him 4 cubits (Greek cubits here) and a span, 6 ft. 8½ in. Now on Greeks, a Mediterranean people and therefore not tall, men of 6 ft., if met with in any quantity, would produce a very different impression from that which they would produce on tall races like the British, among whom 6 ft. is common enough and every one knows individuals of from 6 ft. 3 in. to 6 ft. 5 in.; so 5 cubits for 'most' Indians ought to mean about 6 ft., and Porus would be something over this; 6 ft. 8½ in. is doubtless exaggerated, for Arrian only says ὑπέρ. We can, however, go a little further here. Diodorus makes Porus 5 cubits, and a fine figure of a man (XVII, 88, 4); he also makes another Indian king, Sopeithes, a fine figure of a man, conspicuous among his people for his beauty and in height exceeding (ὑπεράγων) 4 cubits (XVII, 91, 7), i.e. Greek cubits; that is, he was over 6 ft. 1 in. Five Macedonian cubits were therefore roughly the equivalent of 4 Greek cubits or 6 ft. 1 in., which would make the Macedonian cubit about 14 in. long. But this equation of the two cubits is only a rough one; and as, roughly speaking, the bematists' stade was three-quarters of the Attic stade, and as other Macedonian measures ought to correspond, 14 in. may be a little long for the Macedonian cubit; 13½ in. would be nearer the mark; probably it is safest to say that it was somewhere from 13 to 14 in., that being as near as one can get.

This settles the question of the length of the spears of Alexander's phalanx, as well as of the length of the rams used by Demetrius the Besieger and probably other measurements. Because the contemporary Theophrastus gave the length of the longest spears used by Alexander's phalanx as 12 cubits,[1] a common assumption has been that they were some 18 ft. long, which makes nonsense of Alexander's tactics; his phalanx was a very different body from the later Macedonian phalanx with 21 ft. spears described by Polybius. It can now be seen that the longest spears used by Alexander's men were from 13 to

1 *Hist. Plant.* III, 2, 2.

14 ft.;[1] this, of course, has been asserted before,[2] but is now proved.

It is a perpetual trouble to the modern writer on Alexander that he often has no chance of knowing whether the stade of his sources means, in any particular place, the Attic or the Macedonian (bematists') stade. Henceforth he will have the same trouble over the cubit. It follows, too, that there must have been a short Macedonian foot corresponding to the short cubit. I do not recall meeting with it, but that may only mean that I have been reading with my eyes shut.

3. ALEXANDER'S COMMUNICATIONS

This subject has been rather neglected, though there is some information to be got. These communications ultimately grew to an enormous length, but they had the constant feature that Alexander was separated by the sea from his primary bases in Macedonia and Greece; and if it is self-evident that there must have been generals or other officials whose business was to keep the line of land communications open and organised, this must apply to the sea also, a matter which seems usually to have been overlooked.

I will take the sea first, for on that everything else depended. At the beginning of the war it was the business of Antipater in Macedonia to see to the safety of the Aegean;[3] as regards Greece he was the deputy of Alexander, Hegemon of the League of Corinth; as regards Macedonia he was the governor appointed by Alexander, the Macedonian king. This arrangement proved inadequate, and Alexander had to raise a fleet of his own, commanded by Hegelochus, to take the Aegean in hand. By the time Tyre was taken the Persian fleet had broken up; nearly all its bases and much of the fleet were in Alexander's hands or on his side. After the fall of Tyre the Aegean was safe from any organised naval opposition, though piracy entailed constant supervision. How long Hegelochus and his fleet continued to operate is not known; but the Aegean could not again be a theatre of war—and it was war that Hegelochus' appointment had envisaged—while the communica-

---

1 Theophrastus in the passage cited is using a Macedonian source; see Tarn, *op. cit.* p. 16 n. 1.

2 D. G. Hogarth, *J. Philol.* XVII, 1888, p. 5, was, I think, the first to question the traditional view of Alexander's sarissae; he pointed out that the lancers must have used them with one hand, and made them 14 ft., a good guess.

3 Arr. II, 2, 4. See App. 7, p. 202 n. 4.

tions across it, especially the transport of reinforcements, largely composed of Greek mercenaries, for the ever-growing needs of the army in Asia, required a standing organisation. This had become to some extent an administrative matter; and at some date unknown—it is hard to dissociate it from Alexander's delegation to Harpalus of the general financial control everywhere—Alexander transferred Philoxenus, his financial superintendent of Asia Minor north and west of Taurus, from his office and put him in control of the sea communications between Asia Minor and the West. The Persian fleet had compelled Alexander himself to cross by the Dardanelles; but with that fleet removed, it was obviously much easier to ship troops and their impedimenta from Greece, and probably to some extent from Macedonia also, direct to Ephesus at the head of the Royal Road which they would have to follow, rather than to march them by the long overland route through Thrace to Sestos. Philoxenus' office was an entirely new kind of command, which is probably why only one modern writer has recognised it,[1] though our texts are plain enough; he was ὁ τῶν ἐπὶ θαλάττη πραγμάτων Ἀλεξάνδρου στρατηγός,[2] or in abbreviated form ὁ τῶν ἐπὶ θαλάττη στρατηγός;[3] obviously Ἀλεξάνδρου formed no part of the actual title, which must have been ὁ τῶν ἐπὶ θαλάττη πραγμάτων στρατηγός 'General of the affairs at sea'.[4] The story in Plutarch's *Life* of Alexander, in which the above abbreviation occurs, is told again, with some slight variants, in Plutarch's youthful *de Alexandri Fortuna*, which he seemingly wrote straight off without much consultation of sources;[5] in this (*Mor.* 333A) he gives the title as ὁ τῆς παραλίας ὕπαρχος, which merely gives the rough sense and is not the actual title,[6]

---

1 I gave it in 1926 (*C.A.H.* VI, p. 285), but could not add references. Since then O. Leuze, *Die Satrapieneinteilung in Syrien*, 1935, p. 437, has also given it correctly though very briefly, to illustrate Menes' position. Berve on Philoxenus (II, no. 793) is quite inadequate and often wrong, as he omits the material evidence. H. Bengtson, in his long study of Philoxenus, *Philol.* XCII, 1937, p. 126, also fails to understand Philoxenus' real office, though he sees that it was some new thing. See further p. 174 n. 1.

2 Plut. *Mor.* 531 A.   3 Plut. *Alex.* XXII.

4 For πραγμάτων in this sense cf. the Seleucid office ἐπὶ τῶν πραγμάτων, minister for affairs. Philoxenus' title may recall the old English phrase 'the sea-affair'.

5 See Tarn, *A.J.P.* LX, 1939, p. 56.

6 It might be a reminiscence of the Persian office; Mentor had been σατράπης τῆς κατὰ τὴν Ἀσίαν παραλίας, Diod. XVI, 52, 2, cf. 50, 7, and Memnon had commanded the fleet καὶ τῆς παραλίου ξυμπάσης, Arr. II, 1, 1. Bengtson *op. cit.* argues that παραλία meant the Ionian satrapy; but he does not make Philoxenus satrap of Ionia, or satrap at all. He says, p. 142, that in

as is shown by the use of the word ὕπαρχος. There was no such office as 'hyparch' in Alexander's time, and the use of the word in the Alexander-historians has nothing to do with its meaning in the later Seleucid political organisation as the governor of a hyparchy; they used it as a vague term for one exercising any sort of command or control, when they did not know how, or did not wish, to specify it more accurately; in Arrian the word is often applied to native chiefs or rulers.[1] Philoxenus' real title can only have been στρατηγός; he supplies the earliest instance of the use of this word in a sense not entirely military, which in Ptolemaic Egypt developed into its use for the civil governor of a nome. Philoxenus must, however, have had warships at his disposal, if only for protecting transports and supply ships against pirates;[2] his squadron must have formed one of the nuclei of that Imperial Fleet (we shall meet another such nucleus in Phoenicia) which existed when Alexander died. That his personal headquarters must have been in or near Ephesus, probably at its port, seems obvious;[3] it was at Ephesus that the Royal Road, or rather the most important branch of it, came to the sea, and Ephesus must have been as much the natural port of entry for Asia Minor as it was later when under Roman rule. As regards ports, Alexander as Hegemon of the League of Corinth could use those on the Greek side of the Aegean; and the Greek cities on the Asiatic side, who were his free allies (see App. 7), must have given him the use of their harbours, or his expedition would shortly have come

---

Alexander's time ὕπαρχος meant *Unterstatthalter*. Arrian's *Anabasis* shows that it did not mean that to Ptolemy, which is conclusive; his *Diadochoi* may show that Hieronymus knew of such a meaning later, but that is not in point. See next note.

1 Arr. IV, 7, 2, ὕπαρχος contrasted with σατράπης; but Mazaeus and Arsites the satraps are each called ὕπαρχος, IV, 18, 3; I, 12, 8, just as two Indians are called satraps, V, 20, 7; VI, 16, 3. The following are called ὕπαρχοι: IV, 1, 5, the great Bactrian barons (so IV, 21, 1, the Sogdian barons and IV, 21, 9, Chorienes); in India, IV, 22, 7, chiefs or rulers generally (so IV, 28, 6); IV, 22, 8, Astes, chief of Peucelaïtis; V, 20, 6, the 'bad' Porus; *ib.* 7, the chief of the 'free' Assaceni; V, 29, 4, Arsaces; VI, 17, 5, ὁ τῶν Πατάλων ὕπαρχος (Curtius' Moeris). In τὰ μετὰ Ἀλέξανδρον fr. 1 (no. 156, p. 840, Jacoby) Arrian twice uses ὕπαρχος for a second-in-command or subordinate: § 3, Meleager of Perdiccas, § 5, Cleomenes of Ptolemy.

2 Escorting merchantmen with warships was well known: *I.G.* II, 808a, 37 (326 B.C.).

3 His troops, if any, would of course be quartered outside. Bengtson, *op. cit.* made Sardis his seat; but it is too far inland, and is merely a deduction from the worthless story, Polyaen. VI, 49 (*post*).

to an end. Philoxenus must have had such control of the actual ports, and presumably of the shipping, as was necessary for the proper maintenance of the vital communications.

But a quite unfounded legend has been built up round Philoxenus, which asserts that he had jurisdiction over free Greek cities.[1] Berve (I, p. 248; II, no. 793) quotes Polyaenus VI, 49, which I shall come to. Ehrenberg (n. 1 *below*, p. 18), who follows him, states that it was 'characteristic of the position of Rhodes that men guilty of political misdeeds were taken as prisoners to Sardis by Philoxenus', citing Plutarch, *Phocion* XVIII = Aelian *V.H.* 1, 25. There is no mention in Plutarch or Aelian of Philoxenus or political misdeeds, nor do they say or suggest that anyone was taken from Rhodes to Sardis by anybody; all they say (which may or may not be true) is that Phocion procured the release of four men who were in prison at Sardis 'for something or other', ἐπ' αἰτίαις τισί; one was a sophist from Methymna, one an Imbrian, and two Rhodians (brothers). To turn to Polyaenus VI, 49. Three men murdered Hegesias, tyrant of Ephesus; Philoxenus, Alexander's ὕπαρχος Ἰωνίας, threw troops into Ephesus, caught the men, and sent them as prisoners to Sardis, i.e. to the satrap of Lydia whose seat Sardis was; they escaped, but one was caught by 'the Lydians' and sent to Alexander for punishment, but Alexander opportunely died. It is a silly story, for it presupposes that Alexander was supporting a tyrant in Ephesus and desired to avenge his murder, a thing quite impossible; and as it stands it has no chance of being true. It would, *a priori*, be conceivable that, while Alexander was in India, a man should seize power in Ephesus and that both Menander, satrap of Lydia, and Philoxenus should wink at it; but as Menander and Philoxenus were *not* among the numerous satraps and officers whom Alexander on his return removed or executed for oppression

---

1 Started by Beloch, *Gr. Gesch.*[2] IV, 1, 14 n. 2; elaborated by Berve, I, p. 250, II, no. 793, and by V. Ehrenberg, *Alexander and the Greeks*, 1938, pp. 10, 18. I have failed to understand exactly what Bengtson means in his article cited p. 172 n. 1. He says (p. 140) that Philoxenus 'überwachte' the Greek cities, and had 'Aufsicht' over them; but he also says (p. 141) that the Greek cities of Aeolis, Ionia, and Caria, with Rhodes, were included in Philoxenus' 'Amtsbezirk', and compares his position with that of Cleomenes in Egypt, who was acting satrap. In his book, however (*Die Strategie in der hellenistischen Zeit*, 1, 1937), which is later, he is quite definite: Philoxenus governed the Greek cities of Asia Minor as Alexander's στρατηγός (pp. 34 *sqq.*, 215), till Alexander in his 'last years' put them under satraps (p. 216), a statement apparently copied from Bickermann, see App. 7, 1, pp. 220 *sqq.*

of subjects or other misfeasance, the idea is untenable.[1] And there was of course no such office as hyparch of Ionia; there was no such official in Alexander's reign as a ὕπαρχος (pp. 172 *sq.* nn.), and no such political division as Ionia, the word being only a popular expression.[2] Even if anyone should desire to take the story at its face value, there is nothing in it even to suggest that Philoxenus had jurisdiction over Ephesus or any other Greek city, though the author of it was ignorant of Philoxenus' real office. But in fact the story is as valueless as many others in Polyaenus. That writer compiled his collection of 'stratagems' or tricks in a great hurry, to be an aid to Verus on his Parthian expedition, and took material, good or bad, wherever he could get it without any discrimination;[3] sometimes the setting of an item shows that it goes back to some known historian or other known work; more often it does not. For all this he cared nothing; his aim was to collect 'stratagems', true or false, and the story in VI, 49 is given solely for the trick by which the murderers are said to have escaped from Sardis.

There is no evidence therefore for the belief that Philoxenus had jurisdiction over free Greek cities; the idea would probably never have been put forward had his real position been understood. His only two genuine recorded acts are that, when Harpalus rebelled against Alexander, he sent men to Athens to demand, in Alexander's name, Harpalus' surrender[4] (or, as we should say, his extradition), and he sent others to Rhodes to demand the surrender of Harpalus' confidential slave,[5] who had fled thither and was needed as a

1 At some time there were tyrants in Ephesus, as Baton of Sinope wrote a book, of which little is known, περὶ τῶν ἐν Ἐφέσῳ τυράννων, Athen. VII, 289 C. If Hegesias really existed, he might have seized power after Alexander's death, as did Polemon at Mylasa (Inscr. of Theangela, Rostovtzeff, *R.E.A.* XXXIII, 5), or he might have lived in that disturbed period of Lysimachus' rule which saw other tyrants in Ionia, some supported by Lysimachus himself. But the scanty fragments of Baton (Jacoby III A, no. 268) do not mention Hegesias.

2 On the distinction between Ἰωνία and Ἴωνες see App. 15, p. 292 n. 1.

3 One cannot speak of Polyaenus' 'sources', any more than one could have spoken of the 'sources' of Athenaeus' vast collection of snippets if he had not (fortunately) given the reference for nearly every item; Polyaenus did not, but every item is a separate thing just like those in Athenaeus. He must have used (among other things) Alexandrian collections, his quickest way; but that has nothing to do with the ultimate origin of any story.

4 Hypereides κατὰ Δημοσθένους col. 8; Plut. *Mor.* 531 A; Paus. II, 33, 4.

5 Paus. *ib.* This shows that Alexander had no garrison in Rhodes at the time, or the slave could not have sought refuge there; see App. 7, p. 215 n. 4.

witness; as he controlled all the sea transport, he was the proper official to do this.

After Alexander had occupied Syria, Babylon, and Susa, the sea communication between Phoenicia and the west became of importance alongside of the earlier line or lines between Asia Minor and the west, and Alexander sent Menes the Bodyguard to take control of the new line.[1] Arrian says he was sent to the sea, ἐπὶ θάλασσαν, as ὕπαρχος of Phoenicia, Syria, and Cilicia;[2] there was no such office,[3] and Arrian's vague use of ὕπαρχος has already been noticed (p. 173 n. 1). His orders were to take with him to the sea, ἐπὶ θάλασσαν, a sum of 3,000 talents, and to remit to Antipater what he needed for the war against Agis. Subsequently, when Alexander sent home his Thessalian cavalry, who had sold their horses in Ecbatana, he wrote to Menes to provide warships for them when they reached the sea to take (or perhaps 'escort') them as far as Euboea;[4] it is noteworthy that the Thessalians are sent by the long sea-route rather than marched on foot the length of Asia Minor, and the orders to Menes show that he had warships at command; he must, like Philoxenus, and for the same reason, have had a squadron under him which served as another nucleus of the later Imperial Fleet. Both these orders to Menes relate to sea transport, and both, together with some other passages,[5] show that Menes' post was on the sea-coast, with his headquarters presumably in one of the Phoenician harbour towns; and if he was on the coast, possessed warships, and saw to naval transport, his office was the control of the

1 I gave this correctly in 1926 (*C.A.H.* VI, p. 283), but could not add the evidence. Since then Leuze has seen it independently, *op. cit.* pp. 436 *sq.*

2 Arr. III, 16, 9, ὕπαρχον Συρίας τε καὶ Φοινίκης καὶ Κιλικίας.

3 Leuze, *op. cit.* pp. 435–44 had no difficulty in destroying the two modern views on the matter, (*a*) that Menes was a satrap (Beloch and others), (*b*) that he was a financial superintendent (the majority of writers, including Berve). The latter view is quite unfounded, and hardly merited so lengthy a discussion; it would have sufficed to say: (1) that there is no evidence; (2) that when Arrian means a financial superintendent he says so, III, 5, 4; 6, 4; *and* (3) that a Bodyguard was much too important a person to be turned into a tax-collector. Leuze, p. 437, suggested that in Arr. III, 16, 9 some source really called Menes ὕπαρχον τῆς παραλίας Συρίας κ.τ.λ., τῆς παραλίας (cf. Plut. *Mor.* 333 A) having fallen out. It is possible enough.

4 Arr. III, 19, 6, ἐπιμεληθῆναι ὅπως ἐπὶ τριηρῶν κομισθήσονται ἐς Εὔβοιαν.

5 Arr. IV, 7, 2, return ἀπὸ θαλάσσης of the generals who had escorted ἐπὶ θάλασσαν Menes and the money and the Thessalians; *ib.* Menes comes ἀπὸ θαλάσσης to Bactra, bringing reinforcements, on which passage see the Note at the end of this Appendix.

sea communications with Phoenicia and the Gulf of Issus, just as Philoxenus controlled those with Asia Minor. The fact that Menes was called by the vague title ὕπαρχος, just as Philoxenus (whose real title is known) is by some writers, there being in Alexander's day no such official as an ὕπαρχος, merely shows once again that some Greek writers did not know what to call this new kind of command. Menes was really, like Philoxenus, a general (στρατηγός) in charge of a very important sector of communications.

I come to Alexander's communications on land. We cannot envisage anything in the nature of a definite chain; rather we must think of occasional garrisons here and there along the route, with a general in control of a large section who occupied a central position and had a mobile field force. Only one *organised* attempt to cut his communications is known (*below*), allowing that it is uncertain whether, when Darius did cut his communications before Issus, it was done by accident or design; but there was always the chance of a rising in his rear, like those of Satibarzanes in Aria and Spitamenes in Sogdiana. He had to think of the transmission of reinforcements, arms, and orders, but he had an advantage over a modern army in the matter of commissariat: his small force could and did live on the country, and supplies for the next advance were collected in each satrapy as it was conquered. His main line of communications of necessity followed the great trans-Asiatic through route which is so well known—the Royal Road across Asia Minor which joined the route from Phoenicia round the 'fertile crescent' to Babylon (later to Seleuceia); from Babylon it ran by Ecbatana and Bactra to Taxila, and so on to Pātaliputra on the Ganges.

Antigonus had charge of the important section across Asia Minor, with his headquarters at Celaenae in Phrygia on the Royal Road; this explains why Alexander left behind him the man who was to be, and perhaps already was, the best of his generals, and why Antigonus occupied the central position of satrap of Phrygia, whose capital Celaenae was. Alexander, in his haste to meet Darius, had neglected the northern part of Asia Minor, and must have known that he was leaving behind him a thoroughly bad bottle-neck where the road ran between Cappadocia and the Isaurians of the Taurus, both unconquered; he evidently trusted Antigonus to keep the road open. After Issus, that part of the Persian army which had retreated into Cappadocia attempted, with Cappadocian help, to cut the bottle-neck, and Antigonus after a hard struggle defeated the attempt;[1] he never had force enough

1 Curt. IV, 1, 34–5, from the 'mercenaries' source'; see § G, pp. 110 *sq.* and my text (Lydia in Curtius is a mere slip for Phrygia). Modern writers,

to remove the double threat from north and south, but he kept the
road open till Alexander died, when Perdiccas at once got rid of the
bottle-neck by using the Imperial army to conquer both Cappadocia
and Isauria.

The section east of Asia Minor through the heart of the Persian
empire was, as has always been known, in charge of Parmenion, till
then Alexander's second-in-command, who had his headquarters at
Ecbatana, the old capital of Media; he had a strong force, for Media,
populous and important, was subject to incursions by the unconquered
tribes of the Elburz and the Zagros. One would suppose that, being
so far north, he must have had a lieutenant in Damascus to keep in
touch with Menes on the Phoenician coast; but Syria was a quiet sector,
and the satrap of Syria may have done the work. There is, I am told, a
modern belief (I have seen nothing published) that there was in
Hellenistic times a direct route from Ecbatana through Asia Minor,
cutting out the long detour southward to Babylon made by the Persian
road, and I suppose that Parmenion's position so far north might be
quoted in support of this; but if any such route did exist it was later
than Alexander, for the Thessalians from Ecbatana were not sent
home through Asia Minor but were shipped from Phoenicia, showing
that Ecbatana's communications were still those of the Persian period.
After Parmenion's death, it seems that his second-in-command,
Cleander, Coenus' brother (Vol. 1, pp. 48, 64), was put in charge of
this section of Alexander's communications; he was still in charge when
Alexander returned from India and executed him.[1]

Here knowledge ends. It is not known who replaced Cleander, and
nothing is known about the next sector of communications to the east,
which must have been managed from Bactra; perhaps the satrap of
Bactria-Sogdiana, who already had quite enough to do, was in charge.
It is not known, either, how Alexander kept open his communications
between Alexandria of the Caucasus and Taxila through the difficult
countries of the Paropamisadae and of Gandhāra; some garrisons and
fortified points are heard of, but Alexander in India, as many things
show, was really for a time lost to the west, and it may be that he had
no organised communications at all after crossing the Hindu Kush.
He used the large and friendly city of Taxila as an advanced base for

myself included, have neglected this, and so cannot explain why Antigonus,
almost unnoticed in Arrian's *Anabasis* (for Ptolemy had no desire to praise
his great opponent), should suddenly appear after Alexander's death as a
person of such importance.
1 On Cleander and his position see App. 16, p. 305.

the invasion of the Punjab, and as he left Craterus, his second-in-command, behind on the Jhelum, Craterus may have been intended to take charge of his communications with Taxila; but Alexander soon reached the limits of possibility in that hostile and hard-fighting land, and any arrangements he made were only a sketch which was never completed. But, until he quitted Bactra to invade India, his communications obviously worked very well.

NOTE

As I have been writing on Menes, I must notice the much discussed corruption in Arrian IV, 7, 2. Among the reinforcements which Alexander received at Bactra there came to him (manuscript reading) Βῆσσός τε ὁ Συρίας σατράπης καὶ 'Ασκληπιόδωρος ὁ ὕπαρχος ἀπὸ θαλάσσης, καὶ οὗτοι στρατιὰν ἄγοντες. This passage and the various views taken of it have been discussed at great length by Leuze, *op. cit.* pp. 444–56. It has been generally held to be corrupt, which seems certain enough, but Leuze argues that it is not; he accepts Βῆσσος,[1] and refuses to identify Asclepiodorus with the known satrap of Syria. I do not myself like emending a text if any sense can be made of it; but this one as it stands is mere nonsense. I am not going through Leuze's tremendous examination, for certain things are quite clear. In Arr. III, 6, 4, and again in IV, 13, 4, that is, *both before and after* the date of the events given in IV, 7, 2, Asclepiodorus is mentioned as satrap of Syria; it is therefore impossible that in IV, 7, 2 that satrap can have been any one but Asclepiodorus, and therefore the unknown name Βῆσσος falls out (as it ought to do, for it has only got in from the mention of the real Bessus just before and just after the passage in question) and the name Asclepiodorus replaces it, anything else being impossible. Leuze has two objections to this. One is that in III, 6, 4 Asclepiodorus has a patronymic and in IV, 7, 2 he has not, so the one in IV, 7, 2 might be another man. This argument is misconceived, for there is no patronymic in IV, 13, 4 either. Arrian has no rule about patronymics, and many characters who are often mentioned sometimes have the patronymic and sometimes not, just as occurs to him; he has, however, a tendency to give the patronymic the *first* time, as here. The second objection is that in IV, 13, 4 Asclepiodorus is called, not σατράπης, but 'Ασκληπιοδώρου τοῦ Συρίας σατραπεύσαντος; he had therefore died, or possibly been dismissed, before IV, 7, 2, because (says Leuze) σατραπεύσας means ex-satrap (pp. 449, 454), (i.e. one who had once held the office but had finished doing so). I cannot throw such weight on an aorist participle; had Arrian meant ex-satrap, he would have said τοῦ πρόσθεν σατραπεύσαντος or something of the sort, as he does elsewhere, e.g. VI, 15, 3, Τιρυάσπην τὸν πρόσθεν σατράπην. Asclepiodorus then replaces Bessus, leaving a blank for a name, which must be the name of some one called a ὕπαρχος who brought an armed force 'from the sea', i.e. from overseas, and who joined the satrap of Syria (whose troops would not have come from overseas) for the march to Bactra. That the name must be Menes, who is called ὕπαρχος and who (after he was

[1] Berve has now followed him, *Klio*, XXXI, 1938, p. 138 n. 4.

sent to the coast) is never mentioned except in connection with the sea, is obvious; no one else is known who would fit. The passage in IV, 7, 2 then should read Ἀσκληπιόδωρός τε ὁ Συρίας σατράπης καὶ Μένης ὁ ὕπαρχος ἀπὸ θαλάσσης. This is the emendation made by Schmieder in 1798 and adopted in Abicht's edition of the *Anabasis*; it seems to me so necessarily right that I cannot help wondering what all the discussion has been about.

4. THE CARDACES

Arrian in his account of the battle of Issus says that on each side of the Greek mercenaries who formed the centre of Darius' line was posted a force called Cardaces;[1] they are never mentioned again in the Alexander-story. What were they? It was once supposed that they represented an attempt by the Persians to form a professional heavy infantry, since Arrian calls them hoplites; but there is no evidence for this, and there is no reason for rejecting the explanation of the name given in the text of Strabo.[2] According to this, Cardaces was the name given to the young Persians who were doing their training in the use of arms, in hunting, and in other open-air pursuits designed to make them physically fit; it corresponds therefore more or less to the Greek 'ephebes', though the training was different. The Cardaces were trained together at a centre (εἰς ἕνα τόπον), of which there were doubtless a number; their regular military service began at 20, but that service, like their training, was as cavalry or archers, not as spearmen serving on foot. What then had happened was that the Persian command, with no passable infantry

1 Arr. II, 8, 6, τῶν Καρδάκων καλουμένων. It was therefore a name for some special body.
2 Strabo XV, 3, 18 (734), καλοῦνται δ' οὗτοι Κάρδακες, ἀπὸ κλοπείας τρεφό-μενοι. κάρδα γὰρ τὸ ἀνδρῶδες καὶ πολεμικὸν λέγεται. Meineke in his edition rejected the whole passage as an interpolation in the text, but I cannot follow this sweeping excision. There is no reason for rejecting the name Cardaces, which, as will be seen, fits the circumstances of its mention by Arrian, or the words κάρδα γὰρ κ.τ.λ. These words, however, must clearly follow directly after Κάρδακες, which they explain, and what must therefore be rejected as an interpolation are the words ἀπὸ κλοπείας τρεφόμενοι, which not only do not belong here but which make nonsense; no one would ever say that certain people were called 'manly warriors' because they lived by thieving, and Strabo's account of the boys' training shows that they did not live by thieving, but very much the reverse; they were well fed by the State, and each had to bring any game he killed into the common stock. Whether Strabo's interpretation of κάρδα be right or wrong seems immaterial for my purpose; it was doubtless what was believed. Corn. Nepos XIV, 8, 2, calls the Persian Cardaces a tribe, genus; this is a mere misunderstanding.

but the Greek mercenaries and Darius' foot-guard, the μηλοφόροι, had armed a body of youths under 20 as infantry and had put them in line. It shows how hard up for men the Persians at Issus were; Darius' army in that battle, the Greeks apart, was only his home and household troops, i.e. the Persians proper, and it is quite possible that, as Curtius says, he was actually outnumbered.[1] The Cardaces on the Persian left had to prolong the Persian line to the hills, all the Persian horse being massed on the right; they thus had to face Alexander himself, who with the Companion cavalry was as usual on his own extreme right. It was unavoidable, for the Greeks had to be opposite the phalanx, and there were none to spare for anything else. The Persian command did what it could: a column of light-armed troops was thrown out along the foothills past Alexander's right in the hope that this threat to his flank and rear might prevent him charging (but he drove them off before the battle began); and the Persian archers were posted in front of the Cardaces in the hope that they might break up a possible charge.[2] It was an axiom that cavalry could not make a frontal attack on an unbroken line of heavy-armed spearmen, as the Persians had learnt to their cost at Plataea; if Arrian be right, Alexander did perform the feat of riding through hoplites, but their line may have been disordered by the flying archers. It seems likely, however, that Callisthenes was for once right in calling the Cardaces peltasts,[3] a very different matter; his account of the Persian line is very clear. In any case, Alexander's charge took him right through both archers and Cardaces, and the youths naturally were not used as infantry again. The real problem of Issus is why the Persians, with their insufficient infantry, ever fought an infantry battle which depended on holding a line from the hills to the sea; but the temptation was great, for they were across Alexander's communications, and if they could have held the line his chance of conquering Asia would have been ended.

The name Cardaces reappears a century later. At Raphia in 217 Antiochus III had a corps of 1,000 men called Cardaces, commanded by a Galatian and brigaded with formations of archers and javelin-men,[4] but these had nothing to do with the Cardaces of Issus; they were

1 For references see § G, p. 106, from the 'mercenaries' source'. Curtius' own figures are as ridiculous as Arrian's.
2 Arr. II, 10, 3, ἐντὸς βέλους and ὡς... ὀλίγα πρὸς τῶν τοξοτῶν βλάπτεσθαι, shows that the archers were opposite Alexander, though there is no formal statement.
3 Fr. 35 (Jacoby II, no. 124) = Polyb. XII, 17, 7, ἐχομένους τούτων (the Greeks) τοὺς πελταστὰς συνάπτοντας τοῖς ὄρεσιν.
4 Polyb. v, 79, 11; 82, 11.

certainly barbarian mercenaries of some sort, for Antiochus settled them in a military settlement.[1] Why they were called Cardaces is unexplained; but if that word did mean, or at any rate was supposed to mean, 'manly warriors', as Strabo says, the men might have adopted it themselves as a fancy designation.

5. THE BATTLE OF GAUGAMELA[2]

This Appendix considers the evidence for the battle as described in my text. Arrian's account is not always clear as to details or as to the exact sequence of events. He is following Ptolemy's account, but may not always have understood it; and some valuable help can be got from Curtius (§ G, pp. 109 *sq.*), who used both Ptolemy and the 'mercenaries' source'. As a battle, Curtius' description is an impossible confusion, and he contradicts himself too often for it to be worth notice; but he has preserved some true items, wherever he may put them, and without him certain things in Arrian would hardly be intelligible. Diodorus' account is mostly useless rhetoric; he does not use Ptolemy, but has preserved an occasional item from the 'mercenaries' source'. There is, however, apart from mere nonsense, a definite element in Curtius, Diodorus, and Plutarch which has nothing to do with either of our good sources, Ptolemy or the 'mercenaries' source', and which points to some well-known but thoroughly incompetent account in circulation. In this account Darius is on his own left,[3] so as to stage a duel between him and Alexander, given by Diodorus; there is much confusion between the two wings;[4] Mazaeus at the very start sends 1,000 horse to plunder Alexander's camp[5] (taken from the charge of the Persian Guard later); in Diodorus the plundering is done by the 'Scythians' and Cadusians,[6] in Curtius by 'Scythians' in one place (IV, 15, 18) and by

1 Letter of Eumenes II (published by M. Segre, *Clara Rhodos*, IX, 1938, pp. 190 *sqq.*), οἱ κατοικοῦντες ἐν Καρδάκων κώμῃ; see M. Rostovtzeff, *Soc. and Econ. Hist.* pp. 645, 648, and p. 1477 nn. 59–61. Segre suggested that they were Galatians. There is no reason why Antiochus should not have settled Galatians in his kingdom, for some Macedonian king settled Galatians, 'impigros cultores', in Macedonia, Livy XLV, 30, 5; but Galatians must have been swordsmen, and could hardly have been brigaded with light-armed troops.

2 See Addenda.   3 Diod. XVII, 59, 2; Curt. IV, 14, 8.

4 Curt. IV, 15, 2; Plut. *Alex.* XXXII *sq.* throughout, see App. 22, p. 352.

5 Curt. IV, 15, 5; Diod. XVII, 59, 5; Plut. *Alex.* XXXII.

6 XVII, 59, 5.

Bactrians in another (15, 20); but in 15, 12, where he has the 'Scythians' in their right context, he has tacked Cadusians on to them, showing the same source as Diodorus.[1] Finally, Parmenion calls on Alexander for help *twice*.[2] It is not worth speculating what this source was; Plutarch twice names Callisthenes, but he may not be entirely responsible. What matters is to see what the two good sources have to say.

The Persians had tried an infantry battle at Issus, and failed. They could not have fought another had they wished, not having the infantry; at Gaugamela they relied solely on cavalry (and chariots). Arrian says they were drawn up in depth;[3] but their line must have been somewhat longer than Alexander's, for when in his advance he inclined to the right to avoid being outflanked he became outflanked on his left, as is shown by the charge of the Persian Guard; they started from Darius' centre, but hit Alexander's line well to the left of his centre. Arrian's reference to the Persians' first line[4] shows that there were two; one can see what they were. Darius was in the centre, as the Great King always was, and all the troops who can be identified as infantry, except the Persian archers (who were stationed between the squadrons of the Persian cavalry proper),[5] were with him; the only effective foot he had were 2,000 Greek mercenaries and his bodyguard of spearmen, the μηλοφόροι,[6] whom Arrian (III, 11, 7) calls the only troops who could stand up to the phalanx. It cannot be made out from the captured battle-order (Arr. III, 11, 3 *sqq.*) what other infantry there was, for it often only gives nationalities; but what was in the centre is given as some Carian settlers; Mardians and Uxians, who were hillmen; Babylonians, who were unwarlike, and Sitaceni (? Sittaceni); doubtless this is typical. As the Persian cavalry Guard[7] and the Indian horse were also in the centre, but were free to charge, and as the course of the battle shows that the Parthian and Persian horse in the line were also free to act, it is clear that Darius' army was composed of a first line of cavalry alone with a second line of infantry behind them, most of them untrained formations, largely hillmen, who were of doubtful use

1 Taken from some real connection between the two, Arr. III, 19, 3.
2 Curt. IV, 15, 6; 16, 2; Plut. *Alex.* XXXII *sq.*   3 III, 11, 5, ἐς βάθος.
4 III, 14, 2, τῆς πρώτης φάλαγγος.
5 III, 11, 3, Πέρσαι, ἱππεῖς τε ὁμοῦ καὶ πεζοὶ ἀναμεμιγμένοι.
6 In III, 11, 7, Arrian calls them τοὺς ἅμα αὐτῷ Πέρσας, but in 13, 1 correctly οἱ μηλοφόροι Πέρσαι; so Diod. XVII, 59, 3. Their number is nowhere given; on the analogy of the cavalry Guard one would naturally think of 1,000.
7 Arr. III, 11, 6, τὴν Δαρείου ἴλην τὴν βασιλικήν; so Curt. IV, 14, 8, 'delectis equitum'. The number 1,000, Diod. XVII, 59, 2, from the 'mercenaries' source'; also their commander was called (the Persian equivalent of) chiliarch.

in a pitched battle. When Alexander's charge broke the line, the trained men did their best, and held up the phalanx long enough for Darius to escape; the Greeks lost a quarter of their force,[1] and few of the μηλοφόροι survived.[2] But, except for this, we shall be concerned only with the Persian cavalry line. The two ends of that line were made as strong as possible by extra bodies of horse being stationed in front of them; on their left, facing Alexander, the number was 2,000—1,000 mailed Saca cataphracts and 1,000 Bactrians with them[3] in front of the Bactrian horse who formed the end of the line; on their right, before the Syrian horse at the end of the line, were Cappadocians and Armenians, probably 2,000 also, though the number is not given. Certainly Alexander thought he might be surrounded; this is shown by his order to the mercenaries who formed his second line. He had formed two flanking columns (ἐς ἐπικαμπήν) extending backward from each end of his first line; and he ordered the mercenaries, if the army was surrounded, to form front to the rear (III, 12, 1), thus, with the two flanking columns, completing a square.[4] We may suppose that this order was given before he drew out his army, when he would see from the Persian dispositions that they had no intention of trying to surround him; what in fact they meant to do was to try to turn both his flanks. He had made the flanking column on his right very much stronger than that on his left; it is natural to think of an offensive and a defensive wing, but in fact at the start the Persians seized the offensive on both wings, and his flanking columns may show that he expected this. He may have expected too that the main attack would be made against his own person, as at the Granicus; whether he understood the power of the mailed Saca cataphracts, or even knew of them, cannot be said. As it turned out, the column on the right was only just strong enough, while the weaker column on the left was a danger; but he had not men enough to be strong everywhere, just as the Persian command could only use what it had got. Time was vital to both sides, as doubtless both com-

1 Arr. III, 23, 9, those who finally surrendered in Hyrcania were some 1,500. The 2,000 of III, 16, 2, merely repeats their number before the battle.
2 *Id.* III, 16, 1, τῶν μηλοφόρων καλουμένων οὐ πολλοί (survivors).
3 *Id.* III, 11, 6, has the Sacas (no number) and 1,000 Bactrians brigaded with them (συντεταγμένοι, III, 13, 3). Curtius IV, 12, 7 gives 2,000 Sacas but mentions no Bactrians. His 2,000 is obviously meant for the whole brigade, which makes 1,000 Sacas and 1,000 Bactrians. Diodorus XVII, 59, 5 does give the number of the Sacas as 1,000, presumably from the 'mercenaries' source'.
4 This order is also given by Curtius IV, 13, 32. As it does not come in Diodorus, who did not use Ptolemy, it comes from Ptolemy.

mands understood: the Persians had to win with their powerful cavalry wings before Alexander broke their line, and Alexander had to break their line before his left gave way.

One of Curtius' principal contributions (see also § G, pp. 109 *sq.*) is that he shows that Mazaeus commanded the Persian right wing (IV, 16, 1, 4) and Bessus the left (IV, 15, 2); without this, the battle and what followed it can hardly be understood, but it is not given by Arrian, which may mean that it was not given by Ptolemy, though he must have known. Curtius got it from the 'mercenaries' source'; this is certain, for Diodorus, who used that source but not Ptolemy, gives Mazaeus' command also.[1] Arrian, i.e. Ptolemy, also omits the honour with which Alexander at Babylon received Mazaeus,[2] the man who had come near defeating him. It is one of the worst lacunas in Arrian's book; his narrative supplies no reason for Alexander's attitude to Mazaeus later or for Bessus' revolt, and our debt to Curtius is considerable.

Curtius also helps to explain the fight on Alexander's right flank (Arr. III, 13, 2 *sqq.*). In Arrian the battle opens with τοὺς προτεταγ-μένους τοῦ εὐωνύμου, that is, the Saca horse and the 1,000 Bactrians brigaded with them, riding round Alexander's right flank and attacking the flanking column; Menidas with his mercenary horse meets but cannot hold them; Alexander sends in the Paeonians and Cleander's mercenaries (infantry), who check them for the moment; Bessus in reply sends in all the rest of the Bactrians.[3] The Sacas, thus reinforced, break through into Alexander's 'τάξις' (III, 13, 4); Alexander suffers heavy loss (πλείονες) but finally 'the Macedonians' drive them out of the τάξις;[4] Curtius, who has an abbreviated version of Ptolemy here, may be right in saying that Alexander felt nervous (IV, 15, 13). At this point both Arrian and Curtius break off to describe the abortive charge of the chariots; this must therefore be Ptolemy's order, and it shows that the charge of the chariots was timed to take advantage of the temporary success of the Sacas and Bactrians and to drive it home. The question here is the meaning of 'the τάξις'; it could mean Alexander's formation generally, i.e. that the Sacas broke through the flanking column and got in on the rear of the Companions, or it could mean that they broke into the ranks of the Companions. The second meaning is the correct one; had they broken through the flanking column further to the rear, they must have encountered the lancers,

1 XVII, 59, 5; 60, 5, ὁ τοῦ δεξιοῦ κέρατος ἡγούμενος.
2 Given by Curtius alone, V, 1, 17. Not in Diodorus.
3 Arr. III, 13, 4, Βάκτριοι οἱ ἄλλοι.
4 *Id.* III, 13, 4, ἐξώθουν ἐκ τῆς τάξεως. Therefore they had got in.

while just afterwards the lancers appear as an intact force; also 'the Macedonians' who drove the Sacas out of the τάξις were the Companions, there being no other Macedonians at all on that flank.[1] There is also a discrepancy between Arrian and Curtius about the Bactrians; after the check to the Sacas administered by the Paeonians and Cleander's force, Arrian says that Bessus sent in all the rest of the Bactrians, οἱ ἄλλοι, as we have seen, while Curtius' narrative implies that it was only part. Both writers agree that, following on the charge of the chariots, Alexander sent Aretes and the lancers against the Sacas, and both agree that the Saca-Bactrian column was 'frightened' of them,[2] which means that the lancers gained a good deal of ground; it is clear from Arrian's fuller narrative (Curtius does not give the Saca break-in) that the lancers were sent against them after the Companions had driven them out of the τάξις and while they were still in confusion. Aretes in turn was driven back, says Curtius, by the Bactrians (IV, 15, 20); this is a mistake, for it implies that Bessus had still some Bactrians under his hand, while in fact all had been sent in previously. Curtius' various confusions about the Bactrians in his account are not worth unravelling; but the point is that a few lines on (IV, 15, 19 and 21) he calls the men who checked Aretes Persians, and that is certainly correct; the Persians were on the right of the Bactrians in the line, Arr. III, 11, 3. Arrian omits the checking of Aretes, but shows that something has been omitted by his statement (III, 14, 2) that those horsemen who went to the help of the force which was encircling Alexander's right wing left a gap (τὸ διέχον) in Darius' line; the horsemen he alludes to are Curtius' Persians, who also left a gap in the line (*rarior acies*). What happened, then, was that, the Bactrians being all in, Aretes was checked and driven back by an attack from the next force in the line, the Persian horse. Arrian's allusion is correct, but would not be comprehensible without Curtius, garbled as he is.

Curtius supplies one more omission in Arrian about the fight on the flank. There was still in Alexander's flanking column one very important force whom Arrian does not mention again, the Agrianians. Curtius IV, 15, 21 shows that it was the Agrianians who in turn checked the successful Persian horse.[3] The battle on the flank then was an

---

1 The lancers were not Macedonians (App. 1, IV, p. 157). And in any case they were not yet engaged.
2 Arr. III, 14, 3, ἐφοβήθησαν; Curt. IV, 15, 18, 'territis'. It presumably means that they were more or less in confusion.
3 Curtius here makes the Agrianians cavalry. He knew well enough they were light-armed infantry, VIII, 14, 24, and often; so he must have mis-

indeterminate affair, swaying to and fro, and still undecided when the decision had fallen elsewhere; hence the Bactrian cavalry, when the battle was over, were able to get away as a unit in good order (Arr. III, 16, 1, ὡς τότε ἐν τῇ μάχη ξυνετάχθησαν), and Bessus could claim that he personally had not been defeated.

The rest is plain sailing. On the left, Mazaeus' cavalry drove in or broke through the weak flanking column, had the Thessalians in bad trouble, and was able to attack from the flank and immobilise the two nearest battalions of the phalanx, whereon the Persian Guard, followed by the Parthians and Indians, charged through the phalanx from front to rear, cutting those two battalions off from the rest; but the steadiness of the phalanx and Darius' foolish order to his Guard (*post*) prevented Mazaeus from developing his success quickly enough. For Alexander had got the Companions free of the mêlée on the right flank in time, though possibly only just in time; and his charge, which must have been beautifully calculated, broke the Persian line in time, though again perhaps only just in time. He had taken a chance on his left flank, believing that he could decide the battle before it gave way; and he had done so. But the honours he paid to Mazaeus suggest that it was a near-run thing, much nearer than the Ptolemy-Arrian account lets us see. What one does not know is how the charge of the Persian Guard was so well synchronised with Mazaeus' success on the flank.

As to that charge, Arrian nowhere says that it *was* the Guard; he only says, III, 14, 5, 'some of the Persian horse'. But as all the rest of the Persian horse proper were on Darius' left next the Bactrians and were otherwise engaged, and as the Guard was with Darius (Arr. III, 11, 6), and as of the troops who followed them in this charge the Indians were with Darius and the Parthians (Parthava) were further to his right (III, 11 4), and as the charge hit Alexander's left wing pretty far to his left, no other body of horse but the Guard is possible.[1] Arrian does not say why the Guard, after cutting the phalanx in half, did not take it in rear, as Hannibal's heavy cavalry was to take the legions in rear at Cannae, but just rode on to the camp. Again Curtius explains (see further § G, p. 110): the 'mercenaries' source' knew that Darius

understood something in Ptolemy's text, and put it down in the careless way he had with things he considered unessential. Now Arrian, III, 12, 2, describing Alexander's flanking column, says ἐχόμενοι τῆς βασιλικῆς ἴλης τῶν ᾿Αγριάνων ἐτάχθησαν οἱ ἡμίσεες; and if this be what Ptolemy wrote, Curtius *may* have read it as 'the Royal squadron of the Agrianians'. I do not say he *did* so read it.   1 III, 15, 1 also implies this.

had ordered the Guard to rescue his family,[1] and they threw away the best chance of the day from a mistaken sense of loyalty to their worthless king. One hopes that the story of Sisygambis refusing to return to Darius may be true.

How Alexander, when Parmenion's appeal for help reached him, cut the Persian Guard off from retreat is in Arrian left obscure; but as he could not ride across the front of the charging phalanx, he must have ridden right round the rear of his own army. Ptolemy-Arrian's description (III, 15, 2) of the desperate fight between the Companions and the Guard could not be bettered (Ptolemy presumably was in it); it is the more notable that he says that the Persians, who may have been outnumbered,[2] broke *through* the Companions,[3] not away from them; for the second time in the battle the Companions had substantial losses.[4] No wonder Alexander rated Persians highly.

Whether Alexander was actually outnumbered in this battle cannot possibly be determined. The figures for Persian armies in the Alexander-historians, except some of those for particular formations, are worthless; analogies from Parthian armies contain far too many unknown factors to be of any use. Our certainties are, that the Saca-Bactrian column on the Persian left, on which so much depended, only numbered 2,000 men; that Alexander decided the battle by the charge of some 2,000 horse; and that the other great charge of the day, that of the Persian Guard, was made by 1,000 horse, with perhaps a similar number following them. These things do not agree with any very great numbers for the Persian cavalry, though they must have outnumbered Alexander's 7,000 horse. But Alexander had, all told, 47,000 fighting men, all useful; it is not very likely that the Persians had so many. They probably outnumbered Alexander on a count of heads, as Diodorus and Curtius assume; but many of the heads belonged to undisciplined hill tribesmen, brave and efficient, no

1 Curt. IV, 14, 22 gives Darius' order, in a speech; I have noticed elsewhere (§ G, p. 94) Curtius' habit of inserting into speeches bits of real information which should normally have come in the narrative. Darius' order must be from the 'mercenaries' source', for Diodorus XVII, 59, 7, though he attributes the capture of Alexander's camp to the Sacas, says that the aim of the capture was to free the female prisoners (see § F, p. 74).

2 The Guard alone were heavily outnumbered; but the strength of the Parthian and Indian horse who followed them is unknown.

3 Arr. III, 15, 3, διεξέπεσον διὰ τῶν ἀμφ' Ἀλέξανδρον.

4 What they were may depend on the number of reinforcements subsequently received at Susa, which is unknown; one cannot trust Diodorus' 500 (XVII, 65, 1). See generally App. 1, IV, p. 159 n. 1.

doubt, in their own mountain warfare, but of little use against trained troops on the flat.

The latest examination of the ground[1] follows Herzfeld's suggestion in identifying Gaugamela, where Darius' camp was, with the mound Tel Gōmel on the Khazir river, and puts the battle near Keramlais on the plain between the Tigris and the Khazir south of the old route from Nineveh to Arbela (Erbil), where Droysen put it, though he thought that Keramlais was Gaugamela. This cannot be wrong; consequently the distances in Arrian between the battlefield and Arbela must be discarded. The real distance from Erbil to Tel Gōmel is barely 30 miles, with perhaps another 6 to Keramlais; but Arrian gives the distance, in one place to the Khazir (III, 8, 7) and in another for Alexander's pursuit from the battlefield to Arbela (III, 15, 5), as 600 stades (either 75 or 56 miles). Elsewhere he does give a variant for Alexander's pursuit, 500 stades (VI, 11, 5), which if the bematists' stade be taken would reduce it to slightly under 47 miles; but that is still too great a variation from the real distance, some 35 miles, to be upheld, even if large allowance be made for deviations. It is evident that we do not possess the bematists' figures; and as neither Ptolemy nor Aristobulus gave the distance (VI, 11, 5), Arrian has fallen back on quite inaccurate stories.[2] A pursuit of 35 miles, after such a battle, would be strenuous enough for the horses; and in fact, between battle and pursuit, the Companions alone lost 500 horses (III, 15, 6).

One point emerges from the two cavalry charges at Gaugamela. Both were successful in cutting through the enemy line by taking advantage of gaps; and the charge of the Persian Guard, looking at the nature of the opposition, may have been the greater feat of arms of the two. But whereas the Persian line broke, Alexander's did not, which illustrates the enormous advantage to cavalry in ancient warfare of having a background of perfectly steady infantry.[3] Alexander of course was helped by Darius' flight, and those who will may call it part of his luck that his opposite number was an inefficient coward. But it may be doubted whether even the most efficient and determined of generals, in Darius' place, though he might have broken Alexander's personal charge with his 15 elephants, could, with his scarcity of good infantry, have held up the battalions of the phalanx who followed him long

1 Sir A. Stein, *Geog. Journal*, C, 1942, p. 155, with map.
2 The figure of 600 stades may belong to the incompetent but widely circulated account (p. 182 *ante*) which can be traced in Diodorus, Curtius, and Plutarch.
3 Cf. Tarn, *Hellenistic Military Developments*, p. 64.

enough to enable Mazaeus to develop his success, unless, like Cyrus at Cunaxa, Alexander had been killed. But then an efficient general, with the warning of Issus before him, would never have fought a pitched battle like Gaugamela; he could have found a better use for his splendid cavalry.

6. THE BATTLE OF THE HYDASPES

(All references are to Arrian unless otherwise stated)

There are certain difficulties in Arrian's text relating to this battle; evidently he himself did not always understand it clearly.

(1) How many battalions of the phalanx actually fought against the elephants? This battle gives the conclusive proof that after Bactra the phalanx was raised to seven battalions (see App. 1, 11, pp. 142, 147) and all were present at the battle. Four offer no difficulty. Two, those of Cleitus the White and (formerly) of Coenus, the latter now commanded by Antigenes, crossed with Alexander[1] 150 stades upstream above his and Porus' camps,[2] and were in the battle. Two others, those of Polyperchon and Alcetas, were left with Craterus in the camp and under his command, facing Porus' camp (v, 11, 3), and were not in the battle. The other three, those of Meleager, Attalus, and Gorgias, were left on the bank ἐν μέσῳ, between the camp (Craterus) and Alexander's crossing-place (v, 12, 1); and it is these three which require explanation. A casual reading of Arrian would lead any one to suppose that these three took no part in the hardest battle Alexander's infantry ever had, and that two battalions only, Cleitus' and Antigenes', fought against the elephants; this cannot be right. The order given to these three commanders in Arrian[3] was to cross in turn, κατὰ μέρος, with their forces divided, διελόντας τὸν στρατόν, whenever—I will leave what follows for a moment. The order, so far, shows that the three battalions were not together, but were strung out along the bank in different places, obviously to meet Porus if he tried to slip a force across the river between the camp and Alexander's crossing-place, and that they

1 Arr. v, 12, 2; on Antigenes see App. 1, 11, p. 146.
2 150 stades, v, 11, 2, could be some 18½ or 13¾ miles, according to whether the Attic or the bematists' stade be used. There is no doubt that he crossed upstream, though only Frontinus, 1, 4, 9, actually says so.
3 V, 12, 1: τούτοις (the three commanders) διαβαίνειν παρηγγέλλετο κατὰ μέρος, διελόντας τὸν στρατόν, ὁπότε ξυνεχομένους ἤδη ἐν τῇ μάχῃ τοὺς Ἰνδοὺς ἴδοιεν.

were to cross one by one, whenever (I now complete the order)—
whenever they should see the Indian army fully engaged. This is a flat
contradiction of κατὰ μέρος, and cannot be right; they were to cross
one after the other, not all at a given moment; the last part of the order
was never given, and is due to some confusion with the real orders
given to Craterus, set out by Arrian in minute detail just before it.
Whether the mistake be that of Arrian or another (it cannot be
Ptolemy's, but could be Aristobulus') Arrian's narrative follows it up;
he does not mention these three commanders again, and leaves the
reader to suppose that they and their battalions were among the forces
which crossed with Craterus when the battle was practically over.[1]
Yet in Arrian's account of the end of the battle, v, 17, 7, *before* Craterus
crossed Alexander had a large force of heavy infantry, enough to
surround, or help to surround, the Indian cavalry and at the same time
(the elephants having retreated) attack the Indian infantry from all
sides; the three battalions in question must therefore have been with
him.

One can see what happened. After Alexander crossed, he turned
downstream toward Porus' position; he would thus pass in turn the
three battalions strung out on the other bank. Each of them, as he came
level, became useless where it was, as Porus could no longer attempt to
cross there even if he wished to, and would cross in its turn, κατὰ μέρος,
and join Alexander; he had more than ample transport and would have
sent some of his boats back for them. The ἡγεμόνες who crossed at
the end with Craterus were only Polyperchon and Alcetas. This is
what must have happened, but how Arrian's mistake in Alexander's
order came about is obscure. Alexander then, as v, 17, 7 requires, had
five battalions of the phalanx in action against the elephants, not two.
This also happens to be common sense.

(2) The next difficulty is the famous crux connected with Alexander's
battle-line as drawn up after he crossed the river for his advance towards
Porus' position; I give the text in a note.[2] It has led to some absurd
theories about the 'Royal hypaspists', who were simply the hypaspists;
I have gone through the evidence in detail in App. 1, iii. What has

---

1 v, 18, 1, Κράτερός τε καὶ οἱ ἄλλοι ὅσοι τῆς στρατιᾶς τῆς Ἀλεξάνδρου ἐπὶ
τῇ ὄχθῃ τοῦ ποταμοῦ ὑπολελειμμένοι ἡγεμόνες ἦσαν...ἑτέρων καὶ αὐτοὶ
τὸν ποταμόν. 'The other commanders' were really only Polyperchon
and Alcetas.

2 v, 13, 4, τῶν δὲ πεζῶν πρώτους μὲν τοὺς ὑπασπιστὰς τοὺς βασιλικούς,
ὧν ἡγεῖτο Σέλευκος, ἐπέταξε τῇ ἵππῳ· ἐπὶ δὲ τούτοις τὸ ἄγημα τὸ
βασιλικόν· ἐχομένους δὲ τούτων τοὺς ἄλλους ὑπασπιστάς, ὡς ἑκάστοις αἱ
ἡγεμονίαι ἐν τῷ τότε ξυνέβαινον.

happened to Arrian's text is simple enough (how it happened is another matter): the hypaspists are given twice over and the phalanx has fallen out. The battle-line was very much that of Issus and Gaugamela: from right to left, first Alexander's own cavalry, then the hypaspists, then the phalanx, with the light-armed on either flank; the only difference is that this time, having for tactical reasons massed all his cavalry on the right, he had no cavalry on the left of the phalanx. In our text as it stands, ἐχομένους δὲ τούτων is ungrammatical; it should be the singular, τούτου, as in III, 11, 9. Again, ἡγεμονίαι (the plural) has no meaning; for only one corps has been mentioned, the hypaspists, in which the battalions could rotate,[1] so either it should be ἡγεμονία (singular) or something has been left out. The word ἑκάστοις shows that something has been left out; and that what has been left out is the phalanx is obvious. If we compare the official description of Alexander's line at Gaugamela (III, 11, 9),[2] and also the description at Issus (II, 8, 3), there can be no doubt what Ptolemy wrote: τῶν δὲ πεζῶν πρῶτον μὲν ἐπέταξε τῇ ἵππῳ τὸ ἄγημα τὸ βασιλικὸν καὶ τοὺς ἄλλους ὑπασπιστάς, ὧν ἡγεῖτο Σέλευκος, ἐχομένας δὲ τούτων the battalions of the phalanx, ὡς ἑκάστοις αἱ ἡγεμονίαι ἐν τῷ τότε ξυνέβαινον, the word ἑκάστοις referring to the hypaspists *and* the phalanx, which explains the plural ἡγεμονίαι—in each formation the battalion whose day it was had the post of honour on the right. How the double description of the hypaspists got in, and how the second description τοὺς ὑπασπιστὰς τοὺς βασιλικούς, which is complete in itself, came to oust the phalanx, I do not know; it does not seem likely to have arisen from Arrian having inserted both of two different sources. But the confusion is plain enough, and so is the meaning.

(3) In v, 14, 1 the forces which crossed the river with Alexander are given as: infantry, not much short of 6,000, cavalry 5,000. The cavalry is correct enough for a round figure; he had four hipparchies of 1,000 each,[3] 1,000 Dahae, horse-archers, and the cavalry *agēma*, 300 (taking the paper totals). The actual enumeration in v, 12, 2 gives only three hipparchies, that of Coenus, which played such a prominent part in the battle (v, 16, 3; 17, 1), being omitted, doubtless through some con-

---

1 The squadrons of the Companion cavalry held the ἡγεμονία in turn, I, 14, 6; this passage, v, 13, 4, shows that the battalions of the phalanx and the hypaspists did the same. It meant the post on the right, I, 14, 1.

2 III, 11, 9, ἐχόμενον τῶν ἱππέων πρῶτον τὸ ἄγημα ἐτέτακτο τῶν ὑπασπιστῶν καὶ ἐπὶ τούτῳ οἱ ἄλλοι ὑπασπισταί· ἡγεῖτο δὲ αὐτῶν Νικάνωρ (II, 8, 3, ὧν ἡγεῖτο Νικάνωρ).

3 See App. 1, IV, for these various numbers.

fusion with the battalion of the phalanx (Antigenes') still called by Coenus' name; but the total agrees well enough with the facts. But by no possibility can the infantry be reduced to 6,000. Taking paper totals, Alexander had the hypaspists, 3,000; two battalions of the phalanx, Cleitus' and Antigenes' (once Coenus'), 3,000; Agrianians, probably 1,000;[1] archers, at least 2,000;[2] and the enumeration in v, 13, 4 adds javelin-men, who like Coenus' hipparchy are omitted from the enumeration in v, 12, 2; if Balacrus' τάξις be meant, and it does not appear what else it could be, that is another 1,000. That makes a paper total of 10,000, even neglecting the possibility of a third chiliarchy of archers; the various formations must, looking at the enormous reinforcements received by Alexander at Bactra, have been at least brought up to strength, or thereabouts, for the invasion of India, and they cannot have been reduced to 6,000 in Gandhāra; if he had had losses on that scale before reaching Taxila, he could never have reached the Beas, let alone have desired to go farther. No reason is apparent for Ptolemy writing down the figure in this way; unless it be, not Ptolemy, but some very old mistake in the text, no longer traceable.[3] He consistently used propaganda figures over losses, writing down Alexander's and writing up those of the Persians for the honour and glory of Alexander; but this cannot be propaganda, for it would merely have increased the honour and glory of his rival Seleucus by making him help to vanquish the elephants with far fewer men than there really were. The figure seems to me inexplicable.

I have now given three mistakes, textual or substantial, in Arrian's account of the preliminaries of the battle with Porus, all relating to the infantry. The errors are plain enough; I do not know the explanation of any of them.

(4) I must now turn to the cavalry battle, of which there have been so many fanciful reconstructions; I gave the correct translation of

---

1 Originally 1,000, Arr. I, 6, 6. Berve I, p. 138, cuts them down to 500, depending on Diodorus' list; but this list (see App. I, IV, pp. 156 *sqq.*) comes from the 'mercenaries' source', which, outside the Greek troops, often did not know Alexander's real numbers. They cannot have been less than a chiliarchy, from the work they did. Berve admits that in 327 they were 1,000 again, for the MSS. of Arr. IV, 25, 6 give τοὺς Ἀγριᾶνας τοὺς χιλίους. This is, however, an impossible expression; read ὄντας ἐς χιλίους, as in Arr. v, 16, 4 (of the 1,000 Dahae). Geier read ἐς χιλίους.

2 Two chiliarchies 'of the archers', IV, 24, 10, might perhaps be held to imply three altogether.

3 As, for example, if some one else's figure for the cavalry has replaced Ptolemy's figure for the infantry in our text.

Alexander's orders to Coenus in *C.A.H.* vi, p. 408, but could not add the necessary notes. Of older writers, the only one who took the trouble to translate these orders correctly was that careful scholar Adolf Bauer in 1898;[1] since I wrote, U. Wilcken has also given them correctly;[2] but that did not prevent the subsequent appearance at other hands of the wildest of all reconstructions. I shall have to go through Arrian's text.

Porus' battle-line was infantry covered by elephants, but only in the centre part; on his left his infantry extended far enough beyond the elephants for horse-archers to be able to attack them; he had part of his cavalry on either flank. Alexander's primary problem was that he and his cavalry could not go near the elephants;[3] he could not help his infantry, save by defeating Porus' cavalry, and to do this he had to draw them away from the elephants. He had all his own cavalry massed on his own right. In Arrian, the time-sequence of what happened is arranged thus. (1) v, 16, 3, Alexander sends off Coenus with orders, when the Indian cavalry shall charge him (Alexander), to take them in rear; I shall come back to this. (2) 16, 4, he sends the horse-archers to attack the infantry of Porus' left, outside the elephants, presumably with long-range fire. (3) 16, 4, he himself begins to ride toward Porus' left wing, i.e. the cavalry on Porus' left, hoping that if he hurries he will catch them still in column, κατὰ κέρας, before they shall have deployed into line.[4] (4) 17, 1, meanwhile (ἐν τούτῳ, a vague expression)

1 *Festgabe für Max Büdinger*, Innsbruck, 1898, p. 71.
2 *Alexander der Grosse*, 1931, p. 171.
3 Arrian has stressed the fact throughout that horses will not approach elephants unless trained to them: v, 10, 2; 11, 4; 15, 6; 16, 2.
4 Arr. v, 16, 4 (latter half). καὶ αὐτὸς δὲ τοὺς ἑταίρους ἔχων τοὺς ἱππέας παρήλαυνεν ὀξέως ἐπὶ τὸ εὐώνυμον τῶν βαρβάρων, κατὰ κέρας ἔτι τεταραγμένοις ἐμβαλεῖν σπουδὴν ποιούμενος, πρὶν ἐπὶ φάλαγγος ἐκταθῆναι αὐτοῖς τὴν ἵππον. The imperfect παρήλαυνεν must have its full force. παρελαύνειν ἐπὶ in the sense of 'ride toward' is a common usage of Xenophon's (see Liddell and Scott, *s.v.*); this, apart from the mistake of fact in applying κατὰ κέρας to Porus' *left* wing, shows that Arrian is not here transcribing Ptolemy but is writing in his own person. Another thing which shows this is that this is the only passage in which Arrian, instead of talking of the hipparchies, includes the Iranian cavalry under the term 'Companion cavalry'; elsewhere they are distinguished, obviously because Ptolemy did so. I see no reason to suppose that those parts of Arrian's description which are not from Ptolemy are from Aristobulus; it cannot be shown that Arrian used Aristobulus in his battle pieces. An attempt was made long ago by R. Schubert, *Rh. Mus.* LVI, 1901, p. 543, to separate what he believed to be the Ptolemy and Aristobulus strata in the account of this battle; it was not a success.

the Indians have collected all their cavalry from everywhere (πάντοθεν) into one body (which means that Porus had brought the cavalry from his right wing round to his left) and the whole body charges Alexander's advancing cavalry. (5) 17, 1, Coenus, as ordered, takes the Indian horse in rear.

Arrian's arrangement will not do. The horse-archers (2) were sent off before Coenus (1), or he would have blocked them.[1] (3) is demonstrably wrong. The words from κατὰ κέρας to the end of the sentence (p. 194 n. 4) are no part of Ptolemy's description; the *left* wing was never in column, as here assumed, though the right wing was, on its way round to the left. The words before κατὰ κέρας are correct, but they do not mean that Alexander charged the Indian cavalry,[2] for his orders to Coenus show that he was not going to charge, but was going to make the Indian cavalry charge *him*, to get them well away from the elephants and give Coenus the opportunity of taking them in rear. But if he was going to make the Indian cavalry, a weaker force than his own, charge him, they had at any rate, as we shall see, to be all massed opposite him *before* he gave Coenus his orders. The word παρήλαυνεν then does not refer to charging;[3] to take it in that sense would make it impossible to explain how Coenus, with 2,000 horse, had room to get round and take the Indian cavalry in rear. As to (4), one can hardly say that Arrian is wrong, for ἐν τούτῳ might mean anything; but it hardly suggests, as must have been the case, that Porus had already massed all his cavalry on his left before Alexander gave Coenus his orders.[4]

Those orders[5] have been much misunderstood.[6] Alexander had four

---

1 U. Wilcken, *op. cit.* p. 171, said correctly that Alexander held Coenus back; but he makes him held back too long.

2 As it has often been taken to mean, from the author of the forged letter in Plut. *Alex.* LX to Wilcken, *loc. cit.*

3 This is certain, because the word and the phrase in 16, 4 merely repeat the same word and phrase in 16, 2, *before* the orders to Coenus: ἐπὶ τὸ εὐώνυμον κέρας τῶν πολεμίων παρήλαυνεν, ὡς ταύτῃ ἐπιθησόμενος, 'he began to ride towards the Indian left, *as if* he was going to charge it (but he was not)'. ὡς is common enough in Arrian in this sense.

4 Wilcken, *loc. cit.* makes Alexander's charge the reason why Porus brought his cavalry round from the right. This cannot be correct.

5 16, 2 *sq.* ἐπὶ τὸ εὐώνυμον κέρας τῶν πολεμίων παρήλαυνεν, ὡς ταύτῃ ἐπιθησόμενος. Κοῖνον δὲ πέμπει ὡς ἐπὶ τὸ δεξιόν, τὴν Δημητρίου καὶ τὴν αὐτοῦ ἔχοντα ἱππαρχίαν, κελεύσας, ἐπειδὰν τὸ κατὰ σφᾶς στῖφος τῶν ἱππέων ἰδόντες οἱ βάρβαροι ἀντιπαριππεύωσιν, αὐτὸν κατόπιν ἔχεσθαι αὐτῶν.

6 See *ante*, p. 194. Mistranslation and the forged letter have played their part in some modern versions; even Alexander's main problem, that

hipparchies in the battle, those of Hephaestion, Perdiccas, Coenus, and Demetrius, besides the *agēma*. He sent Coenus with two hipparchies, his own and Demetrius', ὡς ἐπὶ τὸ δεξιόν, which is not 'to Porus' right', as given in the forged letter of Alexander's in Plut. *Alex.* LX, but 'as if (he were going) towards Porus' right';[1] that is to say, he was to move away from Alexander leftward; the Indians might suppose that he was going to support the horse-archers. The order continues that, when the Indian cavalry should see the body of cavalry facing themselves, κατὰ σφᾶς (σφᾶς is the Indian cavalry), and should attack it, Coenus was to swing round (to his own right) and take them in rear; this he did (fully described in 17, 1 *sq.*). The point of the order is the word ἰδόντες; why does Alexander say 'when the Indian cavalry shall see the body of my cavalry facing them', τὸ κατὰ σφᾶς στῖφος,[2] when they had been watching him the whole time? ἰδόντες goes closely with στῖφος, and means 'when the Indians see how small my own στῖφος is after you (Coenus) have gone'. The orders show that Alexander was certain that the Indian cavalry, a weaker force than his own, would attack him. The only way he could be certain was if he knew that he could make them do so. And he made them do so by showing them that all he had with him after sending off Coenus was the *agēma* and two hipparchies, a weaker force than their own.[3]

I have alluded more than once to Alexander's letter on the Hydaspes battle in Plutarch *Alex.* LX as being a forgery. Kaerst long ago laid down the right principle, that we cannot just take the Alexander-letters on trust as authentic sources;[4] every letter has to be examined separately and has to prove its claim to be genuine. This principle has sometimes been neglected or challenged,[5] but has never been shaken; and though many have accepted the Plutarch letter, it has only led them to wrong

---

horses will not approach elephants unless trained to them, has sometimes been neglected, in spite of the trouble Arrian took to rub it in (p. 194 n. 3).

1 Porus' right, not Alexander's; proved by the reference just before to Porus' left.

2 στῖφος has already been used to mean the body of cavalry with Alexander, v, 15, 2.

3 Wilcken, *loc. cit.* understood Coenus' orders, but has neglected the words πέμπει ὡς ἐπὶ δεξιόν. His arrangement provides no inducement for the Indian cavalry to charge Alexander.

4 J. Kaerst, *Philologus*, LI, 1892, p. 602; LVI, 1897, p. 406; so *Gesch. d. Hellenismus*, I³, p. 545–6.

5 E.g. E. Pridik, *De Alexandri Magni epistularum commercio*, 1893; Th. Birt, *Alexander der Grosse*, 1924, pp. 267, 449 n. 28, 458 n. 20; Berve I, p. 44 n. 2.

reconstructions. For though Kaerst himself only said that this letter was probably (*wahrscheinlich*) not genuine,[1] the matter is certain. The earlier part of the letter, Alexander's preparations for crossing the river, has been carefully done from good sources and would pass muster; but the statement about the actual battle shows that the writer had before him Alexander's order to Coenus exactly as Arrian gives it, and misunderstood it exactly as so many modern scholars have done, making Coenus attack Porus' right wing. Arrian's words are Κοῖνον δὲ πέμπει ὡς ἐπὶ τὸ δεξιόν, κελεύσας κ.τ.λ. The words of the letter are Κοῖνον δὲ τῷ δεξιῷ προσβαλεῖν κελεῦσαι. Only a trifling discrepancy, says Berve,[2] defending the letter. Only a wretched little Greek particle of two letters; but it happens to make the whole difference between sense and nonsense,[3] just as an iota once made the whole difference between God and man. The letter, however, has its uses. The writer was earlier, probably far earlier, than Arrian, and could not have read him; but he did read the words ὡς ἐπὶ τὸ δεξιόν, and must therefore have read them in Ptolemy. We thus have a valuable proof that Arrian here copied Ptolemy verbatim; very probably we have Alexander's own words. What puzzles me, however, about this letter is why the forger wrote it. The forged letters of Alexander all serve some purpose, usually propaganda; but, so far as can be seen, this letter can never have been any good to anybody as propaganda for anything.

The only other point to mention about the battle is the century-old controversy as to whether Alexander's camp was at Jhelum or Jalalpur; the best and most recent exposition of the Jhelum theory is that of B. Breloer,[4] while more recently the late Sir A. Stein has made a strong case for Jalalpur.[5] No one who has not studied the ground at first hand can presume to offer an opinion, save on one point. Arrian refers to a 'notable' bend in the river[6] at the promontory from which Alexander started to cross, several miles upstream from his camp; this suits

1 *Gesch. d. Hellenismus*, I[3], p. 458 n. 1.
2 Berve I, p. 44 n. 2, 'nur ganz geringe Diskrepanzen'. So Birt, *op. cit.* p. 449 n. 28, 'geringfügig'.
3 Because (*a*) there was no cavalry on Porus' right to attack, and (*b*) Coenus could neither ride along the front of the elephant line nor attack it.
4 B. Breloer, *Alexander's Kampf gegen Poros*, 1933, who also criticises Stein's article in the *Geographical Journal* (see n. 5).
5 Sir A. Stein, *Geog. J.* LXXX, 1932, p. 32; amplified in *Archaeolog. Reconnaissances in North-Western India and South-Eastern Iran*, 1937, in which he in turn criticises Breloer.
6 v, 11, 1, ἄκρα ἦν ἀνέχουσα τῆς ὄχθης τοῦ Ὑδάσπου, ἵνα ἐπέκαμπτεν ὁ ποταμὸς λόγου ἀξίως.

Jhelum, but will not suit Jalalpur; on Stein's map the bend is very slight and certainly not 'notable'. I asked him if there was any chance, from the nature of the ground, of the river having radically altered its course at this point; he said 'No'. The question, however, will never be settled till the site of Bucephala be located and identified by excavation;[1] the chances of this being done are probably small.

[1] The evidence is conclusive that Bucephala stood on the east side of the river, and not, as so often stated, on the west side; see App. 8, 1, pp. 236 *sq.*

Appendices 7–8: CITIES

7. ALEXANDER AND THE GREEK CITIES OF ASIA MINOR

HISTORIANS were once practically unanimous in believing that Alexander did restore freedom to the Greek cities of Asia Minor and that they became his free allies; and the dominant opinion was that he united them to the League of Corinth. Of recent years both these beliefs have been strongly attacked. The two questions must not be mixed up; the first one is far the more important, for it involves one of the great principles affecting Alexander's career, while the second is merely a matter of machinery. I must first, therefore, consider the main question: did Alexander *restore* their original freedom to these cities, or did he treat them, not as free allies, but as conquered territory, *giving* autonomy to this one or that one arbitrarily and as an act of grace on his part? It is the vital distinction between giving them *back* something to which they were entitled, and *giving* them something to which they had no claim but which he might sometimes give if he felt benevolent. I may say at once that, to me, the latter view (the new view) is misconceived and unsupported by evidence.

I. THE POLITICAL POSITION OF THE CITIES

For practical purposes the new view took shape in Dr Bickermann's article of 1934;[1] some subsequent writers seem to suppose that it settled the matter, and little has since been added. The article was one eminently fitted to attract those who did not consider it carefully; what it sought to prove was that Alexander treated the Greeks of Asia exactly as he treated conquered Asiatics and that they merely became part of his Empire of Asia. For were it otherwise, says the writer (pp. 352 *sq.*), there must have been a contract between Alexander and the cities; and he does not find one. I have found it very hard to make out when Bickermann is talking of the position *de jure* and when of the position *de facto*; but it seems to boil down to this, that actions on Alexander's part which were in reality the removal of *de facto* hindrances to the

---

1 E. Bickermann (now Bikerman), 'Alexandre le Grand et les villes d'Asie', *R.E.G.* XLVII, 1934, p. 346.

de facto enjoyment by these cities of a pre-existing freedom are represented by Bickermann as arbitrary gifts or grants of freedom. This is the theory that has to be examined; but first there are some preliminary matters to be considered.

The first is, that all our information comes from the years 334 and 333 B.C., prior to the battle of Issus; and the dominant fact of these years, which must never be lost sight of, was simply that there was a war on. Alexander was attacking the Persian empire; *we* know that he conquered that empire, but *he* did not know it at the time; he believed that he could defeat the Persians, but all he *knew* was that he was going to attack superior forces and that he could not afford to give anything away. All his measures of this period, therefore, were primarily war measures; they were taken with one eye on the war, and with regard to their effect on the war; they cannot be used to construct far-reaching theories. He himself had not as yet any definite intention of conquering the whole Persian empire; that came later. He crossed the Dardanelles as leader of the Panhellenic war against Persia which Isocrates had preached and Philip II had planned; two years later, after Issus, he stated that his reason was to punish Persia for all the wrong she had done to Greece, from Xerxes to Ochus;[1] whether he had this in mind at the start does not appear. But, whatever his reason, it was a necessary consequence of the mere fact of war that any enemies of Persia, like the democracies in the Greek cities of Asia Minor, must *ipso facto* become his friends.

Now what was a Greek city? It was, from its beginning, a State, a State free and independent, the cities in Asia or elsewhere no less than those in old Greece. (I will consider presently what 'freedom' means.) How, juridically, could it lose its freedom? In no way except by its own act.[2] Certainly not by destruction by a conqueror; still less by occupation, physically or notionally, by a conqueror.[3] Three instances will suffice as proof—Thebes, Mantinea, Mitylene. Alexander destroyed Thebes, and physically the city vanished from the earth; but when Cassander rebuilt it and collected into it again the scattered Thebans,

---

1 His letter to Darius, Arr. II, 14, 4 *sqq.*
2 That is, if it was still a city-state. A city could be swamped by penetration by 'barbarians' till it ceased to be a πόλις at all and became an Asiatic town with perhaps a few Greeks still living in it; there are instances.
3 A. Heuss, *Stadt und Herrscher des Hellenismus*, 1937, p. 223 n. 1, I think saw this, though he expressed it rather differently. This book, though it does not deal with Alexander, contains in Part 2, chap. 2, a good deal that is useful for my subject.

its liberty revived, and nobody had any doubt that Thebes was (except for being weaker) exactly in the same position as before, a free and independent Greek city, as its subsequent history showed. Bickermann, who believed that a city *could* lose its freedom by conquest, says that the freedom of the old Thebes was extinguished by Alexander;[1] where then did the freedom of the revived Thebes come from? He did not consider that question. It was not a gift from Cassander, as on his reasoning it should have been. Cassander had no power in the matter at all, and could not 'give' anything; he was not master of Boeotia or of any part of it; there is no evidence that it was even his ally. He merely persuaded the Boeotians to let him rebuild Thebes,[2] which involved their surrendering the Theban territory which they had occupied. No alternative explanation is possible; the freedom of the old Thebes had never been extinguished, but juridically still existed in its people; once the obstacle to the actual revival of that freedom was removed, it revived automatically.[3]

Mantinea was conquered and broken up into villages by the Spartans 14 years before Leuctra, each village being under Spartan domination. After Leuctra, with Sparta temporarily helpless, the villages threw off the Spartan yoke and came together into a city again. The freedom of the new Mantinea was juridically that of the old city revived.

Mitylene, when Alexander appeared in Asia, had exiled its oligarchs,[4] joined Alexander,[5] become a member of the League of Corinth,[6] and, like some other coastal towns, had accepted a temporary garrison from

1 P. 370: 'La liberté ne s'éteint ici (cities of old Greece) que quand la cité cesse d'exister. Tel fut le cas des Thébains.'
2 Diod. xix, 54, 1, πείσας τοὺς Βοιωτούς.
3 Diodorus xix, 54, 1 (Hieronymus) says Cassander ἀνέστησε τὴν πόλιν; there was continuity.
4 Arr. ii, 1, 4, τοὺς φυγάδας κατιέναι. There had, therefore, been banishments.
5 Arr. *ib.* συμμαχία with Alexander and στῆλαι.
6 The στῆλαι, and *O.G.I.S.* 2. A summary of this, the usual, view in Berve I, pp. 245 *sq.* Doubts have been expressed by V. Ehrenberg, *Alexander and the Greeks*, 1938, pp. 19 *sq.* on the ground that the συμμαχία is (stated to be) an alliance with Alexander only and not with the League; he believes that the formula for joining the League was that of the στῆλαι at Tenedos, Arr. ii, 2, 2, πρὸς Ἀλέξανδρον καὶ τοὺς Ἕλληνας. But it is not known whether the ἡγεμών may not have had power to make treaties in his own name, and it is not known if the Tenedos formula was the rule or the exception, or if Arrian was merely abbreviating. In any case, *O.G.I.S.* 2 seems to me conclusive.

Alexander as a protection against the Persian fleet.[1] In 333 the Persian admiral Pharnabazus besieged it and compelled it to surrender on terms which provided that it should renounce its treaty with Alexander, become Darius' ally according to the Peace of Antalcidas (merely a fine phrase for subjection), and recall the exiled oligarchs, the pro-Persian faction; he made one of these exiles, Diogenes, tyrant and re-imposed the tribute to Persia,[2] and Mitylene was no longer free *de facto*. Subsequently, how is unknown, the Athenian soldier of fortune, Chares, got possession of the city; Alexander's admiral Hegelochus 'took it away' from him, and brought the city over to Alexander by agreement, ὁμολογίᾳ,[3] that is, an agreement made with the restored democracy; whereupon not only did the city's freedom automatically revive, but also—proof of this—its membership of the League of Corinth; this is shown by the fact that when in 324 Alexander promulgated his decree for the return of the exiles, which only applied to the cities of the League,[4] it applied, as *O.G.I.S.* 2 shows, to Mitylene.

The general principle proved by these instances, though it was known to Alexander, is hardly noticed by Bickermann, except in the already quoted remark (p. 370) that Thebes' liberty was 'extinguished' by its physical destruction; he gives no reason for this, except to quote (p. 370, cf. p. 357) a remark of Cyrus in Xenophon's romance the *Cyropaedia* that when a city was taken by force the persons (σώματα) and property (χρήματα) of the inhabitants belonged by universal custom to the victor, which, even if true, is not in point.[5] What Bickermann really

---

1 Arr. II, 1, 4, τοὺς ξένους τοὺς παρ' Ἀλεξάνδρου σφίσι κατὰ συμμαχίαν ἥκοντας. All Alexander's garrisons in seaports at this period, while the Persian fleet was in being, were protective only, except at Chios, where *someone* had to stop the slaughter *somehow*. See p. 216.

2 Arr. II, 1, 4 *sq.*   3 Arr. III, 2, 6.

4 Because Antipater was to be executant, Diod. XVIII, 8, 4. Alexander's orders to Craterus when sent to take Antipater's place, Arr. VII, 12, 4, which must correspond to the functions Antipater had been exercising, show that one of Antipater's duties had been to 'supervise (or "lead", ἐξηγεῖσθαι) the freedom of the Hellenes', i.e. to manage the League; he had no authority in Asia, but he was concerned with the islands in the League equally with the cities of the Greek mainland; thus during Pharnabazus' activity it was Antipater's admiral who was sent to protect the islands, Arr. II, 2, 4, ὡς εἶναί τινα ταῖς τε νήσοις φυλακήν κ.τ.λ.

5 Xen. *Cyr.* VII, 5, 73. νόμος here plainly means 'custom', not 'law', and 'une loi éternelle' is not a translation of νόμος... ἀίδιός ἐστι; when Bickermann (p. 360) talks of 'les règles du droit grec de la guerre', he is talking of a thing which never existed; 'law' implies a body or a person to legislate. I take it that σώματα τῶν ἐν τῇ πόλει must here mean the inhabitants, though σώματα usually means slaves.

does is to attempt to draw a distinction, which does not exist, between the Greek cities in Greece and in Asia Minor. When Alexander arrived, the Greek cities of Asia, unlike those of Greece, were, he says (p. 353), not free, but were subjects of Darius III by virtue (not of conquest but) of a pact, the Peace of Antalcidas. He means that they were not free *de jure*; for the Peace of Antalcidas, he continues, was their 'loi constitutive du droit', which regulated 'le statut international des cités grecques'. It was nothing of the kind. The Greek cities of Asia had never renounced their freedom, the only method by which, juridically, they could lose it; *they* were not parties, let alone consenting parties, to the Peace of Antalcidas. Indeed, strictly speaking, there were no parties to that peace; the Great King dictated terms, and Sparta accepted them, as did her opponents, and abandoned the Greek cities of Asia to Persia. Those cities did not fight, for the disparity of strength was too great; but the mere fact that they submitted to *force majeure* as the only alternative to ruin did nothing to alter their juridical position. Sparta had purported to give them away; but they were not hers to give.

I turn now to the Greek conception of freedom. Freedom, to a city in old Greece, had meant that the city was a Sovereign State; that it was not subject to a foreign master, and that it had the right to manage its own affairs, not only internal but also external (foreign policy and war), without interference from anybody; and such, in theory, the conception of freedom remained throughout. Persian rule over a city had been an obstacle to a city exercising its rights, but had not impaired those rights *de jure*; consequently, when Alexander removed the obstacle, i.e. Persian rule (which was a physical act, the expulsion of a garrison or what not, and was expressed as Alexander *restoring* the city's freedom), all the free rights were still there and, with the removal of the obstacle, became exercisable again by the city, including the right to a foreign policy. A distinction was once attempted by Bruno Keil[1] between ἐλευθερία and αὐτονομία; he argued that the former meant external freedom and the latter internal freedom, and that both words were necessary to express complete freedom and sovereignty; and that this was why, in formal documents like the King's Peace, both ἐλευθερία and αὐτονομία are mentioned. Wilcken strongly supported this view; all his instances are earlier than Alexander, and he got rid of literary texts which mention αὐτονομία alone by saying that the writers wrote

---

1 Bruno Keil, *Gercke-Norden*, III², p. 318; see U. Wilcken, *S.B. Berlin*, XVIII, 1929, pp. 4 *sq.*, esp. p. 4 n. 2.

like that *aus Bequemlichkeit* (for convenience).[1] But after Alexander there are so many cases of the two words, ἐλευθερία and αὐτονομία, being used as equivalent to one another and interchangeable that Wilcken's view, even had it been valid for the earlier period,[2] was certainly so no longer; there are cases in city decrees,[3] where *Bequemlichkeit* can have no place, and there are so many instances from those books of Diodorus which depend on Hieronymus of Cardia[4] that we can only suppose that to Hieronymus, whose authority will not be questioned, both words meant the same thing. Did then Alexander's reign mark a change? Was there, let us ask, a change in the idea of Greek freedom, so that henceforth it meant internal freedom (rendered as αὐτονομία) alone? And could this be supported by the fact that the two words are still, very occasionally, used together in formal documents?[5] We shall see that both the actual happenings and the meaning of αὐτονομία negative any such supposition; it will follow, therefore, that the view of Bruno Keil and Wilcken, that ἐλευθερία and αὐτονομία meant different things and that, to express complete freedom, the two must be conjoined, cannot be maintained;[6] and it will follow further

1 Wilcken, *loc. cit.*
2 I have not investigated the earlier period, but there is certainly a case in Thucydides (III, 46, 5, the debate on Mitylene) of the two words being interchangeable. Diodotus says ἥν τινα (a city) ἐλεύθερον καὶ βίᾳ ἀρχόμενον εἰκότως πρὸς αὐτονομίαν ἀποστάντα χειρωσώμεθα—a city once free but subsequently ruled by force, which revolts to get freedom. He is meaning Mitylene, and to call αὐτονομίαν here 'the right to manage its internal affairs' makes no sense; the word is used merely by *variatio* to avoid the jingle ἐλεύθερον—ἐλευθερίαν in the same clause.
3 Instances are *O.G.I.S.* 228, l. 8, ἐλευθέραν = *O.G.I.S.* 229, l. 10, αὐτονομίαν (Smyrna, same transaction); *O.G.I.S.* 223, ll. 22, 26, αὐτονομία = Ditt.³ 442, l. 14, ἐλευθέραν (Erythrae, near to it in time).
4 E.g. Diod. XIX, 74, 1, ἐλευθεροῦν = αὐτονομία; 75, 4, ἐλευθερίαν = αὐτονομίαν; XX, 102, 1, ἐλευθεροῦν = αὐτονομία, in each case in the same sentence and about the same transaction; XX, 45, 1, 4, 5, ἐλευθερία twice and αὐτονομία twice, all relating to the same transaction. See also Plut. *Demetrius* VIII (from Hieronymus), where ἐλευθερώσοντα = τοὺς νόμους αὐτοῖς καὶ τὴν πάτριον ἀποδώσοντα πολιτείαν, i.e. ἐλευθερία = αὐτονομία and δημοκρατία. Cf. Polyb. XVIII, 51, 9, αὐτονόμους = τῆς ἐλευθερίας.
5 *Milet* 123, l. 1 (official list of stephanephoroi), ἐλευθέρα καὶ αὐτόνομος; App. *Samn.* 10 (proposal for treaty between Pyrrhus and Rome), ἐλευθέρους καὶ αὐτονόμους. See p. 205 n. 1.
6 This view has already been rejected by Berve I, p. 229 n. 2, and by Heuss, *op. cit.* p. 221, both following a Frankfurt dissertation by F. Nolte, 1923, which I have not seen and only know from Wilcken's criticism, *loc. cit.*; I do not know therefore what arguments Nolte used to support his view, which accords with my own conclusion, 'dass Autonomie allein schon

that, when the two words are found together in a treaty or other formal document, it is merely a case of the kind of tautology,[1] only too well known to every lawyer, where expressions are duplicated or triplicated *ex abundanti cautela*. And this is common sense.

For what does αὐτονομία mean? We sometimes get a fuller expression in its place. In Alexander's order to Alcimachus (*post*) it is τοὺς νόμους τοὺς σφῶν (ἑκάστοις ἀποδοῦναι); in the treaty between Rome and Philip V[2] it is νόμοις χρῆσθαι τοῖς ἰδίοις; it can be represented by νόμοις χρωμένους τοῖς πατρίοις.[3] These phrases mean *all* the laws of the city, not only some of them; a city whose αὐτονομία was restored had the right to *all* its laws, as aforetime. But in many cities, probably in all, the laws provided for the conduct of foreign policy; they provided who was the treaty-making organ, who could declare war, and so on; αὐτονομία then, juridically, included external freedom, the right to a foreign policy; that is, ἐλευθερία and αὐτονομία *are* the same thing. Besides the cases given in p. 204 nn. 4, 5, there is a passage in Polybius which practically identifies them;[4] and in the well-known formula αὐτόνομος ἀφρούρητος ἀφορολόγητος, ἐλεύθερος could be substituted for αὐτόνομος.[5] It is worth noting, too, that Strabo XIV, 2, 5 (652) calls Hellenistic Rhodes αὐτόνομος, not ἐλεύθερος, and the reference to the Colossus shows that he is referring to a time when Rhodes was as independent as any monarchy.

But the restoration by Alexander of complete freedom to a city, juridically speaking, might not necessarily mean that it became possible, in actual fact, for that city to exercise all its rights—for example, to make war on its neighbour, which was what foreign policy had too often meant to Greek cities. Even before Philip's League of Corinth there had been cases of cities, certainly free—for instance some of

den ganzen Freiheitsbegriff ausdrückt'. I do not, however, agree with his further conclusion that ἐλευθερία was only a *Schlagwort* (catchword, propaganda word).

1 A passage like the proclamation of Philip V to the Eleans (Polyb. IV, 84, 5) is one long tautology; so is *O.G.I.S.* 228, l. 5, ἐλευθέραν εἶμεν καὶ ἀφορολόγη-τον, where the former term, on any view, includes the latter. A good instance is Polyb. XXI, 19, 8–9, Eumenes II before the Senate after Magnesia says: 'Rhodes demands the freedom, ἐλευθερίας, of the Greek cities of Asia; but if they are to be freed, ἐλευθερωθεισῶν, it will increase her power and diminish mine; for the words ἐλευθερία and αὐτονομία will tear all (Greeks) away from me, not only τοὺς ἐλευθερωθησομένους but also those formerly my subjects.' Here αὐτονομία is quite superfluous.

2 Polyb. XVIII, 44, 2; XV, 24, 2 *sq.*   3 *Id.* IV, 25, 7.

4 *Id.* XXI, 19, 8 *sq.*; see n. 1, *above*.

5 *Id.* IV, 84, 5, edict of Philip V.

those in Sparta's Peloponnesian confederacy, or some of those in the Boeotian confederacy—who in practice were unable to conduct a foreign policy of their own and had to follow that of Sparta or Thebes; and in Philip's League the Greek cities had surrendered their foreign policy, nominally to the League, actually to Philip. In the same way, though Alexander restored to the Greek cities of Asia the old right (among other things) to a foreign policy, his mere existence and enormous power made it impossible in practice for cities in his sphere to exercise it. Cities outside his sphere, like Byzantium, Heracleia in Bithynia, Callatis, continued steadily to exercise theirs, and Byzantium was ultimately to destroy Callatis in the bad old way; cities in old Greece, once they had torn up the Covenant of the League of Corinth, again exercised theirs when they could, with various vicissitudes; but for some time no city in what had been Alexander's sphere, except Rhodes, ever managed to do so. Things that lie dormant have a habit of looking dead; and doubtless in many cases, as regards the smaller cities, what came to matter to the city was not its juridical rights, but absence of interference with its daily life, the absence of a garrison and of the hated φόρος. But a thing that is only dormant is *not* dead, and the dormant juridical right to a foreign policy was kept alive by many things—the habit of communicating with kings by means of the city's own ambassadors, everlasting boundary disputes and arbitrations with other cities, the examples of their kin elsewhere, in Sparta, Achaea, Aetolia and above all Rhodes; and after the first two or three generations of the royal houses of Alexander's Successors had come and gone, the dormant right began to come to life again in the old cities of Asia.

Two instances may suffice. When in 246–245 B.C. Seleucus II was fighting for his life and crown against Ptolemy III, and the Greek cities of Asia were divided as to who was the rightful heir, Smyrna exercised as much foreign policy as any one could desire; she was much more than Seleucus' ally, she was pretty nearly his Viceroy in Asia Minor, confirming grants of land made by his father, engaging him to make new grants, and making promises in his name which involved expenditure by his Treasury.[1] And in 196 B.C., in the hey-day of the reign of Antiochus III, Miletus and Magnesia on the Maeander, instead of arbitrating a boundary dispute, went to war about it in the old way and were finally reconciled by a number of Greek cities, including several

---

1 *O.G.I.S.* 229, III, decree of Smyrna; apart from συμμαχία (l. 93), note the regular occurrence of verbs compounded with συν-: συναύξων, συνδιατηρῆσαι (twice), συνέχειν, συντεθεῖται; the decree might almost be a letter of one king to another. Expenditure by Seleucus' Treasury: ll. 106, 107, ἐκ βασιλικοῦ.

of the smaller cities of Asia, all just as if Antiochus III did not exist.[1] What might have happened had Rome not appeared on the scene can only be guessed.

One more preliminary point. Nearly all Greek cities of the time were, as Aristotle said of Plato's Ideal State,[2] two cities, oligarchs and democrats, who normally lived in a state of tension; Rhodes again, owing to the wisdom of her oligarchic (or rather perhaps aristocratic) rulers—their measures to care for the people and to alleviate poverty[3]— was an exception, as came out clearly in the great siege of 304. Normally the bulk of a city's population were democrats. But in Asia the Persians had kept oligarchies (or sometimes tyrants) in power in the cities, and to the people these men had become something more than mere oligarchs; they were quislings, pro-Persians, the friends of the enemy. Persian rule itself was not oppressive, but doubtless that of the quislings was, for they were living above a volcano; they were in fact Persian garrisons, and were not likely to pay any very scrupulous attention to the city's laws. Freedom and oligarchy *could* be perfectly compatible, witness Rhodes again; but to the ordinary man in the Greek cities of Asia freedom from Persia without the abolition of the oligarchies would have been a mockery.

The stage is now set, and we can turn to what Alexander did do; and we fortunately possess clear evidence in his own orders to Alcimachus. When he sent Alcimachus to take over the Greek cities of Aeolis and Ionia which were still under 'the barbarians', he ordered him to abolish the oligarchies, put the democrats in power, give *back* (ἀποδοῦναι) to each city its own laws, and abolish the tribute paid to Persia.[4] In fact, everything else would have followed automatically upon the abolition of the quisling governments, a simple and obvious war measure, for they acted in effect as Persian garrisons. We have here therefore the genesis of the later stock phrase αὐτόνομος, ἀφρούρητος, ἀφορολόγη-τος, 'own laws; no garrison; no tribute'. I have already explained that 'own laws' implied full freedom, external as well as internal; and

1 Ditt.³ 588.
2 Arist. *Pol.* II, 5, 1264a, 24; cf. VIII (v), 11, 1315a, 31, a city generally consists of two parts.
3 Strabo XIV, 652 *sq.* Perhaps Rhodes should be called an aristocracy rather than an oligarchy; Strabo says δημοκηδεῖς καίπερ οὐ δημοκρατούμενοι. But Rhodes was an exception to most rules. See Rostovtzeff in *C.A.H.* VIII, p. 634, who calls her 'an aristocracy disguised as a democracy'.
4 Arr. I, 18, 2, τὰς μὲν ὀλιγαρχίας πανταχοῦ καταλύειν ἐκέλευσε δημοκρατίας δὲ ἐγκαθιστάναι καὶ τοὺς νόμους τοὺς σφῶν ἑκάστοις ἀποδοῦναι καὶ τοὺς φόρους ἀνεῖναι ὅσους τοῖς βαρβάροις ἀπέφερον. This is the crucial passage on the question here being examined.

'freedom' in these cities meant to them democratic government.[1] This suited Alexander very well; he knew that the democracies in every city were Persia's enemies and therefore his friends, whether of choice or of necessity. But this order was not meant only for Alcimachus' private ear; Alexander was laying down his policy, and consequently he must have issued a general proclamation in the same sense, so that in every city where the democrats took to self-help they would know just where they stood; any other course is unthinkable. It follows, at any rate as regards Aeolis and Ionia, that when Bickermann says (p. 359) that what he calls the 'capitulation' of the Greek cities 's'effectuait générale-ment à la merci du vainqueur', and (p. 364) that Alexander treated the cities 'non en "hégémôn" hellénique mais en "Seigneur de l'Asie"' he is entirely mistaken; he does not appear to understand the position of the oligarchs in the cities, and it is hardly worth remarking that in 334 and 333 Alexander was not Seigneur de l'Asie and did not claim to be.[2]

I shall come back to this, but first I must emphasise the word ἀποδοῦναι in Alexander's order to Alcimachus, for it is conclusive against Bickermann's thesis that Alexander gave the Greek cities of Asia liberty as a *gift*, a thesis for which, as we are going to see, he produces no relevant evidence save a mistranslation of this word. ᾿Αποδοῦναι means to give back, or restore, to some one something to which he has a just claim, something he has once had and has lost. Greeks distinguished it most carefully from δοῦναι, to give;[3] but Bickermann does

---

1 ἐλευθερία and δημοκρατία are sometimes even linked together as two facets of one thing: *O.G.I.S.* 222, l. 15; 226, l. 8; Ditt.³ 409, l. 38; cf. Plut. *Dem.* VIII, cited p. 204 n. 4.

2 He only claimed to be after Darius' death; see Vol. I, p. 37. The claim in his answer to Darius' first letter, after Issus, Arr. II, 14, 8, if it be a claim— ὡς οὖν ἐμοῦ τῆς ᾿Ασίας ἁπάσης κυρίου ὄντος—was only put in to ensure that Darius would fight; but there is the usual ambiguity in Arrian's use of ὡς, which could equally well mean 'as being' or 'as if I were'.

3 For official documents see the use of the two words in Ditt.³ 292-5. But there is a famous instance in history, when Philip II offered to *give* Halonnesos to Athens and Athens refused to receive it unless he *gave it back*: [Demosth.] (VII) περὶ ᾿Αλοννήσου, 2, Philip proposes to give it, δίδωσιν; he sees (5) that you will have the island just the same ἄν τε λαβῆτε ἄν τ' ἀπολαβῆτε, and (6) what does it matter to that unjust man μὴ τῷ δικαίῳ ὀνόματι χρησάμενον ἀποδοῦναι ὑμῖν ἀλλὰ δωρεὰν δεδωκέναι? But to Athens the distinction was vital, as it was in Alexander's case. Heuss, *op. cit.* pp. 217–18, collected, for another purpose, a great number of instances of liberation from the generation after Alexander, i.e. that of Ptolemy I; the verbs used—ἀποδίδωμι, ἀποκαθίστημι—all mean 'restoring'; there is not a single instance of 'giving'. Ptolemy-Arrian *once* has 'give' in connection with Greeks: I, 19, 6, Alexander released the Milesians

not distinguish; he treats both words as meaning 'to give'. On p. 363 he puts side by side two passages in Arrian (Ptolemy), Alexander's orders to Alcimachus, where the verb is ἀποδοῦναι, and the gift (to be presently considered) to the Lydians of the use of their own laws, where the verb is ἔδωκε,[1] and translates both verbs by 'rendit'. 'Rendre' could be an ambiguous word, but its use in two consecutive sentences to translate two very different Greek words shows that Bickermann observed no distinction between them; and that he treated both as meaning 'to give' is shown, not only by the whole argument of his paper, but more precisely on p. 370, where (n. 4) he translates ἀπέδοσαν by 'donner'. It is to be noted that Ehrenberg (*op. cit.*), who follows Bickermann throughout on the question here discussed and speaks of his 'important discovery',[2] on p. 19 renders ἀποδιδοῖ by 'given' and on p. 11 translates ἔδωκε by 'gave back'.

I might really stop here, for with this simple mistranslation the whole basis of Bickermann's study has gone; but, looking at the support this article has attracted, it will be better to go through his other arguments *seriatim*.

Bickermann claims (pp. 371–2) that the cities themselves acknowledged that their liberty was merely a favour of their ruler (Alexander); as evidence for this he adduces two inscriptions, which must be carefully considered. The first is a decree of Colophon, unpublished when he wrote in 1934;[3] it was found in the American excavations of 1922 and

καὶ ἐλευθέρους εἶναι ἔδωκεν; this is correct, for it refers only to the men who had fought against him and were prisoners of war, liable to be sold as slaves; it had nothing to do with the position of the city-state of Miletus. Arrian himself (and not only Ptolemy) is correct in his use of ἀποδίδωμι, see τὰ μετὰ ᾿Αλέξανδρον, Jacoby II, no. 156 fr. 5, ὑμῖν δὲ τοὺς πατρίους νόμους ἀποδοὺς ἐν ἐλευθερίᾳ πολιτεύειν ἀπέδωκεν. (Who ὑμῖν were is unknown; Rhodes was a conjecture of Koehler's.)

1 Arr. I, 17, 4, Σαρδιανοὺς δὲ καὶ τοὺς ἄλλους Λυδοὺς τοῖς νόμοις τε τοῖς πάλαι Λυδῶν χρῆσθαι ἔδωκε καὶ ἐλευθέρους εἶναι ἀφῆκεν.

2 V. Ehrenberg, *op. cit.* (English translation of an unpublished German original), p. 13: 'What Alexander was giving was a privilege...granted to each city separately according to his own arbitration (read "arbitrarily" as on p. 51) as a favour and a gift'; so pp. 15, 34, 51. Bickermann's 'important discovery' is pp. 13 n. 1, 34 n. 3.

3 Bickermann (p. 371 n. 7) only said of this decree 'signalée par Ch. Picard, *Ephèse et Claros* (1923), p. 635', where Picard refers to it as showing that the two cities of Colophon 'songèrent à s'entourer d'un nouveau rempart les unissant l'une à l'autre'. Ehrenberg, *op. cit.* p. 14 n. 1, Heuss, *op. cit.* (p. 200 n. 3) p. 219 n. 3, and Bengtson, *Die Strategie in der hellenistischen Zeit*, I, p. 35 n. 3, only repeated Bickermann's reference; on their dates of publication, they could probably do nothing else.

1925 with other inscriptions, and was published in 1935.[1] It is a long document authorising the building of a wall; I give the preamble, lines 6–8, other than formal parts, in a note.[2] Bickermann cited part of this (p. 371 n. 7), from παρέδωκεν to Ἀντίγονος, and said, without discussion, that it showed that the Colophonians 's'aperçoivent parfaitement que leur "autonomie" sous Alexandre...se fondait exclusivement sur la faveur du prince'; in other words, though he *translates* παρέδωκεν correctly as 'concédé', he *treats* it as though it were ἔδωκεν, a grant, as he had treated ἀπέδωκεν. It needs a little more care than that. The preamble runs 'in order that it may be clear that the people, since King Alexander and (subsequently) Antigonus conceded to it its freedom, is jealous to safeguard in every way its ancestral repute (or honour), be it enacted', etc. What were the circumstances? L. Robert has shown,[3] past any question, that the date of the decree must lie between Antigonus' proclamation of freedom in 314 and his assumption of the crown in 307/6, probably therefore after the peace of 311. That means that the draftsman of the decree had his mind very full of Antigonus, while Alexander in 334 was rather ancient history. We have not the exact wording of Antigonus' famous proclamation,[4] but it applied to *all* Greek cities, both those who had lost their freedom *de facto* and whom he was liberating and those who had not; it could not therefore have talked of *restoring* freedom, but must have been so framed as to suit both classes; the Colophonian draftsman in turn had to find some word to represent this and used παρέδωκεν, 'conceded', and though it was hardly the right word for Alexander, Alexander was so to speak thrown in, for at any rate παρέδωκεν was not ἔδωκεν. There is nothing here at all about an arbitrary grant by Alexander; the Colophonians understood well enough that they were in the enjoyment of their ancestral freedom,[5] which (as I have already shown by other instances) had never been juridically lost.

1 B. D. Meritt, *A.J.P.* LVI, 1935, p. 358.
2 L. 6, ὅπως ὁ δῆμος φαίνηται, ἐπειδὴ παρέδωκεν αὐτῶι Ἀλέξανδρος ὁ βασιλεὺς | τὴν ἐλευθερίαν καὶ Ἀντίγονος, κατὰ πάντα τρόπον φιλοτιμούμενος δια|φυλάττειν τὴν τῶν προγόνων δόξαν, ἀγαθῆι τύχηι κ.τ.λ.
3 *Rev. Phil.* LXII, 1936, p. 158. He had not to consider the question I am considering.
4 All we know is the summary of this part of the proclamation in Diod. XIX, 61, 3: εἶναι δὲ καὶ τοὺς Ἕλληνας ἅπαντας ἐλευθέρους, ἀφρουρήτους, αὐτονόμους.
5 This is the ancestral δόξα the people were jealous to safeguard; references in city decrees to fathers or ancestors always imply the idea of freedom, the πάτριος πολιτεία.

The other inscription is the well-known letter of some Antiochus to Erythrae.[1] (Whether it be Antiochus I or II has been much disputed; I incline to Antiochus I, but it is not material here.) I give the relevant part of the text below[2] for easy reference; the correct translation is this (Antiochus speaking): 'Since (your envoys) have shown that, in the reigns of Alexander and Antigonus, your city was autonomous[3] and untaxed...and since We see that these (i.e. Alexander and Antigonus) decided (or "judged") rightly (i.e. that Erythrae was free), and since We ourselves wish not to be behind-hand in well-doing (towards you), We will help you to maintain your autonomy and We agree that you shall be (or "shall remain") free of all taxes, including the Galatica.' The meaning is perfectly clear throughout, except for the words ἀφορολογήτους εἶναι συγχωροῦμεν; if Erythrae was actually being taxed at the time of the appeal to Antiochus, they mean 'We agree that you shall be tax-free' (in future); if the city was not being taxed at that time, they mean 'We agree that you shall remain tax-free';[4] and it is not known whether Erythrae was, or was not, being taxed at the time. The crucial word of course is κρίναντας, for κρίνειν was the regular word for a king's decision;[5] it means that, on some occasion, Alexander gave judgement that Erythrae *was* free, a very different thing from Bickermann's theory that he *granted* freedom to this or that city at his own whim. It is a pity that Welles, having correctly given the

1 *O.G.I.S.* 223; C. B. Welles, *Royal Correspondence in the Hellenistic Period*, 1934, p. 78, no. 15, who gives all the editors and literature.
2 Ll. 21–8: καὶ ἐπειδὴ οἱ περὶ Θαρσύνοντα καὶ Πυθῆν καὶ Βοττᾶν ἀπέφαινον διότι ἐπί τε ᾿Αλεξάνδρου καὶ ᾿Αντιγόνου αὐτό[ν]ομος ἦν καὶ ἀφορολόγητος ἡ πόλις ὑμῶν...θεωροῦ[ν]τες τούτους τε κρί[ναν]τας δικαίως καὶ αὐτοὶ βουλόμενοι μὴ λείπεσθαι ταῖς εὐερ[γεσ]ίαις, τήν τε αὐτονομίαν ὑμῖν συνδιατηρήσομεν καὶ ἀφορο[λογ]ήτους εἶναι συγχωροῦμεν τῶν τε ἄλλων ἁπάντων καὶ τῶν εἰς τὰ Γαλατικὰ συναγομένων.
3 I am translating αὐτόνομος as 'autonomous' and not as 'free' lest I should seem to be pressing the translation in my own favour; but in fact at this time (whatever happened later) the word, as I see it, was indistinguishable from ἐλεύθερος, 'free'; see *ante*, pp. 204 *sq.* and nn.
4 An excellent case of συγχωρεῖν, followed by the present infinitive, meaning 'we agree that you shall *remain*', 'shall be as before', is Polyb. xv, 24, 2 *sq.* The Thasians agree to hand over (παραδοῦναι) their city to Philip εἰ διατηρήσοι αὐτοὺς ἀφρουρήτους, ἀφορολογήτους, ἀνεπισταθμεύτους, νόμοις χρῆσθαι τοῖς ἰδίοις, i.e. if they can remain in their present position; his general replies συγχωρεῖν τὸν βασιλέα Θασίους ἀφρουρήτους, ἀφορολογήτους, ἀνεπισταθμεύτους, νόμοις χρῆσθαι τοῖς ἰδίοις, using the identical words.
5 Welles, *op. cit.* p. 83, note to 24–5, κρίνειν is 'technical in the sense of a royal "decision"', with some references.

meaning of κρίνειν, should then have translated θεωροῦντες τούτους τε κρίναντας δικαίως as 'since we see that their policy was just', for there is much difference between a policy and a decision or judgement; and it is an even worse pity (for every one naturally turns to his book) that he should have headed this letter (p. 78) 'Letter of Antiochus II to Erythrae granting the city autonomy' when even his own translation shows that there is not one word from beginning to end about a *grant* of autonomy by anybody.[1]

How now does Bickermann treat this letter, which he adduces in support of his theory that the Greek cities acknowledged that their liberty was merely a favour of their ruler? The Erythraean ambassadors, he begins (p. 372), have told Antiochus that 'leur ville fut autonome sous Alexandre et Antigone'; he omits ἀφορολογήτους, and omits the crucial κρίναντας passage altogether, and goes straight on 'comme nous désirons n'être pas surpassés en bienfaits, nous maintenons votre autonomie et vous accordons l'exemption des impôts'; this last phrase takes on a very different colour from the previous omission of ἀφορο-λογήτους, and 'nous maintenons', 'we maintain', is a very different thing from συνδιατηρήσομεν, 'we will help you to maintain'. Then follows his conclusion: one sees that the Erythraeans perceived perfectly, like the Colophonians, that their 'autonomie', under Alexander no less than Antiochus, 'se fondait exclusivement sur la faveur du prince'. There is not a word in the Greek text, or even in Bickermann's version of it, to bear this conclusion out; the Greek text of the whole letter contradicts it flatly.

I must return here for a moment to Bickermann's 'merci du vainqueur' (p. 208 *ante*). He argues (p. 361) that, were it otherwise, we ought to hear of treaties of συμμαχία made with separate cities, and we never do. It is true that we never do, though we hear of agreements, ὁμολογίαι or συνθῆκαι;[2] and Bickermann is entitled to say that the juridical position between Alexander and the old Greek cities of Asia was never formally regulated (assuming always that they did not become members of the

1 Welles, *op. cit.* p. 83, note to 26, says of συνδιατηρεῖν: 'In 1, 54–5 and 62, the verb is used of a new grant, and that must be the sense here.' 1 is *O.G.I.S.* 5, Antigonus' letter to Scepsis; the word συνδιατηρεῖν does not occur in it, and there is nothing in it about a new grant; some word (? συνδιαφυλάσσειν) may have fallen out after 'verb'. συνδιατηρεῖν is common enough and its meaning is not in doubt; Welles translates it correctly, in spite of his note. He concludes that note by saying: 'It is as if Antiochus preferred to assume that autonomy had always been in the city's possession.' Antiochus did not assume; he knew it was so, and wrote accordingly.

2 Arr. III, 2, 6, ὁμολογία; 1, 26, 3, ξυνθέμενοι.

League of Corinth, see *post*). I agree that it was not; but why should it have been? Alexander did not need it; provided there were democratic governments in the cities they *had* to help him if he so desired, συμμαχία or no συμμαχία. The cities did not need it; Alexander had given them back their freedom, and for his own sake he would have to take order with any quislings who returned, as he did. The question is immaterial to the main issue, whether the liberty of the cities was a gift from Alexander or not. I must repeat that all our information comes from the war years 334 and 333; the Exiles Decree of 324, an entirely new development, has nothing to do with the matter, and indeed no one has ever claimed that it had or could have;[1] besides, it only concerned the League cities. In the years 334 and 333 Alexander was not thinking about the juridical position but about the practical one. A state of things was coming into being in Asia Minor which was entirely without precedent; the position was fluid, and outside the known constitutional forms. Alexander on the one hand was feeling his way, as he always did, taking each question as it arose, and on the other was occupied with two overriding military problems: he wanted to get on as quickly as possible to meet Darius, and he had to deal with a quite active Persian fleet operating on his communications, a fleet which he could not meet at sea. Both these problems would be solved if the Greek cities became free, that is, if his friends the democrats came into power; it would start the break-up of the Persian fleet,[2] as it did, and would safeguard his rear against the quislings who depended on that fleet. (He had some luck, for he could not guess that Darius would help to hamstring his own fleet by recalling the troops on board; at the same time it was the speed of his advance which compelled Darius to take that step.) Many cities freed themselves from their oligarchs or garrisons,[3] though Alexander sometimes put the democrats in power by force, or a show of force, as at Mitylene and Chios; but it is clear that where force was used it was to turn out the oligarchs, virtually Persian garrisons, where the democrats could not do it themselves; the one exception is Miletus, held by Darius' mercenaries, who made the citizens fight.[4] But this was not treating the cities 'en Seigneur de l'Asie'.

It is not known what the powers of the Hegemon of the League

1 Discussed at length by A. Heuss, *Hermes*, LXXIII, 1938, pp. 134–41.
2 Arr. I, 20, 1; see further Vol. I, p. 19.
3 Ehrenberg, *op. cit.* p. 11, says that 'most of the Greek cities surrendered to Alexander only when no other chance was left'. What this statement means I do not know.
4 Perhaps unwillingly: Glaucippus attempted a compromise, Arr. I, 19, 1.

of Corinth were in wartime; but (quite apart from any question whether Alexander was στρατηγὸς αὐτοκράτωρ or not) they must have included every power necessary for the successful prosecution of a war—Philip could be trusted to see to *that*—and if Alexander had to use force, which could only happen where the oligarchs were still, or were again, in control, he could undoubtedly do so as Hegemon of the League; for it cannot be supposed that either Philip or Alexander would have sanctioned in the League Covenant any such restriction on the military powers of the Hegemon (i.e. himself) as would compel him to leave in his rear a walled city, probably with a harbour, controlled by partisans of Persia. We have seen that the absence of separate treaties of alliance between Alexander and the democracies in the Greek cities of Asia made no difference to the actual position, which was all that Alexander cared about; what is not known is whether he himself personally desired that the Greek cities should be free. It is possible enough,[1] and he would certainly regard their freedom as good propaganda for Greece itself; but his primary reason can only have been the war motive which I have outlined above. It cannot be supposed that, as yet, he had in mind any of those ideas of human brotherhood which distinguished his last years; these can only have grown gradually as he matured and gained greater knowledge and experience of his world.

I have said that the cities, when free, had to aid him. A city which, by its geographical position, was involved in a war between Macedonia and Persia could only remain neutral if it were strong enough to withstand the inevitable attack from one side or the other;[2] and that no city was strong enough to do, not even Rhodes. Rhodes enforced her neutrality against Antigonus in 304; it is very doubtful if she could have done so against Alexander. But it is worth considering the confused story of what did happen to Rhodes, the key to the Aegean, the vital station which might keep asunder the Greek and the Phoenician-Cyprian halves of the Persian fleet. It has been supposed that she remained anti-

1 Diodorus (XVII, 24, 1), after praising Alexander's φιλανθρωπία and εὐεργεσία towards the Greek cities of Asia, says that he had begun the war against Persia in order to free the Greeks, προσεπιλέγων ὅτι τῆς τῶν Ἑλλήνων ἐλευθερώσεως ἕνεκα τὸν πρὸς Πέρσας πόλεμον ἐπανῄρηται. The statement is Diodorus' own, taken from XVI, 91, 2, where Philip, after sending Attalus and Parmenion on in advance to Asia Minor, orders them to free the Greek cities. This might be true of Philip, as the business of his advance force was to secure bridgeheads; but Diodorus' statement cannot be true of Alexander.

2 One Greek phrase for neutrality, οἱ διὰ μέσου or ἐκ τοῦ μέσου, well expresses the idea of being liable to be shot at by both sides.

Macedonian till after Issus,[1] which is impossible (*post*). Certainly the
island is not mentioned in the tradition till after Issus: when the Persian
fleet broke up, she sent ten ships to aid Alexander against Tyre.[2] But
she had accepted Alexander's garrison; I say 'accepted', for had there
been fighting, some trace of it must have survived in the tradition,
owing to the great importance of the island. But the garrisons Alexander
left in the maritime towns were only for protection against the Persian
fleet, and so Rhodes must have received her garrison when the other
maritime cities did, that is, while the Persian fleet was still in being and
active, though there is no information on the point. But the extraordinary thing is that, so far as is known, Rhodes retained her oligarchic
government, the only oligarchy left; it differed greatly from other
oligarchies, as I have mentioned, and Alexander must have recognised
the fact. It means that Rhodes can never have been anti-Macedonian
or assisted Persia; and though Curtius is doubtless right in saying that
Rhodes did not *actively* join Alexander and give him the use of her
harbour till the Persian fleet had broken up,[3] she must in the earlier
period have acted with sufficient correctness to convince Alexander
that there was no question of any hostility to him. In 331, after the
Persian fleet had broken up, Alexander withdrew the garrison from
Rhodes at the same time as that from Chios;[4] and the later story, already
known to Diodorus (xx, 81, 3), that he deposited his (supposed) will
at Rhodes for safe custody, though untrue, points to known good
relations between Alexander and the city such as Diodorus describes,
for otherwise the legend could not have selected Rhodes. The same
thing is shown by Plutarch's story[5] that the cloak which Alexander
wore at Gaugamela over his armour, and which he always did wear in

1 Berve I, 247 *sq.*, followed by Ehrenberg, *op. cit.* p. 18.
2 Arr. II, 20, 2. 3 Curt. IV, 5, 9, after the fall of Tyre.
4 Curt. IV, 5, 9. Curtius' detailed statement, IV, 8, 12, that the garrisons of
   Chios and Rhodes were withdrawn in 331 must be correct; it presumably
   comes from the 'mercenaries' source', and, in fact, they were no longer
   needed. Some, however, have followed Diodorus, XVIII, 8, 1, who says the
   Rhodians expelled their garrison soon after Alexander's death. He, however, only has a one-line statement, sandwiched in between the connected
   events of Peithon's victory over the mutineers in the Farther East and the
   Lamian war; it is brought in à propos of nothing at all, and may well be a
   later insertion; if it be Diodorus' own statement, it may suggest that book
   XVIII, like XVII (§ F, p. 80 n. 1), never had a final revision. The statement
   cannot be true, because Harpalus' confidential slave fled to Rhodes
   (Paus. II, 33, 4), which shows that, towards the end of Alexander's life,
   Rhodes was not in his hands, despite the mention of Philoxenus (*post*).
5 *Alex.* XXXII, σοβαρώτερον τῇ ἐργασίᾳ.

battle, was a gift from the city of Rhodes; it was of very special workmanship, the maker being named. The belief of some writers that Rhodes was subject to an official of Alexander's, Philoxenus, is a mere mistake, unsupported by evidence and due to their misunderstanding of Philoxenus' position (see App. 3).

Rhodes then, as so often, seems to have occupied a somewhat special position. As to Alexander's relations with another city, Chios, on which so much has been written, there is no need for me to examine them here, for the central fact is simple: Chios was almost in a state of anarchy, with the two factions slaughtering each other, and Alexander, as any other decent man would have done, intervened to stop the horror without waiting to inquire if he was legally entitled to do so. It has no bearing at all on Alexander's position with regard to the Greek cities generally, any more than has his action at Ephesus, where he had stopped his friends from murdering their opponents.[1]

I must now consider that part of Bickermann's theory on which he lays so much stress, that Alexander treated the Greek cities like conquered Asiatics; and here I must first return for a moment to Sardis and the Lydians. Arrian (Ptolemy) says that Alexander gave, ἔδωκε, to Sardis and the Lydians generally the right to use the ancient νόμοι of the Lydians, and set them free (i.e. from Persian rule).[2] Lydians had never been 'free', in the Greek sense; so far as Greeks knew, they had always been under the despotic rule of some king, most recently that of the kings of Persia, and with Persia's rule removed they automatically became subject to Persia's conqueror; their position was entirely different from that of a Greek city-state. Consequently, anything that Alexander did for them, or for any Asiatics, really was a gift, an act of grace, as Ptolemy quite correctly says, and whatever he gave them he could give on his own terms; he did in fact garrison the all-but-impregnable Sardis and appointed a satrap of Lydia, though that satrap had to take account of native νόμοι. (In fact, every satrap who desired to govern decently must have done the same thing.) Bickermann (p. 363) put together this passage and Alexander's order to Alcimachus, already considered, and by means of the mistranslation which I have examined made these two totally different statements mean the same thing; and on this fundamentally wrong foundation he built up the theory, not merely that any liberty which the Greek cities had was a gift, an act of

1 Arr. I, 17, 11 *sqq.* One may agree with Arrian that Alexander ἐν τῷ τότε εὐδοκίμει.
2 Arr. I, 17, 4, set out p. 209 n. 1. I suppose νόμοι does mean 'laws' here (king's rescripts); but it would probably include 'customs'.

grace, from Alexander (this has already been examined), but that Alexander treated Greeks and Asiatics alike, that is, that he treated Greeks like conquered Asiatics, as part of his Asiatic empire. To him, every city that joined Alexander was 'conquered'. Of this I have said enough already; it remains to look at the reasons adduced for saying that Alexander treated Greeks like Asiatics.

The first is that, in Asia, Alexander destroyed some Greek cities. Before looking at the three alleged cases, it may be well to ask, supposing this were true, how would it show that Alexander treated Greeks like Asiatics? Greek cities had often enough destroyed other Greek cities: Thebes had destroyed Plataea and Orchomenus, Sparta had destroyed Mantinea as a city, Croton had wiped out Sybaris; were they treating the cities they destroyed as part of their 'empire'? What they were really doing was carrying the barbarous customs of Greek warfare one step further, a step which always aroused popular feeling. If Alexander's destruction of Thebes was not treating Greeks like Asiatics, how could the (supposed) destruction of Halicarnassus be that, seeing that both were due to the same cause, very desperate resistance? But I had better look now at Bickermann's three instances (p. 360), Halicarnassus, Gryneion, Lampsacus.

Two questions can be asked about Halicarnassus: what does its 'destruction' mean, and what sort of a city was it? I have shown elsewhere (§ F, p. 73) that we possess two authoritative accounts of the siege, that of Arrian (Ptolemy) from the point of view of the besiegers and that of Diodorus (the 'mercenaries' source') from the point of view of the besieged, which supplement each other; the 'besieged' were Darius' garrison, i.e. the Persian satrap Orontobates with his troops and Memnon with some of Darius' Greek mercenaries; it does not appear that the townspeople, Greek or Carian, were resisting Alexander. Arrian says that the besieged fired the town; Alexander extinguished or tried to extinguish the fire,[1] and then destroyed the town himself,[2] which as it stands is nonsense. Diodorus naturally omits the firing of the town by the besieged, and merely says that Alexander destroyed it;[3] he adds that Alexander surrounded the citadel of Salmacis, which the Persians still held, with a wall and ditch, while Ptolemy adds that he left a garrison *in* the town,[4] presumably to besiege Salmacis, which he could not have done had the town been destroyed. Clearly what happened was that the garrison tried to destroy the town and Alexander prevented it, but cleared a space round Salmacis for his siege works. The 'destruction'

1 Arr. I, 23, 3 *sqq.* 2 *Ib.* 23, 6, ἐς ἔδαφος κατασκάψας.
3 Diod. XVII, 27, 6. 4 Arr. I, 23, 6, φυλακὴν ἐγκαταλιπών.

of Halicarnassus was then at most a very partial affair, largely due to the Persian garrison; Alexander did *not* sell any of the inhabitants, who had not been fighting against him, and the Mausoleum remained to be one of the seven wonders of the Hellenistic world.

But what sort of a 'Greek' city was this Halicarnassus, in any case? Its Anatolian name shows that, when Greeks first settled there, they settled in what was already an Anatolian (in this case Carian) town, as they did in Miletus, Ephesus, and many other places on the seaboard of Asia Minor. At first the Greeks got the upper hand, and the city ranked as one of the six cities of the Dorian Hexapolis, from which, however, it was expelled before Herodotus' time;[1] but his story that this was due to one man's peculation is most improbable, and the supposition, first voiced by Grote, that it happened because the place was ceasing to be Greek and becoming Carian is certainly correct; Herodotus himself, though half a Carian, never lived or worked there. For by the fifth century, though the Greeks may have retained Greek organisation in their own community,[2] the town was really in the hands of a family of Carian dynasts, that of Mausolus, one of whom, the famous Artemisia, commanded its contingent at Salamis; if it be true that the Greek and Carian organisations were working side by side, the phenomenon seems unique,[3] but the Greeks were losing ground, for in 460 they revolted to try to recover their autonomy.[4] In the fourth century the Persian king made a member of the Carian dynasty, Hecatomnus, satrap of the new Carian satrapy, and he set up his βασίλειον in Halicarnassus, though he subsequently transferred it to the religious centre of Caria, Mylasa;[5] his son Mausolus II brought the βασίλειον back to Halicarnassus[6] and enlarged the town greatly by synoecising into it six very populous towns of the Leleges,[7] who reinforced the already dominant Carian element, and it became the satrapal seat of Mausolus' dynasty.[8] There is, I think, no certain case, and only one possible one,[9] of a native βασίλειον being set up in a Greek or Greek-controlled city; and though Halicarnassus in Alexander's time probably still contained

1 Herod. I, 144.
2 This depends on Michel 451. It seems a curious sort of organisation.
3 See Swoboda, *Staatsaltertümer*, p. 90 (in Hermann's *Lehrbuch*⁶), again from Michel 451.
4 Bürchner, 'Halikarnassos' in PW.   5 Strabo XIV, 7, 23 (659).
6 Diod. XV, 90; Vitruv. II, 8, 11.
7 Strabo XIII, 1, 59 (611), εὐανδρησάντων.   8 Strabo *ib.*
9 The earlier Parthian kings seem for a time to have made Hecatompylos their capital, but whether it was Seleucus' foundation or the older Median town seems uncertain.

a Greek element, it was essentially a Carian town. What happened after him is not material here.

Halicarnassus then does nothing to prove Bickermann's case. His second instance, Gryneion (p. 360), does even less. He says that the people of Gryneion, 'ville éolienne', were sold as slaves like the Tyrians. So they apparently were; but it was done by Philip's general Parmenion in his capacity as commander of Philip's expeditionary force, and has nothing to do with Alexander, whether at the moment (we do not know) Philip was still alive or not;[1] Parmenion was still exercising his independent command, for as soon as Alexander was in the saddle he recalled him, for other reasons. That is decisive, and it is hardly necessary to consider what sort of a place Gryneion was. It had been a Greek πόλις once, one of the eleven Aeolian cities of Herodotus;[2] but it is known that many Greek settlements in Aeolis failed,[3] and Gryneion was one of the places which after Salamis Xerxes presented to Gongylus of Eretria.[4] He must have lost it, for it subsequently appears as one of the numerous little places which in the Athenian tribute-lists of the Confederacy of Delos were assessed at 1,000 drachmae, practically the lowest assessment known.[5] At the end of the century, when Athens' arm weakened, Gongylus' younger son recovered it, and Xenophon found him in possession of both Myrina and Gryneion.[6] The Athenian assessment shows that in the fifth century Gryneion had lost whatever importance it may have had, except for its temple; Strabo calls it a πολίχνιον of Myrina,[7] and Pliny refers to it as a 'has-been';[8] it is difficult to suppose that, when Parmenion took it, it had more than a Greek nucleus. The fact that it had a famous temple of a pre-Hellenic Anatolian god, Graecised as Apollo, with an old (ἀρχαῖον)

---

1 Diod. XVII, 7, 9. He leaves it uncertain whether Philip was actually still alive or not, and there is no other evidence.
2 Herod. I, 149.
3 Strabo XIII, 3, 6 (622). See Wilamowitz, *Der Glaube der Hellenen*, I, p. 81.
4 Xen. *Hell.* III, 1, 6.
5 These lists were conveniently collected in *S.E.G.* v; see now B. D. Meritt, H. T. Wade-Gery, and M. F. Macgregor, *The Athenian Tribute Lists*, I (1939). The lists give no help as to whether a place was Greek, semi-Greek, or native; but they are conclusive for its relative importance or unimportance at the time.
6 Xen. *Hell.* III, 1, 6, cf. *Anab.* VII, 8, 8. Unfortunately in *Hell.* III, 1, Xenophon gives little indication of what towns in Aeolis were Greek and what native; he calls every inhabited place a πόλις indiscriminately.
7 Strabo XIII, 3, 5 (622).
8 Pliny V, 121, 'Fuit et Grynia'.

oracle,[1] has no bearing on the matter, for the temple must have had its own separate organisation.

Bickermann's third instance is merely that Alexander *meant* to destroy Lampsacus, for which he cites Pausanias' story,[2] there being no other evidence. The story is that the people of Lampsacus sent their fellow-citizen Anaximenes, the historian, to plead for them; Alexander meant to destroy Lampsacus and, when he found out why Anaximenes had come, swore that he would refuse whatever he asked, whereon Anaximenes said 'Destroy Lampsacus'. Did Alexander cross the Hellespont to play at children's games? The story is only one of the many fables so common in the Alexander-story. The form of Pausanias' previous sentence implies that Lampsacus set up Anaximenes' statue at Olympia in his honour as an *historian*; it is clear that there was nothing on the statue-base to say that he had once saved Lampsacus, for Pausanias disconnects that story from the statue.

There is then no evidence for the statement that in Asia Alexander destroyed some Greek cities. Ehrenberg, however (*op. cit.* p. 15), who has adopted these stories from Bickermann to illustrate Alexander's way of dealing with 'refractory' cities, has added a fourth case, Tralles, merely because, after Halicarnassus fell, Alexander is said to have sent his siege-train to Tralles (which had in fact joined him of itself).[3] He was bound to send his siege-train to Tralles; it was the nearest station to Halicarnassus on the Royal Road which Parmenion was to follow with the siege- and baggage-trains while he himself with a flying column went southward.

Bickermann's second argument (p. 349) for his thesis that Alexander treated Greeks like Asiatics is that Greek cities were subject to Alexander's satraps. There is no mention anywhere of such a thing, and it has always been supposed that they were not; and there is a piece of evidence which is conclusive that they were not, the case of Aspendus.[4] Aspendus was traditionally a foundation of Argos,[5] a strong and populous place; it was a Greek city, and Alexander treated it as such, but, like most places in Pamphylia, it must have contained a native element; even in the third century it easily admitted aliens to citizenship.[6] It also

---

1 Strabo XIII, 3, 5 (622); for the temple see also *O.G.I.S.* 229, l. 85, 266, l. 18; Welles, *Royal Correspondence*, no. 57, l. 32; Jessen, 'Gryneios' in PW.

2 Paus. VI, 18, 2 = Jacoby II, no. 72 (Anaximenes), T. 6. The words ὑπελείπετο δὲ 'Αναξιμένης τοσάδε ἐς μνήμην do not mean that the story was Anaximenes' own, and Jacoby does not include it among the fragments.

3 Arr. I, 18, 1.   4 Arr. I, 26, 2–27, 4.   5 Strabo XIV, 4, 2 (667).

6 For this inscription see A. Wilhelm, *Neue Beiträge*, IV, p. 61; M. Segre, *Aegyptus*, XIV, 1934, p. 253.

contained a pro-Persian element, and was rearing a stud of horses for Darius. The people made an agreement with Alexander (ξυνθέμενοι), which they broke after he passed on; he returned, they submitted to mercy, and he punished them by putting them back into the position they had occupied under Persian rule: they were subjected to his satrap and the φόρος was reimposed. If Greek cities generally had been subject to his satraps, this would not have been a punishment; it would have been the normal course,[1] and would have been done on his first visit; also he could not have made a συνθήκη with a subject city.

Bickermann, however (p. 350), claims to find express evidence of a Greek city being subject to a satrap of Alexander's in a well-known inscription;[2] he does not consider the inscription, but merely states as a fact that in 326/5 the Greek city of Gambreion formed part of the Lydian satrapy, though the most certain thing about this inscription is that it does not mention Gambreion, which moreover is not in Herodotus' list of the Greek cities of Aeolis. As, however, the stone was found at Gambrei, Gambreion *is* probably the city in question, though there is no certainty; and though the Caïcus valley, in which Gambreion stood, was more usually reckoned to the Mysian satrapy, it *could* have been at this time in the Lydian, of which Menander was satrap, for the boundary between the two satrapies is known to have varied at different times.[3] Xenophon says that in his day Gambreion was under the rule of a renegade Greek, to whose father Xerxes had presented it;[4] but as Xenophon calls every place in Aeolis, Greek or native, a πόλις, this throws no light on its quality. But if it be the town of the inscription in question, we must suppose that by Alexander's day it ranked as a Greek πόλις, as it did a century later;[5] for it seems certain that the inscription does refer to some Greek πόλις, whatever it was. It is a lease by one private person to another of a piece of land, locality unknown, dated in the eleventh year of Alexander, Menander being

1 Heuss, *op. cit.* p. 20 n. 2, saw this obvious fact, as did Bengtson, *Philol.* 92, 1937, p. 140 n. 56. It is not answered by Ehrenberg, *op. cit.* p. 15 n. 1. Subsequently, however, Bengtson in *Die Strategie in der hellenistischen Zeit*, I, 1937, p. 216, said that Alexander in his 'last years' put the Greek cities of Asia Minor under satraps, a statement copied from Bickermann.

2 Ditt.³ 302. There is a misprint in Bickermann's references, p. 349 n. 1.

3 See Ernst Meyer, *Die Grenzen der hellenistischen Staaten in Kleinasien*, 1925, pp. 2 *sq.*, 8 *sq.* There may be confirmation of an extended Lydia at this time in Arrian I, 17, 7: Menander's predecessor Asander was satrap Λυδίας καὶ τῆς ἄλλης τῆς Σπιθριδάτου ἀρχῆς; for if τῆς ἄλλης meant only Ionia, one would have expected the formula already used in I, 12, 8, Σπιθριδάτης ὁ Λυδίας καὶ Ἰωνίας σατράπης.

4 Xen. *Hell.* III, 1, 6.   5 Ditt.³ 1219.

satrap and Isagoras prytanis.[1] Prof. Rostovtzeff showed long ago that it was a lease of King's Land;[2] and as all King's Land belonged to Alexander and was under his satrap, the transaction was properly and completely dated by Alexander's regnal year. But why the dating by Isagoras also? At a later time, the eponymous magistrate of many Greek cities in Asia was called prytanis, and there are at least two cases of this in Aeolian Greek cities just after Alexander's death;[3] Isagoras then was eponymous magistrate of some Greek city, whether Gambreion or another. What could a Greek city have had to do with a transaction in King's Land? Only one answer is possible: Gambreion must have been the registration centre for the district in which lay the piece of land leased. There is no direct evidence that the Persian empire had a system of land registration, though it must have had, for it could never have been managed without one;[4] and Alexander must have retained in substance the Persian system, as he did the Persian satraps, for he can have had no time in his brief life to set up a new system; that was left for the Seleucids to do, though there is no need to discuss here how far their system[5] was the Persian system and how far modified by themselves.

This lease, therefore, does not show that a Greek city was subject to Alexander's satrap.

Bickermann's last reason (p. 349) is that Alexander dealt with Greek cities in Asia as his personal possession; the sole evidence adduced for this statement is the story,[6] given by Plutarch and Aelian, that Alexander offered to give to Phocion one of four cities in Asia, whichever he might choose. Neither writer calls them *Greek* cities; this addition, 'ces villes grecques', is Bickermann's own. Whether or no this story be an echo of Artaxerxes' alleged gift of the *revenues* of certain towns to Themistocles (which does at least make sense, Themistocles being on the spot), or an echo of Xerxes' gifts of land and towns to Demaratus

---

1 Βασιλεύοντος Ἀλεξάνδρου, ἔτει ἐνδεκάτωι, Μενάνδρου σατραπεύοντος, ἐπὶ πρυτάνιος Ἰσαγόρου.

2 M. Rostowzew, *Studien zur Gesch. des römischen Kolonats*, 1910, p. 267.

3 *O.G.I.S.* 2, l. 37 (Mitylene), 8, l. 103 (Eresus); later in Ephesus, Colophon, Methymna, Teos, Temnos, Pergamum, Phocaea. Note how in the case of the letter of Antigonus I to the Eresians (*O.G.I.S.* 8, l. 103) the Eresians, who were not his subjects, put on their official copy their own dating, Πρότανις Μελίδωρος, for convenience of reference.

4 See Rostovtzeff, *Soc. and Econ. Hist.* p. 1033.

5 W. L. Westermann, *Class. Phil.* XVI, 1921, p. 12; Rostovtzeff in *C.A.H.* VII, p. 167, and *Seleucid Babylonia*, p. 71; Tarn, *Hell. Civ.*², p. 121. See *O.G.I.S.* 225.

6 Plut. *Phocion*, XVIII; Aelian, *V.H.* ĭ, 25.

of Sparta and Gongylus of Eretria,[1] it is certainly both untrue and foolish, for to give a town in Asia to a citizen of Athens resident in Athens has not, and cannot have, any meaning; and quite apart from that, Alexander is never recorded to have given so much as an estate in Asia, however small, to any of his Macedonian friends or generals, let alone to a Greek, though this was done by later rulers. I propose, however, to examine this story; this will show that it is a demonstrably late invention, and will, I hope, throw even more light on Bickermann's 'Greek' cities than has already been done.

The four towns in Plutarch's list are Elaia, Gergithos, Kios, and Mylasa; Aelian substitutes Patara for Gergithos. It will be seen that the first three in Plutarch's list (I have rearranged his order) belong to what in Achaemenid times was Mysia, while Mylasa was far away in Caria, and conditions in the two countries differed considerably; Carians easily became hellenised and intermarried with Greeks—Herodotus, and perhaps Themistocles,[2] had Carian mothers and there was plenty of Carian blood in Miletus—while Mysians apparently did not; the numerous small Greek settlements in Mysia often came to little on account of native pressure (Strabo XIII, 622 says there were once about thirty, but 'not a few' had died out), and after the destruction of Smyrna Cyme was the only one of importance. There was evidently more than one version of the Phocion story, and the original presumably gave four places all together and therefore in Mysia, the name Mylasa having become substituted later for some other name, as e.g. Myrleia; but I will take Plutarch's story as it stands.

ELAIA was not Greek at all; it is not, as from its position if a Greek settlement it must have been, in Herodotus' list (I, 149) of the Greek cities of Aeolis, and in the Athenian tribute-lists of the Confederacy of Delos already noticed it is more usually, though not always, referred to as 'Ελαία παρά Μύριναν, which shows its unimportance; it was one of a number of little places, some unknown, which were assessed for tribute at (practically) the lowest figure, 1,000 drachmae; many of the towns and places, like the tribes, in these lists are not Greek, but the lists do not distinguish. It was practically unknown till the Attalids made it the port of Pergamum and began to hellenise it; their acquisition of the place cannot be earlier than Eumenes I (263–241),[3] and its enlargement[4] must, like that of Pergamum, be essentially due to Attalus I.

1 Xen. *Hell.* III, 1, 6.   2 The famous epitaph, however, calls her Thracian.
3 Ernst Meyer, *op. cit.* p. 97.
4 Strabo XIII, 3, 5 (622), λιμένα ἔχουσαν καὶ ναύσταθμον τῶν 'Ατταλικῶν βασιλέων.

Like many other places when they began to become hellenised, it took
to itself a foundation legend from the heroic world: it was founded by
Menestheus, who led the Athenian contingent against Troy,[1] and whose
name, in compliment to Athens, thus appears at both ends of the
Mediterranean.[2]

No *polis* named GERGITHOS ever existed. Herodotus (v, 22) knew
of an Anatolian people or tribe called Gergithes, who lived in Aeolis;
Strabo amplifies this by saying that their town, called after the Persian
fashion αἱ Γέργιθες, 'the Gergithes', was in the territory of Cyme, where
in his day there was still a place (τόπος) called Gergithion.[3] Prior to
Xerxes' reign the Gergithes went northward[4] and occupied a stretch of
country between Ilium and Lampsacus, part of the tribe being ultimately
in the territory of each city;[5] when Xerxes went from Ilium to Abydos
he passed on his left Rhoeteum and Dardanus and on his right the
Gergithes.[6] Here they built a town, which they fortified; Xenophon
calls it indifferently τὴν Γέργιθα or τὴν τῶν Γεργιθίων πόλιν (*Hell.*
III, 1, 15, 19, 22); Strabo shows it was not a πόλις, a term used indiscriminately by Xenophon for every inhabited place. This is where the
tribe was in Alexander's day; but Attalus I destroyed their town there
(Strabo calls it a χωρίον) and moved the people to the head of the
Caïcus valley, where he settled them in a village or native town (κώμη)
which became known as Gergitha.[7]

KIOS probably *was* a Greek settlement at the start, for Pliny (v, 144)
says that Miletus founded it as an outlet for the Phrygian trade. But it
disappointed expectations, and in the fifth century was both small and
barbarised (which does not mean that no Greeks remained there, but
that they had been swamped by the natives); in the Athenian tribute-
lists it is one of the many insignificant places assessed at 1,000 drachmae,

1 Strabo XIII, 3, 5 (622).
2 In Spain, Strabo III, 1, 9 (140); in South Italy, VI, 1, 10 (261).
3 Strabo XIII, 1, 19 (589).
4 'Went northward': this follows from the subsequent notes and from
  Strabo XIII, 1, 19 (589), who says they came from the Gergithes of Cyme.
  As the *name* remained in Cyme's territory, some part of the tribe may
  have remained behind.
5 Ilium: ἡ Γεργιθία (χώρα) in Ilium's territory, *O.G.I.S.* 221, II, l. 24 (with
  Dittenberger's note 7, which must be right)=Welles, *op. cit.* no. 10, l. 6.
  Lampsacus: in Strabo's day, XIII, 1, 19 (589), there was still a place, τόπος,
  called Γεργίθιον in Lampsacus' territory. Of course city territories might
  vary at different times.
6 Herod. VII, 43. The map to ch. II in A. H. M. Jones, *Cities of the Eastern
  Roman Provinces*, 1937, puts them *south* of Ilium, which must be a slip.
7 Strabo XIII, 1, 70 (616).

and Herodotus calls it 'Mysian Kios',[1] which, as no other Kios is known, means that it had become a Mysian town. All through Alexander's reign it was in the hands of a Persian dynast, Mithridates, uncle of the founder of the kingdom of Pontus, who ruled there from 337 to 302.[2] While he lived, the place was never in the Hellespontine (formerly Mysian) satrapy; this is shown by the fact that when in 318 Antigonus drove out the satrap of that satrapy, Arrhidaeus, he fled for refuge to Kios, i.e. to Mithridates.[3] Subsequently, Mithridates became Antigonus' vassal,[4] and the town, which he had presumably enlarged, in due course became hellenised and of more consequence, and in the usual way adopted as its founder either Heracles[5] or his companion Kios;[6] but Alexander never had anything to do with Kios, and it was never his to give away, had he so wished.

MYLASA in Caria was in the fifth century B.C. a purely Carian village, distinguished as a centre of the Carian religion; it had an old shrine of the Carian Zeus common to three tribes, Carians, Lydians, and Mysians, in which no other peoples participated.[7] In the troubles of the Ionian revolt, the Carians, hearing that a Persian column meant to attack 'their cities', ambushed and destroyed it under the lead of a man of Mylasa, showing again that Mylasa was a Carian community.[8] It never in fact even acquired a Greek foundation legend of the usual type. As regards the fourth century, Strabo has a good deal to say about the place; he calls it a κώμη,[9] a word he correctly uses to mean, not only a village, but a native town which had no *polis* organisation; it was the birthplace and seat (βασίλειον) of the Carian satrap Hecatomnus,[10] father of the Mausolus who transferred the βασίλειον to Halicarnassus.[11] It has been claimed that in Mausolus' time the larger Carian towns, at any rate, were 'completely hellenised', and in support of this a well-known inscription from Mylasa,[12] containing three decrees ranging from 367–366 to 353–352, has been cited as having been 'passed in full constitutional form and recorded in Greek'.[13] I am afraid that in fact these documents show the exact opposite. They reveal no trace of a

---

1 Herod. v, 122, Κῖος ἡ Μυσίη.
2 Diod. xx, 111, 4; see Ernst Meyer, *op. cit.* pp. 157 *sqq.* and Beloch, *Gr. Gesch.*[2] IV, 2, pp. 214 *sq.*
3 Diod. XVIII, 72, 2.   4 Diod. xx, 111, 4.
5 Heracles κτίστης on coins.   6 Strabo XII, 4, 3 (564).
7 Herod. I, 171; Strabo XIV, 2, 23 (659). It had not even a town-name; it was τὰ Μύλασα.
8 Herod. v, 121.   9 Strabo *ib.*   10 Strabo *ib.*
11 See p. 218 *ante* on the incompatibility of βασίλειον and πόλις.
12 Ditt.[3] 167.   13 A. H. M. Jones, *op. cit.* p. 30.

polis organisation; they record decrees, but these are dated, not by any city magistrate, but by the year of Artaxerxes the king, 'Mausolus being satrap'; the decrees are passed by the Mylaseans in *ecclesia*, but no proposer is named, as he must have been in a Greek decree; all the proper names are Carian, and, above all, a decree of the *ecclesia* is not valid until ratified by 'the three tribes', presumably the Carians, Lydians, and Mysians who shared the temple. What we really have here is an interesting glimpse of the developing native organisation of a Carian town; it is known from the case of Sardis[1] that a large native Anatolian town had some method of holding meetings and passing resolutions or 'decrees', but the method by which such an *ecclesia* was constituted is unknown. Any one who doubts that these decrees of Mylasa belong to a Carian town should compare with them a decree of the neighbouring Greek city of Iasos,[2] evoked by the same occurrence and passed about the same time in similar circumstances. Iasos, too, was subject to Artaxerxes and to the satrap Mausolus, but its decree is totally different; it is passed by βουλή and δῆμος in the usual form and dated not by the king but by the eponymous Greek magistrate of the city; it names all the usual Greek magistracies and their holders, and there are tribes and prytanies with long lists of Greek names. Of course there is the fact that the Mylasa documents are written in Greek; but what this shows is, not that Mylasa was a Greek πόλις, but that hellenisation was (as is known) beginning in Mausolus' satrapy. Mausolus has often been treated as a helleniser before Alexander, and we may here have an instance, but no one who is familiar with the fortunes of the Greeks in inner Asia later will attach too much importance to the use of Greek in official documents; it was the first thing any native town did when it started to hellenise itself or to be hellenised by some ruler,[3] and there are cases enough of the use of Greek, which was a conquering tongue, in places where there can have been no Greeks to speak of.[4] In

1 Ditt.[3] 273.   2 Ditt.[3] 169.

3 A good instance is the decree of Anisa in Cappadocia, Michel 546, on which see Fr. Cumont, *Rev. E.A.* xxxiv, 1932, p. 135 and *C.A.H.* xi, p. 608; Tarn, *Bactria and India*, p. 19; M. Rostovtzeff, *Soc. and Econ. Hist.* pp. 840, 1533 n. 120 (with further literature).

4 Beside the well-known phenomena from Parthia—the Avroman leases, coin legends, and other documents—I will cite here two Greek documents from Georgia, which was quite outside the Greek sphere. One, *C.I.L.* iii, 6052, from Mexeta (Tiflis), of Vespasian's time, has long been known; the other is a substantial funerary inscription in Greek and Georgian from Armazi near Tiflis, third quarter of the second century A.D.: G. Tseretheli, *A bilingual inscription from Armazi*, Bulletin of the Marr Institute of

the reign of Antiochus I or II a synoecism took place at Mylasa[1] (it was probably then that it became a Greek *polis*), and in due course we reach the marble-built πόλις ἀξιόλογος known to Strabo;[2] but all this has nothing to do with Alexander.

I need not pause over Aelian's PATARA. It was a Lycian town of the Lycian League, first hellenised, how far is not known, by Ptolemy II.[3]

It is now self-evident that the date of the Phocion story is much later than Alexander's time; for that story presupposes, first that the name Elaia was, at the least, generally known, which shows that it cannot have originated earlier than the reign of Attalus I, and secondly that the position of Kios in Alexander's reign had been completely forgotten, which might make it even later. It was pure invention; there may once have been more versions than the two now extant.

Such are the four 'Greek' cities which, according to Bickermann, Alexander dealt with as his personal possession. But I am afraid that any town is what he wants it to be at the moment. Besides those already noticed, on p. 363 Mallos is a Greek city (descendants of Argives); on p. 364 it is a native Cilician town. On p. 349 Mylasa is a Greek city; on p. 369 it is contrasted with a Greek city, Priene, as being 'une ville provinciale'. On p. 369 the Greek Aspendus in Pamphylia becomes 'ces Pisidiens'; on p. 371 the κατοικία Naulochos in Priene's territory is 'une ville libre du royaume asiatique', after he has spent many pages in declaring that there was no such thing.

At the end of the article Bickermann brings in the Seleucids and the notorious remark of Antiochus III,[4] so often misunderstood; this need not be considered here, for what any Seleucid did is no evidence for Alexander, with whom alone I am concerned. I have been through this article in great detail, partly because those who have accepted it have added no fresh arguments, but chiefly because the questions raised are vital for our conception of Alexander; I need not say more than that its failure to prove its thesis is complete.

Languages, History, and Material Culture, XIII, 1942 (in Georgian with a shortened English translation); M. N. Tod, *J.R.S.* XXXIII, 1943, p. 82. Gems with Greek inscriptions have also been found at Armazi: Tsereteli, *op. cit.* pp. 69 *sq.*

1 For this inscription see Ernst Meyer, *op. cit.* p. 128, and for the date L. Robert, *Rev. E.A.* XXXVI, 1934, p. 525.

2 Strabo XIV, 2, 22–3 (658–9).   3 Strabo *ib.*

4 Livy XXXIII, 38, 6; better given, Polyb. XVIII, 51, 9, τυγχάνειν τῆς ἐλευθερίας ... διὰ τῆς αὐτοῦ χάριτος.

II. The League of Corinth

Were the Greek cities on the mainland of Asia Minor joined to the League of Corinth or not?

There is no express evidence for any single city, but the argument from silence means little. No one has ever supposed that the semi-Greek cities in Pamphylia and Cilicia became members of the League; but there would be no difficulty in supposing that it applied only to the cities of the Aegean seaboard, facing old Greece. It could be argued that the reason why there was no treaty of συμμαχία between Alexander and any of these Greek cities was because all were taken up into a greater συμμαχία, the League; but I think the real reason was the one I have already given, that Alexander was sure of the democracies in any case and all his thought was directed to the war.

The arguments for the inclusion of the Greek cities of the mainland in the League were best given by Wilcken.[1] Berve, who followed him, set them out neatly under four heads, with some supplements of his own;[2] I will just run through his four heads.

(1) These cities had ἐλευθερία, αὐτονομία, and freedom from φόρος; so had the cities of the League; therefore these cities were in the League. This is obviously no argument; it would have made every free Greek city from Sicily to the Euxine a member.

(2) Chios was in the League,[3] and was very near the mainland coast. If that coast had not been League territory, the traitors from Chios, who were only exiled from League territory, had an easy refuge close at hand. Some have seen much force in this; I fear I cannot. The escaped traitor would have to take refuge either in a city, which would not risk war with Alexander by declining to hand him over, or in the country, where the satrap of Lydia could pick him up if it seemed worth while. And in fact, under the Peace of Antalcidas, Chios and the adjacent mainland had already, before Alexander, once belonged to two very different political systems.

1 U. Wilcken, *S.B. Berlin*, XVI, 1922, pp. 105 *sqq*. Wilcken, however, was afterwards convinced by Ehrenberg's study, and agreed that they were not in the League: *S.B. Berlin*, XXVIII, 1938, p. 302 n. 5.

2 Berve I, p. 250.

3 Ditt.³ 283. I have not been convinced by Ehrenberg's long argument to the contrary, *op. cit.* pp. 23–9; the inscription is clear enough on this point, though some have managed to disbelieve it. Alexander's title βασιλεύς has no more to do with the matter than British allusions to 'Kaiser Wilhelm' or 'the Kaiser' in 1914–18; what else could Alexander call himself or the Chians call him?

(3) is the *pompe* of Ptolemy II, the real argument, which I shall come to; and (4) turns on Philoxenus, whose position has been more misunderstood than that of any other figure in the Alexander-story; I have explained his real office, stated clearly enough in our sources, in App. 3. What Berve says is that the superintendence of the internal relationships of two sets of communities, the mainland cities and the Island Greeks, the latter of whom were in the League, was exercised by the same official, Philoxenus; therefore the mainland cities were probably in the League also. But the only evidence he can produce for this supposed position of Philoxenus is two worthless stories, dealt with in App. 3, which have no chance of being true; and his theory shatters both on Philoxenus' real position and on the powers and duties of Antipater, for which see p. 202 n. 4.

Against the inclusion of the mainland cities in the League I may refer to the very long argument in Ehrenberg's study already cited. I am not going through it, for I am not arguing that they *were* included; the part relating to the *pompe* of Ptolemy II will be noticed presently. But the study is not conclusive, though Wilcken thought otherwise; and, apart from its refinements in the matter of the Island Greeks, which I cannot accept, it is spoilt by the author's belief in Bickermann's 'important discovery', which is mixed up with the question of the League.

I turn to the *pompe* of Ptolemy II, described by Callixenus;[1] whether my date, 279–278, or Otto's, 271–270, be correct—one of the two it must be—is immaterial here. What is material is that the *pompe* was quite certainly a *triumph*,[2] and as such would be expected to refer to past events and not to future ones; and what has to be considered here is the appearance in the procession of a figure of the city of Corinth wearing a golden diadem and standing on a wheeled platform which was followed by women representing 'the cities of Ionia and the other Greek cities of Asia and the Islands, as many as had been under Persian rule'.[3] On the same wheeled platform with Corinth were figures of

1 Athen. v, 197 c *sqq.*
2 W. Otto, *Beiträge zur Seleukidengeschichte*, 1928, pp. 6 *sqq.*, *Zeit. d. 6 Ptolemäers*, 1934, p. 83 n. 6; Tarn, *Hermes* LXV, 1930, p. 447 n. 2, *J.H.S.* LIII, 1933, pp. 59 *sq.*; F. Caspari, *Hermes* LXVIII, 1933, p. 407; E. Kornemann, *Die Alexandergesch. d. K. Ptolemaios I*, 1935, p. 225 n. 22; cf. Tarn, *Bactria and India*, p. 194.
3 Athen. v, 201 D, Κόρινθος δ' ἡ πόλις παρεστῶσα τῷ Πτολεμαίῳ ἐστεφάνωτο διαδήματι χρυσῷ... τῇ δὲ τετρακύκλῳ ταύτῃ ἠκολούθουν γυναῖκες ἔχουσαι ἱμάτια πολυτελῆ καὶ κόσμον· προσηγορεύοντο δὲ πόλεις, αἵ τε ἀπ' Ἰωνίας καὶ ⟨αἱ⟩ λοιπαὶ Ἑλληνίδες ὅσαι τὴν Ἀσίαν καὶ τὰς νήσους κατοικοῦσαι ὑπὸ τοὺς Πέρσας ἐτάχθησαν.

Alexander and Ptolemy I, and two gods, Priapus and Arete, whose meaning is obscure. The single MS. of Athenaeus describes Corinth as παρεστῶσα τῷ Πτολεμαίῳ, for which Wilamowitz conjectured παρεστῶσα τῷ Ἀλεξάνδρῳ. Wilcken in 1922, adopting this conjecture and taking the passage to mean that the Greek cities of Asia were following Alexander and Corinth, thought that this must mean that in Alexander's reign these cities belonged to the League of Corinth, though he felt it strange that Ptolemy II should be alluding to such a long-past political combination. The belief that the reference is to the League of Corinth has been followed by several writers; were it so, *cadit quaestio*. But Ehrenberg must be right in his view[1] that there is no reference to the League of Corinth. Certainly he begins his examination with a mistake in his reconstruction of the position of the figures on the wheeled platform (see the plan on his p. 7); it is certain from Athenaeus' παρεστῶσα that Corinth stood *beside* (i.e. had some intimate connection with) either Ptolemy or Alexander, while he makes her stand in a back row *behind* Alexander, which is not only wrong but meaningless. But he has done service in pointing out that, as Athenaeus says, the women who represented the Greek cities were not following either Alexander (as Wilcken took it) or Ptolemy, but the wheeled platform on which they two and Corinth stood; and that seems to justify him (p. 8) in saying that the *pompe* cannot settle the question of how Alexander dealt with and organised the 'released Greek cities', though I should hardly agree with his positive conclusion that the passage under examination shows 'the general tendency to connect the house of the Ptolemies, as whose protagonist Alexander figured here as elsewhere, with the Greek world, with the mother country, with the Islands, and with the cities of Asia Minor'. Long ago I referred to this figure of Corinth as symbolic of the headship of the Greek world;[2] but this concept depended on the figure referring (as I then thought and said) both to the League of Corinth in the past and to the plans of the Ptolemies for the future, and I should hardly maintain this to-day either.

For there is one item in Callixenus' account to which neither I nor, as far as I know, anyone else has ever paid proper attention: Corinth wears the diadem.[3] This can only mean that Corinth was, or symbolised, a Sovereign State.[4] But that was not true of 'present day'; whether in

1 *Op. cit.* pp. 2–8.   2 Tarn, *Antigonos Gonatas*, 1913, p. 371.
3 Athen. V, 201 D, ἐστεφάνωτο διαδήματι χρυσῷ.
4 The diadem symbolised sovereignty, and Corinth's diadem had nothing to do with the turreted mural crown which later became the distinguishing sign of the Fortune of a city; the figure in the *pompe* was not the Fortune

279–278 or 271–270, Corinth was merely a garrison town of Antigonus Gonatas. It was not true of the past; Alexander's League of Corinth was not a State at all, let alone a Sovereign State; it was only a confederacy of States. And it cannot refer to the future; for whatever the exact aim of the Ptolemies—of that policy of Ptolemy I, Ptolemy II, and Arsinoe II, which culminated in the Chremonidean war—it was certainly not to make of some Greek combination a Sovereign State alongside of their own. So far as I can see, therefore, Callixenus' reference to Corinth is an insoluble crux, which cannot be used to prove or disprove anything unless or until someone shall find a convincing explanation of Corinth's diadem. I have none to offer myself.

So far, then, those who believe that Alexander joined the Greek cities of Asia Minor to the League of Corinth have failed to prove their point. Those who believe that he did not have failed also, but then they do not require to prove anything; the burden of proof lies on their opponents. But there are three things yet to notice which seem to me to invite us to accept the negative view. One is that the cities of the League had to, and did, furnish contingents of troops for the war, while the cities in Asia Minor furnished no troops. The second is that Antipater, Alexander's deputy in the Presidency of the League, though responsible (seemingly) for the safety of the islands of the Aegean (p. 202 n. 4 *ante*), had no authority on the mainland of Asia. And the third is the general course of the history after Alexander's death. When he died, the League cities of old Greece at once tore up the Covenant of the League of Corinth and formed a new Hellenic League, with which they fought the Hellenic (Lamian) war; but we hear nothing throughout of any of the cities of Asia Minor. Later, Antigonus I and his son Demetrius, who acted politically as one person, got enough control to re-form the League of Corinth, with Demetrius in Alexander's seat; and, though Antigonus claimed to stand in Alexander's place and imitated his measures, the Greek cities of Asia Minor were not included in the new League, though Antigonus and his son were in a position to include them had they wished. Instead, Antigonus founded in Asia Minor two very peculiar Leagues, the Ilian and the Ionian, to include the cities of Aeolis and Ionia. Some used to believe that these two Leagues were creations of Alexander's; it is certain that they were not. For *three* of these peculiar Leagues, all strongly resembling one another

of Corinth but Κόρινθος ἡ πόλις. When Miss P. Zancan, *Il monarcato ellenistico*, 1934, p. 12, called Corinth's diadem *diadema turrito* she was mixing up two quite different things.

and resembling nothing else in Greek history,[1] appear after Alexander's death—the Ilian, Ionian, and Island Leagues; and as it has long been quite certain that it was Antigonus and Demetrius who founded the League of the Islanders, Antigonus must also have founded the Ilian and Ionian Leagues, as the three cannot be separated. And if Alexander had brought the Greek cities of Aeolis and Ionia into the League of Corinth, Antigonus could not have gone back on that when Demetrius re-formed that League.

The probabilities then seem very strongly in favour of the view that the Greek cities of Asia Minor were not in the League of Corinth; I have accordingly adopted that view in this book.

I may conclude with one general remark, which applies to both parts (I and II) of this study. Much of the trouble has arisen from Continental scholars finding it impossible to believe that Alexander did not *organise* these cities in some way or other; the League of Corinth was an obvious guess, and if that was rejected there seemed nothing for it but Bickermann's theory that the cities were included in the general organisation of the Asiatic empire. But a Greek of the time would have seen nothing strange in these cities not being included in any organisation but being left as separate units; indeed, he would have thought it the natural thing, and I agree with him. We only have evidence from two war years, the first two; and Alexander had everything he wanted at the time if his friends in the individual cities were in power. What he might have done later, had he lived and been compelled, as he would have been compelled, to turn his mind seriously from conquest and exploration to administration, is useless speculation.

8. ALEXANDER'S FOUNDATIONS

I. The Cities generally

There is much more to say on this matter than can be found in the usual books. The difficulties of the subject are considerable, the margin of uncertainty often substantial, the sources of confusion numerous. The first of them is that almost every classical writer uses πόλις (or *oppidum*) for every kind of collection of dwellings; Strabo is less inaccurate than most, but even he can be bad enough; the only writer

---

1 I listed the chief peculiarities briefly in *Hell. Civ.*[2] 1930, p. 66. For details see Swoboda's *Staatsaltertümer*.

who can be relied on to use πόλις and other technical terms correctly is Isidore of Charax, because he is reproducing the Parthian survey. This has led, not only to extraordinary places being included among Alexander's cities, but to much confusion in regard to military colonies; these often grew into cities later, and later writers call them πόλεις because *in their own day* they were. The second is that, as time passed, the tendency to attribute to Alexander many things which he never did grew stronger and stronger till at the end, with the coming of Islam, it burst all bounds; probably hardly any Byzantine writer is worth anything here except Stephanus, who often preserved old material; even under the Roman Empire quite impossible places were attributed to Alexander, like Dion and Gerasa in Transjordania, or attributed themselves to him without any known reason, like Apollonia in Pisidia. A third source of trouble has been that no one who has written on the subject has understood that, as Alexander's cities in the East all had the same official name, Alexandria, there naturally grew up for daily use a series of popular names, or nicknames, which largely ousted the official names altogether from the literature we possess;[1] some lost official names have now been recovered from Oriental literatures, together with other valuable information, and more will doubtless come to light. There are also the difficulties that some cities which are recorded to have been ordered, or even begun, were probably never finished; that Alexander certainly intended, and in two cases at least (Alexandria Troas and Ilium) promised, to build or refound cities which had not been taken in hand when he died; and perhaps I may add the amount of corruption in the lists we possess. A few things are certain. The statement that he founded over seventy cities[2] is a gross exaggeration. The first city he built was the great Alexandria by Egypt. Every one of his cities was named Alexandria. And nearly all his cities were east of the Tigris. The reason is obvious. Between the Aegean and the Tigris he had plenty of existing cities, Greek, Phoenician, Syrian, Babylonian; between the Tigris and India hardly a couple. Of the three principal writers on this subject, Droysen,[3] in his famous Appendix, collected almost every scrap of material then known about every inhabited place which any one had ever connected with Alexander; it is still a useful corpus of references, and his outstanding ability occasionally made his judgement truer than that of his successors, in spite of the

1 I have explained the system of nicknames fully in *Bactria and India*, pp. 13–16.
2 Plutarch, *De Alexandri fortuna*, I, 328 E.
3 *Hellenismus* III, 2, pp. 189 *sqq.* (2nd German ed. 1877).

increase in knowledge since. Berve[1] is practically Droysen pruned and trimmed. Tscherikower[2] did good service by emphasising the importance of the military colony, and sometimes his criticism is valuable; but much has been learnt about the Farther East since he wrote. I did a good deal for some of the cities of the Farther East in *Bactria and India* and in a subsequent article on Alexandria-Termez,[3] but much remains to be done; Alexandria in Makarene, for example, has had to have a study to itself.[4] Both Berve and Tscherikower declined to consider that valuable Hellenistic document, the list of Alexandrias in the Alexander-Romance, which I hope to get on to its proper footing.

I take first those cities which are certain. There are six which, with whatever vicissitudes, are represented by towns to-day: Alexandria by Egypt, Alexandria in Aria (Herat), Alexandria in Arachosia (Ghazni), Alexandria in Margiane (Merv), Alexandria on the Oxus in Sogdiana (Termez), Alexandria Eschate on the Jaxartes (Chodjend). There are seven others which, though not represented by towns to-day, existed (or were represented) well down into Greek history: Alexandria in Susiana, twice refounded, at the then mouth of the Tigris, Alexandria-Prophthasia in Seistan, Alexandria-Bactra, Alexandria of the Caucasus, Alexandria Bucephala on the Jhelum, Alexandria Iomousa on the Chenab, and Alexandria in Makarene. It is curious that this number, thirteen, should be the number given for the original list in the Romance; but this is mere coincidence, for they are not the same thirteen. Two things will be noticed at once: that all these, except Alexandria in Egypt, are east of the Tigris, and that all bore the name Alexandria.

I must run through this list: Alexandria in Aria,[5] like Alexandria by Egypt, needs no comment.

Alexandria in Arachosia was certainly Ghazni, as Droysen saw, and not Candahar, as usually given since. I have dealt with this at length elsewhere.[6]

Alexandria in Margiane (Merv)[7] has often been doubted, and Berve omits it altogether; the reason has been that, in spite of the perfectly

1 *Alexanderreich* I, pp. 291 *sqq.*
2 V. Tscherikower, 'Die hellenistischen Städtegründungen von Alexander den Grossen bis auf die Römerzeit', *Philol. Supp.Bd.* XIX, Heft 1, 1927.
3 Tarn, 'Two Seleucid Studies: II. Tarmita', *J.H.S.* LX, 1940, p. 89. Referred to as 'Tarmita'.
4 Part II of this Appendix.
5 Isidore 15 (the Parthian survey); Strabo XI, 8, 9 (514), 10, 1 (516); XV, 2, 8 (723); Pliny VI, 61, 93. These writers show that it was not Artacoana.
6 Tarn, *Bactria and India*, pp. 470 *sq.* See p. 249 *post.*
7 Pliny VI, 47; the Syriac version of the Romance list (*post*).

plain evidence about the city, it is not recorded that Alexander was at Merv. This is immaterial; even if he were really never there in person, could he not give orders? I have considered the destruction and re-foundation (by Antiochus I) of Alexandria-Merv, and its place in a much larger story, in 'Tarmita' (p. 234 n. 3); but there are two points to add. One is that, as the early Seleucids never used the Alexander-name, and as no Macedonian ruler was active on the north-eastern marches between Alexander and Antiochus I (293–280 in the East), who refounded this city as an Antioch, the Alexander-name can only have got there through Alexander himself; the other is the explicit testimony of the Hellenistic Romance list to the existence of this Alexandria.

That Alexandria on the Oxus in Sogdiana, given by Claudius Ptolemy (VI, 12, 6), was the modern Termez, is a very recent discovery, the key having been supplied by the Tibetan translator of a Sanskrit work;[1] the native name of the place was Tarmita. The Alexandria there was destroyed when Alexandria-Merv was destroyed; it was refounded by Antiochus I as Antioch Tarmata or Tharmata at the same time as Antioch-Merv, and subsequently refounded by Demetrius of Bactria as a Demetrias; the native name, as was usual, finally came back again, medieval Termedh, modern Termez. I have given the complete story and references in my 'Tarmita'; I need only add that, now that this Alexandria is established, it can be recognised in the lists in Stephanus and the Romance (*post*), and is probably referred to in Plutarch, *Mor.* 328F, on which see part III of this Appendix. Possibly it will be detected elsewhere.

The foundation and completion of Alexandria on the Jaxartes are given by Arrian;[2] it was destroyed when the Alexandrias at Merv and Tarmita were destroyed and was rebuilt by Antiochus I as Antioch 'in Scythia', i.e. in 'Saca-land beyond Sogd'; for the story see my 'Tarmita'. I may note here, as it will recur, that Sogd was, properly speaking, not the whole of the *political* division known to Greeks as Sogdiana, but was the country between the Oxus and the mountains north of Samar-cand; the country between these mountains and the Jaxartes (Syr Daria), belonging to a different water-system, was to Persians 'Saca-land beyond Sogd', as on the Hamadan gold plate of Darius I,[3] but Greeks wrongly called it Scythia, hence the appearance of this Alexandria as

1 S. Lévi, *Journ. Asiatique*, 1933, p. 271 n. 1.
2 Arr. IV, 1, 3; 4, 1.
3 S. Smith, *J.R.A.S.* 1926, p. 435; E. Herzfeld, *Memoirs of the Arch. Survey of India*, XXXIV, 1928; Tarn, *Bactria and India*, Index, *s.v.* Sogd.

Alexandria 'in Scythia' in the Romance list, and that of Antioch 'in Scythia' noticed above.

Alexandria in Susiana at the mouth of the Tigris, successively an Antioch and the famous trading port Charax of Hyspaosines, requires no comment; details are given in the usual books.

Alexandria-Prophthasia on the Hamun lake in Seistan, subsequently the capital of that East Parthian realm of the Surens which finally attained to such extension and power under Gondofares, has been very fully treated by me elsewhere, to which I must refer.[1] The Alexander-name dropped out of Greek literature, but was preserved by Pan-ku in the *Ch'ien-han-shu* (Annals of the Former Han). A fresh examination of the passage in Plutarch (*Mor.* 328 F) which, alone in Greek literature, indicates this city's importance will be found in part III of this Appendix.

Alexandria-Bactra.[2] Again the Alexander-name, which shows that Alexander refounded Bactra as an Alexandria, would have dropped out of Greek literature but for Stephanus and the Romance list. It is given by Ssu-ma Ch'ien in the *Shi-ki*, chap. 123, and by Fan-ye in the *Hou-han-shu*.[3]

Alexandria of the Caucasus, known to the peoples about it as 'the Greek city',[4] is better known than any Alexandria except the Egyptian.[5] For its locality see App. 6 to my *Bactria and India*;[6] the evidence from literature is complete, but the excavation being carried on at Begram has still to speak.

Alexandria-Bucephala on the east bank of the Jhelum was important later as the capital of the Indo-Greek king Hippostratus,[7] and is mentioned as late as the *Periplus*. Those modern books which do not leave its position ambiguous all place it on the west bank, though every Alexander-historian we possess, with one exception, is indeterminate, merely saying that Nicaea and Bucephala stood one on each side of the river; the one exception, the Metz Epitome, places it on the east bank. I have not troubled to trace the origin of this modern error, copied by one writer from another for a long time, because it is immaterial, since Claudius Ptolemy is conclusive that it stood on the east bank. In VII, 1, 45 he gives a list, not complete, of towns between the Indus and

1 Tarn, *Bactria and India*, pp. 14 (not Farah), 49, 347 (O-ik-san-li), 482.
2 No. 11 in Stephanus' list (*post*).
3 The Chinese references are given in my *Bactria and India*, p. 115 n. 1.
4 Tarn, *Bactria and India*, p. 341; part III of this Appendix.
5 Its foundation, Arr. III, 28, 4; IV, 22, 4.
6 Cf. the remarks of Sir J. Marshall, *J.R.A.S.* 1941, p. 87.
7 Tarn, *Bactria and India*, pp. 318, 326 *sq.* But see Addenda.

the Jhelum, i.e. west of the Jhelum; he follows this in 46 and 47 with a list of the towns east of the Jhelum, between that river and the Jumna; his list, which runs from west to east, begins with Bucephala (on the Jhelum), Sagala (between Jhelum and Chenab) and Iomousa (on the Chenab), and ends with Mathurā (modern Muttra) on the Jumna. There is no doubt what he means, but in our text the sense has been obscured by the list beginning περὶ τὸν Βιδάσπην. So much I have given before,[1] but I did not indicate, as I should have done, that Ptolemy's meaningless περί is only a corruption in the text for παρά. Confusion of these two prepositions in later Greek is not uncommon; I gave a complicated instance of it in *Bactria and India*, p. 235 n. 1, and for another quite obvious case of περί displacing παρά in one of our texts see *post* (III, p. 259). Of course the towns of Ptolemy's list did not all lie *beside* the Jhelum; they were strung out from the Jhelum to the Jumna; but to say of a list of names that it was παρά (beside) a certain river, when in fact only one member of the list was, is a known usage; see Diod. XVIII, 5, 4 (the Gazetteer), where a string of satrapies are said to lie παρὰ τὸν Τάναϊν, though in fact only the first satrapy of the list, Sogdiana, did so.

For Alexandria-Iomousa see my *Bactria and India*, pp. 246 *sq.* But I was, I think, wrong to equate it with the Alexandria at the junction of the Chenab and the Indus on the strength of Ptolemy's co-ordinates, for several reasons: that town was only ordered to be built (Arr. VI, 15, 2) and it is not known that it was ever finished; the position is too far south for a genuine Greek city of the eastern Punjab; and Ptolemy's co-ordinates, always an uncertain guide in the East, slope the whole of his list progressively too far to the southward, till they bring Mathurā (Muttra), whose position is accurately known, almost down to the Vindhya mountains. Iomousa was probably the Alexandria on the upper Chenab, which *was* completed, Arr. V, 29, 3.

Last comes Alexandria in Makarene, a city which explains many things. The investigation here is of necessity a long one, and I have relegated it to part II of this Appendix.

These thirteen Alexandrias seem to be the only ones of which anything is really known. But before going on, the problem of Alexandria κατ' Ἴσσον in Syria, the modern Alexandretta, has to be considered. The formal evidence that this Alexandria was founded by Alexander is late and bad;[2] but it does not appear how else this city could have gôt there. That he did not found it after the battle of Issus is certain, and is

1 Tarn, *Bactria and India*, pp. 245 *sq.* and 245 n. 3, 246 n. 1.
2 It is all given in Droysen, *op. cit.* p. 200.

common ground to everybody; had he done so, it would have been the first city he founded and its foundation must have been mentioned, whereas it is certain, from the amount of story and legend which gathered about its foundation, that his first city was Alexandria by Egypt.[1] For he knew, while in Syria and Egypt, that he had not yet met the real strength of the Persian Empire, and till after Gaugamela he did not *know* that he could conquer it; but he knew that Egypt was practically impregnable, or could be made so, and he founded his city there to be (among other things) the capital of the empire he had already conquered. On the other hand, it is certain that Alexandria by Issus did not attribute itself to him in Roman times, for the name is Hellenistic, as is shown by its occurrence in Strabo[2] and the Romance list, which is Hellenistic (*post*); and that list supplies good, though not impeccable, evidence that it was founded by Alexander. The view that it was probably founded by Antigonus or Seleucus is impossible; neither they nor any Successor ever used the Alexander-name.[3] Berve merely says 'possibly Alexander's' but does not consider it. Droysen, who did consider it, naturally saw that it must be later than Gaugamela, and suggested that it was founded from Media, India, or Babylon, which at least makes sense. I can only see one possibility. After Gaugamela, Alexander sent Menes the Bodyguard from Susa to the coast to take charge of his sea-communications between Syria, Phoenicia, and Cilicia and Greece (App. 3, p. 176), and this was the occasion and purpose of its foundation, on Alexander's order. But this, though the only possible guess, is still a guess only; a satisfactory solution of the problem is not possible.

There were other Alexandrias, built or ordered, but there is little that can be made out about them. Alexandria-Nicaea on the west bank of the Jhelum, and Alexandria in Babylonia,[4] were certainly completed, and both appear in the Romance list, but that is all; it is just possible

1 So too Tscherikower, *op. cit.* p. 143, though qualified as 'die erste grosse Gründung'.
2 Strabo XIV, 5, 19 (676), in a list: Rhosos, Myriandros, Alexandria, Nicopolis, Mopsuestia.
3 Tscherikower, p. 59 says probably Antigonus or Seleucus; A. H. M. Jones, *Cities of the Eastern Roman Provinces*, 1937, p. 198, says probably Seleucus 'who Appian says founded many towns in honour of Alexander'. Appian *Syr.* 57 does not say 'many', but he does profess to give two, which show that his statement is a worthless blunder: one is a supposed Alexandropolis in India (see *post* on this form) and the other Alexandria Eschate on the Jaxartes.
4 Arr. VII, 21, 7.

that there is a later indication of the existence of Nicaea.[1] Two more Alexandrias in India were ordered or begun;[2] they never appear again, and if finished, which may be very doubtful, were probably swept away in Chandragupta's conquest. Alexandria in Carmania[3] certainly existed, and must have been Alexander's foundation; but the history of that province, so far as it can be recovered or guessed, centres entirely on the sea-port Harmozia-Zetis-Omana, precursor of the later Ormuz.[4] There may perhaps have been an Alexandria in Mygdonia,[5] but no connection with Alexander appears, and if it existed it had nothing to do with the battle of Gaugamela, which was not fought in Mygdonia. A 'city' in the Paropamisadae, one day distant from Alexandria of the Caucasus, is attributed to Alexander;[6] it can, at best, only have been a military settlement, whoever settled it; there was a good deal of settlement later in the Paropamisadae.[7] I have said quite enough elsewhere[8] about the absurdities given by Curtius, Justin, and others concerning the Indus Delta, including Pliny's delightful Xylinepolis (a native ξυλίνη πόλις), which took in Droysen, Berve and Tscherikower.

I come now to the problem of the name of Alexandria Troas, a city founded by Antigonus as an Antigoneia and then refounded by Lysimachus, who in modern works is generally said to have renamed it.[9]

1 Tarn, *Bactria and India*, p. 328.
2 One at the confluence of Chenab and Indus was ordered, Arr. VI, 15, 2. Of the second, in the country of the Sogdi, Arrian VI, 15, 4 says ἐτείχιзεν and νεωσοίκους ἐποίει—imperfects, not aorists.
3 Named in both Pliny VI, 107 and Ptolemy VI, 8, 14.
4 Tarn, *Bactria and India*, App. 12.
5 It depends solely on a very unsatisfactory passage in Pliny, VI, 42, where he mixes up Mygdonia and Arbelitis. Droysen, *op. cit.* pp. 208 *sq.*, argued for a foundation near Arbela after Gaugamela, but is not convincing. The Armenian version of the Romance list (*post*) gives an Alexandria ἐπὶ Μεσοποταμίας, which might be Alexandria in Mygdonia; but the whole question of this town is so confused that the verdict must be 'not proven'.
6 Diod. XVII, 83, 2, reading ἄλλην πόλιν with Florentinus for the absurd ἄλλας πόλεις. Diodorus is referring to the first foundation of Alexandria of the Caucasus, not to Alexander's invasion of India; so the place might have been the Νίκαιαν πόλιν (the name used proleptically) of Arr. IV, 22, 6. It is obvious that Alexander did not found another πόλις so close to Alexandria.
7 Tarn, *Bactria and India*, p. 99.   8 *Ib.* p. 244.
9 The material passage is Strabo XIII, 593; Lysimachus synoecised Ilium, ὅτε καὶ 'Αλεξανδρείας ἤδη ἐπεμελήθη, συνῳκισμένης ἤδη ὑπ' 'Αντιγόνου καὶ προσηγορευμένης 'Αντιγονείας, μεταβαλούσης δὲ τοὔνομα. μεταβαλούσης shows the city changed its name itself; ἐπεμελήθη here means refounded, it having just been used of Ilium where the refounding is described.

It is impossible to believe that *one* Successor, just *once*, used the Alexander-name, especially as elsewhere Lysimachus used his own, and, as a matter of fact, Strabo says nothing of the sort; he says that the city changed its name itself. How could it possibly do this? There is only one explanation. Alexander must have promised to found a city there (probably to refound an existing community) as he promised Ilium, but he did not live to do it. Antigonus did found it, but called it by his own name; the people felt cheated, and when Lysimachus refounded it he allowed them to take the name which they felt they ought to have had, the Alexander-name; it was good policy and good propaganda on his part. Strabo's own explanation, that it was felt, ἔδοξε (or that Lysimachus felt) that the Successors should use Alexander's name, is merely a faulty generalisation, whether on his part or on that of his source, from the real fact, viz. that *in this particular case* it was felt (or Lysimachus felt) that Antigonus should, *in the circumstances*, have used, or permitted the people to take, the Alexander-name. As to Alexander's promise, it is recorded that, when master of his Empire, he had made a similar promise to Ilium in writing;[1] and as Lysimachus attended to Alexandria Troas before Ilium, Alexander's promise to that community, though not recorded, is certain. Indeed one can say when it was made. For the promise is confirmed by the strange fact that the city is sometimes called Alexandria on the Granicus,[2] or 'in Granicus',[3] though the river Granicus was far away; the identity of Alexandria on or in the Granicus with Alexandria Troas is certain.[4] As cities do not stand *in* rivers, and as, moreover, this city did not stand *on* the Granicus, the real phrase can only have been '*of* the Granicus', and means that Alexander's promise was made after his victory on that river; it was thus earlier than his promise to Ilium, which was why Lysimachus attended to Alexandria first, and the city adopted 'of the Granicus' as its nickname, to perpetuate its connection with the victory.[5] This is why both the lists we possess (*post*) give Alexandria Troas among Alexander's foundations; it is usually called a mere blunder, but the reason is plain if one attends to the evidence.

1 Strabo XIII, 593.   2 App. *Syr.* 29, ᾽Αλεξάνδρειαν τὴν ἐπὶ Γρανίκῳ.
3 Some later versions of the Romance list (*post*) have ἐν Γρανίκῳ.
4 Appian and Livy are describing the same Roman operation, both presumably from Polybius; in Livy, XXXV, 42; XXXVII, 35, the three cities concerned are called Smyrna, Lampsacus and Alexandria Troas; in Appian, *Syr.* 29, they are Smyrna, Lampsacus and Alexandria on the Granicus. This is conclusive. See Tscherikower, p. 16 n. 30.
5 *Mutatis mutandis*, the same usage occurs in English titles bestowed for victories: Lord Nelson of the Nile, Lord Kitchener of Khartoum, etc.

I must now turn to our two lists, and I will take the later one, that of Stephanus, first. It gives eighteen Alexandrias, which I copy here: (1) Alexandria the Egyptian,[1] (2) Alexandria Troas, (3) Alexandria in Thrace πρὸς τῇ Λακεδαιμονίᾳ, which he founded 17 years before Alexandria in Egypt, (4) πόλις Νεαρτῶν, a people of the Ichthyophagi, on the periplus to India, (5) A. in Opiane κατὰ τὴν Ἰνδικήν, (6) πάλιν Ἰνδικῆς, (7) ἐν Ἀρίοις, (8) in Cilicia, (9) in Cyprus, (10) πρὸς τῷ Λάτμῳ τῆς Καρίας, (11) κατὰ Βάκτρα, (12) in Arachosia, (13) in Makarene, (14) among the Sorianoi, an Indian people, (15) in Arachosia, ὁμοροῦσα τῇ Ἰνδικῇ, (16) κατὰ τὸν μέλανα κόλπον, (17) in Sogdiana παρὰ Παροπαμισάδαις, (18) on the Tanaïs.

Of these, (1), (2), (7) and (18) need no further comment; (5) is Alexandria of the Caucasus;[2] (6) and (14) are two of the Indian Alexandrias (the Sorianoi are unknown); (8) is Alexandria κατ᾽ Ἴσσον; (11) is Alexandria-Bactra; (12) is Alexandria-Prophthasia in Seistan, which was often, though not always, part of the political Arachosia; (15) is Alexandria-Ghazni; (17) is Alexandria-Termez on the Oxus in Sogdiana; (13), and (16) with it, are dealt with in part II of this Appendix. All these, except (16), are known; four problems remain: (3), (4), (9) and (10).

(9) is simple. The Romance list (p. 243) shows that it has nothing to do with Cyprus; it is the Alexandria ἐπὶ Κύπριδος ποταμοῦ of the version C′, which is merely Alexandria at the mouth of the Tigris, Τίγριδος having been corrupted into Κύπριδος.

(4) is not difficult. In Diodorus XVII, 105, 1 various MSS., for Ὠρειτῶν and Ὠρεῖται, give the forms Νεωριτῶν, Νεωρητῶν, Νεωρειτῶν, Νεωρίται, Νεωρεῖται; while 'in 104, 5, for Ὠρείτιδος, there are variants Νεωτερίδος, Νεωτερίδας. Νεαρτῶν therefore is merely a further corruption of the first set of corruptions given above, and the people meant are the Oreitae. The suggestion that Νεαρτῶν means the Oreitae is very old, and Droysen, *op. cit.* p. 235 n. 1, called it *unbedenklich*; but he does not seem to have known the variants in the MSS. of Diodorus which prove it. The place cannot be Alexandria in Makarene, as this Alexandria is given as (13), and the confusion of the Oreitae with the Fisheaters of the coast,[3] and the reference to the voyage to India, make it certain enough that the port of this Alexandria is meant; but the port was not an Alexandria, though a passage in Diodorus has been taken to mean that it was (p. 253). The whole

1 ἤτοι Λίβυσσα, ὡς οἱ πολλοί. 2 Tarn, *Bactria and India*, App. 6.
3 This confusion goes back to Cleitarchus: Pliny VII, 30= Cleit. fr. 27. So Pliny VI, 95, Ichthyophagos Oritas.

notice in Stephanus is greatly confused, but one can see what it was meant to represent.

(3) is another queer confusion; seventeen years before the foundation of Alexandria by Egypt Alexander was a child, and even a Byzantine knew that Thrace was nowhere near Lacedaemonia. The figure means when Alexander was 17 years old; the reference to Alexandria by Egypt must come from a statement that this was the only Alexandria he founded before the Egyptian one; and the two statements have telescoped. What it refers to is not any Alexandria, but the Alexandro-polis in Thrace which he is said to have founded when 16,[1] and which will be considered later. I have considered 'Lacedaemonia' elsewhere in connection with other passages of the same import, which point to a border tribe called Lacones (Λακόνες) in Macedonia.[2]

(10) is insoluble, though a conjecture might be hazarded. Heracleia-Latmos in Caria, famous for its great fortifications, was never an Alexandria; Pleistarchus renamed it Pleistarcheia, but after his brief rule the name Heracleia came back.[3] Now Strabo and Ptolemy knew of a Heracleia in Northern Media, which in Pliny VI, 48 is attributed to Alexander; he *could* have founded it after his return from India, and if so the full name must have been Alexandria-Heracleia; and some one *may* have confused Heracleia in Media with the better-known Heracleia in Caria. But no reason is apparent for this, and it would be a very long shot; more likely 'Latmos' conceals some word now irrecoverable.

Stephanus then, out of eighteen Alexandrias, gave two places which were Alexander's but not Alexandrias, (3) and (4); one named Alexandria which could hardly be called his, (2); one which has merely suffered a textual corruption, (9); and two, (10) and (16), which are now irrecoverable. Giving his two in India the benefit of the doubt, that means that he has got twelve right out of eighteen. This is not too bad altogether for his date, and he has done good service in preserving the name of Alexandria in Makarene, and also the Alexandria-name of Bactra; but it does not compare well for accuracy with the Hellenistic list given in the Romance, which must now be examined.

The original list of Alexandrias in the Romance belongs to about the middle or the latter half of the first century B.C. (p. 245). Droysen, pp. 246 *sq.*, did his best with what he had, but far too little was then known; Berve and Tscherikower ignored this list altogether. Kroll's notes on p. 146 of his edition of A′ are extremely useful;[4] but more is

---

1 Plut. *Alex.* IX.   2 Tarn, *J.H.S.* LIV, 1934, p. 34 n. 42.
3 Steph. Byz. *s.v.* Πλεισταρχεία.
4 W. Kroll, *Historia Alexandri Magni*, 1926.

known now than when he wrote. The original list is said both by A′ and the Syriac version to have contained thirteen names; but our earliest version of the Romance, A′, though it says that Alexander founded thirteen cities 'which are still inhabited and at peace to-day', only gives nine.[1] One need not notice the statement 'inhabited and at peace'; it is only the author (or compiler) of the Romance speaking and is not likely to be any part of the original list.[2] The original list is older than A′, as A′ already has two corrupt names. In the later versions of the Romance some names have become impossibly corrupt; this will be noticed later. The history of this list of Alexandrias has been an exact parallel to the history of the list of Alexander-questions in the Romance, which I have examined fully elsewhere;[3] and, as in that, no deductions can be drawn from the *order* of the items, which varies greatly in different versions.

The nine names in A′ are as follows: (1) Ἀλεξάνδρειαν τὴν ἐπὶ Βουκεφάλῳ ἵππῳ; (2) Α. τὴν πρὸς Πέρσας; (3) Α. τὴν ἐπὶ Πώρῳ; (4) Α. τὴν ἐν Σκυθίᾳ; (5) Α. τὴν ἐπὶ τοῦ Τίγριδος ποταμοῦ; (6) Α. τὴν ἐπὶ Βαβυλῶνος; (7) Α. τὴν πρὸς Τρωάδα; (8) Α. τὴν ἐπὶ Σούσοις; (9) Α. τὴν πρὸς Αἴγυπτον. Of these (1) is of value as giving the Alexander-name of Bucephala and (3) as giving that of Nicaea on the Jhelum, there being no doubt about the identity of (3).[4] (7) and (9) are obvious. (4) is Alexandria on the Jaxartes (see pp. 235 *sq.*). (5) is Alexandria in Susiana at the mouth of the Tigris, the later Charax Spasinu; in the version in C′ Τίγριδος ποταμοῦ has become corrupted into Κύπριδος ποταμοῦ, from which is derived the Alexandria in Cyprus of Stephanus' list (p. 241).[5] (6) is A. in Babylonia. This leaves two names, (2) and (8), which are corrupt. I will take (8) first.

There was only one Alexandria in Susiana, that at the mouth of the Tigris, which has already been given; ἐν Σούσοις therefore is corrupt, and is obviously ἐν Σόγδοις, among the Sogdians, the confusion of these two names being known elsewhere;[6] that Σόγδοις must be right here is

---

1 III, 35 (p. 146 Kroll).
2 The Syriac version, which is later than A′, says 'Alexander built 13 cities, some of which are flourishing to this day, but some are laid waste'. I quote this version throughout from E. A. W. Budge, *The History of Alexander the Great, being the Syriac version of Pseudo-Callisthenes*, 1889.
3 Tarn, *Bactria and India*, pp. 429–31.
4 It celebrated the victory over Porus (Kroll). The Syriac version (p. 245) has 'in the dominion of King Porus'.
5 Droysen suggested this, but doubtfully. I can see no room for doubt.
6 In Ps.-Call. A′, III, 33, 22 (p. 143 Kroll) Philip's satrapy is called τὴν Βακτριανὴν καὶ Σουσιανήν; Σογδιανήν is certain. In Dexippus (Jacoby II A,

shown by the Syriac version (p. 246), which gives as its ninth Alexandria, 'A. which is in the country of Sôd, that is to say Samarkand'; Sôd is Sogd, on which term see p. 235. Whether the word Samarkand here refers to the Alexandria in question or to the land of Sôd I do not know; in any case Alexander did not found Samarcand, later so famous— that is a later legend. The only city Alexander founded in the land of Sogd was Alexandria-Termez on the Oxus (p. 235), mentioned by Claudius Ptolemy; Alexandria-Chodjend on the Jaxartes was not in Sogd but in 'Saca-land beyond Sogd', and has already been given in our list as A. in Scythia. (8) therefore is certainly Alexandria-Termez.

This leaves (2), A. πρὸς Πέρσας, which dates the original list; I may add that no one writing before 1938 could have explained this name. There was of course no Alexandria in Persis, and Ausfeld's emendation,[1] which Kroll adopted, A. ἐν Πιερίᾳ κατ᾽ Ἴσσον (it would at least have to be A. κατ᾽ Ἴσσον ἐν Πιερίᾳ) was only a counsel of despair; it has no chance of being correct, for κατ᾽ Ἴσσον could not be omitted, and in fact the Armenian version does give· an Alexandria κάττισον (p. 246). The city is A. πρὸς Παρσίους (or Πάρσους), Alexandria of, or near, the Parsii (or Parsi);[2] that is, Alexandria-Ghazni. The corruption of the half-forgotten Παρσίοι into Πέρσαι was inevitable; the two names had a common root and origin, and were indeed the same word, the Parsii having originally been a Persian sept; and a later version of the Romance, C', gives a name here which exhibits a halfway house in the process of corruption, Περσίαν. These Parsii were members of the Massagetae confederacy, and were sometimes called Massagetae by late writers;[3] and the Alexandria εἰς (or *apud*) Μασσαγέτας

---

no. 100, fr. 8, § 6) the geographical order of the satrapies, which run Carmania, Persis, Σογδιανῶν, Babylonia, Mesopotamia, and the fact that the Σογδιανοί have been named two lines before, make von Gutschmid's emendation of Σουσιανῶν for Σογδιανῶν certain.

1 *Der griech. Alexander-Roman*, 1907, p. 121 n. 12.
2 For the Parsii, see my *Bactria and India*, pp. 292 *sqq.*; for their later history, that book *passim*. The preposition πρός occurs three times in the list in A', (2), (7), (9); and (9) shows that the compiler figured Greek Ghazni as standing in the same relation to the Parsii as Greek Alexandria stood to Egypt; and as for some purposes that Alexandria was not regarded as part of Egypt, this shows that the compiler understood the position of an autonomous Greek city of the Farther East under foreign rule. This greatly strengthens my view that the original compiler probably got his information from the Greek historian 'Trogus' source'.
3 Tarn, *Bactria and India*, p. 469, an examination of Stephanus' Ἀραχωσία· πόλις οὐκ ἄποθεν Μασσαγετῶν. Ausfeld, *op. cit.* pp. 122, 213, made

which occurs several times in later versions of the Romance has nothing to do with the Caspian steppes but is Alexandria of the Parsii again, which confirms my identification (if it needed confirmation). I rescued the Parsii from the shades in my *Bactria and India*, and was able to give a good deal of their history: they took part in the great invasion of Parthia and Bactria from the steppes in 130–129 B.C., but instead of going on into India with the Saca peoples they turned north through Arachosia along Alexander's route, occupied Ghazni and Cabul, and formed a realm which, at first subject to the East Parthian (Suren) rulers of Seistan, attained independence and considerable power under Spalirises and his son Azes, both called Great King of Kings, who about 30 B.C. destroyed the last two Greek kingdoms in India; by A.D. 19 the kingdom of the Parsii had been conquered by the Parthian Gondophares, and the name Parsii vanishes. As to dates, the Parsii reached Cabul some time before 87 B.C.[1] and had therefore occupied Ghazni earlier; the compiler of the original Romance list of Alexandrias presumably therefore got this name for Ghazni from the historian of the Farther East whom I had to call 'Trogus' source' (cf. p. 244 n. 2), for he wrote about 85 B.C.; no possible source later is known, and after A.D. 19 the name no longer corresponded to any reality. The date of the original Romance list therefore is first century B.C., either in the middle or the latter half of the century, and the list is one of the Hellenistic documents embedded in the Romance as we have it (see App. 22, p. 363), like Alexander's *Testament* and the Letter to the Rhodians, known to Diodorus, and one version of Alexander's questions to the Gymnosophists.

We now have to find, from other and later versions, the four Alexandrias missing[2] from the list in A'; the Syriac version, the only one which professes to give all the thirteen names, is much the most helpful, though in fact it only gives 12, not 13, for its no. 3, Alexandria the Great, is obviously a duplicate of its no. 13, Alexandria by Egypt. Taking its numeration, seven of its Alexandrias, beside the Egyptian, appear in A', viz. (1) Bucephala; (4) A. 'in the dominion of King Porus' (Nicaea); (5) A. 'in the land of Gelênîkôs' (apparently Granicus);

Alexandria by the Massagetae the same city as Alexandria on the Jaxartes. This is impossible; A. on the Jaxartes is given in the list in A' (no. 4), and it stood in the country of the Sacaraucae (Tarn, *ib.* pp. 80, 291), not of the Massagetae, with whom Alexander never had anything to do.

1 Tarn, *ib.* p. 472; cf. pp. 50, 332. 87 B.C. means the death of Wu-ti.
2 Kroll's suggestion (p. 146) was ἐν Γρανίκῳ, εἰς Μασσαγέτας (both of these are already in A'), πρὸς Ὀρείτας, and κατὰ Ξάνθον (which is inexplicable).

(6) A. 'in the country of the Scythians'; (7) A. 'on the shore of the sea (or river)', which can only mean A. on the Persian Gulf at the mouth of the Tigris; (8) A. 'which is near Babylon'; (9) A. 'which is in the country of Sôd' (i.e. Sogd, see p. 244 *ante*). We then, in (10), (11) and (12), get three of the four missing names. (10) is A. 'which is called Kûsh, that is Balkh', i.e. Bactra, given in Stephanus' list. (11) is A. 'which is called Margenîkôs, that is to say Môrô (Merv)', which incidentally supports Curtius' form Margania (p. 248). (12) is A. 'which is upon the farther bank of the rivers in the country of the Indians'. There was only one Alexandria in India which could be connected with more than one river, and that was Alexandria of the Caucasus, at or about the junction of the Panjshir and Ghorband rivers;[1] incidentally, the words 'farther bank' show that the compiler of this list lived somewhere west of the Hindu Kush. There is still one other town in the Syriac list, (2) A. 'the fortified Rôphôs (?)'; this must stand over for a moment, with the remark that *position* in a list is no guide.

We now have three of the missing towns, Bactra, Merv, and Alexandria of the Caucasus; the fourth is uncertain. Of the names which occur in various versions, three—ἐν Γρανίκῳ (p. 240), εἰς Μασσαγέτας (pp. 244 *sq.*), ἐπὶ Κύπριδος ποταμοῦ (p. 243)—have already been identified with towns in A'; three, κατὰ Ξάνθον,[2] and the 'apud Origala' and 'apud Sanctum' of Valerius, are too corrupt to make anything of; the A. περὶ Μεσοποταμίας of the Armenian version has already been noticed (p. 239 n. 5). Two remain that are possible candidates for the vacancy. One is the A. πρὸς Oreitas of C', Valerius, and Leo, i.e. A. in Makarene (11, *post*). The other is the κάττισον (A. κατ' Ἴσσον) of the Armenian version, which, as Kroll suggested, may be the origin of the corrupt κρατίστη of C' and Leo; if so, κρατίστη might in turn have given rise to the 'A. the fortified', no. 2 of the Syriac version, though this would be a long shot, and I cannot explain Rôphôs. It will be noticed that two versions, C' and Leo, give *both* A. in Makarene and A. by Issus. I see no way of deciding which of these two came from the original list; probably in course of time one or more towns not in the original found their way into this or that version.

1 Tarn, *Bactria and India*, App. 6; subject of course to excavation.
2 Ausfeld, *op. cit.* p. 122, no. 19, identified κατὰ Ξάνθον with 'apud Sanctum' and called both words corruptions of 'Ιαξάρτην. But A', which must be nearest to the original, does not mention the Jaxartes; there is only one way in which it *could* be mentioned, and A' calls Alexandria on the Jaxartes A. in Scythia; the Syriac version supports this.

Taken as a whole, then, the merit of the Romance list is that it helps to confirm the existence of Alexandria-Bactra, Alexandria-Merv, and Alexandria-Termez, and gives the Alexander-names of Bucephala and Nicaea on the Jhelum.

At a first glance it may look as if Alexander meant to found an Alexandria in each satrapy of the East to be the seat of government; but this view cannot be maintained. There were three Alexandrias in Bactria-Sogdiana, or four if Merv be reckoned in, and two in Aria-Drangiana; there was no Alexandria in Persis or in the Parthia-Hyrcania satrapy, while it is doubtful if there was one in Media and more than doubtful if there was one in Mesopotamia; the one in Babylonia was on the extreme outskirts of the satrapy, which continued to be governed from Babylon. It is only occasionally that we can be sure that any particular Alexandria was meant to be a seat of government. Some were founded to promote trade, like Alexandria in Makarene, to tap the spice-land of eastern Gedrosia; Alexandria-Termez, which stood where the great trade-route from the north crossed the Oxus; and Alexandria of the Caucasus, gateway for the trade between India and the west. Alexandria on the Jaxartes was meant to be both the centre of a fertile country (so probably also Alexandria-Merv and Alexandria-Prophthasia in Seistan) and for the defence of the Jaxartes crossing against nomads;[1] speaking generally, Alexander hoped that his cities might convert nomad and hill peoples to agriculture.[2] But probably his dominant motive throughout was to strengthen the remoter parts of his Empire with Greek cities and all that they implied as a mainspring of his policy of the fusion of races.

A word must be said in conclusion about Alexander's military colonies,[3] as he undoubtedly started the system in Asia. He did settle a number, but military colonies are difficult to identify, as so many merely kept the name of the native village in or near which they were founded; and even where there are helps to identification, such as the settlers giving to their settlement the name of their home-town or the name of the official who had actually settled them, the possibility of dating a settlement to any particular king is not too common, thougn, speaking

1 Arr. IV, 1, 3 records these two objects, which is exceptional.
2 Arr. *Ind.* 40, 8. On Alexander's care for agriculture in Macedonia see Arr. IV, 25, 4, and Alexander's fragmentary decree from Philippi as to bringing some waste land into cultivation, published by J. Coupry, *Inscriptions hellénistiques de Philippes* (see *C.R. Ac. I.* 1938, pp. 185 *sq.*). See further p. 254 n. 7.
3 On military colonies generally, Tarn, *Bactria and India*, pp. 6–12, which will give the literature.

generally, it can be said that the Graeco-Macedonian colonisation of Asia was carried out by means of the military settlement rather than the city and that a great deal of it was Seleucid. We know that Alexander founded a chain of such settlements in Bactria-Sogdiana as a bulwark against the nomads,[1] and at any rate ordered or began another group in northern Media to bridle the tribes of the Elburz.[2] Curtius makes him found six others in Margania, which may mean Margiane;[3] the details of the interlocking are good and ought to represent something real, but he makes them face *south* and east, which as regards Alexander's day has no meaning. Tradition gave Alexander two such settlements in the Paropamisadae, the 'town' a day's march from Alexandria of the Caucasus (p. 239 n. 6 *ante*) and a 'town' among the Cadrusi, wherever they lived;[4] but there was a good deal of settlement in this province later, and these two places are not likely to be Alexander's; looking at the large force he left in Bactria and the re-foundation of Alexandria of the Caucasus, he could hardly have left more fighting men behind with India to conquer. The men left at various places in Gandhāra were all military garrisons *ad hoc*, except at Arigaion in Swat; this has been claimed as a 'foundation', but in fact he only restored the native population and left there a few men quite unfit, ἀπόμαχοι,[5] and the men in a military colony had to be ready to fight. Lastly, Nikephorion at the junction of the Chabur with the Euphrates has been ascribed to Alexander;[6] but it is not known that the term νικηφόρος was ever applied to, or used by, Alexander,[7] and the form of the name shows that the place belongs to a class, like Dokimeion, Zenodotion, Menedemion, in which the settlement took the name of the official who settled it; and no official of Alexander's named Nikephoros is known. Doubtless the place was Seleucid.[8]

Lastly come the three places called Alexandropolis. The one in Thrace was a native town or village in which Alexander, during Philip's life-time, settled συμμίκτους, people of different races;[9]

1 Eight, Strabo XI, 9, 4 (517); seven or twelve, Justin XII, 5, 13.
2 Polyb. X, 27, 3, κατὰ τὴν ὑφήγησιν τὴν Ἀλεξάνδρου.
3 Curt. VII, 10, 15. In the list of Alexandrias in the Syriac version of the Romance (p. 246) Merv is called Margenîkôs, which may show that Margania was a known variant for Margiane, another instance of Curtius' curious knowledge.
4 Pliny VI, 92, usually mistranslated; see Tarn, *Bactria and India*, p. 99 n. 6.
5 Arr. IV, 24, 6 *sq*.
6 Isidore 1, κτίσμα Ἀλεξάνδρου βασιλέως (his own remark, not from the Parthian survey); Pliny VI, 119.   7 It occurs in the Romance.
8 App. *Syr.* 57.   9 Plut. *Alex.* IX.

Stephanus (no. 3) calls it an Alexandria, which implies that Alexander founded it as a Greek πόλις. Certainly he did nothing of the sort; to have founded a city bearing his own name while his father lived would have been a declaration of independence, the clearest act of rebellion known to the ancient world.[1] It was, as Plutarch's συμμίκτους implies, a military colony (which could be settled by a subject) which later attributed itself, possibly with truth, to Alexander and took his name. The name Alexandropolis then belongs to a class of names, like Dionysopolis, Macedonopolis, etc., which all indicate military colonies.[2] This shows that the two places in the East called Alexandropolis were also military colonies, apart from the fact that Alexander, all of whose cities were officially named Alexandria, could not possibly have changed the name in just two cases. Whether Alexandropolis in Parthyene[3] was right in attributing itself to Alexander cannot be said; but the third Alexandropolis is of great interest. I have elsewhere straightened out the deep-seated confusion in Isidore 18 and 19,[4] and it is now certain that Isidore's Alexandropolis is Candahar, and that Candahar was therefore not a city founded by Alexander, but a military colony which attributed itself to him. The attribution may well be correct, but whether the name Candahar represents Iskander is at best doubtful; the suggestion that it represents Gundofarr (Gondophares), the Parthian Suren who ruled a realm greater than Arsacid Parthia, is quite as likely to be true.

II. Alexandria in Makarene

The thirteenth Alexandria in Stephanus' list is Ἀλεξάνδρεια ἐν Μακαρηνῇ ἣν παραρρεῖ ποταμὸς Μαξάτης, Alexandria in Makarene beside which flows the river Maxates; whether ἣν refers to the city or the province will be considered later. Long ago, Salmasius darkened counsel by changing the two unknown words Makarene and Maxates to Sakasene and Jaxartes, which he happened to have heard of; for this sort of thing there is less than nothing to be said, but Droysen and

---

1 For the classical example see Tarn, *Bactria and India*, p. 208.
2 A reviewer of *Bactria and India* in *J.R.A.S.* 1941 took me to task (p. 68) for saying that the name Alexandropolis meant a military colony. There is no explicit statement, as I had said. But the evidence here given for Alexandropolis in Thrace is, to any one who understands the Hellenistic world, conclusive that it could not have been a *polis*; it was therefore a military colony, as indeed Plutarch implies, there being no third possibility. The other two places follow.
3 Pliny VI, 113.   4 *Bactria and India*, pp. 470 *sq*.

Tscherikower (p. 147) have followed him. The city was in fact the capital of eastern Gedrosia, a country whose history is most obscure. The Persians had tried to govern it from western Gedrosia, an impossible task owing to the mountains and deserts which separated them; they were in fact two different countries.[1] Three eparchies of Gedrosia and/or Carmania are known from the Peutinger Table—Pantyene, Tazarene, Thybrassene, all apparently inland districts;[2] Makarene is a properly formed eparchy name and was certainly an eparchy of Gedrosia, for it is the same word as the modern Makran; the story will show that it included the littoral and the southern portion of eastern Gedrosia, or part of it. Tomaschek, though he wrote long before the discovery of the eparchy system, rightly saw that Makarene must be part of Gedrosia.[3] The city must be identical with 'Alexandria of the Oreitae' of most modern and three ancient writers;[4] but Alexandria of the Oreitae, whose foundation (without any name) is recorded by Arrian, has itself been the subject of much confusion, Arrian himself not being any too clear; Droysen (p. 233) made two cities of it, while Berve (p. 295), who anyhow knew Tomaschek, managed to make Alexander found four cities in this one small country. I may mention that, as Makarene was an eparchy and the eparchy system was Seleucid, we know (it could not be deduced from the Alexander-historians) that this Alexandria was existing in Seleucid times, at any rate.

I must now go through Arrian's story.[5] The last Indian people Alexander met after leaving the Indus delta were the Arabitae or Arbitae or Arabies or Arbies, east of and about the river Arabis (Hab), which was the boundary, ethnologically and linguistically, between India and Ariana.[6] West of the Arabis, Alexander first crossed a barren tract and then entered the country of the Oreitae or Oroi; Arrian uses

1 On the natural division of Gedrosia into two parts and the greater importance of the eastern part see Kiessling, 'Gedrosia' in PW.
2 See Tarn, *Bactria and India*, p. 442.
3 Tomaschek, 'Alexandreia' (10) in PW.
4 The lists of Stephanus (p. 241) and of the Romance (p. 243), and also Diodorus (*post*), give the Alexander-name.
5 Arr. VI, 21, 3 to 22, 3.
6 Nearchus gives it all clearly. Arr. *Ind.* 21, 8; 22, 10: the Arabies are the last Indian people; the Arabis is the boundary between them and the Oreitae; 25, 2, the Oreitae are not Indians but have another language (repeated in Pliny VI, 95) and laws, though some Indian customs; some live along the coast, some inland (ἄνω); the boundary on the coast between them and the (stone-age) Fisheaters is called Malana (Malan), and (24, 1) is west of the Tomeros (Hingol). The Oreitae therefore were Iranians.

both names,[1] but they do not signify two different sources.[2] This people, a sept of the Gedrosii, who lived west and north of them, were Iranians,[3] perhaps somewhat mixed; they are sometimes referred to in general terms as Gedrosians.[4] Their country was essentially the plain watered by the Purali river and some other streams, the only plain of any size in Eastern Gedrosia, though they extended farther westward across the river Hingol; the story may indicate that this plain, or anyhow its northern extension, was better cultivated and perhaps more fertile than to-day.[5]

In the Oreitae-land (Arrian continues) Alexander came to a village named Rhambakia and thought the country looked a good place for a city, but there is nothing to show that, as some modern writers (including Stein) assume, he (or rather Hephaestion for him) founded an Alexandria at Rhambakia.[6] Going westward, he met the Oreitae and Gedrosii holding a pass[7] between their two countries; they surrendered. There is no word, so far, of Alexander going into the land of the Gedrosii or crossing the Hingol-Nal; what follows still passes in the land of the Oreitae, east of that river. He made Apollophanes satrap of the Oreitae, and left Leonnatus with a strong force at a town named Ora, obviously the capital of the Oreitae-Oroi, to support the satrap (who was therefore at Ora) and to 'synoecise the city', τὴν πόλιν.[8]

1 Long and short forms of personal names are known both in Iranian and other tongues (examples in my *Bactria and India*, p. 496); and there are instances in the East of long and short names of peoples, like Sogdiani—Sogdi, Susiani—Susii (cf. Susiana—Susis).

2 Because both forms occur in Arr. VII, 5, 5, where a change of source is impossible.

3 See p. 250 n. 6. 'Indians' in Arr. *Anab.* VI, 21, 3 is a mere mistake.

4 E.g. in Ptolemy Apollophanes is called satrap of the Oreitae, Arr. VI, 22, 3, in Nearchus of the Gedrosians, Arr. *Ind.* 23, 5. So Arr. VI, 22, 2 has Oreitae where, in the same story (p. 252 n. 2 *post*), Curtius IX, 10, 5 has Gedrosii. See also Plut. *de Alex. Fortuna*, I, 328 D, referred to p. 254 n. 9.

5 On the country see the late Sir Aurel Stein, 'On Alexander's route through Gedrosia', *Geog. J.* CII (Nov.–Dec. 1943), p. 193 and his map. He has made it certain that the Arabis river was the Hab, not the Purali.

6 The words in Arr. VI, 21, 5, Ἡφαιστίωνα μὲν δὴ ἐπὶ τούτοις ὑπελείπετο, do not mean that Hephaestion was left to found a city at Rhambakia (else it must have been attributed to him and not to Leonnatus in the crownings at Susa, Arr. VII, 5, 5) but that he was left in military control; for as soon as the Oreitae surrendered, Hephaestion rejoined Alexander, bringing τοὺς ὑπολειφθέντας back to the στρατιά at Ora, VI, 22, 3.

7 On this pass see Stein, *op. cit.* p. 216.

8 Arr. VI, 22, 3. The phrase ἐν Ὤροις can only mean a town named Ora; if it were meant for 'in the Oreitae country', as Droysen contended, it would

There has been no mention before of any πόλις, and as a matter of Greek τὴν πόλιν can only refer to Ora, which is therefore the place where Alexander's new Alexandria was founded; this is shown by Arr. VII, 5, 5, where the list of gold crowns can only be originally from the *Journal* and is authoritative: Leonnatus, after the weddings at Susa, is crowned, first for shielding Alexander at the Malli town, and secondly because he had defeated the rising of the Oreitae after Alexander's departure καὶ τἆλλα καλῶς ἔδοξε τὰ ἐν Ὤροις κοσμῆσαι, i.e. the building and settling of the Alexandria. Ora cannot be identified with Rhambakia, because Hephaestion went from one to the other (p. 251 n. 6); neither can Rhambakia be identified; but both must have stood in the northern and more fertile part of the plain of the Purali, as does Bela to-day.[1] Rhambakia was only a village, not the Oreitae capital; and as this Alexandria is called by Arrian (VI, 22, 3) a synoecism —Alexander's only recorded synoecism—it must have taken in Rhambakia and the other places as its 'villages' (*demes*). The reason why, when the pass to the west lay open, Alexander returned for a time into the Oreitae country is curious, but is given by both Arrian and Curtius, both presumably from Ptolemy: the Oreitae were so democratic that they could not even surrender to superior force without calling an assembly, doubtless at Ora, and Alexander gave them time to do so.[2]

This Alexandria was founded both to be the capital of Eastern Gedrosia and to develop the spice trade, which must already have existed in some form; immediately after the reference to Leonnatus at Ora, Arrian VI, 22, 4 *sqq.* gives Aristobulus' description of the barren country west of the Purali plain as a spice-land, and Greeks were crazy about 'spices'. The idea that this one little country could support two full-blown Alexandrias should never have been started; but obviously this Alexandria, founded for trade, had to have a port, and this port must be considered. Diodorus has two different stories about the

---

have had to be ἐν τοῖς Ὤροις. This town Ora is mentioned again in Arr. VI, 24, 1 = Strabo xv, 723 (Aristobulus, fr. 49, Jacoby), where the distance is given from Ora to the βασίλειον of Gedrosia, which is conclusive that Ora was a town; so also in Arr. VII, 5, 5. Droysen was worried over the town Ora in Swat; he could not know that it was only one of the Iranian names then common in N.-W. India.

1 Further than this Stein (*op. cit.* p. 215) did not attempt to locate Alexandria, but said there were some large mounds in the Bela district. He did not know of Ora, and took Rhambakia to have been the capital.

2 Arr. VI, 22, 2, ξυγκαλέσαντες τὸ πλῆθος; Curt. IX, 10, 5: 'Liber hic populus, concilio habito, dedidit se.' Incidentally, this refutes Cleitarchus' story of the massacre.

Oreitae side by side; in the first, Alexander enters the Oreitis, massacres the people, and founds Alexandria; in the second he enters the Oreitis and receives the people's submission, followed by an account of the Iranian custom of exposing the dead;[1] it is one of many proofs that his book XVII never had a final revision (§ F, p. 80 n. 1). The first version says that Alexander wanted to found a city near the sea; he discovered a sheltered harbour, and near it a well-adapted position, τόπον εὔθετον, in which (i.e. in the τόπος εὔθετος) he founded a city, Alexandria.[2] The τόπος εὔθετος is obviously Arrian's 'good place for a city', and Diodorus is thus far correct, except that Alexandria was probably not *near* the sea; but it is the statement that Alexander wanted to found a city beside the sea, together with a misunderstanding of Diodorus, which is responsible for the idea of a second Alexandria. The harbour in question, the port of the new Alexandria, can only have been Cocala, which must already have been a port of some sort, as Nearchus was able to repair some ships there (Arr. *Ind.* 23, 8); there too he met Leonnatus (*ib.*), a meeting which could not have been pre-arranged, and which therefore meant that Leonnatus was settling the harbour-town as well as the city, things for which he was afterwards honoured. Cocala therefore must have been at or near the mouth of the Purali, which to-day reaches the sea at an inland gulf and is well sheltered (Diodorus' ἄκλυστον) by a long spit of land between it and open water (see Stein's map). It is noteworthy that Nearchus' log, while it mentions (Arr. *Ind.* 22, 8) that he put into the mouth of the Arabis (Hab) and also (*ib.* 24, 1; 25, 1) into the mouth of the Hingol (Tomeros), does not mention the mouth of the Purali; that is because he anchored, not in the river-mouth, but off the sheltered port there, Cocala. No doubt the port would have become one of Alexandria's 'villages'. Attempts have been made to bring in here the sixteenth Alexandria in Stephanus' list, that on the Black Gulf, κατὰ τὸν μέλανα κόλπον, by identifying the name with Nearchus' Μάλανα΄(Malan); but Malan is much too far away (see Stein's map), and the equation μέλανα—Μάλανα

---

1 The first version, XVII, 104, 5–8, is shown by the massacre to be from Cleitarchus. The second version, 105, 1, is from Diodorus' main source in book XVII, Aristobulus (see § F), as is shown by Aristobulus giving the Iranian custom again elsewhere, Strabo XV, 1, 62 (714).

2 Diod. XVII, 104, 8, παρὰ θάλατταν ἐφιλοτιμήθη κτίσαι πόλιν καὶ λιμένα μὲν εὑρὼν ἄκλυστον πλησίον δ' αὐτοῦ τόπον εὔθετον ἔκτισεν ἐν αὐτῷ πόλιν ᾿Αλεξάνδρειαν. This is Cleitarchus copying from and misunderstanding or partially garbling Aristobulus; what Aristobulus must have said was that Alexander saw that his new city must have communication with the sea.

is a mere jingle of sound, one word Greek, one native of some sort. No one knows where the Black Gulf was.[1]

To return to the river Maxates (p. 249 *ante*). One might guess it to be the unrecorded name of the Purali, flowing past Alexandria; but the name of the Purali was probably Hydaspes,[2] and we do not know that Alexandria stood on the river. There seems to be a more probable interpretation, that the river flowed past, i.e. bounded, Makarene. Makarene must have included the whole of the Oreitae country, for a single tribe would not be divided between two eparchies; and Nearchus says that the Oreitae extended across the Hingol to Malan (Arr. *Ind.* 25, 1). Now a river, given on some maps as Mashkai,[3] comes down from the north-west to join the Hingol-Nal below the small plain of Jau; if this were the Maxates, then the Oreitae extended across the Hingol-Nal as well as across the lower Hingol, which would mean that the spice-land was in the Oreitae country, as the story rather demands. It would also explain why the Oreitae tried to hold the already mentioned pass against Alexander, a senseless procedure if it was his way out of their country; they were defending the valuable spice-land.

I have considered elsewhere the later developments in eastern Gedrosia as evidenced by coin finds,[4] but I may note here that Alexandria in Makarene and its port explain some obscure later allusions to Gedrosia. Stephanus called Barygaza 'a port of Gedrosia',[5] implying sea-trade between the two; Pliny says that Alexander 'forbade the Fisheaters to live on fish',[6] which means the establishment, or attempted establishment, of agriculture by some ruler;[7] 'Patalene in Gedrosia'[8] probably refers to trade with the Indus mouth. Most important, however, is Plutarch's statement[9] that the Gedrosians performed the tragedies of Sophocles and Euripides, which implies a Greek πόλις

---

1 Not the well-known Black Gulf north of the Thracian Chersonese.
2 See Kiessling, 'Hydaspes' (2) in PW, and my *Bactria and India*, p. 100; the last river of Iran to the eastward, Vergil's *Medus Hydaspes*.
3 On Stein's map it is called Pao.
4 *Bactria and India*, pp. 93 *sqq.*, cf. p. 260.
5 Stephanus *s.v.* Barygaza.   6 Pliny VI, 95.
7 This is connected with the statement that Alexander taught the Arachosians agriculture, Plut. *de Alex. Fort.* I, 328 c. This cannot refer to Seistan, and I suggested before that it was a mistake for 'Gedrosians'; but it could be literally correct, if it be true that he settled some Arachosians in this Alexandria or its harbour town, Curt. IX, 10, 7. On his care for agriculture see p. 247 n. 2.
8 Marcianus I, 32 (*G.G.M.* I, p. 534).   9 *De Alex. Fort.* I, 328 D.

in Gedrosia with (as every πόλις would have) a theatre.[1] I have taken much trouble over this most interesting chapter in Plutarch,[2] as much of it comes from a good source and relates to Graeco-Bactrian times; but the only explanation I could find before for this particular statement was far-fetched[3] and must be abandoned. It can now be seen that Plutarch is referring specifically to Alexandria in Makarene, though he speaks of a later period than Alexander's. It has been seen, from the eparchy name Makarene, that the city was in existence in the Seleucid period; and it must have been existing in Parthian times, else how did Vergil get the name *Medus Hydaspes* for the Purali, and why did he give it?

III. PLUTARCH, *DE ALEXANDRI FORTUNA AUT VIRTUTE* I, 328 F

In this part of the above work Plutarch is dealing with the effects of Alexander's career on the East, and among other things he gives a list of five Greek cities,[4] obviously important ones, which but for Alexander's conquests would not have existed; and anyone reading the passage for the first time would be pulled up short by the name Prophthasia (p. 236). This city occurs, like other hardly known places, in itineraries and geographers' lists, but this is the only passage in Greek or Latin literature which even so much as hints at its importance, though the fact has become known from Chinese sources.[5] Plutarch's list, therefore, is not a random one, and has to be explained. I dealt with it in *Bactria and India*, pp. 48 *sq.*, on the basis that 'the collocation of names, if not the whole passage, must go back to' the Greek historian of the East whom I had to call 'Trogus' source' and who wrote about 85 B.C.; and I said that the only possible explanation of the four names (those other than Alexandria in Egypt) was that they represented 'the four civilised kingdoms which at the beginning of the first century B.C. occupied

1 On theatres in the east, Tarn, *Bactria and India*, p. 17; on Sophocles *ib.* p. 382.
2 *De Alex. Fort.* I, chap. 5. See Tarn, *Bactria and India*, pp. 48–50, 81 n. 9, 94, 260, 318, 380 and n. 4, 382, 482; *A.J.P.* LX, 1939, p. 57. See also part III of this Appendix.
3 *Bactria and India*, p. 94.
4 Alexandria by Egypt, Seleuceia on the Tigris, Prophthasia, Bucephala, Alexandria of the Caucasus. The MSS. text (328 F) reads: οὐκ ἂν εἶχεν Ἀλεξάνδρειαν Αἴγυπτος οὐδὲ Μεσοποταμία Σελεύκειαν οὐδὲ Προφθασίαν Σογδιανὴ οὐδ' Ἰνδία Βουκεφαλίαν οὐδὲ πόλιν Ἑλλάδα Καύκασος περιοικοῦσαν αἷς ἐμποδισθεῖσαν ἐσβέσθη τὸ ἄγριον καὶ μετέβαλε τὸ χεῖρον ὑπὸ τοῦ κρείττονος ἐθιζόμενον.
5 Tarn, *Bactria and India*, p. 347, cf. p. 204 n. 1.

what had once been Greek Asia east of the Euphrates, nomads being omitted', nomads of course meaning the Yueh-chi.[1] This must be right as far as it goes, there being nothing else that will fit, and no possible date but the one I gave, soon after 87 B.C.; but it does not go far enough. Meanwhile Mr J. E. Powell, in an article noticed in App. 16,[2] has criticised this and has sought to maintain, by a drastic rewriting of Plutarch's text, that Plutarch *did* write at random. I need not trouble about the rest of his criticism, though he *has* detected an obvious slip-up in my proof-reading; but he has done me the service of sending me back to Plutarch's text, which is what has to be considered.

Powell first says: 'It is self-evident that Καύκασος here is as corrupt as the words that follow it.' It is anything but self-evident, seeing that Plutarch shortly before had used the word Καύκασος by itself to denote the city Alexandria of the Caucasus.[3] He goes on: 'Were it (Καύκασος) sound, a proper name parallel with ᾿Αλεξάνδρειαν and the rest would be required for πόλιν ῾Ελλάδα, and παροικοῦσαν (so Reiske) must have been absent. The text was originally a generalising conclusion such as οὐδὲ πόλιν ῾Ελλάδα ἑκάστη γῇ βάρβαρος παροικοῦσαν, ἧς ἐμπολισθείσης κτλ.' The statement that each barbarian land had a Greek city 'beside' it is something quite new to me; but he has in effect asked, as is necessary, 'Why no proper name?', and I suppose ἧς ἐμπολισθείσης, which at least construes, means 'which (land) being urbanised'; only, if so, the verb would have to be πολίζω, not ἐμπολίζω. I think I had better leave this reconstruction alone for the present—I shall come to the restoration of the text later—and begin at the beginning; we may find, incidentally, that Powell's difficulties do not exist.

I have given many instances in these Appendices of the trouble Hellenistic writers took to avoid a jingle of sound, especially the same word twice in a sentence[4] (I presume that this was taught in the schools of rhetoric, and nearly every writer had had some training in rhetoric); naturally I have not made a search through Plutarch, but if an example from him be needed I give one in a note.[5] Now Plutarch, in the passage

1 For all this and the proofs see my *Bactria and India*, pp. 48 *sq*. and cross-references.
2 'The sources of Plutarch's Alexander', *J.H.S.* LIX, 1939, p. 236 n. 3.
3 *De Alex. Fort.* I, 328 E, Βάκτρα καὶ Καύκασος προσεκύνησε.
4 Most modern men do this automatically.
5 Plut. *Alex.* XXVI, ὑπεξέφερε τὴν φιλονεικίαν ἀήττητον, where ἀήττητον is substituted for the regular term ἀνίκητον (on which see App. 21) to avoid the jingle with φιλονεικίαν, which is here used in its good sense (see L. and S. *s.v.*) of φιλονικίαν, desire for victory. Another case of ἀήττητος being used for ἀνίκητος, and for the same reason, is Diod. XVII, 51, 3.

under examination, was faced by the necessity of getting into one sentence four cities named Alexandria, while he wanted to, or thought he ought to, use the word 'Alexandria' once only. He used up his 'Alexandria' at the start for the Egyptian capital, and got over the next two, Alexandria in Seistan and Alexandria on the left bank of the Jhelum, by using their nicknames, Prophthasia and Bucephala; this left him with Alexandria of the Caucasus, which, like Alexandria by Egypt, had no nickname, so he had to use a paraphrase and wrote Καύκασος πόλιν Ἑλλάδα. There could be no mistake as to which city was meant; but why did he use this particular paraphrase, 'Greek city'? The answer is, because it was already known, and probably well known. When the Chinese general Wen-chung was in the Paropamisadae, his interpreters gave him, as the name of this city, not Alexandria but Ἰωνακὴ πόλις; this he took to mean, not 'the Greek city' but 'a city called Ἰωνακή', which word he transliterated into Chinese as its name;[1] this shows that, to the people round about, Alexandria of the Caucasus was commonly known as 'the Greek city'. (Another Greek foundation in the East, presumably Antioch-Bushire on the Persian Gulf, was also locally known as 'the Greek city', and the phrase found its way into Claudius Ptolemy.)[2] Plutarch then, knowing that Alexandria of the Caucasus was known as 'the Greek city',[3] naturally used this for his paraphrase, merely changing the antiquated word Ἰωνακή, in use in the East, into the common Ἑλλάδα.

I will leave the corrupt text which follows the word Ἑλλάδα for a moment, and will take another phrase: οὐδὲ Προφθασίαν Σογδιανή. It has usually been supposed that Σογδιανή is a mere mistake for Δραγγιανή, and so I took it before; I thought the blunder might show that Plutarch had not the list at first hand, or that he was writing in haste, careless of minutiae.[4] I am satisfied now that this will not do; he *was* writing in haste, but I do not think that any serious writer, however excited over his subject, would say 'Newcastle in Cumberland' on the ground that Northumberland and Cumberland both end in -umberland. Another point arises. I had said 'the four civilised kingdoms, nomads being omitted', nomads meaning the Yueh-chi. Why should the Yueh-chi be omitted, seeing that it was not going to be long before there was little enough difference in civilisation between them

---

1 Tarn, *Bactria and India*, pp. 341, 418.
2 Ptol. VI, 4, 2, Ἰωνακὰ πόλις; see Tarn, *Bactria and India*, p. 418.
3 His historical source, which was a generation earlier than Wen-chung, must have noticed this; it means the name 'Alexandria' was lost.
4 Tarn, *Bactria and India*, p. 48 n. 5; *A.J.P.* LX, 1939, p. 56 n. 88.

(i.e. the Kushans) and the eastern Parthians? I propose therefore now, instead of taking the easy course of saying that Plutarch made a mistake, to retain the MSS. reading Σογδιανή and see whither it leads us.

As Prophthasia was not in Sogdiana, something has fallen out of the text; what Plutarch must have written was οὐδὲ Προφθασίαν [Δραγγιανὴ οὐδὲ *x*] Σογδιανή, a copyist's eye having jumped from the one -ιανή to the other. As *x* cannot be the word Alexandria, what was it? The city has to be the Yueh-chi capital and to be in Sogdiana, and it has to owe its origin to Alexander or Alexander's career. Alexandria-Bactra is excluded, for it was not in Sogdiana, though it became the Yueh-chi capital. But it did not do so till much later; when Chang-k'ien visited the Yueh-chi in 128 B.C., Ssu-ma Ch'ien says that they were still north of the Oxus (i.e. in Sogdiana) and adds that subsequently they had their capital there; Pan-ku corroborates this.[1] Of the cities in Sogdiana, Alexandria (subsequently Antioch) on the Jaxartes, if it still existed, was much too far to the north, for the Yueh-chi had already conquered Bactria; and it is not known that Samarcand (Maracanda), later so famous, was ever a Greek city. There was only one city in Sogdiana that was both a foundation of Alexander's and that could, from its position, have been the first capital of the Yueh-chi north of the Oxus mentioned by Ssu-ma Ch'ien, and that was Alexandria on the Oxus (Termez). It stood where the main route from the north, which the Yueh-chi must have followed, came to the river; and across the Oxus the city faced Bactra, or rather the point where the river of Bactra then entered the Oxus, Bactra itself being a little distance from the Oxus; the later transfer of the Yueh-chi capital across the river from this Alexandria to the more important Bactra would have been easy and obvious. This Alexandria had become successively an Antioch and a Demetrias before the Yueh-chi arrived; I have given its history elsewhere.[2] As Plutarch used the nicknames Prophthasia and Bucephala, he probably used the nickname of Alexandria on the Oxus also. We do not know what it was; but as the Antioch which succeeded it was called Antioch Tarmata or Tharmata,[3] which represents the native name of the place, Tarmita, the chances are that the second name of this Alexandria was also Tarmata or Tarmita. As Greek rule had ended about 130 B.C., and Plutarch's source wrote shortly after 87 B.C., it is likely that the name Demetrias had died out and that the city in Yueh-chi hands had resumed the native name Tarmita; though of course there

1 References in Tarn, *Bactria and India*, pp. 277 n. 5, 304 n. 5.
2 'Tarmita', *J.H.S.* LX, 1940, p. 89; and see p. 235 *ante*.
3 In the Peutinger Table and the Ravennate Geographer.

may have been some Greek nickname unknown to us. Plutarch therefore should probably read οὐδὲ Προφθασίαν Δραγγιανὴ οὐδὲ Τάρμιτα (or Τάρματα or some nickname) Σογδιανή, with a bare possibility that for Τάρμιτα should be substituted Δημητριάδα. It follows that, east of the Euphrates, Plutarch is giving, not the four civilised kingdoms, but all the kingdoms or realms into which Alexander's one-time Empire had become divided, five in number, viz. Western (Arsacid) Parthia, Eastern Parthia of the Surens, the Yueh-chi, the Paropamisadae, and what remained of Menander's kingdom east of the Jhelum; and it cannot possibly be coincidence that the names fit. As to the west of the Euphrates, Plutarch could only name Alexandria by Egypt, since at the date in question there was no such thing as a Seleucid kingdom left in Syria, so his source could not name Antioch;[1] had Plutarch been writing at random, he would obviously have done so. Doubtless Plutarch's source explained what he was doing; that, to Plutarch's argument, was immaterial.

I must conclude by looking at the sentence, clearly corrupt, which follows the word Ἑλλάδα; I have given the MSS. words in p. 255 n. 4. Reiske saw the two things that matter, viz. that περι- in περιοικοῦσαν must be παρα-,[2] and that the following verb should be ἐμπολίζω, not ἐμποδίζω. I have given various proposed restorations in the Addenda, none satisfactory; as I see it, the best restoration would be οὐδὲ Καύκασος πόλιν Ἑλλάδα πάροικον, ἐν αἷς ἐμπολισθὲν ἀπεσβέσθη τὸ ἄγριον. πάροικον is both necessary and true, for Alexandria of the Caucasus stood, not *on* the Hindu Kush, but beside it, or as we should say at its foot.[3] Literally translated, the whole passage then runs thus: '[But for Alexander] Egypt would not have had her Alexandria, nor Mesopotamia her Seleuceia, nor Seistan her Prophthasia, nor Sogdiana her Tarmita (or whatever appellative was used), nor India her Bucephala, nor the Caucasus her "Greek city" for a neighbour, in which (countries) what was uncivilised, enclosed within the cities, died out, and what was worse changed, being compelled by what was better to adopt its customs.' This has been Plutarch's theme throughout ch. 5: Alexander as a civilising force.

1 This, which I said before, is quite correct, *pace* Powell's remarks. The dates at the end of his note are mere misunderstandings.
2 I have commented elsewhere on the confusion of περί and παρά in late writers. See the instances given p. 237 *ante*, and in *Bactria and India*, p. 235 n. 1.   3 *Bactria and India*, App. 6.

Appendices 9–14: SOME HISTORICAL ITEMS

9. CARANUS

MANY modern writers, on the faith of Justin, state that Alexander had a half-brother named Caranus, whom he murdered after his accession, the implication being that he was old enough to be a rival, as Justin calls him. There never was any such person.

I take Justin IX, 7, 1–3 first. The first sentence mentions Olympias' grief, *doluisse*, at being repudiated by Philip and at Cleopatra, Attalus' niece, being preferred to her. The next sentence begins *Alexandrum quoque*, where *quoque* shows that what is to come about Alexander's feelings must be connected with Olympias' feelings, i.e. it must relate to Cleopatra. What does come is this.[1] Alexander too feared the brother born of his stepmother, *noverca*, as a rival for the kingship, *aemulum regni*; thus it came about that he quarrelled first with Attalus and then with Philip. No doubt therefore is possible that, so far, *noverca* (stepmother) means Cleopatra and *frater* (brother) means Cleopatra's child; Justin is using some source which made Cleopatra's child a boy. It is on account of the stepmother that Alexander quarrels with Attalus, another proof that 'stepmother' means Cleopatra, Attalus' niece.[2] So far Justin's meaning is clear.

In XI, 2, 3, the same source occurs again in identical language, but Cleopatra's supposed son is named. I put the two passages side by side: IX, 7, 3 'Alexandrum quoque regni aemulum fratrem ex noverca susceptum timuisse'; XI, 2, 3 '(Alexander) aemulum quoque imperii Caranum, fratrem ex noverca susceptum, interfici curavit'. That these identical sentences refer to the same *noverca* and the same *frater* is obvious, as obvious as it is that a baby could not be *aemulum imperii* (though others might use him as a tool) and that a grown man is meant. Justin's source then (I mean the original source, not Trogus) had the following story: Cleopatra bore Philip a son, whom Philip acknowledged and named Caranus; Alexander, whose own mother had been repudiated in favour of Cleopatra, feared Caranus as a rival for the

---

1 'Alexandrum quoque regni aemulum fratrem ex noverca susceptum timuisse.'
2 So Justin XI, 5, 1, where Alexander kills all the relations of his stepmother, can only refer to Attalus and Cleopatra; Attalus was the one person of any importance whom Alexander on his accession did put to death (for treason): Diod. XVII, 5, 2; Curt. VII, 1, 3; VIII, 1, 42; 7, 5.

kingship and so murdered him. Caranus is not mentioned by any other writer; his existence depends on this unknown source of Justin's, which made him Cleopatra's son. That source is valueless, not merely because it implies that Caranus was grown up (*aemulum regni* or *imperii*) but because Cleopatra's infant was not a boy.

In fact, Cleopatra's infant was a girl.[1] Satyrus' statement[2] on the subject has been generally accepted, and is not likely to be wrong; it is good third-century, and moreover Satyrus is professing to give a complete list of Philip's wives[3] and concubines with their children; all Philip's children known to history are included, and Caranus is not among them. The assumption made by some modern writers[4] that Justin's *noverca* was not Cleopatra but was one of these 'wives', whose son Caranus was, requires no confutation in the light of the analysis of Justin given above and of Satyrus' list. But in fact there is fourth-century evidence, much earlier than Satyrus, that Cleopatra's child was a girl. Justin IX, 7, 8–14 comes ultimately from the war of propaganda waged by Cassander and his friends against Olympias and her friends,[5] Olympias declaring that Cassander and his brothers had poisoned Alexander, while Cassander's party retorted that Olympias had procured the murder of her husband Philip—probably the first war of propaganda of which historical record remains. Most of the Justin passage in question is directed to showing Olympias' privity to Philip's murder, but § 12 has nothing to do with Philip; it says that Olympias murdered Cleopatra and her *daughter*.[6] This has generally been taken to be true, and no doubt is; not merely because Olympias, being what she was, would naturally kill her rival when in her power, but because she forced her to hang herself, which was Olympias' way; later she murdered Eurydice in the same manner, and that detail is from

1 There was no time for her to have had a second child, and had she borne twins Satyrus must have said so.
2 Satyrus fr. 5 in *F.H.G.* III, 161=Athen. XIII, 557D: Cleopatra bore Philip a daughter, Europa.
3 These 'wives', if married at all, were only married for the duration of a campaign; divorce merely consisted in Philip saying 'Go', and Athenaeus quotes Satyrus' list to illustrate the thesis Φίλιππος αἰεὶ κατὰ πόλεμον ἐγάμει. When he really did marry a girl of the Macedonian aristocracy (Cleopatra) and sought to put her in Olympias' place, there was a storm which only ended with his death.
4 See Berve II, *s.v.* Κάρανος, 411, and Κλεοπάτρα, 434, with the literature referred to.
5 *C.A.H.* VI, 474; see App. 16, p. 301.
6 'Post haec Cleopatram...in gremio eius prius filia interfecta, finire vitam suspendio coegit.'

Hieronymus.[1] The source of the Justin passage then must lie somewhere between the deaths of Alexander (323) and Olympias (316), when the sex of Cleopatra's infant was doubtless well enough remembered; and as between the two conflicting stories which appear in Justin, viz. that Cleopatra's child was a boy named Caranus, murdered by Alexander (source unknown), and was a girl, murdered by Olympias (source ultimately fourth century B.C.), there can be no doubt that the latter is correct. For completeness, it may be mentioned that Cleopatra's daughter turns up again in the *Heidelberg Epitome*,[2] in which she is a grown woman, Alexander's half-sister, daughter of Philip and Cleopatra his wife and herself called Cleopatra, who successively marries Perdiccas and Ptolemy; this is a confusion with Alexander's full sister Cleopatra, Olympias' daughter, who, as matter of history was offered to, but refused by, Perdiccas and afterwards thought of marrying Ptolemy, but who in Alexander's *Testament* was to be Ptolemy's wife.[3]

Thus Caranus vanishes from history. He never existed, whether as man or baby; his murder is a modern blunder, due to careless reading of Justin. Alexander did commit two murders in his day; there is no need to invent one which he could not have committed.

10. THE GORDIAN KNOT[4]

Every one, as the phrase goes, knows two things about Alexander, even if they do not know who he was: he was the man who wept because there were no more worlds to conquer, and he was the man who 'cut the knot'; cutting the knot has become an English cliché. The

1 Diod. XIX, 11, 7. Arrian III, 6, 5 calls this Cleopatra Eurydice. Wrong proper names are common in many late writers (App. 17, p. 315 n. 2) but I only recall one other case in Arrian (App. 1, 11, p. 145). Was Arrian thinking of the two women whom Olympias caused to hang themselves, and did he by mistake write down the wrong name?

2 Jacoby II, no. 155, fr. 4. The *Heidelberg Epitome* has some affinity with Alexander's *Testament* in the Romance.

3 A', ed. Kroll (*Hist. Alex. M.*), III, 33, 15 (p. 142).

4 Conspectus of modern literature in E. Mederer, *Die Alexanderlegenden bei den ältesten Alexanderhistorikern*, 1936, chap. 11. I have got little from it, as no one has seen the point of the sword story, that it makes Alexander cheat; but I note as a curiosity that Mederer himself calls his supposed act *ritterlich*. I need not do more than mention the theories which have made of Gordium the centre of the earth, or the knot a 'cosmic knot'; see G. Radet, *R.E.A.* XIX, 1917, p. 98, no. 6: 'L'omphalos Gordien', and cf. his 'Alexandre le Grand', p. 64; W. Deonna, *R.E.G.* XXXI, 1918, pp. 39, 141, 'Le nœud Gordien'.

first story does not occur anywhere in ancient literature, whether history, legend, or romance; it is presumably an invention of the medieval or modern world, though I do not know if its origin has been traced. The cutting of the knot is just as untrue.

The story of the Gordian knot is given by four of our five extant Alexander-historians;[1] Diodorus omits it, for it could not have come in the 'mercenaries' source', which he was here following (see § F). Arrian II, 3, gives it as a λόγος, a thing that people say, but he also gives Aristobulus' version,[2] so we have five versions altogether, all differing as to details. It is clear from Arrian that Ptolemy did not give the incident. Now Ptolemy used the *Journal*, and a king's official *Journal* recorded day by day his λεγόμενα καὶ πρασσόμενα,[3] what he said and what he did; the *Journal* therefore must have mentioned the incident, but in some form which Ptolemy thought not worth recording; the *Journal* therefore cannot have given the story of the cutting of the knot, which makes that story suspect from the start. All our four writers agree that, to fulfil the oracle, the knot had to be *untied*;[4] and Alexander's respect for oracles is well known. The knot was formed by the cord which bound the yoke to the pole of the wagon, and all four agree that the difficulty was to find the end or ends of the cord (made of cornel bark), which were hidden.[5] Here agreement ends. The preliminary stories differ greatly. In Arrian it is Midas' wagon and Midas is chosen king; in Justin it is Gordius' wagon and Gordius is chosen king; in Curtius it is Gordius' wagon but Midas is chosen king; in Plutarch Midas is king, but it is not said whose wagon it was. There are differences too about the birds and about what the girl did; and as to the knot itself, Arrian's λόγος and Aristobulus give one knot, Curtius and Justin several, while Plutarch gives one in the oracle and several in fact. But all we really want is what Alexander is supposed to have done.

1 Arr. II, 3–8; Curt. III, 1, 14–18; Plut. *Alex.* XVIII; Justin XI, 7, 3–16. It is also mentioned by Marsyas of Pella, fourth century B.C.: Jacoby II, no. 135, fr. 4. But unfortunately the fragment is too brief to be of any use.
2 Aristobulus fr. 4 (Jacoby II, no. 139)=Arr. II, 3, 7.
3 U. Wilcken, 'Υπομνηματισμοί, *Philol.* LIII, 1894, pp. 80, 110, citing the letter of Pseudo-Aristeas to Philocrates, πάντα ἀναγράφεσθαι τὰ λεγόμενα καὶ πρασσόμενα each day, the entries of the day before being corrected if necessary by the king. This article was the basis of the understanding of what Alexander's *Journal* ('Εφημερίδες) was.
4 The oracle: Arr., ὅστις λύσειε τὸν δεσμόν; Plut., τῷ λύσαντι τὸν δεσμον; Curt., 'qui vinculum solvisset'; Justin, 'nexum si quis solvisset'.
5 Arrian, οὔτε τέλος οὔτε ἀρχὴ ἐφαίνετο. Curtius, 'nodis...celantibus nexus'. Plutarch, τῶν δεσμῶν τυφλὰς ἐχόντων τὰς ἀρχάς. Justin, 'capita loramentorum abscondita'.

Aristobulus makes him draw out the pole to find the end of the cord; he must then have untied the knot, for he sacrificed to the gods who had shown him how to untie it, τὴν λύσιν (Arr. II, 3, 8), and Arrian shows that this is not part of the λόγος. Aristobulus' details suggest that he saw what happened, while the origin of the sword story is mere guesswork, and it can be seen from Ptolemy (see p. 263) that what was recorded in the *Journal* can have been nothing sensational. In Justin and Plutarch Alexander cuts the knots (plural) to get some ends,[1] and then unties the knots; that is, the cutting is not the solution, but merely the preliminary to the untying which follows. In Arrian's λόγος Alexander cuts the knot with his sword, and then says, using the verb used by the oracle, 'I have untied it',[2] that is, he cheats; Arrian safeguards himself, after giving Aristobulus' version, by saying that he personally cannot say what really happened (he had not Ptolemy's guidance). Finally, Curtius makes Alexander cut through the knots (plural) and say 'Who cares how they are untied?'[3] This is Curtius' own cynicism (§ G, pp. 92 *sq.*), further displayed in the next clause, *oraculi sortem vel elusit vel implevit*, which is just 'Who cares?' over again: how can it matter to any sensible man whether Alexander fulfilled the oracle or just dodged it?

On this analysis, Aristobulus has the right version beyond question. This is really shown by Justin and Plutarch, who, though they give the sword story, Plutarch because it is picturesque, Justin because it is derogatory to Alexander, nevertheless both attempt to combine it with the true version that Alexander found the end of the cord and untied the knot, a mere piece of common sense which Ptolemy did not think worth recording.

What then is the origin of the sword story? It cannot be true, because it makes Alexander flout the oracle, which is quite out of character; his respect, or outward respect, for the gods and all their manifestations stands out at every point of his history.[4] But the sword story does more than that. We have seen that Alexander sacrificed to the gods who showed him τοῦ δεσμοῦ τὴν λύσιν; that is, the sword story makes him not only cheat but lie to heaven about it, a flat negation of his whole attitude towards the gods. I have collected six cases of Alexander cheating from our inferior sources, and there is no

1 Plut., πολλὰς ἀρχὰς φανῆναι. Justin, 'latentia in nodis capita invenit'.
2 Arr. II, 3, 7, λελύσθαι ἔφη.
3 Curt. III, 1, 18, 'nihil', inquit, 'interest quomodo solvantur'.
4 See the big collection of instances in O. Kern, *Die Religion der Griechen*, III, 1938, chap. 3, 'Der Glaube Alexanders des Grossen', pp. 38–57.

reasonable doubt that they mostly come from Cleitarchus (§ E, p. 54), though he was not necessarily the inventor; he may merely have been passing on the stories. But Alexander is never recorded to have stooped to cheating by any respectable authority; it would have been utterly out of character. There was however a source to which it would have been in character: the Stoic tradition. To the Stoics, Alexander was bad from the start (see § F, p. 69 n. 1); and the sword story and the cheating and the lying to heaven would have constituted a fine exhibition of his (to them) characteristic vices of τῦφος and ὕβρις, the insolence of a tyrant's pride. It is possible then that this particular story, even if passed on by Cleitarchus (and some of Arrian's λόγοι appear to represent Cleitarchus), was of Stoic origin; and it may be noted that Justin, who also brings in the sword story, had certain affinities with the Stoic tradition (see § H). This explains Curtius. He gave the rival Peripatetic account (see § G) in which Alexander was good at the start, the change in his character occurring after Darius' death, long after Gordium. Except for the difference about the wagon, which may only be Curtius' usual carelessness, he and Arrian are using the same λόγος; both begin with Alexander's πόθος (*cupido*) and in both the sword is the solution. But Gordium is much too early for Curtius to attribute insolence and pride to Alexander; so he omits the sacrifice, says as little about it all as he can, and turns the matter off with his accustomed cynicism, 'Who cares?'

I believe this analysis to be correct. But nothing can now displace the sword story in popular belief.

11. THE DEATH OF BATIS

First, who and what was Batis, who defended Gaza against Alexander? Arrian II, 25, 4 calls him a eunuch, κρατῶν τῆς Γαζαίων πόλεως, i.e. a tyrant of Gaza. The phrase might also suggest an Arab chief, Gaza having once probably been Nabataean;[1] but an Arab chief was not likely to be a eunuch, while a tyrant—one who had seized power for himself—could be; there is a well-known instance.[2] The name Batis, however, is Iranian;[3] that is, the man was a Persian, and if so the eunuch story is almost certainly untrue. Diodorus XVII, 48, 7 says that the

1 Herod. III, 5, 7, 91.
2 Philetairos of Pergamum, θλιβίας ἐκ παιδός, Strabo XIII, 4, 1 (623).
3 R. Marcus in the Loeb Josephus, vol. VI, 1937, p. 468 n. c, citing Justi and L. H. Gray.

city was φρουρουμένην ὑπὸ Περσῶν, and he must be attended to, for he is using the 'mercenaries' source' (see § F); Josephus calls the man φρούραρχος,[1] and when he has no axe to grind over Jewish history he is often well informed about details in the East. Josephus indeed gives his name as Babemesis (with MSS. variants), which has clearly nothing to do with the name Batis and has been explained as Semitic;[2] the suggestion, however, has recently been made that Babemesis may also be Iranian, a corruption of Bagamisa, 'Mithra is god'.[3] This too cannot represent Batis, but it could be a predicate of some sort which has taken the place of the actual name; quite certain instances of this are known.[4] As Dionysius of Halicarnassus only calls the man ἡγεμών,[5] and Curtius IV, 6, 7 has the indeterminate *praeerat urbi*, it seems tolerably certain, so far, that Arrian is wrong, and that Batis was the Persian commander of the garrison of Gaza, who on Alexander's approach had strengthened himself by recruiting local Arabs.

Mr E. T. Newell, however, has recently published, among a number of 'Philisto-Arabian' coins, a drachma, sent to him from Damascus, which has no name or legend on it except the letter *Beth*;[6] following Babelon, he calls it 'Batis?, Dynast of Gaza', though throughout his remarks about it he treats this ascription as hypothetical. There is, indeed, no evidence for it, and he states (p. 50) that 'many other Philisto-Arabian coins provided with the letter *Beth* have been published'. Some Persian satraps sometimes coined, but I think there is no case of a garrison-commander doing so. Newell (p. 51) indeed states that Hegesias gives the man the title βασιλεύς, but this is hardly correct. The Hegesias passage in question[7] is preserved by Dionysius of Halicarnassus, in *de compositione verborum*; some MSS. do give βασιλέα, but the earliest, Parisinus 1741, has Βαῖστ[ι]ν,[8] and both Roberts and Jacoby print Βαῖτιν without discussion; it is obvious that while the corruption of the name into βασιλέα is easy, the converse is almost impossible. Professor Rostovtzeff has accepted Newell's

---

1 *Ant.* XI, 320.   2 See Marcus *loc. cit.*

3 By Marcus *loc. cit.* The numerous MSS. variants in Josephus' transcription of another Iranian name, Barzafarna (*Ant.* XIV, 330), may show that such corruption is likely enough.

4 Tarn, *Bactria and India*, pp. 340 *sq.* where two certain instances are given, one Dr Herzfeld's, one (in effect) Wylie's.

5 Dionysius, *de compositione verborum*, XVIII (p. 186 in Roberts' ed.).

6 *Num. Notes and Monographs*, 82, 1938, p. 49.

7 Jacoby II, no. 142, fr. 5 = Dionysius, *de comp. verb.* XVIII.

8 See the apparatus in Roberts' ed. *ad loc.*

hypothesis;[1] I fear that, in the absence of any evidence, I am unable to do so. If Newell were right, his coin could be used to support Arrian's κρατῶν; but this vague term only means that Arrian had no particulars, i.e. that Ptolemy, from whom his account of the siege is taken, said nothing about Batis' position; if Arrian had meant δυνάστης or τύραννος he would have said so, and I do not see how the 'mercenaries' source'[2] which Diodorus used (and Arrian did not), so well-informed on the Persian side, can be wrong. I will leave Arrian's εὐνοῦχος for the moment, and go on with the story on the basis that Batis was the Persian commander of the garrison, and one of Darius' officers.

Three versions are extant of the story of Batis' death, those of Hegesias, Dionysius of Halicarnassus, and Curtius.[3] Dionysius gives the simplest one: Batis, a man held in repute for good fortune and a fine appearance, was ἡγεμών of the garrison of Gaza; Alexander ordered him, after he was captured, to be tied living behind a chariot and the horses driven at full speed, and so killed him. There is nothing here about Alexander imitating Achilles or sending the chariot round the city; and as it comes in a criticism of Hegesias, it may show that Dionysius tacitly rejected much of Hegesias' story. Hegesias, in the third century B.C., is actually the earliest of our three versions; that however merely shows that the original invention, to which Dionysius' simpler version must stand nearest, was very early. Hegesias invented, or perhaps adopted, the story of a member of the garrison attempting to kill Alexander by treachery,[4] in order to say that Alexander hated Batis for instigating the plot, that is, he rationalises; and he has exhausted the resources of the Greek language in describing Batis' loathsome appearance, though it has been left to modern historians to improve upon this rubbish by calling him a negro.[5] The latter part of

1 *Soc. and Econ. Hist.* p. 1325.
2 On this source see sections F, G and G', *passim*.
3 Hegesias, Jacoby II, no. 142, fr. 5; Dionysius, *de comp. verb.* XVIII; Curtius IV, 6, 26–9. It is not given by Arrian, II, 26–7; by Diodorus, XVII, 48, 7; by Plutarch, *Alex.* XXV, or by Josephus, *Ant.* XI, 325. Justin omits Gaza altogether.
4 He says that the enemy leaders planned to kill Alexander personally, and makes the attempted assassination the outcome of this plan. But the 'plan' is merely taken from the genuine plan of the Persian satraps at the Granicus to kill Alexander himself in the battle, which shows that the story of the attempted assassination is also untrue.
5 Grote, *History of Greece*, 1884 ed., XI, p. 469, 'a black man'; G. Radet, *Alexandre le Grand*, 1931, p. 104, 'un Nègre'. μέλας means sunburnt, like Latin 'niger': Corn. Nepos, XIV, 3, 1, of a Paphlagonian. See Add.

Hegesias' account is one of the most abominable things in Greek literature; but he has no suggestion anywhere that Alexander was imitating Achilles. Curtius, even if he wrote under Augustus, might possibly have read Dionysius *de compositione verborum*.[1] He makes the chariot go round the city, *circa urbem*, and makes Alexander, who is off his head (*ira vertit in rabiem*), rejoice that he is imitating Achilles. But Curtius, who possessed some critical faculty when he chose to use it, has more than this. He emphasises and praises the heroic resistance Batis had made;[2] he omits Hegesias' abominations, though if he likes he can describe horrors with anybody;[3] and he shows clearly enough that he does not believe the story of Batis being dragged alive behind a chariot, though he relates it. For it must be remembered that he said that he copied things which he did not believe;[4] and his statement that, except on this one occasion, Alexander always admired bravery even in an enemy[5] (which can be illustrated from Alexander's treatment of Mazaeus, Porus, and the daughter of the dead Spitamenes), read in the light of his general remark above, shows clearly what he himself thought. It may be noticed in passing that none of our three accounts even suggests that Alexander drove the chariot himself; that statement is another invention of modern writers.[6]

It should be unnecessary to-day to state that the whole story, including the attempted assassination of Alexander, is untrue; Ptolemy was there, and his silence is conclusive. Neither need I repeat that silence was Ptolemy's method of dealing with untrue stories;[7] he never explicitly rejects or argues; the day, it may be hoped, is long past when his silence could be construed as an attempt to save Alexander's reputation.[8] What has to be considered is the source of the story, or rather the source of the chariot story in the simple form given by Dionysius.

It has already been seen that that source has to be very early, earlier than Hegesias; at the same time, no one would have dared to tell the story while Alexander lived. It was not part of the Peripatetic portrait of Alexander, which means that it did not originate in Cassander's circle, for though Curtius gives both the story and also the Peripatetic portrait

---

1 Roberts, *op. cit.* p. 1, puts the date of the *de comp. verb.* conjecturally between 20 and 10 B.C.
2 Curt. IV, 6, 7 and 25.
3 E.g. the torture of Philotas, VI, 11, 12–19.
4 IX, 1, 34: 'Equidem plura transcribo quam credo.' See § G, p. 92.
5 'alias virtutis etiam in hoste mirator'.
6 Grote, *loc. cit.*; Radet, *op. cit.* p. 105.
7 H. Strasburger, *Ptolemaios und Alexander*, 1934, esp. pp. 50, 55.
8 I treated this absurd idea at some length in *C.R.* XXXVI, 1922, pp. 64 *sqq.*

of Alexander (see § G), in that portrait in Curtius Alexander was a model prince down to Darius' death, and the chariot story belongs to a point of time long before that. If Cleitarchus were really the source of the secondary portrait in Curtius, which makes Alexander bad throughout (see § G), it might have been passed on by him; but this would hardly give time for the additions found in Hegesias, which he may have invented himself but may equally well have adopted from someone else. We know that after Alexander's death there was an outburst of literature in the Greek world very unfavourable to him (Ephippus is a specimen); it is probably here that the simple form of the story known to Dionysius started. One point in Hegesias' additions is worth notice, as bearing on Arrian's εὐνοῦχος. He says that Batis' corpulence ἐνέφαινε Βαβυλώνιον ζῷον ἕτερον ἁδρόν, 'indicated (to the onlookers) a second huge-bodied Babylonian creature' (or animal). The reference must be to some lost story earlier in Hegesias; and as animals in Babylonia were presumably no more corpulent than elsewhere, and as corpulence was one of the signs of a eunuch, Hegesias must have told some story about a Babylonian eunuch; the comparison with Batis presently turned Batis himself into a eunuch, and Arrian, having no correct information, repeated the story that Batis was a eunuch.

No one but Curtius gives, or even hints at, the comparison with Achilles. With one exception, the parallels between Alexander and Achilles in our extant literature are harmless, or even laudatory, probably invented by Choerilus of Iasos (see § E'). The exception is Curtius' sneer at the *ignobilis virguncula* Roxane,[1] where he drags in Achilles and Briseis, though he has to admit that Alexander, unlike Achilles, did marry the girl. This is Curtius himself speaking; did he himself then also invent the comparison with Achilles in the Batis story? I think he was too clever to invent a comparison which breaks down at every point; Alexander had not himself killed Batis as Achilles had killed Hector, Alexander did not drive the chariot himself as did Achilles, Hector was dead and Batis living, and while there was point in dragging Hector's corpse round unconquered Troy to announce to the Trojans their coming doom, there was none in dragging Batis alive round the already captured Gaza. Of course Dionysius, having quoted Hegesias, goes on: 'See now how Homer treated a similar theme';[2] but the comparison is his own, and also he is comparing

---

1 Curtius VIII, 4, 25–7.
2 After the end of Hegesias' story, Dionysius (p. 190, Roberts) goes on: ἆρά γε ὅμοια ταῦτ' ἐστὶ τοῖς Ὁμηρικοῖς ἐκείνοις, ἐν οἷς Ἀχιλλεύς ἐστιν

Hegesias and Homer, not Alexander and Achilles, and he is not dealing with substance at all, but merely with its expression in clauses and rhythms. Curtius perhaps *could* have read him, and got a hint; but that is not to say that he did. And there is another reason why I do not believe that Curtius invented the comparison with Achilles for himself: he shows, as has been seen, that he did not believe the chariot story.

It seems therefore impossible to locate the ultimate source of the story of the death of Batis, either in the simple form of the original chariot story or in the form of a comparison of Alexander with Achilles. It merely illustrates what I said before, that we cannot hope to find the sources of everything in the Alexander-story.

12. THE MURDER OF PARMENION

The source from which Curtius drew the considerable number of Macedonian customs which he describes (§ G, pp. 106 *sq.*) is certainly trustworthy; and one of the customs given is that if, in a trial for treason, the accused was condemned to death, it was a law (*lex*) of the Macedonians that his relatives should be put to death also.[1] There was no such thing as 'a law of the Macedonians'; a *lex* in Macedonia, if it had any meaning, could only mean a royal decree; the king was the fount of law, and there was no other legislative body. But it seems most improbable that any former king of Macedonia should have issued a general decree to this effect, and *lex* cannot be taken literally; it must have been a custom (*mos*), come down from a barbarous age—one of the old customs of which Macedonia was full, but none the less binding for being only a custom. The interesting suggestion has been made by Professor C. J. Robinson, Jr., that this old custom relieves Alexander of the guilt of Parmenion's murder:[2] Parmenion's son Philotas having been judicially condemned to death for treason, the father was automatically included in the same (judicial) condemnation. One would be

αἰκιζόμενος Ἕκτορα μετὰ τὴν τελευτήν; καίτοι τό γε πάθος ἐκεῖνο ἔλαττον· εἰς ἀναίσθητον γὰρ σῶμα ἡ ὕβρις· ἀλλ' ὅμως ἄξιόν ἐστιν ἰδεῖν, ὅσῳ διενήνοχεν ὁ ποιητὴς τοῦ σοφιστοῦ. This is Dionysius making his own comparison, not referring to something given in the story he has quoted.

1 VI, 11, 20, 'legem Macedonum veriti, qua cautum erat ut propinqui eorum qui regi insidiati sunt, cum ipsis necarentur'. See VIII, 6, 28; VI, 10, 30 *sqq.*

2 *A.J.P.* LVIII, 1937, p. 109, in a review of Kornemann's *Alexandergeschichte des Ptolemaios I.*

glad to believe this; but it requires examination. All that is recorded on the matter comes from Curtius; in Arrian, Parmenion's death is plain murder (assassination).

Curtius' story is that, after Philotas had confessed under torture but before the army had actually passed sentence (though it was obvious what the sentence must be), those related to Parmenion, mindful of the Macedonian custom, began committing suicide, and Alexander, to stop the panic, issued a decree which suspended the operation of the old custom (*lex* in Curtius),[1] as he presumably had power to do (n. 2, *below*). Philotas was then condemned to death by the army, and Parmenion also (VI, 11, 39), apparently on the strength of an incriminating letter (VI, 9, 13); Philotas was put to death, but Parmenion's death came later, after the trial and acquittal of Amyntas (VII, 2, 11 *sqq.*). That is, to Curtius, Parmenion's condemnation and death depended, not on the old custom, whose operation had been suspended, but on the definite evidence of a treasonable letter. It has never been believed either that there was such a letter or that Parmenion, who was far away, was condemned by the army, since both these things were unknown to Arrian's sources; and it must be noted that, if Curtius acquits Alexander of murder, it is because of these two things and not because of the old custom, whose operation, he says, had been suspended.[2] So far, then, Professor Robinson's suggestion cannot stand. The question came up again later over the Pages' conspiracy, where Curtius relates that the fathers and relatives of the pages on trial were afraid that they also would be put to death under the old custom (VIII, 6, 28). However, having suspended its operation once, Alexander ignored it, and no one (except Callisthenes, who was not a relative and whose case was another matter) was put to death but the pages themselves who were found guilty, VIII, 8, 20; Arrian IV, 14, 3 bears this out. Alexander then, in the Philotas matter, did suspend the old custom, and had suspended it *before* he took any steps about Parmenion; we have therefore reluctantly

1 VI, 11, 20, 'legem de supplicio coniunctorum sontibus remittere edixit'. I take this to mean, not an out and out repeal, but a suspension *ad hoc*; for the custom turns up again later, over the Pages' conspiracy. It makes no difference, as regards Parmenion's case, whether it was suspended or abolished.

2 It is not likely that the powers of a king of the Macedonians were defined; presumably he had every power there was, provided it did not conflict with the rights of the Macedonian people under arms. One must suppose that Alexander had power to suspend or abolish the custom in question; but in any case he had purported to do so, and the custom therefore cannot be pleaded on his behalf at the bar of history.

to conclude that Parmenion *was* murdered, and not merely executed following a judicial condemnation.

The one thing that has made me hesitate a little over this conclusion is that Curtius' whole story, which is very long, is directed to showing that it was *not* murder; and as, except for his summary (see § G, p. 100), he is, after Darius' death, hostile to Alexander and does everything he can to show him in a bad light (see § G), it is strange that he should thus labour to acquit Alexander of a murder charge. He must have been following some particular source here; he had read widely, but the only writer *we* know who might seem at all probable would be Chares, who tried to acquit Alexander of the charge of putting Callisthenes to death;[1] but this would be mere guesswork. Curtius' inconsistency, however, goes further than his portrait of Alexander; it extends to that of Parmenion also. For while in the story here considered he has taken Alexander's part as against Parmenion, elsewhere he praises Parmenion highly: he is the most faithful of the generals, III, 6, 4; Alexander takes his advice both at Issus, III, 7, 8, and before 'Arbela', IV, 10, 17, which is precisely what Alexander did *not* do; in VII, 2, 33 there is a list of Parmenion's excellences, followed by the untrue statement (which Beloch adopted) that Alexander never did anything of much moment without him. There is still one more inconsistency: while in VI, 11, 39 Parmenion is treated as having been rightly condemned, in VII, 2, 34 Curtius leaves this an open question, on the ground that Philotas' confession was obtained by torture; he has quite forgotten his own statement about an incriminating letter. But inconsistencies in Curtius are common enough, and some of the problems they raise are probably insoluble.

13. THE ALLEGED MASSACRE OF THE BRANCHIDAE

I wrote on this story in *C.R.* XXXVI, 1922, p. 63, an article which, I venture to think, made it certain enough that Alexander never met any Branchidae, and to which I may still refer for various considerations which do not need restating. I am treating the main points again, very briefly, for two reasons: the first is that I did not know in 1922 that there was in existence a quite conclusive piece of evidence on the matter, never (so far as I know) yet utilised by any writer on Alexander,

---

1 Chares fr. 15 (Jacoby II, no. 125). Aristobulus, who had not Ptolemy's better information, was here merely following Chares (*ib.*).

which ought to be put upon record; the other is that the question of sources requires fresh treatment, for to show that a story is untrue is only half the battle unless one can also show how it got there.

The story of the supposed massacre, given or alluded to by several secondary writers,[1] is based on a belief that Xerxes had settled the Branchidae in Bactria because to please him they had either sacked, or betrayed to him, the temple of Apollo at Didyma near Miletus, of which they were the priests. Herodotus however (VI, 19), an early and trustworthy witness, has a very different story: the temple and oracle of Didyma had been sacked and burnt to the ground by the Persians in the Ionian revolt in the reign of Darius I, after the capture of Miletus; it follows therefore that, if Herodotus be right, in Xerxes' time there were neither priests nor temple nor treasure at Didyma. Herodotus adds that Darius took the surviving Milesians first to Susa, and then settled them at a place on the Persian Gulf near the then mouth of the Tigris; and this has been confirmed by a massive bronze knucklebone dug up at Susa and published in 1905.[2] It bears an old inscription which shows that it had been dedicated to Apollo, and it was therefore part of the temple treasure of Didyma brought by Darius to Susa. In face of this knucklebone, no one can any longer refuse to credit Herodotus' account, as some have managed to do;[3] and therewith the Massacre of the Branchidae vanishes from history for ever.

I turn to the sources. Ctesias[4] has a story that after Xerxes returned to Sardis he sent one Matakes to sack Apollo's temple at Delphi, which he did. Reuss[5] emended ἐν Δελφοῖς to ἐν Διδύμοις, because Xerxes was in Sardis, and Jacoby[6] accepted this. It seems to me impossible to accept such an arbitrary alteration. I have little respect for Ctesias; but, so far as concerns this story of his, Xerxes still had a large force in Greece and could have sent any orders he wished; and as a later writer

---

1 Curt. VII, 5, 28–35; Diod. XVII, Table of contents κ´; Plut. *Mor.* 557B; Strabo XI, 11, 4 (518); XIV, 1, 5 (634).

2 B. Haussoullier, *Mém. de la Délégation en Perse*, VII, 1905, p. 155. The inscription runs: (1) Τάδε τἀγάλματα (2) [ἀ]πὸ λείο (*sic*) Ἀριστόλοχ[ος (3) καὶ] Θράσων ἀνέθεσαν τ[ῶι (4) Ἀ]πόλλωνι δεκάτην· ἐχά[λκευε] (5) δ' αὐτὰ Τσικλῆς ὁ Κυδιμάνδ[ρο. There is said to be room at the end of line 3 and beginning of 4 for the letters restored. The text has been examined by Bruno Keil, *Rev. Phil.* 1905, p. 335; P. Perdrizet, *R.E.G.* XXXIV, 1921, p. 64, and Ch. Picard, *R.E.G.* XLII, 1929, p. 121, who agrees it was brought from Didyma to Susa by Darius in 494.

3 One need no longer mention those who have thrown over Herodotus or have tried to 'reconcile' good early and bad late evidence.

4 58 (27), Gilmore.   5 *Rhein. Mus.* LX, 1905, p. 144.

6 'Ktesias' in PW, XI, 2 (1922), 2060.

has a story that Xerxes did sack Delphi,[1] no possible argument for the alteration exists. This being so, and Ctesias being out of the question, our earliest source for the Branchidae story is Callisthenes,[2] who said that Apollo had deserted Didyma because in Xerxes' time the Branchidae had medised and sacked the temple; the sacred spring had failed, but had started again in Alexander's time and the Milesians had brought oracles to him at Memphis which hailed him son of Zeus and prophesied the battle of 'Arbela' and the death of Darius III. In Callisthenes, then, the story of the Branchidae cannot be separated from the prophecy, and as Callisthenes must have made up the prophecy himself after Darius' death, he made up the story of the Branchidae at the same time.

In Callisthenes the Branchidae *sack* the temple (σεσύλητο). In Diodorus and Plutarch they *betray* it. In the two Strabo passages they hand over the treasure to Xerxes, but as Strabo in both also speaks of ἱεροσυλία and προδοσία he is combining the two versions, as does Curtius, who makes the Branchidae both sack and betray the temple.[3] Callisthenes is nowhere said to have related the massacre by Alexander, but he is solely responsible for the version which made the Branchidae sack Didyma themselves, and we shall see that he must have related the massacre. As a general thing, these stories of massacres most probably came from or through Cleitarchus (see § E, p. 53); but we find in later writers two different and mutually exclusive attitudes towards Alexander's supposed action, and Cleitarchus cannot have been responsible for both. Strabo XI, 11, 4 (518) glorifies Alexander's action: he kills the Branchidae because he abominates their sacrilege and treachery (μυσαττόμενον). No early writer is known who could have taken this view except Callisthenes, who was committed to writing up Alexander; it cannot be Cleitarchus, for Strabo practically never uses him,[4] and as Strabo elsewhere (XVII, 814) does quote Callisthenes in this connection, Strabo's view of the massacre must be taken from Callisthenes, who therefore did relate it; he had plenty of time, for in Curtius the massacre comes long before the Pages' conspiracy, when Callisthenes was put to death. Callisthenes' theme, then, was that as Apollo had done much for Alexander over the prophecies (Strabo XVII, 814), Alexander must do

1 Paus. X, 7, 1.
2 Jacoby II, no. 124, fr. 14 (a) = Strabo XVII, 1, 43 (814).
3 VII, 5, 28, 'violaverant'; *ib.* 35, 'prodere'.
4 He only once takes anything from him, an account of an Indian procession, Cleitarchus fr. 20 (Jacoby). He has four allusions to him, Cleitarchus frs. 13, 16, 26, 28; the first two are contemptuous enough and show that he considered Cleitarchus a liar. See on this § B, pp. 14 *sq.*

something for Apollo. How now does it stand with Cleitarchus? As Diodorus is lost and Trogus-Justin omits the story, Cleitarchus' view is most likely to be found in Curtius, and Curtius leaves no doubt as to what he himself thought: to visit the sins of the fathers upon the children, centuries later, was sheer cruelty (*crudelitas*).[1] Curtius was a strict moralist, but he did not invent the moral here, for Plutarch[2] uses the story, with others, to point the same moral. If then Curtius here be from Cleitarchus (and Plutarch makes this probable), Cleitarchus had taken a story originally invented to glorify Alexander and had turned it round so as to vilify him. So far as can be seen, he usually did represent Alexander in a bad light (see § E); and here he would have been justified, had not the story been completely untrue.

14. ALEXANDER AND THE GANGES[3]

The Ganges as a great river was unknown to the Greek world prior to Megasthenes.[4] It is often said that it must have been well known in Taxila, as no doubt it was, and that therefore Alexander must have known of it; but his plans and proceedings are conclusive that he, and therefore those about him, even if they had heard the name, knew nothing of the position of the river or its size, for when he turned at the Beas he thought that the eastern Ocean was quite close.[5] It is certain, too, that neither Alexander nor any one in the Greek world before Megasthenes knew anything of the Prasii or 'Easterners', the people of the great kingdom of Magadha, whose capital Pātaliputra (Palibothra) was on the Ganges near Patna[6] and whose new king Chandragupta after Alexander's death was to unite all Northern India into the

1 In 1922 I made the mistake of adopting Ed. Meyer's view, *Kleine Schriften* I, 1910, p. 286 n. 1, that Curtius' account of the Branchidae massacre was intended to glorify Alexander. It now seems to me certain that it was not, though Callisthenes' account probably was.
2 *De sera numinum vindicta*, 557B.
3 This is not a revision of my old article of the same name in *J.H.S.* XLIII, 1923, p. 93, but a new study.
4 I have said enough elsewhere (*J.H.S.* XLIII, 1923, p. 99) about Ctesias' Hypobaros and the 'fluvius alter' of the *Liber de inundacione Nili*.
5 By the time he reached the Beas he had suffered substantial losses, half his army was on his communications with his advanced base, Taxila, and he could no longer find the necessary garrisons without using Porus' troops; this proves that, as he still wished to advance, he must have thought the Ocean quite close. On his numbers, see App. 1, v, p. 168.
6 Strabo xv, 1, 36, 37 (702, 703), both from Megasthenes.

Appendix 14

Mauryan empire. Neither the Ganges nor the Prasii are mentioned by the best of our contemporary sources for Alexander, Ptolemy and Aristobulus; but some inferior sources connect them with Alexander, and it has to be seen how the connection arose. As we are going to find Magadha placed on the wrong side of the Ganges, it may be noticed here that it lay on the west, or south-west, side of the river and that one had *not* to cross the Ganges to reach it.

The first document to consider is the Gazetteer of Alexander's Empire, compiled in the last year of his life;[1] this document, being merely a list of satrapies, or countries equivalent to satrapies, within the Empire, could not deal with countries outside it. In XVIII, 6, 1 the Gazetteer, having listed the satrapies north of the Taurus-Caucasus line of mountains from east to west, turns to those south of this line, taking them also from east to west and beginning with that part of India which Alexander had conquered, and which, as Alexander left it, included more than one satrapy and two kingdoms treated as nominally vassal; India was too complicated a matter merely to list and required rather more explanation than the Gazetteer had already attached to the satrapy of Parthia and was to attach to that of Persis. Unhappily Diodorus, who wrote up India in the text of book XVII (§ F, *ante*, p. 86), has done the same thing himself in the Gazetteer and has made it difficult to reconstitute the original, even if his own remarks were confined to interpolations and if he did not, as I suspect he may have done, make

---

1 Diod. XVIII, 5, 2 to 6, 3 inclusive. See on the date App. 17. I give here the part relating to India, 6, 1 and 2; the words enclosed in square brackets will be shown to be, not part of the Gazetteer, but Diodorus' own additions. 6, 1. Τῶν δὲ πρὸς μεσημβρίαν ἐστραμμένων πρώτη μὲν παρὰ τὸν Καύκασόν ἐστιν Ἰνδική, βασιλεία μεγάλη καὶ πολυάνθρωπος, οἰκουμένη δ' ὑπὸ πλειόνων Ἰνδικῶν ἐθνῶν, ὧν ἐστι μέγιστον τὸ τῶν Γανδαριδῶν ἔθνος, [ἐφ' οὓς διὰ τὸ πλῆθος τῶν παρ' αὐτοῖς ἐλεφάντων οὐκ ἐπεστράτευσεν ὁ Ἀλέξανδρος. ὁρίζει δὲ τὴν χώραν ταύτην καὶ τὴν ἑξῆς Ἰνδικὴν ποταμὸς ὁ (blank), μέγιστος ὢν τῶν περὶ τοὺς τόπους καὶ τὸ πλάτος ἔχων σταδίων τριάκοντα]. ἐχομένη δὲ ταύτης ἡ λοιπὴ τῆς Ἰνδικῆς ἣν κατεπολέμησεν ὁ Ἀλέξανδρος, [παραποταμίοις ὕδασι κατάρρυτος καὶ κατὰ τὴν εὐδαιμονίαν ἐπιφανεστάτη], καθ' ἣν ὑπῆρχε σὺν ἄλλαις πλείοσι βασιλείαις ἥ τε τοῦ Πώρου καὶ Ταξίλου δυναστεία, δι' ἧς συμβαίνει ῥεῖν τὸν Ἰνδὸν ποταμόν, ἀφ' οὗ τὴν προσηγορίαν ἔσχεν ἡ χώρα. ἐχομένη δὲ τῆς Ἰνδικῆς ἀφώριστο σατραπεία Ἀραχωσία καὶ Κεδρωσία καὶ Καρμανία κ.τ.λ. As to readings, παραποταμίοις, which makes no sense, should be ποταμίοις, the clause in brackets being Diodorus quoting Eratosthenes (in Strabo XV, 1, 13 (690)), κατάρρυτος ποταμοῖς. In the last line but one, Florentinus, the most authoritative MS. for this period, has σατραπεία, which is clearly right; another hand has altered it to σατραπείας, but there was never any such thing as 'the Indian satrapy'.

alterations or omissions in the text of the document itself. Naturally the compiler of the Gazetteer took India in the order of Alexander's march. 'India' he begins 'is beside the Caucasus,[1] a great and populous kingdom inhabited by many peoples, of whom the greatest is the people of the Gandaridae.'[2] The Gandaridae here are the people of Gandhāra, a name which in Alexander's day meant the country between the Paropamisadae satrapy and the Indus, though it had once been extended to include Taxila; it is called a kingdom, not a satrapy, because when the Gazetteer was compiled it was, owing to the death of the satrap Philippus, actually under the rule of Taxiles.[3] The next clause says of the Gandaridae 'whom Alexander did not attack because of the number of their elephants'. This is a foolish interpolation of Diodorus' own. He personally believed that the Gandaridae were far away in the east (I shall come to that), and confuses them with the Gandaridae of the Gazetteer (Gandhāra); and he has transferred this story from the eastern Gandaridae to Gandhāra, not seeing that he is writing nonsense, since Alexander had conquered Gandhāra and the Gazetteer had just given it as his. Diodorus' interpolation goes right on to the word τριάκοντα; this seems clear from the words which follow it, ἐχομένη ταύτης, ταύτης being the kingdom of Gandhāra, for these words cannot in the original have been separated from Gandhāra by a long sentence (which I will consider presently). The Gazetteer then, having given Gandhāra, goes on 'Next to this (Gandhāra) is the rest of the India which Alexander conquered'[4]—the description which follows

---

1 The reference to the Hindu Kush and the Gandaridae shows that Ἰνδική here means the Paropamisadae and Gandhāra together, which had formed one satrapy in Persian times (Eratosthenes in Strabo xv, 2, 9 (724); Tarn, *Bactria and India*, p. 100). Alexander had separated the two, and the Gazetteer appears to ignore this; but one has to remember that Diodorus, who is reporting it, had it firmly in mind, as will be seen, that the Gandaridae were far away to the east, and in the Indian section of the Gazetteer has both interpolations and omissions (*post*). This limited meaning occurs again in Diod. xvii, 85, 3.

2 MSS. Τυνδαρίδων, a name otherwise unknown to the ancient world. As they are described as the greatest people of these parts, they were not some obscure tribe, and the usual alteration to Γανδαριδῶν must be correct, for Asoka (5th Edict) regarded the three most important peoples of the North-West as the Cambojas of Kafiristan (Kapisene in the Paropamisadae), the Gandhāras, and the Greeks. The name Gandaridae is merely a Greek version of Gandhāras, the people of Gandhāra; Pliny vi, 48 has the form Gandari.　　　　　3 Arr. vi, 27, 2.

4 Not 'the rest of India, which Alexander conquered' (that would be ἡ λοιπὴ Ἰνδική), but 'the rest of Alexander's conquests in India'.

from ποταμίοις το ἐπιφανεστάτη is obviously Diodorus' own, see p. 276 n. 1—'in which, with many other kingdoms, lies the δυναστεία of Porus and the δυναστεία of Taxiles through which (i.e. through the δυναστεία of Taxiles) there "happens to flow" the Indus, from which the country takes its name'. This ends the Gazetteer on India; there follow the adjoining satrapies in order, from east to west, Arachosia, Gedrosia, Carmania, etc. Certain things call for remark. The last part which I have cited is guaranteed to belong to the Gazetteer by the use of συμβαίνει, 'happens to', to denote a temporary political arrangement, for this usage occurs in two other places in the Gazetteer (App. 17). The Indus in the Gazetteer is not the boundary of India, as it became later in Eratosthenes' geography, or of anything else. The document confines itself to giving what Alexander did conquer, and (as we have it) not all of that; it does not give the Indus country south of the Punjab, or the still existing satrapies of the Paropamisadae and Sind. The Paropamisadae may be included in the general statement that India lies beside the Caucasus, but the omission of Sind and the Indus country must be due to Diodorus; his transcript may be a compression of a longer description. The important thing, however, for the matter I am considering is that, so far, the Gazetteer contains no mention either of the eastern Gandaridae or the Ganges; they were not in the Empire.

I must now look at the sentence at the beginning of 6, 2, from ὁρίζει το τριάκοντα, which I have called an interpolation. It says: 'This country (that of the Gandaridae) is divided from the India that comes next to it by the river [name missing] which is the greatest river in those parts and is 30 stades broad.' This must mean either the Indus or the Ganges.[1] If the sentence belongs to the Gazetteer, it cannot well be the Indus, because to the compiler of the Gazetteer the Indus (we have seen) ran through the δυναστεία of Taxiles and was no boundary of anything; and whether it belongs to the Gazetteer or not, it equally cannot be the Indus because of the breadth. The statements we have as to the breadths of Indian rivers are mostly conventional tokens, but no one gives the breadth of the Indus as 30 stades.[2] Diodorus, however,

---

1 The Ganges is often called the biggest river in India; Strabo xv, 702 says it is admittedly the biggest in the world. That the Indus came next is also often stated. But Diodorus xvii, 85, 3 had said that the Indus was the biggest river in 'Ινδική, which is interesting as showing the use of 'Ινδική with a limited meaning, probably taken from the Gazetteer (6, 1).

2 Ctesias in Arrian v, 4, 2, 40 stades to 100; Arr. v, 20, 9, 15 to 40; vi, 14, 5, perhaps 100 at Patala; Strabo xv, 700, either 100 or 50; Pliny vi, 71, 50.

does elsewhere (II, 37, 2) give the breadth of the Ganges as 30 stades,[1] and, as the unknown river cannot be the Indus, it should be meant for the Ganges; but it bounds Gandhāra, whereas the Ganges is far away. The sentence then, whether the unnamed river should be Indus or Ganges or something else, is all wrong, and cannot belong to the Gazetteer; it is Diodorus' own interpolation, like the preceding sentence about the elephants, and, like that sentence, has originated from Diodorus confounding the Gandaridae of Gandhāra with the eastern Gandaridae. Diodorus' interpolation, then, runs from ἐφ' οὖς τo σταδίων τριάκοντα; as has already been seen, the following words ἐχομένη ταύτης render any other view impossible. There is then nothing in the Gazetteer itself about the Ganges.[2]

The next document to consider is Diodorus on the eastern Gandaridae. When the 'bad' Porus, whose kingdom lay between the Chenab and the Ravi, fled at Alexander's approach, Arrian (v, 21, 2) does not say where he fled to; but it is fairly obvious. He could not fly westward, as Alexander was coming from the west, nor southward, as this would have taken him either to the Malli between the Chenab and the Ravi or to their allies the Oxydracae across the Ravi; both submitted to Alexander, but he never saw or caught Porus. He can only have fled before Alexander eastward and must have crossed the Beas, where Alexander turned back. Diodorus XVII, 90, 1 says that he fled to the Gandaridae;[3] and as Gandhāra is out of the question, Diodorus can only mean that this people, probably a branch of the Gandaridae of Gandhāra, lived across the Beas, the country between the Ravi and the Beas being occupied by the Cathaeans. It agrees with this that in Diodorus XVII, 93, 4 and 94, 1, Alexander having reached the Beas, his next στρατεία is to be against the Gandaridae, and, as he doubts

---

1 Every one else gives far higher figures for the Ganges. Megasthenes (Strabo xv, 702; Arr. *Ind.* 4, 7), not less than 100 stades ὅταν ᾖ μέτριος; reproduced by Mela, III, 68, 10, and Pliny VI, 65 with an added minimum of 70. Solinus 52, 7, 200 to 80; Aelian *H.A.* 12, 41, 400 to 80.

2 Fischer in his edition of Diodorus filled the blank in XVIII, 6, 2 (see p. 276 n. 1) with ὀνομαζόμενος Γάγγης (from II, 37, 1), which is indefensible and merely darkens counsel; I need not refute Ernst Meyer's attempt to defend it, *Klio*, XXI, 1927, p. 183.

3 The statement in Strabo xv, 1, 30 (699) that the kingdom of this Porus was called Gandaris is a mere confusion, whether it really be from Onesicritus (so Jacoby II, no. 134, fr. 21, but doubtfully, see II, BD, p. 477) or not. Kiessling, 'Gandaridae' in PW, made the people of Gandhāra, the Gandaridae, and the Gangaridae three sections of one tribe. But, though there *was* a people called Gangaridae, the use of this name in Curtius and Justin is a mere confusion for Gandaridae; see *post.*

whether the troops will go on, he harangues them about the στρατεία against the Gandaridae (94, 5); but they refuse to cross the Beas, so he gives up his plan. All this is simple history; and as Diodorus is here following his main source, Aristobulus[1] (§ F, pp. 71, 75), the correctness of the name and location of the Gandaridae cannot well be doubted. Arrian v, 25, 1 says that an Aratta people, whom he does not name, lived beyond the Beas, and that one of the reasons why the troops refused to cross that river was a report that this people had a very large number of war elephants. As we have already seen, Diodorus transferred this report about the elephants to the Gandaridae of Gandhāra, whom he confused with the eastern Gandaridae, proof that Diodorus' Gandaridae were the unnamed people of Arrian and that they lived across the Beas.[2] Be it noted that Diodorus does not say that Alexander feared to attack them; he only says that he did not attack them, which was a fact, though due to the mutiny of the army.

So far I have been dealing with history, which knows nothing about the Ganges and furnishes no reason for supposing that Alexander had ever heard of that river. I come now to the legend which made Alexander not only know of the Ganges but reach it. Into Diodorus' historical account is sandwiched, from another source, the story of a mythical ruler, Phegeus (93, 2, 3), who professed to tell Alexander

1 Because in XVII, 93, 1, Diodorus has Aristobulus' form Ὕπανιν for the name of the Beas (on this form see § D, p. 32). Some MSS. have altered it to the more usual Ὕφασιν; but Florentinus, which most scholars have considered the most authoritative MS. for books XVII–XX, has Ὕπανσιν, i.e. Ὕπανιν, whether the sigma has got in from Ὕφασιν or whether some copyist has reversed the last syllable of Ὕπανις. In the only other place where Diodorus mentions this river, II, 37, 4, he has Ὕπανιν, which should be conclusive. In the same way, in XVII, 98, 1, Diodorus uses the form Συδράκαι for the Oxydracae (Kshudraka) of Ptolemy-Arrian; that this is Aristobulus' form is shown by its use in Strabo XV, 1, 33 (701) in a passage which is shown by the use of Hypanis and the allusion to 'Meropid Cos' to be from Aristobulus beyond any question (see § D, p. 32 n. 3); cf. Strabo XV, 1, 8 (687). This is the more certain because Strabo, in a passage from Megasthenes, XV, 1, 6 (687), uses the form Ὑδράκας, presumably Megasthenes'.
2 V. A. Smith, *J.R.A.S.* 1903, p. 685, put the Oxydracae here. It is quite certain that they lived much farther south, between the Ravi and the Beas, contiguous to their allies the Malli west of the Ravi. When Alexander attacked the Malli, those who broke eastward across the Ravi were trying to join their allies, as indeed Arrian VI, 11, 3 suggests; he adds that ὁ πᾶς λόγος, i.e. every one except Ptolemy and Aristobulus, put the Malli town where Alexander was wounded on the wrong side of the Ravi, among the Oxydracae (so Curtius IX, 4, 26).

what lay beyond the Beas: first a desert, twelve days' journey across, and then the river called Ganges; both statements are completely untrue, and leave no doubt that Phegeus is a myth. In this story the Ganges is called 32 stades across, Diodorus' own figure elsewhere being 30;[1] this shows a new source. Phegeus goes on to say that *beyond* the Ganges lived the nation, ἔθνος, of the 'Gandaridae and Prasii', who in the legend are always named together. Curtius, IX, 2, 2–5, also gave the same story about Phegeus, but concluded it with one of his most polished sarcasms (§ G, p. 93), showing that he did not believe a word of it. But the crucial point about Phegeus' story is this. The Prasii ('Easterners'), first revealed to the Greek world by Megasthenes, were the people of the great kingdom of Magadha;[2] not only were they separated by half the breadth of India from the eastern Gandaridae, but Magadha was west and south of the Ganges, and Phegeus' story puts it beyond, i.e. *on the wrong side of*,[3] that river, proof absolute that Phegeus and his story are pure myth.

Phegeus' story is the beginning of the legend which made Alexander reach the Ganges. He reaches it in the forged letter from Craterus to his mother.[4] Next comes Plutarch,[5] who relates as a fact that the kings of the Prasii and of the Gandaritae (Gandaridae) held the farther bank of the Ganges; Alexander greatly desired to cross, but the army refused; he retired to his tent, but finally turned back, having set up altars on the Ganges bank and leaving behind him arms, mangers, etc., greater than usual. This is merely the real story of Alexander turning back at the Beas transferred to the Ganges, with the embellishment, common to the vulgate writers, of the superhuman camp equipment (see § E', p. 62); that it comes from the same source as the Phegeus story is shown both by the Ganges being 32 stades broad and by Magadha being on the wrong side of that river. Finally, in Justin XII, 8, 9, Alexander defeats the Prasii and Gangaridae (Gandaridae) with great slaughter, which ought to mean that he crosses the Ganges; but Justin does not mention the Ganges, and Alexander conquers the Prasii and Gangaridae before reaching the kingdom of Sopeithes (in the Salt

1 Diod. II, 37, 2, and probably XVIII, 6, 2, see *ante*.
2 Megasthenes in Strabo XV, 1, 36 (702) and 37 (703): Prasii, capital Palibothra (Pātaliputra); so in Arr. *Ind.* 10, 5.
3 Diod. XVII, 93, 2, πέραν; Curt. IX, 2, 3, 'ulteriorem ripam'; Plut. *Alex.* LXII, περᾶσαι, ἀντιπέρας. This was the point made in my article of 1923. How it was ever missed is incomprehensible.
4 Strabo XV, 1, 35 (702).
5 Plut. *Alex.* LXII, the worst chapter he ever wrote.

Range) where he yields to the prayers of his army and so turns back, a hopeless confusion from which no deductions can be drawn.

This legend or group of legends sprang from a desire to glorify Alexander by making him reach the Ganges, while keeping what of reality was possible; his turning back at the Beas became a turning back at the Ganges, and the real Gandaridae across the Beas were transferred to the far side of the Ganges; to add verisimilitude, the Gandaridae were bracketed with the greatest people on the Ganges, the Prasii (who are never mentioned alone), though this involved putting Magadha on the wrong side of that river and bracketing two peoples separated by half the breadth of India. Even Justin's absurdity tries to keep some touch with reality; for it names together, as conquered by Alexander, Cathaeans, Prasii, and Gangaridae, and Alexander really had conquered the Cathaeans, between the Ravi and the Beas. One owes a debt to Diodorus for preserving Aristobulus' sober historical statement that the 'bad' Porus fled to the Gandaridae, which in one sense is the key to the matter; for all we have got, so far, is a mere substitution of the name Ganges for the name Hyphasis (Beas). But unfortunately Diodorus was not historian enough to avoid mixing up history and legend; he became confused between the two, and not only inserted the Phegeus story into his historical account, but let the legend affect his history; he gave the (real) eastern Gandaridae a king because the legend did this, though it is clear from Arrian that they were an Aratta people; and in book II, 37, 2 he placed them east of the Ganges, though he amended this in book XVII. He also managed (as we have seen) to get confused by the name Gandaridae occurring in two separate places, in Gandhāra and on the Beas. But his confusions are not difficult to disentangle; the most notable of them is that, having given in XVII, 94 a correct account of the army refusing to cross the Beas, which compelled Alexander to turn back, in 108, 3 he alludes to the army having refused to cross the *Ganges*, the point in the legend elaborated later by Plutarch; the two writers together exhibit the Ganges as merely replacing the Beas.

As the legend or legends about Alexander reaching the Ganges were invented merely to glorify him, it seems clear that they were not invented by Cleitarchus, for, so far as can be made out, this was not at all that writer's intention (see § E, p. 54). They were in fact very late inventions, produced by some person or persons totally ignorant of Indian geography at a time when the very location of Magadha had been forgotten. Justin's statement that Alexander conquered Magadha is merely a transfer to him of the exploit of a much later king, Demetrius of Bactria, who (through his general Menander) did conquer Magadha and take Pātaliputra, a matter well known to Trogus;[1] and we probably possess another transfer from Demetrius to Alexander. Plutarch makes Chandragupta say frequently that Alexander came within a hair's-breadth of conquering Magadha.[2] Alexander did nothing of the sort; neither did Chandragupta ever say what he is made to say. But the sentence is framed most obscurely, and we only know that λαβεῖν τὰ πράγματα, which might have many geographical meanings, here refers to Magadha because of the subsequent reference to the low-born king. We can only make sense of this if we suppose that the saying, and its attribution to Chandragupta, are taken from somebody's statement (which would have been true) that Demetrius had come within a hair's-breadth of conquering the Mauryan empire which Chandragupta had founded and whose kernel was Chandragupta's own kingdom of Magadha. The legends about Alexander and the Ganges cannot then have started earlier than the middle of the second century B.C.; and as at that time no one was taking any interest in Alexander, there can be little doubt that they belong to the period which saw the production of other stories intended to glorify him—his so-called Plans (App. 24), the Embassies which came to him (App. 23), the stories of his intention to conquer and rule the world. These stories all originated during the same period, the middle and later part of the first century B.C., when the Mediterranean world, which ought to have been Alexander's, was Rome's. Livy thundered against the whole literary movement; but I have dealt with this subject elsewhere (§ C, p. 24; App. 24, pp. 396 *sq.*).

We have seen that, in the legend in Diodorus and Plutarch (Justin differs), the events that happened at the Beas were merely transferred to the Ganges, and the Gandaridae on the one river were bracketed with the Prasii on the other, who were misplaced for the purpose. But there was more than this; the legend omitted most of northern India (for the Ganges throughout means the Ganges at Pātaliputra), and made the Ganges the next river to the Beas, only 12 days distant. Now there must have been some intermediate stage in the transfer of the Gandaridae from the Beas to the Ganges—Diodorus for example in one place (II, 37, 2) puts the Gandaridae east of the Ganges without mentioning the Prasii—but there is not the material to recover it. It is, however, obvious that the next river to the Beas, in Phegeus' story,

---

1 Tarn, *Bactria and India*, ch. IV.
2 Plut. *Alex.* LXII, Ἀνδρόκοττος... λέγεται πολλάκις εἰπεῖν ὕστερον ὡς παρ' οὐδὲν ἦλθε τὰ πράγματα λαβεῖν Ἀλέξανδρος, the king (i.e. of Magadha) being low-born, etc.

must once have meant the Sutlej; that the breadths of 30 stades and 32 stades given for the Ganges by Diodorus and the legend respectively can never have been meant originally for the real Ganges,[1] but might quite well have been meant for the Sutlej; and that somewhere in the intermediate stage there was therefore some confusion of the Sutlej and the Ganges, a confusion that might have started with Cleitarchus, whose geography of Asia, where it can be traced (see § B, pp. 14 *sq.*), is as bad as it can be, though he was not responsible for the late legend of Alexander reaching the Ganges. It is noteworthy that Alexander, till he reached the Beas, seems to have known what was ahead of him, but that there his knowledge, and that of his companions, stops; to those with him, the Punjab was a land of four rivers, not five—Jhelum, Chenab, Ravi, Beas; the other three joined the Chenab, and the united stream entered the Indus under that name.[2] This supports the view, which I think very probable, that the Beas had been the one-time Persian boundary[3] (though India had been lost to the Persians before Alexander came), and that one of the reasons why the army mutinied at that particular point was that they had reached the farthest Persian bounds. Though Phegeus and his story are mythical, Alexander must have made enquiries when he reached the Beas and must have heard of the Sutlej, and as he thought the eastern Ocean quite close (p. 275 n. 5), he may really have thought that there was only one more great river between the Beas and his goal;[4] that later legend should have turned this river into the mighty Ganges would be understandable enough,

1 Every breadth given for the Ganges in antiquity was far greater; see p. 279 n. 1.
2 Arr. VI, 14, 4 *sq.*; *Ind.* 4, 8 *sq.* Arrian himself knew there were other rivers between the Beas and the Ganges, *Ind.* 4, 3–6; 8, 5; 10, 5; *Anab.* v, 5, 5.
3 Prof. A. V. Williams-Jackson in *Camb. Hist. of India,* I, p 341. Megasthenes' story (Strabo xv, 687) of some Persian king hiring mercenaries from the Ὑδράκαι (Oxydracae) must belong to a time when Persian rule no longer extended east of the lower Ravi, if indeed it ever did; but this would not be inconsistent with a further extension farther north along the great road.
4 In Alexander's speech at the Hyphasis in Arrian (see App. 15), a late composition full of contradictions, he says (v, 26, 1) that it is not far to the Ganges and the eastern sea, though later (26, 3) he says that there are many warlike nations between the Beas and the eastern sea. The latter was hardly calculated to induce a weary army to go on; but, as to the former, since he really did believe that the eastern Ocean was quite close, then, allowing for the fact that the name Ganges has come in from the legend, there may well have been a tradition that he did say: 'One more river and then the end', and it may have been a true tradition, seeing that it would have been the one effective argument he had.

especially as Megasthenes had named a people Gangaridae on the lower Ganges who could be, and in Curtius and Justin are, confused with the Gandaridae. But nothing can be proved here, for we have the strange fact that no Alexander-writer, and no geographer before Claudius Ptolemy (much of whose information about India came from the Graeco-Bactrian period),[1] so much as mentions the Sutlej; the silence of Strabo, who used both Megasthenes and Apollodorus of Artemita, is a very strange thing. We know, from a much neglected passage of Aristobulus, that when he was there the Indus had left its bed and was running down the Hakra channel;[2] but no one knows how the Sutlej then ran and how it joined the Indus, or even if it did join it; every hypothesis put forward seems open to grave objection. I need not go into this. Very possibly the Sutlej holds the key to the legend of Alexander knowing and reaching the Ganges; but it also itself furnishes an apparently insoluble problem.

1 The names of the Punjab rivers in use, prior to Claudius Ptolemy, all date from Alexander's expedition and reflect the local Prakrit; Ptolemy's names are said to reflect the Sanscrit forms and are therefore from a quite different source. On his information from Graeco-Bactrian times see Tarn, *Bactria and India*, pp. 230 *sqq.*, 243 *sqq.*, and *passim*.

2 Strabo xv, 1, 19 (693)=Aristobulus fr. 35 in Jacoby II, p. 780, taking the MS. reading τὸ ἕτερον; it is unfortunate that Jacoby should have printed Groskurd's arbitrary alteration of τό to τι. See § F, p. 76 n. 6; Tarn, *Bactria and India*, p. 236.

Appendices 15–17: DOCUMENTARY

15. THE SPEECHES IN ARRIAN

(AND SOME IN CURTIUS)

SPEAKING generally, one expects a speech in any ancient historian to be a fabrication, either composed by the historian himself or by a predecessor, or else some exercise from one of the schools of rhetoric which he had adopted. But, very occasionally, one does meet with a speech which is genuine. 'Genuine', of course, does not imply a verbatim report; no such thing was known. It means that the speech *was* made on the occasion referred to, and that some one who heard it remembered and wrote down the gist of what the speaker did say, and perhaps was able to give some striking and (in the literal sense of the word) memorable point or illustration pretty much in the speaker's own words. In that sense, Arrian has preserved one most important speech of Alexander's which is certainly, in substance, genuine, and another of less importance which is probably so; and that ought to be of some interest.

Arrian gives seven set speeches of very different types, four being Alexander's. As regards four of the seven—those of Alexander before Issus and on the Beas, that of Coenus on the Beas, and that of Callisthenes—he only professes to give them as 'thereabouts'; but the speeches of Alexander before Tyre and at Opis are given without such qualification. The seventh (no. 4 *post*) is immaterial.

(1) II, 7, 3 *sqq.*, Alexander's speech before Issus. This is as bad as it can be. It makes Alexander call Persians cowards, the last thing he would have done, and makes him talk about the levy of the Persian empire, which he knew was not there; it ends with an elaborate 'etcetera'.[1] I take it to be part of a school exercise which Arrian adopted because of the allusion to Xenophon.

(2) II, 17, Alexander's speech before Tyre. This is short, sensible, and to the point. All the facts about sea-power are correct, and the prophecy that the rowers in the Persian fleet would not go on fighting for Persia once their cities were in Macedonian hands did come true. But there is no need to suppose that the speech was composed after this had happened; the prophecy is not beyond the powers of calculation of a competent commander. It may be an actual speech made to

1 II, 7, 9, ὅσα τε ἄλλα. . .ἐξ ἀγαθοῦ ἡγεμόνος παραινεῖσθαι εἰκός.

his officers;[1] but more probably, I think, it reflects a manifesto issued by Alexander to the army on the eve of the great siege.

(3) IV, 11, 2 *sqq.*, Callisthenes' speech on *proskynesis* and on the distinction between honours due to men and honours due to the gods. This does not purport to be a record of what Callisthenes actually said;[2] rather, it is a summary of his position, a very capable summary, whether written by Arrian himself or by some one who was present. For just as we know, internal evidence apart, that the 'cloud in the west' speech of Agelaos of Naupactus in Polybius is substantially genuine because the result of his appeal was his election to the Generalship of the Aetolian League, which is a fact, so Callisthenes must have said something of the sort, because the consequence of what he said was that Alexander, though angry enough, at once excused Macedonians from *proskynesis*, which is a fact, and told them to think no more about it;[3] and they did think no more about it, which is a fact also. The speech throws no light on Callisthenes' amazing *volte-face*.

(4) V, 1, 5, the speech of Akouphis of Nysa, which hardly requires notice. This is part of the Nysa λόγος (§ E, pp. 45 *sq.*), and as Arrian gave the λόγος he also reproduced the speech. It is very silly, and probably Akouphis never existed.

(5) and (6), the speech of Alexander at the Beas, V, 25, 3 *sqq.*, and Coenus' reply, V, 27, 2 *sqq.* Some have accepted Alexander's speech as genuine; this is impossible. The speech cannot be separated from Coenus' reply; the two speeches are meant to be a pair, and a similar pair is given by Curtius.[4] But Coenus made no speech, for he was not there; he had been left behind on communications at the Acesines (Arr. V, 21, 1), perhaps already a doomed man, and it was on the Acesines that he died soon after.[5] This means that Alexander's speech is suspect from the start; it is in fact a very late composition, a mere piece of patchwork, and it does not profess to be more than 'the sort of things' which Alexander said.[6] The lateness is obvious. The statement in V, 26, 1 that it is not far to the Ganges cannot be earlier than

1 Arrian here, 18, 1, says ταῦτα εἰπών, as he does of the genuine speech at Opis (*post*), instead of the τοιαῦτα, or ταῦτα καὶ τοιαῦτα, of the speeches of Alexander and Coenus on the Beas and of the speech of Callisthenes.
2 IV, 12, 1, ταῦτα δὴ καὶ τοιαῦτα εἰπόντος.
3 *Ib.*, πέμψαντα κωλῦσαι Μακεδόνας μεμνῆσθαι ἔτι τῆς προσκυνήσεως.
4 Curt. IX, 2, 12 *sqq.* and 3, 5 *sqq.*
5 Arr. VI, 2, 1; Curt. IX, 3, 20 (on the Acesines). As both agree as to the cause (νόσῳ, morbo), the statement must be from Ptolemy.
6 V, 27, 1, ταῦτα καὶ τὰ τοιαῦτα εἰπόντος, the same formula as is used for Callisthenes' speech.

Megasthenes and may be much later, as it seems to be part of the Ganges legend (see App. 14). The statement in 26, 2 that he will show that the Indian Gulf (i.e. the Indian Ocean), the Persian Gulf, and the Hyrcanian Sea (our Caspian) are all connected as being gulfs of Ocean is Eratosthenes' geography, not Alexander's, as anyone can see who troubles to read my analysis in § B and § C. Finally, in 26, 2, there is a reference to one of Alexander's supposed Plans, to circumnavigate Africa from the Persian Gulf and conquer it by coming eastward from the Pillars 'as a consequence of which (οὕτω) all Asia will be ours (an absurdity) and the bounds of my Empire will be those of the earth', τῆς γῆς ὅρους; and the Plans are first-century B.C. (see App. 24). Be it noted also that 'Asia' here means the continent, while its regular meaning in Alexander's day was the Persian empire. The speech is full of mistakes. It is addressed throughout to 'the Macedonians and the allies'; there were no allies on the Beas. The list of conquests in 25, 4 includes Cappadocians and Paphlagonians, who were not conquered till Perdiccas did so after Alexander's death. In 25, 6 the peoples across the Beas are called unwarlike, in 26, 3 warlike, μάχιμα. Very noticeable is the amount which is copied from Alexander's real speech at Opis. The beginning of the list of conquests in 25, 4 (omitting the Cappadocians and Paphlagonians already noticed) runs 'Ιωνία, 'Ελλήσποντος, Φρύγες ἀμφότεροι, Λυδοί; this is an unintelligent copy from the Opis speech, VII, 9, 7, which has 'Ιωνίαν, Αἰολίδα, Φρύγας ἀμφοτέρους, Λυδούς; but whereas the Opis list is strictly correct, for Aeolis could be, and was, spoken of as distinct from Hellespontine Phrygia, just as Ionia could be, and was, spoken of as something distinct from Lydia, the Hyphasis list dates from a time when the real state of Asia Minor under Alexander had been forgotten; the Hellespont, i.e. Hellespontine Phrygia, is one of the two Phrygias next mentioned, and the substitution of the word for Aeolis merely creates a clumsy tautology. Again, in the list of conquests, 25, 5, we get ὁ Τάναϊς, τὰ πρόσω ἔτι τοῦ Τανάϊδος, 'the Jaxartes, the lands beyond the Jaxartes', which is untrue and is an unintelligent bungling of VII, 10, 6, περάσαντα Ὦξόν τε ποταμὸν καὶ Τάναϊν, by some one who no longer knew the facts. In 26, 8, ὑμεῖς σατραπεύετε is taken from VII, 9, 8, ὑμεῖς σατράπαι; 26, 8, ζηλωτοὺς τοῖς ἀπερχομένοις reflects the phrase in the Opis speech ζηλωτοὺς τοῖς οἴκοι, VII, 10, 5. But what clinches the matter as regards the speech on the Beas in Arrian is that Alexander is made to speak to the same audience again the next day (in Curtius it comes in the original speech) and says to them (28, 2) that those who want to go home (nothing had been said about going home) are free to go home and to tell people there that they deserted their king in the midst of enemies. This is the theme of, and is copied from, the last part of the speech at Opis; at Opis it had meaning indeed, but on the Beas it has no meaning at all: no one could have got home, and to diminish still further his already greatly depleted man-power was the last thing Alexander would have wished. We shall find this much more pointedly put by Curtius; for the moment it suffices to remark that scarcely any document we possess is more obviously a late patchwork than the boastful oration which Arrian has put into Alexander's mouth on the Beas. Why he did so is quite obscure.

Alexander's speech in Curtius, ix, 2, 12 *sqq.*, is quite unlike that in Arrian. Alexander is supposed to be talking to the whole army, the possibility of which may be doubted,[1] and the speech was certainly composed by Curtius himself. It was a fact (Arr. v, 25, 1) that the army believed that beyond the Beas were people who possessed an enormous number of war-elephants; and the first half of Alexander's speech is directed to showing that elephants were not an arm to be feared. So far, all that the Macedonians, when they reached the Beas, knew about war-elephants was the desperate battle they had had, face to face, with those of Porus; but Curtius writes as from his own day, when the real use of elephants as flank guards against cavalry, discovered through trial and error by the great Macedonian generals after Alexander's death,[2] had long been forgotten, and their failures when used unintelligently had led to their general abandonment as an arm. Curtius then wrote this speech himself, introducing, as he so often did in his speeches, a real fact which should have come in his narrative, viz. that Alexander himself never used elephants in battle. In the rest of the speech, except the end, the allusions are correct enough, and the statement that they were near the eastern Ocean and the end of the world probably corresponds with what Alexander did think. But at the close Curtius has given, in concise form, the real ending of the speech at Opis,[3] and much more plainly than Arrian does. He therefore knew the end of the Opis speech as Arrian gives it; and as, on any probable dating, he is much earlier than Arrian, and as the main contact between his sources and those of Arrian is that both used Ptolemy (for Curtius' use of Aristobulus is a small matter compared to his use of Ptolemy (see § G)), it follows, not only

---

1 It is, however, recorded that John Wesley once addressed an open-air meeting of 30,000 persons and all could hear him.

2 On the use of elephants in Hellenistic warfare, see Tarn, *Hell. Military Developments*, pp. 92–100.

3 Curt. ix, 2, 34: 'Ite reduces domos; ite deserto rege ovantes.'

that Curtius took the passage in question from Ptolemy, but that the last part of Alexander's speech at Opis as Arrian gives it also came from Ptolemy, a most valuable proof.

The two speeches of Coenus call for little remark. That in Curtius, IX, 3, 5 *sqq.*, was written by Curtius himself; it is rather like a pacifist tract, and gives the impression of having been composed for the sake of the epigram *omnium victores omnium inopes.* The statement that beyond the Beas was another world, unknown even to Indians, is of interest, and bears out what I said (§ G, p. 93; see App. 14, p. 281) about Curtius telling the story of Phegeus with his tongue in his cheek; the statement that the route home by the southern Ocean would be the shorter could not have been written till long after Alexander's day. Coenus' speech in Arr. V, 27, 2 *sqq.* needs little comment. The reference, 27, 5, to the Greeks in the new settlements being discontented shows that it was written after the rising in Bactria and the East which followed Alexander's death, for no one on the Beas could have known whether they were discontented or not; the statement (27, 5) that the Thessalians were sent home from *Bactra* is wrong; the reference to an expedition against Carthage brings us down to the 'Plans' of the first century B.C. The speech was therefore probably composed at the same time as Alexander's speech in Arrian, it cannot be said by whom; Arrian says of both τοιαῦτα εἰπόντος, not ταῦτα (see p. 287 n. 1); both contain too many blunders to have been written by Arrian himself, and certainly they have nothing to do with Ptolemy. The pair of speeches in Curtius are certainly Curtius' own composition; but (Ptolemy being out of the question) what was the connection between the two pairs of speeches which made both Arrian and Curtius select Coenus as the man who answered Alexander, seeing that it cannot be a true tradition, since Coenus was not there? I do not know.

(7) I come now to the speech which is certainly Alexander's, that to the mutineers at Opis (Arr. VII, 9, 1–10, 7).[1] He addresses his audience as Μακεδόνες, but in some places he is speaking to the officers, in others to the men; one may suppose that in the audience were many officers, as well as a considerable number of the mutinous rank and file. On the platform with him were some of the higher officers (Arr. VII,

---

[1] Here again, as in the speech at Tyre (p. 286), Arrian has ταῦτα εἰπών (VII, 11, 1) instead of τοιαῦτα or ταῦτα καὶ τοιαῦτα of the two speeches on the Beas and of the speech of Callisthenes. Fr. Hampl, *Der König der Makedonen*, Leipzig Diss. 1934, among recent writers, said the speech was not genuine (pp. 81 *sq.*), citing the gold crowns and the bronze statues, and the objection about Ionia dealt with presently (p. 292 n. 1); but his examination is quite superficial.

8, 3), Ptolemy naturally among them, and he was accompanied by his Guards, the *agēma* of the hypaspists (*ib.*). That much of the speech we have is genuine, in the sense in which I have defined it—in this case, written down from memory or from his notes by Ptolemy—is certain enough, even if we cannot go the whole way with a modern scholar who has seen in this speech the principal gem (*Glanzpunkt*) of Ptolemy's book,[1] corresponding to Pericles' *Funeral Oration* in Thucydides; but we have already had a conclusive proof that the end of the speech, at least, is from Ptolemy. The speech, however, as we have it in Arrian, contains some insertions made later;[2] I shall come to that.

The speech falls naturally into four sections. Alexander only spoke at all because he was furious, not only at the demand of the mutineers that the whole army, and not merely the unfit, should go home[3] (he had already arrested the principal leaders of the mutiny), but more especially at the shouts from the army of 'Go and campaign with your father Ammon' (Arr. VII, 8, 3; see App. 22, p. 351); the first section of his speech, 9, 1–5, was therefore, naturally and inevitably, given to a description of the benefits conferred on the Macedonians[4] by his father Philip, whom the mutineers were insulting. Equally naturally and inevitably, he goes on to describe the greater benefits which he himself had conferred on the Macedonians (second section, 9, 6–9). It is not what most Englishmen would have said; but Alexander was steeped in Greek culture and thought, and no Greek was ever modest about his own exploits; if he had done something worth doing, he said so; after all, it was true. There is no difficulty about this section. ὑμεῖς σατράπαι implies that he turned to a knot of officers as he spoke; one can speak to a mixed audience and still say something special to one part of it. The difficulty which has been found over the words 'Ιωνίαν and

1 E. Kornemann, *Die Alexandergeschichte des Ptolemaios I*, p. 164. He discusses the speech, pp. 159–64, and decides that it is from Ptolemy; he does not notice the proof from Curt. IX, 2, 34 given above, but he rightly quotes (p. 160) the translation of part of the speech by Wilamowitz, *Staat und Gesellschaft der Griechen*², p. 142—it is the part relating to Philip—as showing that in 1923 Wilamowitz accepted it as genuine, whatever his earlier views may have been.

2 So Kornemann, *op. cit.* p. 162, who cites the marriages and the gold crowns, but does not go further.

3 Arrian gives no reason for this demand. Curt. X, 2, 12 must be right: they were afraid that he meant to fix his seat in Asia permanently.

4 One must accept the view that the words τῷ κοινῷ τῶν Μακεδόνων in 9, 5 have no technical reference to the later κοινόν, but merely mean the Macedonian people. See Kornemann, *op. cit.* p. 161 and n. 143.

Αἰολίδα among his additions to the Empire is only a misunderstanding.[1]

The third section, 10, 1–4, is difficult. Probably 1 and 2, the wounds of the troops and his own, are genuine, but nearly the whole of 3 and 4, beginning with the words γάμους τε, must be a later interpolation; as I see it, the original, after the words πεδίων πάντων which conclude 2, must have continued ὅστις δὲ δὴ καὶ ἀπέθανεν, εὐκλεὴς μὲν αὐτῷ ἡ τελευτὴ ἐγένετο περιφανὴς δὲ ὁ τάφος· οὐ γάρ τίς γε φεύγων ὑμῶν ἐτελεύτα ἐμοῦ ἄγοντος; the last clause is bound to be genuine and that carries the rest of what I have quoted, but everything else in 3 and 4 goes out. This cuts out the sentence about the marriages; it was not true to say to either officers or men that many of their children would be συγγενεῖς (kinsmen) of his own; this was inserted at some time *after* Alexander had finally quelled the mutiny by saying to the army 'I make you all my συγγενεῖς'.[2] In the same way, the sentence about the gold crowns

1 Hampl, *op. cit.* p. 181, objected that the Ionian cities had been declared autonomous by Alexander and so could not be included in his empire, to which Kornemann, *op. cit.* p. 162, replied: 'Auch autonom erklärte Städte wurden Teile des Alexanderreiches.' (On this subject see App. 7, 1.) Both, however, seem to me to have missed the point, which is that Ἰωνίαν is not Ἴωνας. The district called Ἰωνία, the χώρα outside the Greek cities and their territories, though it could be and sometimes was (as here) named separately from Lydia, was under the satrap of Lydia, while the Greek cities of Ionia were not; so, whereas in the speech we normally get for conquered districts the names of *peoples* as Phrygians and Lydians here and Persians, Medes, etc. in 10, 5, we have here the district name, Ἰωνία, and not the name of the people, Ἴωνες, because the latter word meant the Ionian Greeks and it would not have been true to talk of them as 'conquered'. Exactly the same thing applies to Αἰολίδα; it was in the Mysian (Hellespontine) satrapy, but had its own individuality, and Pharnabazus (e.g.) had appointed a sub-satrap to govern it for him, Xen. *Hell.* III, 1, 10. There is one other case in the speech of the district name being used, Καρμανίαν in 10, 7; this was because there was no distinct Carmanian people who could be named.

2 Arr. VII, 11, 7. Kornemann, p. 164, says: 'Bezeichnung der Vornehmsten unter ihnen als συγγενεῖς.' But 'the most eminent among them' cannot be right, apart from the fact that Arrian says ξύμπαντας, 'all'; Alexander could not, in the circumstances of the moment, have started selecting, and the army would not have been satisfied with anything which did not apply to all of them; he was copying Philip (or whatever king it was) when he made the whole of the national Macedonian infantry levy his Companions. There is no difficulty about 'all'. In Scotland, the surname once common to every member of a particular clan is supposed to mean that all the members were considered, or considered themselves, kinsmen of the Chief, in the sense that all were considered as descended with him from a

bestowed upon 'most of you' is a later exaggeration; Arrian's narrative sufficiently shows the rarity of this high honour.¹ The bronze statues of 'most of' the dead in their own houses is another similar exaggeration, which grew out of the statues by Lysippus set μp in Dium of the 25 Companions killed in the first battle, Granicus (Arr. 1, 16, 4). And, on the face of it, the statement that the parents of the dead (all the dead) were relieved from all liturgies and from the εἰσφορά is taken from the similar statement in Arr. 1, 16, 5 about those who were killed at the Granicus,² and is another exaggeration. In fact, the latter half of this third section of the speech is largely one continuous exaggeration, which cannot be ascribed to Alexander; he could not make statements to the mutineers which they would know were untrue.

In the last section, 10, 5 to end, the first thing to notice is that it is nearly all one sentence of enormous length, 22 lines long, and 17 of these, purporting to be a list of Alexander's conquests, come within the framework of a single clause, which runs οἴκοι ἀπαγγείλατε ὅτι τὸν βασιλέα ὑμῶν 'Αλέξανδρον, νικῶντα (17 lines of conquests), οἴχεσθε ἀπολιπόντες. No such sentence could ever have been spoken, with a list 17 lines long separating the verb from its object, and separating the ἄπιτε of line 3 from the ἄπιτε at the end of the speech; it cannot even be transcribed in English, though it could be in German. Much of the list of conquests must come out; and by chance we happen to know for certain that one clause in the list was inserted by Arrian himself, the words κεκτημένον δὲ καὶ Παρθυαίους καὶ Χωρασμίους καὶ 'Υρκανίους ἔστε ἐπὶ τὴν θάλασσαν τὴν Κασπίαν. I have given the story of the people called Chorasmians elsewhere;³ in Hecataeus and

common ancestor (whether they really were or not); and when a strange surname is found in a clan, it arose from the adoption of a stranger into the kin. I can myself recall a case where the exciting circumstances of one such adoption, though made several centuries ago, were still remembered in my lifetime by a descendant of the man and his neighbours.

1 The only gold crowns mentioned as bestowed by Alexander are those in Arr. VII, 5, 4–6, when he crowned the eight Bodyguards (including Peucestas), Nearchus, and Onesicritus; two of these are referred to in Arr. *Ind.* 42, 9. Gold crowns must have been noted in the *Journal.*

2 Kaerst, *Gesch. d. Hellenismus*, I³, 187 n. 2 thought this, but very properly pointed out that there might be difficulties which we had no chance of resolving, nothing being known about the civil obligations of the Macedonian peasant. It is conceivable (I express no opinion) that Arr. 1, 16, 5 was copied from VII, 10, 4, and not *vice versa*, and that, if so, the Greek who made this insertion in Alexander's speech used the terminology he knew, that proper to a Greek city.

3 Tarn, *Bactria and India*, App. 11, p. 478, where the evidence is collected.

Herodotus they were living beside the Parthians (Parthava) and Hyrcanians, but before Alexander's day they had migrated to the country south of the Aral which subsequently bore their name, Kwarizm, where Ptolemy the geographer placed them. Alexander never 'possessed' them or even saw them, and all he knew about them was the visit of their king Pharasmanes, recorded by Aristobulus (Arr. IV, 15, 4); and the sentence I am considering is ultimately taken from the old geography of Herodotus, who shows (III, 17) that at the beginning of the fifth century B.C. the Chorasmians were living beside the Parthava and Hyrcanians. I only know one other instance of the occurrence of this localisation later than Herodotus, and that is also given by Arrian; in his own geographical sketch of the East he says (V, 5, 2) that the Taurus runs ἀπὸ 'Αρμενίων ὡς ἐπὶ Μηδίαν πρὸς Παρθυαίους τε καὶ Χωρασμίους and thence along Bactria to join Paropamisus. He cites for his sketch Nearchus and Megasthenes, who cannot come into question here, and Eratosthenes. It is conceivable that Eratosthenes may have said that the Chorasmians had once lived beside the Parthava; otherwise no reason appears why Arrian should have given this people their fifth-century location. But that in VII, 10, 6 Arrian is quoting from himself in V, 5, 2 is certain, as certain as it is that Alexander never mentioned, or could have mentioned, the Chorasmians in connection with the Parthava. Neither did Alexander say, nor could he have said, that the Hyrcanians extended to the 'Caspian' Sea; he could only have said 'to the Hyrcanian Sea', for in his day 'Caspian' meant something else.[1] But Arrian uses both names indiscriminately, and doubtless used Κασπίαν here to avoid the jingle of 'Υρκανίους and τὴν 'Υρκανίαν in the same sentence.[2]

Once we have the fact that one item in this list of conquests is a later insertion, we need not hesitate to say, as is indeed easy enough to see, that much else must come out. Alexander did not talk of conquering the unimportant Uxii just after mentioning the conquest of Persians, Medes, and Bactrians, nor did he say that he had crossed the Caucasus 'above the Caspian Gates', whatever that may mean; and after alluding to the terrible march across the Gedrosian desert he did not cast back to talk about the Oreitae and the exploits of Nearchus. We have not the material to go into every detail, as we have about the Chorasmians; but a good deal, at any rate, must come out as being a later addition. Possibly what he did say was something like this: 'who had conquered the Persians, Medes, Bactrians and Sacas, who had crossed

1 See § B on the geographical ideas of Alexander and those about him.
2 For his usage, see App. 1, 1, p. 136.

the Caucasus and the Oxus, the Tanais, and the rivers of India, who had reached the southern Ocean and returned through the Gedrosian desert', which would make a manageable sentence; but it is also possible that the whole recapitulatory list is late, and that what actually followed νικῶντα were some general expressions. If, however, Arrian inserted something in the last section of the speech, he certainly was not responsible for the insertions we have found in the third section, some of which are irreconcilable with his narrative. Why he left them in cannot be said. They cannot well be later insertions in his own text. He wrote the *Anabasis* with Ptolemy's book before him; is it conceivable that, before his day, some parts of Ptolemy's text had been 'edited'?[1] I have given the facts; I do not know the explanation.

With this by way of prelude, I may turn to what really matters, the rest of the last section of the speech. That it came through Ptolemy and is genuine is certain enough (p. 290); but, as I see it, its genuineness does not depend upon Ptolemy alone. Consider the circumstances. Alexander was furiously angry when he began to speak, though for a time—more than half of the speech—he held himself in; but his own words worked him up, and before he reached the end of what he wanted to say he was fairly beside himself, and that had happened which was almost bound to happen: his acquired Greek culture had slipped from him like a cloak, as it had done once before, and he was again for the moment pure Macedonian,[2] of the race who said just what they thought and, in his father's phrase, called a spade a spade.[3] No translation of mine can give the force of those last words. 'And now, as you all want to go, go, every one of you, and tell them at home that you deserted your king who had led you from victory to victory across the world, and left him to the care of the strangers he had conquered; and no doubt your words will win you the praises of men and the blessing of heaven. Go.' No Greek, Arrian or any other, ever wrote that.[4] For the emphatic last sentence, the quick curtain at the end of the play, were to Greek minds an abomination; their fieriest speeches shade off at the close, their most moving tragedies end on a quiet note; their very epigrams carry their stings, should such there be, anywhere but in their tails. That Alexander,

1 How many of us, without knowing it, read Shakespeare in some version which prints later emendations as part of the text? How many of those who read Professor Gilbert Murray's wonderful translations of Euripides know that at least one most beautiful chorus owes nearly as much to the translator as to the poet?

2 Before Cleitus' murder, when Alexander had lost control of himself, he ἀνεβόα Μακεδονιστί (Plut. *Alex.* LI).

3 The words are those of Philip II: Plut. *Mor.* 178 B, no. 15.   4 See Add.

after tongue-lashing the mutineers with all the irony at his command, should suddenly end on a single word, would to a Greek have been incomprehensible; but no one who heard it was likely to forget that tremendous ἄπιτε, flung at the men he loved with all the concentrated scorn of the most passionate nature the ancient world ever knew.

Curtius' version of Alexander's speech at Opis, x, 2, 15 *sqq.*, need not detain us; much of it is just complaining. It agrees with Arrian on the state of Alexander's treasury, and this has been said to prove that these two entirely different speeches must have had a common source[1] (which could only be Ptolemy); all it does prove is that they had a common source *for that particular detail*, i.e. that Curtius took it from Ptolemy, as he took the benefits conferred on the Macedonians by Philip, though he compressed them into a single sentence. But there can be no doubt that Curtius composed the actual speech himself, as he did the two speeches on the Beas, for in x, 2, 27 he makes Alexander call the troops *cives*; Macedonians were not 'citizens', and the phrase is copied from the story of Caesar reducing a mutinous legion to obedience by calling them 'Quirites'.[2] The real ending of the speech is of course not in Curtius, as he had already used it for Alexander's speech at the Beas.

16. PLUTARCH'S *LIFE* OF ALEXANDER

Plutarch's *Life* cannot be classed either with the 'good' tradition or with any of the traditions which go to make up the so-called vulgate; it stands by itself. No one has yet made any real attempt to analyse its sources, and it is not likely that any one ever will, for its ultimate sources must have embraced the whole Alexander-literature, whether known or unknown to ourselves; the usual statement that Plutarch used every source, from the best to the worst, is correct, and any one sentence may need an essay to elucidate it, while much cannot be checked at all. Plutarch in youth had written Part I of the *De Alexandri Fortuna* with all the fervour of a young man bent on righting what he considered to be a great wrong; but by the time that the elderly Plutarch, with his

---

1 Kornemann, p. 159, and the authors he cites in n. 139.
2 Tacitus, *Ann.* I, 42; Suet. *Div. Iul.* 70; Appian, *Bell. Civ.* II, 94, 392; Dio Cass. xLII, 53, 3–4; cf. Lucan, *Pharsalia* v, 358. These are all later than Curtius, who is therefore copying from the incident itself, and not from any writer we possess. Caesar's legionaries were Roman citizens, and to call them 'Quirites' was much to the point; Alexander's Macedonians were not citizens of anything, and to have called them 'cives' would have been meaningless. This shows that Curtius is copying.

comfortable sinecure at Delphi, wrote Alexander's *Life*, the fire had burnt low and was half swamped by his much reading.

Certain general ideas, however, emerge from a study of this *Life*; the main one is, that it contains two separate strata. The first is the historical part, which is not always accurate and has some distinct tendencies towards, and even beyond, the bad tradition; but Plutarch was professedly writing biography, not history. The other, more important, is the personal part, Alexander himself and his character; it is this part which constitutes the claim of Plutarch's *Life* to be something better than just another 'vulgate' document. Much of this part is found nowhere else, and a good deal is extremely valuable, though there are stories which are both untrue and silly. There is no chance, in this stratum, of discovering sources; we must be dealing with what originally were stories told by those about Alexander—Court, generals, officials—which were gradually collected and ultimately crystallised. Doubtless they had crystallised long before Plutarch's day; it is in regard to these that the belief that he made much use of Alexandrian biographical material may be true. One radical consideration, however, has never been sufficiently stressed. If we put aside an occasional political party here or there, and the Academic and Epicurean schools of philosophy, who were neutral, Greece was thoroughly hostile to Alexander in life and even more so after his death; and it was Greeks, not Macedonians, who wrote the world's literature. Once the generation which had known Alexander was dead, the Greek opposition, or rather oppositions, had the field to themselves; and this meant much more than the politically minded, for the main feature of the Greek opposition was the bitter hostility of two great philosophic schools, the Stoics and the Peripatetics, who hated Alexander the man even while they adopted his ideas. The Peripatetics, who never forgave him for the execution of Callisthenes, indeed started their attack very soon after Alexander's death, under Cassander's shield; and as soon as Alexandria, where as regards history Peripatetic influence and traditions were powerful, really got going, there was (if we except Eratosthenes) no voice raised in Alexander's behalf (so far as is known) till the Alexander-revival in the first century B.C. (pp. 396 *sq.*), which used him as a stick wherewith to belabour Rome; the only bearing which this revival had on his personal character was in the invention and ascription to him of that megalomania which has so often been treated as true. My object in recalling these matters is to make it clear that, while stories which show Alexander in a bad light but which are not well attested may easily be Greek inventions of any period, stories which show him in a good light, even if we cannot test them, must at any rate be early—they must belong to his lifetime or very soon after—and are, speaking generally, likely to be true; for once he was dead no one had any interest in inventing such stories, while for many years many people had every interest in inventing stories or incidents derogatory to him. This is my own reason for accepting, I hope with all necessary discrimination, a good deal of what Plutarch says about his personal character as true (see especially App. 18), even where it cannot be checked, as Plutarch's history often can be; for a good deal of this personal character is favourable to him, sometimes indeed more so in our eyes than Plutarch in his time can have foreseen. (See Addenda.)

There is one considerable difference between the *Life* and Part I of *De Alexandri Fortuna* which may be noticed. In the latter, Plutarch had impartially attacked both Stoics and Peripatetics,[1] the Stoics for their teaching that Alexander was wholly bad from start to finish, a tyrant full of τῦφος which his *paidagogos* Leonidas ought to have knocked out of him but didn't,[2] the Peripatetics for their highly elaborated doctrine of τύχη, that Fortune which governs human affairs and which had given Alexander his conquest of Persia;[3] what Plutarch had argued was that Alexander was the philosopher in action, a better philosopher through his acts than were the arm-chair critics of these two schools through their words. In the *Life*, Plutarch has discarded the philosopher in action altogether, and has replaced the idea by some very uninspired history, but there is more than that; he still disagrees utterly with the Stoics,[4] but has dropped much of his opposition to the Peripatetics; he uses some Peripatetic material, and even opens the door just a little way to Fortune herself. Obvious Peripatetic material is the uniform portrayal of Callisthenes in a good light, and the introduction of that invented figure the eunuch Bagoas;[5] but more important is Fortune. Twice she helps Alexander: at Issus (xx) she gives him ground on which the Persian cavalry could not act (δύσιππα), though he did

---

1 Tarn, *A.J.P.* LX, 1939, pp. 55–6.
2 Stroux, *Philol.* LXXXVIII, 1933, p. 232; Tarn, *loc. cit.* See § F, p. 69 n. 1.
3 Stroux, *op. cit.* pp. 229 *sq.* and many others; see especially Polyb. XXIX, 21, citing Demetrius of Phalerum περὶ τῆς τύχης.
4 In Plutarch's *Alexander* Leonidas, the villain of the piece to the Stoics, always appears in a favourable light (V, XXII, XXV), and Alexander is free of the characteristic τῦφος (XXVIII, οὐδὲ τετυφωμένος, cf. XLV, ἀτυφοτέραν); see also XL, XLI, his dislike of τὸ τρυφᾶν, a quality not too far removed from τῦφος.
5 See on Bagoas, § G, p. 98 and App. 18.

owe more to his own generalship than to her, and by her help he alights on his feet when he leaps down into the Malli town (LXIII); but she betrays him over the murder of Cleitus (L, δυστυχίᾳ).. Generally speaking, however, he is stronger than Fortune; it is his ambition to overcome her and her power by daring and bravery,[1] and she yields to his plans.[2] One may compare the τύχη of the Peripatetics in Curtius (§ G, pp. 95, 99) and his statement that Alexander was the only man who ever had Fortune in his power.[3]

It accords, too, with the Peripatetic view that Plutarch should represent Alexander as deteriorating in his later years, though he does not formally date the change as does Curtius; rather, to Plutarch, it is a continuing process, brought about in him by the sort of slanders which took up what he really meant and twisted it into something he did not mean,[4] an enlightening statement which rings true enough and which accords with what *would* happen. That Alexander towards the end did grow impatient and irritable, largely as the result of overwork, is highly probable; but Plutarch ends by exaggerating the process even worse than Curtius does. At Babylon, when Cassander laughs at seeing Persians making προσκύνησις, Alexander seizes his hair and bangs his head against the wall (LXXIV); as Curtius (VIII, 5, 22 *sqq.*) tells the same story, for the same cause, about Polyperchon at Bactra, its untruth in either version is patent, the more so as Arrian (IV, 12, 2) says that the man who laughed (it was at Bactra) was Leonnatus, who suffered nothing thereby. In LXVIII Alexander slays a Persian noble with a *sarissa*, a weapon he did not use; the story is invented from the murder of Cleitus, whom Alexander kills with a *sarissa* snatched from one of his Guards. Worst of all, his campaign against the Cossaeans is described as an amusement. The Cossaeans badly needed a lesson; they were across the road between Babylon-Susa and Ecbatana, and let no one through who did not pay blackmail; even the Persian kings had paid, and this people's strength is shown by the fact that, when Antigonus I refused to pay and fought his way through, he nearly suffered a terrible disaster. But to represent Alexander as hunting the Cossaeans for sport as if they were animals,[5] like the Teutonic Knights

1 LVIII, τόλμῃ τὴν τύχην ὑπερβαλέσθαι.
2 XXVI, ἥ τε γὰρ τύχη ταῖς ἐπιβολαῖς ὑπείκουσα.
3 Curt. x, 5, 35, 'fortunae quam solus omnium mortalium in potestate habuit'.
4 XLII, ἀλλ' ὕστερόν γε αὐτὸν ἐξετράχυναν αἱ πολλαὶ διαβολαὶ διὰ τῶν ἀληθῶν πάροδον ἐπὶ τὰ ψευδῆ λαβοῦσαι.
5 LXXII, ὥσπερ ἐπὶ θήραν καὶ κυνηγέσιον ἀνθρώπων.

with their 'ridings in Lettow', goes far beyond any other malicious invention known to us. None of this, however, really affects what Plutarch says about Alexander's character, for the *Life* habitually exhibits statements diametrically opposed to each other, Plutarch being quite inconsistent. For example, in LIX, speaking in his own person, he very properly describes the Massaga massacre, which did take place, as a stain (κηλίς) on Alexander's reputation, while he had previously transcribed, without blinking, Alexander's imaginary order to massacre the prisoners at Persepolis (XXXVII, from a forged letter). He has in fact a good many untrue stories. Some of them are harmless enough, like that of Serapion (XXXIX), untrue because Sarapis, from whom the man is named, was not invented till after Alexander's death; but one is very terrible, the story in XXXV that Alexander once experimented with a boy by drenching him with naphtha and setting him on fire; the untruth, or rather the silliness, of this is demonstrated by the action ascribed to the bystanders, who put out the fire with buckets of *water*, a thing which would have made the naphtha burn more fiercely. I might mention here, though it does not relate to character, chapter LXII of the *Life*, which may compete with a famous chapter in Pliny[1] for the honour of being the worst bit of history the ancient world has bequeathed to us. I mentioned that this or that sentence in the *Life* might require an essay to elucidate it. One statement in this chapter has cost me an Appendix (no. 14), another an article,[2] a third a chapter in a book.[3]

But whatever may be the case with some of Plutarch's sources in the *Life* of Alexander, there has never been any question about one of them, Alexander's (and other peoples') letters or supposed letters; undoubtedly he had before him an Alexandrian collection, or collections, of such letters. I have sufficiently indicated modern opinion about these elsewhere;[4] I myself entirely agree with Kaerst, that every letter has to be separately considered on its merits. Sweeping assertions such as those of Birt and Berve, that all or nearly all the Alexander letters must be taken as genuine, get us nowhere. One has also to consider, as they do not, by what ways genuine letters may have got into circulation. Forged letters are a known feature of Hellenistic literature—it may suffice to recall here the much discussed 'correspondence' between Zeno and Antigonus Gonatas; and of the Alexander letters some are forged, some genuine, one or two may be genuine letters doctored for

1 Pliny II, 67 (167–70).　　　　2 *J.H.S.* LX, 1940, p. 84.
3 Tarn, *Bactria and India*, ch. IV; see p. 155 n. 2.
4 App. 6 p. 196 nn. 4, 5, which will give the references.

propaganda purposes. We have to decide to which category each letter belongs; sometimes it is easy enough, sometimes very difficult.

As I see it, private letters of Alexander, to whomsoever written, dealing with political events are always suspect. But the principal matter, of course, is Alexander's correspondence with Antipater, his governor in Europe, and his mother Olympias; no one doubts that there *was* such a correspondence, and here, as regards Alexander, we have something to go upon. His letters to Antipater would be placed with the archives at Pella, where Cassander would find them later; Olympias would keep his letters to herself. Consequently, when in 317 the great propaganda war broke out between Olympias and the Royalists on one side and Cassander and the Peripatetics on the other, a war which Plutarch (*Alex.* LXXVII) has indicated in outline so accurately, both sides possessed a number of genuine letters of Alexander's which they could use or doctor as occasion served, and both sides could, and did, forge other letters to their hearts' desire, hoping that they would pass muster because everyone knew that they had some genuine letters. There is a good example in Plut. *Alex.* LV, on the Pages' conspiracy and the death of Callisthenes. Both Ptolemy and Aristobulus said that the pages stated that Callisthenes was at the bottom of the conspiracy (Arr. IV, 14, 1); and Ptolemy anyhow, who must have known the facts (*ib.* 13, 7), had not, and never had had, any axe to grind in the matter of the propaganda war, with which he was not concerned. Of the two letters in *Life* LV, the first (Alexander to Craterus, Attalus, and Alcetas) was forged by Cassander's side to show Callisthenes' innocence, and a clumsy job they have made of it; the addressees alone would prove the forgery,[1] and it is worth noting that three men had been selected who were all safely dead. The second letter (Alexander to Antipater) was forged by or for Olympias to uphold her story that the Peripatetics had helped to poison Alexander; the threat in the letter to punish *Aristotle* (τοὺς ἐκπέμψαντας αὐτόν) gives it away completely. But if

[1] No time can be found when Craterus was away from Alexander with only these two generals with him. But apparently not long after, or even during, the Pages' conspiracy Craterus is said to have been sent on an expedition with four battalions of the phalanx, his own (i.e. Gorgias'), Polyperchon's, Attalus', and Alcetas' (Arr. IV, 22, 1), where 'Alcetas' is a mistake for 'Meleager'; the matter is treated in App. 1, II, p. 145. Alcetas had not yet a command; he may not even have been in Bactria. So far as I could see, this is the only time in which Arrian has made the mistake, common enough in some writers, of writing one general's name for another's; it is difficult not to suppose that it is somehow connected with the forged letter, though I do not see how. If it be just a coincidence, it is a strange one.

such political forgeries are clear enough, there must have been among Alexander's genuine letters many on matters indifferent to the contestants which were just set aside. Specimens of such letters in Plutarch are those on Mt Climax (xvii), Issus (xx) and the Saca princess (xlvi), all of them quoted by Plutarch to show that Alexander did *not* mention some extravagant story on the subject; while it is difficult to see why any one should have forged, or wanted to forge, a number of the letters in xli to his generals on little personal matters, though it may be equally difficult to see how they ever got into circulation. The very interesting letter to Aristotle in vii could well be genuine; it could also have been forged to show Alexander's annoyance with the philosopher, but a forgery would probably have said something more direct. Of course a State document like Alexander's letter to Darius (Arr. ii, 14, 4) is on a different footing altogether; Eumenes must have kept a copy, even if he did not transcribe it into the *Journal.*

The letters which Alexander received in return from Antipater and Olympias are of less importance, but we certainly possess one genuine letter of Olympias', the ἰσοβασιλέας letter in Plutarch (xxxix), for it is exactly what any mother of strong character, let alone an Olympias, must have written to a son in Alexander's position. Antipater would naturally keep copies of his letters to Alexander; Olympias probably would not. When Alexander died, Perdiccas presumably got all his papers, which in turn must have passed to Antipater when he was elected Regent of the Empire after Perdiccas' death; he would have taken them back to Pella with him, for there was nothing else he could do with them. Cassander subsequently got everything at Pella, and also got Olympias' papers when he put her to death; one way or another, Cassander got almost everything that survived of, or was connected with, Alexander's correspondence with Antipater and Olympias, whether original letters or copies, whether genuine letters or forgeries; and what he had was doubtless at the service of his Peripatetic friends. But a substantial number of genuine letters of every sort must have perished in the Successors' wars.

It is not my purpose to go through the letters, but merely to indicate the sort of thing we have before us. Forgeries were not confined to the propaganda war I have mentioned; even Strabo (xv, 702) quotes a letter from Craterus to his mother which was invented out of hand by some one, later than Megasthenes, who was committed to the support of the legend that Alexander had reached the Ganges. I mentioned however that some forgeries might be very difficult to detect, and I should like to illustrate this. The much discussed letter in Plutarch lx on the battle with Porus, on which opinion has always been divided, is dealt with in App. 6 and is really a very simple matter; so I will take a forgery which is anything but simple and is also most important, Alexander's letter to Cleomenes in Arrian VII, 23, 6–8; it has nearly always been considered genuine and it took in Arrian, though he was uncomfortable about it, as is shown by his very peculiar running commentary, distinguishing the matters for which he blamed or did not blame Alexander. The letter purports to have been written after Hephaestion's death, at the very end of Alexander's life, when Cleomenes was governing Egypt. It has often been supposed that Alexander had made him satrap;[1] but Alexander had never had a satrap of Egypt, and he certainly would not have appointed a Greek financier from Naucratis to such a very important post; the only Greek he ever made a satrap was Nearchus, who was settled in Macedonia and had been his life-long friend, and even so only got an unimportant province. Cleomenes' position and his powers are defined below, n. 1. The letter orders him to build two ἡρῷα for Hephaestion, one in Alexandria and one on Pharos 'where the lighthouse (πύργος) stands', and orders that Hephaestion's name is to be written on all mercantile bonds or contracts, συμβόλαια; Arrian then changes to *oratio recta*, and the letter makes Alexander say to Cleomenes: If I find the building well done, 'I will pardon any offences you may already have committed, and for the future, however greatly you may sin, you will have nothing to fear from me'.

---

1 For the usual view see Berve II, no. 431, Κλεομένης, with full references. The only writer who actually says that Alexander made Cleomenes satrap is Pausanias, I, 6, 3, ὃν σατραπεύειν Αἰγύπτου κατέστησεν 'Αλέξανδρος, and he is as poor evidence as one could wish for a precise detail of this kind. Ps.-Arist. *Oec.* II, 1352a, 16, says only Αἰγύπτου σατραπεύων, which in a sense is true. What matters is Arrian, τὰ μετὰ 'Αλέξανδρον, Jacoby II, no. 156, fr. 1, 5 (from Hieronymus), who calls Cleomenes ὁ ἐξ 'Αλεξάνδρου τῆς σατραπείας ταύτης ἄρχειν τεταγμένος, that is, he does *not* say that Alexander made Cleomenes satrap of Egypt, but says that he was appointed by Alexander to govern 'this satrapy'; he refers to Egypt as a satrapy because in the line before he has given Ptolemy's appointment (at Babylon) to be satrap of Egypt. Dexippus, Jacoby II, no. 100, fr. 8, merely copies Arrian, ὁ τῶι βασιλεῖ 'Αλεξάνδρωι ἐπὶ τῆι σατραπείαι ταύτηι τεταγμένος. What happened should be clear enough from this. Alexander's governor Doloaspis, who was *not* a satrap, must have died while Alexander was in the East, and the king told the next highest official, Cleomenes, to carry on with the government till he (the king) should be able to attend to the matter—an exact parallel to the cases of Taxiles and Peucestas (App. 17). This would entitle Cleomenes to exercise Doloaspis' powers, whatever they were; obviously he *did* act like a full-blown satrap.

The lesser difficulties, no doubt, can all be explained away. There is no impossibility about Alexander having ordered an ἡρῷον for Hephaestion in Alexandria, the order lapsing with his death. The order about the συμβόλαια seems purposeless and silly,[1] but could be called a later insertion. If the reference to the lighthouse be part of the letter, it would make the letter not earlier than the reign of Ptolemy II;[2] but, though I dislike explaining away difficulties in a text as 'glosses', the clause referring to the lighthouse has certainly got into Arrian's text at a later time, for Arrian could never have written the jingle ἐν τῇ νήσῳ—ἐν τῇ νήσῳ[3] in consecutive lines, and had he found it in the text before him he would certainly have altered the wording. But the last part of the letter, the pardon of Cleomenes and the licence to sin for the future, is something quite different. A common view, I think, is that Cleomenes was making so much money for the Treasury that Alexander threw morality and statesmanship to the winds.[4] In itself, this, though it would contradict everything we know about Alexander, might perhaps have been possible; it was mundane considerations which evoked Luther's *Pecca fortiter*. But, if the circumstances of the time be considered, it was *not* possible. Cleomenes' offence had been oppression of subjects,[5] the one thing Alexander never forgave.[6] He found it going on in some quarters on his return from India, and he struck very hard; he meant to cut out the roots of the evil thing before it could grow.[7] He put four of his Persian satraps to death, made all his satraps disband their private armies (which would include Cleomenes' mercenaries), and—this is the point I want to make—put to death three

1 It means, I suppose, that all business documents were to be dated by Hephaestion's year (i.e. from his death?) in addition to the usual dating.
2 It was the lighthouse which made Mahaffy declare long ago that the letter was a forgery.   3 For Arrian's practice, see App. 1, p. 136.
4 I once followed this; that was due to insufficient study. For defences of Cleomenes, see B. A. van Groningen, *Mnemosyne*, LIII, 1925, p. 101; V. Ehrenberg, 'Alexander und Ägypten', *Beihefte zum alten Orient* 7, 1926, pp. 50 *sqq*. There is a useful list in A. Andréadès, ἡ δημοσία οἰκονομία τοῦ μεγάλου Ἀλεξάνδρου, p. 82, of scholars who have taken various views of Cleomenes.
5 Cleomenes was πολλὰ ἀδικήματα ἀδικήσαντι ἐν Αἰγύπτῳ, Arr. VII, 23, 6. It is the same word as is used for oppression of subjects in Cleander's case (n. 6) and in Arrian's general statement (n. 7).
6 Arr. VI, 27, 5, the thing above all others that held together so many diverse peoples in Alexander's empire was ὅτι οὐκ ἐξῆν ὑπὸ τῇ Ἀλεξάνδρου βασιλείᾳ ἀδικεῖσθαι (the word used of Cleomenes) τοὺς ἀρχομένους ὑπὸ τῶν ἀρχόντων. It is in a parenthesis, and may be from Ptolemy; it follows upon the execution of Cleander.
7 Arr. VII, 4, 3.

generals on his line of communications in Media, Cleander, Sitalces, Herakon.[1] Sitalces was a Thracian and Herakon an unknown man of unknown nationality; let them pass. But Cleander was different. He was of the Macedonian aristocracy; he had played his part in the early days of the invasion, and had commanded a contingent at Gaugamela; he had then been left with Parmenion in Media as his second-in-command, and had killed him on Alexander's order (which means that Alexander trusted him completely); and as he was still in Media when Alexander returned from India, he must have been given Parmenion's place as general in command of that section of Alexander's communications, a most important post. His father's name was Polemocrates;[2] it is an extremely rare name, but it was also the name of Coenus' father;[3] unless we have here some most peculiar coincidence, Cleander was a brother of Coenus,[4] one of the ablest and most trusted of Alexander's generals; in any case, to every Macedonian general in the army Cleander was 'one of *us*'. Apparently his execution led to no difficulties with the other generals, any more than the murder of Cleitus the Black had done: Cleander, like Cleitus, had asked for it; that sufficed. But suppose that, after executing Cleander, Alexander had not only pardoned a Greek financier from Naucratis for the same offence but had licensed him to continue his wrong-doing to any extent he desired. No one but a madman could have done such a thing; the position would have become unthinkable. This is not a mathematical proof that Alexander never wrote this letter; but it should be quite proof enough. If it be asked, why then did Alexander not execute Cleomenes himself, instead of leaving it to be done by Ptolemy a little later, the simple answer must be that he, just back from India and still far away at Susa, did not yet know of Cleomenes' misdeeds; either he had not received complaints before he died, or he had not yet the proofs; it was when, after his death, Ptolemy went to Egypt as satrap that everything came out.

It is perhaps not difficult to see the origin of the forged letter, which could not have been written while Alexander lived; it is one of the numerous attempts to vilify him after his death,[5] and is doubtless

---

1 Arr. VI, 27, 4–5. Cleander's offences, besides sacrilege, are summed up as ἄδικα ἔργα ἐς τοὺς ὑπηκόους καὶ ἀτάσθαλα. Curtius has a lurid account of them, x, 1, 3 *sqq*.

2 Arr. I, 24, 2. 3 Arr. v, 27, 1; Ditt.³ 332.

4 Berve II, no. 422, Κλέανδρος, gives this as a fact. Doubtless it is.

5 Examples are the accusations of excessive drinking (Ephippus and 'Nicobule'), and of many massacres, crystallised in (most probably) Cleitarchus (§ E, pp. 53 *sq*.); and of course the sexual accusations considered in App. 18.

connected with the Hephaestion literature. We know from Arrian that there was a large literature dealing with Hephaestion's death and what came after, much of it anything but favourable to Alexander.[1] Whether Arrian himself read all the versions which he alludes to, or whether (more probably) he got his information from some later monograph on the subject, it must have been in this literature that he found the letter, which took him in; though it remains a problem why he should have given it at length and partly verbatim when he did not normally cite private letters (other than generals' reports).[2] That he found the letter in Ptolemy's book seems to me out of the question;[3] but I incline to believe that it was Ptolemy, not Arrian, who stigmatised Cleomenes as a 'bad man'.[4]

I might have stopped here, but that a theory has recently been put forward by Mr J. E. Powell[5] that Plutarch's *Life* of Alexander can be explained quite simply by supposing that he used two sources and two only, a collection of Alexander's spurious letters[6] and a 'variorum source-book', which he defines as 'an encyclopaedic work in which the divergent versions of each successive event in a large number of historians of Alexander were collected and registered' (p. 234), a new version of the well-known belief that no writer we possess can ever

1 Arr. VII, 14, 2–7. If in this passage such expressions be noted as φθόνου πρὸς αὐτὸν 'Αλέξανδρον, ἀτάσθαλα ἀναγράψαντες, ἐς αἰσχύνην, the origin of the letter will hardly seem doubtful. It is, I suppose, mere coincidence that the word ἀτάσθαλα, rare in prose after Herodotus, is used once again by Arrian (VI, 27, 4) to describe Cleander's misdeeds.

2 Alexander to Olympias in VI, 1, 4, probably genuine (n. 6, *below*), seems about the only exception, though a λόγος, VII, 12, 6 *sq.*, alludes to the Alexander-Antipater-Olympias correspondence.

3 Kornemann's view, *Ptolemaios I*, pp. 177, 194. No reason is given.

4 Kornemann *ib.* p. 94 and authors cited. Arrian's words (VII, 23, 6) are ἀνδρὶ κακῷ καὶ πολλὰ ἀδικήματα ἀδικήσαντι ἐν Αἰγύπτῳ. However, I do not accept Kornemann's further contention (p. 194) that Arrian's running commentary of blame for Alexander, where he twice says ἐγώ, is really Ptolemy blaming Cleomenes. See further p. 308 n. 2.

5 J. E. Powell, 'The sources of Plutarch's Alexander', *J.H.S.* LIX, 1939, p. 229.

6 P. 230, all those Plutarch uses are spurious. The letter to Cleomenes, however, he thinks genuine; I do not understand what he thinks about the letter to Olympias, Arr. VI, 1, 4. Aristotle in the *Liber de inundacione Nili* had said that Ochus had thought that the Indus was the upper Nile, and, as Herodotus was apparently no longer read, Alexander was almost bound to have had this idea in his head when he entered India. Unless then a forger knew this work of Aristotle's (and even then we should have to ask *cui bono?*) the letter, as I see it, must be genuine.

have done any work himself, but always had it done for him by some unknown predecessor who has perished without trace. So far as my knowledge goes, in the whole vast mass of information which we possess about Hellenistic literature there is no indication that such a thing as a source-book on any subject ever existed. Greeks compiled endless ὑπομνήματα, collections of snippets on any and every subject;[1] they wrote elaborate monographs (p. 308), or *Lives* which are practically a number of quotations;[2] they produced works—Athenaeus, though later, is a surviving example—in which masses of material were strung together on a very thin thread of narrative, and which may have taken generations to build up, as a modern handbook may be enlarged out of all knowledge by successive editors; but of source-books in Powell's sense there seems no trace. He seeks to prove his point by saying that Arrian also used the source-book, and that certain resemblances between him and Plutarch show a common source, which can only be the source-book.[3] I need not go through these resemblances, for even if correctly given, which is not always the case, they cannot prove anything, seeing that two writers can use the same source without a source-book. His likeliest instance is that both writers put the death of Callisthenes directly after that of Cleitus, out of chronological order. But in fact Plutarch puts *three* deaths together out of chronological order, not two, those of Philotas, Cleitus, and Callisthenes, because he is collecting illustrations of character, not writing a history; while Arrian, who has given Philotas' death in its right place long before, is, as regards Cleitus and Callisthenes, merely following Ptolemy's order, who must have finished up the domestic events at Bactra in order to go back and treat the military history consecutively without interruption, the sort of thing done by every modern historian who wants to write something better than annals. In his treatment of Alexander's death (p. 232) Powell asserts that the accounts of Plutarch and Arrian are 'as like as two pins', and that both quote the *Journal* 'with no divergence of fact', which is precisely what they do *not* do.[4] But the theory of a

1 I listed some in *J.H.S.* xli, 1921, p. 10. A great number can be found in the index to Müller's *F.H.G.*
2 E.g. Life of Demosthenes by Demetrius Chalcenteros.
3 Powell is really going back to A. Schoene's old study of 1870, *De rerum Alex. Magni scriptorum imprimis Arriani et Plutarchi fontibus* (to which he duly refers), and enlarging it, for Schoene only made Arrian use the same 'Sammelwerk' as Plutarch for the λεγόμενα. Schwartz firmly rejected the whole idea ('Arrianos' in PW), *q.v.*; I thought it was dead.
4 Plutarch and Arrian quote the *Journal* through different intermediaries. This is shown, not by differences in wording, as Daisios 24th A. χιλίαρχος

source-book is always tempting, because, if two secondary writers agree, you can say that they used the source-book, and if they disagree, you can say that they chose different versions from it.

It was unfortunate to bring in Arrian. For, besides the main points of the Alexander-story, he has masses of detail, practically all from Ptolemy, on everyday matters—military formations, names of commanders, names and changes of satraps and other officials; so if he relied on a source-book, that source-book gave the whole of Ptolemy's history, a *reductio ad absurdum*. In fact, the last sentence of Arrian's preface to the *Anabasis* shows by itself that Arrian did his own reading.[1] 'Someone', he says, 'may wonder why I wrote this book when there have already been so many historians of Alexander; well, let him go and read all their books, and read mine, and then wonder.' This is a clear statement that Arrian himself had read the histories he is telling the objector to read; if he only knew them from extracts, he was being dishonest. And it is not much use calling Arrian, of all writers, dishonest.[2]

Powell however (p. 234) does claim that one passage directly proves the existence of the source-book he postulates, Plutarch's long list of the writers who did, and did not, relate that the Queen of the Amazons visited Alexander (XLVI); Plutarch, he argues, did not get at this list for himself. I quite agree; he did not; he took it from some monograph on the Amazons. It is the business of writers of monographs to do this sort of thing; if, to give an instance, Demetrius of Byzantium[3] took thirteen books to relate the crossing of the Galatae to Asia Minor, he must have given minutely every version of every story that had been told about them since Deucalion's flood. Trogus, or Justin, knew a version of the Amazon story in which the Queen bore a name which

---

P. ταξιάρχους, or by differences in outlook (P. more concerned with the fever, A. with the Arabian expedition), for these things come to little; but while in A. the *Journal* begins with the evening of Daisios 16th, with P. it begins with the day Daisios 18th, and Plutarch's account, given in his own words, of what happened between the 16th and 18th differs entirely from the *Journal* for that period as given by Arrian, which therefore Plutarch did not know. See § D, p. 41 n. 5.

1 When he wrote the τὰ μετ' 'Αλέξανδρον, did he get Hieronymus out of *another* source-book?
2 The theory of Kornemann, *op. cit.* that Arrian, VII, 28–30, where Arrian sums up in his own person (ἐγώ throughout), is really Ptolemy speaking, would make Arrian dishonest; but apparently Kornemann did not see the implication.
3 Demetrius ἕβδομος in the Demetrius list in Diog. Laertius V, 83; see Susemihl I, p. 620; Jacoby II, no. 162.

is not her usual one, Thalestris;[1] did Trogus too use a source-book? Arrian has a list (VII, 14, 2–5), already noticed, of many different versions of the reason for Hephaestion's death, which is the same sort of thing, substituting versions for writers, as Plutarch's list in XLVI under discussion; and in this case the title and some fragments of one work professedly dealing with the subject have survived.[2]

I fear that Mr Powell's study does not enable me to add anything to what I have already said about Plutarch's *Life* of Alexander.

17. THE DATE OF THE GAZETTEER OF ALEXANDER'S EMPIRE

In *J.H.S.* XXIII, 1923, p. 93, I isolated that invaluable contemporary document, the satrapy-list or Gazetteer of 'Asia', i.e. of Alexander's empire.[3] It is given in Diodorus XVIII, 5, 2–6, 3 inclusive, with some additions of Diodorus' own, notably about India; most probably it came to him through Hieronymus of Cardia, his basic authority for the greater part of his books XVIII–XX, but whether this be so or not, it represents an official document. I dated it in the last year of Alexander's life; this is correct, but I only gave the evidence very briefly, and I can now give it fully, and also consider a very curious subordinate question to which before I could only give a note but which has since undergone considerable development. I have already had to consider some of the substance of the Gazetteer, both its bearing on the Caspian question (in § B) and on Alexander in India (App. 14); here I am only dealing with its date.

Its date can be ascertained by narrowing down the limits of the dates between which it must lie. As it includes the Indian provinces, it is later than Alexander's return from India, i.e. than 324 B.C. As the Hyrcanian and Caspian Seas are still two separate lakes, it is much earlier than Patrocles, i.e. than *c.* 280 (see § B). As Porus is still alive, it is earlier than 317. The next step is to show that it is earlier than the partition of Triparadeisos in 321, which turns on the three instances it

1 Justin XII, 3, 5, 'Thalestris sive Minythyia.'
2 Ephippus περὶ τῆς ᾿Αλεξάνδρου καὶ ῾Ηφαιστίωνος τελευτῆς, Jacoby II, no. 126. It is possible that the monograph or *Life* which Arrian must have used is the same as the source used by Diodorus which wrote up Hephaestion; see § F, p. 78.
3 The regular meaning of 'Asia' was the Persian empire and from that the Empire of Alexander, who had conquered the Persian empire. I gave a selection of instances in *Bactria and India*, p. 153 n. 1; there are plenty of others in Arrian alone.

contains of the use of the verb συμβαίνειν to signify a temporary political arrangement; this usage does occur elsewhere,[1] but three occurrences close together in one document are striking. I give the three instances. (1) Diod. xviii, 5, 4, the Hyrcanian Sea 'happens to be embraced by Parthia', that is, Hyrcania at the time was under the same satrap as, and so formed part of, the Parthian satrapy, which did not itself extend to the Caspian Sea.[2] This had been the case in the last years of Alexander's life, when both provinces were under the satrap Phrataphernes; the arrangement was terminated at Triparadeisos in 321, when Parthia was given to Philippus (Diod. xviii, 39, 6; Arr. *Diad.* fr. 9, 35 (no. 156 Jacoby)). (2) xviii, 6, 3, 'it has happened that Susiana and Sittacene lie in Persis', i.e. are part of the satrapy of Persis at the moment; I must postpone considering this, but it shows an earlier date than the partition of Triparadeisos, when Peucestas retained Persis but Susiana was given to Antigenes, Diod. and Arr. *ib.* (3) xviii, 6, 2, 'the Indus river happens to run through the realm, δυναστεία, of Taxiles'. While Alexander was in India, Taxiles' kingdom lay east of, and was bounded by, the Indus, which divided it from Gandhāra, west of the river; Alexander made Philippus satrap of Gandhāra,[3] his satrapy extending to the confluence of the Indus and Acesines (Arr. vi, 15, 2). On his murder in spring 324, Alexander sent orders to Eudamus and Taxiles to take charge of his satrapy till another satrap could be sent (Arr. vi, 27, 2); this means that Taxiles became the civil ruler of Gandhāra while Eudamus commanded the army of occupation, as appears from his career in the wars after Alexander's death. The time then when the Indus 'happened to run' through Taxiles' δυναστεία was when Taxiles was governing Gandhāra;[4] this lasted from summer 324 to 321. At the partition of Babylon in 323 Gandhāra (τὴν συνορίζουσαν σατραπείαν) was explicitly left under Taxiles' rule (Diod. xviii, 3, 3); this arrangement ended at Triparadeisos in 321 (Diod. xviii, 39, 6)

---

1 E.g. Polyb. xxi, 26, 2, συνέβαινε γὰρ τότε πολιτεύεσθαι τοὺς Ἀμβρακιώτας μετὰ τῶν Αἰτωλῶν.

2 Fischer's interpolation of ⟨καὶ Ὑρκανία⟩ in the text after Παρθυαία is indefensible; it merely destroys evidence.

3 Arr. vi, 2, 3, where ἐπὶ Βακτρίους means 'toward', not 'up to', Tyriaspes being at the time satrap of the Paropamisadae, Arr. iv, 22, 5.

4 There is an exact parallel in the case of the Ochus river (lower Arius). Strabo xi, 518, says that some say it flows through Bactria, others along its boundary, παρά. Both are correct, but at different times; it was the boundary of Bactria on the west till Euthydemus annexed the provinces of Tapuria and Traxiane across (west of) the river. See Tarn, *Bactria and India*, p. 88.

when Gandhāra was put under Peithon son of Agenor as satrap (see p. 312 n. 6).

So far, then, the Gazetteer has been dated between summer 324 and 321. But there are two statements in it antedating the partition of Babylon, which was made very soon after Alexander's death, in either June or July 323. In the Gazetteer, Media is still undivided; at Babylon it was divided between Peithon son of Crateuas and Atropates. And Armenia is still a satrapy; but at Babylon the fiction of an Armenian satrapy was abolished, and was never revived. The date of the Gazetteer is then between summer 324 and June–July 323, in the last year of Alexander's life.

It remains to consider the Susian satrapy mentioned above. There is no difficulty about it if we keep to the good early evidence, the contemporary and official Gazetteer and Hieronymus of Cardia. Alexander, on his return from India, made Peucestas satrap of Persis, an office he continued to hold for several years after 321. The Gazetteer is conclusive that in the last year of Alexander's life Susiana was temporarily under the same satrap as Persis, i.e. Peucestas; Alexander had had to put to death the satrap Abulites and his son Oxathres,[1] and must have told Peucestas to take charge of Susiana pending the appointment of a new satrap, just as, after Philippus' murder, he had told Taxiles to take charge temporarily of Gandhāra; these arrangements were not disturbed at the partition of Babylon, very soon after Alexander's death, when no one possessed unquestioned authority. But in 321, at Triparadeisos, the position was different; Antipater had just been appointed Regent of the Empire in proper form, there was again a ruler with full and unquestioned authority, and he tied up Alexander's loose ends. Taxiles was removed from his temporary rule over Gandhāra, though not disturbed in his own kingdom, and Peithon, son of Agenor, was appointed satrap of Gandhāra; and Peucestas lost his temporary rule of Susiana and Antigenes was appointed satrap; that Antipater could do this and still leave Peucestas undisturbed in his satrapy of Persis shows that both men knew very well that Peucestas' authority over Susiana had been meant to be, and was, a temporary matter only. Naturally, however, Peucestas did not welcome Antigenes; the circumstances of Antigenes' appointment explain, and are needed to explain, Peucestas' enmity to him when both men were supporting Eumenes of Cardia in his war with Antigonus, an enmity which in our sources is left unexplained.

1 Abulites appointed, Arr. III, 16, 9; he and Oxathres put to death in 324 for governing badly, VII, 4, 1.

A very different view has been put forward in Germany about the Susian satrapy; it neglects entirely the good early evidence, and, starting from the partition of Babylon, has created out of some late material, in part corrupt, a second Coenus, who is called satrap of Susiana and has now attained to the dignity of a biography,[1] though he never existed. I am going to examine this view, for it bears on the dating and trustworthiness of the Gazetteer, and is an excellent example of how *not* to write history. It will be necessary to begin from the partition of Babylon as a background. We have five accounts of this partition,[2] the first part of each giving Perdiccas' appointments, and the second part, where given, being a list of Alexander's arrangements in the East which Perdiccas left untouched; they all go back ultimately to a common source, which can only be Hieronymus. They are Diodorus XVIII, 3, 1–3; Arrian, *Diad.* (τὰ μετὰ 'Αλέξανδρον);[3] Curtius X, 10, 1–4; Justin XIII, 4, 10–24; Dexippus.[4] The first three agree as to the first part of the list; there Curtius stops, and Arrian stops with the remark that there were many provinces which were not distributed [afresh], but which remained under the 'native' rulers appointed by Alexander; Diodorus shows that this applies to all the eastern satrapies, and consequently the word 'native', ἐγχωρίων, has got in by mistake. Arrian and Curtius therefore give no help about the Susian satrapy, but Diodorus, who alone of the three gives the whole list, naturally does not mention it, as Susiana remained as it was when Alexander died, i.e. part of Persis; the presumption then, so far, is that Hieronymus, from whom Diodorus probably took the Gazetteer, did not mention it either. What really have to be considered here are the lists of Justin and Dexippus; the τὰ μετὰ 'Αλέξανδρον of Dexippus (third or fourth century A.D.) is supposed to represent Arrian, but certainly does not always do so. Both Dexippus and Justin give the whole list, and both have the common feature that they introduce into their lists material which comes from the partition of Triparadeisos in 321, a partition of whose details we are well informed.[5] Dexippus has brought in from Triparadeisos Peithon as satrap of Gandhāra[6] and Seleucus as satrap

1 Berve II, p. 218, no. 440.
2 A convenient table of the several versions is given by Beloch, *Gr. Gesch.*[2] IV, ii, 309.
3 Jacoby II, no. 156, fr. 1, 5–7 (from Photius).
4 Jacoby II A, no. 100, fr. 8 (from Photius).
5 Diod. XVIII, 39, 6; Arr. *Diad.* fr. 9, §§ 34 *sqq.* (Jacoby). They are in substantial agreement.
6 Peithon gets τῶν τούτοις (Taxiles and Porus) ὁμόρων, πλὴν Παροπαμισαδῶν, which is from Arr. *Diad.* fr. 9, 36 where at Triparadeisos Peithon

of Babylonia; he has also substituted Neoptolemus, a known figure, for Tlepolemus as satrap of Carmania; there are some other mistakes also.[1] Justin has brought in from Triparadeisos the division of the Hyrcanian-Parthian satrapy, up to 321 ruled by Phratapherness, in the form 'Parthos Philippus, Hyrcanios Phrataphernes', and also the transfer of Stasanor at Triparadeisos from the Arian to the Bactrian-Sogdian satrapy in the garbled form 'Drangae et Arei Stasanori...Sogdianos Soleus Staganor'; and he has some mistakes, assigning Lycia and Pamphylia to their one-time satrap Nearchus instead of (as is certain from the other versions of the list) to Antigonus, and calling Peithon the Bodyguard Illyrius, which must be a corruption.

I can now turn to the sentence in Justin which is responsible for the creation of Coenus II; in the first part of his list, out of place, he has 'Susiana gens Coeno' (xiii, 4, 14). The only Coenus known to history, Alexander's famous general, had died in India (Arr. vi, 2, 1); and it was Beloch[2] who attempted to satisfy Justin's statement by the supposition of a second Coenus, saying that Coenus the taxiarch who died in India was apparently a different person from Coenus the hipparch of the battle with Porus (which is quite impossible),[3] and that the name also

gets τὰ ξύνορα Παροπαμισάδαις; both mean Gandhāra. At Babylon (Diod. xviii, 3, 3) Gandhāra, τὴν συνορίζουσαν σατραπείαν, was left, as Alexander had left it, in Taxiles' hands (τοῖς περὶ Ταξίλην βασιλεῦσι only means Taxiles). Beloch's insertion of Peithon's name in Diod. xviii, 3, 3, shows he did not understand the position; between Alexander's death and Triparadeisos Peithon was still satrap of Sind.

1 Κιλίκων for Λυκίων in Dexippus 8, § 2 (Antigonus' satrapy), Κιλικίας having been given two lines previously, may be a scribe's error, as it is a known confusion; see MSS. of Diod. xviii, 39, 6 (Antigonus' satrapy) and xx, 19, 5, while in xix, 57, 1, Λυκίαν of the MSS. is certainly Κιλικίαν, see *C.A.H.* vi, p. 484 n. 1; also in the Romance, A', iii, 33, 15 (Antigonus' satrapy), with Kroll's note. But Dexippus' interchange of the kingdoms of Porus and Taxiles is another matter. As it occurs also in Alexander's fictitious Testament, some affinity of Dexippus with the Romance has been suggested; but this does not follow, for the same interchange occurs elsewhere. Diodorus has it in xviii, 39, 6 (Triparadeisos) though he gives the two kingdoms correctly in xviii, 3, 3 (Babylon) and elsewhere in xvii and xviii; and Arrian has the same mistake in the partition of Triparadeisos, *Diad.* fr. 9, 36. What it all means I do not know; as the Triparadeisos lists in both Diodorus and Arrian go back to Hieronymus, is it conceivable that Hieronymus made a slip? In any case, it is one more instance of Dexippus introducing material from Triparadeisos into his account of the partition of Babylon.

2 Beloch, *op. cit.* iv, ii, 310 *sq.*
3 Coenus' career can be followed in App. i, ii and iv; see also App. 6.

appeared in the Dexippus fragment (see p. 312), where it had been corrupted into κοινῶς. This was taken up and worked out more fully by Berve (II, p. 218, no. 440), who found a second Coenus not only in Justin and Dexippus, but in Curtius x, 1, 43 and in a highly imaginative restoration by Ausfeld of a meaningless passage in the *Metz Epitome*. I may take Justin first.

Every late writer contains meaningless substitutions of one known proper name for another, though Justin is in a class by himself in this respect (p. 125 n. 2); but this does not apply here, for the corruption in 'Susiana gens Coeno' does not lie in the name Coenus. The complete sentence runs: 'Susiana gens Coeno, Phrygia maior Antigono, Philippi filio, adsignatur.' It has to be explained why Justin wrote 'Susiana *gens*', when all through this the first part of his list he gives names of countries alone, and *gens* adds nothing to Susiana, which is complete in itself. It is also noticeable that he gives the well-known Antigonus his patronymic, though his father was quite undistinguished. There is only one other patronymic in Justin's list: Peithon son of Agenor has his father's name given to distinguish him from the more important Peithon the Bodyguard, the son of Crateuas, and to avoid confusion; and similarly Antigonus' patronymic can only have been given to distinguish his name from some other name with which it might be confused, no other Antigonus being known. We know that there *was* confusion between the names Antigonus and Antigenes;[1] Antigenes then is the other name in question. As we have also seen that *gens* is, at best, suspect, and also that Justin inserted material in his list from the partition of Triparadeisos, the solution of the problem is obvious: Justin wrote 'Susa (or conceivably Susiana)[2] Antigeni Coeni (*sc.* filio), Phrygia maior Antigono Philippi filio'. This relationship makes it certain that my deduction that Antigenes got Coenus' battalion of the phalanx when Coenus was promoted to be hipparch is correct,[3] and it also explains why Alexander put the newly promoted Antigenes in general command of the phalanx for the battle with Porus' elephants: he saw in him something of his father's ability.[4] With this, Coenus II vanishes

1 In Diod. XVIII, 39, 6, ᾿Αντιγένει δὲ τὴν Σουσιανήν, all the MSS. have ᾿Αντιγόνῳ, though Antigenes is quite certain for other reasons. In Plut. *Alex*. LXX Antigenes the One-eyed is Antigonus.
2 For Susa as still the name of the satrapy, see Arr. III, 19, 2.
3 App. 1, II, p. 146. This was deduced without any reference to any relationship between Coenus and Antigenes, which had not then occurred to me.
4 Cf. also Arr. VI, 2, 1, of Coenus, ἐν τοῖς πιστοτάτοις, with Diod. XVIII, 62, 6, of Antigenes, πίστεως βεβαιότητι διαφέρων.

from history; but before coming to Berve's story I had better notice his reference to Curtius.

Curtius x, 1, 43 says: 'iisdem fere diebus (at Pasargadae in 324) litteras a Coeno accipit (Alexander) de rebus in Europa et Asia gestis dum ipse Indiam subegit'; that is, Alexander received a report on what had happened in the West while he was away. 'Litteras a Coeno accipit' means, and can only mean, 'he received a letter (a report) from Coenus', that is, a report made and written by Coenus. Such a thing is impossible. There was only one man who could have made such a report for Alexander, and that was the man whose duty it was to make it, Antipater. Berve,[1] who saw in 'Coenus' his Coenus II, tried to get out of this by saying that Coenus came to Alexander 'und überbrachte ihm Berichte über die Lage in Europa', i.e. Coenus was only a messenger; that is not a translation of Curtius, but a rewriting. It is certain that 'Coeno' here is a mere mistake for 'Antipatro'; I have already mentioned that the meaningless substitution of one known name for another known name in late writers is common enough.[2] In addition, Curtius notoriously has many proper names not found elsewhere, some of which he seems to have invented himself, but he always says who the man was, what office he held, etc.; he does not leave readers to guess. But he says nothing here about 'Coenus', though as he himself has previously recorded Coenus' death (IX, 3, 20) an explanation was desirable; he assumes that the name will be known to readers, as of course Antipater's would have been, and he has written 'Coeno' when he meant 'Antipatro'. I apologise for dwelling on so common a phenomenon.

I come now to Berve's story,[3] or rather Ausfeld's, drawn from the *Metz Epitome* and Dexippus;[4] it would never have been invented but

1 Berve II, p. 218, no. 440.
2 For examples in Curtius, see § G, p. 96. In § H, p. 125 n. 2, I have given a list of quite certain instances from the Hellenistic books of Justin; it is rather startling, for in some cases Trogus, whom Justin is epitomising, gave the name correctly. But every secondary historian seems to contain similar blunders; as a specimen, in Diodorus xviii we get (3, 1) Meleager (all MSS.) for Menander and (12, 1) Philotas (all MSS.) for Leonnatus, besides (39, 6) Antigonus (all MSS.) for Antigenes. Even Arrian's *Anabasis* is not exempt; it has Alcetas for Meleager, IV, 22, 1 (see App. 1, II, p. 145), and Eurydice for Cleopatra, III, 6, 5 (see App. 9, p. 262 n. 1). It is much to be wished that some one would collect all the cases in later Greek writers.
3 Berve II, p. 218, no. 440, Κοῖνος, and p. 57, no. 107, Ἀργαῖος.
4 Jacoby II A, no. 100, fr. 8, 6. Πέρσαι δὲ ὑπὸ Πευκέστηι ἐτάχθησαν· τὴν δὲ Σουσιανῶν (Phot. Σογδιανῶν) βασιλείαν † Ὀρώπιος εἶχεν, οὐ πάτριον

for the passage in Justin already considered. The *Metȝ Epitome*, like many other versions of the Alexander-Romance, gives Alexander's supposed Testament; the variations of this document in different versions of the Romance are endless.¹ It included directions for the allotment of various satrapies; some of these agree with history, some do not. The Susian satrapy is not as a rule one of these,² but the *Metȝ Epitome* has a corrupt sentence which does not seem to occur elsewhere. It runs: 'sit pro Mediis imperator Craterus. excedat item exussannis. Argaeus imperator sit poenis.' No one can restore this convincingly; 'exussannis' is presumably 'ex Susianis'; somebody then is to quit the Susian satrapy, possibly Craterus, possibly Argaeus; 'poenis' looks like the name of a people (satrapy); Paeonibus has been suggested, but is pure guesswork. When Ausfeld³ was attempting to get together, from the various Romance documents, a version of the Testament which should not be too remote from reality, he took this sentence in hand and produced 'excedat item ex Susianis Argaeus; imperator sit pro eo Coenus'. He then explained the name Argaeus by means of the word Ὀρώπιος in Dexippus, saying that what Dexippus must have written was Ἀργαῖος Ὀρώπιος, Argaeus of Oropus, who was therefore at one time satrap of Susiana; and, like Beloch, he read Κοῖνος for Dexippus' κοινῶς. Berve took up Ausfeld's conjecture as though it were a fact and produced the story that, after Abulites satrap of Susa had been put to death by Alexander in 324, Argaeus held the satrapy for a little while and was succeeded by Coenus II, a story of which he says that it 'kann als gesichert gelten'.⁴ That is to say: Alexander's fictitious Testament makes him give certain orders, to take effect if he dies; one of these (which only occurs in one version), being incomprehensible, was rewritten by Ausfeld; Berve took Ausfeld's guess and made of it a series of events which had actually happened and which, he says, may be regarded as well established.

This story, though it has had some acceptance,⁵ ought not to need

---

ἔχων ἀρχήν, ἀλλὰ δόντος αὐτοῦ Ἀλεξάνδρου· ἐπεὶ δὲ τύχη τις αὐτῶι συνέπεσεν ἐπαναστάσεως αἰτίαν φεύγοντι, τότε κοινῶς (Κοῖνος, Jacoby) αὐτῶν τὴν ἀρχὴν εἶχε. Gutschmid's emendation of Σουσιανῶν for Σογδιανῶν is quite certain, for the geographical reasons given App. 8, 1, p. 243 n. 6.

1 The notes to Alexander's διαθήκη in W. Kroll's edition of Aʹ, *Historia Alexandri Magni*, 1926, pp. 138–44 inclusive, will give a good idea of this.
2 With the reservation that I have not seen all the versions of the Romance.
3 A. Ausfeld, *Rhein. Mus.* LVI, 1901, pp. 517, 538.   4 Berve II, no. 440.
5 Lehmann-Haupt, 'Satrap' in PW, 154. It is unfortunate that Jacoby should have printed Κοῖνος for κοινῶς in his text of the Dexippus fragment.

comment. Alexander's fictitious Testament is not historical evidence for anything. Some of the people named in it, like the omnipresent Holkias, unknown outside the Romance,[1] and Phanocrates, general of the upper satrapies, never existed; Argaeus, if the name be not corrupt, is only another of these.[2] Ausfeld's Argaeus of Oropus is impossible for several reasons. A man of Oropus is not 'Ορώπιος but 'Ωρώπιος. Alexander did not bestow satrapies upon unknown Greeks. And, as Beloch saw,[3] the name concealed under 'Ορώπιος must be that of a Persian; no one could have said of a Greek or Macedonian that his satrapy was not hereditary, while in Persia hereditary satrapies were not uncommon. And, as Coenus II has been disproved, his name cannot be concealed under Dexippus' κοινῶς. I am not going to try to emend the Dexippus passage; there has been too much guessing about it already, and the corruption may go deeper than the two words 'Ορώπιος and κοινῶς. The things which are evident are that Dexippus thought that there was something unusual about the state of the Susian satrapy when the generals met at Babylon and that it needed an explanatory paragraph; and his explanation is *not* taken from Arrian, for the Persian satrap whose name is concealed under 'Ορώπιος can only be Abulites, and while in Arrian Abulites and his son Oxathres are put to death for oppression of subjects,[4] the satrap in the Dexippus passage is removed from office on a charge of rebellion; also Arrian would not have called a satrapy βασιλεία. Where Dexippus got his story from does not appear, but the κοινῶς clause at the end, whatever the corruption may be (Droysen's and Müller's ἐκεῖνος is the best of the conjectures), must refer, like the Gazetteer, to the rule of Peucestas, for no one else has been mentioned who can be the subject of ἀρχὴν εἶχε. It is worth notice, in conclusion, that Arrian, in describing the partition of Triparadeisos,[5] makes Antipater give to Antigenes the *whole* of Susiana, τῆς Σουσιανῆς συμπάσης ἄρχειν; this must allude to the fact that when Alexander gave Abulites the Susian satrapy he detached a part of it, called Media Paraetacene, for his son Oxathres, who was executed

---

1 Berve II, p. 283, no. 580 sought to make Holkias historical on the faith of Polyaenus IV, 6, 6, and called him a 'hohe Pezetairenoffizier'. Whatever Polyaenus' story may be worth, his Holkias is not Alexander's supposed friend of the Romance, but one of three ring-leaders of some mutinous soldiery.
2 No Argaeus is mentioned in other versions of the Romance. The only Argaeus known in this period is a 'Friend' of Ptolemy, mentioned once in 310 (Diod. xx, 21, 1). 3 *Op. cit.* IV, ii, 311.
4 Arr. VII, 4, 1, ὅτι κακῶς ἐπεμελεῖτο τῶν Σουσίων.
5 Jacoby II, no. 156, fr. 9, 35.

with his father and on the same charge, and the word συμπάσης suggests that the division of the satrapy had not previously been formally abolished. And this is followed by the statement that Antipater Πευκέσται ἐβεβαίου τὴν Περσίδα; no expression of this sort is used by Arrian of any other satrap, and it emphasises the fact that, though Susiana was taken from Peucestas, Antipater was not touching his original satrapy of Persis, but 'made it sure' to him.

Appendices 18–21: PERSONAL

18. ALEXANDER'S ATTITUDE TO SEX

I REGRET having to write this Appendix, for the title might suggest the worst kind of popular historiography; but it is very necessary to straighten the matter out.[1] What I wrote about it in *C.A.H.* VI is correct, and I have altered nothing; but readers are entitled to ask for the evidence.

The form of the attack made upon Alexander by the Peripatetics is well known: Aristotle had turned out a perfectly good pupil, but he was ruined by his own fortune, his τύχη, and degenerated into a cruel, mean, and sensual tyrant (§ F, p. 69 n. 1). Of our extant writers, Curtius' main portrait (see § G) exhibits the fullest working up of the Peripatetic thesis which we possess, and he knows the exact time of the great change in Alexander's character; it took place in Hyrcania, after Darius' death,[2] and follows immediately after the Queen of the Amazons story and the introduction of the eunuch Bagoas.

As one way of attacking Alexander, the Peripatetic school took his supposed indifference to women and explained it in two different ways. One explanation was given by his contemporary, Theophrastus. As a philosopher, Theophrastus utilised the scientific knowledge acquired by Alexander's expedition, and also gave currency to the most important of his social ideas;[3] but as a man he desired revenge on Alexander for the death of his friend Callisthenes. He branded Alexander as a tyrant,[4] but he did more than that; he suggested that the tyrant was something less than a man. He could not indeed say that he was impotent, for there was no doubt that Alexander IV was his son;[5] but

1 Berve's disquisition, I, pp. 10–11, will show the necessity as well as anything.
2 Curt. VI, 6, 1–8, Alexander's 'continentia' and 'moderatio' change to 'superbia' and 'lascivia', and he gives free reign to his 'cupiditates'. Cf. VI, 2, 1–5.
3 Tarn, 'Alexander the Great and the Unity of Mankind', *Proc. Brit. Acad.* 1933, p. 140 [20] and n. 101; Fr. Dirlmeier, 'Die Oikeiosis-Lehre Theophrasts', *Philol. Supp. Bd.* XXX, 1, 1937, esp. p. 72; Tarn, *A.J.P.* LX, 1939, p. 58. See App. 25, V.
4 In Καλλισθένης ἢ περὶ πένθους; see Jacoby II, no. 124, Kallisthenes, T. 19.
5 The Theophrastus passage (given p. 320 n. 1) obviously cannot have been written during Alexander's lifetime.

he called him semi-impotent,[1] and cited from Aristotle a quasi-scientific explanation of this as caused by drunkenness;[2] and either he or a later Peripatetic, Hieronymus of Rhodes, gave currency to an unpleasant story designed to show that Philip and Olympias had been afraid that their son was a eunuch.[3] Another very different explanation was however given by Theophrastus' younger contemporary, Dicaearchus, whose activity is associated with the rule, after Alexander's death, of his enemy Cassander: Alexander was homosexual. To uphold this, Dicaearchus invented for him a minion, the eunuch Bagoas.[4] The explanations of Theophrastus and Dicaearchus, explanations of a supposed indifference to women which did not in fact exist (p. 324), are mutually exclusive and therefore presumably both untrue. Theophrastus' theory was sufficiently refuted by the existence of Alexander IV; it was repeated later by Carystius of Pergamum and by Hieronymus of Rhodes, but otherwise gained no currency. But Dicaearchus' theory had a long run; and I must first investigate Bagoas, whom some modern writers have taken for a real person.

The only one of our extant writers who features Bagoas is Curtius; Plutarch (*Alex.* LXVII) repeats Dicaearchus' story, but otherwise Bagoas is not mentioned. Curtius locates the change in Alexander's character in Hyrcania, and introduces Bagoas to signalise the change: when Nabarzanes, last of Darius' followers, surrendered to Alexander, he brought with him, says Curtius, Bagoas, the minion of Darius III, who in a short time (*mox*) became Alexander's minion, and induced him to pardon Nabarzanes.[5] It is a silly story; Alexander, who knew all the facts, and who 'never put anything off',[6] would not have needed even a 'short time' to make up his mind about Nabarzanes; while Curtius,

1 Athen. X, 435 A, from the letters of Hieronymus of Rhodes, who quotes Theophrastus as saying ὅτι Ἀλέξανδρος οὐκ εὖ διέκειτο πρὸς τὰ ἀφροδίσια. The story given to illustrate this shows that something physical is meant and not merely frigidity. I am not aware that any modern writer has noticed this passage.   2 *Ib.* 434F.

3 *Ib.* 435 A. It cannot be said whether Athenaeus is here quoting Hieronymus only or continuing Hieronymus' quotation from Theophrastus; the Greek would suit either. The word here translated 'eunuch' is γύννις, a mule.

4 Dicaearchus, *F.H.G.* II, 241 = Athen. XIII, 603 A, B. The name may have been taken from the famous eunuch Bagoas who poisoned Arses and put Darius III on the throne; at the same time, it is conceivable that among the eunuchs of Darius III there *was* one called Bagoas. When I call the Bagoas of Dicaearchus an invented figure, I mean that the part played by this figure in the Alexander-story is an invention, whether a eunuch of that name did exist or not.

5 Curt. VI, 5, 22–3.   6 References, § F, p. 75 n. 4.

in his usual careless fashion, has forgotten that, in his own story, Alexander had already given Nabarzanes his life and he had come in *accepta fide.*[1] Moreover, as Alexander had pardoned Satibarzanes, who (with Barsaentes) was the actual murderer of Darius,[2] he did not need anyone's persuasion to pardon Nabarzanes, who was not a murderer; he put no one to death for Darius' murder (which after all relieved him of the difficulty of dealing with his rival), for though Barsaentes was executed later it was for rebellion.[3]

The other story which Curtius has to tell about Bagoas is that Orxines, for long satrap of Persis and the noblest of the Persians, visited Alexander and gave presents to all his friends except the eunuch Bagoas; Bagoas in revenge accused him of robbing Cyrus' tomb, and Alexander thereupon put him to death.[4] This story is an even clearer fabrication than the other. Orxines indeed existed, but he was very different from Curtius' account of him. While Alexander was in India, Phrasaortes satrap of Persis died, and Orxines usurped the office; his subjects, on Alexander's return, accused him of plundering temples and royal tombs and of putting many Persians to death unjustly; he was convicted (ἐξηλέγχθη) and hanged.[5]

In face of these considerations, the whole of Curtius' account of Bagoas falls to the ground. He was following Peripatetic tradition (see § G); he had to use Peripatetic tools. A strict moralist himself (§ G, p. 93), he was committed to exhibiting Alexander's degeneration in his later period; Bagoas was a godsend to him. In fact, he alludes to homosexuality again in connection with a certain Excipinus, another invented character whose name is neither Greek nor any other known language;[6] though it was left to such writers as Justin (another moralist) and Aelian to produce the absurdity that Hephaestion was Alexander's minion.[7]

Such things merit no notice; but there remains Dicaearchus, whose story of Alexander kissing Bagoas in the theatre amid the applause of the Macedonians is reproduced in Plutarch.[8] The fragment of Dicae-

---

1 Curt. VI, 4, 14; 5, 22.   2 Arr. III, 21, 10, MSS.
3 Arr. III, 23, 4 only says that Nabarzanes came in, not last, but with Phrataphernes and many others. He is not mentioned again; but Alexander never put any one to death who surrendered. For Barsaentes see Arr. III, 25, 8, who is wrong in saying that he was executed for Darius' murder.
4 Curt. X, 1, 22 *sqq.*   5 Arr. VI, 29, 2; 30, 1 *sq.*
6 Curt. VII, 9, 19, MSS.   7 Justin XII, 12, 11; Ael. *V.H.* XII, 7.
8 Dicaearchus in Athen. XIII, 603 B = Plut. *Alex.* LXVII. It is strange that Plutarch did not see how inconsistent this was with everything else he had written.

archus which we have does not name the locality, but as the incident, on the Peripatetic thesis, was after Darius' death, it was somewhere in the Farther East, and Plutarch, in reproducing the story, locates it at the Persian capital (βασιλεῖον) of western Gedrosia. His scene-setting is hopeless; he connects the story with the Bacchic rout through Carmania, whose falsity needs no demonstration to-day (§ E, pp. 46 *sq*.), and makes Alexander, after marching for seven days through Carmania, reach the capital of Gedrosia, which lay in the opposite direction and which he had long left behind. But these absurdities are not the real point; the point is that the story is an anachronism. Alexander kisses Bagoas in a *theatre*,[1] and in Alexander's day there was no such thing as a theatre in Iran, or anywhere east of Asia Minor, though there were plenty later on; but Greeks could not imagine a town without a theatre, and we get exactly the same anachronism elsewhere.[2] The theatre damns the story completely, and therewith the invented figure of 'the eunuch Bagoas' vanishes from history;[3] and with him vanishes the theory which he had been invented to sustain.

It is refreshing to turn to the truth of the matter. The truth is shown by Alexander's rage with Philoxenus, when he offered to buy for him two beautiful boys who were for sale: 'What evil has he ever seen in me', he exclaimed, 'that should make him offer me such shameful creatures?'[4] and he told Philoxenus to tell the dealer to take his wares to hell.[5] Even in late work the same tradition is found: Alexander was courteous to everyone except τοῖς καλοῖς,[6] καλοῖς being a euphemism.

---

1 θέατρον in both writers means a building and not the audience, for Dicaearchus distinguishes the latter as τῶν θεατῶν.

2 Plut. *Alex.* LXXII: when Hephaestion was ill at Ecbatana his physician goes off εἰς τὸ θέατρον. Diod. XVII, 106, 4, at Salmus in Carmania, Alexander σκηνικοὺς ἀγῶνας ἐν τῷ θεάτρῳ ποιοῦντος.

3 The Bagoas who entertained Alexander at Babylon (Aelian, *V.H.* III, 23) is admittedly a different person; but the whole of this section of Aelian is highly suspect.

4 Plut. *Alex.* XXII. τοιαῦτα ὀνείδη means the boys, cf. Callimachus, *Hymn to Delos*, l. 241, Ζηνὸς ὀνείδεα = light-o'-loves. It may be quoted from Sophocles *O.T.* 1494, where Oedipus calls his daughters τοιαῦτ' ὀνείδη on account of their origin.

5 For the stories in Plutarch favourable to Alexander see App. 16, p. 298. J. Kaerst in *Philol.* LI, 1892, p. 602, admitted (p. 616) that these letters in Plut. *Alex.* XXI, XXII are tolerably free from suspicion, and that anyhow this attitude of Alexander's, and generally Plutarch on his chastity, are probably historical. This is noteworthy, for Kaerst did not admit much, and regarded most of the Alexander letters as forged; a good many are.

6 [Plut.] *Mor.* 338 D, μόνοις ὑπερηφάνως τοῖς καλοῖς ἐχρῆτο.

Indeed, the very fount of offence, Athenaeus himself, after quoting Dicaearchus on Bagoas and calling Alexander φιλόπαις ἐκμανῶς on the strength of it (he alleges no other evidence), proceeded to stultify himself, first by quoting a story from Carystius that Alexander had refused to let the son of his host kiss him when the boy's father told him to, and then by adding on his own account that Alexander's continence (ἐγκρατής) was the pattern of what was most becoming (πρεπωδέστατον),[1] showing that truth will out, even in an Athenaeus. But of course the amazing thing is that Curtius, having reproduced the Peripatetic character of Alexander and having done his best to show, by means of Bagoas, that he was homosexual, at the end of his book informs his readers, in plain Latin, that there is not a word of truth in these stories and that Alexander was neither homosexual nor promiscuous.[2] I must refer to my discussion of Curtius in § G.

There is then not one scrap of evidence for calling Alexander homosexual. It is now well established that throughout the Hellenistic period, if you disliked any one, it was common form to make sexual accusations against him, in the hope that some of the mud might stick; and during the Civil Wars the Romans copied this custom wholeheartedly. Seeing what violent opposition Alexander evoked in Stoic, Peripatetic, and literary circles, it is most extraordinary that we get so little of the sort about him. Of promiscuity there is precisely one story. Justin, who on Alexander is as worthless as may be, but who shows occasional affinities with the Stoic tradition (see § H), has managed to assert that he slept with Darius' 360 concubines[3], though even Curtius, with a similar axe to grind, says no more than that they remained in 'the palace',[4] i.e. at Susa. Presumably they did; no one with a grain of humanity could have turned them loose to the alternatives of starvation or prostitution.

And this brings us to the astonishing fact that, so far as trustworthy records go, Alexander, with the world at his feet, never had a mistress. The story of his supposed intrigue with the quite imaginary 'Memnon's widow' is considered in Appendix 20; it breaks down at every point, and it is easy to see how it originated. Even in antiquity no responsible writer believed that a mythical Queen of the Amazons (see App. 19) visited him for the same purpose for which the Queen of Sheba visited Solomon, though Curtius' version is interesting for the light it throws

1 Athen. XIII, 603 B.
2 Curt. X, 5, 32: 'Veneris intra naturale desiderium usus nec ulla nisi ex permisso voluptas.'
3 Justin XII, 3, 10.   4 Curt. VI, 6, 8, 'regiam implebant'.

on Curtius' mentality (§ G, pp. 92 *sq.*). The story of Alexander's intrigue with Cleophis, 'queen' of the Assaceni of Gandhāra who ruled in Massaga, is worse than untrue, it is silly; though, unlike the Amazon and 'Memnon's widow', Cleophis really did exist. She was not, however, a queen, for the Assaceni were part of the Asvaka,[1] one of the 'free peoples' who had neither kings nor queens (if Indians ever were ruled by queens); her son was not king, neither had he died before Alexander came, as Curtius says; every detail in the story is wrong. Her son in actual fact was ἡγεμών, the people's war-leader, and she was merely his mother, a woman with a grown-up son[2] (and a war-leader would not be very young) and also a grand-daughter; few 'romantic inventions'[3] have miscarried worse. Even Curtius[4] only gives the story as what 'some' believed, leaving direct affirmation to Justin.[5] As to the famous story of Thais at Persepolis, no ancient writer says that she was Alexander's mistress, and no writer but Athenaeus even hints at it;[6] if she *was* there, she was there as Ptolemy's mistress (§ E, p. 48), as their sons' ages show.[7] The conclusion is that when Plutarch[8] says that Alexander had known no woman before Roxane except Memnon's widow, he is, so far as our records go, speaking the truth, allowing that the story of 'Memnon's widow' is an undoubted fabrication.

We have now been through the worthless concoctions of the traditions hostile to Alexander; it is time to consider the facts. Plutarch's wide reading had left a very clear impression on his mind of Alexander's attitude toward women:[9] it was not indifference at all, but the expression of a most definite purpose, the subjugation of his body to his mind and will; the body was to be only a servant. The rebellion of the body, Alexander said, sweet at the moment, only led to trouble.[10] A man must be master of himself if he was to be master of others;[11] τὸ ἐρωτικόν

1 Tarn, *Bactria and India*, pp. 169 *sq.*   2 Arr. IV, 27, 2–4.
3 Berve II, no. 435, 'eine Erfindung der romanhaften Tradition'; this is notable, for Berve usually accepts far too much. Cleophis reappears in the Romance.
4 Curt. VIII, 10, 22, 34 *sqq.* Diodorus does not give it.
5 Justin XII, 7, 9 *sqq.*   6 Athen. XIII, 576 D.
7 Ditt.³ 314; Justin XV, 2, 7.   8 *Alex.* XXI.
9 Not only in the *Life* of Alexander and the *de Alexandri Fortuna*, but everywhere; see e.g. *Mor.* 179 E 3, 180 F 19. On the trustworthiness of chaps. XXI and XXII of the *Life*, see p. 322 n. 5 and p. 298 with Addenda.
10 *Alex.* XXII, ἔλεγε δὲ μάλιστα συνιέναι θνητὸς ὤν... ἀπὸ μιᾶς ἐγγινόμενον ἀσθενείας τῇ φύσει καὶ τὸ πονοῦν καὶ τὸ ἡδόμενον.
11 *Ib.* XXI, τοῦ νικᾶν τοὺς πολεμίους τὸ κρατεῖν ἑαυτοῦ βασιλικώτερον ἡγούμενος.

must be τὸ σῶφρον,[1] and the beauty of woman must yield place to the beauty of virtue.[2] But there was more than this; there was something very like compassion for the whole of womankind; in his day they needed it badly enough. His treatment of Darius' family, which so astonished the world, went beyond mere protection; the two girls were not only to be kept safe, but were not to hear or expect or suspect anything wrong.[3] The list of brides at Susa shows that several other girls were being looked after, including the orphaned daughter of his most determined opponent, Spitamenes. His humane treatment of Darius' harem has already been noticed (p. 323); and there is a pretty story of his helping two lovers.[4] When the satrap Atropates sent him a corps of 100 mounted girls armed like men, he sent them home again to be safe from the soldiery.[5] Very notable was his attitude towards rape. Greeks apparently paid little attention to it; it was the universal concomitant of war—*quid enim capta crudelius urbe?*—and, if the Attic stage can be trusted, was by no means unknown at nocturnal religious festivals. But when a Theban woman named Timocleia, the sister of a bitter enemy of his—Aristobulus vouches for the story[6]—was brought before him, charged with murdering a soldier who had raped her, he so admired her courage that he pardoned and released her together with her family; and when, later, he heard that two Macedonians of Parmenion's command had raped certain women, he ordered Parmenion to put them on trial and, if convicted, to kill them like wild beasts (θηρία) destructive to mankind.[7] No one could have invented that story, for no one could understand his action; neither, though the sack of Persepolis in Curtius is an invention, could any one have invented Alexander's order that the women were not to be touched;[8] that order was given *somewhere*.

1 *De Alexandri Fortuna*, I, 332 D.
2 *Alex.* XXI, ἀντεπιδεικνύμενος πρὸς τὴν ἰδέαν τὴν ἐκείνων (some beautiful captives) τὸ τῆς ἰδίας ἐγκρατείας καὶ σωφροσύνης κάλλος.
3 *Ib.*, μήτε ἀκοῦσαί τι μήτε ὑπονοῆσαι μήτε προσδοκῆσαι τῶν αἰσχρῶν.
4 Plut. *Alex.* XLI (Telesippa); repeated *Mor.* 180 F 21, 339 D. As two different names are given for the man, it may perhaps be untrue; yet inventions *favourable* to Alexander scarcely exist.
5 Arr. VII, 13, 2 *sq.*; see App. 19. It has nothing to do with the Amazon story, though it had been mixed up with it before it reached Arrian.
6 Aristobulus, fr. 1, Jacoby = Plut. *Mor.* 259 D–260 D; repeated Plut. *Alex.* XII; for other references see Berve II, no. 751.   7 Plut. *Alex.* XXII.
8 Curt. V, 6, 8, 'cultu et corporibus feminarum abstinere iussit'. I have called attention elsewhere (§ G, p. 94) to Curtius' habit of casually introducing some genuine piece of information in the middle of a lot of rhetoric.

A late writer calls Alexander ἄτρωτον ἐπιθυμίαις, unwounded by desire[1] (which is by no means the same thing as absence of desire);[2] and it may well be true. Our historians naturally represent him as in love with Roxane, for that was the proper thing to say; but it is certain enough that he married her for political reasons,[3] to reconcile her class and end the struggle with the great barons of the north-eastern marches, just as later he married Darius' elder daughter Barsine for political reasons, to fortify his claim to the Empire he had conquered and to give a personal lead to the union he was striving for between Macedonians and Persians. It is probably safe to say that he never cared for any woman except his terrible mother—that is certain—and possibly his adopted mother Sisygambis, who certainly had some influence with him.[4] Perhaps, as the world then went, Theophrastus had some small excuse for his materialistic explanation; but the right of the matter undoubtedly lies with Plutarch—self-conquest. It was the first time that such a thing had appeared publicly on the world's stage; the world could not understand it, and it may have been one, though only one, of the reasons which made Arrian, in the great summing-up which ends his book, say that Alexander was like no other man.[5]

19. THE QUEEN OF THE AMAZONS[6]

When Alexander was on the Jaxartes, he sent envoys to some people of the 'European Scyths', i.e. the Sacas beyond the Jaxartes; these returned to him to Bactra, accompanied by envoys from the 'king of

1 [Plut.] *de Alexandri Fortuna*, II, 339A.
2 Shown by such stories as Plutarch, *Mor.* 180 F 19, and especially *Alex.* XXI, where he calls some beautiful captives ἀλγηδόνες ὀμμάτων. The meaning is not affected if the phrase be quoted from Herod. v, 18 (where the meaning is rather different) or more probably from the story current in Macedonia which Herodotus reproduced.
3 Plutarch alone had some suspicion of this: *Alex.* XLVII, ἔδοξε δὲ οὐκ ἀνάρμοστα τοῖς ὑποκειμένοις εἶναι πράγμασιν. It is noteworthy that Roxane is never mentioned again in any reputable tradition while Alexander lived; contrast the frequent mentions of Olympias and Sisygambis.
4 Ptolemy relates her successful intercession with Alexander for the Uxii, Arr. III, 17, 6.
5 Arr. VII, 30, 2, οὐδενὶ ἄλλῳ ἀνθρώπων ἐοικώς. There is a later, but very different, case in Hellenistic history of a man whom no one could understand, Aratus of Sicyon; apparently Greeks had never seen a neurotic before.
6 Three versions of the story: Diod. XVII, 77, 1 *sqq.*; Curt. VI, 5, 24 *sqq.*; Justin XII, 3, 5 *sqq.*

the Scyths', who offered Alexander his daughter in marriage;[1] Alexander declined her with thanks. That this girl was the origin of the story of the visit of the Queen of the Amazons to Alexander[2] (for of course this story, like most others, had to have some small grain of fact at the bottom of it) seems certain enough from four things: (1) the Queen of the Amazons came to Alexander παιδοποιίας χάριν, as a foreign bride married for political reasons would; (2) Arrian calls the girl βασίλισσα, queen; (3) Pharasmanes' reference to Amazons as being his neighbours; (4) the original place of meeting of the Amazon Queen and Alexander was beyond the Jaxartes.[3] (1) needs no elaboration. (2) At a later time, the unmarried princesses of the Ptolemaic and Seleucid houses were called βασίλισσαι, but, except for the Arrian passage above, I can only recall one other case of the word being used anywhere of an unmarried girl before that time: Alexander ordered that Darius' daughters, when captives, should be called βασίλισσαι,[4] which is not in point. No doubt Arrian's use of the word for a 'barbarian' girl is a glance at the Queen of the Amazons story. As to (3), Pharasmanes king of Chorasmia was in Bactra at the same time as the Saca envoys, and is recorded[5] to have told Alexander that his kingdom bordered on 'the Amazon women'. Of course he had never heard of Amazons, a purely Greek conception, and bad interpreting alone would hardly have produced them. What must have happened was that someone about Alexander, or Alexander himself, was interested in accounts (or the sight) of the nomad girls riding and shooting, and naturally thought of Amazons[6] and asked Pharasmanes if there were any

1 Arr. IV, 15, 1–3. The whole passage, 1–4, has generally been supposed to be from Aristobulus (Kornemann, p. 143). This must be so as regards § 4, what Pharasmanes said; but the two embassies which occupy 1–3 must have been recorded in the *Journal* and so could be from Ptolemy; the authority is good in any case. Alexander's embassy appears in a garbled form in Curtius VII, 6, 12, VIII, 1, 7 and 9, which exhibits the usual later confusion of the two rivers called Tanais; for the name of the envoy, Berdas (Arrian has 'envoys'), which may be invented, some would substitute the known name Derdas, Berve II, no. 250.
2 Suggested, but not worked out, by E. Mederer, *Die Alexanderlegenden bei den ältesten Alexanderhistorikern*, 1936, p. 87. He has collected the literature on previous Greek ideas of the Amazons.
3 Plut. *Alex.* XLVI, ἐνταῦθα.
4 Arr. II, 12, 5, explicitly from both Ptolemy and Aristobulus. The use of the term ἄνασσαι in Cyprus, on which see Sir G. F. Hill, *A History of Cyprus*, I, p. 114, I think has no bearing on the matter.
5 Arr. IV, 15, 4, from Aristobulus (see n. 1 above).
6 The nomad women may have been the origin of the Greek Amazons; literature in Mederer, *op. cit.*

Amazons in his part of the world; and the king, with the usual Oriental desire to please, said 'Amazons? O yes, lots; in fact they are my neighbours.'[1] This would have been quite enough to start somebody calling the Saca girl, who of course could ride and shoot—doubtless the envoys would enlarge on her prowess—an Amazon;[2] and then the story grew like a snowball. Either Polycleitus or Onesicritus (to whom it would have been a godsend) actually originated the story of the Amazon Queen's visit to Alexander;[3] it was taken up and written up by Cleitarchus (*post*), and from him doubtless derive the three versions we possess.

(4) The place of meeting of Alexander and the Amazon Queen is important. Originally, we have seen, it was where it should have been, beyond the Jaxartes. But it is quite clear from Strabo[4] that Cleitarchus transferred the meeting to Hyrcania; and the reason for thinking that our three accounts, which all derive ultimately from a common source (in all three the queen's visit lasts thirteen days), go back, with variations, to Cleitarchus is that all three place the meeting in Hyrcania. What the thirteen days mean I do not know. But the interest of the matter lies in Strabo's statement that Cleitarchus made the queen start on her journey 'from the Caspian Gates and the Thermodon'. Jacoby (II BD, p. 491) says that it is not credible that Cleitarchus should have said this, and that the starting point, Thermodon, must have been confused with the last station on the route, the Caspian Gates. Mederer, who did not understand the geographical questions involved, went further; he said (*op. cit.* pp. 85–6) that the easiest way to get rid of the

1 A prospective tenant, inspecting an Irish shooting, became suspicious when to every question the keeper replied that the birds named were very numerous, and said: 'I suppose you haven't any Encyclopaedia Britannicas here?' 'None have come this year,' replied the Irishman, 'but last year a pair nested on the island.' So Pharasmanes.

2 An interesting confirmation of these nomad Amazons will be found in an article by Professor H. H. Dubs, *Class. Phil.* XXXVIII, 1943, p. 13, entitled 'A Roman influence upon Chinese painting', which records a description of a series of (lost) Chinese pictures illustrating an attack by Chinese troops in the winter of 36–35 B.C. upon the fortress of a Hun chieftain in Sogdiana. The fifth picture showed the chieftain in armour on the battlements, with his consort and the ladies of his harem (who would of course be nomad girls), all shooting valiantly at the attackers; several of the women have been killed. Evidently harem life in Central Asia had its moments.

3 The two earliest names in the list in Plut. *Alex.* XLVI, which also shows that Cleitarchus related the story.

4 Strabo XI, 5, 4 (505) = Cleitarchus fr. 16.

difficulty ('ist am ehesten beseitigt') is to follow Jacoby. But difficulties in texts do not exist to be got rid of; one has to try to understand them. Strabo's context, which ought to have been noticed, makes Jacoby's explanation impossible. Strabo says: 'Cleitarchus says that Thalestris came to Alexander starting from the Caspian Gates and Thermodon; *but* (my italics) the distance from Caspia to Thermodon is more than 6,000 stades.'[1] Were Jacoby right, Strabo could never have written that 'but'. We have already seen that Cleitarchus was totally ignorant of the geography of all this part of Asia, and that he ran the Hyrcanian Sea (our Caspian) and the Black Sea (which the Thermodon entered) together, separated by an isthmus so narrow that it could be flooded from either sea (§ B, p. 15); and there is not the least doubt that Strabo here is quoting him correctly. This Cleitarchean geography occurs again in Curtius VI, 4, 17, where various peoples of northern Asia Minor, Mosyni, Chalybes, Leucosyri (Cappadocians), and with them *Amazonum campi*, the land of the Amazons (whom Greeks located in Asia Minor, about the Thermodon), are located on the Caspian. Strabo then provides one more proof of what has already been proved (§ B, p. 15), that Cleitarchus was utterly ignorant of Hyrcania and the Caspian and the whole of that part of the world, and was consequently not there with Alexander.

I may just finish up the matter of the Amazon Queen. Arrian VII, 13, 2 gives a λόγος that Atropates, satrap of Media, sent Alexander 100 armed girls on horseback, saying they were Amazons; Alexander sent them home again with a message to their queen that he would come to her παιδοποιησόμενος. Mederer (*op. cit.* p. 90) connects this with the Cleitarchus story, which is most unlikely, but immaterial. It is, as Arrian suspected, a true story which has had an Amazonian λόγος subsequently tacked on to it; Atropates sent to Alexander 100 armed girls on horseback, and Alexander sent them home again 'lest they should be violated by the soldiery'.[2] No one living but Alexander could or would have thought of such a thing,[3] and no one could have invented such a reason; had there never been camp-followers before? One recalls that unique event in history when Alexander induced 10,000 of his troops to marry their native concubines.

1 Strabo *ib.*: Κλείταρχος δέ φησι τὴν Θαληστρίαν ἀπὸ Κασπίων πυλῶν καὶ Θερμώδοντος ὁρμηθεῖσαν ἐλθεῖν πρὸς 'Αλέξανδρον· εἰσὶ δ' ἀπὸ Κασπίας εἰς Θερμώδοντα στάδιοι πλείους ἑξακισχιλίων.
2 μή τι νεωτερισθείη κατ' αὐτὰς ἐς ὕβριν πρὸς τῶν Μακεδόνων ἢ βαρβάρων.
3 See generally App. 18.

20. 'BARSINE' AND HER SON HERACLES

In 1921 I wrote an article[1] on this question which was a conclusive proof that the boy Heracles, who in 309 B.C. suddenly appeared in the character of an unknown son of Alexander, was merely a pretender set up by Polyperchon. Once stated, it was so obvious that it secured large acceptance; but there are several reasons besides accessibility for re-stating the proof here. One is that two important matters arising out of the story can be better put—indeed the part played by Aristobulus needed a thorough rewriting; another is the bearing of the story on what I have written in Appendix 18; a third is that for many years yet people will consult Professor Berve's big compendium, and it may be advisable not to seem to be letting his rejection of my proof go by default, though there is nothing to answer.[2] The traditional story, collected from several unsatisfactory notices in late writers,[3] but not given in full by any one of them, is this: among the women captured at Damascus after Issus was Memnon's widow Barsine, daughter of Artabazus, with whom Alexander had a liaison; she bore him a son named Heracles, and she and the boy lived at Pergamum. None of the notices suggest that she remained his mistress, or that the liaison took place at any time other than shortly after the capture of Damascus.[4] I will give as briefly as possible the various points which show that Heracles was not Alexander's son, and will then consider Aristobulus.

(1) By an analysis of six passages in Diodorus, to which I must refer, I showed that Hieronymus of Cardia only knew of one son of Alexander's, Roxane's son Alexander IV.[5] This by itself is conclusive that Heracles

1 *J.H.S.* XLI, 1921, p. 18, 'Heracles son of Barsine.' I refer to this throughout.
2 Berve II, nos. 206, *Barsine* and 353, *Heracles*.
3 Curt. X, 6, 11, a fabricated speech at the council of generals after Alexander's death, attributed to Nearchus. Justin XIII, 2, 7, the same speech, attributed to Meleager. Plut. *Eum.* 1 (from Duris), containing also a garbled account of two of the Susa weddings with the names wrong. Paus. IX, 7, 2, where Cassander, not Polyperchon, is Heracles' murderer. Justin XV, 2, 3, where Cassander is again the murderer (though Trogus *Prol.* XV gives Poly-perchon) and the context connects the murder with the story that Cassander poisoned Alexander. Plut. *Alex.* XXI will be considered later.
4 Berve makes Alexander take Barsine about with him till he reaches Bactria, where he discards her for Roxane. For this there is no evidence.
5 Berve II, p. 168 had to admit this, but said that Heracles, being illegitimate, did not count. Unfortunately he had already said on p. 104 that Alexander's liaison with the captive Barsine was designed to produce an heir to the

was not Alexander's son: (*a*) because Hieronymus had access to the archives at Pella, that is, to the papers of both of the opponents on whom the story of Heracles turns, Cassander and Antigonus, and (*b*) because, as a close friend of Alexander's secretary Eumenes, who wrote the *Journal*, he was in a position to know himself such a simple fact as the number of Alexander's sons.

(2) The traditional story asks us to believe that, during the first 14 years of the great struggle between the Successors, 323–309, a son of Alexander's could, and did, grow up at Pergamum unnoticed and unknown and never be used as a pawn in the game by any one. It is not possible.

(3) Ptolemy, who had been Alexander's friend from boyhood and who used the *Journal*, has no mention of any son of Alexander's born during his lifetime; and, as for most of the time between 315 and 301 he was Cassander's ally and Antigonus' enemy, he must have known through Cassander who Heracles was. He passes over the whole business in silence, his usual way with things he thought untrue; he never explicitly contradicts.[1]

(4) I come to the story of the pretender of 309, given fully by Diodorus xx, 20 and 28; there is no doubt, for the reasons I gave, that the story is from Hieronymus, Diodorus' basic source in books xviii–xx, whatever additions he may make. The story is this. In 309 Polyperchon, though now nothing but a soldier of fortune of little power, still desired to rule Macedonia, then ruled by Cassander, and therefore fetched from Pergamum Heracles, son of Alexander and Barsine, who was brought up at Pergamum and was now 17. He secured the alliance of the Aetolians, raised money, collected an army of 21,000 men, and called upon the Macedonian royalists to help 'the king' to such good purpose that Cassander, fearing wholesale defection, secured an interview with him (Polyperchon), persuaded him that if he succeeded he would merely be the servant of 'others', ἑτέρων, and bribed him with a share of power and the governorship of the Peloponnese to put the boy to death. Now the discarded soldier of fortune could not have raised an army of 21,000 men and enough money for a campaign without some one behind him; and as he got a pretender

throne. He has another similar self-contradiction, on consecutive pages. Curtius had said that three daughters of Mentor were captured at Damascus. On p. 102 Berve says that these were probably ('mögen') daughters of Barsine; on p. 103 n. 2 he says that 'natürlich' they were not. This sort of thing will happen if one tries to write history from bad late sources.

1 See H. Strasburger, *Ptolemaios und Alexander*, 1934, pp. 50, 55.

from Pergamum, which was subject to Antigonus, and as he could not have done this without the permission of Antigonus, who wanted to damage Cassander, there is no doubt who it was. He was in fact merely Antigonus' tool, which explains the support given him by Antigonus' allies the Aetolians; it was Antigonus who supplied him with money to raise an army of mercenaries and who sent him a pretender to be set up against Cassander.

(5) How much did Hieronymus himself know? Antigonus would not leave a full account of the transaction in his *Journal*; and in any case Hieronymus, writing at the court of Antigonus Gonatas, could hardly say straight out that Gonatas' grandfather had committed a fraud. But he himself knew well enough that Alexander had no second son, and he has left two perfectly plain indications about Heracles. The first is the interview between Cassander and Polyperchon, which shows that both men knew that they were dealing with a puppet; what clinches this is that Cassander's statement to Polyperchon that, if he succeeded, he would only be someone else's (i.e. Antigonus') servant[1] persuaded Polyperchon, whereas, had Heracles been Alexander's son, Polyperchon, if successful, would have been the real ruler of Macedonia in the boy's name and Cassander's bribe would have been entirely inadequate. This is conclusive. The second indication is that Hieronymus gave the boy's real age in 309, which was seventeen,[2] i.e. he was born in 326. Issus was fought in 333, and Alexander's son by a temporary liaison with a captive after the battle must have been born in 332; the boy from Pergamum, chosen doubtless for some facial resemblance to Alexander, was six years too young for his alleged parentage; this also is conclusive. Of course the statement in Diodorus' narrative that Heracles was the son of Alexander and Barsine is not from Hieronymus, who knew, as has been seen, that Alexander only had one son and that Heracles was merely a pretender; it is an addition of Diodorus' own,[3] and is taken from the common story. That story goes back to what Polyperchon gave out:[4] Alexander after Issus took a Persian captive named Barsine as mistress and had by her a son Heracles; the two lived

---

1 Diod. xx, 28, 2, ποιήσει τὸ προστατтόμενον ὑφ' ἑτέρων. That 'some one else' means Antigonus is certain; there was no one else concerned in the matter.

2 Diod. xx, 20, 1.

3 That Diodorus often did this is now a commonplace; instances in R. Schubert, *Die Quellen zur Geschichte der Diadochenzeit*, 1914, *passim*, and in Jacoby's article in PW on 'Hieronymos' of Cardia. See also § F and § F'.

4 For this see the analysis in my article.

at Pergamum. He *may* have added that Barsine was Artabazus' daughter; or that may be a later addition.[1]

(6) Barsine the captive is a made-up figure; I analysed her sufficiently in my article. Mentor, not Memnon, did really have a wife named Barsine, for their daughter married Nearchus at the Susa weddings in 324;[2] and Curtius and Diodorus may be following good evidence (the 'mercenaries' source') in saying that a widow of Memnon (unnamed) with a son of hers, presumably under military age, was captured at Damascus;[3] as Memnon had grown-up sons fighting at the Granicus,[4] his widow cannot have been very young (unless she were a second wife). That is all we know. Plutarch is the only writer who identifies Barsine the captive of Damascus with Memnon's unnamed widow;[5] the identification, as I showed, might perhaps be from Duris, who misuses proper names (see n. 1 below), but in any case it is late and valueless; the story that Memnon married his brother Mentor's widow after Mentor's death is a modern invention and does not appear in any tradition, good or bad; it may be remembered that all these people belonged to an older generation than Alexander. What is conceivable is that the name Memnon in Plutarch (Memnon's widow) is a mistake for

[1] It is first mentioned, so far as we know, by Duris (Plut. *Eum.* 1), in a passage which is completely worthless. I must refer to the list of the brides at the Susa weddings, Arr. VII, 4, 4–6. Arrian's citation in one place of a variant from Aristobulus shows that his list is from Ptolemy, and there is no doubt that we have here (part of) the official list from the *Journal*, written by Eumenes, with the true names of the brides, several of them not otherwise known. In it, Ptolemy and Eumenes marry two daughters of Artabazus, named respectively Artakama and Artonis; one may suppose that they knew their wives' names. But Duris, in the passage cited about Barsine the captive, though he makes Ptolemy and Eumenes marry daughters of Artabazus, has the names hopelessly wrong; Ptolemy's bride is called Apama, the only Apama known at the time being Spitamenes' daughter, the wife of Seleucus, who is epigraphically attested, and Eumenes' bride is called Barsine and described as a sister of Barsine the captive. The whole of the Duris passage is therefore quite useless for any purpose. Arrian's official list of brides at Susa has had some rough treatment. Jacoby II, BD, p. 522, on Aristobulus fr. 52, says that the variant cited from Aristobulus by Arrian does not preclude the list of couples being from Aristobulus, reasoning which I do not understand. Berve derives the real Barsine from the imaginary one (see on this p. 334 n. 4). Kornemann, *Ptolemaios I,* p. 89, first admits that Arrian's list *is* from Ptolemy and then follows Berve in saying that Stateira was the real name of Alexander's bride; he treats 'Barsine' as a mere mistake in Arrian's text, and thus manages to make the worst of both worlds.

[2] Arr. VII, 4, 6. [3] Diod. XVII, 23, 5; Curt. III, 13, 4.
[4] Arr. I, 15, 2. [5] Plut. *Alex.* XXI.

Mentor, as it is in Strabo XIII, 610; but no one mentions a widow of Mentor's at Damascus, though his daughters are mentioned. I said quite enough before about this tissue of absurdities.

(7) I come now to the two things that matter, the first being Plutarch's Barsine of the blood royal; Plutarch, after identifying his Barsine the captive of Damascus with Memnon's widow, says that she was of royal blood (Achaemenid) through her father Artabazus.[1] A good deal is known about Artabazus, but nowhere else is royal blood attributed to him; a modern theory has done this, but it is a very improbable one, on the dates.[2] The royal blood belongs to another story altogether, and not to that of Barsine the captive of Damascus who supposedly became Alexander's mistress and who was invented by Polyperchon or, more probably, by Antigonus for Polyperchon to use. This other story can be got at through Justin, who, though worth very little for the *history* of Alexander, can be valuable for tracing a legend. Justin (not from Trogus, see p. 330 n. 3) says that in 309 Cassander killed Heracles, son of Alexander and Barsine, 'who had passed his 14th year'.[3] And here it is as well to bear in mind throughout that there *was* a Barsine who was of royal blood and who was captured after Issus, viz. Darius' elder daughter (on her name, see n. 4 below). Heracles was killed by Polyperchon after, or late in, the campaigning season of 309, which means in the autumn, and as he was 'over 14' this means that, according to this story, he was born in the summer of 323; that is, in this story of Justin's, he was indeed a son of Alexander and Barsine, but the Barsine was Darius' elder daughter, whom Alexander married at the weddings at Susa in 324;[4] hence the lady's 'royal blood'

1 Plut. *Alex.* XXI. 2 See p. 26 n. 21 of my article.

3 Justin XV, 2, 3, 'qui annos XIV excesserat'. The idea once put forward that 14 was the Macedonian throne-age is exploded; see my article. That Justin means precisely what he says, 14 years old, is shown by XXVII, 2, 7, where he says of Antiochus Hierax: 'cum esset annos XIV natus, *supra aetatem* regni avidus' he attacked his brother, though only a boy, 'puer'. Justin therefore did *not* consider 'XIV' the age at which a boy should begin to rule.

4 Barsine was the official name of Darius' elder daughter; that is clear from the official list of the Susa weddings in Arrian VII, 4, 4 (see p. 333 n. 1). The 'vulgate' writers and the Romance call her Stateira, and Berve wrongly listed her as Stateira (II, p. 363, no. 722), actually saying that the name Barsine was due to a confusion with Artabazus' daughter Barsine, i.e. Barsine the captive! The origin of the name Stateira, probably the name used in common speech (§ G, p. 103), seems an insoluble puzzle. Two names for a woman, A ἡ καὶ B, are common enough, the second being her name ἐν τῇ συνηθείᾳ, the pet name used by her family and

in Plutarch. No son of Alexander's wife Barsine is known; but Alexander's wife Roxane did bear a son (Alexander IV) in July 323, and Justin's story, beyond doubt, is originally due to a confusion between Alexander's two wives, as can be seen from Trogus;[1] indeed Justin elsewhere (XIV, 6, 2) calls Heracles a son of Roxane, and it is notorious that in legend Roxane had become a daughter of Darius III well before the end of the third century B.C.[2] What influence, if any, the story of Heracles son of Barsine the queen had on the manufacture of the story of Heracles son of Barsine the captive, beyond supplying Plutarch with his 'royal blood', cannot be said;[3] we rarely know enough to arrange such stories in a tidy time-sequence.

(8) Aristobulus. Plutarch, speaking of Alexander's supposed liaison with Barsine the captive, adds Παρμενίωνος προτρεψαμένου τὸν 'Αλέξανδρον, ὥς φησιν 'Αριστόβουλος, καλῆς καὶ γενναίας ἄψασθαι γυναικός.[4] In my article I suggested that Parmenion's advice really applied to Darius' daughter and that Aristobulus attributed it to the wrong Barsine. This was a mistake; the error does not lie with Aristobulus, but with Plutarch; Aristobulus knew much too much about Alexander (§ D, pp. 40 sq.) to misinterpret Parmenion's advice in this fashion. For we know Parmenion's position. He understood very well what would happen in Macedonia if Alexander died childless, and

intimates; but that seems impossible here, for Stateira was a royal name in the Achaemenid house. Adeia's name was changed to Eurydike ὕστερον, which must mean after her marriage to Philip III (Arr. τὰ μετὰ 'Αλέξανδρον, Jacoby II, no. 156, fr. 9, 23), and Antiochus III changed the name of his bride from Chalcis to Euboea (Polyb. xx, 8, 5), so the idea that Barsine's name was changed when she married is not impossible; but no reason for it is apparent, and it would seem that Arrian must have mentioned it. One might suppose a confusion with her mother's name, *if* it were certain that the name Stateira for Darius' wife in Plut. *Alex.* xxx is correct; but the confusion might be the other way round.

1 The same confusion occurs in Suidas, 'Αντίπατρος: Antipater was regent for Alexander's son, named Heracles.

2 Suidas *s.v.* Δαρεῖος; Syncellus, p. 264B (given as Porphyry in *F.H.G.* III, p. 693, fr. 3 (1), but not so given in Jacoby); and regularly in the Greek Alexander-Romance, *Hist. Alex. M.* ed. Kroll, p. 92 and often. As to the date, see Tarn, *Bactria and India*, App. 3 on the fictitious Seleucid pedigree beginning with Alexander and Roxane daughter of Darius III. One of the things which show that Alexander's *Testament* is much earlier than the Romance itself is that in the *Testament* Roxane is not yet Darius' daughter but only 'the Bactrian', Kroll, p. 142.

3 See, however, the suggestion on p. 336 n. 7.

4 Plut. *Alex.* xxi = Jacoby II, no. 139 (Aristobulus), fr. 11. Jacoby, however, gives Aristobulus too much; what comes before the word Παρμενίωνος is not his.

he had advised Alexander that he ought, before setting out to invade Persia, to marry and beget an heir,[1] sensible advice which Alexander disregarded as he almost always did disregard Parmenion's advice.[2] After Issus Parmenion saw another chance, and advised Alexander to marry Barsine, Darius' elder daughter, as indeed was his obvious course; Alexander refused at the time, though he did marry her later. Aristobulus related this quite correctly; Darius' daughter was γενναία, well-born, and doubtless, as her father and mother are both called very handsome, she was sufficiently good-looking, at any rate for a princess, to be called καλή, beautiful;[3] but Plutarch (or his source), who only knew Darius' daughter as Stateira, took Aristobulus' Barsine, herself a captive, to mean Barsine the captive of Damascus and reproduced what he said accordingly, though it is most improbable that ἄψασθαι was the word Aristobulus used.[4] The supposition that Parmenion after Issus advised a liaison with a captive is merely silly; it is also impossible, for it could not have resulted in what Parmenion wanted, a legitimate heir to the throne. Parmenion's conduct was consistent throughout, and a later incident shows that after Issus he *did* advise Alexander to marry Darius' daughter, and that what I have said is not mere conjecture. For shortly after Issus Darius wrote to Alexander offering, as the price of peace, Asia west of the Euphrates and the hand of his daughter,[5] and Parmenion said that were he Alexander he would accept; and Alexander, though he refused Parmenion's advice and Darius' offer, qualified his refusal of the daughter by saying, in his reply to Darius, that if he wanted to marry her he would do so without Darius' leave,[6] as indeed he did; all this confirms Aristobulus' story. A conqueror in the East normally married the daughter or widow of the conquered, to get a better title to the kingdom than mere conquest; and as, when Alexander deposited Barsine at Susa, he arranged for her and her sister to be taught Greek,[7] there can be little doubt that he meant to marry her all along. The interesting thing is how Aristobulus

1 Diod. XVII, 16, 2.   2 See my article, p. 24.
3 Plut. *Alex.* XXI, after saying how handsome Darius and his wife were, adds τὰς δὲ παῖδας ἐοικέναι τοῖς γονεῦσιν.
4 Not necessarily a deliberate and tendencious alteration; Greeks often quoted very loosely. When a book might mean a big bundle of unindexed papyrus rolls, it was not so easy, even if you had access to it, to verify quotations as it is to-day.
5 Arr. II, 25, 1 *sqq.*   6 *Ib.* 25, 3.
7 Diod. XVII, 67, 1. It may conceivably be from this that Plutarch, or his source, got the statement (*Alex.* XXI) that Barsine the captive was πεπαιδευμένη παιδείαν Ἑλληνικήν.

came to know as much as he did; I have considered this elsewhere (§ D, pp. 40 *sq.*).[1]

(9) I have treated Barsine the captive as a figure invented by Polyperchon or by Antigonus for him. It is, of course, conceivable that, though the statements we have are valueless, Artabazus *did* have a daughter named Barsine who *was* among the women taken at Damascus. It would be quite immaterial if it were so; Barsine the captive as mistress of Alexander and mother of his son would be none the less an invention, and it would have no bearing on the proof of the facts that matter, that Alexander did *not* have a liaison with a captive after Issus[2] and that Heracles of Pergamum (presumably not the boy's real name) was *not* his son.

NOTE ON § 8 *ante* (pp. 335–7)

There is a curious reference elsewhere to Parmenion's advice to Alexander after Issus. Stobaeus III, 5, 41 (ed. O. Hense) has a story which, as Hense prints it, says that some urged Alexander to see Darius' daughters and his wife, who was extremely beautiful, to which he replied that it would be shameful if, after vanquishing the men, he were to be vanquished by the women.[3] I gather from Hense's notes (it is not absolutely clear to me) that this represents the version of the best MS., Escurialis (M) which is eleventh to twelfth century; but another MS., Parisinus (A), fourteenth century, has a very different story. A used to be rated highly; but Hense, p. xxxvi, not only puts it far below M, but says that the scribe of A religiously tries to amend the corruptions in M, but does it badly, *imperite*. As an editor, then, Hense is presumably right to print the text he does; but that does not quite end the matter for the historian. The version of A is that some urged Alexander to see Darius' daughters and marry the beautiful one, and he made the same reply,[4] a very different matter. Now the version of M is pure nonsense. ἡττᾶσθαι is very common in late writers when speaking of a man and a woman, and regularly means either to fall in love with or to feel desire for, and Alexander's saying (hardly likely to be genuine) is a play on the two meanings of the verb: 'I have vanquished the men; I will not be vanquished

---

1 See further on this section (8) the Note at the end of this Appendix.

2 Berve II, p. 103 has made me say in my article that 'Barsine aber sei tatsächlich nur eine Mätresse Alexander's', and p. 104 that Alexander's liaison took place after Parmenion's death. He is quite mistaken in supposing that I ever said anything of the kind.

3 'Αλέξανδρος προτρεπομένων τινῶν αὐτὸν ἰδεῖν τὰς Δαρείου θυγατέρας καὶ τὴν γυναῖκα διαφέρουσαν κάλλει 'αἰσχρόν' ἔφη 'τοὺς ἄνδρας νικήσαντας ὑπὸ γυναικῶν ἡττᾶσθαι'.

4 ἰδεῖν τὰς Δαρείου θυγατέρας καὶ τὴν κάλλει διαφέρουσαν εἰς γυναῖκα λαβεῖν, 'αἰσχρόν' ἔφη κ.τ.λ. A fourteenth-century compilation, the *Rosetum* of Macarius Chrysocephalus, has the same story in garbled form, εἰς γυναῖκα λαβεῖν διαφερούσας κάλλει. (From Hense's notes.)

by the women, as I should be if I desired one of them.' As all that he has been urged to do in M is to see (ἰδεῖν), i.e. interview, the captive women, there is no place for the common meaning of ἡττᾶσθαι; his answer does not belong to what it has been tacked on to. But in the version of A it does belong; he is being urged to marry one of the girls, and his supposed answer is in point. Now suppose that what Stobaeus really gave (he names no source for his extract, a rare thing) was the A version; it could very easily get altered to the M version because of Plutarch, who says that Darius' wife was extremely beautiful and that Alexander never set eyes on her[1] (this might quite well be true, for she died in child-birth soon after her capture); but if the version of M be correct, there is no possibility of the A story growing out of it or being a corruption of it; it is something totally different. The scribe of A, then, (or someone behind him), was deliberately correcting M, just as Hense said, by giving a different tradition, and that tradition either was, or was derived from, the story told by Aristobulus as I have deduced it in § 8 p. 335; note further that the Stobaeus story uses the same verb (προτρε-πομένων τινῶν αὐτόν) as does Aristobulus (Παρμενίωνος προτρεψαμένου τὸν Ἀλέξανδρον). The deduction I have given in § 8 of what Parmenion really said and Aristobulus really wrote is too obvious to need confirmation; but it is interesting to find the result reached turning up in a fourteenth-century MS. of Stobaeus.

21. ΑΝΙΚΗΤΟΣ

The title by which Alexander is known, in the literature which we possess, is ἀνίκητος, 'invincible' or 'unconquered'; its history has not been examined. We are supposed to have two versions of its origin: in one, Plutarch's, Alexander receives the title from Apollo at Delphi; the other, Diodorus', has been supposed to show that he received it from Ammon at Siwah. Plutarch's story (*Alex.* XIV) is that Alexander reached Delphi on one of the forbidden days;[2] the priestess said it was not lawful for her to prophesy, whereon Alexander pulled her towards the temple, and she, as though overwhelmed by his impetuosity, ex-

---

1 Plut. *Alex.* XXI; *de Curiositate* 522 A.
2 I cannot agree with H. W. Parke, *C.Q.* XXXVII, 1943, p. 19, that Plut. *Mor.* 292 F means that, at some time before the fifth century B.C., the antique practice at Delphi of Apollo only prophesying once a year was replaced by once a month. The word ὀψέ seems conclusive that Plutarch means shortly before his own time, when the oracle was dying, and not seven or eight centuries previously; the whole argument shows that the clause ὀψέ...δεομένοις is Plutarch's own, Callisthenes being only quoted for the antique practice. Between once a year and once a month came the bulk of Greek history, with the practice as indicated in Plut. *Alex.* XIV and (seemingly) *Codex Sabbaiticus* 19 (p. 341).

claimed: 'Boy, you are invincible', ἀνίκητος εἶ, ὦ παῖ. Alexander said that that was all the oracle he needed.

Wilcken[1] said it needed no demonstration that Plutarch's story was an invention, since Alexander never was at Delphi. I see no reason for doubting his visit to Delphi. As Diodorus (XVII, 93, 4) knew of this visit and the Pythia's greeting, it must have appeared in literature long before Plutarch; and Plutarch was in a position to check the story. For he was for long a priest at Delphi, and it is incredible that the priests should not have kept a list for themselves, even if not cut on stone, of the great men who had visited the temple or consulted the oracle, just as the temple at Delos kept records, many of which we possess, of the men, famous and obscure, who had visited the temple and made gifts to it; Plutarch's story, whoever first published it, cannot well have originally come from anywhere but the records of the priests of Delphi, for one cannot imagine Plutarch, who is credited with a (lost) collection of oracles and must therefore have studied the records of his temple, relating it, if those records showed that it had never happened. It was from these records that Plutarch must have got his other story of an otherwise unrecorded visit of Cassander to Delphi (*Alex.* LXXIV). Probably too there is other confirmation of Alexander's visit to Delphi. Plutarch makes him visit the place on his way home from the Congress of the League of Corinth at Corinth which elected him Hegemon, and the accounts of the ταμίαι at Delphi show that, subsequently to the autumn meeting of 336 B.C., somebody presented toward the building of the new temple 150 gold Philips, which were expended in the spring of 335; and it does not appear who this could have been but Alexander.[2] It was no great gift for a king; but when Alexander crossed the Dardanelles he was bankrupt, and probably the money represented just what he had with him at the time. The dedication by Craterus of a statue-group of Alexander's hunting at Delphi (Plut. *Alex.* XL) also points to some connection between Delphi and Alexander, and the story (*ib.* III) that Delphi ordered Philip to honour Ammon most of all gods may point to a similar connection, though the statement itself is only part of the story of Olympias and the snake (*ib.* II) and therefore just as untrue; some tradition connecting Delphi and Ammon did however exist, as will appear from Diodorus.

Diodorus (XVII, 51, 3) gives the story which is supposed to make Alexander's title ἀνίκητος originate from Ammon. The story is an

---

1 *S.B. Berlin* XXX, 1928, p. 17 [590] n. 3.
2 Ditt.³ 251 H, col. II, l. 9 (p. 436); see Pomtow's note 15 (p. 437). Olympias in 331 made a gift of gold darics to the temple, Ditt.³ 252, p. 447.

invention, for it has nothing to do with the greeting of the priest of Ammon to Alexander, the only thing which became known to the world (see App. 22, 1); it purports to give part of the response of the oracle, i.e. of what the priest said to him when he entered the inner shrine alone, and what that was no one ever knew. The responses of the oracle which we have, however, though inventions, seem to be early ones, and Diodorus' story existed long before Diodorus, which shows that the story of Alexander's visit to Delphi and the exclamation of the priestess must be early also, for Diodorus' story presupposes it. In Diodorus' story the oracle, after telling Alexander that Philip was not his father, says that the proof of his divine parentage will be the greatness of his success in all he does; for before this he had been invincible but after this he would be for ever invincible, καὶ γὰρ πρότερον ἀήττητον αὐτὸν γεγονέναι καὶ μετὰ ταῦτα ἔσεσθαι διὰ παντὸς ἀνίκητον. Now ἀήττητος and ἀνίκητος mean exactly the same thing, and the only reason for Diodorus using ἀήττητος here is to avoid the jingle of ἀνίκητος twice in the same sentence;[1] and what the oracle is saying is 'You were already invincible, as you will still always be; but you did not before know the reason—your divine parentage.' In other words, Ammon is represented not as conferring a new title but as confirming and explaining a pre-existing one; the allusion in πρότερον is to Delphi, as is clearly shown by what Diodorus says later. For in XVII, 93, 4 he gives as Alexander's reason for wishing still to go forward across the Beas τὴν μὲν γὰρ Πυθίαν ἀνίκητον αὐτὸν ὠνομακέναι, τὸν δὲ Ἄμμωνα συγκεχωρηκέναι τὴν ἁπάσης τῆς γῆς ἐξουσίαν. Diodorus therefore, on whom has been based the theory that the title ἀνίκητος was conferred upon Alexander by Ammon, says specifically that it was not given by Ammon but by the Pythia at Delphi, i.e. by Apollo.

Curtius IV, 7, 27 is too brief to be of any use here: the priest of Ammon, after telling Alexander that Philip's murderers had been punished, 'adiecit, invictum fore'; this adds nothing to Diodorus, and omits what matters.

Two small items may be noted here in passing as showing some connection between Alexander and Apollo which largely escapes us. When, in Carmania, Alexander offered Soteria, his thanksgiving for the safety of Nearchus and the fleet, he sacrificed to Apollo Alexikakos no

---

1 See my remarks, App. 1, 1, p. 136. I have purposely reproduced in my translation the jingle of a twice-repeated 'invincible' to show how impossibly ugly it is. Style was one of the reasons for the Greek dislike of technical terms.

ΑΝΙΚΗΤΟΣ

less than to Zeus Soter;[1] and a story was told that during the siege of
Tyre the Tyrians chained the statue of Apollo, lest he should desert to
Alexander.[2]

In Diodorus, then, the Delphi story is known to the priest of
Ammon; in a later work, the Alexander-history of which a fragment
remains in *Codex Sabbaiticus* 29,[3] that story is transferred bodily to
Ammon.[4] Alexander goes to the temple of Ammon in search of an
oracle, but the priest and the προφήτης (interpreter of the signs given
by the god) say that they are unable on that day to give an oracle, μὴ
δύνασθαι χρηστηριάζειν (it is not actually said to be a forbidden
day); Alexander compels them, and the προφήτης says μειράκιον,
ἀνίκητον εἶ, the words of the Pythia. *Codex Sabbaiticus* has certain
affinities with the Romance; but in the Romance itself the episode again
takes place at Delphi.[5] The Romance sometimes gives valuable information (see App. 22, pp. 363 *sqq.*), and it confirms Alexander's visit to
Delphi, but it has altered the story: Alexander threatens, if the Pythia
will not prophesy, to carry off the tripod as Heracles had done; Apollo's
own voice from the shrine says: 'Heracles, Alexander, was a god and
you are mortal', whereon the priestess says to Alexander: 'The god
has called you Heracles Alexander, which means that you will be
stronger than all men, ἰσχυρότερον πάντων δεῖ σε γενέσθαι.' It
comes to much the same thing, but the introduction of the name
Heracles conjoined in this fashion with Alexander's may show that it

1 Arr. *Ind.* 36, 3; see App. 22, p. 351 n. 5.
2 Diod. xvii, 41, 8; Curt. iv, 3, 22; Plut. *Alex.* xxiv, where the Tyrians
accuse Apollo of 'Alexandrising'. See G. Radet, *Notes critiques sur
l'histoire d'Alexandre*, 1st ser. 1925, p. 51.
3 Jacoby ii b, no. 151, 10. Jacoby put the document not earlier than
c. A.D. 150.
4 Wilcken, *loc. cit.* agrees that it *was* such a transfer.
5 Ps.-Call. A', i, 45, 5. Alexander is on his way from Locris to Thebes, and
reaches a place with an oracle; the text gives Ἀκραγαντίνους (Agrigentum
in Sicily), but the references to τὴν Φοιβηλάλον and to τὸν φοιβηλάλον
τρίποδα ὃν Κροῖσος ὁ Λυδῶν βασιλεὺς ἀνέθετο, together with the locality,
make it certain that Delphi is meant. How Ἀκραγαντίνους got into the
text cannot be said, but there are several parallels (noted separately) which
give inexplicable substitutions of one name for another; such are Curt. viii,
4, 21, where the MSS. give Cohortandus (whatever it may mean) for
Oxyartes; Diod. xvii, 113, 4, where, in a reference to the four Panhellenic
festivals, Ἀμμωνιεῦσι has taken the place of Ἀργείοις (App. 23, p. 377,
cf. App. 22, p. 356); and Diod. xviii, 4, 5, where a word which cannot be
guessed has been replaced by Κύρνῳ (Corsica). Such cases have nothing
to do with the so common instances of one known name (generals, satraps,
provinces) being written for another.

341

is a very late version; it might be connected with the prominence of Heracles ἀνίκητος under the Roman Empire.

On what I have given above, there can be no doubt that Delphi, not Ammon, is the true version of the story. It is also certain enough that the very widespread use of this title among later writers, who make it cover Alexander's whole existence, necessitates some definite and special origin for it. Berve,[1] who saw this, thought that the broken words in Hypereides I, col. 32, 5, pointed at the least to a proposal at Athens in 324 to erect a statue of Alexander as θεὸς ἀνίκητος, and accordingly found the formal origin of the title at that point, as he thought the title must have been given *ex eventu*; but it can be said with confidence that, if Berve's conjecture as to Hypereides' meaning should be correct, the title must, on the contrary, have been already well known. However, though I should be glad to call Hypereides as contemporary evidence for the existence of the title ἀνίκητος—and that he *may* be—I do not feel that enough of the Greek remains to make Berve's particular conjecture as to its meaning more than a conjecture. Certainly I see no reason to believe that the title must have been given *ex eventu*, whether in 324 or any other year. Demetrius of Bactria, who copied Alexander, took the title, not *ex eventu*, but on his earliest coins, that is, *before* his conquest of Northern India; and a number of extant secondary writers could hardly all represent Alexander, as they do, as having borne the title long before 324 unless this had been indicated in some early source.

The instances of ἀνίκητος applied to Alexander which I have, though probably not complete, cover his whole life from conception to death. In the Romance, Nectanebo, after seducing Olympias, speaks of σπέρματα ἀνίκητα.[2] When Philip received the triple news of his Illyrian and Olympic victories and of Alexander's birth, the soothsayers declared that the boy would be ἀνίκητος.[3] The title occurs in various contexts in our secondary writers,[4] apart from the passages in Plutarch and Diodorus already discussed; Curtius took a malicious pleasure in calling Alexander at the Persian Gates 'till then invincible',[5] and some hostile writer made Alexander adopt Persian luxury because he thought himself ἀνίκητος.[6] The word became something like a

---

1 H. Berve, *Gnomon* v, 1929, p. 376 n. 2.
2 Α' 1, 7, 1, σπέρματα ἀνίκητα διαμείνατε.
3 Plut. *Alex.* III.
4 Curt. IX, 9, 23; Plut. *Pyrrh.* XIX, *Alex.* XXVI (ἀήττητος).
5 Curt. V, 3, 22, 'invictus ante eam diem fuerat'.
6 Diod. XVII, table of contents II, ιγ' (not in the text).

proverb,[1] and occurs in poetry;[2] it was even transferred from Alexander to his army.[3] One writer gave a new turn to it by saying that Alexander was not only unconquered in battle but unconquered also by pleasure or toil or the amenities of life;[4] a hostile writer calls his soul unconquerable even in face of death.[5] But the most startling and important use of the word is on the coins of Demetrius I the Euthydemid, who took it as his title,[6] a thing long unexplained, as it was not recognised that this was Alexander's own title; it is perhaps the most unmistakable of the pieces of evidence which show that Demetrius was quite consciously emulating Alexander.

It remains to consider two possible objections to the view here taken. The first, which I owe to a friend, is a suggestion that ἀνίκητος was Heracles' title before it was Alexander's and was merely transferred from him to Alexander. Tyrtaeus does call Heracles ἀνίκητος,[7] but that appears to be the only instance of the title being applied to him which is earlier than Alexander. The inscriptions usually quoted are all later than Alexander,[8] as is the use of Heracles ἀνίκητος under the Roman Empire; this is said to be common, but I have not verified the statement, for obviously cases later than Alexander are not in point. A large number of gods, besides Heracles, were called ἀνίκητος in their day;[9] two of them were so called prior to Alexander,[10] but in the case of these two the word was not used as a title, merely as a statement of fact. The solitary instance in Tyrtaeus is very ancient history; what we want is to know what Heracles' regular title in this connection was nearer to

1 Plut. *de Fortuna Rom.* 326 C, ὅπλοις ἀνικήτοις; [? Pseudo-]Plut. *de Alex. Fortuna* II, 335 A, 337 A, τὸ ἀνίκητον.

2 *Anth. Pal.* VII, 239.   3 Diod. XVII, 9, 3; 16, 2.

4 [? Pseudo-]Plut. *de Alex. Fortuna* II, 339 B, τὸ ἐν ἡδονῇ καὶ πόνοις καὶ χάρισιν ἀνίκητον.

5 Justin XII, 15, 4, 'sicuti in hostem, ita et in mortem invictus animus fuit'.

6 Tarn, *Bactria and India*, p. 132.

7 Tyrtaeus 9 (7), 1: 'Αλλ' 'Ηρακλῆος γὰρ ἀνικήτου γένος ἐστέ.

8 The three given by Gruppe, *Herakles* in PW, Supp. Bd. III, 1001 are *I. Priene* 194, which mentions Sarapis; *C.I.G.* III, 3817, from Dorylaeum; and *J.H.S.* VIII, 1887, p. 504, no. 79, from Mezea near Dorylaeum. These three had been given by Weinreich, *Ath. Mitt.* XXXVII, 1912, p. 29 n. 1, who added *C.I.G.* III, 4966, Heracles Βῆλος, obviously late.

9 The list given by Weinreich, *op. cit.* p. 29 n. 1, from epigraphic evidence, is: Aphrodite, Ares (twice), Harpocrates, Helios (thrice), Zeus Aniketos Helios (five times), Helios Mithras (twice), θεὸς ἀνίκητος often on Mithras reliefs, Dusares; add Ma (p. 15, nos. 66, 67), and Kora (p. 15, no. 16); all I think later than Alexander.

10 Eros (Soph. *Antig.* 781) and Artemis (Pindar, *Pyth.* IV, 161); literary allusions, not inscriptions.

Alexander's day, and at the end of the fifth century that title was not
ἀνίκητος at all, but καλλίνικος. This word for example runs through
Euripides' *Heracles Mainomenos*,[1] and in Heracles' statement in l. 581
that, if he does not kill his children, οὐκ ἄρ' Ἡρακλῆς ὁ καλλίνικος,
ὡς πάροιθε, λέξομαι, the words ὡς πάροιθε show that, in Euripides'
eyes, this must have been Heracles' title for some time. Certainly the
use of καλλίνικος in this connection is older than the tragedians;[2] here
too may be cited its appearance as Heracles' title in the full form of the
common apotropaic formula on the doors of houses, one copy of
which at least is later than Alexander.[3] As a matter of fact, the tragedians
do *not* regard Heracles as ἀνίκητος, invincible; both in Sophocles
(*Trachiniae*, ll. 155 *sqq.*) and Euripides (*Alcestis*, l. 1023) he contemplates
the possibility of failing and never returning. Though Alexander
certainly honoured Heracles, there is no doubt that, the Labours apart,
the later Heracles stories borrowed a good deal from Alexander's career;
and there is nothing in favour of, and much against, any supposition
that Alexander's title was borrowed from Heracles; the converse
would be much more probable, even apart from the fact, which I have
already pointed out, that the very widespread use of this title for
Alexander in secondary writers shows not only that there should be a
good early source behind them, but that the title must have had some
definite and special origin; it cannot merely have been transferred to
Alexander from somebody else by various literary men. And it
remains to be shown that it was ever Heracles' title before it was
Alexander's.

The other possible objection is a view put forward by Mr H. W.
Parke, that the oracle given to Alexander at Delphi is 'obviously a
fictitious doublet of the oracle said to have been given at Delphi to

1 Ll. 581 (cf. 570), 681, 789, 961, 1046.
2 Archilochus 113 (77) Τήνελλα καλλίνικε. χαῖρ' ἄναξ Ἡράκλεες. Τήνελλα
(Hurrah!) was Archilochus' invention; but though the phrase τήνελλα
καλλίνικε became the usual greeting of the Olympic victor, I doubt if it be
correct here, and whether the older punctuation Τήνελλα. καλλίνικε
χαῖρ' ἄναξ Ἡράκλεες be not right. But to Archilochus καλλίνικε meant
Heracles whichever way it be read.
3 Ὁ τοῦ Διὸς παῖς καλλίνικος Ἡρακλῆς | ἐνθάδε κατοικεῖ· μηδὲν εἰσίτω κακόν.
On this formula see O. Weinreich, *Arch. f. Religionswiss.* XVIII, 1915,
pp. 12 *sqq.* If Mr Tod's suggested dating of the copy over the entrance to
the Karafto caves in Kurdistan, i.e. the close of the fourth or the early part
of the third century, be correct (in Sir A. Stein, *Old Routes of Western
Īrān*, 1940, p. 338), then the Heracles who penetrated Asia at Alexander's
heels was still καλλίνικος.

Philomelus'.[1] Parke neglects the fact that the story of Alexander at
Delphi was known to and alluded to by Diodorus; and as the Philomelus story depends on Diodorus alone, then, if we want to talk about
doublets, that story may, *a priori*, just as well be a doublet of the
Alexander-story as vice versa, especially as the supposed incident is
only an excrescence which has no logical place in the career of Philomelus. But in fact the two stories are quite different. Parke's paraphrase of Diodorus XVI, 27, 1[2] is 'when Philomelus was preparing to
use force to compel her (the Pythia) to occupy the tripod, she exclaimed
in exasperation "You can do as you please"'. There is nothing in
Diodorus about 'preparing to use force'; and if the sentence be rendered
accurately, the story takes on quite a different complexion. What
Diodorus says is that Philomelus, having seized the seat of the oracle
at Delphi, ordered the Pythia to prophesy from the tripod in the regular
way, κατὰ τὰ πάτρια. She made some objection, but it is not known
what, the text being corrupt, whereon he threatened her and helped
to compel her by force (συνηνάγκασε, aorist) to mount the tripod. She
called out, against the insolence of the man who was using force to
her, 'You can do as you please'; Philomelus received the words gladly,
and (Diodorus continues) spread the knowledge of them widely, to
show that the god had given him authority to do whatever he liked.
The words are of course ambiguous, and Parke's translation, 'you can
do as you please', gives the ambiguity very well; they can mean 'it is
permissible for you to do as you please' or 'you have the power to do
as you please'; the Pythia meant the second, Philomelus chose to
understand the first. But there are great difficulties in the story, if the
Pythia really uttered these words. συνηνάγκασε means that Philomelus
had his men with him and that together they forced her on to the
tripod, whereon very naturally she cried out. But Parke has overlooked
the earlier account in Diodorus XVI, 25, 3, which shows that she gave
a regular response from the tripod, even if under duress;[3] Diodorus
rubs this in by proceeding to relate the history of the tripod. And this

1 *A History of the Delphic Oracle*, 1939, p. 252, cf. p. 251; cf. also p. 338 n. 2 *ante*.
The references in Diodorus are XVI, 25, 3; 27, 1.
2 XVI, 27, 1. Οὗτος γὰρ κρατῶν τοῦ μαντείου προσέταττε τῇ Πυθίᾳ τὴν
μαντείαν ἀπὸ τοῦ τρίποδος ποιεῖσθαι κατὰ τὰ πάτρια. ἀποκριναμένης
δ' αὐτῆς ὅτι (ταῦτά ἐστι τὰ πάτρια)—there are many suggested emendations—διηπειλήσατο καὶ συνηνάγκασε τὴν ἀνάβασιν ποιεῖσθαι ἐπὶ τὸν
τρίποδα. ἀποφθεγξαμένης δ' αὐτῆς πρὸς τὴν ὑπεροχὴν τοῦ βιαζομένου
ὅτι ἔξεστιν αὐτῷ πράττειν ὃ βούλεται, ἀσμένως τὸ ῥηθὲν ἐδέξατο κ.τ.λ.
3 τὴν Πυθίαν ἠνάγκασεν ἀναβᾶσαν ἐπὶ τὸν τρίποδα δοῦναι τὸν χρησμόν.
There is nothing here about seating her on the tripod by force.

345

is made clear by the words themselves, which are a carefully composed ambiguity in Delphi's best style; the Pythia did not compose them on the spur of the moment while in the grasp of the soldiery. If any part of the story is true, the words of the oracle are most likely to be; and they are quite inconsistent with the story of force and a hasty exclamation, which may have been added by one of Philomelus' enemies.

Even, however, if the whole story be taken at its face value, which I regard as impossible, the differences from the Alexander-story are patent. Alexander came on a *dies non*; Philomelus did not. The Pythia gave her oracle to Philomelus from the tripod, and it was ambiguous; her words to Alexander were neither an oracle nor ambiguous, and were not spoken from the tripod. Philomelus and his men used force; no one can even imagine Alexander using force to any woman,[1] let alone a priestess. Philomelus wanted an oracle for propaganda purposes, and used it as such; Alexander did neither. Lastly (again taking the Philomelus story at its face value), there is, I apprehend, all the difference in the world between a middle-aged woman saying to a young prince: 'Boy, you are irresistible' and her saying to a body of armed soldiery: 'I am in your power.'

I have long had a profound distrust of facile explanations of events as 'doublets'; I have seen too many 'doublets' actually occur in my own personal life,[2] and many people, if they note these things, must have had a similar experience. In history, as in more important matters, the broad way may lead to destruction.

1 See generally App. 18. Certainly Plutarch says βίᾳ εἷλκεν, which probably means that he took her arm and said 'O, come along', or something of the sort. Βίᾳ only signifies 'against her intention'; any display of real force is out of the question.
2 In one 'doublet' in which I took part, the identity of time, place, purpose, and numbers was so exact that no one would believe it without strict proof, which cannot now be given, the other two men who participated being dead. But here is a simple case. In the sixteenth month after the publication of my first book (*Antigonos Gonatas*) Britain declared war on Germany. In the sixteenth month after the publication of my last book (*The Greeks in Bactria and India*) Britain declared war on Germany. Two thousand years hence, some scholar, were this coincidence known, would certainly command general assent if he said that the two books were one.

Appendices 22–25: THE MAIN PROBLEMS

22. ALEXANDER'S DEIFICATION

I AM loth to add yet one more study to what has been written on this subject; but there are still things to clear up, and I must explain what I have written in Vol. I. My primary concern is to try to ascertain what Alexander himself thought about it. , Discussion must naturally centre about three 'moments': his visit to Ammon, the proskynesis scene at Bactra, and the deification in 324 B.C.

I. AMMON

In the long debate between Professor Wilcken and his opponents, Wilcken proved certain things so conclusively that no more need be said about them.[1] These are, that the idea of Alexander's divine sonship came from the preliminary greeting of the High Priest of Ammon[2] and not from a response of the oracle; that he did *not* go to Siwah in order to be called son of Ammon, but merely to consult the oracle about the future, the oracle being regarded as very sure; and that nobody ever knew, and we do not know, what passed when he entered the inner shrine, the oracular responses given by some Greek writers being inventions. That is to say, in my own words, that Alexander got whatever he did get at Siwah, as he had got his title ἀνίκητος at Delphi (App. 21), by an accident which was regarded as inspired, the accident at Siwah being that the priest met and greeted him; and as Alexander had already been crowned Pharaoh at Memphis[3] and as such had become, like every other Pharaoh, the son of Amon-Re, the priest of Ammon, if he did

---

1 U. Wilcken, *S.B. Berlin*, xxx, 1928, p. 576 (the principal article); *ib.* x, 1930, p. 159; *ib.* xxviii, 1938, pp. 298–305. I cite these merely by their dates. See Addenda.

2 Many, including myself, had already taken this view; see a list in J. A. O. Larsen, *Class. Phil.* xxvii, 1932, p. 74.

3 The actual fact is only recorded in Ps.-Call. A', 1, 34, 2, the priests ἐθρόνιζον αὐτὸν εἰς τὸ τοῦ 'Ηφαίστου (Ptah) ἱερὸν θρονιστήριον καὶ ἐστόλιζον ὡς Αἰγύπτιον βασιλέα. (On the Romance see my remarks, p. 363.) It is not actual evidence; but as some of the royal titles are epigraphically attested for Alexander, there must have been a coronation ceremony (see Wilcken, 1928, pp. 577 [4] *sqq.*, esp. n. 5; *Alexander der Grosse*, 1931, pp. 104 *sqq.*) which is further proved by the reference in Arrian to his double paternity, pp. 353 *sq.*

347

come out to greet the new Pharaoh, had no option but to address him as son of Ammon, Ammon being merely Amon transplanted to Siwah with his name modified to mean, or suggest, 'god of the sands'.[1] But this being so, there are several things to be considered.

First, every one has always assumed that the priest spoke to Alexander in Greek; but it is necessary to be sure about this, for it is not what one would naturally expect. The natural supposition would be that the Egyptian priest of an Egyptian god in an Egyptian temple would have spoken Egyptian; and indeed Plutarch (*Alex.* xxvII) knew of 'some' writers—their names and authority are unknown—who asserted that the priest had learnt up a Greek sentence for the occasion and had bungled it, i.e. that he could not speak Greek. Had this been so, Alexander would have had to take his interpreter into the inner shrine with him, which would most probably have meant that everything that passed there would shortly have become public property. Personally, however, I believe Arrian's statement (III, 4, 5) that Alexander merely said he was pleased with what he had heard, and I believe also that he did write to his mother to say that he had heard 'some ineffable (or secret) oracles' which he would tell to her only;[2] as he never saw her again, they never became known. If this is correct, it proves that, as Callisthenes said, he did enter the shrine alone, which means that the priest could speak Greek; this after all was highly probable, for there was regular intercourse between Siwah and Cyrene, whose god Ammon was.

But another assumption, which has been made by every writer I have met with, including Wilcken, is a very different matter. It is that the Greek world had, *prior to Alexander*, identified Ammon with Zeus, and that the two were interchangeable. More is meant by this than just that the two names had become interchangeable, though that is always assumed; we are told that the god at Siwah had become a Greek god or at least an Aegypto-Greek one, and he is habitually called Zeus Ammon; one writer has even gone so far as to say that at Siwah Egyptian and Greek cults were combined and that the god there was a very early

1 Wilcken, 1928, p. 576 [3] n. 1.

2 Plut. *Alex.* xxvII, τινας μαντείας ἀπορρήτους. Kaerst (*Philol.* LI, 1892, p. 612) doubted the genuineness of this letter, but his reasons were far-fetched; there is no cause to do so, and it has since, I think, been generally accepted. If one doubts a letter from a reputable source—and there are forgeries in better sources than Plutarch—then, unless the contents of the letter prove the forgery, one must be prepared to answer the question 'For what purpose could it have been forged?' and here no purpose is apparent.

case of syncretism.[1] But if we ask for evidence for all this, it is not forthcoming. Certainly Ammon had become a god for some Greeks; but that is a very different thing from becoming a particular Greek god. He had become a god of one Greek city, Cyrene,[2] which had already been worshipping an old pre-Dorian ram god, Carneius,[3] and that and the Libyan blood in Cyrene, together with the amount of intercourse between Cyrene in its early days and Egypt, had no doubt made Ammon's path easy for him; but the one-time idea that the head of Ammon on Cyrene's coins is the head of Zeus with ram's horns added is not the case, for the Ammon heads are a perfect medley of types; a Zeus, Lycaeus, does indeed appear on the coins,[4] but not till after Alexander. Ammon was honoured too, at Athens, where he had a cult before 371–370,[5] a temple before 333–332;[6] prominent Greeks had consulted his oracle, which was ranked by Athenians with Delphi and Dodona.[7] But the god always appears as he does at Cyrene, as Ammon alone, a foreign deity whom Greeks had begun to worship, as they did Isis; it is very noteworthy that at Elis a sharp distinction was long maintained between 'the Greek gods' and 'the god in Libya'.[8] There was in fact no such god as Zeus Ammon, and, except for one poet, even the name Zeus Ammon does not occur in Greek literature and in Latin only in passages of no authority many centuries later.[9] The one exception is the poet Pindar, who in one place speaks of Zeus Ammon[10] and in another calls Ammon Lord of Olympus,[11] i.e. Zeus. But this is only the so common Greek habit of calling foreign gods by Greek names, as for example Herodotus calls Amon of Thebes Zeus[12] and Ptah Hermes; no one has ever supposed that this made Amon of Thebes a Greek god or created a deity Zeus Amon, and a piece of poetry would

---

1 V. Ehrenberg, 'Alexander und Ägypten', *Beihefte zum alten Orient* 7, 1926, pp. 37–9.
2 Plato, *Politicus* 257B, Theodorus swears νὴ τὸν ἡμέτερον θεὸν τὸν Ἄμμωνα.
3 E. S. G. Robinson, *Brit. Mus. Coins: Cyrenaica*, 1927, p. ccxl.
4 *Ib.* p. ccxxxix.
5 On the date see now Sterling Dow, *Harvard Theol. Rev.* xxx, 1937, p. 184.
6 Ditt.³ 281, ll. 15, 29; cf. 289, l. 19; 1029, l. 33.
7 Plato, *Laws*, 738C and *Alcib.* II, 148E–149B; Ar. *Birds*, 619, 716. Cf. Strabo XVII, 1, 5 (790).
8 Paus. V, 15, 11.
9 Curt. VI, 9, 18, 'Jovis Hammonis', in an invented and tendencious speech; Gellius, *Noctes Atticae*, XIII, 4, 1, the forged letter beginning 'Rex Alexander, Jovis Hammonis filius'.
10 Pind. *Pyth.* 4, 16 (28) Διὸς ἐν Ἄμμωνος θεμέθλοις.
11 Ἄμμων Ὀλύμπου δέσποτα, all that remains of his hymn to Ammon.
12 Herod. II, 42; IV, 181.

not make a god Zeus Ammon out of two gods with very different origins, functions and cults; what Pindar may have done was to give a hint to Callisthenes (pp. 356 *sqq.*).

The whole matter, however, is somewhat academic, seeing that what Alexander himself thought (and that is what matters) is certain past any argument. When, in Carmania, he at last met Nearchus, he swore to him a great oath that he was gladder to know that he (Nearchus) and the fleet were safe than he had been over the conquest of Asia; and the oath he swore was 'by Zeus of the Greeks and by Ammon of the Libyans'.[1] Nearchus is one of the most truthful writers of antiquity, and wrote not very long after the event (he died in 312); and Alexander's oath is conclusive that, to himself, Zeus and Ammon were two separate deities. There is other evidence also, as that on his return from Siwah to Egypt he sacrificed, not to Ammon, but to 'Zeus the king',[2] and, whatever Pindar may have said, there is no doubt that the first man to identify Ammon with Zeus for practical purposes was Callisthenes. The priest had hailed Alexander 'son of Ammon', for he could do no other, the new Pharaoh being *ex officio* son of Amon-Re;[3] but Callisthenes made him hail Alexander as son of Zeus,[4] and son of Zeus he was called by a large number of flatterers. Alexander never called himself son of either the one god or the other, though there is plenty of worthless assertion that he did.[5] In particular, he is never known to

1 Arr. *Ind.* 35, 8 = Jacoby II, no. 133 (Nearchus), fr. 1, p. 700: τόν τε Δία τῶν Ἑλλήνων καὶ τὸν Ἄμμωνα τῶν Λιβύων.

2 Arr. III, 5, 2, τῷ Διῒ τῷ βασιλεῖ. On V. Ehrenberg's assumption, *op. cit.* p. 40, that this meant Amon-Re, see Wilcken, 1928, p. 596 [23].

3 So Beloch, *Griech. Gesch.*² III, 1, 641: 'Die Priester begrüssten den König als Ammons Sohn, wie es als Herrscher Aegyptens ihm zukam.'

4 Fr. 14 (36) in Jacoby II, no. 124 = Strabo XVII, 1, 43 (814) ὅτι εἴη Διὸς υἱός.

5 These assertions fall into four groups: (1) Callisthenes in Plut. *Alex.* XXXIII, which will be discussed presently. (2) The statements in Curtius. In an invented and tendencious speech, Curtius makes Alexander call himself son of Juppiter Hammon, VI, 9, 18. In another invented speech, VIII, 1, 42, he makes Cleitus say that Alexander called himself son of Juppiter, and also makes Cleitus taunt him with being son of Ammon (the words 'oraculum—respondisse' show this); to Curtius the names meant the same thing. The rest is Alexander's orders to others (IV, 7, 30; VI, 11, 23; VIII, 5, 5). All this comes from one (or both) of the two sources which are concerned to show Alexander in a bad light and which have been discussed in § G. (3) The Romance, in which he calls himself son of Ammon and Olympias four times (see p. 364 nn.). And (4) forged letters in late writers, like the one in Gellius quoted p. 349 n. 9 and that in Eunapius, *F.H.G.* IV, 24, fr. 24, Ἀλεξάνδρου θειάζοντος ἑαυτὸν ἐκ Διός, both of which, as Olympias' answers show, belong to the story-cycle of Olympias and the snake.

have called himself son of Ammon, and to be called son of Ammon by others, as by the Macedonian mutineers at Opis,[1] or by Cleitus on the night of his murder[2] (if that story be true), roused him to fury; and what happened at Opis is important, for the mutineers drew from him a passionate harangue, in which he made no reference to Ammon; he began by recounting the benefits conferred upon Macedonia by his father Philip.[3] He is never even known to have sacrificed to Ammon;[4] once, and once only, he is recorded to have poured a libation to him (there is a difficulty here), but only as one among other deities;[5] there

1 Arr. VII, 8, 3.   2 Plut. *Alex.* L; Curt. VIII, 1, 42.

3 This speech is considered at length in App. 15; it is genuine except for certain interpolations. Alexander always alluded to Philip as his father; the letter to the Samians, Plut. *Alex.* XXVIII, where he calls Philip his 'so-called' father, is an obvious forgery on historical grounds, as Kaerst showed (*Philol.* LI, 1892, p. 613); add to his reasons that Alexander says ἔδωκα for ἀπέδωκα, on which see App. 7, 1, pp. 208 *sq.*

4 Ehrenberg, *op. cit.* p. 40, says Alexander always sacrificed to Ammon on weighty occasions, and gives several references, not one of which mentions sacrificing to Ammon.

5 Arr. VI, 3, 1, when starting down the Hydaspes he poured a libation, standing on the prow of his ship, to the rivers Hydaspes, Acesines and Indus, to Heraclès τῷ προπάτορι and to Ammon, and to the other gods ὅσοις αὐτῷ νόμος (Wilcken, 1928, p. 601 [28] thought that προπάτορι implied that Ammon was πατήρ, but it does not follow, any more than it follows that τῷ προπάτορι belongs to the original account). This *libation* must be distinguished from the earlier *sacrifice* recorded by Nearchus, Arr. *Ind.* 18, 11, when Alexander, his preparations complete, held ἀγῶνες and sacrificed to the gods ὅσοι γε πάτριοι ἢ μαντευτοὶ αὐτῷ (μαντευτοί means the gods to whom Ammon had told him to sacrifice, Arr. VI, 19, 4), and also to Poseidon, Amphritrite, the Nereids, Ocean, and the three rivers; Ammon was not included. The libation to Ammon ought to mean invoking his protection for the fleet, and this might be borne out by Alexander's oath when, on meeting Nearchus in Carmania, he swore by Ammon how glad he was to know that Nearchus and the fleet were safe (Arr. *Ind.* 35, 8); but he gave no thanks to Ammon, for the formal σωτήρια which he sacrificed when he knew that the fleet was safe (Arr. *Ind.* 36, 3) did not mention Ammon, but corresponded to the sacrifice he had offered before the expedition started; he sacrificed to Zeus Soter, Heracles, Apollo the averter of evil (ἀλεξίκακος), Poseidon and the gods of the sea (the rivers naturally drop out); in the first sacrifice Zeus Soter and Heracles would come under θεοὶ πάτριοι, and Apollo must have been a θεὸς μαντευτός. How now does the unique libation to Ammon fit into all this? It does not fit at all. Why did Alexander, just once, thus exhibit in public his connection with Ammon? And why, having invoked him, did he never thank him? I cannot answer these questions; I would sooner believe that, in the libation, Ἄμμωνι is merely one of those strange mistakes in our texts of which several have already been noticed (App. 21, p. 341 n. 5).

is, however, a strange passage in Arrian bearing on the matter of his birth which I shall come to. On the other hand, he acquiesced in people calling him son of Zeus (p. 359), and Callisthenes asserted that he himself once called himself son of Zeus,[1] a passage which has been much quoted because, as Wilcken said very frankly, no other case in any credible writer can be found. A mere glance at the context is sufficient to show what a pitiful untruth Callisthenes' assertion was; and I will take that first.

It comes in Plutarch's account of the battle of Gaugamela,[2] an account taken from some writer who knew next to nothing about the battle; Plutarch twice quotes Callisthenes by name, but as Curtius and Diodorus also made some use of this account (App. 5, p. 182) Callisthenes may not be entirely responsible. In the real battle, Alexander with the Companion cavalry was on the extreme right of his line, Parmenion with the Thessalian and Greek allied horse on the extreme left. I will now go through Plutarch. On the left wing, where Parmenion is, ἐν τῷ εὐωνύμῳ κέρατι κατὰ Παρμενίωνα, the Bactrian horse strongly charge the Macedonians (this really happened on the right wing), and Mazaeus sends a force to seize Alexander's camp (fictitious). Parmenion, upset by these two attacks, sends Alexander a message that he must at once despatch help to the camp (the real message was quite different, and later) which reaches Alexander just as he is going to order 'those about him' to advance (it did reach him when the battle was largely over); Alexander sends back a message to Parmenion explaining to him at some length that he does not understand the first principles of warfare (in fact he went to his help), and proceeds (same sentence) to put on his helmet, which means that he himself had not yet been engaged (he had in fact been fighting the battle of his life). Here follows a digression on Alexander's arms and horses which goes down to the end of XXXII. Book XXXIII returns to the story with 'Thereupon', τότε δέ, i.e. after putting on his helmet, Alexander makes a long speech, πλεῖστα διαλεχθείς, to the *Thessalians* and the other Greeks (i.e. the Greek allied horse), who are therefore supposed to be his personal command but who in reality were Parmenion's and were engaged in a desperate fight at the other end of the battle from Alexander; and when they (the Thessalians) encouraged him[3] with shouts to lead them against the enemy, he raised his hand and 'as Callisthenes says, called on all the gods, praying them, if he were

1 Plut. *Alex.* XXXIII.   2 *Ib.* XXXII, XXXIII.
3 ἐπέρρωσαν. 'Encouraging' Alexander is delightful.

really son of Zeus, Διόθεν γεγονώς,¹ to help and strengthen the Greeks'. If there is a worse farrago of nonsense in the Greek language than all this, I do not know where to find it. There follow Alexander's advance, Darius' flight, Parmenion's call for help (duplicated), and Callisthenes' accusation that Parmenion through jealousy of Alexander had not done his best in the battle, i.e. that he was a traitor. The setting of Alexander's supposed prayer is conclusive that it is pure invention.

Alexander then never, in the credible tradition, called himself son of Zeus; and I must now look at the peculiar passage in Arrian² which has often been taken to mean that he thought he was son of Ammon *before* he went to Siwah, and that he went thither in order to get his divine sonship confirmed. Wilcken has conclusively shown that he had no such intention, but I have never seen the actual passage explained. Arrian first quotes from Callisthenes (fr. 14) the statement, probably true, that one of Alexander's reasons for going to Siwah was because his ancestors Heracles and Perseus had done so before him, and then continues (same sentence) 'and also he was referring something (or some part) of his birth, τι τῆς γενέσεως τῆς ἑαυτοῦ, to Ammon, as the mythology refers the births of Heracles and Perseus to Zeus'. The mention of Heracles and Perseus, who were *sons* of Zeus, shows that γενέσεως here means 'birth' and not 'race, descent'. What then is the meaning of the amazing statement that Alexander, when he went to Siwah, was already referring part of his birth to Ammon? If it were simply 'his birth', as it usually gets translated,³ it would merely be a reference to the story of Olympias and the snake or something of the sort, whose falsity is patent; but that is not what the Greek says.

1 'Son of Zeus' is by no means a certain translation; it could also mean 'Zeus-descended', and be a mere reference to his lineage as an Argead.

2 Arr. III, 3, 1. Ἐπὶ τούτοις δὲ πόθος λαμβάνει αὐτὸν ἐλθεῖν παρ' Ἄμμωνα ἐς Λιβύην, τὸ μέν τι τῷ θεῷ χρησόμενον, ὅτι ἀτρεκὲς ἐλέγετο εἶναι τὸ μαντεῖον τοῦ Ἄμμωνος καὶ χρήσασθαι αὐτῷ Περσέα καὶ Ἡρακλέα.... Ἀλεξάνδρῳ δὲ φιλοτιμία ἦν πρὸς Περσέα καὶ Ἡρακλέα, ἀπὸ γένους τε ὄντι τοῦ ἀμφοῖν καί τι καὶ αὐτὸς τῆς γενέσεως τῆς ἑαυτοῦ ἐς Ἄμμωνα ἀνέφερε, καθάπερ οἱ μῦθοι τὴν Ἡρακλέους καὶ Περσέως ἐς Δία. Ehrenberg has shown that πόθος λαμβάνει does not indicate any particular source, *Alexander and the Greeks*, 1938, ch. 11; but Aristobulus often uses it. Perseus and Heracles (Perseus named first) come from Callisthenes fr. 14 (Perseus named first), but, as will appear, not at first hand.

3 Arrian made the same mistake, for in his summary, VII, 29, 3, he wrote ὅτι δὲ εἰς θεὸν τὴν γένεσιν αὐτοῦ ἀνέφερεν, which must refer to something he had previously written and there is nothing else but the τι τῆς γενέσεως passage. E. Kornemann, *Ptolemaios I*, p. 228 n. 64, called this 'wörtliche Uebereinstimmung'!

'Part of his birth' can only mean that he had, or thought he had, two fathers, which is impossible. But for very many years before Alexander there had always been *one* man in the world who had two fathers, the reigning Pharaoh; he was son of his human father and also son of the god Amon-Re, not mystically but through union of the god with his mother. And Alexander at the moment was the reigning Pharaoh and as such had two fathers in Egypt, the country from which he went to Siwah. Greeks seem to have been puzzled by this Egyptian doctrine; they were accustomed to their own gods having had children by human mothers, but a double paternity worried them; hence the stories of Olympias and the snake and so on.[1] Alexander must have been puzzled also; and if I had to make a guess at what the priest of Ammon told him in the inner shrine—the thing which pleased him and which he kept for his mother's ears alone—it would be that the priest explained to him the spiritual, or mystical, meaning which, one may suppose, must have been held to lie behind the Egyptian doctrine. This would explain why being called a son of Ammon always roused him to fury, so that none of his flatterers dared do it:[2] it was a profanation. And it would explain the extraordinary story of his birth in the Romance; it was told in order to get rid of the double paternity, while safeguarding his claim to be Pharaoh, by making him the son of the last native Pharaoh, Nectanebo, who by magic arts had made Olympias believe that what visited her was the god Ammon himself.[3]

What did Alexander himself think about his relations with Ammon? There are certain indications. He let it be known later that Ammon had advised him to what gods to sacrifice,[4] as Apollo of Delphi had

1 Plut. *Alex.* II, III.
2 It was, however, done by the scurrilous pasquinader Ephippus when Alexander was safely dead, Jacoby II, no. 126, fr. 5. Gorgos the ὁπλο-φύλαξ had once crowned Alexander (Ditt.³ 312, see Jacoby II, BD, p. 439); Ephippus turned this into a story that at Ecbatana Gorgos had ordered the herald to proclaim that he was crowning 'Alexander son of Ammon', which has about as much chance of being true as his statement (fr. 5) that Alexander sometimes dressed up as Ammon and sometimes as the goddess Artemis; for the rest of the story, that Gorgos promised to provide at his own expense 10,000 panoplies and 10,000 catapults and their ammunition for the siege of Athens, is ridiculous on the figures and untrue in fact, since (*pace* Justin XIII, 5, 1, and Curt. X, 2, 2) no attack on Athens was ever contemplated. Ephippus has nothing to do with history, as Schwartz said long ago, *Hermes*, XXXV, 1900, pp. 106 *sqq.*
3 In the version in B′ Nectanebo also dresses the part.
4 Arr. VI, 19, 4 (twice). They must be the θεοὶ μαντευτοί of Arr. *Ind.* 18, 11 (p. 351 n. 5). Cf. the story of his asking Ammon's advice, Arr. VII, 14, 7.

advised Xenophon;[1] that is, he had asked Ammon about the success of his advance into Persia,[2] and Ammon had counselled him. He is twice recorded, before his visit to Siwah, to have felt that he was under divine protection;[3] doubtless, after his visit, he believed that it was Ammon who had protected him.[4] But most important is his saying that God was the common father of all men, but that he made the best ones peculiarly his own.[5] I have examined this at length in App. 25, VI, pp. 435 *sq.*; and, while what called out this statement was a very different matter, the context shows that the second half must be a reference to Ammon; Alexander was 'peculiarly Ammon's own'. But he had to be *made* such by Ammon (ποιούμενον). Sonship therefore does not come into the matter; like Aristotle's 'god among men' (p. 366), his relations with Ammon were such as might be shared by others who were 'best', though meanwhile they were his alone. He thought then that he stood in some special relation to Ammon, the god being his guide, counsellor, protector; further we cannot safely go without knowing, as we shall never know, what the priest of Ammon said to him; but it is tolerably obvious that there was something deeper,[6] and that Alexander felt the relation to be something very serious, even perhaps sacred. He might perhaps have figured it as a spiritual adoption, but the mere fact that two ancient writers, one of slight authority and both in very unsatisfactory passages, do refer to adoption,[7] is not enough to support such a view; what is certain is that the saying of Alexander's which I have been considering negatives any idea that he ever claimed to be a god. Two things I omit here. His supposed wish to be buried at Siwah adds nothing, if true, but is probably only Ptolemy's propaganda to secure the body for himself;[8] and the

1 Xen. *Anab.* III, 1, 6.
2 He must naturally have put much the same question to Ammon as Xenophon did to Apollo (τίνι ἂν θεῶν θύων καὶ εὐχόμενος κάλλιστα καὶ ἄριστα ἔλθοι τὴν ὁδὸν ἣν ἐπινοεῖ καὶ καλῶς πράξας σωθείη), since he got a similar response.
3 The shifting of the wind at Mt Climax, Arr. 1, 26, 2 (see Note at end of this Appendix), and the rain on the way to Siwah, *id.* III, 3, 4.
4 Cf. his appeal to Ammon to protect Nearchus and the fleet (p. 351 n. 5), the only occasion on which he is recorded to have appealed to him (if he really did).
5 Plut. *Alex.* XXVII, ἰδίους δὲ ποιούμενον ἑαυτοῦ τοὺς ἀρίστους.
6 See the suggestion on p. 369 n. 1.
7 Justin XI, 11, 8, 'adoptione'; Plut. *Alex.* XXVIII, τεκνώσεως (a Hellenistic usage); *ib.* L, Cleitus taunts Alexander: 'You have become τηλικοῦτος ὥστε Ἄμμωνι σαυτὸν εἰσποιεῖν ἀπειπάμενος Φίλιππον.'
8 For the circumstances see *C.A.H.* VI, p. 467.

supposed embassy from Siwah to him at Babylon (App. 23, p. 377) is only a mistake, 'Αμμωνιεῦσι in Diodorus XVII, 113, 4 having taken the place of 'Αργείοις in what was obviously a list of the four Pan-Hellenic festivals.[1]

The source of the τι τῆς γενέσεως passage is unknown. The earlier part of Arrian's statement, that about Heracles and Perseus, is from Callisthenes; but this passage is not from Callisthenes, as it speaks of Ammon, not Zeus. The sentence which follows it is from Cleitarchus, as Wilcken for other reasons supposed, for it accuses Alexander of an intention to cheat (ἢ φήσων γε ἐγνωκέναι) and there is a very high degree of probability that all the cases in our tradition which accuse Alexander of cheating—there are several—come from or through Cleitarchus (see § E, p. 54). Wilcken attributed the τι τῆς γενέσεως passage to Cleitarchus also, but I cannot imagine Arrian inserting a bit of Cleitarchus into a sentence from someone else. Arrian must have taken the whole statement, from ἐπὶ τούτοις to ἐς Δία, from one source, and the only possible source seems to be Aristobulus, using Callisthenes for the first part and his own knowledge of Alexander (see § D, pp. 40 *sq.*) for the τι τῆς γενέσεως passage.

So far we have only been dealing with the Egyptian side of things; and the man who was responsible for bringing the matter into the Greek religious sphere was Callisthenes. It is impossible to make out who was with Alexander at Siwah. Ptolemy may or may not have been there; Aristobulus certainly was not; it has sometimes been supposed that Callisthenes must have been, but there is no evidence. Callisthenes did not complete his book earlier than 330–329, i.e. several years later, since he mentions the death of Darius; it cannot be said if he heard the greeting of the priest of Ammon, or was told of it by someone who did;[2] anyhow, he deliberately altered it, and made the priest greet Alexander not as son of Ammon, but as son of Zeus (fr. 14). When he first thought of this, or how much he may have talked before he wrote, is not known, but by the time he completed his book he was

1 Other similar substitutions in our MSS. of an unconnected name, certain but inexplicable, are known; for instances see App. 21, p. 341 n. 5. This is a different matter from naming a wrong general or satrap, which is not uncommon.

2 All with Alexander must have heard the *greeting*; but I have little doubt that τοὺς ἄλλους who, in Callisthenes, fr. 14, heard the *oracles* outside of the inner shrine were not Alexander's party, as Wilcken thought, but those who had consulted the oracle aforetime; R. Vallois, *R.E. Gr.* XLV, 1931, p. 135; E. Mederer, *Die Alexanderlegenden bei den ältesten Alexanderhistorikern*, 1936, p. 55.

deeply committed to Zeus; he had made the Milesians (fr. 14) bring to Alexander at Memphis[1] many oracles from the ruined shrine at Branchidae attributing Alexander's birth to Zeus and foretelling the coming battle at 'Arbela', Darius' death, and the defeat of Agis of Sparta at Megalopolis, and had said that one Athenaïs at Erythrae had also testified to Alexander's high descent (εὐγένειαν), which in the context seems to mean 'divine birth'.[2] Wilcken (1938, p. 299 [4]) called Callisthenes our 'earliest and best source' for what happened at Siwah; and we can believe that he told the truth over two matters: that the priest of Ammon greeted Alexander publicly as son of a god (for he could not have avoided so addressing the new Pharaoh), though he (Callisthenes) altered the god's name; and that Alexander went alone into the inner shrine, for that is confirmed by what Arrian says and by Alexander's letter to his mother. But further than that we need not seek the truth in Callisthenes. He altered the greeting of the priest of Ammon, invented all the Milesian oracles (of course after Darius' death), invented Alexander's prayer at Gaugamela (p. 353 *ante*), made Parmenion a traitor, and falsified the history of the destruction of the Branchidae temple and invented the story of Alexander's massacre of the Branchidae (App. 13). One can check his method over the story of Mt Climax.[3] Alexander had regarded the shifting of the wind which enabled him to go safely along the beach as a divine intervention on his behalf,[4] which was understandable enough; but Callisthenes (fr. 31) altered this to a statement that the sea recognised its lord and went back as though making a *proskynesis* (i.e. to a god). Possibly he had in mind Xenophon's statement[5] that, when Cyrus and his army waded across the Euphrates which had never been forded before, the river obviously (σαφῶς) yielded him passage because he was going to be its

1 The discussion whether the Milesian oracles making Alexander son of Zeus could have reached Memphis before Alexander quitted Egypt is meaningless, for the Milesian envoys are said to have also brought to Memphis the prophecies of Arbela, Darius' death, etc.; no distinction is made, and the words εἰς Μέμφιν are therefore as fictitious as the rest of the story.
2 Athenaïs is said to be 'like the ancient Sibyl of Erythrae', which Strabo elsewhere (XIV, 645) more or less explains by saying that, like the ancient Sibyl, she was a prophetess, μαντική, 'in the same manner'. But he also calls her 'another Sibyl'; was she supposed to be a reincarnation of the first one, and like her to prophesy in some peculiar fashion? In any case she is the κορυβαντιώσαις γυναιξί of Timaeus *ap*. Polyb. XII, 12b.
3 See Note at end of this Appendix.
4 Arr. I, 26, 2, οὐκ ἄνευ τοῦ θείου, ὡς αὐτός τε καὶ οἱ ἀμφ' αὐτὸν ἐξηγοῦντο.
5 Xen. *Anab*. I, 4, 17 *sq*.

king (i.e. Great King), and this was taken as a sign from heaven (though unfortunately the river guessed wrong).

Callisthenes' reasons for changing Ammon to Zeus—or, if one pleases, treating Ammon as a form of Zeus—are hardly obscure. The so common statement that he was Court historian and wrote under Alexander's eye, and could only therefore write what Alexander wished, is entirely devoid of any serious foundation; he wrote what he himself wanted to write, but he wanted to write what *he* thought Alexander would like, a very different matter. He is reported to have said that Alexander's fame would depend, not on what Alexander did, but on what he (Callisthenes) wrote;[1] he is also reported to have said that Alexander's divinity would depend, not on Olympias' lies, but on what he (Callisthenes) might choose to write and publish;[2] but this latter statement has been doubted—a doubt I share—and I am not using it. But Strabo, who had some critical faculty, said of Callisthenes' account of what happened at Siwah that, while some of it was worthy of belief, some was mere flattery;[3] and that is true. For Callisthenes had an axe to grind; he wanted to persuade Alexander to rebuild his native city, Olynthus. He therefore set to work to flatter him by making him a son of Zeus, as his ancestor Heracles had been, and was followed by the 'philosopher' Anaxarchus[4] and a number of poets (see § E') and others, who all treated him as a son of Zeus; how soon this began cannot be said, but it was in full swing at Bactra. Probably, as Aristotle's pupil, Callisthenes despised barbarians and their gods; his long speech in Arrian IV, 11, 2 *sqq.*, though not genuine, may correctly represent his ideas about Asiatics. It was more respectable to turn Ammon into a Greek god, as well as being more plausible, for the pedigree of the Argead kings went up to Zeus through Heracles and Dionysus; and though Alexander honoured Heracles as his ancestor and never mentioned Zeus, still Zeus might be expected to interest himself in the Argead line, and, in vulgar parlance, give them a leg up. What Alexander thought about it all we do not know; the one decently attested story remaining shows him being sarcastic to one of his flatterers,[5] like Antigonus Gonatas later. But so long as talk con-

---

1 Arr. IV, 10, 1, ὅτι ὑφ' αὐτῷ εἶναι ἀπέφαινε καὶ τῇ αὐτοῦ ξυγγραφῇ ᾿Αλέξανδρόν τε καὶ τὰ ᾿Αλεξάνδρου ἔργα.

2 *Id.* IV, 10, 2.   3 Strabo XVII, 1, 43 (813).

4 Arr. IV, 9, 7–9; 10, 6 *sq.*; Plut. *Alex.* XXVIII, LII.

5 The ichor story. Aristobulus (fr. 47 = Athen. VI, 251 A) represented Dioxippus as saying to Alexander, when bleeding from a wound, 'That is "ichor, such as flows in the veins of the blessed gods"' (*Iliad* E, 340). Plutarch (*Alex.* XXVIII; also *de Alex. Fortuna* II, 341 B, but the latter is

fined itself to Zeus and left out Ammon (who to him was a serious matter), he let it go on. Whether he *could* have stopped it, even by wholesale banishment of the 'flatterers', may be doubted; but as he did not attempt to, he possibly thought that some day it might have its uses. The idea that he himself took steps to spread the knowledge of his divine sonship is again entirely unsupported by any serious evidence.

II. BACTRA

So far, then, what we have got is that Alexander never called himself either son of Ammon or son of Zeus, and refused to allow others to call him son of Ammon but tolerated them calling him son of Zeus, the ancestor of his line, though he might be ironical on the subject; of any question of actual divinity there is, so far, no trace. We come now to the second 'moment' of the enquiry, the scene at Bactra when he attempted to introduce *proskynesis* (prostration), the usual Persian ceremony for those approaching the Great King, as Alexander now was. The Achaemenid kings had not been gods,[1] and when a Persian made *proskynesis* to his king he was not worshipping him; it was a ceremony and no more. But to Greeks, and presumably to Macedonians, prostration did import worship; man did not prostrate himself except to the gods,[2] and one tradition even said that a Greek had once

probably not Plutarch) makes Alexander say to some flatterer: 'This, you see, is blood, and not "ichor, etc."' (quoting Homer's line). Evidently we have here two halves of the same story, Athenaeus only giving part of what Aristobulus said; in the full story, it was obviously Dioxippus, not Alexander, who quoted Homer's line, and Alexander snubbed him by saying: 'It's not ichor, it's blood.' The story then is from a good source (Aristobulus). The very different version in Diogenes Laertius IX, 60 may be neglected, as it makes Anaxarchus exactly the reverse of what he is known to have been from Arrian and Plutarch (see last note). There is a variant of the ichor story, for what it may be worth, in Curtius VIII, 10, 29 and Seneca, *Ep.* 59, 12, 'the pain of my wound shows I am mortal'.

1 For the contrary view see L. R. Taylor, *The Divinity of the Roman Emperor*, 1931, chap. 1 and App. 1; Calvin W. McEwan, *The Oriental Origin of Hellenistic Kingship*, 1934, pp. 17 *sqq.* There is no relevant Persian evidence, and the examination of Aeschylus' much discussed use of θεός in the *Persae*, as applied to the Persian king, by A. S. F. Gow, *J.H.S.* XLVIII, 1928, pp. 134 *sqq.*, is valid; briefly, θεός is merely metaphorical. See further, M. P. Charlesworth, *Harvard Theol. Rev.* XXVIII, 1935, pp. 8–16. There is the same use in English; if we say of a man 'money is his god', it does not mean that he performs cult acts before a bundle of Treasury notes.

2 Aesch. *Agam.* 925 combined with 919–20; Xen. *Anab.* III, 2, 13; Arr. IV, 11, 3. Aeschylus and Xenophon are explicit enough. Curtius VIII, 5, 9 *sqq.*

been put to death for making *proskynesis* to the Persian king.¹ I need not describe the scene at Bactra. When the attempt to introduce prostration for Greeks and Macedonians as well as Persians was made, the Macedonians showed anger, and worse: one general burst out laughing. The first Greek called upon was Callisthenes; he refused, and told Alexander that he must confine Asiatic customs to Asiatics. Alexander dropped the idea, and no more was ever heard of it.²

What did it all mean? There have been various theories. The commonest, I suppose, has been that it was a continuation of what happened at Siwah and meant that Alexander now desired to be recognised publicly as the god he already was; and it has been customary to point out that Lysander and Clearchus had already received divine honours from Greeks. But it is certain enough that the honours said to have been paid to Lysander by some Ionian cities—sacrifices, altars, paeans— even if true, did not amount to deification, and Clearchus, the cruel tyrant of Heracleia, never was in point.³ Two other theories may be

takes it for granted that *proskynesis* would mean that Alexander was a god; he may have been reproducing the tone of the poetasters examined in § E′, whom he had probably read; and though Callisthenes' speech in Arrian is not genuine, it may very well represent Callisthenes' state of mind. Of course, προσκυνεῖν, both before and after Alexander, is used of many forms of humbling oneself before a superior (see Gow, *op. cit.*, Charlesworth, *op. cit.*), but that does not negative the meaning of 'worship'; the fact that many Englishmen have told some girl that they worshipped her does not prevent the word properly meaning the worship of God.

1 Timagoras: Hegesander in Athen. VI, 251 B, cf. 253 F. But Plut. *Artax.* XXII gives a different reason; both, however, could be true.
2 Miss Taylor, *op. cit.* took our two accounts of the attempt to introduce *proskynesis* to be two separate attempts made in two different ways at two different banquets; we are only told, she says, that *one* method failed and was abandoned, and she contends, without any evidence, that therefore the other one continued indefinitely. But our accounts are only different versions of the same thing, like our different versions of the conversation which led up to the murder of Cleitus, who was only murdered once.
3 The story about Lysander (Plut. *Lys.* XVIII) is explicitly taken from Duris, a most untrustworthy author who wrote a century and a half after the event; and the whole story has been doubted on other grounds (Fr. Taeger, *Hermes* LXXII, 1937, p. 358 n. 4). No cult of Lysander is known, and the honours said to have been paid to him, even if true, are expressly classed by Aristotle (*Rhet.* I, 5, 1361a, 27) as (human) τιμαί proper to be paid to benefactors; on this and the cult of benefactors, see Charlesworth, *op. cit.* pp. 8 *sqq.* As to Clearchus, who called himself son of Zeus (not the same thing as a god), his townspeople humoured him because it was not safe to do otherwise; one might as well cite people who just called themselves gods, like Empedocles, or the crazy Sicilian doctor Menecrates (App. 25,

set aside. One is that of P. Schnabel, that *proskynesis* was made, not to Alexander, but to a statue of him standing on an altar among the hearth-gods; it never secured acceptance, and was killed years ago.[1] The other, that of Professor L. R. Taylor,[2] sprang originally from Schnabel's theory, and was that, though Persians did not actually worship the Achaemenid king, they did worship his *daimon* (i.e. his *fravashi*), and that what was worshipped at Bactra was Alexander's *daimon*. It has always seemed to me an impossible theory, and though Miss Taylor subsequently restated it with some modifications,[3] I remain content with my original examination of it[4] and with Professor A. D. Nock's review of her book in the same sense.[5] Certainly a *Parthian* king, early in the second century B.C., possibly Phriapitius, called himself a god, θεός, on one of the 'beardless' coins,[6] and, since Miss Taylor wrote, Greek inscriptions from Susa[7] have shown that, towards the end of the first century B.C., the Parthian king Phraates IV was called a god by Greeks and had a *daimon* (*fravashi*) whom Greeks spoke of with respect; but all this is merely one of the numerous Parthian borrowings from the Seleucids,[8] and has no conceivable bearing on the Achaemenid kings or on Alexander.

There is, however, a view which stands on a different footing. Wilcken in his history of Alexander said that the idea that Alexander was using *proskynesis* as a roundabout method of getting himself recognised as a god must be rejected altogether; what he was doing was trying to get Greeks, Macedonians, and Persians all on the same level in the interest of his policy of fusion[9] (which indeed he had already begun when he made Mazaeus satrap of Babylonia). I wish very much that I could believe this; it would simplify matters greatly. But

v, p. 433). Doubtless Alexander knew that Philip's statue had been carried in a procession after those of the twelve Olympians (Diod. XVI, 92, 5); but no one knows what that really meant, and nothing came of it.

1 All necessary references in Tarn, *J.H.S.* XLVIII, 1928, p. 206.
2 *J.H.S.* XLVII, 1927, p. 53, and *Class. Phil.* XXII, 1927, p. 162.
3 In *The Divinity of the Roman Emperor*, chap. I and App. II.
4 Tarn, *J.H.S.* XLVIII, p. 206.
5 *Gnomon* VIII, 1932, p. 513.
6 Wroth, *Brit. Mus. Coins: Parthia*, pp. xxix, 5.
7 *S.E.G.* VII, 12, 13.
8 So Cumont, *C.R. Ac. Inscr.* 1930, p. 216 [11]. It seems very obvious; see, however, McEwan, *op. cit.* p. 20 n. 134. The title on the θεός coin must have been taken from the neighbouring Antimachus the Euthydemid, Tarn, *Bactria and India*, p. 92; but the Euthydemids were a Seleucid offshoot.
9 *Alexander der Grosse*, 1931, p. 158.

Alexander *must* have known how Greeks and Macedonians regarded *proskynesis*, as indeed the careful staging of the attempt to introduce it shows; and if he knew this, I do not see how the scene could mean anything but a preparation for his recognition as a god, which, since Greeks, Macedonians, and Persians were all involved, would mean the god of his Empire. It was certainly a political matter, as Wilcken says, primarily in the interest of his fusion policy, but perhaps already with some dim idea of what was to take place later at Opis; but deification it must have meant, and we have to try to see what was in his mind, for certainly he never thought that he was either a god or the son of one. What made him contemplate being the god of his Empire? Certainly not Ammon; that was his own private matter, too serious, perhaps too sacred, for the public gaze, as his fury with the mutineers at Opis showed; besides, his relations with Ammon had nothing to do with divinity. Was it the fact that in Egypt he was not only king but god? The general opinion, with which I agree, has been that Egypt did not influence him at all; there is no sign of it in the tradition. Was it because Callisthenes, and a number of flatterers, had made him a son, and not merely a descendant, of Zeus? It has sometimes been thought that Callisthenes was responsible, as Timaeus said;[1] and as Alexander tolerated the flattery, might this not have been to accustom people beforehand to the idea of divinity? There are two reasons against this: one is that all the talk was directed to vanity and ostentation, so to speak, and could have nothing to do with any policy; the other, which seems conclusive, is that being a son of Zeus, which was all that Callisthenes had asserted, did not make anybody a god. We have to distinguish carefully here between what came before and what came after Alexander, precisely as had to be done in the matter of the identification of Ammon and Zeus; and, prior to Alexander, a son of Zeus and a god were very different things. Certainly *some* sons of Zeus by human mothers—Heracles, Dionysus, the Dioscuri—had become gods; but they had had to be *made* gods, to be raised to heaven; there were sons of Zeus, like Perseus, who never became gods at all. *After* Alexander, in the third century B.C. and later, there are plenty of cases where no distinction is drawn between being the son of a god and a god;[2]

---

1 Timaeus in Polyb. XII, 12b: αἰγίδα καὶ κεραυνὸν περιθέντα θνητῇ φύσει δικαίως... τετευχέναι τούτων ὧν ἔτυχεν.

2 E.g. Timaeus, *loc. cit.*, and the stories, true or false, from Satyrus, Hegesander, and Phylarchus collected in Athenaeus VI, 250 F to 251 C; also Philodemus περὶ κολακ. in Jacoby II, 124, T. 21, Callisthenes ἀπεθέου τὸν Ἀλέξανδρον.

but that is another matter. There is possibly one such case in Alexander's lifetime, though much later than Bactra. When, at Athens in 324, Demades proposed that Alexander should be made a god, θεός,[1] Demosthenes is said to have given a contemptuous assent: 'Let him be the son of Zeus and of Poseidon too if he likes'; but the evidence for this saying is not good,[2] and it is clear that Demosthenes fought hard against the proposal;[3] he may have assented at the end, as being the lesser of two evils, but the form of words he is said to have used is too uncertain for deductions to be drawn from it. Naturally all the talk by others about his being son of Zeus has no bearing on Alexander's own character, nor is there any reason to suppose it affected him any more than it affected the character or actions of Antigonus Gonatas that some poet once addressed him as, 'Son of the Sun and god'[4] and got well snubbed; and it seems an entirely insufficient reason for a desire to be, or a feeling that he ought to be, the god of his Empire.

I attach some importance to the Romance here, i.e. Pseudo-Callisthenes A', which was the origin and basis of all the versions, however extravagant they might grow later. It is a document put together from many components, of different dates and origins and not by any means always consistent with one another. It has been called the last debased version of the Cleitarchean tradition, but, as has been seen (Part I), there was no such tradition, and there seem to be only two traces of Cleitarchus in the work: Ptolemy shielding Alexander in the (Malli) town (III, 4, 14) and the abominable quibble with which Alexander broke his word in order to secure the murderers of Darius (II, 21, 22–6); this is the same quibble and breach of faith which Cleitarchus ascribed to him over the Massaga massacre (see § E, p. 54). The Romance, A', has to be taken on its merits. Parts are Hellenistic: Alexander's Testament and the Letter to the Rhodians were known to Diodorus (XX, 81, 3), and the list of the Alexandrias can be dated to the first century B.C. (App. 8, 1, p. 245); the version of Alexander's questions to the Gymnosophists cannot be later, and might be earlier, than the second century B.C.;[5] it has long been agreed that the description of Alexandria contains much that is valuable; and the most famous of all the Romance stories,

---

1 Athen. VI, 251 B; Ael. *V.H.* v, 12.
2 Hypereides *in Demosth.* col. XXXI. Hypereides was concerned in this speech to put everything Demosthenes said or did in the worst light, and I have not much confidence in the form of words he gives.
3 Timaeus, *loc. cit.*   4 Plut. *Mor.* 360 C.
5 Tarn, *Bactria and India*, pp. 429 *sq.*

though it does not occur in A′, was evidently known in the middle of the third century B.C.[1]

To get at the kernel of A′ one must strip off many detachable components—the metrical prophecies, the pointless stories of Alexander's visits in disguise to the camp of Darius and to Candace, the marvels which fill the long letter to Aristotle (the only marvels in the work), the Testament, and those letters which exhibit a scheme, making Alexander call himself son of Philip and Olympias up to Darius' death and son of Ammon and Olympias after it. This leaves a kernel which, setting aside the fanciful itinerary and battles, contains a good deal that is of interest—items that may be old and good, and occasionally even serious history; for example, it gives very clearly the fact that Craterus was sent to take Antipater's place (III, 31, 1). But what concerns me here is the matter of deification. As Alexander really became a god for certain people in 324 B.C., one would expect the Romance, of all works, to treat him as divine; but the main thread of the narrative does exactly the opposite.[2] It has already been seen how the narrative got over the Egyptian double paternity by making Alexander a son of Nectanebo masquerading as Ammon (though the double paternity does crop up in a letter);[3] and thenceforth Alexander lays stress throughout on the fact that he is only a mortal man (usually θνητός, once φθαρτός), a fact of which Delphi also reminds him;[4] and near the end he prays to Zeus that he may live to finish his work, 'but if thou hast decreed that I shall die, then receive me too, a mortal, as a third (mortal)',[5] which the text explains to mean that, as Dionysus and Heracles were among the gods for their works, so he too thought himself worthy, for his works, to share the home of the gods after death.[6] But there is more than this:

[1] In Teles περὶ πενίας (O. Hense, *Teletis reliquiae*[2], p. 33 = Stobaeus, ed. Hense, V, 33, 31, p. 816) occurs the phrase (p. 43), εἶτα, ὡς ᾿Αλέξανδρος, ἀθάνατος γενέσθαι. This has nothing to do with deification, as is shown by the words following, εἰ δὲ καὶ τούτου τύχοι, οἶμαι, ἵνα Ζεὺς γένηται ἐπιθυμήσει; it can only mean therefore that Alexander's journey to the Well of Life at the world's end in search of immortality was known *c.* 240 B.C., and if, as is probable, Teles here be Bion, the story was known as early as the second quarter of the third century.

[2] He is never a god, but occasionally calls himself son of Ammon: i.e. in two letters in the Testament, and once in the narrative, I, 30, 4. I have remarked that the work is not consistent; alongside the terrible story of Darius' murderers (above), we get cases of almost quixotic chivalry.

[3] In a letter to the Tyrians, I, 35, 5, he calls himself son of Ammon and of Philip.   4 I, 45, 3. That it is Delphi, see App. 21, p. 341 n. 5.

[5] III, 30, 15, δέχου κἀμὲ τρίτον ὄντα θνητόν.

[6] *Ib.* 16, ἄξιον τοῖς θεοῖς συνέστιον γενέσθαι.

in a perfectly serious passage—would that we knew whence it came—
the writer makes Alexander refuse an offer of deification, and on very
peculiar grounds. Rhodogune and Stateira in a letter address him as
ἰσόθεος, and offer to get the gods of Persia to make him a σύνθρονος
of Zeus;[1] Alexander refuses their offer of deification, saying: 'I decline
these divine honours; for I was born a mortal subject to death and
I must beware of such things, since they endanger the soul.'[2] Now the
historian Timaeus, in the third century, had written of Callisthenes
that he deserved what he got, for he had made of a man a god and had
done all in his power to destroy Alexander's soul;[3] and here the
Romance writer makes Alexander refuse deification on the ground that
it would endanger his soul. The reference to Timaeus is plain enough,
and the other parallels in language between the two passages are so
close[4] as to leave no doubt that the Romance writer wrote with
Timaeus' book unrolled before him; and what he is really doing is
commenting on Timaeus and saying: 'Callisthenes did not succeed in
doing anything of the sort.' I do not want to press this further than
I ought; but it shows, at the very least, that one man in antiquity, with
a good knowledge of Timaeus and presumably therefore of other
historians also, did not believe that Callisthenes' attempt to make
Alexander son of Zeus had anything to do with the historical fact of
Alexander's deification.

It seems then that anything we have met with so far—Ammon,
Callisthenes, Alexander's entourage—is quite insufficient to account
for the fact that at Bactra he thought of becoming the god of his Empire
as a help to carrying out his policy of fusion, not to mention the fact
that in 324 he was deified by and for certain people at his own request.
Something else then has to be sought which put the idea of deification
firmly into his head; and there can be little doubt what it was. Isocrates
had written to Philip that if he conquered the king of Persia nothing
would be left for him but to become a god;[5] and Alexander, who had
not only read Isocrates' *Philippus*[6] but was following his advice in

---

1 II, 22, 9 *sq.*
2 II, 22, 12. Παραιτοῦμαι τὰς ἰσοθέους τιμάς· ἐγὼ γὰρ ἄνθρωπος φθαρτὸς
  γεγένημαι καὶ εὐλαβοῦμαι τὸ τοιοῦτον· κίνδυνον γὰρ φέρει τὸν περὶ ψυχῆς.
3 *Ap.* Polyb. XII, 12b: διεφθαρκότα τὴν ἐκείνου ψυχὴν καθ' ὅσον οἷός τ' ἦν.
4 See my comparison of the two passages on p. 7 of Mr M. P. Charlesworth's
  article 'The Refusal of Divine Honours', *Papers of the Brit. School at
  Rome*, XV, 1939, p. 1, with his remarks.
5 Isoc. *Ep.* 3.
6 Benno von Hagen, *Philol.* LXVII, 113; Wilcken, 1928, p. 578 [5] n. 3,
  'gründlich gekannt'.

another matter,[1] could not fail to have known of this. That is one thing; the other is Aristotle's famous remark about the θεὸς ἐν ἀνθρώποις, the 'god among men'. This will have to be considered; but first I want to emphasise that both Isocrates and Aristotle were referring to *politics*, and nothing but politics; in each case godship is only the end of a chain of *political* events or ideas. And the scene at Bactra had a political purpose: indeed one might even say that all the innumerable deifications of Hellenistic kings later had a political purpose too.

I turn to Aristotle. It has long been supposed that when he spoke of 'a god among men' he had Alexander in mind; but this has been denied by Dr Ehrenberg in a long and interesting study,[2] and I must give my reasons for not accepting his view. Aristotle, in the passage in question in the *Politics*, has been speaking of that form of State in which the 'best' men bear rule. Is then, he asks,[3] the lawgiver to make laws to suit the best men or the majority? Perhaps, he says, he should consider the interests of all the citizens; for rulers and ruled are all alike citizens. But if (he continues, 1284a 3) there be a single man, or more than one man, who shall so surpass the rest of the citizens in excellence and political capacity that no comparison would be possible, such cannot merely be a part of the State, for it would be unjust to them to put them on an equality with those they so surpass, 'for such a man would truly be as a god among men' (note the change from plural to singular). 'Whence it follows that concerning them there is no law; for they themselves are law.'[4] Ehrenberg's argument, p. 74, is that the phrase 'god among men' is applied to the qualified Few no less than to the qualified One; the passage deals with two forms of constitution, not only monarchy but aristocracy as well. This is true of the passage generally; but actually, for the phrase 'god among men', Aristotle makes a sudden change from the plural to the singular, as though he were not calling the Few 'gods among men', and then returns to the plural again; this must mean *something*, and as Aristotle

1 *Phil.* 106, Isocrates advised Philip to build cities in Asia and settle in them the homeless mercenary population. Alexander did.
2 V. Ehrenberg, *Alexander and the Greeks*, ch. III.
3 *Politics*, III, 13, 1283b 37.
4 ἀδικήσονται γὰρ ἀξιούμενοι τῶν ἴσων, ἄνισοι τοσοῦτον κατ' ἀρετὴν ὄντες καὶ τὴν πολιτικὴν δύναμιν· ὥσπερ γὰρ θεὸς ἐν ἀνθρώποις εἰκὸς εἶναι τὸν τοιοῦτον. ὅθεν δῆλον…κατὰ δὲ τῶν τοιούτων οὐκ ἔστι νόμος. αὐτοὶ γάρ εἰσι νόμος. The phrase 'a god among men', or something equivalent, is older than Aristotle (Ehrenberg, p. 73 n. 1), but this seems to me immaterial; you can apply a known phrase to a particular individual.

could so easily have written τοὺς τοιούτους for τὸν τοιοῦτον had he wished, it is fair to suppose that he did not wish, i.e. that he had some individual man in mind.[1] To continue with his text. Aristocracy is dropped almost at once, and with 1284b35 there begins the discussion of monarchy alone, which is introduced (1284b 30) by a repetition of the 'god among men' idea; Aristotle starts afresh by asking what is to be done with the man of surpassing excellence, and answers his question by saying: 'One cannot rule over such a one, for that would resemble a claim to rule over Zeus'; the only way is for every one to obey him gladly as king. In one place, then, the man of surpassing excellence is spoken of as being 'as a god' and in the other is compared to Zeus; it comes to the same thing, and in the second passage aristocracy (the Few) has been left behind and is not mentioned. It seems to me impossible therefore to accept Ehrenberg's conclusion, which is (pp. 74, 81 *sqq*.), not merely that we are under no necessity to connect Aristotle's idea of kingship with Alexander, but that it is not permissible to do so; it is certainly permissible enough, but the necessity I leave for the moment. Indeed I am not sure that there is not a very different reason which would invalidate Ehrenberg's argument from aristocracy. We have seen that Alexander contemplated that Ammon's favours might be extended to any of 'the best' (i.e., other men), though the man he had in mind was, of course, himself; even so Aristotle speaks of 'the best' in the plural, but makes the actual statement about being as a god in the singular, τὸν τοιοῦτον; he therefore, like Alexander, may be supposed to have had a certain individual in mind, and if so there can be no doubt who that individual was.

Before I go on I may draw attention to a very strange passage a little further on in Aristotle. In 1286a 30 *sqq*. he says that the populace (ὄχλος) is apt to judge more rightly than a single man; for the single man may be mastered by anger (i.e. lose control of himself) and so go wrong, but all the populace will not be mastered by anger at the same time. As the falsehood of this last statement is palpable—he had only to recollect the temper of the Athenian populace over the mutilation of the Hermae and in the matter of the generals after Arginusae, to go no further into crowd psychology—he must have had in mind some overmastering example of a single ruler (i.e. a king) losing his self-control; and I suggest that it is an obvious reference to the supreme instance of loss of self-control in the world he knew, Alexander's

---

1 It could, of course, be said that it is only a generic singular; but my feeling is that such a use would be strange in a passage where everything else both before and after it is in the plural.

murder of Cleitus. That would mean that when writing this part of the *Politics* he had Alexander in his mind.

Now there happens to be external evidence as to what Aristotle meant by the 'god among men', which Ehrenberg did not consider; I do not know if any one else has, but I have not met it. It occurs in the περὶ .βασιλείας of Diotogenes the 'Pythagorean'.[1] I have considered the date of Diotogenes elsewhere;[2] it cannot be *later* than shortly after the death of Demetrius the Besieger, and the language shows that it is almost bound to be earlier, during Demetrius' hey-day; that is, it belongs to the generation after Aristotle. In the passage in question, Diotogenes is arguing that as God is to the universe, so is the king to the State; the king (like God) need render no account to anybody, 'and since he himself is animate law, he has been figured as a god among men'.[3] This is an unmistakable reference to the θεὸς ἐν ἀνθρώποις passage in Aristotle which I have been considering,[4] and shows that Diotogenes interpreted the 'god among men' as a reference to a king; and in Aristotle's lifetime there was only one king possible, Alexander. I do not say that Diotogenes' interpretation is absolutely conclusive; but it is so early that it must carry great weight, and I see no reason to doubt it. I cannot therefore accept Ehrenberg's contention that it is not necessary to suppose that Aristotle had Alexander in mind; the several reasons I have given seem to show clearly enough that he had.

Alexander then could have got from Aristotle the idea that the one man of surpassing excellence, when he arrived, would necessarily be as a god among men; and as he certainly had no doubt of the identity of that man, the only question would be if he knew Aristotle's idea. I do not see much room for doubt. I am not considering the question of the date of the *Politics*, because it seems to me obvious that whatever ideas Alexander got from his tutor Aristotle were got, not from Aristotle's books, but from Aristotle himself during the three years of their association at Mieza. It is, for example, simple fact (see § B) that

1 Stobaeus IV, 7, 61 (p. 263 Hense).
2 Tarn, 'Alexander the Great and the Unity of Mankind', *Proc. Brit. Acad.* 1933, p. 152 [32] n. 33; see *post*, App. 25, III, p. 410 n. 1.
3 Stobaeus *ib.* p. 265, ὁ δὲ βασιλεὺς ἀρχὰν ἔχων ἀνυπεύθυνον, καὶ αὐτὸς ὢν νόμος ἔμψυχος, θεὸς ἐν ἀνθρώποις παρεσχαμάτισται. This last word seems to be a ἅπαξ λεγόμενον.
4 Because in Diotogenes, as in Aristotle, the person to whom the phrase is applied is himself 'law', which precludes the idea that Diotogenes is referring to some earlier case of the use of the phrase θεὸς ἐν ἀνθρώποις; indeed one has only to look up Ehrenberg's instances (p. 73 n. 1) to see the impossibility.

when Alexander reached the Caspian, and when later he reached India, he had Aristotle's geography in his head; but, with his known interest in Asia from boyhood (Plut. *Alex.* v), he did not get that geography, as we have to do, from reading the *Meteorologica* and the (original of the) *Liber de inundacione Nili.* It is in fact recorded that at Mieza he did learn Aristotle's views on politics and ethics,[1] and if Aristotle talked to him about politics at all, kingship was not a thing that he could possibly have omitted;[2] it was the most obvious of all subjects in which to instruct Philip's heir. Alexander was 16 before he left Mieza; and, apart from his unusual ability, the training of a prince has to begin earlier than that.

Alexander then, long before his visit to Siwah, long before the activities of Callisthenes, had learnt from the two chief political thinkers of his youth, Isocrates and Aristotle, something which looked like the necessary deification of the man who stood out above all others (Aristotle) or was conqueror and ruler of Asia (Isocrates); the latter he in fact was when at Bactra, and pretty obviously the former also. But the point is that he got this solely as a *political* idea from political thinkers; it had nothing in any way to do with religion. Just as, probably, he never thought of *not* invading Persia, that being his inescapable heritage from Philip, so perhaps he never thought of *not* becoming a god when the conquest was completed; Isocrates and Aristotle had appeared to him to treat it as the natural and inevitable thing. At Bactra, in the interests of his own policy of fusion, he made a preliminary attempt at becoming the god of his Empire; it failed completely. He had, as he was to show at the Beas, a strong sense of what was possible and what was not, and he at once dropped the idea of becoming the god of his Empire for good and all and ever; nothing more is ever heard of it. The policy of fusion had to get along without it.

---

1 Plut. *Alex.* VII, "Ἔοικε δὲ 'Αλέξανδρος (at Mieza) οὐ μόνον τὸν ἠθικὸν καὶ πολιτικὸν παραλαβεῖν λόγον. It was inevitable even without express testimony. It does not of course mean the *books* known as the *Ethics* and the *Politics.* The further reference to Alexander learning 'esoteric doctrines' which Aristotle published later is on a different footing and need not be discussed here. If modern views of Aristotle's development be correct, it could hardly (if true) refer to the *Metaphysics*; but it may be permissible to wonder if the kind of religious mysticism which has been deduced concerning the lost περὶ φιλοσοφίας (J. Bidez, *Un singulier naufrage littéraire dans l'antiquité*, 1943, pp. 32–54) may have influenced Alexander's ideas of his relationship with Ammon.

2 So W. S. Ferguson, *Greek Imperialism*, p. 122: Aristotle must have talked to Alexander about his political theories and the 'god among men'.

III. 324 B.C.

In 324, at Susa, Alexander was faced by a new problem. In old Greece there was a mass of exiles from every city, many of them democrats exiled by Antipater or his governments. Some had taken service as mercenaries with Alexander's satraps while he was in India; when he made the satraps disband their private armies, they had returned to Greece with their arms and without occupation. The position in that overcrowded country had become difficult; at best the exiles were a focus for every kind of discontent, at worst a possible menace. Alexander saw that, if he were to have the peace in his world (not merely in his Empire, for Greece was not in his Empire) which soon after he was to pray for at Opis, the exiles must be restored to their cities and their cities must receive them. But his difficulty was that the cities were those of the League of Corinth, and as its President he had sworn to the Covenant of the League, which forbade him to interfere in the internal affairs of the cities; yet it was very necessary to interfere. In these circumstances he issued to the cities of the League[1] a decree ordering them to receive back their exiles (which he had no constitutional power to issue) and also a request for his own deification (which probably came first); for the Covenant bound Alexander the king but did not, and would not, bind Alexander the god, and he could therefore set it aside without losing his self-respect. To us this may seem a quibble, but no one can say it was a quibble to him, or that his careful observance throughout life of the outer forms of religion meant that they were nothing to him but forms. It has been objected that deification did not actually give him any new powers, but that is not the point; he had all the power he wanted, but he had not the right to use it; and to be a god gave him a juridical standing in the cities which he could not otherwise have got, for there was no place for a king in the constitution of a Greek city. The cities of the League granted his request and deified him,[2] thereby (in form) condoning his breach of the Covenant; for while Alexander was thinking of a way of escape

---

[1] To the cities of the League only, for Antipater was to be executant, Diod. XVIII, 8, 4, and he had no authority on the mainland of Asia; see App. 7, 1, p. 202 n. 4. The Greek cities of Asia Minor, who were not in the League (App. 7, II), were not affected. See p. 371 n. 2 *post*.

[2] The story that at Athens he became a particular god, Dionysus, has long been exploded; see A. D. Nock, 'Notes on ruler-cult I–IV', *J.H.S.* XLVIII, 1928, p. 21. Some had rejected it before; e.g. Ed. Meyer, *Kleine Schriften*, I, 1910, p. 331; P. Perdrizet, *R.E.A.* XII, 1910, p. 227 n. 6. There was a good deal of difference between becoming a god and becoming a particular god.

from the Covenant which bound him, the cities and States of the League were thinking primarily of the exiles decree, which hit some of them hard, notably Athens and Aetolia, and was disturbing to them all; and they were hoping to appease Alexander by granting his request for deification, which by comparison seemed to them of little importance. Calling him a god did not mean that they were going to worship him; no cult of him was set up anywhere, and in fact there is no sign that, Egypt apart, anybody ever did worship him till after his death; the first known case is that of Eumenes and his Macedonian troops in the Alexander-tent. His request for deification, then, was a limited *political* measure for a purely political purpose, and nothing else. It is well known that some scholars have long believed this,[1] while others have strenuously denied it; I trust that what I have written in this study will show that the view which I follow is not only true but inevitable. His deification showed that he meant to stand above parties and factions, for many of the exiles, banished by Antipater or by the governments he supported, were Macedonia's enemies; it also showed that he had no intention of adopting Aristotle's view that such as he were above the law and that he could break the Covenant of the League at his pleasure. That his deification was purely political seems to be further supported by two facts: one is that he never put his own head on his coinage, as he must have done had he been a god in the sense in which many of the kings who followed him were gods; and the other is that his request for deification did not (so far as is known) extend to the Greek cities of Asia Minor, who were his free allies and who were not members of the League of Corinth.[2] There may have been no exiles problem there; but had there been he could have settled it without being their god, for he was not bound to them by any covenant which forbade him to interfere in their internal affairs. His deification, therefore, in 324 B.C., like his preliminary attempt at Bactra, was entirely a political matter, but this time limited to the cities of the League of Corinth; and it only remains to consider two modern objections to this view.

1 Ed. Meyer, *Kleine Schriften*, I, pp. 283 *sqq.*, 312, 331; W. S. Ferguson, *Amer. Hist. Rev.* 1912, p. 32; *Greek Imperialism*, 1913, pp. 147 *sqq.*; *C.A.H.* VII, 15.
2 See App. 7, II. Wilcken, who so long championed the view that they were in the League of Corinth, finally abandoned it, 1938, p. 302 [7] n. 5, and in doing so he left it open (*ib.*) whether Alexander's request for deification was directed to them also or not. It seems certain that it was not; there is no evidence that the request was sent to any mainland city of Asia Minor, and the reason against it given p. 370 n. 1 *ante* should be conclusive; also no mainland city took any part in the Larmian war.

Professor Berve's pupil A. Heuss has put forward the view,[1] if I understand him rightly, that a political *Herrschaft*—say kingship—was always compounded of two independent elements, a political and a religious, and that you cannot abolish the religious element and make the political element do the work of both. He said there was warrant enough for this view in history, but did not say what it was; as I understand the matter, one need go no further than the Macedonian and Epirote monarchies to see that Heuss' view is untenable, and that there were plenty of kings whose kingship had no religious element; indeed I doubt if one could find any king in Alexander's day and in his sphere whose kingship *had* any religious element, putting aside Egypt and the little priest-kings of Asia Minor. Heuss makes a point that the deified kings (he includes Alexander) never mention their divine powers in their letters to the cities, where one would expect it. Why one should expect it I cannot imagine, seeing that they never mention their temporal powers either, any more than is ever done by kings or presidents to-day.

The other objection is one made in 1931 by Wilcken in his *Alexander der Grosse*. After discarding offhand the view that Alexander's deification in 324 was a political measure (though he had taken the scene at Bactra to be a political measure) he said (p. 201) that both the decree for the recall of the exiles and Alexander's request to the Greek cities of the League for deification had their roots in Alexander's psychology, and that that psychology was not only an outcome of his amazing success but was connected with, or conditioned by, his desire and plans for world-dominion; for he had been conscious for years that he *was* the son of Zeus-Ammon (p. 198) and history will go wrong if it neglects this inner religious experience. I trust I have given full weight to Alexander's inner religious experience (Ammon), fuller, possibly, than, even if not quite in the same way as, my predecessors; but this can have nothing to do with his deification in 324. There are several things to be said about Wilcken's view; the first and most obvious is that he has refuted it himself by his repeated statement that, as was indeed the fact, Alexander's request for deification in 324 was confined to the Greek cities of the League of Corinth, who were not even his subjects; what has that to do with the psychology of world-rule? The second is that, before it is possible to talk of Alexander's plans for world-dominion, some one has got to refute my demonstration (App. 24), based on evidence, that his supposed plans in that behalf are a late invention;

1 *Stadt und Herrscher des Hellenismus*, Klio, Beiheft XXVI, 1937, pp. 188 *sq.*

this has never been done, and I greatly doubt if it can be. As to Alexander's psychology in the matter of deification, I should be sorry to claim exact knowledge; but I have been considering it throughout this study, and as there is no reputable evidence that he ever called himself the son of any god, let alone a god, or that he even alluded to the descent of his line from Zeus, it is only fair to suppose that he did not believe that he was a god or even the son of one; and if those about him called him a son of Zeus, or even intimated that he ought to be a god, that has no bearing on his own thoughts or beliefs. Wilcken made one other point: his deification in 324 cannot have been political, or the Greek cities would never have granted it in the casual way they did. Certainly the cities did not take it to be a political move; but the only sign of casualness, I think, is the contemptuous remark attributed to Demosthenes, which is none too certain (p. 363 n. 2). I have already explained why the cities granted deification; but, quite apart from that, no city could afford to refuse. There was a great struggle at Athens over the proposal, but Demosthenes finally gave in, and those who desired appeasement and peace carried the day; Sparta, bled white at Megalopolis, was helpless; and probably most of the cities, great and small, acted as they did largely through fear of Alexander, for the moment that that fear was removed by his death they tore up the Covenant of the League of Corinth and started war against Macedonia, led by Athens, who punished Demades for having moved the proposal that Alexander should be a god.[1]

NOTE ON MOUNT CLIMAX (p. 357)

In Arrian I, 26, 1 Alexander's safe passage is called οὐκ ἄνευ τοῦ θείου; in Strabo XIV, 3, 9 (666) it is said to have been due to τύχη. There has been needless argument as to which version is due to Ptolemy and which to Aristobulus (on this see E. Mederer, *Die Alexanderlegenden*, p. 2 n. 3; Kornemann, *Ptolemaios I*, p. 108). Arrian is certainly from Ptolemy, his main source, for Ptolemy mentions Alexander's divine guidance elsewhere, for example, the two snakes on the way to Ammon (Vol. I, p. 43 n. 2), and both instances alike rest on quite ordinary events; travellers in the desert, we are told, often see snakes gliding away before them, and the natives regularly used (Strabo, χρῶνται) the short cut by the beach at Climax, and could have told Alexander when the water was safe for wading. Equally the factual part of Strabo's account must be from Aristobulus, whom he uses so freely (see § D). But Aristobulus never uses τύχη; that is Strabo's own insertion. Plutarch (*Alex.* XVII) has managed to combine both views, θείᾳ τινι τύχῃ; none of the later notices, fully given by Mederer, add anything.

1 Athen. VI, 251B; Aelian, *V.H.* V, 12.

373

What brought the matter into prominence was simply Callisthenes' story (fr. 31) of the sea making *proskynesis* to Alexander, i.e. recognising him as divine, the point being, not what Alexander did, but what the sea did. Mederer's statement that the incident belongs to a well-known *Wundertypus* is not in point here, for in all his instances but one the water itself does nothing; the Red Sea was not making *proskynesis* to Moses, or the Jordan recognising Joshua as its lord; the only real parallel is the Euphrates recognising Cyrus as its future king (Xen. *Anab.* I, 4, 18), which I gave in *C.A.H.* VI. I have not met anywhere with the thing I want, a good modern account of the coast and of what the sea actually does, and it has not been possible for me to make a proper search. That in shallow waters the wind will play tricks with the tide is, I suppose, a commonplace; I have seen it myself quite appreciably delay or accelerate the tide in the upper Cromarty Firth. But the Mediterranean is almost tideless, and our sources do not refer to a tide.

23. THE EMBASSIES TO BABYLON

Every embassy naturally appeared in the *Journal*, and the only ones at Babylon from foreign States or peoples which can be relied on are the four given by Arrian VII, 15, 4, from Ptolemy—Libyans, Bruttians, Lucanians, Tyrrhenians—for all of which, unless perhaps the Tyrrhenians, good reasons are apparent. *A priori*, one might have expected an embassy from Carthage, but Arrian gives it only as a λόγος, which means that it was not in Ptolemy and therefore not in the *Journal*; for if Ptolemy gave the embassies at all, he could not have given the unimportant ones and omitted the important one, which moreover might have been very material to himself as king of Egypt. What have here to be considered are the embassies given by our extant writers (other than Ptolemy-Arrian). They have of course been attributed to Cleitarchus; in fact, they are not only a fabrication but a very late one.

We possess three lists: a λόγος in Arrian VII, 15, 4–5; Diodorus XVII, 113, 2 *sqq.*; Justin XII, 13, 1; it is to be regretted that Curtius' list is lost. Arrian's λόγος gives Carthage, Ethiopians, European Scythians, and Celts and Iberians who came to ask for friendship; this, it says, was the first time that their names, i.e. Celts and Iberians, had been known to Greeks and Macedonians. (As regards Celts, this is of course untrue.) Justin gives Carthage and the other African states (*civitates*), also the states of the Spaniards (*Hispaniarum*), of Gaul (*Gallia*), of Sicily, of Sardinia, and some (*nonnullas*) states of Italy. Diodorus gives the races (ἐθνῶν) and cities and dynasts of Asia, and many of those of Europe and Libya (Africa): from Libya, the Carthaginians, Libyphoenicians, and all the dwellers along the coast as far as the Pillars of Heracles; from Europe, the Greek cities and the Macedonians (Μακεδόνες), the Illyrians and most of the dwellers along the Adriatic, the Thracian tribes and the Galatae who dwelt near them (πλησιοχώρων) and whose race (or tribe, γένος) then first became known to the Greeks. I will omit for a moment what follows in Diodorus, and will consider these names. The Celts of Arrian's λόγος and the Galatae of Diodorus have the same rubric, 'unknown to Greeks heretofore'; they therefore have a common source and are the same people. But the Celts of Arrian's λόγος are closely coupled with the Iberians (Spaniards), and Justin couples the Spaniards with *Gallia* (Gaul); it follows that all three lists are interconnected, and are therefore presumably taken from, or are portions of, one and the same original list, though in the versions we have there may be additions or omissions or mistakes. It follows further that Diodorus' Galatae, who have played such a part in discussions of the date of Cleitarchus, have nothing to do with that author or his date, but are simply *Gallia*, Gaul; they are *not* the Celts of the Danube whom Alexander had met, πλησιοχώρων being merely an erroneous insertion of Diodorus' own, and they are *not* the Galatians of Asia Minor; the fact that the other two lists couple the Celts or *Gallia* with the Spaniards is conclusive. No such country as Gaul (or Spain either) existed in Alexander's day, or for long after; the name is very late (first century B.C.). Another name that is very late indeed is Diodorus' Μακεδόνες. The Macedonians in 323 B.C. could not have sent an embassy to their own king, even had they wished to, for they had no way of doing it; they had no means of corporate expression[1] except through Alexander himself, who *was* the Macedonian State. Diodorus' statement must belong to a time when the real situation in Macedonia had been forgotten, that is, to a time a good deal later than the end of Macedonian independence in 168 B.C. What Justin's Sardinia is supposed to mean I do not know. No time is known when there was a Sardinian *civitas*; in Alexander's day the island was a Carthaginian possession. Sardinia may have replaced some other name,[2] or may have come in from some version of the supposed plan for the conquest of the Mediterranean which named the island. Finally, Diodorus' expression τῶν ἀπὸ τῆς Ἀσίας ἐθνῶν καὶ πόλεων ἔτι δὲ

---

1 The power of the army, i.e. the people under arms, to judge in trials for treason or murder does not bear on this; the army had no voice in foreign politics, or in any political matter except choosing, or confirming, a new king when the throne was vacant.

2 As e.g. Κύρνος (Corsica) has in Diod. XVIII, 4, 5.

δυναστῶν πολλοί is the well-known formula for the Seleucid Empire,[1] much later than Alexander.

The document which gave the embassies here discussed was then a very late one, and two things show what it was. While Arrian's λόγος and Justin relate to Europe and Africa alone, Diodorus' fuller account brings in Asia also, and his mention of all three continents shows that, as he says, the whole οἰκουμένη is meant;[2] in fact, this is tacitly assumed also by Arrian's λόγος and by Justin, for both state that the embassies made Alexander *seem* to be lord of the whole earth[3] (for the reason see below); that is to say, the original document was composed for this purpose. The second thing is that Diodorus and Justin agree that the original document included all the states or peoples of North Africa, Diodorus adding 'as far as the Pillars', while Arrian's λόγος and Justin agree that it included Spain and Gaul; it follows that these embassies are connected with Alexander's supposed plan (see App. 24) to conquer the coast of North Africa as far as the Pillars, and Spain and Gaul also. The two documents, then, the Embassies and the full final version of the Plans, belong to the same period, a period when those who composed them no longer knew enough about Alexander's own day to avoid a number of anachronisms. One thing, however, is clear: whoever put the Embassies document together knew nothing about the alleged embassy from Rome to Alexander. The Plans and the Embassies were invented, undoubtedly in the first century B.C., simply for the honour and glory of Alexander (see App. 24, p. 393), but the embassy from Rome and Alexander's prophecy (the two cannot be disconnected) were invented somewhat later, to glorify Rome rather than the Macedonian king; the only *terminus ante quem* for this story is that one writer who gave it, Aristos (he was not likely to have been the original inventor), was earlier than Strabo.[4] If I were compelled to define dates more closely, I should connect the Plans and Embassies with the age of Pompey and Caesar, when Alexander had become the fashion, and the Roman embassy with Octavian's final victory *terra marique* (§ C, pp. 24 *sq.*). This cannot be very far wrong, and indeed as regards the Embassies there is something

1 *O.G.I.S.* 229, l. 12.
2 Diod. XVII, 113, 1, ἐξ ἁπάσης σχεδὸν τῆς οἰκουμένης ἧκον πρέσβεις.
3 Arr. VII, 15, 5, καὶ τότε μάλιστα αὐτόν τε αὐτῷ ᾿Αλέξανδρον καὶ τοῖς ἀμφ᾽ αὐτὸν φανῆναι γῆς τε ἁπάσης καὶ θαλάσσης κύριον. Justin XII, 13, 2, 'ut cunctae gentes velut destinato sibi regi adularentur'; 13, 3, 'velut conventum terrarum orbis acturo'.
4 This story and its date have been discussed at length in § C, pp. 21–4.

very like proof. For Arrian's λόγος gives as the reason for Alexander seeming to be lord of the world that the states who sent embassies entrusted to him the task of settling their differences one with another; this is what Pompey actually did,[1] and of course Alexander must do no less than the Roman had done.

I come now to the part of Diodorus' account which I deferred considering. After his list of embassies he goes on to say how Alexander dealt with them, and what he has to say relates not to the foreign embassies, but exclusively to those from *Greek cities*; this comes from some good source (*post*) and is doubtless true, for it is certain that many Greek cities did send envoys to Alexander at Babylon (Arr. VII, 23, 2). Diodorus says that Alexander had a list of the envoys and divided them into five classes: those who came about sacred things, those who brought gifts, those who came about boundary disputes, those who came about ἰδιωτικά, which probably means special questions of some kind (not 'internal affairs', which would be δημόσια and which were not Alexander's business), and those who objected to the return of the exiles (as it is known for example that Athens did about Samos and Aetolia about Oeniadae). All this is plain sense. Alexander first interviewed the envoys who came about sacred things; the description given is Eleans, men from Ammon ('Αμμωνιεῦσιν), Delphians, Corinthians, and then Epidaurians and others. It is obvious that in the original the first four names must have represented those who conducted the four Panhellenic festivals; Olympia, Pythia, Isthmia are explicit, but the word that should have represented the fourth festival, the Nemea, (presumably 'Αργείοις), has fallen out and been replaced by 'Αμμωνιεῦσιν, who can have no place in a section professedly dealing with Greek cities. How the word has come to replace 'Αργείοις in Diodorus' text cannot be said; but our texts contain other replacements of the sort quite as extraordinary and inexplicable[2] and I must leave it at that. I may mention, however, that the reason of the four Panhellenic festivals being given was this. The συνέδριον of Demetrius' revived League of Corinth of 303 was to hold its meetings in peace-time at the four Panhellenic festivals.[3] It has long been supposed that the League of Philip and Alexander did the same, though it is not actually recorded.[4] Diodorus here shows

1 Plut. *Pomp.* xxxix.
2 For some certain instances see App. 21, p. 341 n. 5.
3 *S.E.G.* I, 75 II, l. 18: οὗ ἂν οἱ στεφανῖται ἀγῶνες ἄ[γ]ωνται.
4 Originally suggested by Droysen; see Kaerst's discussion, *Rh. Mus.* LII, 1897, pp. 526–9. The discovery of *S.E.G.* I, 75 enormously increased the probability.

that Alexander's League of Corinth did so hold its meetings and was doing so up to (just before) his death.

Diodorus, then, has run two things together, the document already considered which gave the fictitious embassies, and a detailed and perfectly straightforward account of the embassies to Babylon from the Greek cities, not given elsewhere, which has nothing to do with the document aforesaid; it is part of Diodorus' own narrative. That narrative, we have seen (§ F, pp. 71, 75, and *passim*), was (after Gaugamela) based primarily on Aristobulus, with an admixture of Cleitarchus, but no use of Cleitarchus can be detected later than the Bacchic rout in Carmania, and much of the subsequent narrative has been shown to be from Aristobulus beyond question (§ F, pp. 77 *sq.*). There is little doubt therefore that Aristobulus was the source of Diodorus' valuable account of the Greek embassies and their division into classes by Alexander, which in turn throws some light on his capacity for detail.

24. ALEXANDER'S SUPPOSED PLANS AND THE 'WORLD-KINGDOM'

The question is whether these plans are Alexander's, or a late forgery. They are given in Diodorus XVIII, 4, 2–5, and one of them has for some time been the sole support for the German belief in Alexander's 'world-kingdom', which means his alleged desire for world-conquest; for Ammon's supposed promise[1] to him of the dominion of the earth is now well known to be merely an age-old formula, a promise made by Amon-Re to every Pharaoh, the small with the great, and a phrase which echoed on meaninglessly under the Ptolemies.[2] In a paper written in 1921[3] I discussed at length the setting of Diodorus' story; it will suffice to give it here very briefly before considering the plans themselves.

1 It is supposed to have been one of the responses of the oracle to Alexander, i.e. one of the things which the priest told him when he entered the inner shrine alone. But I regard it as well proven now that no one ever knew what he did hear in the inner shrine. See App. 22, 1.

2 When in a petition in Egypt the petitioner ended by praying that the reigning Ptolemy might have the dominion of the whole earth, it meant precisely what the conclusion of an English petition means, 'and your petitioner will ever pray et cetera', that is, just nothing at all.

3 'Alexander's ὑπομνήματα and the "World-kingdom"', *J.H.S.* XLI, 1921, p. 1.

In Diodorus XVIII, 4, 1 Craterus, on his way to Macedonia with the 10,000 veterans he was taking home, is said to have brought with him written orders, ἐντολὰς ἐγγράπτους, 'which Alexander had given to him to carry out, but on Alexander's death his Successors decided that they should be dropped'. This is simple history; the orders to Craterus are known (Arr. VII, 12, 4) and they were not in fact carried out. Diodorus continues (4, 2) '*For* Perdiccas had found in the king's ὑπομνήματα his plans, ἐπιβολάς, many and great, entailing unparalleled expenditure'; and as these also were dropped, the word 'for' is a formal identification, by Diodorus, of Craterus' orders and the plans. This, however, need not be considered, as we possess both the orders and the plans and they have nothing to do with each other; what Diodorus' identification does, or should do, is to make us suspicious of his story. The story goes on (4, 2) that Perdiccas thought that these plans should be dropped; but (4, 3) not wishing to take the responsibility himself, he referred the matter to the Macedonians, which means the army, and they (4, 6), seeing that the plans were both monstrous in scale, ὑπερόγκους, and hard to carry out, δυσεφίκτους, decided that every one of them should be dropped. The story is impossible, for at least two of the plans, (2) and (5), involved matters of high policy, and that was no concern of the Macedonians. The Macedonian people in arms, the army, had authority in two classes of cases only. They confirmed the succession of a new king and could elect a king or regent when the throne was vacant,[1] and they were the judges in capital cases, in trials for murder or treason, the king in the latter being virtually a party;[2] but over policy they had no voice, and there is not a remark or an incident anywhere to suggest that they had. And Perdiccas, who had just been having trouble, verging on civil war, with the Macedonian infantry, was not likely to purport to bestow upon them a new and unheard of power, a thing which he himself was not in a position to do and which was unknown to every subsequent king of the Macedonians. If the army wanted to make its voice heard on any matter outside its customary competency, it could only do so by mutinying. Three such mutinies are known: on the Beas, and over the

---

1 They forced the illegitimate Philip Arrhidaeus on the generals, thus diminishing the position of Alexander IV; they made Antipater regent and Antigonus Doson king.
2 Curt. VI, 8, 25, from a compilation of Macedonian customs (§ G, p. 106); confirmed by many trials under Alexander and the Successors, as those of Philotas; Hermolaus and his fellow-conspirators; Eumenes, Alcetas and their friends; Olympias; Sibyrtius; Nicanor.

marriage of Eurydice to Philip III, it got what it wanted; the third mutiny, that at Opis, failed.

The setting then of Diodorus' story is not one to inspire confidence, and in particular the reference of the plans by Perdiccas to the army cannot be true and could not have been written by a contemporary like Hieronymus, familiar with Macedonia and its customs. The next question is, what is the meaning of Alexander's ὑπομνήματα? It is a word of many meanings. Among other things, it can mean a king's *Journal*;[1] and an attempt has accordingly been made to equate it here with Alexander's official *Journal*.[2] This is out of the question; a king's *Journal* only recorded λεγόμενα καὶ πρασσόμενα, things said and done, i.e. past; it had no place for plans for the future. It was once usual to call these ὑπομνήματα Alexander's *Memoirs*; some men of note in antiquity did write their *Memoirs*.[3] In 1921 I thought the word might have its commonest meaning, a collection of extracts or stories on this or that subject; I rather had in mind some Alexandrian collection of kings' plans. Diodorus himself (1, 4, 4) used the word of anything which could be called historical records, even of paintings (1, 66, 5) as is also done in *I.G.* ii², 677; his own use of the word is wide and vague. Recently the meaning 'memoranda' has come into prominence from papyri,[4] and Wilcken, in an article written in 1937 to which I shall often have to refer, took this view;[5] he thought that Diodorus' ὑπομνήματα were Alexander's official memoranda, presumably kept for him by Eumenes, concerning future things which could find no place in the *Journal*, that being only a record of events. Doubtless Alexander, or Eumenes for him, did write down memoranda for the future; most people do. But it is not very important what the form of the document which Diodorus calls ὑπομνήματα really was, and I am not going to dogmatise about it; it was a document of some sort, containing plans which Diodorus attributed to Alexander, and the question whether they were his plans or not (and that *is* important) can only be decided by analysing them.

A word, however, must first be said about Hieronymus. Most of the modern literature on Alexander has been written in Germany, and German scholars of an older day had no doubt that these plans were

1 U. Wilcken, *Philol.* LIII, 1894, p. 80.
2 H. Endres, *Rh. Mus.* LXXII, 1917–18, p. 437.
3 Pyrrhus and Aratus of Sicyon are instances.
4 E. Bickermann, *Arch. f. Papyrusforschung*, IX, 1930, pp. 165 *sqq.*
5 U. Wilcken, 'Die letzten Pläne Alexanders des Grossen', *S.B. Berlin*, XXIV, 1937, p. 194 [5].

not genuine; Niese and Beloch rejected them out of hand, and Wilamowitz called them fantastic,[1] which is the right word. But for a generation or more in that country it had, down to 1939 (I know nothing later), been an article of faith that Diodorus' description of the plans came from Hieronymus and was therefore true without any question; and this was Wilcken's position in his article of 1937. I have traced this belief as far back as I can, but I have found no one who has given, or even attempted to give, any proof for it; there is nothing but opinion and assertion, derived from the unquestioned fact that, Agathocles apart, the basis and much of the detail (but by no means all of it) in Diodorus books XVIII–XX are from Hieronymus. In *J.H.S.* 1921 I gave an analysis of the opening sections of XVIII which no one has attempted to refute; I need not repeat it, but the matter stands thus. The opening of XVIII, 5 shows that Diodorus is here settling down to follow a new source, and the Gazetteer, XVIII, 5–6, is certainly from Hieronymus, subject to some insertions of Diodorus' own, on which see App. 17. But XVIII, 2, 4 throughout, all of XVIII, 3 which is not the satrapy list (that is Hieronymus), i.e. parts of 3, 1 and of 3, 4–5, and XVIII, 4, 6–7, mostly contradict Hieronymus, and are a patchwork. Consequently it cannot be affirmed offhand that XVIII, 4, 2–5 (the plans) are Hieronymus rather than part of the surrounding patchwork; it would be necessary to show first that 4, 2–5 *could* be from Hieronymus (it has been seen (p. 379) that 4, 3 cannot be), that is, that they do not exhibit material which he could not have known, and secondly that they contain nothing later than Alexander's death. We are therefore thrown back once again on an analysis of the actual plans.

I will now give the plans as Diodorus gives them; he says that he is only giving the greatest and most memorable of them, but we cannot go behind his text.

(1) The completion of Hephaestion's pyre.[2] This might be true, were it not that Diodorus himself (XVII, 115) had already described the completed pyre, an elaborate and costly work of art. Diodorus, however, in XVII had made use of some work, perhaps a monograph, perhaps a *Life*, which 'featured' Hephaestion and gave several things about him which are quite untrue (Arrian perhaps used it also),[3] and

---

1 'Alexander der Grosse' in *Reden aus der Kriegszeit* 5, XI (1916), p. 18.
2 The word used for 'completion', συντέλειαν, is in this sense late Hellenistic and largely confined to Polybius, who uses it freely. But it need not have been in the original; with rare exceptions, Diodorus covers over all his sources with his own style and language.
3 On this source see § F, p. 78 (Diodorus) and App. 16, p. 306 (Arrian).

Diodorus may have taken his description of the pyre from this work. No one can say how the matter of the pyre really stands; in any case, (1) can hardly be called a plan, and is quite immaterial.

(2) The conquest of the Mediterranean basin. This will be considered in detail.

(3) The building of six temples in six named places. The first three, Delos, Delphi, and Dodona, already possessed famous old temples. Nothing in the tradition connects Alexander with either Delos or Dodona; as to Delphi, Apollo's temple was already being rebuilt when Alexander ascended the throne, and he had given a modest subscription toward it before he crossed to Asia.[1] The other three were to be in Macedonia. The first he was to build, to Zeus at Dium, was an existing temple famous for its sanctity (Livy XLIV, 6 and 7); the second, to Artemis Tauropolos in Amphipolis, was the religious centre of Amphipolis (Livy XLIV, 44) and must from the name have been old.[2] The third is called to Athena ἐν Κύρνῳ (Corsica). What name is concealed behind Κύρνῳ cannot be said; Κύρρῳ, a little place near Pella (Thuc. II, 100), has been suggested, in which case it might refer to Athena Alkis of Pella; but the real name need not have been in the least like Κύρνῳ.[3] Omitting Κύρνῳ, this plan then attributes to Alexander the design of building five temples which already existed. It cannot mean pulling down and rebuilding, for the temple at Delphi was in process of being rebuilt; and it cannot mean temples to some god other than the principal god in each place, for the gods at Dium and Amphipolis are named. The only way to salve it would be to say that κατασκευάσαι here means, not 'build', but 'equip, furnish', i.e. adorn; and this is impossible, for Diodorus has used the same verb twice again in the Plans, the meaning 'build' in each case being unmistakable; had he therefore, in the plan under consideration, meant 'equip', he *must* have used some other verb. On the face of it, this plan is pure nonsense. (On Κύρνῳ see Addenda.)

(4) πόλεων συνοικισμούς. Only one synoecism of Alexander's is recorded, that of Alexandria in Makarene (Arr. VI, 22, 3, see App. 8, II).

1 Ditt.³ 251 H, col. II, l. 9 (p. 436); see Pomtow's n. 15, p. 437.
2 Tauropolos was an old goddess in the Aegean; this seems to follow from Euripides' *Iphigeneia in Tauris* 1450 *sqq.* There was a shrine of hers on the island of Icaria near Samos (Strabo XIV, 639), from which island must have come the colonists of the island on the Arabian side of the Persian Gulf, who named that island Icaros and brought Tauropolos with them (*id.* XVI, 766); the colonisation could only have been Alexander's (Arr. VII, 19, 5) or early Seleucid. See Addenda.
3 For some similar instances, see App. 21, p. 341 n. 5.

But doubtless he did mean to found more cities; so let this plan pass as genuine.

(5) Interchange of peoples between Europe and Asia. Alexander may have intended to send more European settlers to his new cities in Asia; but Europe must primarily mean Greece, and that he should have intended to settle Asiatics in Greece, already hopelessly overcrowded and moreover not his, is impossible. But in any case this 'plan' is later than Alexander, for it quotes Theophrastus; it will therefore be more convenient to consider it in another place (App. 25, V, p. 429).

(6) To build a great temple at Ilium. This is genuine enough, Strabo XIII, 1, 26 (593); but it is curious that the plans omit the other two temples which Alexander is known to have intended to build, that to Zeus at Sardis, Arr. I, 17, 5, and the rebuilding of E-sagila, the great temple of Bel at Babylon destroyed by Xerxes, Arr. III, 16, 4; VII, 17, 1 *sq.*

(7) To construct a tomb for Philip at Aegae like the Great Pyramid. This plan, which is very late, will be considered presently together with (2).

So far, the survey is not very hopeful. One plan genuine (6) and one possibly so (4); one possibly genuine, but hardly a plan (1); one made up later than Alexander's death (5); one meaningless (3); and a general setting which cannot be correct. It remains to be seen what information (7) and (2) can supply.

In 1937 Wilcken published an article, to which I have already referred,[1] on the principal plan (2), the conquest of the Mediterranean basin, in which, starting from the belief that the Plans are from Hieronymus, he sought to found this particular plan better by going through various points in Alexander's career which, he thought, led up to it or pointed to it. I fear that, as I see it, this argument did nothing to confirm the plan; but anything pertinent will be noticed in its place. This article led me to publish in 1939[2] an analysis of two of the plans, Philip's tomb (7) and the conquest plan (2); the former was quite new, the latter, I trust, a considerable improvement on my analysis in 1921, in which I had still talked about Cleitarchus. What now follows here is a second edition of my article of 1939, with the omission of things already noticed in this Appendix and with various additions and corrections.

I begin with the last plan in the Diodorus list: Alexander intended to build for his father, Philip, a tomb like the greatest of the pyramids of

1 *S.B. Berlin*, XXIV, 1937, p. 192[3].
2 Tarn, 'Alexander's Plans', *J.H.S.* LIX, 1939, p. 124.

Egypt, which people reckon among the seven wonders of the world.[1]
(The lists of the seven wonders are Hellenistic, and Diodorus' reference
to these is his own addition, repeated from his description of the
Pyramids, 1, 63, 2.) That παραπλήσιον here means 'like'—i.e. in
shape—and not merely 'as big as', is certain.[2] To explain this fantastic
'plan' I start from two lines in Lucan,[3] on the death of Pompey: why
should Pompey's corpse be tossed on the waves

> Cum Ptolemaeorum manes seriemque pudendam
> Pyramides claudant indignaque Mausolea.

H. Thiersch, in a notable article[4] which seems never to have got into
circulation among historians, called attention to these lines and to
then current mistranslations of them; they certainly refer to *burials*—
'Seeing that the Manes of the Ptolemies and their shameful line are
buried in pyramids, disgraceful tombs'[5]—and the main point, burial, is
given in the latest translations of Lucan.[6] That Lucan, through his uncle
Seneca, was in a position to know a good deal about Egypt is not in
doubt. Thiersch collected all that is known of the tombs of the first
four Ptolemies, and it shows that their tombs were not pyramids; he

---

1 Diod. XVIII, 4, 5: τοῦ δὲ πατρὸς Φιλίππου τάφον πυραμίδι παραπλήσιον
μιᾷ τῇ μεγίστῃ κατὰ τὴν Αἴγυπτον, ὃς ἐν τοῖς ἑπτά τινες μεγίστοις ἔργοις
καταριθμοῦσιν.
2 Παραπλήσιος means 'like'. Like in size is always π. τὸ μέγεθος (instances
in Dindorf's Stephanus, the fullest thing); so π. τὴν ἡλικίαν, π. τὸν
ἀριθμόν, but τὸν ἀριθμόν *can* be omitted if ambiguity be impossible, as
παραπλήσιαι νῆες in a battle. I went through Diodorus' book 1 (Egypt),
and he is very careful to avoid ambiguity: eighteen instances of π. alone
as 'like'; one case, 21, 5—Isis makes a model of each of Osiris' limbs—
which could be ambiguous, as a model need not be life-size, so he writes
π. τὸ μέγεθος; while of the second pyramid (64, 2) he says, τῇ μὲν τέχνῃ
παραπλησίαν τῇ προειρημένῃ (the first) τῷ δὲ μεγέθει πολὺ λειπομένην.
This excludes any idea of ambiguity in the passage I am considering; the
tomb is to be of pyramid shape, *and* is also to rival the Great Pyramid in
size, because of the mention of that particular pyramid.
3 *Pharsalia* VIII, 696 *sq.* See Addenda.
4 H. Thiersch, 'Die Alexandrinische Königsnekropole', in *J.D.A.I.* xxv,
1910, p. 55.
5 Line 697 does not mean tombs of two different sorts, Egyptian and Greek,
for Lucan could not have called Greek tombs 'disgraceful'; the *indignitas*
lay in Greek kings being buried in native tombs.
6 MM. Bourgery et Ponchont, 1929: 'quand les mânes des Ptolemées, une
honteuse ligne, sont enfermés sous des pyramides et de scandaleux
Mausolées'; J. D. Duff, Loeb ed. 1928: 'though the dead Ptolemies and
their unworthy dynasty are covered by pyramids and mausoleums too
good for them'.

consequently assigned the pyramid tombs of the Ptolemies mentioned by Lucan to the later Ptolemies without specifying more closely, as indeed follows from Lucan, who could hardly have called the early Ptolemies 'shameful'. The earliest possibility of a Ptolemaic pyramid tomb would then be that of Ptolemy V Epiphanes (died 181); but the known history of Epiphanes and of his successor Ptolemy VI Philometor, who would have built the tomb, hardly suggests Egyptianising, and more probably the first pyramid tomb would have been that of Philometor (died 145), built by his successor Euergetes II, whose Egyptianising policy is known. In any case, these tombs cannot have begun *earlier* than 181, and it was from them that the 'plan' to build a pyramid tomb for Philip was taken. This plan then is certainly later than 181, and probably later than 145. And this is also common sense; for Alexander's own culture was Greek, not Egyptian; he was not a megalomaniac; and the man who forbade Deinocrates to carve Mt Athos into a bust of himself was not going to build another Great Pyramid at Aegae.

I do not think that the Semitic custom of the *naphshā* gives any help in dating the first Ptolemaic pyramid tomb. The *naphshā* was a memorial placed beside a tomb, and is said to have represented the soul or personality of the deceased;[1] Greeks called it a μνημεῖον,[2] but it must not be confused with the tomb itself which held the body. It took many forms, but at some period the form of a pyramid rather came into vogue, presumably under the influence of Egypt. Thiersch (*op. cit.* p. 69) refers to a number of pyramids, known from archaeology, in the countries near Egypt; I do not know if they are tombs or memorials, but most seem to be of Roman times and do not therefore affect the chronology question.[3] The earliest pyramids used for this purpose (memorials) which I have met with in the East are those before the great μνημεῖον at Modin which Simon the Maccabee (143–142 to 135) built for his

1 S. A. Cook, *The Religion of Ancient Palestine in the Light of Archaeology*, 1930, p. 19.
2 So translated in a Nabataean bilingual: Cook *ib.* p. 19 n. 3. μνημεῖον could mean any funeral monument which was not a tomb; Josephus calls Simon's monument at Modin (below) a μνημεῖον, and Plutarch, *Mor.* 821 D, uses the word for the stupas erected by the cities who, in the legend, divided up Menander's ashes (see Tarn, *Bactria and India*, p. 264). But in Hellenistic Greek μνημεῖον more often meant the actual tomb, e.g. Ditt.³ 1234, LXX *Genesis* xxiii, 6, 9, etc., and commonly in the Gospels.
3 The Ethiopian pyramids are much older, and are I imagine quite a separate matter.

parents and brothers.¹ If they are really the first, it might be argued that Simon was influenced by the new custom started in Egypt with Philometor's tomb; but I am not familiar with Oriental archaeology, and there may be earlier cases. There is certainly said to have been an earlier case in the West: Diodorus says that Hiero of Syracuse (*c.* 275–215) built 'tombs of many pyramids',² and if Hiero adopted this Semitic custom he presumably took it from Carthage. The *naphshā* pyramids then do not help us to decide whether 145 was the date of the first appearance of the Ptolemaic pyramid tombs; 181 must remain open, while on the other hand it would satisfy the Lucan passage just as well if they did not begin till (say) the death of Euergetes II in 116.

However that may be, the 'plan' to build a pyramid *tomb* (τάφος) for Philip is later, perhaps much later, than 181, and clearly originated in Alexandria. Hieronymus therefore cannot be the source of the document called Alexander's ὑπομνήματα, any more than he can have been the origin of the story of Perdiccas referring the plans to the Macedonian army; and as the plans are a single document, the principal plan, that for the conquest of the Mediterranean basin, cannot be genuine unless the claim that it be so be strictly proved. Of that plan there are two versions, in Diodorus and Curtius, and Wilcken has said very frankly: 'For those of us who are convinced of the genuineness of the Diodorus tradition, it follows...that Curtius' account must also be genuine.'³ Nothing turns on the fact that Curtius attaches *his* plan to the meeting of Alexander and Nearchus in Carmania, while Diodorus makes *his* plan discovered after Alexander's death; for there is nothing to show at what time the Diodorus plan is supposed to have been thought of or written down. I take Curtius first.

Curtius⁴ begins by saying that Alexander desired⁵ to *know* more (conquest is not mentioned). He decided, after conquering all the maritime region towards the east, to go from Syria to Africa, to be hostile to Carthage (or, being hostile to Carthage), and then march

---

1 *I Macc.* xiii, 27 *sqq.*; Jos. *Ant.* XIII, 211. The pyramids of Helena of Adiabene, cited by Cook, *op. cit.* p. 19 n. 1, are much later.

2 XVI, 83, 3, τάφους πυραμίδων πολλῶν.   3 *Op. cit.* p. 203 [14].

4 Curtius X, 1, 16–18: 'Rex cognoscendi plura cupidine accensus....Ipse animo infinita complexus statuerat, omni ad orientem maritima regione perdomita, ex Syria petere Africam, Carthagini infensus, inde Numidiae solitudinibus peragratis cursum Gadis dirigere—ibi namque columnas Herculis esse fama vulgaverat—Hispanias deinde adire...et praetervehi Alpes Italiaeque oram, unde in Epirum brevis cursus est. Igitur' he orders his governors in Mesopotamia to build 700 septiremes, i.e. heptereis.

5 'Cupidine' is doubtless meant to represent his πόθος, so often mentioned in Arrian.

through the solitudes of Numidia to Gades, where report said the Pillars of Hercules stood, then go to Spain and sail past the Alps[1] and the shore of Italy, whence there is a short passage to Epirus (i.e. from Brindisi or thereabouts). He therefore ordered his governors in Mesopotamia to build 700 septiremes at Thapsacus in Syria and bring them [down the Euphrates] to Babylonia.[2] This alone should suffice to discredit the story; for if you are going from Syria to Gibraltar you do not begin by bringing your fleet from Syria to the Persian Gulf. The writer is ill-informed; he thinks Gades (Cadiz) is in Africa, while the Pillars (Gibraltar and Ceuta) are not in fact (as he puts them) at Cadiz. But let that pass. The passage from Brindisi to Epirus belongs to much later history; but let that pass also. The number of the heptereis is merely ridiculous; no war-fleet in Hellenistic times even remotely approached 700—nothing much over 300 is known, let alone such a number of heptereis; the largest recorded number of these, true or false, is 37 in what is probably the navy list (on paper) of Ptolemy II.[3] And Alexander always operated with forces comparatively small, but highly trained and efficient. However, Antony and Octavian together did have more warships than 700 at sea in 31 B.C., and there are real battles in which the numbers are vastly exaggerated, like first Salamis and Issus; so let that pass also. But two things cannot pass: the actual septiremes (heptereis) and the name *Alpes*.

I gave the date of the hepteres very briefly in 1921, as being well known, but I was too optimistic, and must therefore now do it in full; the facts which show that it was invented eight years after Alexander's death really are from Hieronymus, this time. When in 315 Antigonus started to create a fleet in Phoenicia to get the command of the sea,[4] Ptolemy had previously carried off all the Phoenician ships to Egypt;[5] he got nothing larger than quinqueremes, for at Salamis in 306 his largest vessel was a quinquereme.[6] Demetrius, however, at Salamis, in addition to quinqueremes and quadriremes, had ten hexereis (sixes)

1 In my 1921 article this was wrongly given as crossing the Alps. Wilcken pointed this out (*S.B. Berlin* 1928, XXX, p. 593 [20] n. 1), and I appreciate the courteous manner in which he treated it; I daresay it astonished him as much as it did myself. The error was *against* myself; it made the earliest possible date of the Curtius passage a little too early.
2 This story grew out of the fact that Alexander really did have a few ships brought down the Euphrates from Thapsacus, Arr. VII, 19, 3.
3 Athen. V, 203 D. On Callixenus' figures here see Tarn, *Antigonos Gonatas*, p. 456.
4 Diod. XIX, 58, 1. This and all the Diodorus passages in this paragraph are from Hieronymus.
5 *Id.* XIX, 58, 2.   6 *Id.* XX, 49, 2.

and seven heptereis (sevens).[1] Antigonus in 315 is said, in Diodorus' text, to have built, besides quinqueremes and quadriremes, three ἐννήρεις (nines) and ten δεκήρεις (tens);[2] but the δεκήρης did not in fact appear till after, possibly even generations after, 306,[3] and it is certain that these two words are either corrupt or one of Diodorus' slips in transcription. This is shown, not merely by the sudden and impossible jump in the figures (for progress in the power of warships went step by step), but by a comparison with Demetrius' fleet at Salamis given above: the ten 'δεκήρεις' are clearly the ten ἑξήρεις (sixes) of Salamis, and the three 'ἐννήρεις' are three of Demetrius' new ἑπτήρεις (sevens), which were the largest ships he had in the battle and which played such a part in it.[4] Read then in Diodorus XIX, 62, 8, ἑξήρεις δὲ δέκα ἑπτήρεις δὲ τρεῖς. Diodorus explicitly says that Antigonus' shipbuilding was not yet finished; and four more heptereis were built before Salamis. The hepteres then was invented by (or for) Demetrius in 315, and was the vessel which started that extraordinary race in shipbuilding between himself and his son on the one hand and the Ptolemies on the other, which I have described fully elsewhere.[5] It is certain that Alexander never had anything larger than a quinquereme,[6] and that Pliny's statement, taken from a quite unknown writer Mnesigeiton,[7] that Alexander invented all the classes of warships from sevens to tens,[8] is merely untrue, as are so many items in his lists of 'inventors'.

The appearance of the name Alps (*Alpes*) in Greek (and Latin) literature is very late.[9] In the fifth century, Herodotus did not know that these mountains existed; he gives a river Alpis as a tributary of the Danube, running in from the south, but it has nothing to do with the

1 Diod. XX, 50, 2 *sq.*   2 *Id.* XIX, 62, 8.
3 Tarn, *Mariner's Mirror*, 1933, p. 69. Ptolemy II had none, Athen. V, 203 D.
4 The heavier sevens and sixes crushed Ptolemy's right while the thirty Athenian quadriremes turned it. Some day I must collect the evidence that the quadrireme was the fastest ship of the line.
5 *Hellenistic Military and Naval Developments*, 1930, pp. 132 *sqq.*; *Mariner's Mirror*, 1933, pp. 69 *sqq.*
6 See H. Droysen, *Griech. Kriegsaltertümer* in Hermann's *Lehrbuch*, II, 2, p. 272 n. 3, and E. Luebeck, *Das Seewesen der Griechen und Römer*, I, p. 17 n. 6. Both naturally rejected as worthless the statements in Pliny and Curtius.
7 E. Bux, 'Mnesigeiton' in PW. Not given in Susemihl.
8 Pliny VII, 208.
9 See generally J. Partsch, 'Alpes' in PW. and 'Die Stromgabelungen der Argonautensage' in *Berichte d. sächs. Akad. d. Wiss.* 71, 1919, Heft 2, pp. 11 *sq.*; M. Cary and E. H. Warmington, *The Ancient Explorers*, 1929, pp. 121 *sqq.* (Cary).

mountains; and it must be remembered that in Alexander's day he was no longer much read, and that both Alexander and the most learned man in his train, Callisthenes, were ignorant of him.[1] Also Pseudo-Scylax, whose sources are mainly fifth century, knows nothing of the Alps, mountains or name. In the fourth century, Ephorus, whose ideas about Celts were shadowy and unreal, knew nothing of either mountains or name, as is shown by their absence from Pseudo-Scymnus;[2] they did not exist either for Heracleides Ponticus late in the century.[3] Even as late as the last quarter of the third century, Apollonius Rhodius, though librarian at Alexandria, knew nothing of any such mountains at all,[4] and there is nothing to show that even Eratosthenes knew of them either; and if the view that there is a great deal of Eratosthenes running through Pseudo-Scymnus be correct,[5] the ignorance of Pseudo-Scymnus on the matter becomes very material. The Alps and their name were unknown to Greeks generally prior to the Hannibalic war,[6] and even after Hannibal's crossing knowledge penetrated very slowly, for when after Cynoscephalae Pseudo-Lycophron wrote the *Alexandra*—the most probable year is 196–195[7]—though he had heard of the mountains he had not yet got the correct name; he called them Salpia.[8] The name *Alpes* first appears in extant Latin literature with the elder Cato,[9] and does not appear in extant Greek literature till Polybius.[10] But even Polybius, though personally

1 For Alexander see Vol. 1 p. 86; for Callisthenes, App. 13.
2 If the 'pillar of the north' in Ps.-Scymnus, ll. 188 *sqq.* be really some dim hearsay of the Alps (more it cannot be, *pace* Cary, *op. cit.* p. 121), it shows anyhow that nothing was *known*. On this, and the 'Hercynian rock' of Apollonius Rhodius, see Partsch, *op. cit.* (*Ber. sächs. Akad.*), p. 11.
3 E. Wikén, *Die Kunde der Hellenen von dem Lande und den Völkern der Apenninenhalbinsel bis* 300 *v. Chr.*, 1937, p. 142.
4 IV, 627 *sqq.*: he makes the Argo sail through from the Po into the Rhone. See on this story Partsch, *op. cit.* (*Ber. sächs. Akad.*), pp. 9 *sqq.*
5 U. Hoefer, *Rh. Mus.* LXXVII, 1928, p. 127.
6 See Partsch, *op. cit.* (both works). Massiliote traders must have known something; but the secrecy they observed about their trade routes (Cary, *op. cit.* pp. 124 *sq.*) shows that they did not talk.
7 Ziegler's date in PW., after a very long examination. The exact year is not material here. See A. Momigliano, *J.R.S.* XXXII, 1942, p. 53, who supported the early dating, and my remarks, § C, p. 29.
8 *Alexandra* 1361. Doubts have been expressed if Salpia be the Alps, see Momigliano, *op. cit.* p. 58 n. 24. They do not affect my argument.
9 Servius on *Aen.* X, 13.
10 Polyb. III, 47, 6 *sqq.* shows that one or more writers had (naturally) written on Hannibal's passage of the Alps before him; it does not appear whether in Latin or Greek.

acquainted with the Alps, gave them wrongly as a simple chain running east to west,[1] while Curtius' words *praetervehi Alpes* imply express knowledge of the *Maritime* Alps, which means Roman knowledge; the earliest literary allusion to them is in Pliny,[2] though they were known long before that. The word *Alpes*, then, in the Curtius passage leads to much the same conclusion as does the pyramid-tomb for Philip, a date not earlier, and possibly a good deal later, than 196–195.

It might perhaps be contended that the name *Alpes* was interpolated by Curtius or an intermediary source, and the word *septiremes* by some intermediary source (not by Curtius, in whose day the hepteres had long been forgotten). But then the 'genuineness' of the Curtius passage would be gone; for if late interpolations be once admitted without any reason, there is no stopping-place; the whole passage might be a fabrication, and we are just where we were before.

I will now leave Curtius (I shall return to him later) and turn to Diodorus.[3] He says that Alexander's plan was to build 1,000 warships larger than triremes in Phoenicia, etc., for *the* military expedition against Carthage and the other peoples who bordered on the sea in Libya, Spain, and the contiguous country on the sea as far as Sicily (this would include Rome), to prepare harbours and docks suitable for such a force, and to make a road along the coast of Libya as far as the Pillars. (The road shows that an army as well as a fleet was contemplated.) As the 700 warships of Curtius have now become 1,000,[4]

1 III, 47–8; see Cary, *op. cit.* p. 122.
2 Partsch, *op. cit.* (PW.), col. 1601; Pliny, III, 47, 135.
3 XVIII, 4, 4, χιλίας μὲν ναῦς μακρὰς μείζους τριήρων ναυπηγήσασθαι κατὰ τὴν Φοινίκην καὶ Συρίαν καὶ Κιλικίαν καὶ Κύπρον πρὸς τὴν στρατείαν τὴν ἐπὶ Καρχηδονίους καὶ τοὺς ἄλλους τοὺς παρὰ θάλατταν κατοικοῦντας τῆς τε Λιβύης καὶ Ἰβηρίας καὶ τῆς ὁμόρου χώρας παραθαλαττίου μέχρι Σικελίας, ἀκολούθως δὲ τῷ τηλικούτῳ στόλῳ λιμένας καὶ νεώρια κατασκευάσαι κατὰ τοὺς ἐπικαίρους τῶν τόπων, ὁδοποιῆσαι δὲ τὴν παραθαλάττιον τῆς Λιβύης μέχρι στηλῶν Ἡρακλείων. I have followed Wilcken in transposing the last two clauses, as against Fischer's arrangement; but it makes no difference to what I have to say.
4 Wilcken, *op. cit.* p. 205 [16], made them two separate fleets, though the 700 were to be brought from the Persian Gulf. Such numbers of warships belong to the realm of phantasy. Certainly Alexander had a flotilla of 1,000 vessels when he started down the Hydaspes, Arr. VI, 2, 4, but most of them were only native boats carrying supplies. Was this the origin of Diodorus' 1,000 warships? Or was it Aristobulus' innocent remark (a mere measure of size) that the harbour to be built at Babylon was to be big enough to take 1,000 warships, Arr. VII, 19, 4? Diodorus' 1,000 warships turn up again in Justin XIII, 5, 7 (the Lamian war), who says that Alexander had ordered them to be built for an attack on Athens.

the origin of the Diodorus passage must be later than that of the Curtius passage (we shall come to an even more decisive reason for this), for in the growth of a story numbers grow but never diminish; this alone would make it pretty difficult to call the Diodorus passage a plan of Alexander's. Moreover, this enormous number of ships for an expedition against countries of which Carthage alone possessed a navy shows that, to the writer, Carthage had the reputation of being, or of having been, a very great maritime Power; and this reputation only dated from the battle in which she destroyed the fleet of her secular rival, Syracuse, in her war against Pyrrhus, long after Alexander's day; before that she had only been on a level with Syracuse. The phrase '*the* military expedition' of course imports a known thing, not a new proposal, showing again that the passage is later than the Curtius passage and who knows what else. Wilcken attempted to meet this particular point by a theory that the idea of an expedition against the west originated when Alexander was at Susa, or even earlier, when he met Nearchus in Carmania.[1] Of course, if the Curtius passage, and therefore *a fortiori* the Diodorus passage, exhibit late material, this theory falls to the ground, but, apart from that, it is a difficult theory on its merits; for it is incredible that Alexander could have been occupied (*beschäftigt*) with such an expedition for over a year, and have begun preparations (*Ausarbeitungen*) for it, without Ptolemy of the Staff knowing; there were only seven Bodyguards at the time, and Ptolemy, Alexander's personal friend from youth, was one of the most important. And Ptolemy certainly knew nothing about it, not merely because he did not mention it in his history, but because, had he known of such a plan, he would have eagerly proclaimed the fact, seeing that it would have justified his own advance westward in Africa, his annexation of the Cyrenaica.

But what seems to settle the matter, if it needs settling any further, is the word ὁδοποιῆσαι, which means 'to make a road' and means nothing else; and in this case its conjunction with the preparation of harbours and docks for Alexander's στόλος shows that a military road is meant, a road to assist the advance of the land portion of the στόλος. Now we possess a vast amount of information about Alexander, true and false, but he is never recorded to have made a military road, or indeed a road of any kind.[2] No Hellenistic king, so far as I know, is recorded to have made a road of any kind. Possibly in Asia they did make some additions to existing roads for civil purposes, but I only

1 Wilcken, *op. cit.* (1937), pp. 197, 205 [8, 16].
2 See Rostovtzeff, *Soc. and Econ. Hist.* p. 133.

recall one case in which this is even a probable deduction, and that is in the outlying province of Ferghana on the Jaxartes, which was never conquered or ruled by Alexander: Chang-k'ien in 128 B.C. crossed it on 'postal roads', and it is probable, though not certain, that these roads were made by Euthydemus or by some Seleucid rather than by the Persians.[1] Of new military roads nothing is ever heard. Putting aside, as not here material, anything that may have been done in Persian or pre-Persian Asia, there was one nation, and one only, which prior to Diodorus' time made military roads, and that was the Romans. They did more than make them; such roads were a great instrument of their policy. Alexander's plan to make a military road is a statement that he was going to do as the Romans did; it cannot have been written *before* Rome's entry into the world of the eastern Mediterranean with her victory over Philip V at Cynoscephalae in 197, when Greeks first became acquainted with Roman methods, and it is not likely to antedate the Via Egnatia (after 148), the first Roman road to be constructed east of the Adriatic; indeed the first Greek writer (so far as is known) to mention Roman road-making was Polybius.[2]

But there is a further point about this road. Diodorus' text shows clearly that Wilcken is right in saying that the plan was to go right round the coast of the western Mediterranean as far as Sicily, and that the attempt to confine this plan to North Africa is wrong.[3] This being so, why was Alexander only going to make a road along the south coast of the Mediterranean and not along the north coast also? Why stop short half-way? I cannot do much more than pose the problem, but the answer *ought* to be that it was because the writer knew of the 'Heracles-road': Alexander's ancestor, Heracles, had already made the rest of the road,[4] running from Spain and Gaul through Liguria to Italy and passing between the sea and the Maritime Alps in the Ligurian section,[5] a section known from Polybius to have actually existed in his time.[6] No doubt there really was a very old mercantile route;[7]

1 Tarn, *Bactria and India*, pp. 474 *sq.*
2 Polyb. xxxiv, 12 (= Strabo vii, 7, 4 [322]); iii, 39, 8 (if genuine).
3 *Op. cit.* p. 194 [5].   4 Diod. iv, 19, 3 *sq.*
5 *Ib.* διεξιὼν τὴν ὀρεινὴν τὴν κατὰ τὰς Ἄλπεις. This is always interpreted as *crossing* the Alps, I suppose because of διελθὼν τὰς Ἄλπεις in § 4. It seems to me an impossible translation; 'going through the mountain country which is over (or "on" or "through") the Alps' is nonsense; it is 'which is by (or "at" or "near") the Alps'.
6 It is the first of Polybius' four ὑπερβάσεις, διὰ Λιγύων τὴν ἔγγιστα τῷ Τυρρηνικῷ πελάγει; Strabo iv, 5, 12 (209).
7 Schulten, *Tartessos*, p. 28.

Heracles in the story turned it into a military road,[1] long before the Roman road through Liguria, the Via Iulia Augusta, was constructed by Augustus (12 B.C.). The Heracles-road is mentioned twice in antiquity, by Diodorus (*loc. cit.*) and, much later, in [Aristot.] *de miris auscultationibus* 85, who gives the name 'Heracles-road'.[2] In both cases it is a matter of dispute whether the source be Poseidonius or Timaeus;[3] it seems to me to be very much guesswork,[4] and also to assume that there can have been no other authors who wrote on the West. In any case the Heracles-road is much later than Alexander; and an item drawn from his career appears in Diodorus' story of Heracles.[5] That the Alexander-road and the Heracles-road are connected inventions seems clear; but in the absence of any certain date for the first ascription of the northern road to Heracles, it seems impossible to say what the actual connection was.

It should now, however, be abundantly clear that the document called Alexander's ὑπομνήματα, which embodied the plans given by Diodorus, is not Alexander's, but is a very late document, which cannot be *earlier* than some point in the second century B.C., and might of course be later; it must, however, be Hellenistic, because of Diodorus' own date, and the pyramid tomb for Philip shows that it first saw the light in Alexandria. It does contain one plan, the building of a great temple at Ilium, which is certainly true, and another, the synoecisms, which may be true; but any forger would naturally put in something genuine, if he could, to give verisimilitude to the rest, just as there are said to be some genuine old bits worked into that famous modern forgery, the 'tiara of Saitaphernes'. The plan for the conquest of the Mediterranean basin by Alexander belongs, in essence, not to the sphere of history at all, but to that of the incipient Alexander-Romance, which in its full form later made him carry it out by conquering both Rome and Carthage and sailing out through the Pillars. The Romance was already beginning in the late Hellenistic period, and several things which

1 Diod. IV, 19, 3, ὡδοποίησε... ὥστε δύναθαι στρατοπέδοις... βάσιμον εἶναι.
2 ὁδὸν Ἡρακλείαν καλουμένην.
3 For *de miris ausc.* see Gercke, 'Aristoteles' in PW. Schwartz, 'Diodoros' (38) in PW. col. 676, said Diodorus IV, 19 was from Poseidonius; Laqueur, 'Timaios' (3) in PW. col. 1177, says from Timaeus.
4 I can hardly believe, for example, that Diod. IV, 19, 1–2 on Alesia was written before Caesar's siege; Timaeus was not the only Greek who used absurd derivations.
5 IV, 19, 1: Heracles, having conquered Spain, hands it over to the natives to rule, τοῖς ἀρίστοις τῶν ἐγχωρίων. This is Alexander handing over the eastern Punjab to the conquered Porus (*post*).

Appendix 24

became embodied in the full story appeared earlier than the reign of
Augustus (see App. 22, p. 363); but I have already considered the
Romance (pp. 363–5).

It remains to ask how the plan for the conquest of the Mediterranean
basin grew up, and why it grew up. I will take the former question
first. In 1921 I thought that the embassies which are said to have come
to Alexander at Babylon had played a part here, because of Arrian's
statement that they made Alexander *seem to be* lord of the whole earth;[1]
but I am now satisfied that the Embassies (see App. 23) and this Plan
were parallel inventions, made with the same purpose but probably
not connected with each other. I now think that Alexander's schemes,
real and alleged, of exploration were the important factor, and I must
look at these. When he turned back at the Beas he *abandoned* a hard-
won conquest: he formally handed over the Punjab east of the Jhelum
to Porus,[2] who became completely independent in fact[3] and was
Chandragupta's chief supporter[4] when he expelled the last Macedonian
generals from India and set up the Mauryan empire. The abandonment
of the eastern Punjab was a turning-point in Alexander's career, for,
once he had quitted India, he made no more conquests, but turned his
thoughts to exploration instead. He tried to explore the coast of his
own province[5] of Gedrosia, to help maritime trade; and when he died
he had two explorations in hand, the Caspian and the coast of Arabia.
The Arabian expedition was no more intended to be a *conquest*[6] than

1 Arr. VII, 15, 5, φανῆναι γῆς τε ἁπάσης καὶ θαλάσσης κύριον. No embassies
came from the sea, and Arrian is making the connection himself. On the
earlier history of the phrase *terra marique* see Momigliano, *op. cit.*; but a
post-Augustan writer like Arrian was bound to think of Augustus' very
special appropriation of it.
2 Arr. V, 29, 2, Πώρῳ ἄρχειν προσέθηκεν; VI, 2, 1, βασιλέα ἀπέδειξε. Cf.
Glotz-Roussel-Cohen, *Histoire ancienne* IV, i, 1938, *Alexandre et le démembre-
ment de son empire*, p. 243: 'jouit d'une complète indépendance'.
3 Diod. XVIII, 39, 6. Eudamus, though he subsequently killed Porus and
took his elephants (Diod. XIX, 14, 8, presumably in the war with Chandragupta), was apparently not stationed in Porus' territory (Arr. VI, 27, 2);
my remark that he was (*Bactria and India*, p. 259) is a slip.
4 *Cambridge Hist. of India*, I, p. 471; Tarn, *Bactria and India*, p. 46.
5 The satrap of Gedrosia had submitted long before, Arr. III, 28, 1; that the
Oreitae of eastern Gedrosia did not recognise their satrap's submission
does not affect what I have written. The orders to the fleet to *explore* the
Gedrosian coast are given by Arrian, *Ind.* 32, 11.
6 Wilcken, *op. cit.* p. 195 [6], agreed that it was not to be a conquest, but
envisaged the occupation of certain points as harbours or stations; the
difficulty is that Alexander had not attempted to do this in his own

394

the Gedrosian, though army and fleet were to keep together, as had been intended in Gedrosia: the *Journal* calls it a πορεία[1] and a πλοῦς,[2] not a στρατεία; Alexander himself was going with the fleet, not with the army;[3] and the preliminary dispatch of Hiero and Anaxicrates[4] to try to get round the peninsula from different sides shows the importance he attached to its *circumnavigation*. A story was told that, after Arabia, he meant to circumnavigate Africa and enter the Mediterranean through the Pillars;[5] as he knew nothing of the size of Africa or of Herodotus' story of a Phoenician circumnavigation which took three years, the story has some chance of being true,[6] though he could hardly have gone in person.

But projects of exploration by a naval and military force will, in literature, pass with the greatest ease into projects of conquest. The (supposed) projected circumnavigation of Africa became a plan for conquering North Africa from the Pillars eastward.[7] The real plan of exploring the Arabian coast, known from the *Journal*, became, in the Curtius passage already discussed (x, 1, 16; see p. 386 *ante*), the conquest of that coast;[8] and that passage exhibits a (supposed) projected circumnavigation of the Mediterranean in actual process of passing into the conquest of the Mediterranean basin. In that (the Curtius) passage, Alexander begins by wanting to know (i.e. explore), not to conquer, and army and fleet are to proceed along the coast of North Africa as along that of Gedrosia or Arabia. Then come the vague words *Carthagini infensus*, which might mean fighting his way, if necessary, through Carthaginian territory or might mean the conquest of Carthage. But after reaching Spain the army (i.e. any idea of conquest) drops out altogether and we only have the fleet, the original circumnavigation plan: he is to sail past the Alps and the coast of Italy to Epirus—no

Gedrosia, where it was badly needed. Arrian vii, 20, 3 (from τό τε μέγεθος to the end) is, as a comparison with vii, 20, 8 shows, only Hiero's report, and throws no light on Alexander's intentions.

1 Arr. vii, 25, 2. 2 *Ib*. 25, 2, 4, 5.
3 *Ib*. 25, 2, ἅμα οἱ πλέοντες.
4 For Anaxicrates see Tarn, *J.E.A.* xv, 1929, p. 13.
5 Plut. *Alex.* lxviii (no mention of conquest).
6 It has been suggested to me that this story must have been invented after the voyages of Polybius and Eudoxus down the Atlantic coast of Africa [say perhaps rather after Poseidonius, in the Eudoxus story, had told of a Gades ship doubling the Cape]. But as Alexander certainly thought of the circumnavigation of Arabia for himself, he *could* equally well have thought of that of Africa; he had no idea of its size.
7 Arr. v, 26, 2; vii, 21, 1.
8 'Omni ad orientem maritima regione perdomita.'

further word of the army. We see here vague and undefined military operations in Africa being superimposed upon a plan, true or false, for the circumnavigation of the Mediterranean by the fleet; and this presently develops into the full-blown plan for the conquest of the Mediterranean basin given by Diodorus. That the Diodorus passage is later, perhaps much later, in origin than is the already late Curtius passage, and has merely grown out of it, is surely now self-evident.

The plan in Diodorus which I have been discussing is then far later than Alexander, and my second question is this: allowing that these schemes of conquest grew up, as the Romance grew up, to glorify Alexander's memory, *why* was a document which contained this plan as its chief item put forward in the late Hellenistic period as being Alexander's? The answer is not difficult. I do not know if Diodorus' language means that Alexander was to conquer the Mediterranean littoral only or the countries round that sea—North Africa, Spain, Gaul, Italy; but even if the former meaning be the right one, the carrying out of the plan would have put Alexander in possession of what was to be the (territorial) kernel of the Roman State (Rome itself apart). He was to have what Rome in fact did have—γῆς καὶ θαλάσσης σκῆπτρα καὶ μοναρχίαν,[1] as Pseudo-Lycophron had already written about Rome after Cynoscephalae, a prophecy which was to attain its full significance when Augustus appropriated the phrase *terra marique* to himself (see § C, p. 25 n. 3). Now Livy, in a famous disquisition,[2] set himself to consider what would have happened had Alexander attacked Rome, and in the course of it he referred to certain 'very unimportant Greeks', *levissimi ex Graecis*[3]—would that he had named them[4]—who had gone on asserting repeatedly (*dictitare solent*) that Rome could not have faced Alexander; one at least of them had made unpleasant remarks about Carrhae,[5] and between them they stung Livy's patriotism to the eloquent panegyric we possess on the Rome of Alexander's day. The words *dictitare solent* show that Livy was dealing with a circle of ideas spread over a certain period of time, not with a single utterance; the

---

1 *Alexandra*, 1229. Arrian made the connection, p. 394 n. 1 *ante*.
2 Livy IX, 17–19.
3 Livy IX, 18, 6. Jacoby, *F.Gr. Hist.* II, no. 88, T. 9 prints this passage among his testimonia for Timagenes, which is quite unwarranted; that Livy meant Timagenes has never been anything but guesswork, and 'dictitare solent' *cannot* refer to a single writer.
4 This helps to show how much of Hellenistic literature has perished without trace. For one possibility see Tarn, *Bactria and India*, p. 51.
5 'Qui Parthorum quoque contra nomen Romanum gloriae favent.' 'Gloria' in this context cannot refer to anything before Carrhae.

reference to Carrhae, 53 B.C., shows that the time we are dealing with may be called the middle of the first century B.C. This was the circle of ideas from which came the story of Rome's embassy to Alexander;[1] this was the circle of ideas in which the document giving Alexander's 'plans' saw the light; and this was the reason why that document attributed to him a plan for the conquest of the kernel of the Roman State. We can almost hear one of the *levissimi* speaking: 'So you Romans have now got the Mediterranean and its coasts, the sceptres of land and sea—γῆς καὶ θαλάσσης σκῆπτρα. Well and good. But if Alexander had lived, those sceptres would have been his—here's his plan—and where would you have been then?'

There is one further point. The importance of this 'plan' is that it has become the sole support of the belief in Alexander's 'World-kingdom' (p. 378); and the 'plan' itself affords no historical basis for such a belief. What the 'World-kingdom' exactly means to those who use the word I have never known.[2] In antiquity, Alexander was going to conquer either the οἰκουμένη,[3] or Europe, Asia and Africa,[4] or the world up to the bounds of Ocean;[5] but also Diodorus called his actual realm the 'world',[6] as others used similar expressions of the realm of this or that Roman Emperor.[7] In modern times, any idea of further conquest has seemed to serve, but I fancy the οἰκουμένη is usually meant, though it has been common enough to call his actual kingdom a *Weltreich*,[8] as the Roman Empire gets called a World-State. It is all hopelessly vague. I have sometimes been told that it is impossible for me to believe that Alexander dreamt of the unity of mankind, as I do,

---

1 On the ascription of this embassy to Cleitarchus see § C, pp. 21 *sqq.*; on the embassy itself App. 23, p. 376, which shows that the story must be later than the document which gave the other fictitious embassies.

2 Professor Berve, *Klio*, XXXI, 1938, p. 168, promised a study of Alexander's *Weltherrschaftsgedanken*.

3 That is the meaning of the Diodorus plan. The *word* is used in Diod. XVII, 113, 1.

4 Arr. IV, 7, 5 shows that there was such a story. The same story is told of Pompey (Plut. *Pomp.* XXXVIII) and of Caesar (Plut. *Caes.* LVIII); which of the three stories came first I do not know.

5 *Id.* V, 26, 2.

6 Diod. XVIII, 50, 2, τὰ ὅλα. The context shows clearly what is meant.

7 *I.G.R.R.* I, 901, Augustus is τὸν πάσης γῆς καὶ πάσης θαλάσσης ἄρχοντα; *ib.* I, 772, Alexander Severus is δεσπότης γῆς καὶ θαλάσσης καὶ παντὸς ἀνθρωπίνου γένους. So in Pliny, III, 39, Italy is chosen by the gods to be 'una cunctarum gentium in toto orbe patria'.

8 Most recently, e.g. V. Ehrenberg, *Alexander and the Greeks*, 1938, pp. 39, 61, 83, 'empire of the world'.

without also believing that he desired to conquer the world, as I do not. That is merely a confusion of thought; but it is a conceivable *theory* that, if he both believed that all men were brothers, and also desired that the peoples of the world he knew, whether in his Empire or not, should live in unity and concord (see App. 25, VI), then he must have desired to bring all peoples under his rule in order to promote their unity. But the few facts known afford no support to such a theory. He never even possessed the whole Persian empire; when he died, a huge and contiguous block of territory was still unconquered:[1] Bithynia and Paphlagonia;[2] Cappadocia and Pontus, the realm of Ariarathes; the whole of Armenia, the fiction of a satrap of Armenia being abandoned by his generals the moment he was dead.[3] Cappadocia-Pontus is especially important, because under a Persian dynast this large kingdom flanked, and threatened, Alexander's sole line of communication across Asia Minor, and after Issus it cost Antigonus three battles to keep the communications open (§ G, pp. 110 *sq.*); yet those who believe that the 'plans' are his have also to believe that, while after his death Perdiccas saw that his first task must be to remove this threat, Alexander himself never thought about it and proposed instead to go off to the farthest West. But the vital matter is that, as already mentioned, when he quitted India he *abandoned* the eastern Punjab, though it had cost him hard fighting, and formally handed it over to Porus,[4] while he himself turned his thoughts to exploration, not conquest; those who wish to rule the world do not of themselves give away hard-won provinces. All these things are pointers which point away from Alexander having held any ideas of unlimited conquest; there is no evidence that he did hold any such ideas, and there is one fact, the eastern Punjab, which is to me conclusive against it. It is, I suppose, open to anyone, who so desires, to believe that Alexander *must* have wished to conquer and rule all the world or any further part of it; but he must realise clearly that, in the present state of our knowledge, such a belief is only a speculation from the land of dreams and has nothing to do with history.[5]

1 Later times remembered this very well; see the Livy-Trogus speech of Mithridates (Justin XXXVIII, 7, 2), which enumerates all these countries.
2 Paphlagonia became independent when Calas was killed in Bithynia (references in Berve II, no. 397); his successor Demarchus was not satrap of either country.
3 No satrap of Armenia was appointed at either Babylon or Triparadeisos.
4 Arr. VI, 2, 1 explicitly mentions a formal ceremony.
5 A view has been put forward (C. A. Robinson, Jr., *A.J.P.* LXI, 1940, p. 411; LXIV, 1943, p. 296) that Arr. IV, 15, 5 *sq.* means that Alexander at Bactra told Pharasmanes of 'his plan of world-conquest'. The passage has

25. BROTHERHOOD AND UNITY

I. THE BACKGROUND

Somewhere between the middle of the fourth century B.C. and the early third century there took place a great revolution in Greek thought. For long, prior to that revolution, Greeks had divided the world they knew into Greeks and non-Greeks; the latter they called barbarians, men who said 'bar-bar', that is, men whose speech could not be understood; generally speaking, they regarded barbarians both as enemies and as inferior people to themselves. But in the third century we meet with a body of opinion which discarded this division; it held that all men were brothers and ought to live together in unity and concord. Few modern writers have had any doubt as to who was the author of this tremendous revolution; it was Zeno, the founder of the Stoic philosophy. But there are several passages in Greek writers which, if they are true, show that the original author was not Zeno but Alexander. Until recently, these passages received very cavalier treatment; some scholars either simply discarded them as unhistorical or else said that it was only a case of late writers attributing to Alexander ideas which they had taken from Stoicism,[1] while others whittled them down to make of them a mere expression of Alexander's policy of fusion, which will be noticed in § VI. The first attempt at a thorough treatment of them was in a lecture I gave before the British Academy in 1933;[2] I give the subsequent literature, so far as known to me, in a note.[3] What I am trying to do in

no reference to world-conquest. What Alexander is supposed to have said (it does not follow that he did say it) is that he could not at that time accept Pharasmanes' offer to guide him to the Euxine, as he must next conquer 'the Indians' (i.e. those whom Darius I had ruled), which would give him all 'Asia' (i.e. the Persian empire, its regular meaning); he would then return to Greece and make a naval and military expedition to the Euxine (i.e. reduce the unconquered northern provinces of Asia Minor, once Darius', and remove the Cappadocian bottleneck). The whole thing refers to the completion of the conquest of Darius' empire, which he did not live to achieve.

1 Kaerst, 1³, 1927, p. 501, who has had a good deal of acceptance.
2 Tarn, 'Alexander the Great and the Unity of Mankind', *Proc. Brit. Acad.* XIX, 1933, p. 123.
3 W. Kolbe, *Die Weltreichsidee Alexanders des Grossen*, 1936; M. H. Fisch, 'Alexander and the Stoics', *A.J.P.* LVIII, 1937, pp. 59, 129; U. Wilcken, 'Die letzten Pläne Alexanders des Grossen', *S.B. Berlin*, XXIV, 1937, pp. 199, 200 [10–11]; H. Berve, 'Die Verschmelzungspolitik Alexanders des Grossen', *Klio*, XXXI, 1938, p. 135; Tarn, 'Alexander, Cynics, and Stoics', *A.J.P.* LX, 1939, p. 41.

this Appendix is to clarify this somewhat involved subject for readers; merely to reprint my own studies would not serve the purpose, though I draw upon them freely where advisable. I have also, I hope, improved upon my earlier treatment of these ideas of Alexander's; they merit all the consideration one can give to them, for they were probably the most important thing about him, and they do more than anything else to negative the stupid but widespread belief that the man whose career was one of the great dividing lines of world-history was a mere conqueror. I am postponing Alexander himself, that is to say the meaning and bearing of the Greek passages to which I have referred, to the end of this study (§ vi), so as to get all the preliminary considerations out of the way first; but there is no reason why anyone who prefers should not read § vi first. I may, however, for the reader's convenience, indicate here very briefly the conclusion to which this study leads. In 1933 I referred everything about Alexander to a single idea; it can now be seen that what we possess relates, I will not say to three ideas, but to an idea which had three facets or aspects, and these must be distinguished, though they are closely interconnected. The first is that God is the common Father of mankind, which may be called the brotherhood of man. The second is Alexander's dream of the various races of mankind, so far as known to him, becoming of one mind together and living in unity and concord, which may be called the unity of mankind. And the third, also part of his dream, is that the various peoples of his Empire might be partners in the realm rather than subjects. The keynote of the whole is the conception of Homonoia, a word which will run through this study. It means 'a being of one mind together'; it was to become the symbol of the world's longing for something better than everlasting wars. There is no word in English to translate it. It signifies far more than its Latin translation *concordia* or our 'concord'; 'to live in concord' can be satisfied by the negative meaning 'to live without quarrelling', a thing that can be done by people of very different mentalities and outlooks. 'Unity' might pass, but is too vague; the English political catchword of a generation ago, a 'union of hearts', is better, but hearts are not minds; so I shall keep the Greek word Homonoia throughout.[1]

By way of introduction to the matter under consideration I had better indicate briefly Alexander's background, the notions ruling the

1 It has other meanings which do not come in question here, such as a political Entente, something less than συμμαχία, Alexis fr. 244 Kock (II, p. 386), Ditt.³ 434–5, 1, 32; it is even used for a κοινόν of villages, Sir W. M. Ramsay, *J.H.S.* IV, 1883, pp. 386–8. See generally Tarn, *Hell. Civ.*² p. 84.

world of thought when he appeared. I need not go into details of what happened before Aristotle, for Alexander himself started his career with Aristotle's ideas in his head, and outgrew them in the light of his own experience and not by reading the works of Greek Sophists, if indeed those works have any bearing on the matter. There are some expressions in earlier literature, principally in the Sophists, which have been taken to show that this or that man thought of something better than a hard and fast division of humanity into Greeks and barbarians, friends and enemies;[1] but this comes to very little, if it comes to anything at all,[2] for there is no doubt that when a Greek before Alexander talked of 'all men', or used some equivalent expression, what he meant was 'all Greeks';[3] the barbarian did not count. A Herodotus might suggest that Persians possessed courage and organising powers; a Xenophon, when he wanted to portray an ideal shepherd of the people, might choose a Persian king as shepherd of the Persian people; but Greeks did not want a shepherd, and all Herodotus got for his pains was the nickname ὁ φιλοβάρβαρος, friend of barbarians. Of course, pretty well all we know comes from Athens (even Herodotus worked there), and it may be that the views of cities like Miletus or Cyrene, whose citizen bodies had a good deal of barbarian blood, were not precisely the same; but they have left us no information. All that needs to be said is that the expressions to which I have referred, if they *do* mean anything—I do not think they do—had no importance for history,[4] for in the fourth century the whole thing was swept aside by

1 Max Mühl, *Die antike Menschheitsidee in ihrer geschichtlichen Entwicklung*, 1928 (an excellent book), has made the most of this that can be made, pp. 3–12.
2 See the lengthy note 6 to my lecture of 1933 (on p. 29, l. 14, for 'Athenian' read 'Greek'). The fragments of the sophist Antiphon περὶ ὁμονοίας cannot in my opinion refer to all mankind, though this has been claimed for them; I agree with J. Mewaldt, *Genethliakon W. Schmid*, 1929, pp. 81–3, that this cannot be made out.
3 The use of 'all men' for 'all Greeks' is common enough; I give one or two proven instances. Compare Isocrates, *Panegyr.* 56, Heracles ἅπαντας ἀνθρώπους εὐεργέτησεν, with *Philippus*, 14, τὴν φιλανθρωπίαν—ἣν εἶχεν (Heracles) εἰς τοὺς Ἕλληνας (only two stories of his benefiting non-Greeks seem known and both are later than Alexander). Compare again the two passages from Lysias cited by E. Skard, *Zwei religiös-politische Begriffe: Euergetes-Concordia*, 1932, p. 43, one of which speaks of 'Greeks', the other of 'all men'. There is another clear case in Diod. XIII, 26, 3: Athens has made the law of suppliants respected παρὰ πᾶσιν ἀνθρώποις, i.e. throughout the Greek world. So to-day people say 'Everybody thinks' or 'the whole world knows', when what they mean is their own circle.
4 Even Mühl admits (*op. cit.* p. 11) that any idea of a common humanity in this period was not a factor in history.

the dominant idealist philosophies. Plato and Aristotle left no doubt about *their* views. Plato, who boasted that Athenians were pure Greek and not half-breeds at bottom (μιξοβάρβαροι) like some cities,[1] said that all barbarians were enemies by nature; it was proper to wage war upon them, even to the point of enslaving or extirpating them.[2] Aristotle agreed, and added that all barbarians were slaves by nature, especially those of Asia; they had not the qualities which entitled them to be free men, and it was proper to treat them as slaves.[3] His ideal State cared for nothing but its own citizens; it was a small aristocracy of Greek citizens ruling over a barbarian peasantry[4] who cultivated the land for their masters and had no share in the State—a thing he had seen in some Greek cities of Asia Minor.[5] Certainly neither Plato nor Aristotle was quite consistent; Plato might treat an Egyptian priest as the repository of wisdom, Aristotle might suggest that the constitution of Carthage was worth studying; but their main position was clear enough, as is the impression Alexander must have got from his tutor Aristotle.

Aristotle's older contemporary Isocrates was however important, from his extension of the use of Homonoia. Homonoia had begun by meaning the natural unity of the family,[6] but had early become extended to mean unity in the city, the natural unit of Greek political and social life. The Greek world, whatever its practice, never doubted that in theory unity in a city was very desirable;[7] but though the word Homonoia was in common use among Greeks in the fourth century, it chiefly meant absence of faction fights,[8] and this rather negative meaning lasted in the cities throughout the Hellenistic period, as can be seen in the very numerous decrees in honour of the judicial commissions sent from one city to another, which are praised because they tried to

1 *Menexenus* 245 D.
2 Plato, *Rep.* V, 470 C–471 A. Aristotle agreed, *Pol.* I, 8, 1256b, 25.
3 Arist. *Pol.* I, 2, 1252b, 9, ὡς ταὐτὸ φύσει βάρβαρον καὶ δοῦλον ὄν, III, 14, 1285a, 20 (Asia); fr. 658 Rose (Plut. *Mor.* 329B) τοῖς βαρβάροις δεσποτικῶς χρώμενος... ὡς ζῴοις ἢ φυτοῖς.
4 *Pol.* IV (VII), 10, 1330a, 25 *sqq.* On this non-Hellenic basis see W. L. Newman, *The Politics of Aristotle*, I, p. 125.
5 As the Pedieis at Priene, the Mariandyni at Heraclea, the Phrygians at Zelea. See Swoboda, κώμη in PW Supp. Bd. IV, 962.
6 H. Kramer, *Quid valeat ὁμόνοια in litteris Graecis*, 1915, pp. 45–9. See also Chariton's story about the temple of Homonoia in Miletus, cited by Zwicker, 'Homonoia' in PW, 2266.
7 Xen. *Mem.* IV, 4, 16, ὁμόνοιά γε μέγιστον ἀγαθὸν δοκεῖ ταῖς πόλεσιν εἶναι. See further on the classical period Kramer, *op. cit.* p. 18 and *passim*.
8 See the long *negative* list in Isocrates, *Panath.* 259.

compose internal discord.[1] There was hardly a trace as yet of the more positive sense which Homonoia was to acquire later—a mental attitude which should make war or faction impossible because the parties were at one; and Isocrates extended the application of the word without enlarging its meaning. He took up a suggestion of the sophist Gorgias and proposed to treat the whole Greek world as one and the futile wars between city and city as faction fights—to apply Homonoia to the Greek *race*.[2] For this purpose he utilised Plato's idea (it was much older than Plato) that the barbarian was a natural enemy,[3] and decided that the way to unite Greeks was to attack Persia: 'I come', he said, 'to advocate two things: war against the barbarian, Homonoia between ourselves.'[4] But somebody had to do the uniting; and Isocrates bethought him of Heracles, benefactor of the Greek race, and urged King Philip of Macedonia, a descendant of Heracles, to play the part.[5] But if Philip was to be Heracles and bring about the Homonoia of the Greek world, the way was being prepared for two important ideas of a later time: the essential quality of the king must be that love of man, φιλανθρωπία, which had led Heracles to perform his labours,[6] and the essential business of the king was to promote Homonoia;[7] so far this only applied to Greeks, but if its meaning were to deepen it would still be the king's business. The actual result of all this, the League of Corinth under Philip's presidency, was not quite what Isocrates had dreamt of.

This then was the background against which Alexander appeared.

---

1 Tarn, *Hell. Civ.*[2] 1930, p. 84.   2 Kramer, *op. cit.* pp. 38 *sqq.*
3 *Panegyr.* 184, *Panath.* 163.   4 *Panegyr.* 3.
5 *Philippus* 114, 116; Skard, *op. cit.* pp. 56–7; Kaerst I[3], pp. 142–9; U. Wilcken, *Alexander der Grosse*, 1931, pp. 30–3. Whatever view Greeks took of Macedonians, in their eyes Philip ranked as a Greek, for his forbears had long been admitted to the Olympian games. What that meant is shown by no Roman being admitted, so far as is known, till the time of Augustus (J. Jüthner, *Hellenen und Barbaren*, 1923, p. 69).
6 In *Philippus* 114 Isocrates called on Philip to show φιλανθρωπία like Heracles. On the development of φιλανθρωπία generally see S. Lorenz, *De progressu notionis* φιλανθρωπίας, 1914, pp. 14, 35 (with the necessary correction made by Mühl, *op. cit.* p. 120 n. 55, that the Cynics before Alexander knew nothing of any general love of humanity), and S. Tromp de Ruiter, *Mnemosyne*, LIX, 1931, p. 271. On φιλανθρωπία as the characteristic virtue of a Hellenistic king see Kaerst II[2], p. 321 and references, and cf. F. Schroeter, *De regum hellenisticorum epistulis in lapidibus servatis quaestiones stilisticae*, 1932, pp. 26 n. 1, 45.
7 Isocrates, *Nicocles* 41, lays down the principle: χρὴ τοὺς ὀρθῶς βασιλεύοντας... τὰς πόλεις ἐν ὁμονοίᾳ πειρᾶσθαι διάγειν.

The business of a Macedonian king was to be a benefactor of Greeks to the extent of preventing inter-city warfare; he was to promote Homonoia among Greeks and utilise their enmity to barbarians as a bond of union; but barbarians themselves were still enemies and slaves by nature, a view which Aristotle emphasised when he advised his pupil to treat Greeks as free men, but barbarians as slaves. And this is what has to be kept in mind when we come to consider how far Alexander advanced beyond it for himself.

II. THE CYNICS

Before following the further development of the Homonoia concept, which ultimately almost became a symbol of the world's longing for something better than everlasting war, it may be well to say what is necessary about a subordinate matter which stands by itself, the supposed relation of Alexander's ideas to those of the Cynics of his day. The suggestion of some relationship between him and the Cynics, in some form or other, is old; the shape it has taken in the most recent work dealing with the matter[1] has been that Onesicritus the Cynic managed in his book to attribute to Alexander Cynic cosmopolitanism (I dislike using this horrible word, but there is no other in English which gives the meaning). I have said enough about Onesicritus elsewhere,[2] and there is no need to repeat it; but it may be advisable to state plainly once again that Alexander could neither have borrowed Cynic cosmopolitanism, nor have had it attributed to him, for the simple reason that there was no such thing, quite apart from the fact that Alexander himself never contemplated a 'World-State'. One has read of Cynic cosmopolitanism till one is weary—that man was a citizen, not of this or that country, but of a World-State which knew no countries; but it does not seem to have occurred to any one to investigate the matter. The evidence against it is conclusive, and all I need do here is to give it; but no doubt Cynic cosmopolitanism will continue to figure in books for many a long year.

And first, what was Cynicism? It was not a *philosophy* like those of the four schools, with a body of doctrine; it was a way of life, a mode of thought,[3] and was entirely *negative*; you were to discard everything on which civilisation had been built up, and often enough, unless you

1 M. H. Fisch, *A.J.P.* LVIII, 1937, pp. 129 *sqq.*
2 Tarn, *A.J.P.* LX, 1939, pp. 47 *sqq.*
3 Well brought out by D. R. Dudley, *A history of Cynicism*, 1937, pp. 7 *sqq.*

were a Crates or a Demonax, you ended by finding nothing at the
bottom but mere animalism. It never *constructed* anything, anything
which affected men otherwise than as individuals; Cynicism and
universalism are a contradiction in terms. This was what so puzzled
Zeller; he, like others, took Cynic 'cosmopolitanism' for granted, but
could not reconcile it with Cynicism as he knew it.[1]

Three things are commonly quoted in support of Cynic 'cosmopolitanism'—certainly there is nothing else—and I will take first those
two which are remarks attributed to Diogenes by Diogenes Laertius;
no Cynic but Diogenes himself comes in question. The historical
Diogenes of Sinope, founder of Cynicism, became the subject of a
legend which made of him the ideal philosophic saint; it is very difficult
to disentangle the real man from the legendary figure, and many of the
sayings attributed to him and of the stories told about him, like those
which made him meet Alexander, are merely figments of the legend.[2]
I will assume, however, that he did make the two remarks in question.
The first was when somebody asked him where he came from, i.e. from
what city, and he replied κοσμοπολίτης,[3] literally 'I am a citizen of,
or in, the universe'. The circumstances were that the dominant party
in Sinope had wrongfully accused and imprisoned his father, who had
died in consequence, and had driven Diogenes himself into exile;[4] and
when asked what his city was, the exile in effect replied 'I have none'.
I will come to the actual meaning presently. The word so far as is
known was never again used by any Greek, for Lucian's reference to
the remark in his skit on Diogenes differs;[5] it occurs twice in Philo,
but he was a Jew. Had it come into use as a catchword, it must, like
other philosophical catchwords, have found its way into the tradition.

1 *Socrates and the Socratic schools* (Eng. trans.), p. 276.
2 It will suffice to refer to the long examination by Kurt von Fritz, 'Quellen-
untersuchungen zu Leben und Philosophie des Diogenes von Sinope',
Philol. Supp. Bd. XVIII, 1926, though even he hardly goes far enough.
Diogenes-legends went on being manufactured for centuries (Epictetus
has some new ones), like Alexander-legends in India, where new ones
have originated even under British rule.
3 Diog. Laert. VI, 63, ἐρωτηθεὶς πόθεν εἴη, κοσμοπολίτης ἔφη.
4 Dudley, *op. cit.* p. 21, from Mr C. T. Seltman's unpublished paper
'Diogenes of Sinope, son of the banker Hikesias'. This paper, on the
coinage of Sinope, was read at the Numismatic Congress in 1936; a brief
résumé appeared in the *Transactions* of that Congress, p. 121, and in
Proc. Camb. Philol. Soc. CXLII–CXLIV, p. 7; a more detailed synopsis is
given by Dudley, *op. cit.* pp. 54–5.
5 *Vit. auct.* 8: Diogenes calls himself παντοδαπός and says τοῦ κόσμου
πολίτην ὁρᾶς. For what he *did* mean see next page.

The second remark, which gives the meaning of the word, has invariably been quoted without its context,[1] a bad habit; the first clause, down to λέγων, has always been omitted, and πολιτεία ἐν κόσμῳ has been mistranslated as World-State or some equivalent expression. What the Greek says is this: 'Diogenes laughed at things like long descent and fame, saying that they were merely ornaments which concealed the evil that was behind them; the one true (or real) citizenship was that in the universe.' The πολιτεία ἐν κόσμῳ, then, has to be something which either gets rid of claims to fame and long descent altogether or else renders them meaningless; and no form of State, even world-wide, would prevent people being proud of their pedigrees or prevent some men being of greater repute than others. There has never been any reason to doubt Epictetus' interpretation, however much it may have been neglected. How, he asks (III, 22, 47), does a man live without city or home? Well, the god sent a man (Diogenes) to show you. 'Look at me', he said; 'I have no home, no city, no possessions, no family; I have only the earth and the sky.' That is the 'citizenship in the universe', and that is the meaning of κοσμοπολίτης.[2] He was free of the earth and the sky;[3] it mattered nothing to him where or how he lived; one place, as Epictetus says (III, 24, 66), was as good as another, whether he lived as a free man in Athens, a captive among pirates, or a slave in Corinth. Plutarch, in his treatise *On Exile*, makes his exile say exactly the same thing: the bounds of our country are the earth and the sky (αἰθήρ); there none is an exile, none a stranger, but all men are fellow-citizens with one another.[4]

The third thing that is supposed to support the idea of Cynic 'cosmopolitanism' is that Diogenes wrote a *Politeia*, an ideal State. Certainly in the third century B.C. a work existed called Διογένους Πολιτεία. Little is known of its contents. It said that knucklebones

---

1 Diog. Laert. VI, 72, εὐγενείας δὲ καὶ δόξας καὶ τὰ τοιαῦτα πάντα διέπαιζε, προκοσμήματα κακίας λέγων· μόνην δὲ ὀρθὴν πολιτείαν εἶναι τὴν ἐν κόσμῳ.

2 Much of the trouble has arisen from the assumption that, because κοσμοπολίτης is the same word as the modern 'cosmopolitan', it must have the same meaning. Yet instances of such change of meaning are legion.

3 I cannot refrain from quoting de Musset's lines about Brutus after Philippi, when all was lost; weary of earth

'il contemplait les cieux;
Il n'avait rien perdu dans cet immense espace;
Il lui restait encore son épée et ses dieux.'

4 Plut. *Mor.* 601 A–B, the whole passage, which is too long to quote.

should be current coin and that weapons of war were useless;[1] it probably advocated community of women;[2] it may have contained a defence of incest and parricide, but this suggestion may only be based on the tragedies attributed to Diogenes, which again may not be his. There is no description anywhere of what the book was, but Plutarch says that its basis (ὑπόθεσις), like those of the States of Plato and Zeno, was Lycurgus' Sparta,[3] and it must therefore have depicted, not anything cosmopolitan, but a small State with narrow limits, as did Plato, and Zeno in his early *Politeia* (on which see § iv). It is therefore neither evidence nor argument for Cynic cosmopolitanism, even if Diogenes did write it.

But it is quite uncertain if he did, or whether it is one of the numerous Hellenistic works attributed by their authors to well-known names. The evidence stands thus. The Stoic Cleanthes (262–230) asserted that it was written by Diogenes, and praised it.[4] His successor Chrysippus (230—Olympiad 208–204) referred to it as by Diogenes in six different works, and also praised it.[5] Philodemus in the first century B.C. made his Stoic protagonist admit that some in his day, τινὲς τῶν καθ᾽ ἡμᾶς, did not think it genuine, but made him appeal for its genuineness to 'library catalogues and libraries',[6] which means no more than (say) it means to-day that in any library you will find the *de Fluviis* bound up in any edition of Plutarch. There was then a Stoic tradition from the middle of the third century that the work was genuine. On the other hand, Satyrus, who lived and worked in Alexandria in the latter part of the third century, asserted that Diogenes wrote nothing at all,[7] as did Sosicrates of Rhodes, who may or may not have worked at Alexandria, in the second century;[8] while Sotion of Alexandria (*c.* 200–170 B.C.) gave a short list of Diogenes' works which differed considerably from the orthodox list given by Diogenes Laertius but

1 Philodemus, περὶ Στωϊκῶν, *P. Herc.* 339 P, col. xiv, l. 1, in W. Crönert, *Kolotes und Menedemos* (vol. 6 of Wessely's *Studien zur Palaeographie und Papyruskunde*, 1906), p. 61; Athen. iv, 159c.
2 Dudley, *op. cit.* p. 36.   3 Plut. *Lycurg.* xxxi.
4 *S.V.F.* i, 590=Philodemus *ib.* col. xiii, l. 21.
5 Philodemus *ib.* cols. xiii, l. 26–xiv, l. 29. Dudley, *op. cit.* pp. 25 *sq.*, may be correct in saying that Chrysippus 'attested' its genuineness, but Diog. Laert. vii, 34, which he cites, refers only to the *Politeia* of Zeno.
6 Philodemus *ib.* col. xiii, ll. 12 *sqq.*, αἵ τ᾽ ἀναγραφαὶ τῶν πινάκων αἵ τε βιβλιοθῆκαι. Crönert left it open whether this meant Callimachus' *Pinakes* or only Cynic, or Stoic, lists; surely, had the former been meant, it must have been ἀναγραφή.
7 Diog. Laert. vi, 80, and on Satyrus' date Gudeman, 'Satyros' (16) in PW.
8 Diog. Laert. *ib.*, and on Sosicrates' date Laqueur, 'Sosikrates' in PW.

which did not include the *Politeia*.[1] Satyrus and Sotion were Peripatetics; Satyrus wrote semi-popular biographies, including *Lives* of the philosophers, while Sotion and Sosicrates wrote *Successions* of the philosophers. Nobody supposes that Satyrus investigated the question of the authenticity of Diogenes' *Politeia* for himself; he repeated his statement from some one before him.[2] There was then at Alexandria a Peripatetic tradition from the middle of the third century that the *Politeia* of Diogenes was a forgery. Neither the Stoic nor the Peripatetic tradition can be traced further back than the middle of that century.

The current explanation of the problem, as given by von Fritz (*op. cit.* pp. 55–7) and adopted by Dudley (*op. cit.* pp. 25 *sq.*), is that Diogenes' *Politeia* was genuine, but that in course of time the Stoics became ashamed of it; and as they now desired to attach themselves to Socrates by means of a fictitious succession Socrates—Antisthenes—Diogenes—Crates—Zeno (this is true), they, or rather Sotion, committed a fraud by omitting the *Politeia* from among Diogenes' works. The explanation is impossible. If Stoics wanted to commit a fraud of this sort, it can only have been after Chrysippus' death (Olympiad 208–204 B.C.), for he was all-powerful in the school and regularly assumed the genuineness of the book; but Chrysippus' contemporary Satyrus had already asserted that Diogenes wrote nothing at all, i.e. that the *Politeia* was not his. This seems conclusive against von Fritz's explanation, apart from the fact that he does not explain why a Peripatetic at Alexandria, where it is not known that there ever were any Stoics, should lend himself to a Stoic fraud.[3] As a fact, the Stoics did, later on, try a somewhat similar fraud at Pergamum by means of the Stoic librarian Athenodorus, who was detected;[4] and if they could not bring off such a thing at Pergamum, with the library there in their hands, they had no chance at Alexandria, where they had no following. It is unfortunate that it is not known how Callimachus catalogued the work in his *Pinakes*, which would probably have sufficed to settle the

1 Diog. Laert. VI, 80; Susemihl I, p. 498; Stenzel, 'Sotion' (1) in PW.
2 Gudeman, *op. cit.*, suggested Callimachus. But that is unfortunately guesswork.
3 von Fritz, *op. cit.* p. 57, says that first the Stoics (meaning here Satyrus and Sosicrates) denied that Diogenes ever wrote anything at all, and then found it safer to attribute to him some works of their own invention (Sotion). But (*a*) Satyrus was not a Stoic, and it is not known that Sosicrates was; (*b*) Sotion was not a Stoic and comes in date *between* them. This theory, therefore, cannot be supported.
4 Diog. Laert. VII, 34; Susemihl II, p. 246.

matter; we merely have the two opposed traditions, the Stoic that it was genuine, the Peripatetic that it was not; neither side possessed the modern technique for detecting forgeries, and no decision is possible. This reinforces what, as we have seen, is clear from the work itself, that the Διογένους Πολιτεία furnishes no evidence in favour of Cynic 'cosmopolitanism'. But if I were compelled to give an opinion on the genuineness or otherwise of the work, I should follow Alexandria; for, while the early Stoics had an axe to grind in the matter, the Peripatetics, which means Alexandrian learning, had not. If the work *was* a forgery, it was doubtless put together on the lines of, and presumably from, Zeno's early *Politeia*.

It is quite clear in any case that neither did Alexander borrow Cynic 'cosmopolitanism' nor could it have been attributed to him; for there was no such thing.

III. Homonoia and the Line of Kingship

I must now return to the consideration of Homonoia, taking it up from where it was left at the end of § 1. We saw that part of the background against which Alexander appeared was that it was (in theory) the business of a Macedonian king to promote Homonoia, but only among Greeks; barbarians were still enemies and slaves by nature. I must now leave Alexander for a moment and take up the connection of Homonoia with kingship after his time, and, so far as the fragmentary nature of our material permits, follow this down the line of kingship, just taking the salient points, and see to what it leads.

Kingship after Alexander became so important that for some time there was hardly a philosopher who did not write a treatise upon it, giving his views of the theory of kingship and the duties of a king. Nearly all this literature has perished; but among the debris we happen to possess some illuminating fragments from two otherwise unknown writers, Diotogenes and an author whose work passed as that of an ancient Pythagorean, Ecphantus.[1] Both are called Pythagoreans, and there is no reason to doubt this; they were certainly not Stoics, and it is important to note in this respect that they wrote in Doric. They belong to the early third century, when the theory of kingship was still in the constructive stage; Diotogenes was contemporary with Demetrius

---

1 These fragments, preserved by Stobaeus, IV, 7, 61–6, have been discussed by E. R. Goodenough, *The Political Philosophy of Hellenistic Kingship*, Yale Class. Studies, I, 1928, p. 55, a study to which I am much indebted.

the Besieger.[1] The theory of Pseudo-Ecphantus comes to this: as the king, who is Living Law (that idea is Aristotle's),[2] corresponds upon earth to the divine ruler of the universe, and as in an earthly State existence is impossible without fellowship and love, it is the king's business to promote these things as a copy of the Homonoia of the universe (meaning the heavens).[3] The theory of Diotogenes is very similar. The king, who is Living Law, bears the same relation to the State as God does to the universe; for the State, formed by the harmonising together of different elements, is an imitation of the order and harmony of the universe; therefore the king must harmonise the

1 Apart from the doctrine of these writers, which points to the early third century, there seems definite evidence for the date of Diotogenes in Stob. IV, 7, 62 (p. 268 Hense). The king must not, in overweening pride, hold aloof from the troubles of other men and rank himself near to the gods; this is Demetrius the Besieger, who was notorious for his inaccessibility to his subjects (τὸ δυσόμιλον καὶ δυσπρόσοδον, Plut. *Dem.* XLII), his pride (*ib.*), and acting·the god (on the whole matter see Tarn, *Antigonos Gonatas*, pp. 90–1; K. Scott, *A.J.P.* XLIX, 1928, p. 226). But (the fragment continues) his appearance, walk, and carriage, and also his ἦθος, must strike beholders with awe and wonder; this again is Demetrius (on his appearance and ἦθος see Plut. *Dem.* 11), whom strangers followed merely to gaze upon (Diod. XX, 92, 3). The parallels in phrasing are numerous; besides ἦθος, cf. Diotogenes κατακοσμαθῆμεν καταπεπλαγμένως with Diodorus κεκοσμημένην and Plutarch ἔκπληξιν, and the summary of the whole effect as εὐπρέπειαν in Diodorus and ἐπιπρέπῃαν in Diotogenes. This use of Demetrius as the illustration for kingship shows that Diotogenes was his contemporary, or nearly so; for one of the extraordinary things about Demetrius was that (professed historians apart) no one, not even legend, took any further notice of him once the generation which had known him was dead. Indeed, the language shows that Diotogenes most probably was writing this during the time of Demetrius' power and prosperity. The question has been raised whether the Pythagorean ascription and Doric dialect of these writers might not have been adopted 'in order that the treatises might not be taken as criticisms of contemporary actuality': A. D. Nock, *Harvard Theol. Rev.* XXXIII, 1940, p. 312 n. 54.

2 *Pol.* III, 13, 1284a, 13: αὐτοὶ γάρ εἰσι νόμος (of the παμβασιλεύς, the θεὸς ἐν ἀνθρώποις). Goodenough, p. 85, derives the conception from Persia, which might have played a part in its extension from the παμβασιλεύς to every king; but Diotogenes' words in 61 (p. 265 H), αὐτὸς ὢν νόμος ἔμψυχος, θεὸς ἐν ἀνθρώποις παρεσχαμάτισται, admit of no doubt that he is explicitly quoting Aristotle. See App. 22, II, pp. 366–8.

3 Stob. *ib.* 64, the whole fragment, especially p. 275 H: συνεστάναι γὰρ χωρὶς φιλίας καὶ κοινωνίας ἀμάχανον....ἃ δ' ἐν τᾷ πόλει φιλία...τὰν τῶ παντὸς ὁμόνοιαν μεμίμαται· ἄνευ δὲ τᾶς περὶ τὰς ἀρχὰς διατάξιος οὐδεμία ἂν πόλις οἰκοῖτο.

State.¹ Both then agree that, whether a good disposition of the State be called Harmony or Homonoia, it is the king's business to bring it about; and a writer of a later time, Musonius, alludes to this view as having been widespread.² But the kings whom these two authors had in mind were the Hellenistic monarchs, who ruled over subjects of many races, Greeks and barbarians; and the subjects whose unity the king is to promote are implicitly taken throughout to be *all* his subjects without distinction.³ Now the last thing we saw in this connection (p. 403) was Isocrates urging Philip of Macedon to bring about Homonoia between the Greek cities in order to attack Persia; and here are two writers saying in effect that the king must promote Homonoia between the Greeks and the barbarians over whom his arm reached; that is, Homonoia has ceased to be confined to Greeks and has been extended to include men of any race. Certainly this was not the discovery of these two obscure writers; and as both say much the same thing, something of importance must have happened between Isocrates and themselves.

The next landmark is Iambulus,⁴ author of the best-known of the Greek communistic Utopias, situated upon the Islands of the Sun somewhere in the Indian Ocean. Iambulus is later than Megasthenes and earlier than Aristonicus, that is, between about 290 and 133 B.C.; but he belongs to the constructive period and ought therefore to be

1 Stob. *ib.* 61 (p. 265 H): ἔχει δὲ καὶ ὡς θεὸς ποτὶ κόσμον βασιλεὺς ποτὶ πόλιν, καὶ ὡς πόλις ποτὶ κόσμον βασιλεὺς ποτὶ θεόν. ἃ μὲν γὰρ πόλις ἐκ πολλῶν καὶ διαφερόντων συναρμοσθεῖσα κόσμω σύνταξιν καὶ ἁρμονίαν μεμίμαται· and the king, being a god among men, must (p. 264) harmonise the state, ⟨ποτ⟩ τὰν αὐτὰν ἁρμονίαν συναρμόζεσθαι.

2 Stob. *ib.* 67 (p. 283 H): εἴ περ δεῖ αὐτόν, ὥσπερ ἐδόκει τοῖς παλαιοῖς, νόμον ἔμψυχον εἶναι, εὐνομίαν μὲν καὶ ὁμόνοιαν μηχανώμενον, ἀνομίαν δὲ καὶ στάσιν ἀπείργοντα, ζηλωτὴν δὲ τοῦ Διὸς ὄντα καὶ πατέρα τῶν ἀρχομένων, ὥσπερ ἐκεῖνον.

3 The king binding all his subjects together in κοινωνία represents the idea that only a king, above and outside all divisions among his subjects, could bind Greek and barbarian together. It is allied to the Hellenistic doctrine of the king as benefactor of all men, so common later but already expressed for the third century by Pseudo-Aristeas, 281: ὡς θεὸς εὐεργετεῖ τὸν ὅλον κόσμον, οὕτως καὶ σὺ μιμούμενος ἀπρόσκοπος ἂν εἴης.

4 Diod. II, 55–60; Susemihl, *op. cit.* I, p. 324; E. Rohde, *Der griechische Roman²*, 1900, pp. 241 *sqq.*; W. Kroll, 'Iambulus' in PW; R. von Pöhlmann, *Gesch. der sozialen Frage und des Sozialismus in der antiken Welt*, 3rd ed., by F. Oertel, 1925, I, pp. 404–9; II, p. 570 n. 3; Tarn, *J.R.S.* XXII, 1932, pp. 140, 147; J. Bidez, *La cité du monde et la cité du soleil chez les Stoïciens*, Paris, 1932, pp. 39 *sqq.* Probably Iambulus was not the author's real name.

third-century.[1] I need not dwell on his Utopia for its own sake, since its chief importance for my subject lies in the use made of it by Aristonicus; but since it has been claimed as Stoic,[2] and as, if this were so, it would have no business in the line of kingship, I must run through its main features. The people were divided into systems, each system being ruled by a governor whose power was seemingly absolute[3] but who had to die at a given age. Wives were held in common. Slavery was unknown, and each member of each system in turn filled every office, from servant to governor; this was rendered possible by the islands bearing crops all the year round, some of them without human aid. The people worshipped Heaven and the Sun, and buried corpses in the sand of the sea-shore; and they prized Homonoia above all things[4] and lived in perfect unity and concord. The one thing in this Utopia which is Stoic is the absence of classes; nothing else is, not even the equality of the people; for as every one in turn filled every office, circumstances were identical for all, and no Stoic ever claimed that 'equality'—a spiritual matter—meant similar conditions of life.[5] Filling every office in turn has nothing to do with Stoicism; Iambulus took it from Aristotle, who had met the idea somewhere and had criticised it.[6] Absence of slavery was not a Stoic tenet—one wishes it had been; the compulsory death of the governor at a certain age has nothing to do with the Stoic doctrine of voluntary suicide, but was taken from an old tradition at Ceos and other stories of the sort;[7] community of wives does not really represent the promiscuity of Zeno's early *Politeia*, and

1 Later than Megasthenes, as he knows of the Ganges' mouth. The scene is set in the time of one of the three great Mauryas; but as Rohde, p. 241 n. 1, rightly says, that proves nothing. On an attempt, due to a mistake, to date Iambulus in the first century B.C. see Tarn, *C.Q.* XXXIII, 1939, p. 193.

2 Susemihl I, p. 325; Rohde, pp. 258–9, who elaborates it; Bidez, *op. cit.* p. 46; Kroll, *loc. cit.* (practically). I wrongly followed this in *Hell. Civ.*[2], p. 113. No deduction can be drawn from the apparent absence of things like law-courts and temples, as we do not know what the full account may have contained. Not Stoic: Tarn, *Proc. Brit. Acad.* 1933, pp. 141 *sqq.*; Rostovtzeff, *Soc. and Econ. Hist.* 1941, p. 1523 n. 81.

3 Diod. II, 58, 6, τούτῳ πάντες πείθονται.

4 *Ib.* 58, 1, τὴν ὁμόνοιαν περὶ πλείστου ποιουμένους.

5 Chrysippus' comparison of the world to a theatre, which was common to all but in which each had his own place (*S.V.F.* III, fr. 371), implies an acceptance of differences in circumstance, since some seats were of necessity better than others. So Zeno's acceptance of Antigonus as ἴσον καὶ ὅμοιον (*ib.* I, fr. 24) implies that all men were not ὅμοιοι. Iambulus carried equality to the point of general similarity in body.

6 *Pol.* II, 2, 1261a, 35 *sqq.*; IV (VII), 9, 1328b, 24 *sqq.*

7 Ceos, Strab. X, 5, 6 (486). List of similar customs, Rohde, p. 247.

could have been taken from Plato or from some 'nature-people', like Aristotle's 'Libyans of the interior'.[1] Crops growing of themselves were not Stoic, but were taken from stories of the golden age.[2] Stoics did not worship Heaven or the Sun, or for that matter any other of the popular gods; their reverence—one cannot call it worship—was given to the Supreme Power, that Universal Law who was also Destiny and Nature, Providence and God. And lastly, though the careless disposal of corpses may correspond to Stoic doctrine, similar views about the unimportance of burial were held by at least three other philosophic schools.[3] Iambulus in fact has made his own patchwork, and has taken his material wherever he found it; the circular animals with four eyes and four mouths[4] are obviously taken from the circular men with four legs and four arms of Plato's *Symposium*, the edible reeds which wax and wane with the moon[5] are taken from Aristotle's similar statement, long disbelieved but now proved true, about the Suez sea-urchin. What we do get, however, in the statement that above all things the people prized Homonoia, is, once again, the connection of Homonoia with kingship; for Diodorus' account compares the governors to kings.[6] It is a pity that this account—all that we have of Iambulus—is imperfect (for example, it does not say how the several systems were co-ordinated); it does not say that the duty of the governor was to maintain the much prized Homonoia, though it must have been. But the connection is clear; and absolute governors or kings have no place in the earlier Stoic theory (§ IV).

In 133 B.C. Rome purported to take over the kingdom of Pergamum; a slave rising at once broke out, and Aristonicus, who claimed to be the natural heir to the throne, raised a national revolt against Rome and threw in his lot with the slaves, to whom he promised freedom. His mixed following—Greeks, Asiatics of Asia Minor, mercenaries and slaves of many nationalities—gave Rome so much trouble that one can see that there was an idea behind them, and it is known what it was; they are called *Heliopolitai*,[7] citizens of the Sun-State, and the Sun-

---

1 *Pol.* II, 3, 1262a, 19. Other cases from 'nature-peoples': Tarn, *Hell. Civ.*[2], p. 320 n. 1.
2 Plato, *Pol.* 272A; Dicaearchus, *F.H.G.* II, p. 233, fr. 1.
3 Stoics: *S.V.F.* I, fr. 253; III, fr. 752; and see Rohde, pp. 259–60. It was also the view of the Cynics (Diogenes in Cicero, *Tusc. Disp.* I, 43, 104), the Cyrenaeans (Theodorus in Cicero *ib.* 102) and Epicurus (Usener, *Epicurea*, fr. 578). 4 Diod. II, 58, 2–3.
5 *Id.* II, 59, 8. 6 *Id.* II, 58, 6, καθάπερ τις βασιλεύς.
7 Strabo XIV, 1, 38 (646): πλῆθος ἀπόρων τε ἀνθρώπων καὶ δούλων ἐπ' ἐλευθερίᾳ κεκλημένων, οὓς Ἡλιοπολίτας ἐκάλεσε.

State was that of Iambulus.[1] Aristonicus was using Iambulus as an inspiration to his followers, and the kingdom he meant to set up was the kingdom of Homonoia; probably not Iambulus' unworkable Utopia, but something on the lines of the equality and absence of slavery which he had preached, and naturally without distinctions of race. It is the only occasion in antiquity on which Homonoia was to extend, not merely laterally—from one race to another—but vertically, to the depths of the slave world; and the moving spirit of it was a king.[2] Rome put an end to the attempt.

The next landmark is the Greek prophecy about Cleopatra embedded in the third book of the Sibylline Oracles,[3] emanating from one of her Greek supporters in her war with Octavian. Put briefly, it says that after she has hurled Rome down from heaven to earth she will then raise her up again from earth to heaven and inaugurate a golden age in which Asia and Europe shall alike share; justice and love shall reign upon earth, and with them Homonoia, which 'surpasses all earthly things'.[4] That is to say, Cleopatra is to end the long traditional feud of East and West by reconciling the two sides, Asia and Europe, and making them of one mind together. Whether she herself ever thought of this is not material to my subject; what matters is that the prophet

1 Pöhlmann, *op. cit.* (1, p. 406 in the 3rd ed.), was the first to see that the name referred to Iambulus' State, and not (as Mommsen thought) to Heliopolis in Syria; see also H. M. Last, *C.A.H.* IX, 1932, p. 104. The proof that this is right is that Aristonicus' following included many slaves, to whom he had promised freedom (last note), and Iambulus is the one Greek writer of whom we are certain that he envisaged both a Sun-State and a State without slaves. On what Aristonicus exactly meant see Oertel in Pöhlmann[3], II, p. 570 n. 3; Tarn, *J.R.S.* XXII, p. 140 n. 5. M. Rostovtzeff, *Soc. and Econ. Hist.* pp. 808, 1523 n. 81, has recently made an alternative and interesting suggestion that Strabo's *Heliopolitai* refers, not to Iambulus, but to the Oriental Ἥλιος Δικαιοσύνης, who protected the wronged. But, apart from the slave question, would a Sun-cult have made men fight as did the men of all sorts and conditions who followed Aristonicus? R. admits that in any case Aristonicus must have promised his followers 'all sorts of blessings and a happy life'.

2 The slavery question shows that Aristonicus' inspiration was not Stoicism, i.e. Blossius (as Bidez thinks, *op. cit.* p. 49), precisely as Cleomenes III did not get his ideas from the Stoic Sphaerus; indeed, how could one philosophy produce two such utterly diverse objectives? What moved Blossius was doubtless sympathy with the under-dog and perhaps a family tradition of hostility to the Roman Optimates (*C.A.H.* IX, p. 21). See also on Blossius, Dudley, *J.R.S.* XXXI, 1941, p. 94.

3 *Orac. Sibyl.* III, 350–361, 367–380; see Tarn, *J.R.S.* XXII, 1932, pp. 135 *sqq.*

4 l. 375: ἡ πάντων προφέρουσα βροτοῖς ὁμόνοια σαόφρων.

naturally attributes the establishment of Homonoia, of international unity and fellowship, to a monarch. The connection of universal Homonoia with kingship had never been stated so sharply before; but the prophecy gives us more than that. Any picture of any golden age is bound to make of it an era of peace and goodwill; but this prophecy depicts at some length a golden age of *righteousness*, and Homonoia is its central feature; this means that the central feature of any golden age could henceforth hardly fail to be the reconciliation and the unity of mankind. Perhaps there were other prophecies of the sort among the 2,000 which Augustus burned later.

But though Augustus might burn prophecies, his whole work was in a sense directed to making a beginning in carrying out what could be carried out of the Cleopatra prophecy.[1] Romans now claimed to form a third class beside Greeks and barbarians, though Greeks only admitted this later.[2] But the two peoples had one thing in common: both were weary of the long-continued civil wars and the misery they brought; and if, for Greeks, the longed-for peace and reconciliation must come from a monarch, it was hardly less so for Romans. For Homonoia, under its Latin name *Concordia*, had come to Rome as a goddess late in the fourth century B.C.;[3] and although, prior to Augustus, *Concordia* seems only to have meant to Romans what Homonoia had meant to Greeks before Isocrates—cessation of quarrelling between the orders in Rome itself, the best remedy being a foreign foe—still they had managed to connect the establishment of *Concordia* with kingship, with the mythical kings of legend, Romulus[4] and Numa.[5] To both nations, therefore, Augustus was the man who should do what he did begin to do. He was the Saviour and Benefactor and father of mankind, to the Greek cities of the Diet of Asia[6] no less

---

1 Appian, *Bella Civ.* I, 24, links together the advent of the principate and of Homonoia. A bronze coin of Antoninus Pius (*B.M. Coins, Alexandria*, Pl. XXI, no. 1167) represents Tiber and Nile holding hands, with legend Τίβερις ὁμόνοια; but it cannot, of course, be connected with the Cleopatra prophecy.

2 Jüthner, *Hellenen und Barbaren*, pp. 62, 79.

3 In 304 B.C.: A. Momigliano, *C.Q.* XXXVI, 1942, p. 111.

4 Dion. Hal. II, 3; the section is a treatise on τὴν τῶν πολιτευομένων ὁμοφρο-σύνην.

5 Plut. *Numa* XX, the whole chapter.

6 Two decrees of the Koinon of Asia: *S.E.G.* IV, 490, about 9 B.C., and *B.M. Inscr.* IV, no. 894, about 2 B.C. See also *Sardis*, VII, i, no. 8, l. 101: πατρὸς...τοῦ σύμπαντος τῶν ἀνθρώπων γένους; the king as father of mankind has grown out of the idea of the king imitating or representing

than to Roman poets; the Saecular Games, with their mixture of Latin tradition and Greek form, are the end of the bad old times and the beginning of a new era; and for Vergil in the *Aeneid* (VI, 791–4) Augustus will bring to pass the age of gold, an age which could no longer be confined to one people but must definitely be an age of reconciliation and unity. A new age did in fact begin, an age of progressive unity between the various peoples of the Mediterranean world. How far this may really have been due to Augustus and how far to the actions of many obscure men and women I need not inquire; I am talking primarily about theory. But the theory was, I think, expressed in that temple to the Imperial Concord[1]—*Concordia Augusta*—which Tiberius vowed as a private man and dedicated when Emperor. *Concordia Augusta* is a common phrase on the Imperial coinage; it may occasionally have a political meaning[2]—something perhaps like the *Concord of the Provinces* on Galba's coinage[3]—but usually it merely refers to the domestic felicity of the Emperor, precisely as one of the earliest uses of Homonoia in Greek had been to express family affection.[4] But I do not think that Tiberius took 17 years over a temple to celebrate the fact that Augustus lived happily with his wife; the temple of the Imperial Concord was to enshrine the spirit of a new age, an age of goodwill and unity.

I need not go through the Roman Empire, or relate how the Roman franchise was steadily extended till early in the third century every fully free provincial of whatever race was made a Roman citizen, or how this raised the juridical standing of the provinces till finally Diocletian abolished Italy's privileged position and the whole Empire stood on an equal footing. All I want to notice is that there were men who fully realised what the Empire had done; and perhaps I may quote from Claudian's great eulogy[5] of the Rome of the Emperors, the swan-song of the Western Empire when the Goth was already at the gates.

the Deity as 'father of gods and men', an idea which, apart from Ps.-Ecphantus and Diotogenes, is plainly stated by another writer of that group, Sthenidas (Stob. IV, 7, 63, p. 270H): the king must be μιματὸς νόμιμος τῷ θεῷ. See § VI, p. 436 n. 4 (on p. 437).

1 Dio Cass. LV, 8, 9; LVI, 25; Suet. *Tiberius*, 20; *C.I.L.* I², p. 231, *Fasti Praenestini* under Jan. 16 of A.D. 10. A full description in Sir J. G. Frazer, *The Fasti of Ovid*, II, pp. 238 *sqq.*; p. 240, the goddess of the temple was named *Concordia Augusta*, 'no doubt in compliment to Augustus'.

2 H. Mattingly, *Coins of the Roman Empire in the British Museum*, I, p. ccxxv.

3 *Ib.* pp. cciv, 309.   4 Kramer, *op. cit.* pp. 45–9.

5 Claudian XXIV (*De consulatu Stilichonis*, bk. III), l. 130. I briefly paraphrase lines 150–9.

It is this Rome, he says, who has cared for the human race and given it a common name; who has taken the conquered to her bosom like a mother, and called them not subjects but citizens; who has united distant races in the bonds of affection. To the peace which she has brought to us we owe it, every one of us, that every part of the Empire is to us as a fatherland; that it matters nothing if we drink of the Rhone or of the Orontes; that we are all one people. That is the last verdict on the Rome of the Emperors, the proudest boast perhaps that any man in any empire ever made: we are all one people. My theme has been that it was the business of monarchs to promote Homonoia, unity and concord, among all their subjects; whatever the faults of individual rulers, it would seem that monarchy, taken as a whole, *had* tried to promote it.

The belief that it was the business of kings to promote Homonoia among their subjects without distinction of race thus travelled down the line of kingship for centuries; but the belief, it will be remembered, had no beginning, for nobody will suppose that it began with writers so obscure as Diotogenes and Pseudo-Ecphantus. It must clearly have been connected with some particular king at the start, and that king has to be later than Isocrates and Philip and earlier than Diotogenes and Demetrius. It would seem that only one king is possible; we should have to postulate Alexander at the beginning of the line, even if there were not a definite tradition that it *was* he. This means that when, in § VI, we come to examine Plutarch's, or rather Eratosthenes', statement that Alexander's purpose was to bring about Homonoia between men generally, we can start with a strong presumption in favour of its truth.

IV. ZENO AND THE STOICS

We have seen that it was the business of kings to promote Homonoia among their subjects without distinction of race, and that the idea began with, and went back to, Alexander; it must now be considered what the Stoics thought about it, and whether their view of Homonoia was such that the ideas given as Alexander's *could*, as some have supposed, have really originated with Stoicism and merely been attributed to Alexander by later writers. It will appear that the difference is too great for this to have been possible.

The first thing is to get clear the distinction between the earlier and the later Zeno, between the Zeno who wrote the treatise generally called Zeno's *Republic* (I prefer to keep the Greek term *Politeia*) and the Zeno who ultimately envisaged the universe as one great city of gods and men—all men without distinction of race, though of course there were bad men in the world as well as good, the common Greek distinction of φαῦλοι and σπουδαῖοι. There has been much confusion of the two things, which I once shared, due partly to the confused and fragmentary nature of our information and partly to a certain passage in Plutarch which I shall come to; and I do not recall ever seeing the matter clearly put, though I do not claim to have read anything like all the modern literature on Stoicism. No one, however, doubts that, whatever threads may have contributed to form the great Zeno of a later day, his *Politeia* was a very early work;[1] and in fact, when he wrote it, he was, like many other philosophers, obsessed by the idea of Lycurgus' Sparta. The attraction of that cruel and narrow slave-State for Greek philosophic thought is one of the abiding mysteries, even if it were (as it was) idealised. Plutarch has left the invaluable information that the basis (ὑπόθεσις) of Zeno's *Politeia* was Lycurgus' Sparta;[2] it was therefore, at best, a very limited State, no further advanced, if as far, than the very limited ideal State of Aristotle. What seems known about it is this. You could go abroad from Zeno's State,[3] which implies other States or countries beside it. Men and women were to dress alike;[4] there was community of women, or more accurately complete promiscuity,[5] and each citizen was to love all the children as though he were their father,[6] which implies a quite small community. Instead of the normal mixture of good and bad men, there was a hard and fast division between the worthy, σπουδαῖοι, and the unworthy, φαῦλοι; only the worthy were citizens,[7] and had free speech;[8] the unworthy were like the Helots at Sparta, and Zeno said: 'If the unworthy speak

1 Diog. Laert. VII, 4; Philodemus περὶ Στωϊκῶν, P. Herc. 339 (P.), in W. Crönert, *Kolotes und Menedemos* (vol. 6 of Wessely's *Studien zur Palaeographie und Papyruskunde*, 1906), p. 55, νέου καὶ ἄφρονος ἔτι.

2 Plut. *Lycurg.* XXXI.

3 *S.V.F.* I, fr. 268 = Diog. Laert. VII, 33, ἀποδημίας ἕνεκεν, the ordinary word for going outside the bounds of your own State.

4 *S.V.F.* I, fr. 257 = Diog. Laert. VII, 33.

5 *S.V.F.* I, fr. 269 = Diog. Laert. VII, 131, τὸν ἐντυχόντα τῇ ἐντυχούσῃ χρῆσθαι. Some modern books talk of community of wives, which is wrong; there were no wives. Greeks believed in an original stage of promiscuity, Clearchus, *F.H.G.* II, 319; see Tarn, *Hell. Civ.*[2] pp. 319–20.

6 *S.V.F.* III, 728 = Diog. Laert. VII, 131.

7 *S.V.F.* I, fr. 222 = Diog. Laert. VII, 33. This meaning has been doubted, but is plain enough. Kaerst, *Studien zur Entwicklung und theoretischen Begründung der Monarchie im Altertum*, p. 73, took it as I do.

8 *S.V.F.* I, fr. 228.

against the worthy, shall he not suffer for it?'[1] One other known item, which I shall come to later, may or may not belong to the early *Politeia*; but the above gives its outline, and makes it tolerably obvious that such a State had nothing to do with the later Stoic Homonoia. No wonder later Stoics heartily disliked the *Politeia*, and could only say of it (which was true) that Zeno had not always been Zeno.[2]

I now come to the passage in which Plutarch, who as we have seen knew well enough what Zeno's *Politeia* was, has managed to create a great difficulty. In *de Alexandri Fortuna* I, 6 (329 A), preparatory to the introduction of the long quotation from Eratosthenes which is so important for Alexander's ideas (see § VI), he speaks of ἡ πολὺ θαυμαζομένη πολιτεία τοῦ Ζήνωνος, Zeno's greatly admired (or most wonderful) *Politeia*, and as only one *Politeia* of Zeno's is known, the early work we have been considering, Plutarch has been taken to refer to this. It is quite certain that he does not. He could not have called Zeno's early *Politeia*, which excited such animadversion, ἡ θαυμαζομένη; and he sums up the Politeia he is referring to as one in which men are not to live divided into different States and peoples, each under its own particular laws, but (329 B) one of which all men are to be citizens and all are to be one people,[3] with a common life, a common order, and a common law, like a herd of cattle grazing together.[4] That this is Zeno's (later) city of gods and men, his cosmopolitan World-State, is certain enough, and one must suppose that Plutarch is using 'Politeia' here in a general sense and not as the title of Zeno's book of that name. The World-State apparently had no fixed name; Chrysippus,[5] Areius Didymus,[6] and Poseidonius[7] called it a σύστημα and Cicero[8] a city; there is no reason why Plutarch should not have called it a 'politeia', but it is confusing.

It is not the only passage to name 'Zeno's *Politeia*' which is confusing. In the early *Politeia* there was promiscuity, as we have seen;

---

1 *S.V.F.* I, fr. 228: οὐκ οἰμώξεται;
2 Philodemus in Crönert, *op. cit.* pp. 55 *sqq.* Ζήνων γὰρ οὐκ ἦν ἀεί is col. XV, 15.
3 δημότας, members of the same demos.
4 ἀγέλας συννόμου. The 'human herd' was a Cynic idea, not Stoic; and this comparison is not from Zeno but is Plutarch having a hit at the Stoics; cf. Diog. Laert. VII, 173, where the poet Sositheos accuses Cleanthes of driving men like cattle, βοηλατεῖ.
5 *S.V.F.* III, frs. 527, 528.
6 *S.V.F.* III, fr. 527 = Stob. *Ecl.* I, p. 184, 8 (W.).
7 Poseidonius, *de mundo*, II, p. 391 b.
8 *De leg.* I, 7, 23; *de nat. deorum*, II, 62, 154.

but the same writer who relates this also states that Zeno 'in the *Politeia*' said that the wise man would marry and beget children;[1] as the two statements are mutually exclusive, the one about marriage must belong to the later World-State, here again called the *Politeia*. Really, were it not for the list of Zeno's works in Diogenes Laertius, we might almost suppose that Zeno wrote *two* books called Πολιτεία. Again, Cassius the Sceptic, among others, is said to have stated that 'in the *Politeia*' Zeno prohibited the building of temples, law-courts, and gymnasia *in the cities*;[2] and as the early *Politeia*, if modelled on Sparta, cannot well have included more than one city, no wonder some writers[3] have attributed this to the World-State; I have no idea myself to which it belongs. It is not very important; but Eros *is* important. Athenaeus[4] cites one Pontianus as saying that Zeno thought that Love was the god of φιλία and Homonoia, and also provided freedom but provided nothing else; *therefore* in the *Politeia* Zeno said that Love was the god who co-operated in securing the safety of the city. 'Therefore' clearly relates to Love providing freedom, and the latter part of the passage is plain enough: Zeno is referring to the (original of the) story that follows in Athenaeus (561 E), which says that the Spartans, before marshalling their battle-line, used to sacrifice to Eros because safety (σωτηρία) lay in the φιλία which held the battle-line together. The *Politeia* mentioned by Pontianus is then clearly the early *Politeia*, modelled on Sparta, and we see why 'Eros' provides safety; but what can Love as the god of Homonoia—the Stoic Homonoia—have to do either with Sparta or with the early *Politeia*? This conception ought to belong to the World-State; and is it conceivable that Zeno, having once got hold of the idea of Love holding a State together, should have dropped it in his later period, when one would have expected him to broaden out the idea in relation to the World-State? I would suggest,

---

1 *S.V.F.* I, 270, γαμήσειν, ὡς ὁ Ζήνων φησὶν ἐν Πολιτείᾳ, καὶ παιδοποιήσεσθαι.
2 *S.V.F.* I, fr. 267 = Diog. Laert. VII, 33; cf. *ib.* frs. 264, 265.
3 As for example Kaerst II[2], p. 125 n.
4 Athen. XIII, 561 C. Ποντιανὸς δὲ Ζήνωνα ἔφη τὸν Κιτιέα ὑπολαμβάνειν τὸν Ἔρωτα θεὸν εἶναι φιλίας καὶ ὁμονοίας, ἔτι δὲ καὶ ἐλευθερίας παρασκευαστικόν, ἄλλου δὲ οὐδενός. διὸ καὶ ἐν τῇ Πολιτείᾳ ἔφη τὸν Ἔρωτα θεὸν εἶναι συνεργὸν ὑπάρχοντα πρὸς τὴν τῆς πόλεως σωτηρίαν. I adopt Kaibel's suggested transposition of ἐλευθερίας and ὁμονοίας, which is certain both from 561 D and from the sense. The later Stoic definition of Love (*S.V.F.* III, 716) was thoroughly bad, but they did connect it with φιλία—μὴ εἶναι συνουσίας ἀλλὰ φιλίας; see Diogenes Laertius VII, 130, the whole section. It is evident however that in the Athenaeus passage, whatever Zeno meant by Love, it was something greater than, and to be distinguished from, φιλία.

though diffidently (one can get no certainty), that Pontianus is summarising Zeno's whole attitude to Eros; he first gives, as a general statement, Love as the god of φιλία and Homonoia (from the World-State), and then gives the provision of σωτηρία (which would not apply to the World-State) as a special case, taken from the early *Politeia*.

But whatever may be the difficulty in reconstructing Zeno's early *Politeia* from our sources, one thing is clear enough in broad outline: something had happened to bring about a great change of mind in Zeno between his early and his later period. Plutarch says plainly what it was—Alexander. Zeno's World-State, he says, was as it were a dream or image of a philosophic 'well-ordered' State, εὐνομίας... πολιτείας, and Alexander supplied the ἔργον to Zeno's λόγος,[1] the deed which lay behind the word, if we use the obvious (too obvious) translation. What we should have expected Plutarch to say was, the reality behind Zeno's dream; there is a difficulty, which I shall come to (p. 422 n. 2), about λόγος here meaning 'word', and it is an unnatural term to apply to Zeno's vision. But ἔργον, to Plutarch, did mean 'deed', for the reality to him was just 'deeds'; the argument of the whole treatise *de Alexandri Fortuna I* is that Alexander was as good a philosopher through what he *did*[2] as were the philosophers who ran him down through what they thought and taught. Plutarch is certainly too materialistic, but many modern writers have taken an even more materialistic line; they do not doubt that Plutarch was right about Alexander, but they say that what affected Zeno was Alexander's *Empire*, or sometimes even that World-Empire which he has been supposed to be going to conquer.[3] To myself, Alexander's Empire is no explanation at all. One man conquers a large number of races and brings them under one despotic rule; how could another man deduce from this that distinctions of race are meaningless and that the universe is a harmony in which all men (and Zeno included the slaves) are brothers? The two

---

1 *De Alex. Fort.* 329 B, τοῦτο Ζήνων μὲν ἔγραψεν ὥσπερ ὄναρ ἢ εἴδωλον εὐνομίας φιλοσόφου καὶ πολιτείας ἀνατυπωσάμενος, Ἀλέξανδρος δὲ τῷ λόγῳ τὸ ἔργον παρέσχεν.

2 For an elaboration of 'what he did' see note 147 to my lecture of 1933, and cf. *A.J.P.* LX, 1939, p. 57.

3 Wilamowitz, *Staat und Gesellschaft der Griechen*², p. 190, 'unter dem Eindrucke der Alexandermonarchie'. Kaerst II², p. 125: 'Die innere Beziehung der stoischen Weltstaatsidee zum Weltreiche Alexanders ist schon im Altertum selbst erkannt worden.' Zeller, *Stoics, Epicureans, and Sceptics*, p. 327 (Eng. trans.). J. Kargl, *Die Lehre der Stoiker vom Staat*, 1913, p. 16. J. Jüthner, *Hellenen und Barbaren*, 1923, pp. 48, 50. W. Kapelle, *Klio*, xxv, 1932, p. 87 n. 3.

things have no point of contact; besides, if it were true, why did nobody ever deduce any world-embracing ideas from Darius' huge empire? It has accordingly been suggested that what Zeno took from Alexander was his cosmopolitanism. Unfortunately no trace of cosmopolitan ideas can be found in Alexander from beginning to end, as will be seen more clearly in § VI; a desire that the various races should live together in unity and harmony is a very different thing from abolishing race and treating all mankind as one people, as a cosmopolitan World-State. Certainly, in a very notable passage in the treatise in question, Plutarch, speaking in his own person, might appear to be attributing to Alexander Zeno's own cosmopolitanism; but he treats it as something which Alexander would have wished to carry out had he lived. What he says[1] is that Alexander's expedition was no raid to plunder and destroy; 'rather, he wished to show that all earthly things were subject to one *logos*[2] and one polity (πολιτεία, probably "constitution" rather than "State") and that all men were one people, and he demeaned himself accordingly;[3] and, but for his premature death, one law would have illumined (lit. gazed at) all men and they would have managed their affairs with reference to one justice as being their common (source of) light. But as things happened, that part of the world which never saw Alexander remained sunless',[4] i.e. without that light. The reference to Stoicism throughout, with its one polity for all men and its Universal Law, is obvious; we get the same phraseology which Plutarch had already used of Zeno's World-State in 329B (p. 419 *ante*). But the

---

1 *De Alex. Fort.* I, 330D: ἀλλ' ἑνὸς ὑπήκοα λόγου τὰ ἐπὶ γῆς καὶ μιᾶς πολιτείας, ἕνα δῆμον ἀνθρώπους ἅπαντας ἀποφῆναι βουλόμενος, οὕτως ἑαυτὸν ἐσχημάτισεν· εἰ δὲ μὴ ταχέως ὁ δεῦρο καταπέμψας τὴν Ἀλεξάνδρου ψυχὴν ἀνεκαλέσατο δαίμων, εἷς ἂν νόμος ἅπαντας ἀνθρώπους ἐπέβλεπε καὶ πρὸς ἕν δίκαιον ὡς πρὸς κοινὸν διῳκοῦντο φῶς. νῦν δὲ τῆς γῆς ἀνήλιον μέρος ἔμεινεν, ὅσον Ἀλέξανδρον οὐκ εἶδεν. See the interesting use made of this passage by Dr A. A. T. Ehrhardt, *Journ. of Theolog. Stud.* XLVI, 1945, p. 45. I owe this reference to Professor N. H. Baynes.

2 λόγος is difficult. It cannot be 'word' here, and never means 'law', which anyhow comes soon after it; and it must have the same meaning as Zeno's 'λόγος', p. 421 n. 1 *ante*, and Cleanthes', p. 424 n. 1. The best I can suggest is 'principle', the inner principle of the construction of the universe.

3 The reference seems to be to his adoption of the dress of the conquered. But here again Plutarch, as we saw before, may be too materialistic.

4 Ehrhardt makes this refer to Alexander as the Sun of Righteousness. I think this goes rather far. The ἥλιος may not be Alexander at all; it may be τὸ δίκαιον, Justice, already equated with the φῶς. But, of course, it is Alexander who brings τὸ δίκαιον; and if the reference be indeed to him, I would sooner take it as Alexander the bringer of (the light of) civilisation, which has been one of Plutarch's themes throughout this essay.

passage does not bear on the historical Alexander; it is only Plutarch giving free rein to his imagination of what might have been: had Alexander lived, there would have been no need for Zeno, for what Zeno was in fact to do would have been already done by Alexander himself.[1]

To return to the historical Alexander, whose ἔργον, deeds, lay behind Zeno's λόγος (? principle). Only one explanation of Plutarch's phrase now remains possible: what lay behind Zeno was not so much Alexander's doings as Alexander's ideas,[2] and the foundation of Zeno's World-State was Alexander's declaration that all men are brothers, a declaration which transcended all differences of race. One could of course pass from this to the idea of a World-State, as Alexarchus (§ v) did even before Zeno, though Alexander himself did not do so. But Zeno was too big a man merely to copy, and he gave to Alexander's dream of the Homonoia of the various peoples so different a shape that any theory that Alexander's ideas were attributed back to him from Zeno (which is what I am concerned with in this section) is impossible. To Alexander, it was the business of a king, as has been seen (§ iii), to bring about Homonoia; to Stoics this was not, and could not be, any one's business (let alone that of kings, whom they disliked), since Homonoia already existed, as it always had done. For one thing about the Stoic World-State, from Zeno to Epictetus, was certain: it was, and always had been, a unity, a harmony, by the decree of the Divine Power; for the universe was the expression of Himself, and He Himself *was* Homonoia.[3] Stoics had several names for this unity—Homonoia,[4] harmony,[5] sympathy;[6] but whichever term they used, the World-State, which was co-terminous with the universe, was in harmony together and had been so from the start. The harmony, the Homonoia, *was* there; 'It is Thou', says Cleanthes in his great hymn to the Divine

---

1 Plutarch, who did not like Stoics, may not have been averse to making out that they owed more to Alexander than they really did.
2 Note that Plutarch goes straight on here to Eratosthenes on Alexander's ideas.
3 *S.V.F.* ii, fr. 1076 (Chrysippus).
4 Zeno uses the word, *ib.* i, fr. 263, and it is implied in i, fr. 98. For Chrysippus, it must follow from his statement that God was Homonoia (last note), but the contents of his two books περὶ ὁμονοίας are unknown. See generally E. Skard, *Zwei religiös-politische Begriffe, Euergetes-Concordia*, 1932, pp. 85–6. Later the Homonoia of the heavenly bodies became a common-place: Dio Chrys. xl, 35 *sqq.*
5 Cleanthes' *Hymn*, l. 16 (p. 424), and in Poseidonius.
6 Poseidonius; see also *S.V.F.* ii, frs. 475, 534.

Power, 'It is Thou that hast made this harmony.'[1] And what God had once made it was not for men to make over again. It was the business of kings to bring about Homonoia, but it was not the business of a Stoic; for him Homonoia had already been brought about by the Deity, and all that was required was that men's eyes should be opened that they might see it. There were plenty of men who did not see it— men who set up little earthly States,[2] men who did bad actions;[3] but the business of the earnest Stoic was not to tackle the consequences of bad actions, to smooth away discord or promote unity; his business was to educate the individual man[4] and teach him to think aright. For if you could get all men to think aright, all other things would be added unto you: discord and wrong, national States and slavery—these things would automatically vanish and there would remain only the unity and concord of mankind, which had really been there all the time, though men could not see it. That is the irreconcilable opposition between Stoicism and the theory of kingship, between the belief that unity and concord existed and you must try to get men to see it, and the belief that they did not exist and that it was the business of the rulers of the earth to try to bring them to pass.

Besides this opposition of ideas between Stoicism and kingship, I have mentioned that Stoics disliked kings, and it may be well, in conclusion, to be clear about their attitude towards kingship, for it has been widely believed that the early Stoics thought kingship the ideal form of government. They certainly did not; their World-State grew out of the πόλις and was a πόλις, and knew one king only, that Universal Law which was God and 'king of all things both divine and human'.[5] The belief that the early Stoics thought kingship the ideal form of government was started by Kaerst in 1898,[6] chiefly on the

1 *S.V.F.* I, fr. 537 (Cleanthes' Hymn to Zeus), ll. 16, 17:
ὧδε γὰρ εἰς ἓν πάντα συνήρμοκας ἐσθλὰ κακοῖσιν,
ὥσθ' ἕνα γίγνεσθαι πάντων λόγον αἰὲν ἐόντα.

2 Chrysippus, *ib.* III, fr. 323, called these merely προσθῆκαι—appendages, or accidents—of the World-State, due to men's lack of the sense of fellowship, κοινωνία.

3 Cleanthes' *Hymn*, l. 13: the acts of bad men cut across the universal harmony and are no part of it.

4 *S.V.F.* III, fr. 611, τὸ παιδεύειν ἀνθρώπους.

5 *S.V.F.* III, fr. 314, cf. frs. 327, 329.

6 *Op. cit.* (*Stud. zur Entwicklung*, etc.), p. 67, using the relations of Zeno, Sphaerus, and Persaeus with kings. Kaerst's quotation here from Stobaeus (cf. Suidas, βασιλεία 1), which he calls Stoic, is from one of those lost treatises περὶ βασιλείας which every school wrote.

strength of the friendship between Zeno and Antigonus Gonatas, though he also cited[1] some passages from Roman Imperial times which are not evidence for the early Stoa. But the acts of individual Stoics are not evidence for Stoic theory;[2] you can be the personal friend of a man with whose politics you disagree, and the friendship between Zeno and Antigonus was a matter of personal liking and of ethics, i.e. the philosophy of conduct. Kaerst repeated his belief in his History[3] and gave three references, which do not bear on the matter, for or against; there is in fact no evidence. Zeno said that the σπουδαῖος would not rule others;[4] but Chrysippus said that the philosopher would not shirk a throne if it came to him (i.e. as a duty);[5] and of course kings had to be educated like other people, which was why Zeno sent Persaeus to Antigonus and why Chrysippus recommended the 'philosopher behind the throne' who would be the king's companion, συμβιώσεται βασιλεῖ.[6] The frequent references in Stoic literature to the 'kingly man', βασιλικός, or to the wise man as being a king, are merely a method of indicating the possession of those virtues and qualities which, men believed, a king ought to have; a king, said Chrysippus, is one who has βασιλικὴν ἐπιστήμην[7] (and not merely one who sits on a throne). Let me give a couple of third-century quotations to show what Stoics at that time thought about kingship. The much discussed Stoic Sphaerus had been the tutor, and remained the friend, of Cleomenes III of Sparta; but pretty well everything we *know* about him[8] is connected with education, which to every Stoic was of the first importance; and if, as he probably did, he helped Cleomenes' revolution, about which there was nothing especially Stoic, it was because he was Cleomenes' friend, and not because Cleomenes was a king. For Sphaerus, of whom so much has be*r*n made in this connection, has left on record his opinion of kingship at large: being taken to task for saying that Ptolemy IV was not a king, he said: 'Very well; being what he is (i.e. a worthless creature) he *is* a king.'[9] Contempt for kingship cannot go further. Chrysippus[10] said

---

1 Kaerst, *op. cit.* p. 66 n. 1.
2 Sphaerus and Blossius have sometimes been cited as such evidence. For Sphaerus see below; for Blossius, § III, p. 414 n. 2.
3 II², p. 308 and n. 1.
4 *S.V.F.* I, fr. 216, οὔτε βιάζει οὔτε δεσπόζει.
5 *Ib.* III, fr. 691.   6 *Ib.*   7 *Ib.* III, fr. 618.
8 For a recent reconstruction, in Kaerst's sense, of what Sphaerus *might* have been doing at Cleomenes' court, see F. Ollier, *Rev. E.G.* XLIX, 1936, p. 536.
9 *S.V.F.* I, fr. 625.   10 *Ib.* III, fr. 693 = Plut. *Mor.* 1043 E.

that if the wise man wanted to make money (a thing which the Stoic sage in Stoic eyes had no business to want) the three best ways were, to go to a king, to sponge on his friends, or to prostitute his wisdom;[1] he said elsewhere that the wise man would willingly go to a king for the money he would make[2] (a thing Chrysippus himself refused to do). Plutarch missed the savage sarcasm of this, and was puzzled as to why Chrysippus said it when he had so often said that the wise man did not need money.[3] Of course it was all explained away later,[4] as other inconvenient sayings in other religions have been.

Stoics in fact regarded earthly constitutions as of value solely in so far as, and in proportion as, they might in their eyes approximate to that Divine Reason which was king of the universe; hence at different periods, in the changing circumstances of the world, they gave their preference to different forms of government, as for example when they changed over from the Roman oligarchy to Roman emperors. But it seems clear that the earlier Stoics thought little of kingship as a form of government.

V. Between Alexander and Zeno

We have seen that it was impossible that Alexander's ideas should have originated with Stoicism and merely been attributed to him by later writers; and, before coming to Alexander himself, I may notice briefly one matter which reinforces that conclusion, viz. that two men appear to have been influenced by Alexander's ideas prior to Zeno; it is not necessary for me to prove this, but it may be of interest. The first is the philosopher Theophrastus. The relevant dates are that Theophrastus, Aristotle's pupil, succeeded him as head of the Peripatetic school in 322 and died in 288, while Zeno began to teach in Athens in 301. Zeno however did not become Zeno all at once; time has to be allowed for him to write his early *Politeia* and to acquire intellectual influence, which prior to his friendship with Antigonus Gonatas was a slow matter; while, though Theophrastus did overlap Zeno, the man who during the ten years rule at Athens of Demetrius of Phalerum (316–307 B.C.) had been, intellectually, all-powerful in Athens and had inspired

---

1 τὸν ἀπὸ σοφιστείας, a word invariably used in a bad sense, which therefore gives the meaning of the whole saying; cf. Plut. *Mor.* 1047 F, where Chrysippus classes together going to a king to make money and σοφιστεύειν ἐπ' ἀργυρίῳ.

2 *S.V.F.* III, 691 = Plut. *Mor.* 1043 B–E.

3 Plut. *Mor. ib.*   4 Stob. *Ecl.* II, VII, 11 m., p. 109 Wachsmuth.

Demetrius' laws was not likely in his old age to begin borrowing ideas from the strange newcomer from Cyprus, half Phoenician by blood, even if there was as yet anything to borrow. What I have to notice is Theophrastus' doctrine of οἰκείωσις; he used it as the foundation of ethics, but I am only concerned with the doctrine itself. The word was a rare one; it occurs once in Thucydides (IV, 128), of some troops 'appropriating' to themselves the property of a defaulting ally, but in Theophrastus it signifies promoting οἰκειότης, which means a binding together of human beings either by kinship, or by φιλία (friendship, or love in the non-sexual sense), or by both. Theophrastus' teacher Aristotle had, as already noticed, set a hard and fast line of division between Greek and barbarian; Theophrastus suddenly came out with a statement, amazing in Aristotle's pupil, that all men are kin one to another and are bound together by φιλία. We possess two fragments of his on the matter, which are practically identical.[1] The Porphyry fragment traces the progress of φιλία from the family, where it originated, to the kin and thence to the city, then on to the race or nation, and finally to mankind; it concludes 'and thus we lay it down that all men are kin and friends to one another'.[2] The Stobaeus fragment traces the progress of φιλία in exactly the same way. What Theophrastus is saying is that the foundation of ethics was those primitive natural affections which extended their range step by step till they finally became love of humanity.

1 One is a named fragment of Theophrastus περὶ εὐσεβείας in Porphyry *de abstinentia* III, 25 (Nauck), first identified by J. Bernays, *Theophrastos' Schrift über Frömmigkeit*, 1866, pp. 96 *sqq*. The other is an extract in Stobaeus II, 7, 13 (p. 120 W.) headed Ἀριστοτέλους καὶ τῶν λοιπῶν Περιπατητικῶν περὶ τῶν ἠθικῶν. Despite the heading, the identity of the Stobaeus extract with the Porphyry passage is so clear that it also must be from Theophrastus, as Spengel said long ago; I need not discuss this, as Fr. Dirlmeier, 'Die Oikeiosis-Lehre Theophrasts', *Philol. Supp. Bd.* xxx, 1, 1937, has now shown at minute length that both fragments *are* from Theophrastus and that the οἰκείωσις doctrine was his, and his alone, till at some later time the Stoics adopted it. He says (p. 49) that οἰκείωσις is not even mentioned by any Stoic before Chrysippus, but what we know of the early Stoics is so fragmentary that I doubt if that means much. It is, however, unfortunate that von Arnim in *S.V.F.* should have printed under 'Zeno' the fragment I, 197, τὴν δὲ οἰκείωσιν ἀρχὴν τίθενται δικαιοσύνης οἱ ἀπὸ Ζήνωνος, for it has led to some misunderstanding; οἱ ἀπὸ Ζήνωνος does not mean Zeno—that would be οἱ περὶ Ζήνωνα—but 'the Stoic school which derived from Zeno'; we get the full phrase in I, 216, Ζήνωνι καὶ τοῖς ἀπ' αὐτοῦ Στωϊκοῖς φιλοσόφοις.

2 οὕτως δὲ καὶ τοὺς πάντας ἀνθρώπους ἀλλήλοις τίθεμεν οἰκείους καὶ συγγενεῖς.

Theophrastus was a very learned man on several subjects; he belonged to a school whose method was to collect facts, or what they thought were facts, and draw deductions from them; one can see from the colossal list of his lost writings, as well as from his surviving *History of Plants*, that he too collected facts on the grand scale. It seems unlikely that a man with that type of mind would initiate a revolution in thought at once so simple and so far-reaching; and, as far as I know, no one has ever supposed that he did. His sources have been sought for; the sophist Antiphon has of course been put forward (Mewaldt); rather a favourite has been Empedocles' attraction and repulsion (Max Mühl, Dirlmeier), which is as different as light from dark. It is not worth going into this; really, the unknown man who wrote the heading of the Stobaeus fragment did better when he made Theophrastus' source Aristotle himself,[1] for Aristotle *had* extended φιλία from the city to the race.[2] The common sense of the matter is that something had happened between Aristotle and Theophrastus, and that can only be Alexander. Theophrastus' work, in material matters, regularly reflects the results of Alexander's expedition;[3] but, apart from this, his progress of φιλία, from the family to all mankind, runs a parallel course to that which, as matter of history, was taken by the Homonoia concept (§ III, *ante*); this too began as family unity, and was extended in succession to the Greek city, the Greek race (by Isocrates), and finally by Alexander to all the peoples of the world he had to do with (§ VI). I find it difficult myself to believe (though it can only be put as a probability) that Theophrastus' extension of φιλία to all men was not connected with Alexander's statement that all men were brothers and with his dream that they might be united in Homonoia (see § VI); for though Alexander did not use the word φιλία, men who were of one mind together could not be other than friends; Homonoia and φιλία were only two aspects of the same thing.

1 A modern attempt has been made, but without foundation, to take the idea back to Aristotle. See n. 101 to my lecture of 1933; I need not repeat.

2 *Nic. Eth.* VIII, 1155 a, l. 18: φιλία is naturally implanted in birds and beasts καὶ τοῖς ὁμοεθνέσι πρὸς ἄλληλα καὶ μάλιστα τοῖς ἀνθρώποις, which means that, as beasts *of the same species* are friendly to one another, so are men *of the same race* (e.g. Greeks). Even this much was a great concession for Aristotle; it was a parallel to Isocrates on Homonoia.

3 Theophrastus as a man was personally hostile to the memory of Alexander because of the execution of Callisthenes, and showed it (App. 18). But as a philosopher his aim was the pursuit of knowledge; his feelings did not influence his attitude towards learning, and he regularly reproduced the new knowledge which Alexander acquired or caused to be acquired for the Greek world.

Though I put this as a probability only, there seems to have been one Greek, at any rate, who thought the same thing as myself. I must refer back to my study of Alexander's supposed plans (App. 24) and to the fifth plan, for interchange of populations between Europe and Asia. Its falsity in fact is plain (*ib.* p. 383); but what concerns me here is the reason given for it in Diodorus' list. The plan was to transfer Asiatics to Europe and Europeans to Asia, so that he (Alexander) might, by means of mixed marriages and the ensuing relationships (ταῖς οἰκειώσεσιν), bring the two continents to Homonoia and to the affection (φιλία) of those who are akin.[1] The writer of this took the mixed marriages from Susa and Homonoia from Alexander's prayer, but for the rest he is quoting from Theophrastus. This does not depend merely on the use of Theophrastus' word οἰκείωσις. The Porphyry fragment of Theophrastus, after φιλία has been extended to all mankind, says οὕτως δὲ τοὺς πάντας ἀνθρώπους ἀλλήλοις τίθεμεν οἰκείους καὶ συγγενεῖς. That is, in Theophrastus we get, in one passage, the three words φιλία, οἰκείους, and συγγενεῖς combined, and in the plan we get the same three words, φιλίαν, οἰκειώσεσιν, and συγγενικήν, again combined; that the writer who composed the plan had Theophrastus in mind and was using his language, i.e. quoting loosely for the *sense*, can hardly be doubted. Two things follow: that the 'plan' is later than Theophrastus and so cannot be Alexander's (this was already certain), and that the writer who composed the 'plan' believed, as I do, that Theophrastus' doctrine of universal φιλία was taken from Alexander and so could be used to illustrate Alexander's intentions.

The other man I want to notice is Alexarchus, a son of Antipater and younger brother of Cassander. He was a philologist[2] and a dreamer, and has duly been called either mad or comic; a recent study has argued that what was the matter with him was schizophrenia,[3] or say roughly dual personality. In any case I propose to take him seriously, for some curious evidence exists which shows, either that he was still remembered and more or less copied in Greek Bactria in

---

1 Diod. xviii, 4, 4, ὅπως τὰς μεγίστας ἠπείρους (Europe and Asia) ταῖς ἐπιγαμίαις καὶ ταῖς οἰκειώσεσιν εἰς κοινὴν ὁμόνοιαν καὶ συγγενικὴν φιλίαν καταστήσῃ.

2 γραμματικός: Aristos of Salamis, Jacoby ii, no. 143, fr. 4. Possibly identical with the Alexarchus of Plutarch *de Iside et Osiride* 365 E, who wrote on curious religious names under an alphabetical arrangement; but I cannot trace Plutarch's authority, one Ariston ὁ γεγραφὼς Ἀθηναίων ἀποικίας.

3 O. Weinreich, *Menekrates Zeus und Salmoneus*, 1933, pp. 14, 76.

165 B.C., or that we have to deal with a very peculiar *triple* coincidence,[1] a thing which is possible but which is not too easy to believe. Cassander, who ruled Macedonia from 316 onwards, and was good to his brothers, gave Alexarchus some land on the neck of the Athos peninsula, where he could found a city and dream in peace under Cassander's shield. There he founded and settled a large city called Ouranopolis, the 'city of Heaven'; doubtless it was founded very soon after 316, the period of Cassander's three great foundations, Cassandreia, Thessalonica (Salonica), and Thebes; as the city was 30 stades round,[2] it must have been a synoecism on the model of Cassandreia and Thessalonica, whether it took in Sane, Acroathon, or what not. Alexarchus' own position is obscure; no one calls him a king, and Clement of Alexandria (which probably means Aristos) treated him as a private man;[3] I suppose that he was honoured as κτίστης, and had some position, under Cassander's protection, resembling that of Demetrius of Phalerum at Athens at the same time. Ouranopolis must have been an ordinary enough city, save for its name, for Ptolemy the geographer (v, 5, 6) mentions another Ouranopolis in Pamphylia, and this must have been a colony from Alexarchus' city, for two men could not have hit upon that amazing name independently; Alexarchus' city had therefore founded a colony for his brother Pleistarchus, whose short-lived kingdom included Pamphylia, just as many Greek cities were to found colonies for the Seleucids.[4] Ouranopolis in Macedonia is never mentioned in subsequent history;[5] it may be chance, or the synoecism may have broken up after Cassander's death or the extinction of his dynasty; other cases of the break-up of a synoecism are known. Ouranopolis means 'city of Heaven'; but Alexarchus struck a strange coinage,[6] on which the people of the city are called, not (as would have been normal) Ouranopolitai, citizens of Ouranopolis, but Ouranidai, 'children of Heaven'. This word shows what Alexarchus was doing; he had set up a little World-State in miniature, a good many years before Zeno appeared. His coins figure the Sun, Moon, and Stars,

---

1 Tarn, *Bactria and India*, p. 210, cf. p. 92.
2 Strabo VII, 331, fr. 35; Athen. III, 98 D.
3 Clem. Alex. *Protr.* IV, 54 gives first βασιλεῖς who called themselves gods, and then private persons, among them Alexarchus, for whom he cites Aristos. Cf. Weinreich's table, *op. cit.* p. 92.
4 Tarn, *Bactria and India*, p. 6.
5 What Pliny's 'nunc sunt Uranopolis', etc. means (IV, 37) I do not know. Hardly Pliny's own day.
6 B. V. Head, *Hist. Numm.*[2] p. 206; *B.M. Coins, Macedon*, pp. 133, cxxxii; F. Imhoof-Blumer, *Monnaies grecques*, pp. 96 *sqq*.

primarily as being the natural and universal gods[1]—they were gods
even to the rationalist Euhemerus, his contemporary[2]—but doubtless
they also symbolised himself, his consort, and his citizens, for the stars
were obviously children of Heaven,[3] while it is recorded that he called
himself the Sun,[4] which means a world-ruler. His coins also figure as
a type the daughter (in the mythology) of Ouranos, Plato's great
Aphrodite Ourania[5] or 'Heavenly Love', symbolising the love which
pervaded the universe. Now it was proper for a World-State, like an
ideal State, to have a language of its own, like the world before the
Tower of Babel[6]—Plutarch gives an instance of an ideal State which
had;[7] besides, speaking with 'tongues'—strange words—gave to
Greeks a suggestion of divine inspiration;[8] and Alexarchus the philologist did create a special language. Why he did so, however, is none
too clear. It has been suggested that it was proper for a god to have a
language of his own;[9] that is a possible explanation. It could no doubt
be treated as just a game, as children invent private languages to
mystify their elders. But, though there is no sign that any one ever
used it but Alexarchus himself, I think he invented it as a language for
the World-State of his dream, just as people to-day amuse themselves
by inventing 'universal' languages, like Esperanto or Ido. We possess
a letter of his written to the magistrates of Cassandreia in this extraordinary speech;[10] no one has ever read it, or ever will.[11] But the preamble is plain enough; instead of the usual form, 'Alexarchus to the
magistrates of Cassandreia, greeting', it runs 'Alexarchus to the chief
men of the Brethren, all hail (literally, "rejoicing")'.[12] There was

1 Plato, *Cratylus* 397C; Diod. VI, 1, 2; Plut. *Mor.* 377 F.
2 Diod. VI, 1, 7. For his date, p. 432 n. 3.
3 Cf. *S.V.F.* III, fr. 337.
4 Aristos, fr. 4: ἑαυτὸν κατεσχημάτισεν ἐς Ἥλιον.
5 Plato, *Symp.* 180 D. See on her L. R. Farnell, *Cults of the Greek States*, II,
   pp. 659 *sqq.*, though I doubt her being a ruler, p. 678.
6 Genesis xi, 1: 'And the whole earth was of one language.'
7 *Mor.* 370B, μίαν πολιτείαν ἀνθρώπων μακαρίων καὶ ὁμογλώσσων ἁπάντων.
8 Christ-Schmid, *Gesch. d. gr. Lit.*[6] II, 1, 116, on γλώσσαις λαλεῖν. Naturally
   I need not consider the later phenomena in the *N.T.* and their vast literature.
9 Weinreich, *op. cit.* p. 14.   10 Athen. III, 98 E.
11 For a detailed attempt at decipherment see Weinreich, pp. 108 *sqq.*;
   but our text must be full of corruptions, seeing that one of the three words
   of the preamble has been corrupted. Greeks could not read it themselves;
   Athenaeus, III, 98 F, says that even the Pythian Apollo could not do *that.*
12 Ἀλέξαρχος ὁ μαρμων πρόμοις γαθεῖν. For the corrupt ὁ μαρμων, which
   has to be a word in the genitive plural, Wilamowitz read Ὁμαιμέων,
   Schweighäuser Ὁμαίμων. The sense is certain; I prefer Ὁμαίμων, as slightly
   closer to the MS.

nothing to make the mixed population of Cassandreia brethren of the presumably mixed population of Ouranopolis;[1] and I see nothing for it but a belief on Alexarchus' part that, in his dream-world, all men were members of his World-State and all men were brothers. But no one is likely to suppose that that simple man thought of all that for himself; it is probably as near a proof as one is likely to get in this sort of inquiry that Alexander did think of all men as brothers and did put forward ideas which led Alexarchus, as later they led Zeno, to the idea of a World-State, though Alexander did not think of or desire such a thing himself.

Alexarchus was the first ruler who is known to have called himself the Sun, an idea which was to receive such an extension later. I need not consider that here, or Zeno's star-citizens either; but a word must be said about Alexarchus' choice of Ouranos as the supreme deity. Alexander (§ vi) had said that God was the common father of all men—God, not Zeus, for the inclusion of the barbarian (non-Greek) world would have made a specifically Greek god meaningless; and following upon this comes the curious phenomenon that three men of Cassander's circle,[2] all contemporaries whose connection with each other depended on their connection with Cassander—Alexarchus his brother, Euhemerus his friend,[3] Theophrastus whose bitterness against Alexander had led him to carry his school over to Cassander as being Alexander's enemy—all made of Ouranos, Heaven, the deity who united the universe, and not any specifically Greek god. In the mythology Ouranos stood at the beginning of all things before the gods were; he had the great advantage of not being a cult-god in Greece and having no worship, so that any one could make of him what they wished; he would fit in equally well for Greeks and non-Greeks. We find in this circle a whole group of related ideas, which can be definitely dated to the period between Alexander and Zeno, though the priorities as between the different members cannot be ascertained. Theophrastus made all men united in kinship (οἰκειότης) and also made them sons of Heaven;[4] Alexarchus made them all brethren and sons of Heaven,

---

1 In a later age, cities *which had the same founder* sometimes called themselves 'brothers' on their coins. This has nothing to do with the fourth century B.C., and anyhow Cassandreia and Ouranopolis had not the same founder.

2 Done at greater length in my lecture of 1933.

3 For Euhemerus' date, often put too late, see Appendix to my lecture of 1933. Weinreich, *op. cit.* p. 14, calls him Cassander's 'Court philosopher', which is going rather far.

4 In the Porphyry fragment (p. 427): κοινοὺς ἁπάντων δείκνυσι γονεῖς οὐρανὸν καὶ γῆν.

and had the idea of a World-State which he called the city of Heaven; in his World-State Love (Aphrodite Ourania) played some conspicuous part, while in Theophrastus the natural love of the members of a family for one another was extended till it embraced the whole human race, and he did in one place call it Aphrodite (Cypris).[1] Euhemerus made of Heaven the first ruler to unite the whole human race in a World-State,[2] and the gods of his Ideal State were those of Alexarchus' coinage, the 'natural' deities Sun, Moon, and Stars,[3] while Aphrodite too had some part to play; in this he obviously connects with Alexarchus.[4] Our fragmentary tradition does not say that he called the members of his Ideal State brothers, but he did say that Zeus, when he reunited men in a universal State, joined them together in *amicitia*,[5] which is Theophrastus' φιλία. Euhemerus then connects with both Theophrastus and Alexarchus; but behind all three stood *something*—the same something—which influenced them all and which was later than Aristotle; and it does not appear what else that could have been but Alexander.

*   *   *   *   *

I ought to notice here Weinreich's very different theory about Alexarchus, *op. cit.* Though he has much that is useful, his main object is an attempt to show that Alexarchus was one of the troop (χορός) of Menecrates Zeus and in it played the part of the Sun, though Athenaeus (VII, 289 A *sqq.*) mentions neither Alexarchus nor the Sun in his list of those who went about with Menecrates in the character of his subordinate gods, all of them men whom he claimed to have cured of epilepsy on condition that they should become his slaves, δοῦλοι. This theory about Alexarchus seems impossible, if only on the dates. Menecrates already called himself Zeus when he wrote his (undated) letter[6] to Agesilaus of Sparta (reigned *c.* 399–360), and as he cannot have called himself Zeus till he had acquired a great reputation as a physician, he must have been middle-aged at least by, and perhaps long before, 360. He did visit Philip II (reigned 359–336), but his reception[7] was

---

1 See Dirlmeier, *op. cit.* p. 89 n. 1.   2 Jacoby I, no. 63, fr. 7.
3 *Ib.* fr. 2 = Diod. VI, 1, 2. Euhemerus called these gods ἀϊδίους καὶ ἀφθάρτους, which shows, as his date shows, that no question of Stoicism comes in; for to Stoics no god was ἀΐδιος or ἄφθαρτος except the Supreme Power, *S.V.F.* I, fr. 536.
4 Weinreich, *op. cit.* p. 15, made Alexarchus the reverse of the medal whose obverse was Euhemerus.
5 Jacoby, *ib.* fr. 23.   6 Plut. *Ages.* XXI; *Mor.* 191 A, 213 A.
7 Hegesander in Athen. VII, 289 C *sq.* = *F.H.G.* IV, 414; Aelian, *V.H.* XII, 51.

not of a kind calculated to make him stay in, or return to, Macedonia. On the other hand, in 323 (death of Alexander) Cassander, the eldest son of Antipater's numerous family, was as yet an undistinguished young man and none of his highly eligible sisters were as yet married; if Alexarchus existed when Menecrates visited Macedonia he was only a child. The earliest possible date for the foundation of Ouranopolis, i.e. for Alexarchus calling himself the Sun, is 315; by that time Menecrates, if still alive, must have been a very old man and his pantomime a thing of the past. But even if it were not so—even if we could suppose that Menecrates visited Macedonia again about 315 (for curing Alexarchus of epilepsy was a necessary condition of the theory)—would Cassander, of all men, have allowed a member of his family, one of the noblest in Macedonia, to become a slave (δοῦλος) to a crazy Sicilian doctor? A question, as Shakespeare says, not to be asked.

VI. ALEXANDER AT OPIS

What I have been discussing in this Appendix must be carefully distinguished from Alexander's so-called policy of fusion (*Verschmelzungspolitik*). That policy [1] has always been clear enough; it was a material thing, a thing every one could see—the appointment of Iranians to satrapies or other offices, a mixed army, mixed populations in the new cities, and mixed marriages, including those of himself and of his higher officers at Susa. It came into conflict with the idea of nationality; it had begun to break down during his lifetime—he had to remove or hang several Iranian satraps—and broke down completely once he was dead; the great generals, except Seleucus, repudiated their Asiatic wives, while the Greeks in the eastern cities, mostly mercenaries, rose in a body and tried to get back to Europe. What I am discussing is an idea, an immaterial thing which had not taken corporeal shape by the time he died—a dream, an aspiration, an inspiration, call it what you will—an idea with three facets or aspects, all closely connected; the component parts will be distinguished later. There were points at

---

1 Berve has defined it (*Klio*, xxxi, p. 136) thus: 'die Anerkennung einer fremden Bevölkerung als gleichwertiges Element, und der daraus entspringende Wille, aus rechtlich gleich zu stellenden Volksgruppen durch blutmässige Verbindung eine unauflösliche Einheit zu schaffen.' This is too theoretical for the known facts; many of Alexander's men married women whose peoples were not *rechtlich gleich* with their own. But Berve was trying to show, against the evidence, that the intermarriages were confined to Persians or anyhow Iranians.

which the fusion policy impinged on this idea—perhaps it could be called the first actual step towards putting one part of it into practice—and our sources, as will appear, sometimes do not distinguish the two things sufficiently clearly, while some modern writers have managed to squeeze everything into that policy; indeed the author of the latest, and in some ways the fullest, account of the policy of fusion, by too much insistence on the mixed marriages and the children to be born of them, has succeeded in giving the impression that what Alexander really wanted was to rule an empire of half-castes.[1] With this much of prelude I can now turn to Alexander's ideas, as shown in the four passages which have to be examined.[2] The first three relate to the scene at Opis and to what may be called the unity of mankind, or possibly the unity of peoples; the fourth, which is not connected with Opis, relates to the brotherhood of man. I will take the fourth passage first.

Plutarch (*Alex.* XXVII) begins by telling the story of Alexander's visit to Ammon and the priest hailing him as son of the god. He continues that Alexander had been pleased with some things said by Psammon, a philosopher in Egypt, and especially with his saying that God was king of all men;[3] but that he himself, when considering these matters, reached a more philosophic conclusion (φιλοσοφώτερον, i.e. wiser or better) and said that God was the common father of all mankind but that he made the best ones peculiarly his own.[4] This, on the face of it, is a plain statement that all men are brothers, and, if true, is the earliest known, at any rate in the western world. Wilcken did not believe that this is its meaning; but before I come to his criticism,[5] there are two things which may be got out of the way. In the second clause of Alexander's saying Plutarch obviously saw a reference to the priest hailing him son of Ammon; so Wilcken took it, and so I once took it. But, whatever Plutarch thought, all that the passage demands

1 Berve, *op. cit.*

2 (1) Arrian VII, 11, 8 and 9, the scene at Opis and Alexander's prayer; most is from Ptolemy, but two items are from a λόγος. (2) A fragment of Eratosthenes; part is given in Strabo 1, 4, 9 (66), and part, relating to the scene at Opis, in Plutarch, *de Alex. Fortuna* 1, 6 (329 B); how much is Eratosthenes will be considered. (3) A passage in Plut. *ib.* 330 E, almost certainly from Eratosthenes. (4) Plut. *Alex.* XXVII, source unknown.

3 ὅτι πάντες οἱ ἄνθρωποι βασιλεύονται ὑπὸ θεοῦ.

4 αὐτὸς περὶ τούτων φιλοσοφώτερον δοξάζειν καὶ λέγειν, ὡς πάντων μὲν ὄντα κοινὸν ἀνθρώπων πατέρα τὸν θεόν, ἰδίους δὲ ποιούμενον ἑαυτοῦ τοὺς ἀρίστους.

5 U. Wilcken, *S.B. Berlin*, XXIV, 1937, pp. 199, 200 [10, 11], to which I shall often have to refer. I fear that his criticism in these pages contains nothing to make me alter my views.

is that there must be a reference to Ammon; and as it should now be clear that Alexander never called himself, or thought that he was, son of Ammon (App. 22, 1), the reference is not to sonship but to his relations with Ammon generally. I have considered these already (App. 22, p. 355); they were something that was very serious, perhaps even sacred. But these relations did not preclude others, if 'best', from standing in the same relation to the god as he did. One may feel doubtful about Psammon in Plutarch's story; but it makes no difference, for what he is supposed to have said is good Aristotle,[1] which Alexander would have known in any case. I can now consider the first clause. Wilcken had no doubt that Alexander did say it, but said that it does not matter if he did; it was a mere commonplace, which must have been current among Greeks ever since Homer's πατὴρ ἀνδρῶν τε θεῶν τε, Zeus the father of gods and men; so far from the saying meaning the brotherhood of man, Alexander is at pains to separate God's children into two classes. But if we read Alexander's saying in its context, as I have given it, it seems clear that the first clause is the important one, not the second. Alexander knew his Homer well, and had he wanted to quote him he would have quoted correctly and not inserted the word κοινός, but that is not the real point. The point is, what called out Alexander's expression of opinion? He was soaked in Aristotle's ideas, a matter too often neglected, and he must have known how Aristotle interpreted Homer's phrase:[2] it meant, says Aristotle, that Zeus was *king* of gods and men, divine ruler of the world.[3] That is what Plutarch put in Psammon's mouth; that is the sense in which Homer's phrase is interpreted in three of the later treatises περὶ βασιλείας—Zeus is *king* of the universe;[4] and that was the view which

---

1 See n. 3 below.
2 He had made some annotations on the famous copy of the *Iliad* which Aristotle had revised for him and which he carried about in Darius' casket (Strabo XIII, 1, 27 (594), σημειωσαμένου τινά). Query: were they made while he was Aristotle's pupil?
3 Arist. *Pol.* I, 12, 1259b, 10, ἡ δὲ τῶν τέκνων ἀρχὴ βασιλική . . ., 12, διὸ καλῶς Ὅμηρος τὸν Δία προσηγόρευσεν εἰπών 'πατὴρ ἀνδρῶν τε θεῶν τε', τὸν βασιλέα τούτων ἁπάντων πατέρα εἰπών; i.e. πατήρ does not really mean father, as is obvious, seeing that in Homer some gods and many men are not descended from Zeus. M. P. Nilsson, *Arch. f. Rel. Wiss.* XXXV, 1938, p. 160, rendered πατήρ by *Hausvater*.
4 The fragments of these three treatises περὶ βασιλείας are given in Stobaeus IV, 7 (H.) and headed ὑποθῆκαι περὶ βασιλείας. They have nothing to do with Stoicism, as they are written in the Doric dialect; there is no need to doubt Stobaeus' statement that all are Pythagorean. Diotogenes can be dated to the reign of Demetrius the Besieger (see § III, p. 410 n. 1) and all

Alexander was criticising. That is to say, he was in effect answering, and going beyond, Aristotle, as he is known to have done in some other matters also (see for example p. 439 *post*), and that is why Plutarch says that he said something wiser (φιλοσοφώτερον); he went beyond God as king and ruler and made him the common *father* of all men. That he added that he himself had been specially honoured seems to me not to affect the matter in the least. What we have got, if I may use modern language without offence, is the whole difference between God the Ruler of the universe and God the Father. Before Alexander, every Greek for centuries had known the Homer passage without any-one deducing anything from it; after him, the Stoics took up and amplified his idea of the brotherhood of man, and we have seen (§ v) two men whom it affected who are earlier than Zeno. It is possible that we possess another very early reference to, and therefore con-firmation of, this saying of Alexander's. Megasthenes, in his version of the meeting between Alexander and the gymnosophists, makes the Indian Dandamis say to him 'If you are son of Zeus, *so am I*';[1] and it does not appear what else Megasthenes could have had in mind, for this is much earlier than the earliest Stoic enunciations of the fatherhood of God by Cleanthes[2] and Aratus of Soli.[3]

I turn now to the idea of the unity of mankind, the three passages which relate to the scene at Opis; and it will be best to begin with Eratosthenes. Strabo 1, 4, 9 (66), from ἐπὶ τέλει to the end of book 1, is explicitly from Eratosthenes. E. Schwartz[4] showed long ago that Plutarch, *de Alexandri Fortuna* 1, 6, must be from the same author; I know of no one who has contested this, and it seems quite certain,[5] as the two passages overlap, though Schwartz gave too much ol Plutarch to Eratosthenes. The Strabo passage does not say who it was

three belong to the same group. All three writers argue that the king on earth must imitate the divine ruler of the universe: Diotogenes fr. 62, p. 270, θεόμιμόν ἐντι πρᾶγμα βασιλῆα; Sthenidas of Locri, fr. 63, p. 271, μιματὰς νόμιμος τῶ θεῶ; and Ps.-Ecphantus, fr. 64, p. 272, οἷα τύπος τῶ ἀνωτέρω βασιλέως; and two of them, Diotogenes and Sthenidas, specifically quote Homer's πατὴρ ἀνδρῶν τε θεῶν τε as the object of imitation, but they quote it as meaning the *king* above, the ruler of the universe; there is nothing about this the principal god being *father* of anybody or anything, or any reference to 'father' in the fragments. This bears out what Aristotle had said and shows how Greeks of the early third century understood Homer's phrase.

1 Arr. VII, 2, 3.　　2 *Hymn to Zeus*, l. 4.　　3 *Phainomena*, l. 5.
4 *Rhein. Mus.* XL, 1885, pp. 252–4.
5 Followed by Susemihl, 1, p. 411 n. 13 and by Kaerst, II², p. 124 n. 1, and I think generally.

who advised Alexander to treat Greeks as friends and barbarians as enemies; Plutarch shows it was Aristotle, and indeed we know where it came from: Aristotle in the *Politics* had criticised some who said that good men were really free and bad men were really slaves[1] (whom he himself equated with barbarians),[2] and Alexander, as Eratosthenes says, was in turn criticising Aristotle. Otherwise the Strabo fragment of Eratosthenes is simple. Alexander transcended the old hard and fast distinction of Greek and barbarian, in itself a sufficiently amazing thing, and said that the real distinction between men was not race but whether they were good men or bad; in this way, the passage continues, he kept the spirit of Aristotle's teaching by abandoning the letter of it. There is a question whether this last part of the passage (from ὥσπερ δι' ἄλλο τι to the end) is also from Eratosthenes, as Schwartz thought, or is Strabo himself speaking, as several other writers have supposed;[3] it is not important for my purpose, but it is certainly Eratosthenes, for it is favourable to Alexander, while on the only occasion on which Strabo, speaking in his own person, alludes to Alexander, he uses the term of abuse, τῦφος, which the Stoics regularly applied to him.[4]

Turning now to the Plutarch passage, *de Alex. Fortuna*, I, 6, Schwartz gave the whole section to Eratosthenes. The first part, that dealing with Zeno's Πολιτεία, must however be Plutarch himself speaking, because of the antithesis ἔργον : λόγος; this runs all through *de Alex. Fortuna* I and is of the very essence of Plutarch's argument, while the hit at Zeno in comparing his citizens to cattle grazing together (I suppose we should say 'a lot of robots') is surely from Plutarch himself,[5] who did not love the Stoics. Eratosthenes begins at the words οὐ γὰρ ὡς Ἀριστοτέλης in 329B and goes down to τοὺς γάμους καὶ τὰς διαίτας in 329C; what follows, to the end of 6, is Plutarch mixing up Eratosthenes with other matter. The statement that Alexander told all men to regard the οἰκουμένη as their fatherland is merely an attribution to him of Stoic cosmopolitanism, which is certainly wrong. The statement that for all men the camp was to be their acropolis and guardhouse has nothing to do with the scene at Opis, where it would have been utterly meaningless; if Alexander ever said anything of the sort, which

1 *Pol.* I, 6, 1255a, 39.
2 *Ib.* I, 2, 1252b, 9.
3 W. Hoffman, *Das literarische Porträt Alexanders des Grossen*, p. 16, and writers there cited.
4 Strabo xv, 1, 5 (686), τετυφωμένον ταῖς τοιαύταις εὐτυχίαις.
5 See § IV, p. 419 n. 4.

seems unlikely, it must have been connected with the mixed army and the policy of fusion, to which policy the last phrase of the section, the mixed marriages, clearly relates. On the other hand, the statements that Alexander said that the good are the real kinsmen and the bad the real strangers, and that the good man is the true Greek and the bad man the real barbarian,[1] are Plutarch repeating in his own words what Eratosthenes had said as recorded in the Strabo passage. Eratosthenes himself, be it noted, had already brought in the policy of fusion by his allusion to the Susa marriages; they were in fact the point at which that policy most closely touched those ideas of Alexander which are being considered.

Having thus got the limits of the Eratosthenes fragment, we may now consider what it comes to. Aristotle, he says, had told Alexander to behave to Greeks as a leader,[2] to barbarians as a master, treating the Greeks as friends and relatives and the others as animals or plants; had Alexander done this, his leadership would have come to nothing but wars and banishments and internal conflicts. But Alexander knew better than Aristotle, and said that the real distinction between men was not one of race but whether they were good or bad, there being good and bad in every race. For 'he believed[3] that he had a mission from God to harmonise[4] men generally (κοινός) and to be the reconciler of the world,[5] bringing men from everywhere (τὰ πανταχόθεν) into a unity (εἰς ταὐτό) and mixing their lives and customs, their marriages

---

1 τὸ μὲν Ἑλληνικὸν ἀρετῇ τὸ δὲ βαρβαρικὸν κακίᾳ τεκμαίρεσθαι.

2 ἡγεμονικῶς refers to his being Hegemon of the League of Corinth.

3 ἀλλὰ κοινὸς ἥκειν θεόθεν ἁρμοστὴς καὶ διαλλακτὴς τῶν ὅλων νομίζων,...εἰς ταὐτὸ συνενεγκὼν τὰ πανταχόθεν, ὥσπερ ἐν κρατῆρι φιλοτησίῳ μίξας τοὺς βίους καὶ τὰ ἤθη καὶ τοὺς γάμους καὶ τὰς διαίτας.

4 ἁρμοστής here is not 'governor', but is formed directly from ἁρμόζειν and means 'harmoniser', 'one who brings about Homonoia'; Stoics used ἁρμονία and ὁμόνοια indifferently for the disposition of the universe (§ IV, p. 423 ante), and for common speech see Plut. Mor. 144 C, where ἁρμόζεσθαι is specifically used for 'to bring about Homonoia'. In the same way διαλλακτής is not 'arbitrator', but is formed directly from διαλλάσσειν and means 'reconciler'. ἁρμοστής in this sense seems to be a ἅπαξ λεγόμενον, but διαλλακτής had already been used in the sense of 'reconciler' by Aristotle: in Ath. Pol. 5 Solon is called κοινῇ διαλλακτήν, where the meaning 'arbitrator' is impossible on the facts (see C.A.H. IV, p. 50). The double occurrence in one phrase of words thus formed would alone suffice to show that it is genuine, for no literary forger could have done anything of the sort.

5 τῶν ὅλων without qualification can only have its usual meaning, 'the world'. There is one passage, Diod. XVIII, 50, 2, where it means Alexander's Empire, but that meaning depends solely on the context.

and social ways, as in a loving-cup'.[1] I would call special attention to
the extraordinary phrase 'Reconciler of the World', and to the unique[2]
reference to a loving-cup as an illustration of it; and to explain this
I must turn to the scene at Opis.[3] I may say at once that the explanation
is simply that Eratosthenes' loving-cup did actually exist; it was the
great krater on Alexander's table at Opis.[4]

After the mutiny at Opis and the reconciliation between Alexander
and the Macedonians, Alexander first sacrificed to his accustomed gods,
doubtless a thanksgiving for the reconciliation, and then passed on to a
greater reconciliation; he gave a vast banquet, traditionally to 9,000
people,[5] in order to emphasise that the long war was now over and

1 I have not met with any explanation of the loving-cup, κρατὴρ φιλοτήσιος
(see Athen. XI, no. 106); but the analogy of drinking healths (Tarn, *J.H.S.*
XLVIII, 1928, p. 211; cf. G. Macurdy, *A.J.P.* LIII, 1932, p. 168) shows
what it was. If *A*, the host, desired to toast *B* and *C*, he poured into a cup
two ladles of wine, saying 'of *B*' and 'of *C*', and drank it. But if he
desired to join his guests in a loving-cup, then besides the ladles for *B* and *C*
he poured in a third ladle, saying 'of *A*', and all three drank from the cup,
in which they had all, so to speak, been mixed.
2 No other reference to the use of the loving-cup as an illustration is given
in the long article φιλοτήσιος in Dindorf's Stephanus. It is just possible
that Aristophanes may have referred to it in *Peace* 996, where Trygaeus
prays to Peace to mix the Greeks again 'in the juice of friendship', μῖξον δ'
ἡμᾶς τοὺς Ἕλληνας πάλιν ἐξ ἀρχῆς φιλίας χυλῷ; but, looking at *Frogs*, 943,
it seems much more likely that the usual (metaphorical) rendering, 'a taste
of φιλία', is the correct one.
3 Described, Arr. VII, 11, 8 and 9, from Ἀλέξανδρος δέ to the end. It is a very
short account for so important an event; for the reason see p. 443 *post.*
Except for the two items from a λόγος (n. 5 below; p. 441 n. 1), the account
is Ptolemy's, for it cannot be separated from Arrian's account of the
weddings at Susa; and that account can only be from the *Journal* through
Ptolemy, for it is (part of) an official list of the brides, as is shown by their
names and pairings being correctly given (see App. 20, p. 333 n. 1, cf. p. 334
n. 4); corruptions came in soon enough. Also the weddings and the banquet
are regularly combined in the tradition; Eratosthenes refers to γάμους in
the loving-cup, and Plutarch (or Eratosthenes again) applies the word
φιλοτήσιον to the weddings, 329 E. Kornemann, p. 164, cf. p. 219, gave the
account of the banquet to Ptolemy; and there is really no one else it could
be. For Ptolemy as the source of (the genuine parts of) Alexander's
speech at Opis see my App. 15, pp. 290 *sqq.*
4 I made the identification *A.J.P.* LX, 1939, p. 66; but there is more to be
said about that.
5 The number is from a λόγος in Arrian; but Ptolemy confirms the enormous
size of the gathering by using the strange phrase θοίνην δημοτελῆ. δημοτελής
meant primarily 'at the people's expense' and so came to mean 'national',
in the sense in which we call Bank Holiday a national holiday; neither

that the world with which he was concerned was at peace; the banquet concluded with all the guests making a libation together,[1] which led up to and was followed by his prayer. Arrian's account of the scene and the prayer is, as has been seen, from Ptolemy; Eratosthenes' references go back to some eyewitness (see *post*) who was not Ptolemy. That this extraordinary scene, unparalleled I fancy before or since, was, as it happened, the culminating point of Alexander's career is certain, though no one may have realised it at the time, since it could not be foreseen that he would die next year. The number of guests, all of whom were seated, would necessitate many tables; Alexander's own would be the largest and most prominent, and on it stood the krater Ptolemy mentions, which contained the wine for the libation;[2] it was said to have been of enormous size. Presumably on the other tables would be smaller kraters of wine, otherwise all the guests could not have joined in the libation, as they did; notionally, the other kraters were all part of Alexander's krater and the other tables part of his table, separate tables and kraters being mere machinery necessitated by the great number of guests.

Ptolemy says that at Alexander's own table were seated Macedonians, Persians, some Greek seers, some Magi (presumably Medes), and those representatives of 'the other peoples' (i.e. other than Macedonians or Persians) who, through being distinguished for this or that, ranked highest in dignity;[3] that is, the most prominent men from every race in his Empire and from at least one people not in his Empire, Greeks,[4]

meaning is applicable here, for the gathering was multi-national. There was no word for this in Greek, as there is none in English; Ptolemy did his best by using a word which might mean (as we should say) 'everybody was there', instead of something obvious like μεγίστην. The great number of guests is confirmed by Ptolemy troubling to remark that all were seated, meaning thereby that one would suppose that such a number could not be seated, but that many would have to stand.

1 From the same λόγος. Eratosthenes (*post*) shows it is correct, apart from the fact that nothing else *could* have happened if the host were a Macedonian.

2 There is a valuable description of this krater, which is doubtless correct, in Ps.-Call. A′, III, 29, 9. It was a silver krater of enormous size which had originally belonged to the Great King; it was found in the palace at Susa, and was used by Alexander ἐν τῷ μεγάλῳ δείπνῳ, ὅτε τὴν θυσίαν ἐποιησάμεθα τῶν Σωτηρίων (i.e. the conclusion of peace). The great banquet which followed after the sacrifices is the one I am discussing.

3 The usual meaning of πρεσβευόμενοι. They were not 'envoys'.

4 For the modern theory that the old Greek cities of Asia Minor were in his Empire see App. 7, 1. Few theories have ever been so ill-founded.

sat at his own table. All those at his table (οἱ ἀμφ᾽ αὐτόν) drew for themselves wine from the krater on his table; those at the other tables must have done the same from their kraters (which notionally would be part of Alexander's krater), for the whole assembly made one libation, i.e. at the same time. At an ordinary Macedonian banquet or dinner (not at a Greek one) the signal for the libation after the meal was given by trumpet,[1] and it is known that Alexander followed the Macedonian custom;[2] the signal therefore at Opis was given by trumpet, which also enabled any one outside the banquet to associate himself mentally, if he so desired, with the act of worship involved.[3] The libation, Ptolemy says, was led by the Greek seers and the Magi, not by Alexander or any Macedonian; and it is to be wished that we knew to what god it was made. The ἀγαθοῦ δαίμονος of the private Greek dinner-party is out of the question. The Magi were notoriously strict upholders of their own religion, and could hardly have led a libation to a Greek god; the formula, one supposes, must have been phrased in such a way that every people there could have seen in it the supreme deity of its own religion, and with this agree Alexander's saying that 'God' (and not Zeus or another) was the common father of mankind, and Eratosthenes' statement that he thought his mission was from God, θεόθεν. What is certain is that no witness of the scene could ever have forgotten the sight of that great krater on Alexander's table and people of every nationality drawing wine from it for their common libation; this in turn shows that that krater was Eratosthenes' loving-cup, in which men from everywhere were mixed, as though notionally it contained portions of wine named for each one of them. Eratosthenes does not say that it *was* a loving-cup; he says '*as if* in a loving-cup', because the assembly did not *drink* the wine themselves; it was poured out to heaven in a solemn act of worship. Eratosthenes' account then must go back to an eyewitness, one who had seen that krater; guesses as to who it might have been are useless, except that it was certainly not Ptolemy. But Eratosthenes used the metaphor of the loving-cup to illustrate the phrase 'reconciler of the world'; that phrase then also belongs to, or depends on, the scene at Opis, and may ultimately go back to the same eyewitness; indeed it is conceivable (I will put it no higher) that Alexander used the occasion to proclaim his mission.

1 Tarn, *J.H.S.* xlviii, 1928, p. 210, and passages there cited.
2 Chares, Jacoby ii, no. 125 fr. 4 (16). Add to my references (previous note) that the trumpeter is mentioned at the dinner at which Cleitus was killed; Plut. *Alex.* li.
3 This from Chares, fr. 4.

The culminating point of the whole scene was Alexander's prayer, to which the libation led up; it does not appear how the two can be separated. We have a formal version of the prayer in Arrian from Ptolemy, who heard it, and also an informal reference to it in Plutarch.[1] Plutarch has been using Eratosthenes off and on in this part of the *de Alexandri Fortuna* since 329 B (he is referred to by name in 330 A); and this passage, which conjoins the two key-words of the prayer, ὁμόνοια and κοινωνία, and in the same order, and thus relates to the scene at 'Opis, must, it seems, be from Eratosthenes and therefore ultimately from some one who heard it; but the passage (which I shall come to) does not do more than give the tenor of the prayer, though it helps to elucidate it. *A priori*, one would expect that the prayer to which such a scene led up as its culmination would have contained more than the fourteen words which are all that Ptolemy gives. It almost certainly did. Ptolemy was truthful over facts (though not always so over figures), and the prayer was a fact and so had to be given; but by the time he wrote his history he had long parted company with Alexander's ideas, and he would hardly say more than he could help about a scene with which he had small sympathy and a prayer which was the condemnation of his own methods of rule. But there is another matter. No prayer could possibly *begin* by asking for 'the other good things' (a commonplace formula)[2] before the real object of the prayer had been stated; it is almost certain therefore that what we have is only a brief summary or paraphrase. But we have no means of going behind the words we have, and must take them as they are. It is fortunate therefore that, as Eratosthenes must also go back to some one who, like Ptolemy, was there, we can add to Ptolemy's factual account the interpretation given by Eratosthenes or rather perhaps by his ultimate source.

Two translations of the prayer as given by Arrian[3] are grammatically possible, and both are equally true to the Greek. We can read it: Alexander 'prayed for the other good things and for Homonoia between, and partnership in rule between, Macedonians and Persians'. This is the usual rendering, often enough turned merely into a prayer for the joint rule of Macedonians and Persians, thus enabling writers to say that there is nothing to the scene at Opis at all but the policy of

1 *De Alex. Fort.* I, 330 E: πᾶσιν ἀνθρώποις ὁμόνοιαν καὶ εἰρήνην καὶ κοινωνίαν πρὸς ἀλλήλους παρασκευάσαι διανοηθέντα.
2 See, for example, the ritual prayer in Diod. I, 70, 5.
3 VII, 11, 9, εὔχετο δὲ τά τε ἄλλα ἀγαθὰ καὶ ὁμόνοιάν τε καὶ κοινωνίαν τῆς ἀρχῆς Μακεδόσι καὶ Πέρσαις.

fusion.[1] Or we can read it: Alexander 'prayed for the other good things, and for Homonoia, and for partnership in the realm between Macedonians and Persians'; and two things show that this rendering is the correct one. He *could* not have prayed for a joint rule of Macedonians and Persians; it had no meaning. His two realms, Macedonia and 'Asia', were not two Empires but one, united in his own person as equally ruler of both; he was alike king of the Macedonians and Great King of 'Asia', the one-time Persian empire, and while he lived there could be no talk of any other rule in the joint Empire but his own. And we shall see that Homonoia in the prayer has to stand alone as a substantive thing, and not merely be tacked on to the words 'Macedonians and Persians'.

All this is borne out by the Eratosthenes passage I have referred to (p. 443 n. 1); it has already been seen (§ III, p. 417 *ante*) that we start with a strong presumption in favour of its truth. The passage says this: Alexander's intention (διανοηθέντα) was to bring about for all men Homonoia and peace and partnership (or fellowship) with one another. The κοινωνία πρὸς ἀλλήλους of this sentence shows that the κοινωνία τῆς ἀρχῆς of the prayer does mean partnership in the realm and not partnership in rule. Peace must have been included in the prayer, for in one aspect the whole scene celebrated the end of the war and the return of peace. Finally, the Homonoia of all men towards each other—all becoming of one mind together—shows that the Homonoia which Alexander prayed for was not meant to be confined to Macedonians and Persians. It is hard to believe that in the actual prayer Homonoia was not defined; for it is Homonoia between all men which is signified by Alexander's claim to a divine mission to be the harmoniser and reconciler of the world, that Homonoia which for centuries men were to long for but never to reach.

The prayer was the culminating point of, and cannot be separated from, the libation; and this being so, there is one more question to ask— what peoples were included in the prayer for Homonoia? In 1936 Professor Kolbe claimed that the prayer must have included all the peoples of the Empire;[2] he was on the right tack, but he supported his view solely from the fusion policy—Iranian satraps, mixed army, mixed marriages—and he made the 'other peoples' share in the ἀρχή in the sense of rule, *Herrschaft*; and though he said (p. 18): 'Der

1 Most recently Berve, *Klio*, XXXI, 135 *sqq*.
2 W. Kolbe, *Die Weltreichsidee Alexanders des Grossen*, 1936. The title, and the epilogue (p. 21), show that this study really belongs to the literature of the 'World-kingdom'.

Gedanke einer allgemeinen Weltverbrüderung ist geboren', his world-brotherhood did not follow from anything which he had been saying about the scene at Opis, and seemingly only meant that all men were alike to be subjects in Alexander's 'World-kingdom'. It was not too difficult therefore for Wilcken to discard a conclusion which had not been properly founded.[1] Now, however, that Eratosthenes' loving-cup is seen to have actually existed and that consequently Erastosthenes also is referring to the scene at Opis, many of the old arguments have lost their meaning.[2] That the Homonoia for which Alexander prayed was meant to include more than Macedonians and Persians, more even than the peoples under his rule, seems certain enough, for Eratosthenes calls the people mixed in the loving-cup τὰ πανταχόθεν, people from everywhere, and again πᾶσιν ἀνθρώποις, all men.[3] But one can get much the same thing from Ptolemy-Arrian also. This account mentions the leading men of the 'other peoples' seated at Alexander's table, and states that the libation was led by Greek seers and Magi; and the Greek seers, at the least, show that the participants were not confined to Alexander's Empire. Indeed there must have been plenty of Greeks among the guests, for there were many whom, if the guests numbered anything approaching 9,000, he could not have failed to invite: leading figures like Eumenes and Nearchus, his very important Greek technicians, including Aristobulus (§ D, pp. 39 *sqq.*), the philosophers and poets at his court. But he was not ruler of the Greek world; he had no Greek subjects, unless in Cilicia. With part of that world he had no political connection at all; with another part the connection was only that he was Hegemon of the League of Corinth; the Greek cities of Asia were his free allies (App. 7, 1); with Thessaly alone his relations were somewhat closer, but the fact that he was the elected head of the Thessalian League no more made him *ruler* of Thessaly than Aratus of Sicyon was ruler of the Achaean League. But, besides Greeks, there was another people outside of Alexander's Empire who could not fail to have been represented. If anything like 9,000 people were invited to a banquet whose ostensible object was to celebrate the restoration of peace, representatives of his own armed forces must have been included; and, if so, he could not possibly have omitted the Agrianians, that favourite and indispensable corps to whom he had already paid such

1 *Op. cit.* p. 199 [10] n. 1.
2 For example, Berve, *op. cit.* p. 161 n. 1.
3 It is, of course, too late for 'all men' to mean 'all Greeks' (on which see § 1, p. 401 n. 3 *ante*), even if the context did not, as it does, render such a meaning impossible here.

marked honour in the presence of the whole army;[1] and the Agrianians were not his subjects or even his allies, but just northern 'barbarians'.

I must turn for a moment to Wilcken's already noticed criticism. It is, of course, indisputable, as he said, that only two peoples, Macedonians and Persians, are named in the prayer; that is, in the version Arrian gives, which, we have seen, cannot be more than a summary or paraphrase. However, this is Wilcken's foundation, and as such I take it; and, that being so, it is easy enough to see the reason. Alexander was praying primarily for the reconciliation of the two sides in the great struggle; and Macedonians and Persians are named because they were the protagonists, the leaders, the peoples who had supplied the two rival monarchs. But just as he took advantage of a great gathering, invited primarily to mark the end of the war, to promulgate certain new ideas of his own, so his prayer that Macedonians and Persians might live in partnership (or fellowship, κοινωνία) was only part· of his prayer for the reconciliation of all men in Homonoia. Wilcken, however, has a very different interpretation: the object of Alexander's prayer, which was confined to Macedonians and Persians, was that these two peoples should keep the peace while he was absent conquering the West. This of course depends on Alexander's supposed plan for the conquest of the western Mediterranean basin, which Wilcken believed to be genuine but which, I trust, I have shown to be a demonstrably late invention (App. 24). Wilcken continued that participation of Greek seers and Magi in the sacred ceremony confirms the fact that no peoples other than Macedonians and Persians were meant to be included. About the Magi I cannot dogmatise. They would probably be Medes, and apart from that Alexander could not have left out his wife's Bactrian kinsfolk, the great barons of the north-eastern marches who had cost him such labour to overcome and reconcile; and though I cannot say that the word 'Persians' here could not have included Medes and Bactrians, as it often did in common parlance, still we are not dealing with common parlance, and I cannot recall any *formal* document or occasion on which it does so. But putting that aside, Wilcken's state-

1 Arr. VI, 2, 2: for his voyage down the Hydaspes he took on his transports all the hypaspists and the *agema* of the Companion Cavalry, and also his two favourite corps of light-armed, the Cretan archers, who were at least Greeks, and the Agrianians, who were 'barbarians', while the Macedonian phalanx had to march on foot; this may have been one of the many grievances of the phalanx which came to a head in the mutiny at Opis. The Agrianians were the subjects of Alexander's friend Longarus, and can hardly be called 'allies'; I imagine the nearest parallel to his recruitment of them would be Britain's recruitment of Gurkhas for the Indian army.

ment about Greeks is surely misconceived. If there was one racial distinction more vigorous and vital than another in Alexander's day it was that between Greeks and Macedonians; and though a century later the distinction may have died out in the Farther East, it remained lively enough in the Aegean world till the end of Macedonia's independence. What the Greeks do show has already been indicated. Wilcken's final suggestion was that the representatives of the 'other peoples' were only there as *witnesses*. This, as he means it, is flatly contradicted by Eratosthenes and by the λόγος in Arrian; and one might well ask, why summon representatives from the greater part of the known world to witness a simple political arrangement? But in another sense, everyone there save Alexander himself was both participant and witness—witness to the first tentative enunciation of one of the most important ideas ever put forward in a world which regarded perpetual warfare as an inevitable rule. Before leaving Wilcken, I must notice one point of much interest: he said he had never met a really good explanation of the difficult phrase κοινωνία τῆς ἀρχῆς, taking ἀρχή to mean 'rule'. Neither have I, and I venture to think I never shall; the explanation is that ἀρχή does not mean 'rule'. I may note in conclusion that he passed over 'Reconciler of the World' in silence, which is perhaps better than recent attempts to explain it away.[1]

It seems to me then to be proved as clearly as a difficult question of this sort in antiquity is ever likely to be proved that Alexander did think of, and hold, the ideas which I have ascribed to him; and now that the examination of our texts is ended, it should be possible to be a little more precise about what those ideas were. We have really been dealing, as I mentioned by anticipation in § 1, with three things, though I cannot call them three ideas; all are interconnected, and they are rather three facets of a single idea. The first is the statement that all men are brothers; Alexander was the first man known to us, at any rate in the West,[2] to say so plainly and to apply it to the whole human race, without distinction of Greek or barbarian. The second thing is his belief that he had a divine mission to be the harmoniser and reconciler of the world, to

1 Berve, *op. cit.* pp. 166, 167 n. 1, connects it with Alexander's supposed plan for interchange of populations between Europe and Asia, on which see App. 24, p. 383 and § v, p. 429 *ante*. Kolbe, *op. cit.* p. 14, gets out of it by translating ἁρμοστής by *Schirmherr*, protector, which the word never means, and διαλλακτής by *Scheiderichter*, arbitrator, which makes nonsense of the following metaphor of the loving-cup; on the meaning of these two words see p. 439 n. 4 *ante*.

2 I have read somewhere that he was anticipated by a Chinese philosopher, but I do not remember by whom. Nothing came of it.

bring it to pass that all men, being brothers, should live together in Homonoia, in unity of heart and mind. This was a dream, or an inspiration; it was something which had come to him and was struggling for expression; he gave it expression for the first time at Opis, tentatively, in the form of Homonoia between all men, and one who was there crystallised it in the metaphor of a loving-cup in which all men were mixed. It would seem that his application of this idea was not so much to humanity generally as to the world he himself knew and lived in—not only to the peoples of his Empire, but also to those outside it and in particular to the Greek world, alike the most important, the most civilised, and the most quarrelsome of the peoples with whom he had to do. There is no question of his having had any cut and dried plan; indeed it is unlikely that he had any plan at all, though the recall of the exiles may conceivably have been meant as a first attempt to do something about it. It was, and was to remain, a dream, but a dream greater than all his conquests. Many have dreamt his dream since; but the honour of being the first remains his. But no one has ever seen how it could be made a reality; least of all perhaps do we see it to-day. It is not at all likely that he saw it either; but, being Alexander, he would, had he lived, have tried to do *something* to outlaw war, and would have failed as the world has failed ever since. The third thing of the three which I mentioned was the desire, expressed in the libation and prayer at Opis, that all the peoples in his realm should be partners and not merely subjects; had he lived, this was a thing which he probably would have attempted. The policy of fusion may have been meant as a step towards this idea of partnership, as partnership itself was to be a step towards the fulfilment of his dream.

Hardly any one at the time could understand what he meant. One philosopher after his death, Theophrastus, did get hold of some sort of idea derived from the brotherhood of man and used it theoretically (§ v); one small ruler, Alexarchus, was affected, and was promptly called mad; but the world had to wait for a generation for a man who should be big enough himself to understand Alexander. The tradition that behind Zeno lay Alexander is true enough, but not merely in the somewhat material shape in which it has reached us; what lay behind Zeno was not so much Alexander's career as Alexander's ideas. Zeno's great city of the world took up and was founded on Alexander's idea of a human brotherhood, but as regards the unity of mankind in Homonoia Zeno took his own line; while Alexander thought he had a mission to bring it about, Zeno said that Homonoia was there already and always had been, if only men's eyes could be opened to see it. In practice it made little difference, for a mission to men was necessary in either case, and Zeno and his followers tried to carry that out; but there was a clear difference in theory. We can perhaps trace, in the third century B.C., some slight influence of Alexander's dream on Greeks, whether it came through Zeno or however else: the Greek remained as quarrelsome as ever, but he began to have an uncomfortable feeling that he ought not to be. As to the partnership in the Empire of its different peoples, that to Zeno had no meaning; in his World-State there were neither empires nor races. But this happened to be an idea which Alexander's generals could and did grasp as a practical matter, and they made up their minds to have nothing to do with it; the day he died it vanished like the morning mist.

But the mist returns, and more than a century later this idea of Alexander's came back; it came back in the empire of Northern India set up by Demetrius the Euthydemid, who, like the great Cleopatra, was half Macedonian and half Greek. The evidence that Demetrius was quite consciously copying Alexander—that he meant to be a second Alexander, as he very nearly was—seems conclusive; and his Indian empire can hardly be called the rule of Greeks over Indians, for it was an empire in which both peoples participated, a kind of partnership or joint commonwealth; there is evidence enough for the *fact*, though we know too little of the *form*. I have told the whole story elsewhere;[1] here I need only mention that Demetrius tried to put into practice one of the things for which Alexander prayed, and fell because his ideas were too advanced for many of his Greek subjects to follow.

1 *Bactria and India*, ch. IV *passim*, esp. pp. 131–2 (on ἀνίκητος see further App. 21 *ante*) and 181 (where for 'joint rule', six lines from the bottom, read 'partnership in the realm'); also parts of ch. VI, esp. pp. 258, 260; also pp. 411 *sq*.

ADDENDA

P. 6. In *Meteorologica* III, 2, 372a, 29 Aristotle says he has only met with two instances of the moon-bow (white rainbow) in more than fifty years, and I think such phrasing implies not much over fifty years. In 334/3 he would have been fifty-one; so, as I see it, the *Meteorologica* cannot be much later than that.

P. 21 n. 5. I follow Jan's text (Teubner, 1870), merely substituting the old suggestion 'e fama' for the meaningless 'et fama' which he prints. His text included the words 'hic iam plus quam e fama' in the bracket; later he doubted (Introduction, p. xxxv). Mayhoff's later edition (Teubner, 1906), followed by the Loeb edition, takes these words out of the bracket, thus making 'hic' refer to Theophrastus. To my mind this is impossible; 'hic' *must* refer to the writer last mentioned, i.e. Cleitarchus, and is intended to differentiate him from Theopompus.

P. 57 n. 7 (cf. pp. 84, 105), Alexander's fight with the river. Possibly the name Acesines is correct after all; for the combined stream of the Hydaspes and the Acesines is called Acesines (Arr. VI, 14, 5), and *perhaps* the worst trouble for the ships was below the actual junction (Arr. VI, 4, 4 *sqq.*).

P. 136 n. 2. Another case of Arrian using κατά for 'up-stream', and for the same reason, is VII, 19, 3, τὸ ναυτικὸν κατὰ τὸν Εὐφράτην ποταμὸν ἀναπεπλευκὸς ἀπὸ θαλάσσης τῆς Περσικῆς.

P. 182. See a forthcoming study by G. T. Griffith in *J.H.S.* entitled 'Alexander's generalship at Gaugamela'.

P. 236. For a possible objection to the view that Bucephala was Hippostratus' capital see R. B. Whitehead, *Num. Chron.* 1940, p. 110.

P. 259. Bernardakis in the first Teubner edition (1889) gave παροικοῦσαν (Reiske) αἷς ἐμπολισθεὶς ἀπεσβέσθη (Reiske) τὸ ἄγριον κ.τ.λ., which I cannot construe. Nachstädt in the second Teubner edition (1935) gave παροικοῦσαν, αἷς ἐμπολισθείσαις (Reiske) ἐσβέσθη τὸ ἄγριον κ.τ.λ., which probably is intended to mean 'by which (cities), founded as cities in their midst'; but, if so, it should be πολισθείσαις, 'being made cities', for the only attested meaning of the rare verb ἐμπολίζειν is 'to enclose within a city', and one cannot in an emendation assume that a word has an otherwise unknown meaning. F. C. Babbitt, in the Loeb edition, vol. IV (1936), read παροικοῦσαν, οἷς ἐμπολισθεῖσιν (Babbitt) ἐσβέσθη κ.τ.λ., and translated it 'for by the founding of cities in these places savagery was extinguished', which, like the other versions I have cited, does not give the meaning of ἐμπολίζειν. If, as seems inevitable, Reiske was right in substituting ἐμπολίζειν for ἐμποδίζειν, *something* has got to be enclosed in the cities; I have tried to meet this in my own version (p. 259), where τὸ ἄγριον (in a wild state, uncivilised) refers to the local 'barbarians', numbers of whom were certainly included in every Greek city in the East, whether Alexander's or later.

Addenda

P. 267 n. 5. The meaning of μέλας as 'swarthy' or 'sunburnt' was not given in Liddell and Scott[8]; the ninth edition gives 'dark, swarthy', citing Plato *Rep.* 474 E, Demosth. 21, 71. But for Hellenistic Greek the meaning 'sunburnt' is certain: LXX, *Song of Solomon*, 1, 5, the girl says Μέλαινά εἰμι ἐγὼ καὶ καλή ('black but comely') and then explains (1, 6) ἐγώ εἰμι μεμελανωμένη, ὅτι παρέβλεψέ με ὁ ἥλιος.

P. 295 n. 4, ἄπιτε. Greeks used this word when the speaker of a funeral oration dismissed the mourners: ἀπολοφυράμενοι (or some equivalent) ἄπιτε, 'and now, having mourned the dead, you may depart'; see Thuc. II, 46, Plato *Menex.* 249 C, [Demosth.] 60, 37. But this very different usage does not invalidate anything I have said.

P. 298. Some, if not all, of the sayings of Alexander utilised by Plutarch must go back ultimately to the *Journal,* which recorded λεγόμενα no less than πρασσόμενα (see p. 263). Birt, *Alexander der Grosse*, p. 458 n. 20, must be right as to this.

P. 347 n. 1. The article by G. de Sanctis, 'Gli ultimi messaggi di Alessandro ai Greci', *Riv. Fil.* LXVIII, 1940, p. 1, was not accessible to me till this Appendix was in proof. I have seen no reason to alter anything I have written. Another recent article, by F. Oertel, 'Zur Ammonsohnschaft Alexanders', *Rhein. Mus.* N.F. 89, 1940, pp. 66–74, agrees with Wilcken on the importance of the greeting at Ammon.

P. 382. Herodotus IX, 105, mentions a village near Carystus named Κύρνος; but Euboea is not Macedonia.

P. 382 n. 2. On the island Icaros in the Persian Gulf see M. N. Tod, *J.H.S.* LXIII, 1943, p. 112.

P. 384 n. 3. It is possible to translate 'indigna' as 'unmerited'; to us it may seem more pointed. But I doubt if that was Lucan's point here. What he cared about (I think) was burial or non-burial (great importance was attached to burial): Pompey was not buried, his murderers were; the words 'pudendam' and 'indigna' are just mud thrown at the murderers in passing. 'Pyramides' and 'Mausolea' must be identical, in spite of -que, just as in the previous line the dead Ptolemies and their dynasty *are* identical, in spite of -que.

P. 397 n. 2. O. W. Reinmuth, 'Alexander and the world-state', in *The Greek Political Experience*, 1941, pp. 109–24, thinks that Alexander probably did have the idea of the unity of mankind, but meant to carry it out by a union of all races under one political organisation, i.e. a world-state.

INDEX

To index every occurrence of words that run throughout the book, such as Alexander, Greeks, Persians, or some ancient authors, would be worse than useless; in such cases I have tried to give only what is important. A. = Alexander throughout.

Alexandrias, the, list of (*cont.*)
  (17) Alexandria in Sogdiana on
    the Oxus (Termez), 235, 241,
    247, 258; also called Alexandria
    'among the Sogdians', 243–4,
    or 'in the country of Sôd
    (Sogd)', 244. Probably called
    Alexandria Tarmita or Tarmata,
    258
  (18) Alexandria Troas (promised
    but not built by A.), 233, 239–
    40, 241, 243; also called Alex-
    andria 'of the Granicus', 240,
    245
  Very doubtful are two on the
    Indus, 239, 241, and Alexandria
    in Mygdonia, 239, or in Meso-
    potamia, 246; for Alexandria
    'in Thrace', 241–2, *see* Alex-
    andropolis. Inexplicable are
    Alexandria 'near Latmos in
    Caria', 241–2, Alexandria 'on
    the Black Gulf', 241, 253, and
    some late corruptions, 246
Alexandropolis in Thrace, 242,
  248–9; in Parthyene, 249; near
  Sacastene (Candahar), 249
Alexarchus, 423, 429–34; his miniature World-State, 430–3; affected by A., 432, 448
Alpis, river, 388
Alps, 387–90; Maritime Alps, 390,
  392, 395
Amazons, 308, 327–8; Queen of the,
  83, 92, 103, 125, 132, 308, 319,
  323–4, 327–9
Ammon, 36–7, 54, 70, 123; worshipped by Greeks, 349; identified with Zeus later, 348, 350,
  358; priest of, 347–8, 354; his
  greeting to A., 350, 357, 435;
  Ammon's alleged promise to
  A., 378; alleged grant of invin-
  cibility, 338–42; A. as supposed
  son of Ammon, 98, 291, 347–8,
  350–1, 353, 354 and n., 356,
  359, 364, 435–6; his real relations with Ammon, 351 n.,
  354–5, 359, 362, 436

Ἀμμωνιεῦσι, 341 n., 356, 377
Amon-Re, 347–50, 354, 378
Amphipolis, 33 n., 382
Amphitrite, 351 n.
Amyntas, phalanx-leader, 74, 94–5,
  142, 145, 271; writer, 39 n.
Anatolian, 218–19, 224, 226
Anaxarchus, 57, 358
Anaxicrates, 16 n., 395
Anaximenes, 20, 220
Andromachus, 159, 167
Antigenes, 142, 146–7, 190, 193; son
  of Coenus, 146, 314; satrap,
  310–11, 314, 317
Antigone, 48
Antigoneia, 239
Antigonus I, 95, 114, 141, 146, 151,
  162, 225, 238, 239–40, 299, 311,
  313; on communications, 110–
  11, 177, 398; satrap, 110; his
  agēma, 163; shipbuilding,
  387–8; proclamation of free-
  dom, 210; founds the Ilian,
  Ionian, and Island Leagues,
  231–2; name confused with
  Antigenes, 314. *See* 'Heracles'
Antigonus II Gonatas, 65 n., 168,
  231, 300, 332, 358, 363, 425
Antigonus III Doson, 379 n.
Antioch, Bushire, 257; Merv, 235;
  'in Scythia', 235, 258; in Syria,
  259; Tarmata or Tharmata,
  235, 258; at Tigris mouth, 236
Antiochus I, 12, 17, 19, 50, 235
Antiochus I or II, 211–12, 227
Antiochus III, 181, 206–7, 227, 335 n.
Antiochus (a chiliarch), 150
Antipater, 42, 96, 124, 142, 147,
  155–6, 176, 364, 370–1, 429;
  his powers and duties, 171,
  202 n., 229, 231, 315; corre-
  spondence with A., 301–2;
  regent, 311, 317–18, 335 n. 1,
  379 n.
Antiphon (sophist), 401 n., 427
Antisthenes, 408
Antony, 48, 114, 387
Aornos, 51–2, 58, 76
Apama, 333 n.

Index

Diodorus (*cont.*)

mary, 128–9, 132; appreciation, 87. On A. at Ammon, 339–40; return from Ammon, 37; list of A.'s troops, 156–9, *and see* Argyraspids. On the siege of Halicarnassus, 73–4, 217; on Gaugamela, 74, 182, 185; on the Gandaridae, 280 and n., 282; on Persepolis, 47–8; on Hyrcania, 87–91; on ἀνίκητος, 339–41; on Philomelus, 345. Preserves the Gazetteer, 7, 8, but makes interpolations, 276–9. Gives the fictitious embassies, 23, 374–8, but also the Greek ones, 377; preserves A.'s supposed Plans, 378–98, *see* Plans

Diogenes Laertius, 405, 407, 420

Diogenes, tyrant of Mitylene, 202

Diogenes of Sinope, 405–7; his *Politeia*, 406–9

Diognetus, 39

Dion (in Transjordania), 233

Dionysius of Halicarnassus, 22, 266–9

Dionysopolis, 249

Dionysus, as A.'s ancestor, 358; his Indian expedition, 45–6, 52, 57, 104–5; supposedly imitated by A., 49, 55–6, 60; altars on the Jaxartes, 50, 62; κῶμος to, 46–9, 76, 84, 322

Dioscuri, 56–7, 362

Diotogenes, 368, 409–11, 416n., 417, 436n.; his date, 410n.; quotes Aristotle, 368, 410 n. 2

Dioxippus, 83, 358n., 359n.

Dium in Macedonia, 293, 382

Diyllus, 63n., 78, 83, 87, 115

Dodona, 349, 382

Dokimeion, 248

Doloaspis, 303n.

Doric dialect, 409, 410n., 436n.

Dorylaeum, 343n.

Drangiana, 161, 166, 247, 257

Dryden, *Alexander's Feast*, 47

Duris, 107, 333 and n., 360n.

Dusares, 343n.

Ecbatana, 104, 153, 176, 178, 299

Egypt: place, 37, 59, 151, 238, 387; empire, 19, 29, 173, 384; no satrap of, 303n.; A. in, 350, 354, 362, 372. *See* Alexandria (8)

Egyptian custom, 385–6; language, 348; priest, 402; Egyptians, 95

ἑκατοστύς, 160–1

Elaia, 223–4, 227

Elburz Mts, 104, 178, 248

Eleans, 159, 377

Elis, 349

Embassies, the, 25, 87, 126, 356, 374–8, 394

Empedocles, 360n., 428

Ephesus, 172–5, 216, 218

Ephialtes, 73

Ephippus, 4, 269, 305n., 354n.

Ephorus, 389

Epictetus, 133, 406, 423

Epicurean school, 69, 297

Epidaurians, 377

Epirote monarchy, 372

Epirus, 387, 395

Eratosthenes. Affinities with the Academy, 69; as geographer, 7, 11–13, 17, 88, 91, 278, 288, 294; as critic, 44–5, 51–2, 58, 97, 131, 297; on A.'s flatterers, 58–9; on A.'s ideas, 419; how much of the sources is E., 437–9; A. as harmoniser and reconciler, 439; the loving-cup, 440 and nn., 441 n. 2, 445, identified, 440, 442; E.'s account of the scene at Opis, 441–2, and A.'s prayer, 443–5

Erbil, *see* Arbela

Eriguios, 119

Eros, 343n., 420–1

Erythrae, Erythraeans, 211–12, 357

E-sagila, 77, 383

Ethiopia, 51, 374

Etruscans, 23

Euakes, 164n.

Euboea, 176

Eudaimones, 88

Eudamus, 310, 394n.

Euhemerus, 431–3

Index

Index

Xenophon, 35, 202, 224, 286, 355, 357, 359n., 401
Xerxes, 47–8, 200, 219, 222, 224, 273–4, 383
Xylinepolis, 239

Yueh-chi, 256–9

Zagros Mts, 178
Zarangian horse, 164
Zariaspa, 32n.
Zeno, 123n., 300, 399, 408, 417, 427n., 432, 437, 448–9; friend of Antigonus Gonatas, 300, 425–6; his early *Politeia*, 407, 409, 412, 417, described, 418–20, 438; his later World-State, 418–20, 422–4, 448; its basis, 423; no fixed name, 419; his

change of mind due to A.'s ideas, 421–3; their influence on him, 421–3, 448, but had limits, 448; difference between Stoic Homonoia and that attached to kingship, 423–4
Zenodotion, 248
Zeus, 349–50, 358, 364–5, 367, 373, 382–3, 432–3; 'father of gods and men', 436 and nn.; Zeus Ammon, 348–50, 372; Aniketos Helios, 343n.; Carian, 225; 'Zeus the king', 350; Lycaeus, 349; Soter, 341, 351n.
Zeus, sons of, 56, 274, 360n., 362; A. as son of, 350, 352–3, 356, 358–9, 363, 373, 437
Ziobetis, river, 87, 104
Zonus, river, 13n.

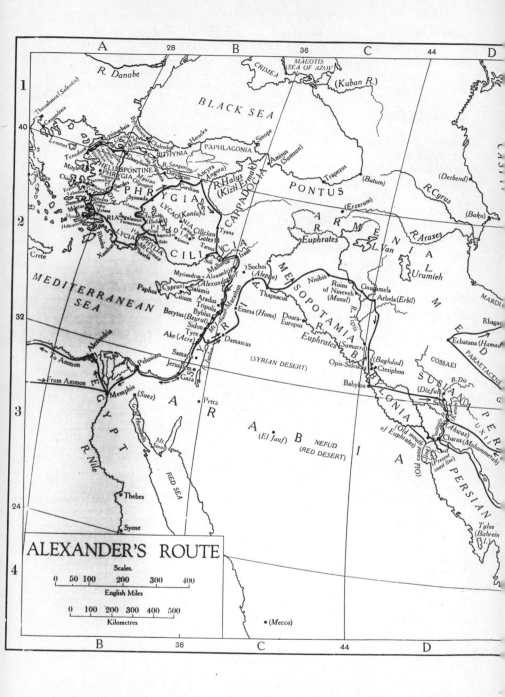

ALEXANDER'S ROUTE

Scales.

0 50 100   200   300   400

English Miles

0 100 200 300 400 500

Kilometres

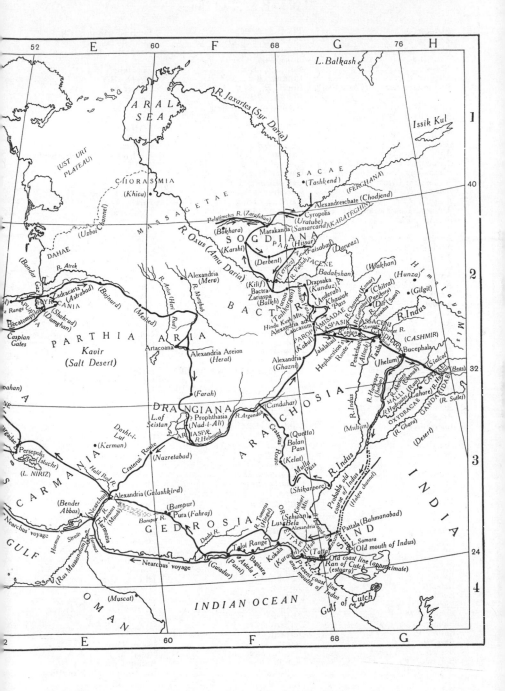

INDEX TO MAP

Indus, probable old course of, G 3
Indus, *R.*, G 2, 3
Isaura, B 2
Ispahan, D 2
Issik Kul, H 1
Issus, C 2
Istachr, E 3

Jalalabad, G 2
El Jauf, C 3
Jaxartes, *R.* (Syr Daria), FG 1
Jerusalem, B 3
Jhelum, *R.*, G 2, 3
Jordan, *R.*, B 2, 3

Kabul, G 2
Kaoshan Pass, G 2
Karateghin, G 2
Karshi, F 2
Karum, D 2, 3
Kavir (Salt Desert), E 2
Kelat, F 3
Kerman, E 3
Khawak Pass, G 2
Khiva, F 1
Kilif, F 2
Kirthari Mts, F 3
Kizil Ermak, *R.*, BC 1, 2
Kokala, F 3
Konia, B 2
Kuban, *R.*, C 1
Kunduz, G 2
Kurachi, F 3

Lahore, G 3
Lampsacus, A 1
Laranda, B 2
Lebanon, *Mt,* BC 2
Lebedus, A 2
Lemnos, A 2
Lus-Bela, F 3
Lycaonia, B 2
Lycia, B 2
Lydia, AB 2
Lysimacheia, A 1

Maeotis, BC 1
Malli, G 3
Mallus, B 2
Marakanda (Samarcand), F 2
Marathus, C 2
Mardi, D 2
Marmora, Sea of, AB 1
Massaga, G 2
Massagetae, EF 1, 2
Mecca, C 4
Media, DE 2
Mediterranean Sea, AB 2
Memphis, B 3
Merv, F 2
Meshed, E 2
Mesopotamia, C 2
Miletus, A 2
Minab, *R.*, E 3
Mitylene, A 2
Mohammerah, D 3
Mosul, C 2
Mulla Pass, F 3

Multan, G 3
Murghab, *R.*, F 2
Muscat, E 4
Mylasa, A 2
Myndus, A 2
Myriandrus, B 2
Mysian Olympus, B 2

Nad-i-Ali, F 3
Nazretabad, EF 3
Nearchus' voyage, DEF 3
Nefud, C 3
Nile, *R.*, B 3
Nineveh, Ruins of, C 2
Niriz, *L.*, E 3
Nisibis, C 2

Ohind, G 2
Oman, E 4
Opis-Seleucia, D 2
Oreitae, F 3
Oxus, *R.* (Amu Daria), FG 1, 2

Pamphylia, B 2
Panjkora, *R.*, G 2
Paphlagonia, B 1
Paphos, B 2
Paraetacene, D 2
Paraetacene, FG 2
Parium, A 1
Paropamisadae, G 2
Parthia, E 2
Pasargadae, E 3
Pasitigris, *R.*, D 2, 3
Pasni, F 3
Pattala, G 3
Pelusium, B 3
Pergamum, A 2
Perge, B 2
Persepolis, E 3
Persian Gulf, DE 3
Persis, DE 3
Petra, B 3
Peukelaotis, G 2
Phaselis, B 2
Phrygia, B 2
Pisidia, B 2
Polytimetus, *R.* (Zarafshan), FG 2
Pontus, C 1
Priene, A 2
Prophthasia, F 3
Pura, F 3

Quetta, F 3

Ras Mussendam, E 3
Ravi, G 2
Red Desert, C 3
Red Sea, BC 3
Rhagae, D 2
Rhodes, B 2

Sacae, G 1
Sagalassus, B 2
Salamis, B 2
Salonica, A 1
Samara, *L.*, G 3
Samarcand, F 2

Samaria, B 2
Samarra, C 2
Samos, A 2
Samsun, C 1
Sangarius, *R.*, B 1
Sardes, B 2
Sehwan, F 3
Seistan, *L.* of, F 3
Shahrud, E 2
Shikarpore, G 3
Sialcot, G 2
Side, B 2
Sidon, B 2
Sinai, *Mt,* B 3
Sinope, B 1
Smyrna, A 2
Sochoi?, C 2
Sogdiana, FG 2
Soli, B 2
Suastos, *R.*, G 2
Suez, B 3
Susa, D 2
Susiana, D 2, 3
Sutlej, *R.*, GH 3
Swat, *R.*, G 2
Syene, B 3
Synnada, B 2
Syria, BC 2, 3
Syrian Desert, C 2

Taloi Range, F 3
Tapuria, E 2
Tarsus, B 2
Tashkend, G 1
Tashkurgan, F 2
Tatta, F 3
Taxila, G 2
Tenedos, A 2
Teos, A 2
Termessus, B 2
Termez, F 2
Thapsacus, C 2
Thebes, B 3
Thessalonica, A 1
Tomeros, *R.*, F 3
Trapezus, C 1
Tripolis, B 2
Troas, A 2
Tyana, B 2
Tylos, D 3
Tyre, B 2

Uratube, G 2
Urumieh, *L.*, D 2
Ust Urt Plateau, E 1
Uxii, D 3
Uzboi Channel, E 1, 2

Vakhsh, *R.*, FG 2
Van, *L.*, C 2

Wakhan, G 2

Xanthus, B 2

Zadracarta, E 2
Zarafshan, *R.*, FG 2
Zelea, A 1